RUN WILD ™

Published by
ARCHAIA ™

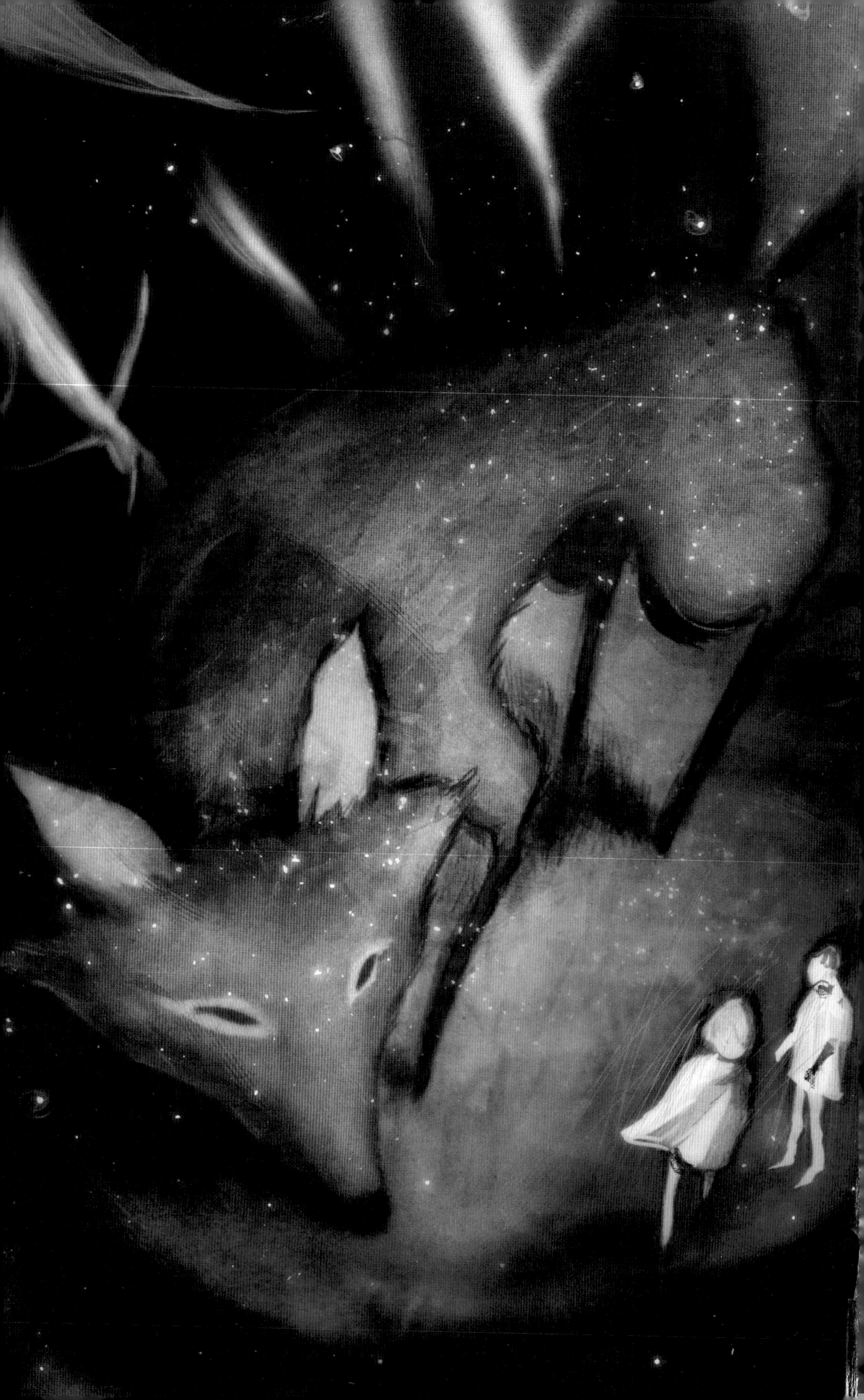

RUN

written by
K.I. ZACHOPOULOS

illustrated by
VINCENZO BALZANO

lettered by
DERON BENNETT

WILD™

Archaia • Los Angeles, California

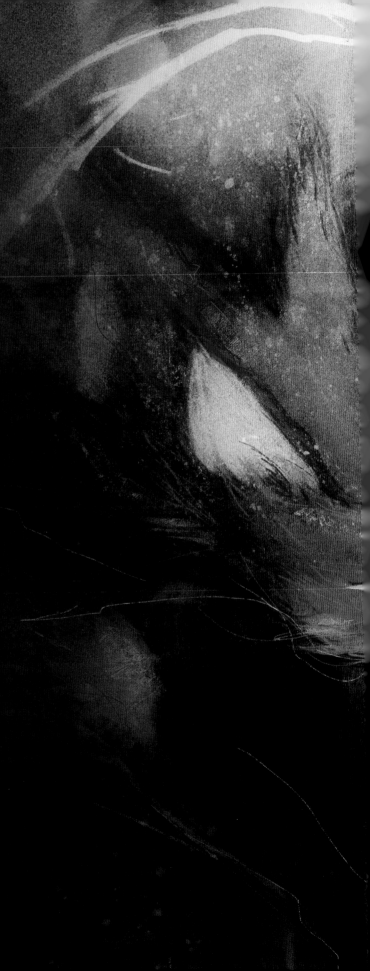

cover by
VINCENZO BALZANO

designer
JILLIAN CRAB

assistant editor
SOPHIE PHILIPS-ROBERTS

editor
SIERRA HAHN

with special thanks to **Whitney Leopard**

ROSS RICHIE...CEO & Founder
MATT GAGNON......................................Editor-in-Chief
FILIP SABLIK...................President of Publishing & Marketing
STEPHEN CHRISTY.....................President of Development
LANCE KREITER...............VP of Licensing & Merchandising
PHIL BARBARO...VP of Finance
ARUNE SINGH......................................VP of Marketing
BRYCE CARLSON................................ Managing Editor
SCOTT NEWMAN......................Production Design Manager
KATE HENNING................................Operations Manager
SIERRA HAHN.. Senior Editor
DAFNA PLEBAN.........................Editor, Talent Development
SHANNON WATTERS......................................Editor
ERIC HARBURN...Editor
WHITNEY LEOPARD......................................Editor
CAMERON CHITTOCK.....................................Editor
CHRIS ROSA.......................................Associate Editor
MATTHEW LEVINE..............................Associate Editor
SOPHIE PHILIPS-ROBERTS.....................Assistant Editor
GAVIN GRONENTHAL..........................Assistant Editor
MICHAEL MOCCIO.............................Assistant Editor
AMANDA LaFRANCO.........................Executive Assistant
KATALINA HOLLAND.......Editorial Administrative Assistant
JILLIAN CRAB..................................Design Coordinator
MICHELLE ANKLEY...........................Design Coordinator
KARA LEOPARD..............................Production Designer
MARIE KRUPINA.............................Production Designer
GRACE PARK............................Production Design Assistant
CHELSEA ROBERTS...................Production Design Assistant
ELIZABETH LOUGHRIDGE..............Accounting Coordinator
STEPHANIE HOCUTT...................Social Media Coordinator
JOSÉ MEZA.................................. Event Coordinator
HOLLY AITCHISON...........................Operations Coordinator
MEGAN CHRISTOPHER.......................Operations Assistant
RODRIGO HERNANDEZ......................Mailroom Assistant
MORGAN PERRY....................Direct Market Representative
CAT O'GRADY..................................Marketing Assistant
LIZ ALMENDAREZ.........Accounting Administrative Assistant
CORNELIA TZANA...........................Administrative Assistant

ARCHAIA™

BOOM! Studios, 5670 Wilshire Boulevard, Suite 400, Los Angeles, CA 90036-5679. Printed in China. First Printing.

ISBN: 978-1-68415-024-3, eISBN: 978-1-61398-701-8

For my daughter, Lorena;
it takes all kinds to make a world.
—K.I. Zachopoulos

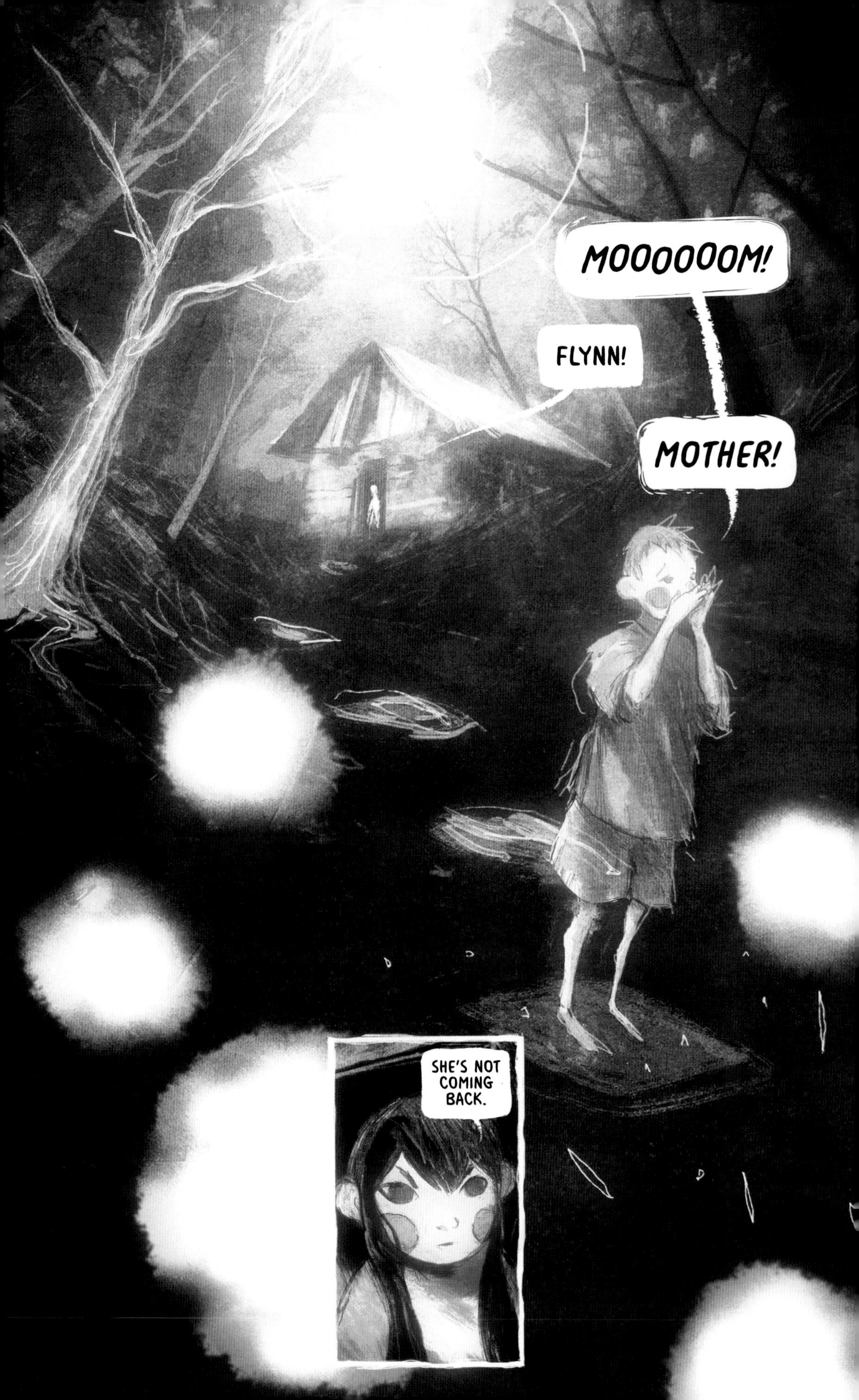
MOOOOOOM!
FLYNN!
MOTHER!
SHE'S NOT COMING BACK.

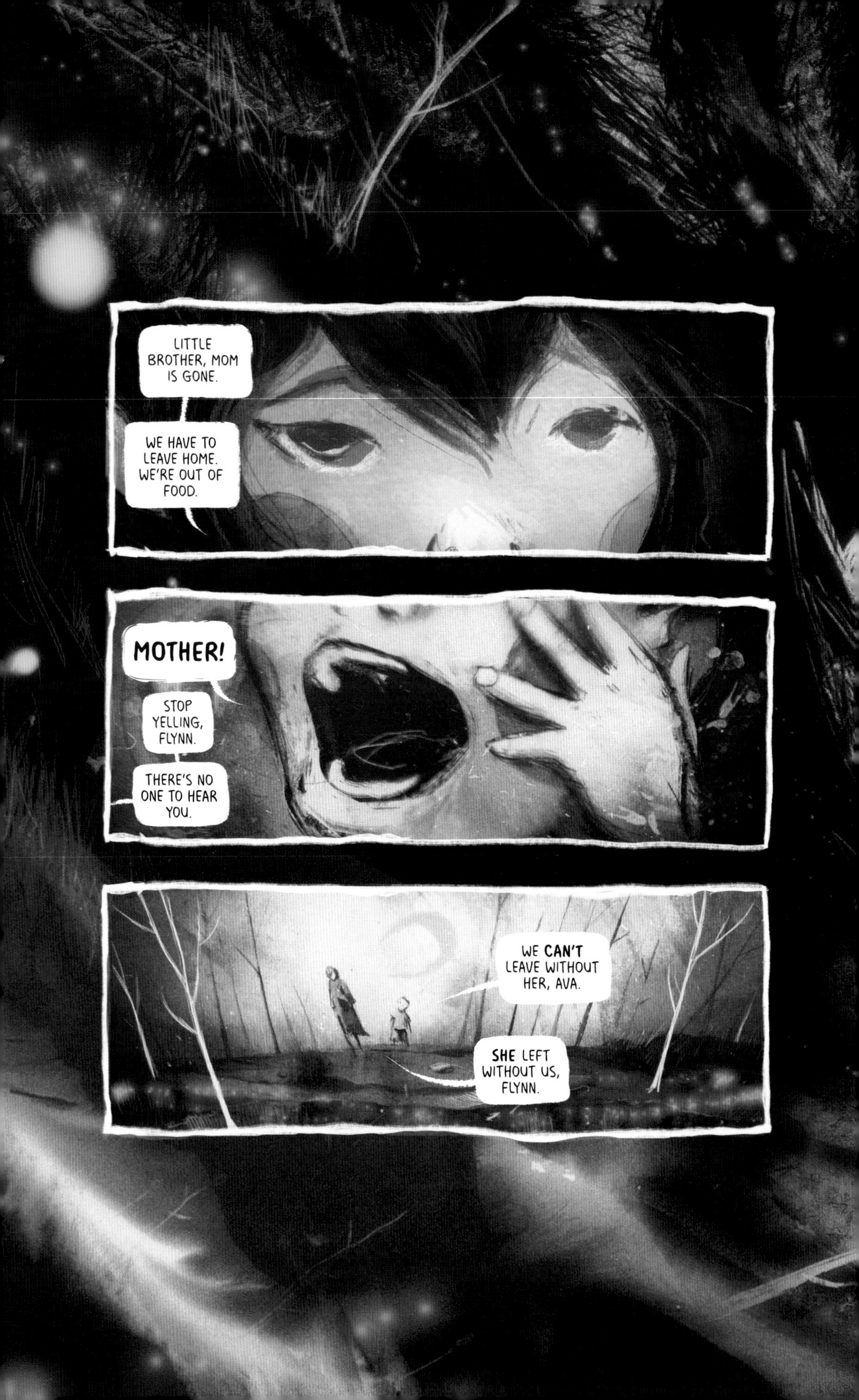
LITTLE BROTHER, MOM IS GONE.
WE HAVE TO LEAVE HOME. WE'RE OUT OF FOOD.
MOTHER!
STOP YELLING, FLYNN.
THERE'S NO ONE TO HEAR YOU.
WE CAN'T LEAVE WITHOUT HER, AVA.
SHE LEFT WITHOUT US, FLYNN.

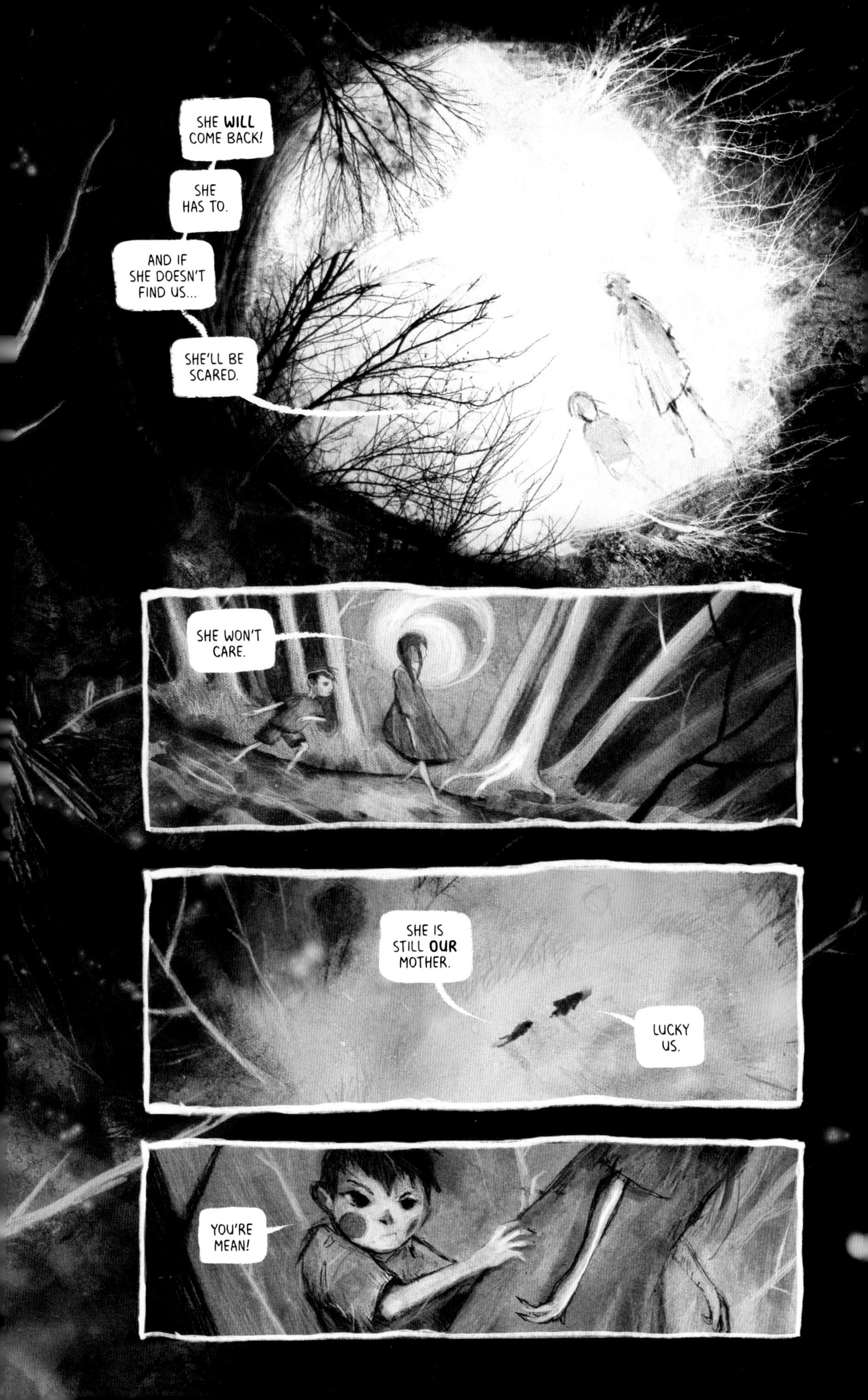
SHE WILL COME BACK!
SHE HAS TO.
AND IF SHE DOESN'T FIND US...
SHE'LL BE SCARED.
SHE WON'T CARE.
SHE IS STILL OUR MOTHER.
LUCKY US.
YOU'RE MEAN!

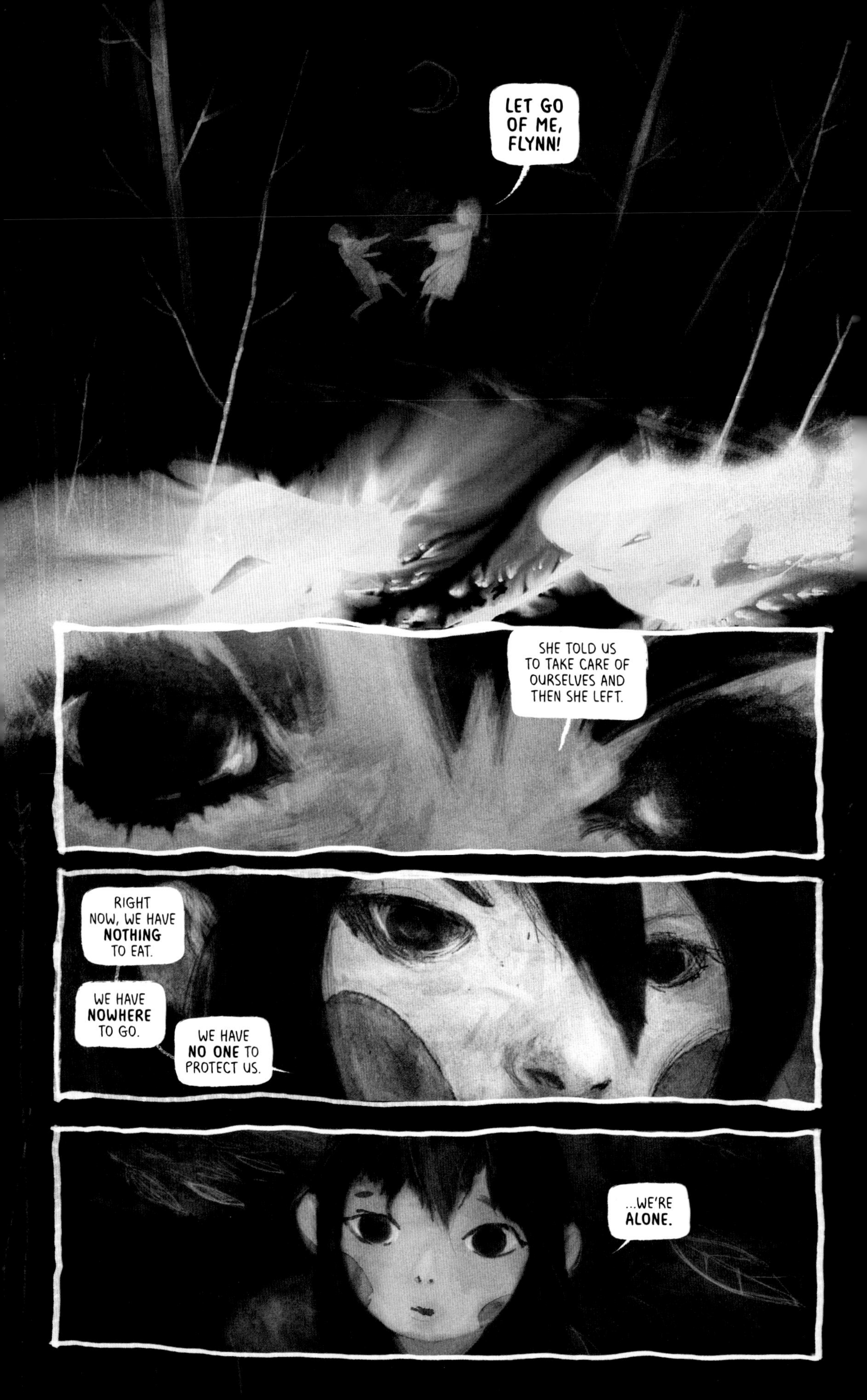
LET GO OF ME, FLYNN!
SHE TOLD US TO TAKE CARE OF OURSELVES AND THEN SHE LEFT.
RIGHT NOW, WE HAVE **NOTHING** TO EAT.
WE HAVE **NOWHERE** TO GO.
WE HAVE **NO ONE** TO PROTECT US.
...WE'RE **ALONE.**

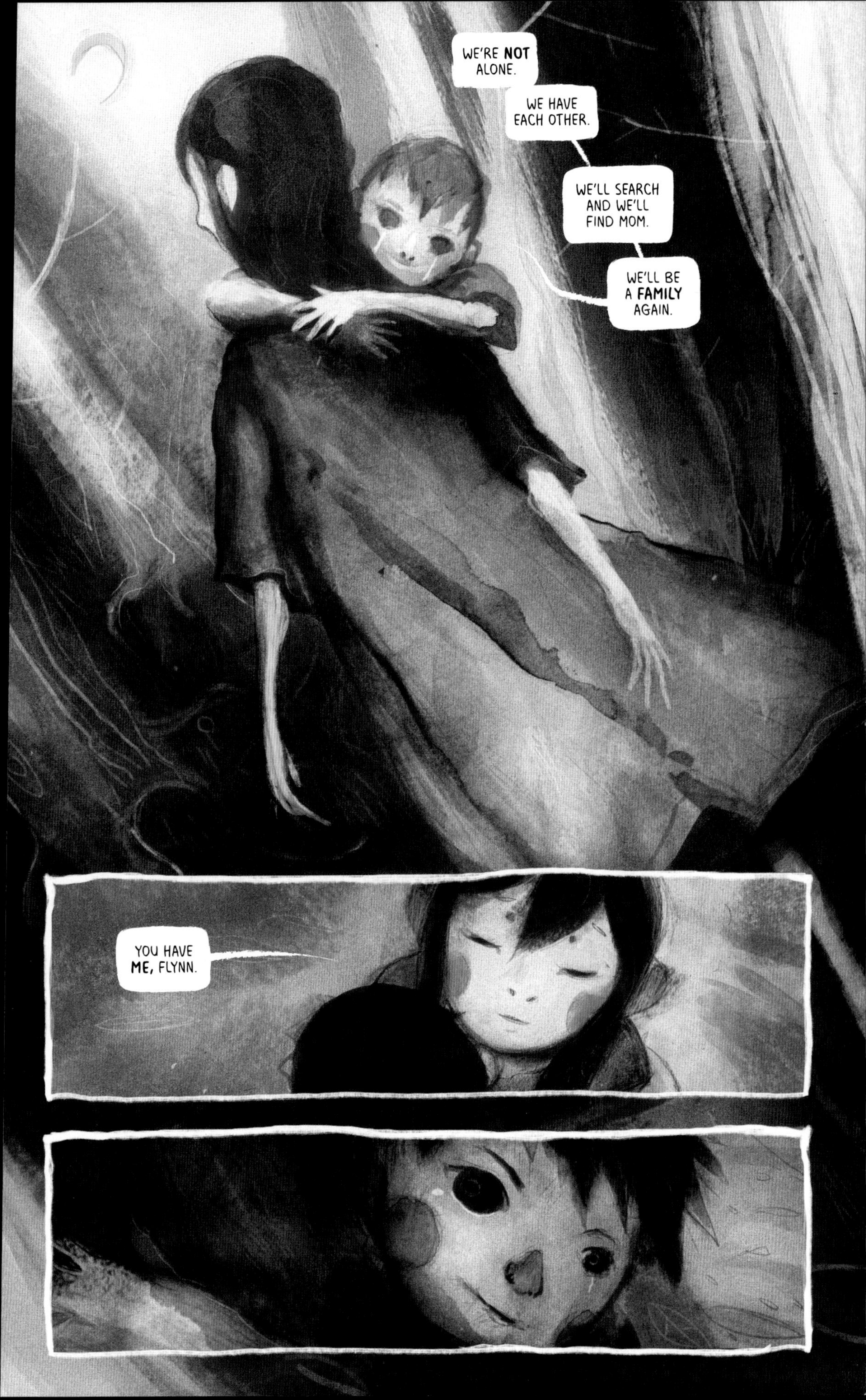
WE'RE **NOT** ALONE.
WE HAVE EACH OTHER.
WE'LL SEARCH AND WE'LL FIND MOM.
WE'LL BE A **FAMILY** AGAIN.
YOU HAVE **ME,** FLYNN.

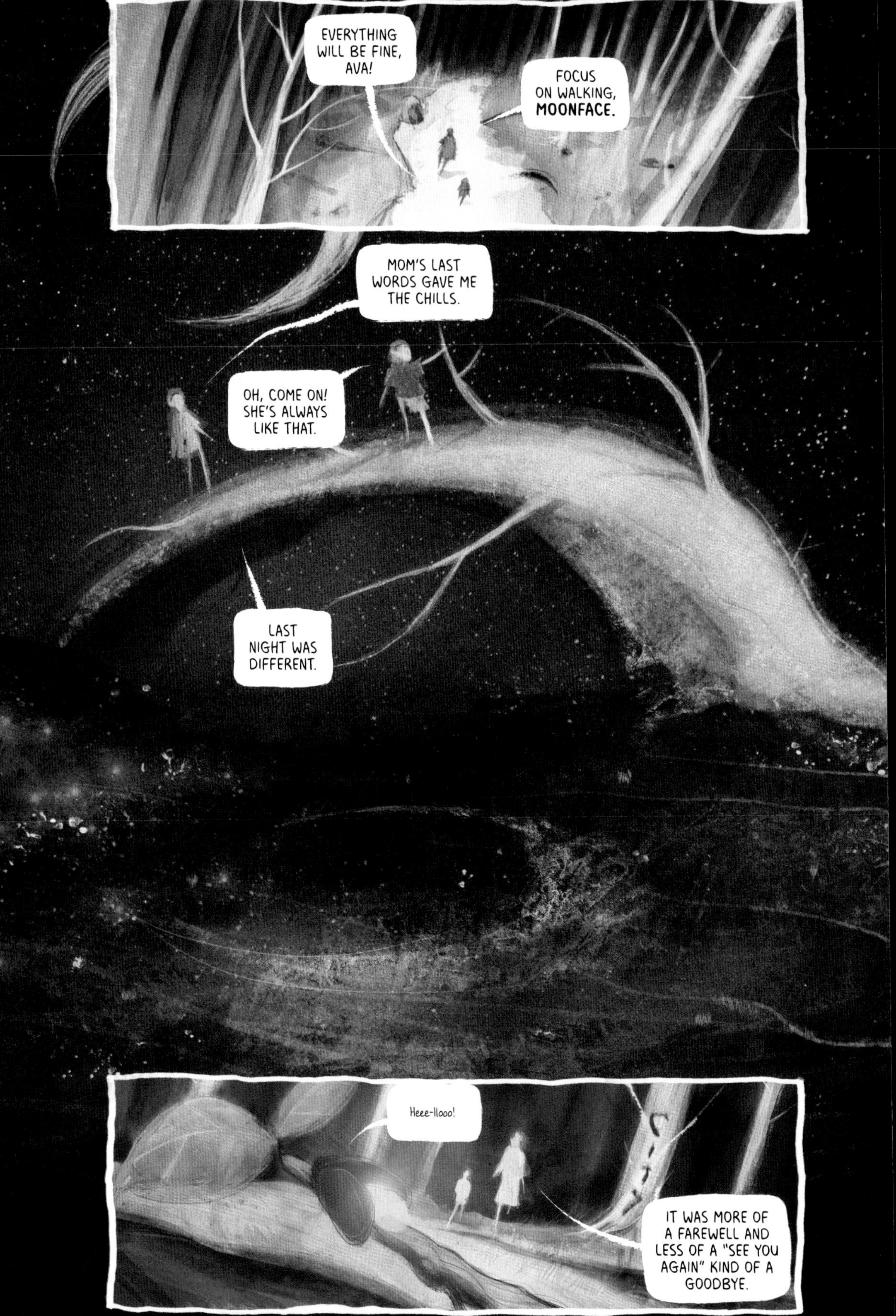
EVERYTHING WILL BE FINE, AVA!
FOCUS ON WALKING, **MOONFACE.**
MOM'S LAST WORDS GAVE ME THE CHILLS.
OH, COME ON! SHE'S ALWAYS LIKE THAT.
LAST NIGHT WAS DIFFERENT.
Heee-llooo!
IT WAS MORE OF A FAREWELL AND LESS OF A "SEE YOU AGAIN" KIND OF A GOODBYE.

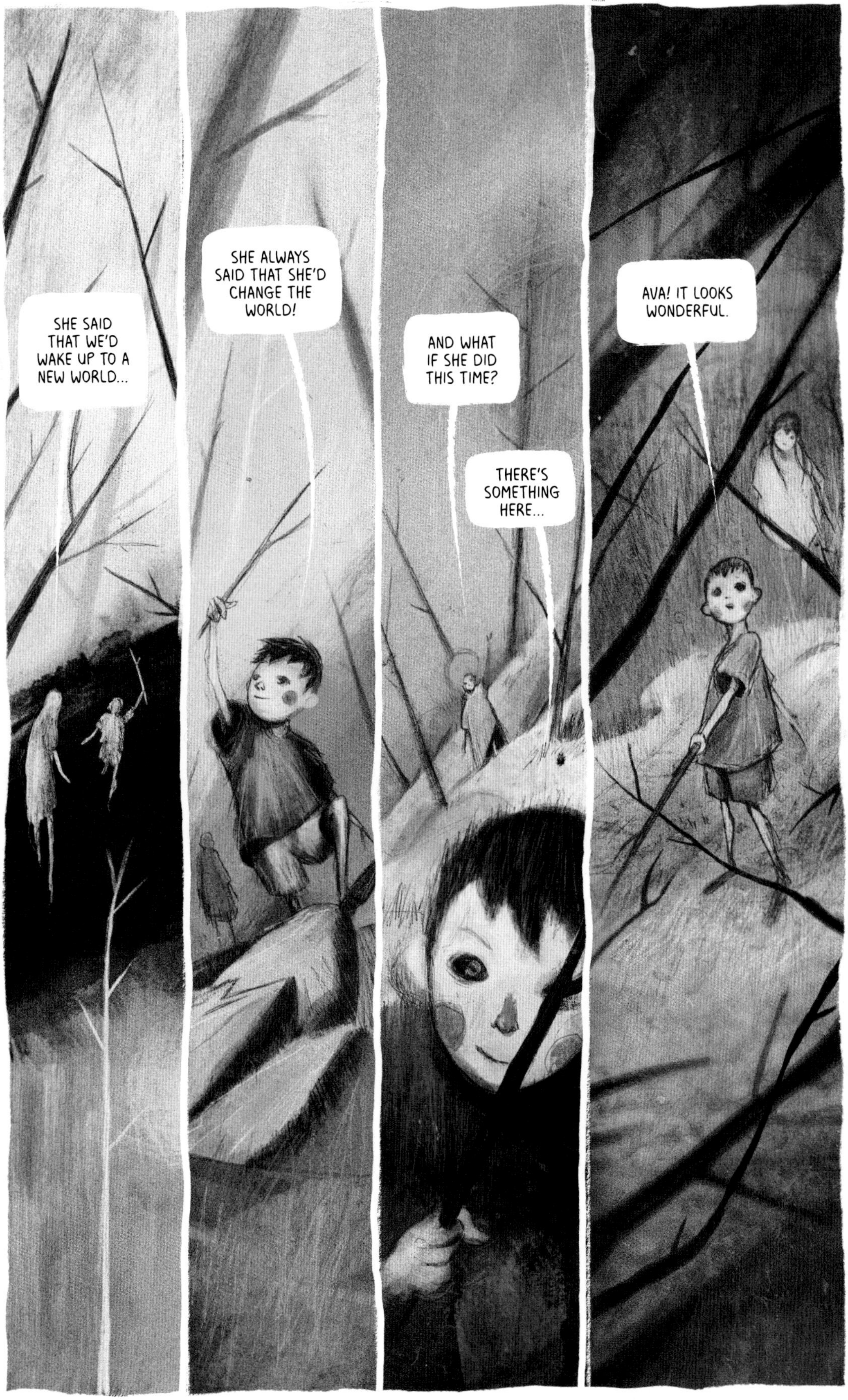
SHE SAID THAT WE'D WAKE UP TO A NEW WORLD...
SHE ALWAYS SAID THAT SHE'D CHANGE THE WORLD!
AND WHAT IF SHE DID THIS TIME?
THERE'S SOMETHING HERE...
AVA! IT LOOKS WONDERFUL.

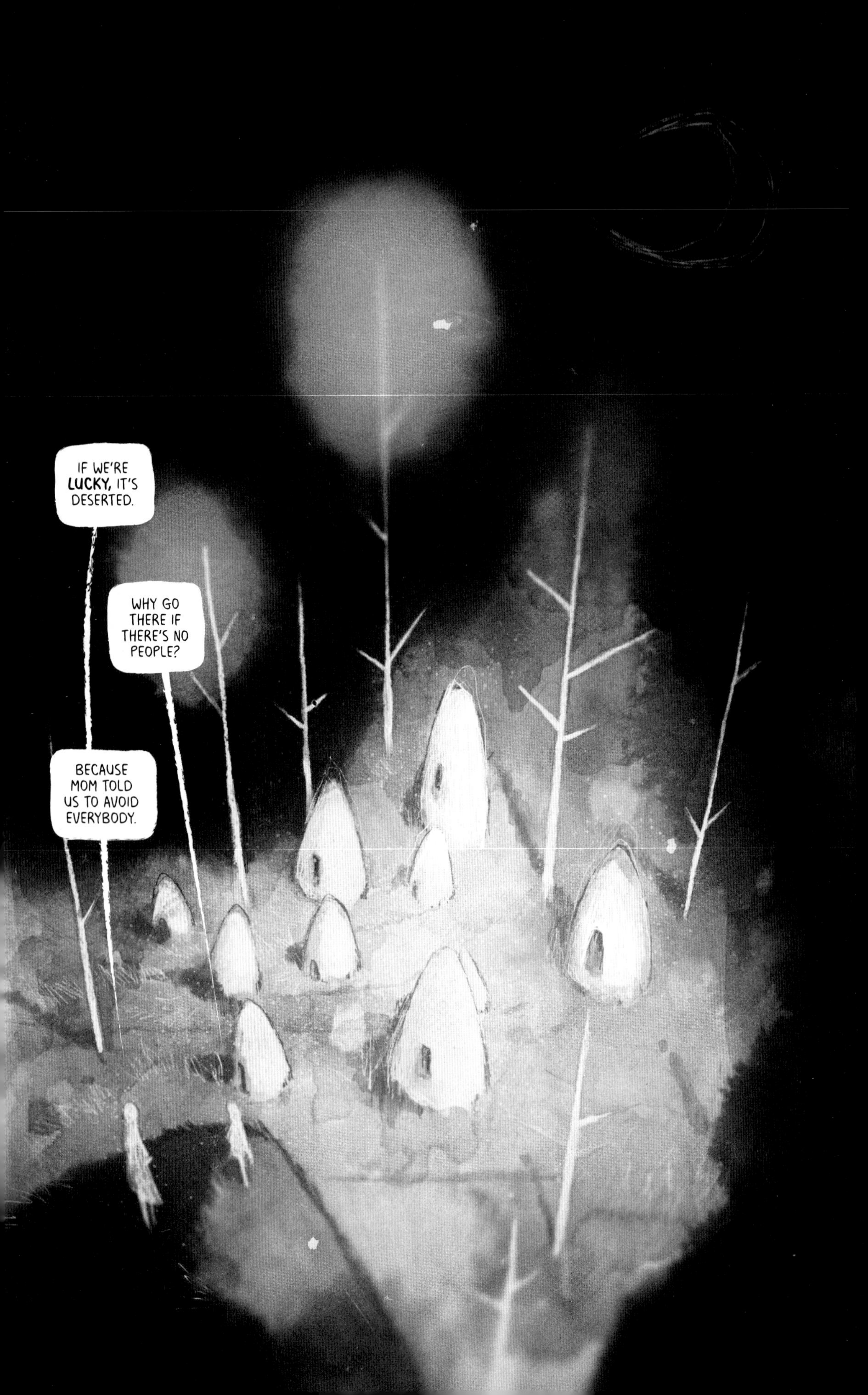
IF WE'RE **LUCKY,** IT'S DESERTED.
WHY GO THERE IF THERE'S NO PEOPLE?
BECAUSE MOM TOLD US TO AVOID EVERYBODY.

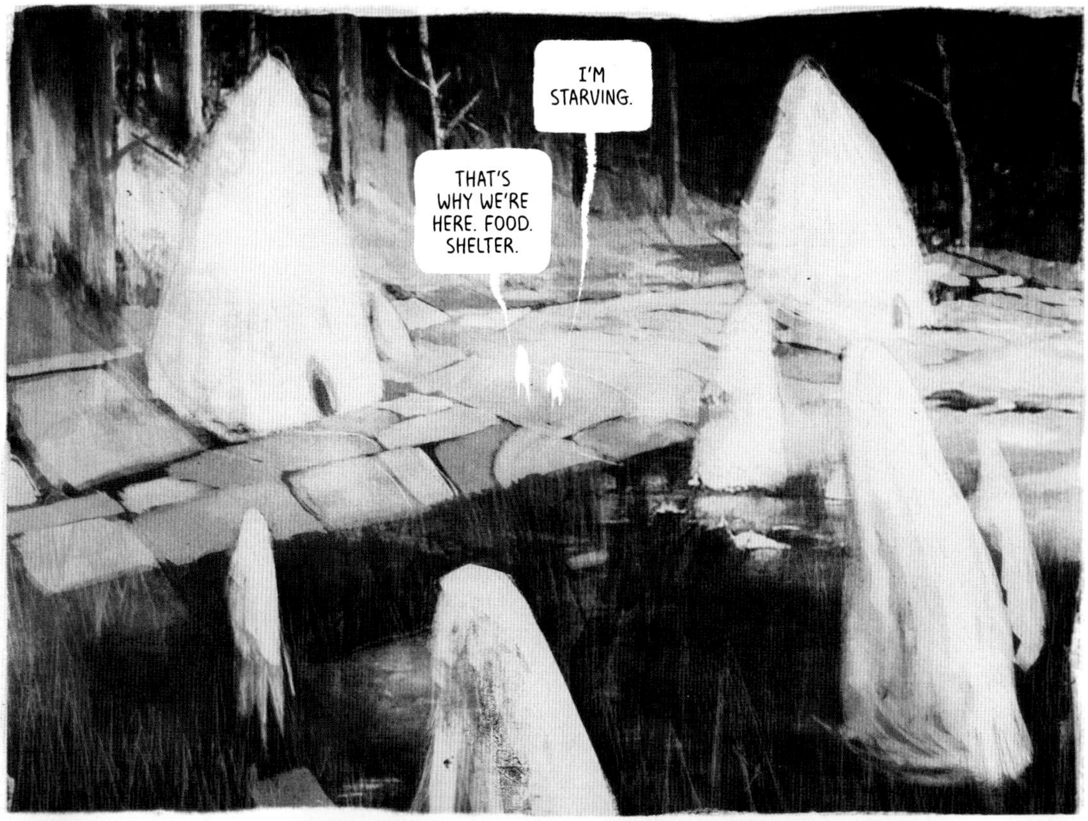
I'M STARVING.
THAT'S WHY WE'RE HERE. FOOD. SHELTER.

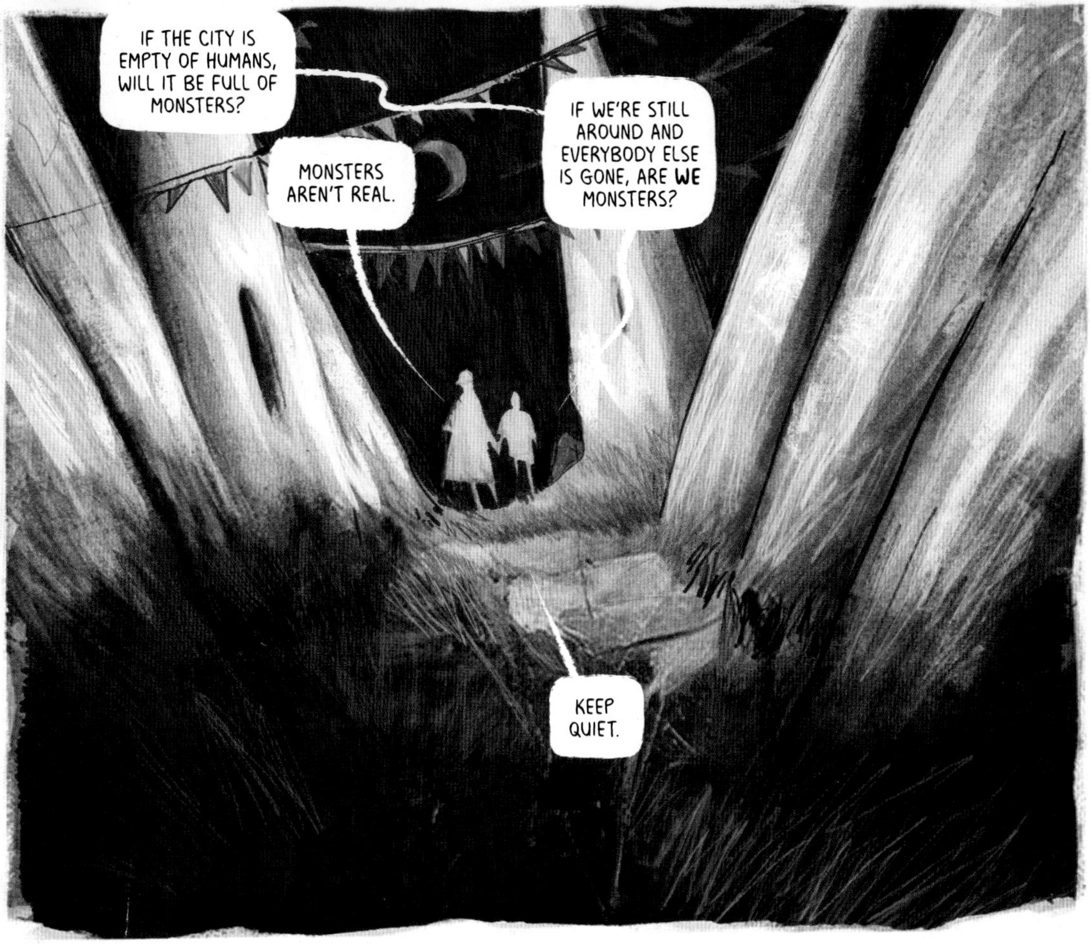
IF THE CITY IS EMPTY OF HUMANS, WILL IT BE FULL OF MONSTERS?
MONSTERS AREN'T REAL.
IF WE'RE STILL AROUND AND EVERYBODY ELSE IS GONE, ARE **WE** MONSTERS?
KEEP QUIET.

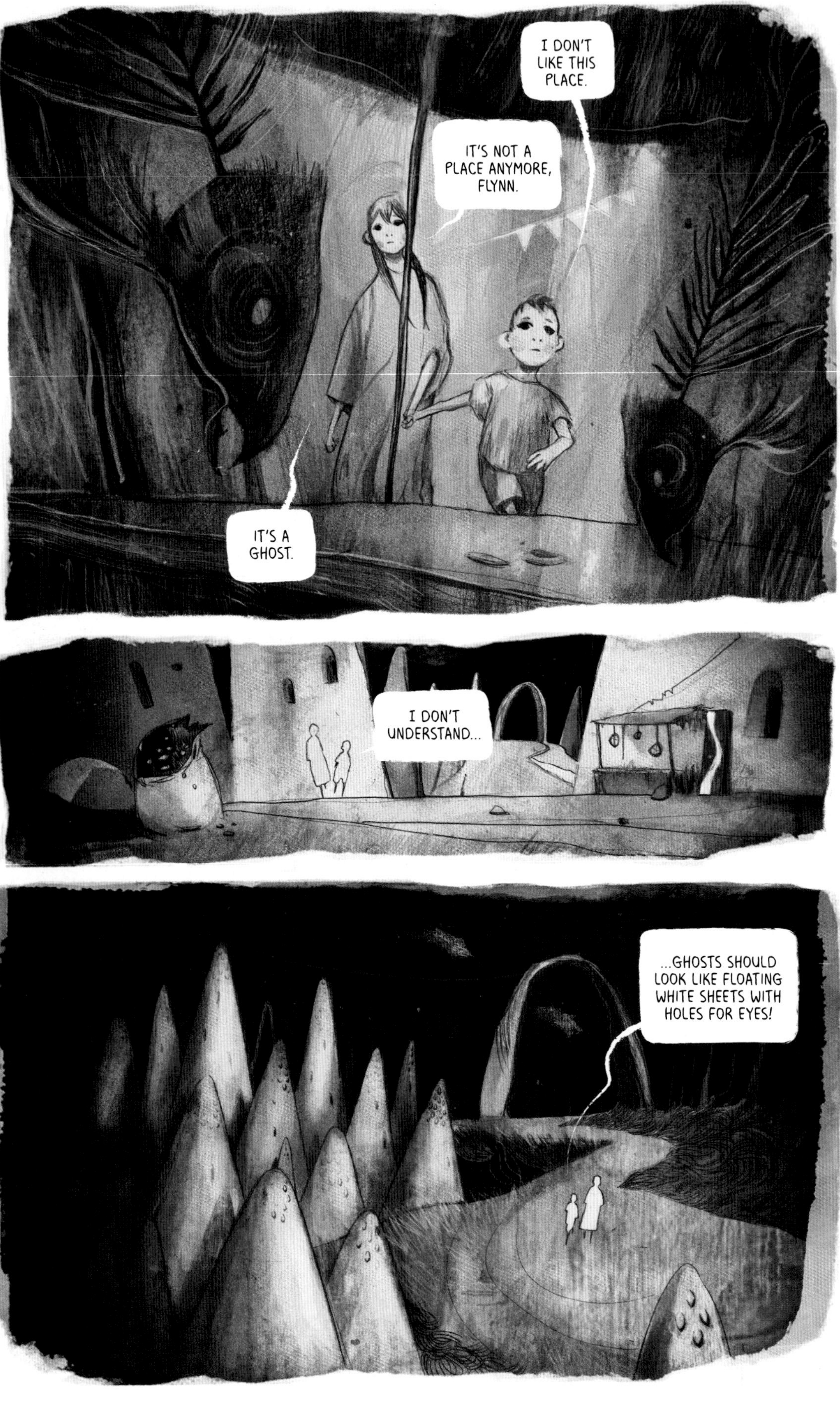
I DON'T LIKE THIS PLACE.
IT'S NOT A PLACE ANYMORE, FLYNN.
IT'S A GHOST.
I DON'T UNDERSTAND...
...GHOSTS SHOULD LOOK LIKE FLOATING WHITE SHEETS WITH HOLES FOR EYES!

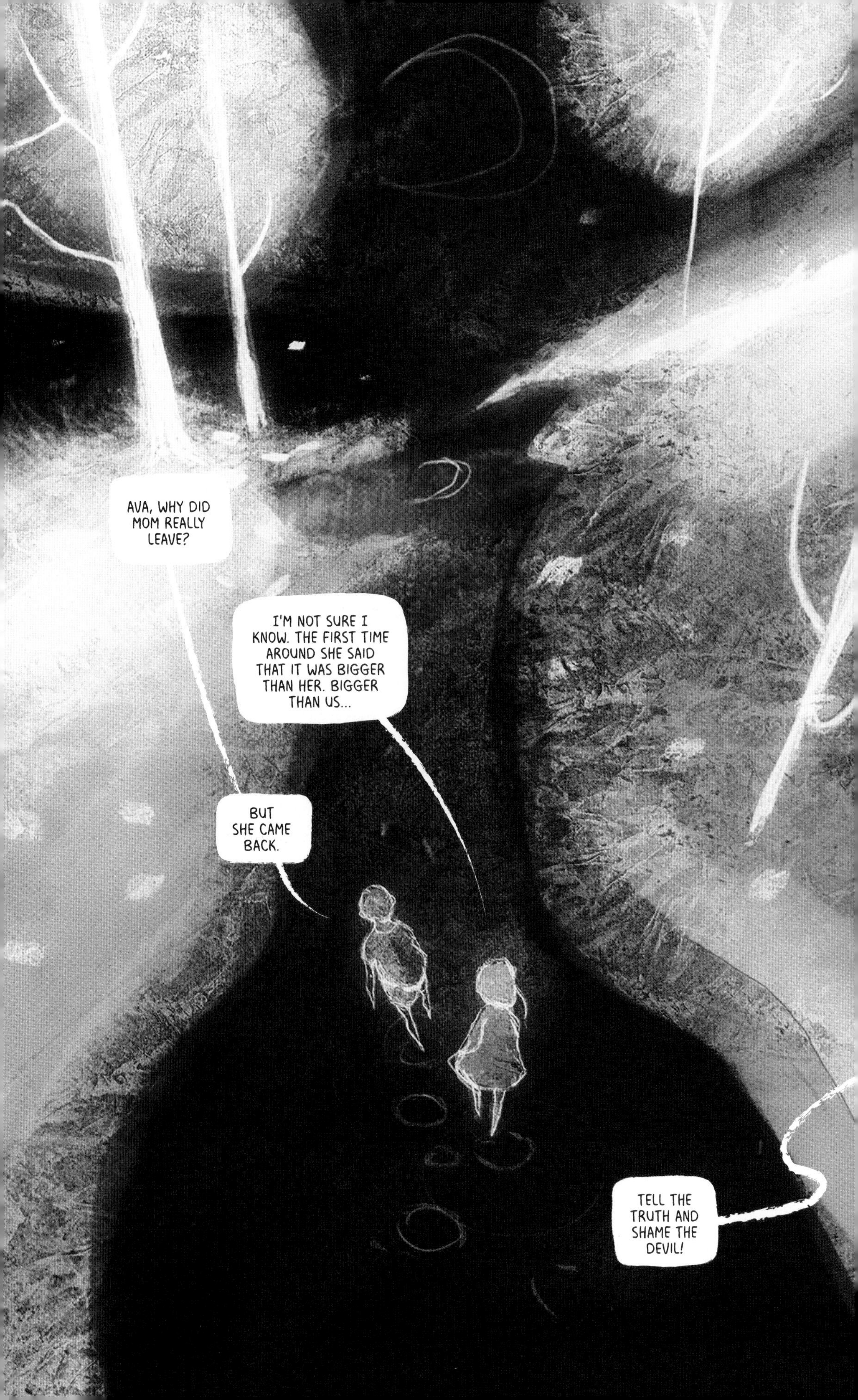
AVA, WHY DID MOM REALLY LEAVE?
I'M NOT SURE I KNOW. THE FIRST TIME AROUND SHE SAID THAT IT WAS BIGGER THAN HER. BIGGER THAN US...
BUT SHE CAME BACK.
TELL THE TRUTH AND SHAME THE DEVIL!

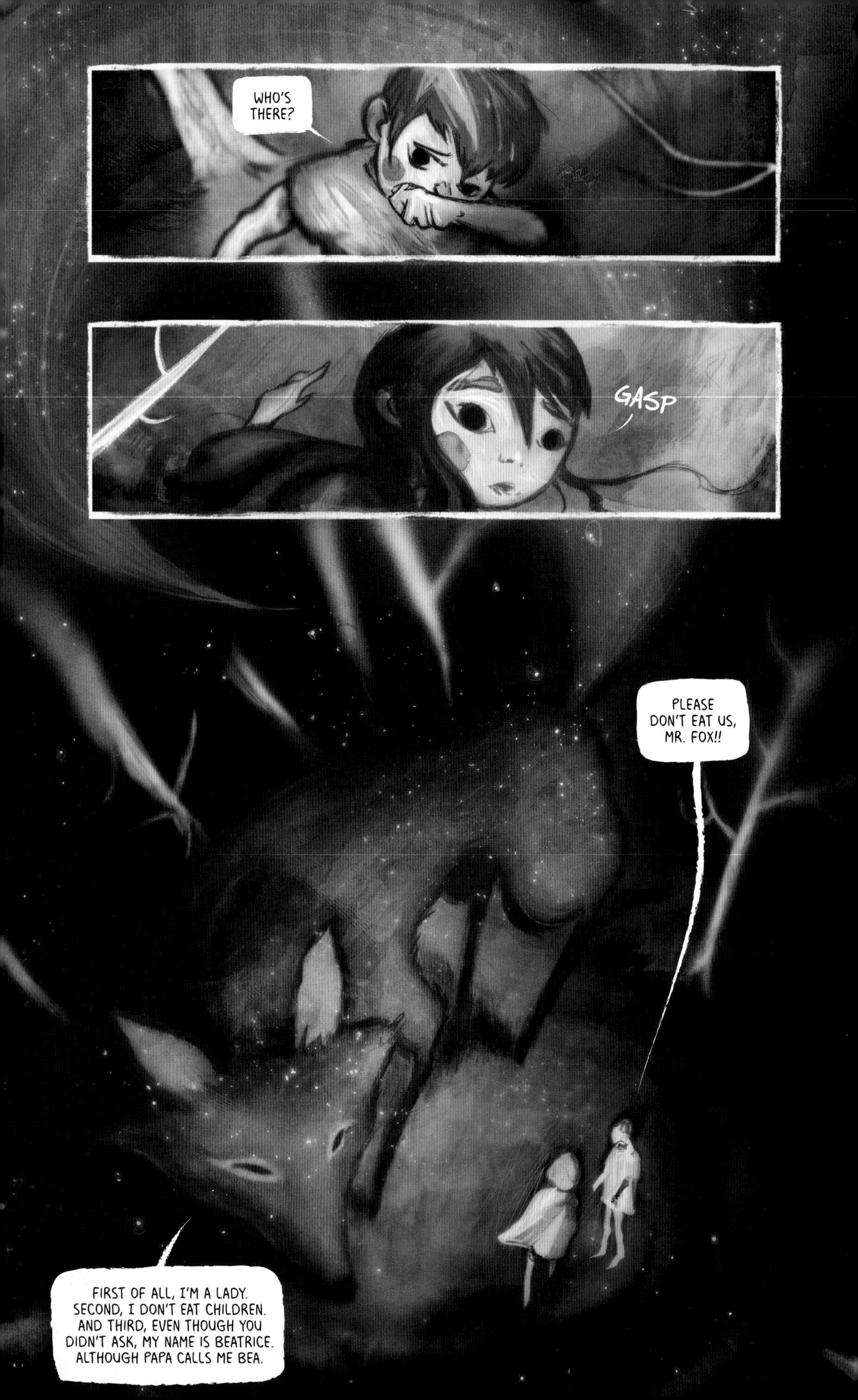

WHO'S THERE?
GASP
PLEASE DON'T EAT US, MR. FOX!!
FIRST OF ALL, I'M A LADY. SECOND, I DON'T EAT CHILDREN. AND THIRD, EVEN THOUGH YOU DIDN'T ASK, MY NAME IS BEATRICE. ALTHOUGH PAPA CALLS ME BEA.

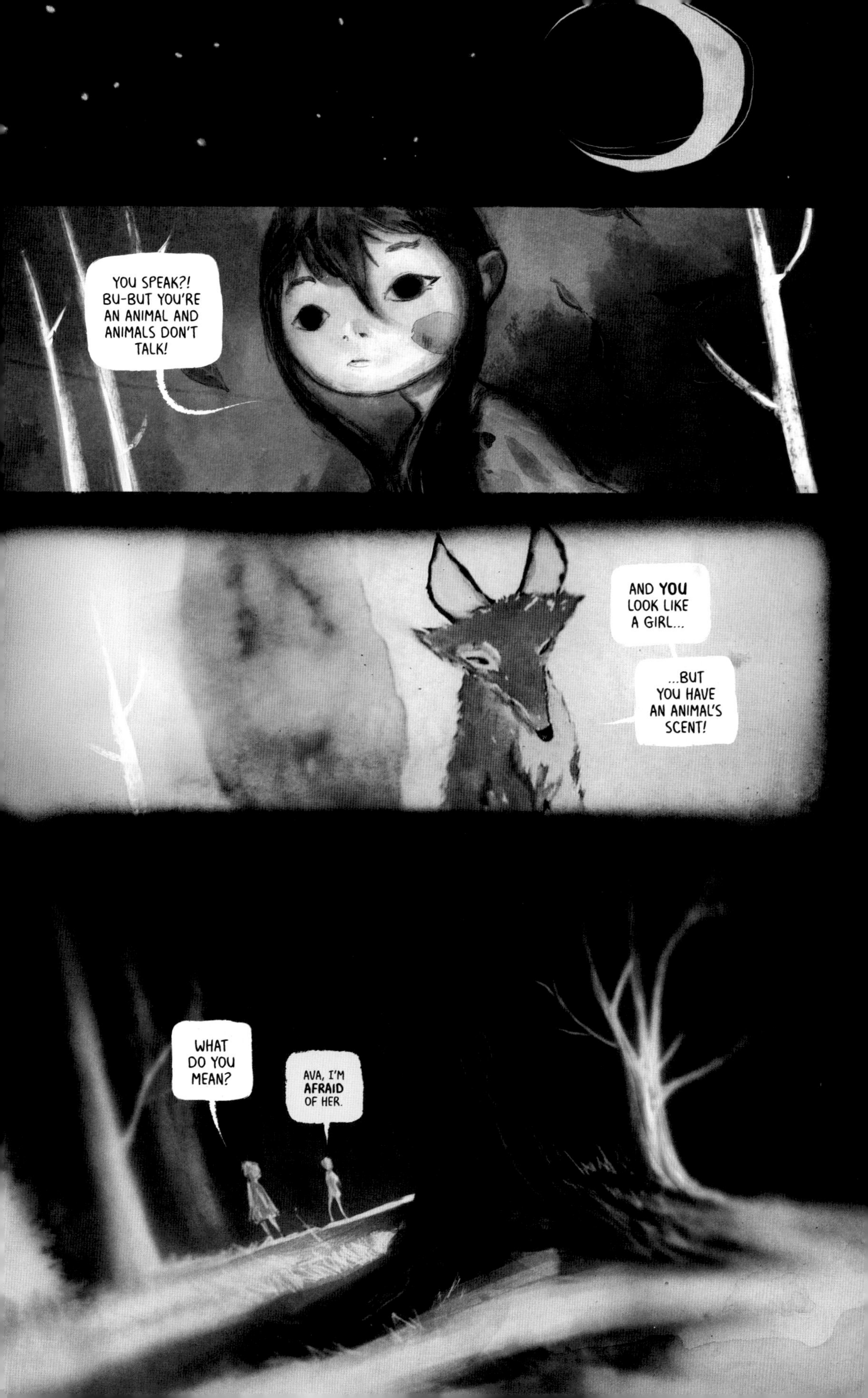
YOU SPEAK?! BU-BUT YOU'RE AN ANIMAL AND ANIMALS DON'T TALK!
AND **YOU** LOOK LIKE A GIRL...
...BUT YOU HAVE AN ANIMAL'S SCENT!
WHAT DO YOU MEAN?
AVA, I'M **AFRAID** OF HER.

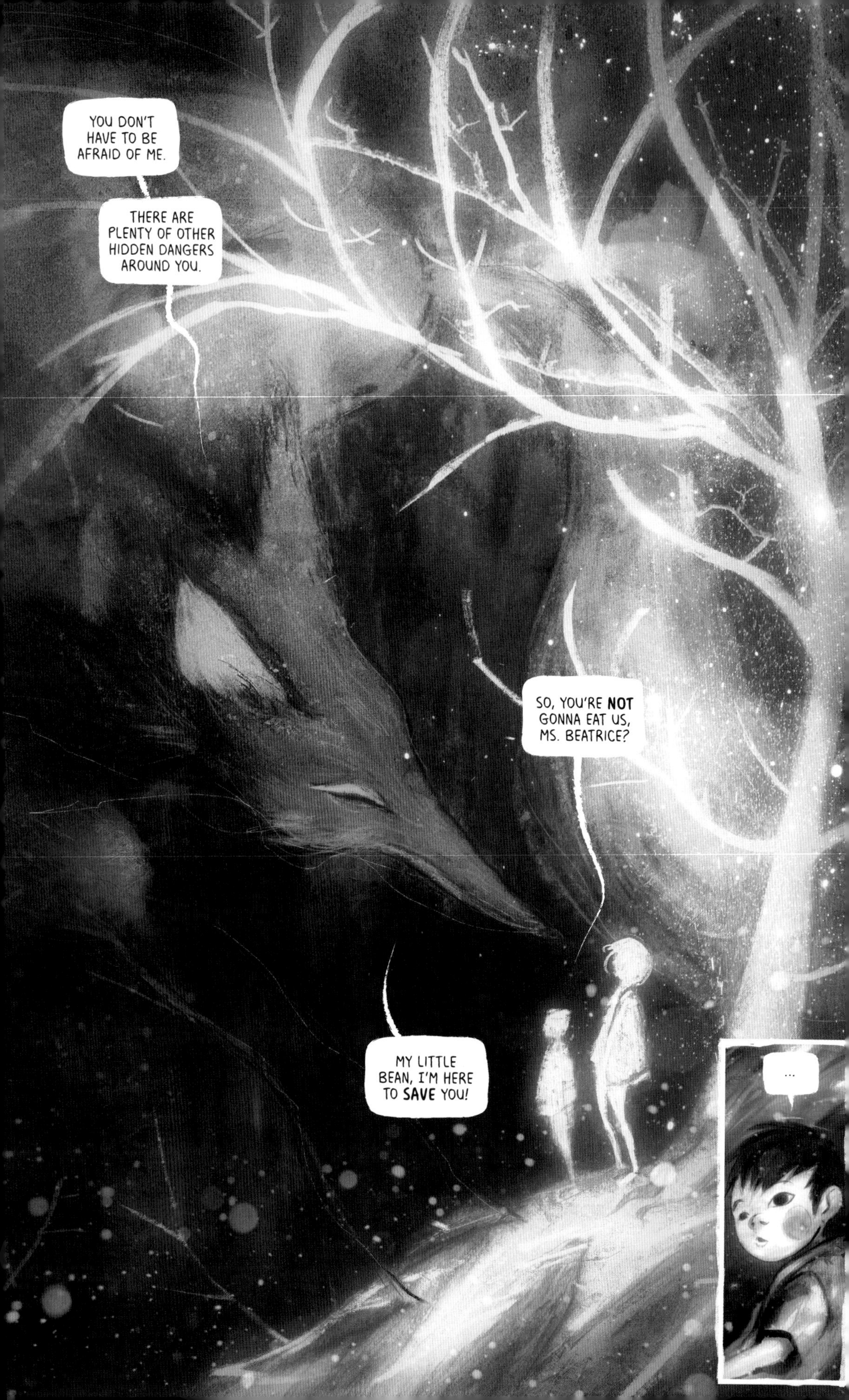
YOU DON'T HAVE TO BE AFRAID OF ME.
THERE ARE PLENTY OF OTHER HIDDEN DANGERS AROUND YOU.
SO, YOU'RE **NOT** GONNA EAT US, MS. BEATRICE?
MY LITTLE BEAN, I'M HERE TO **SAVE** YOU!
...

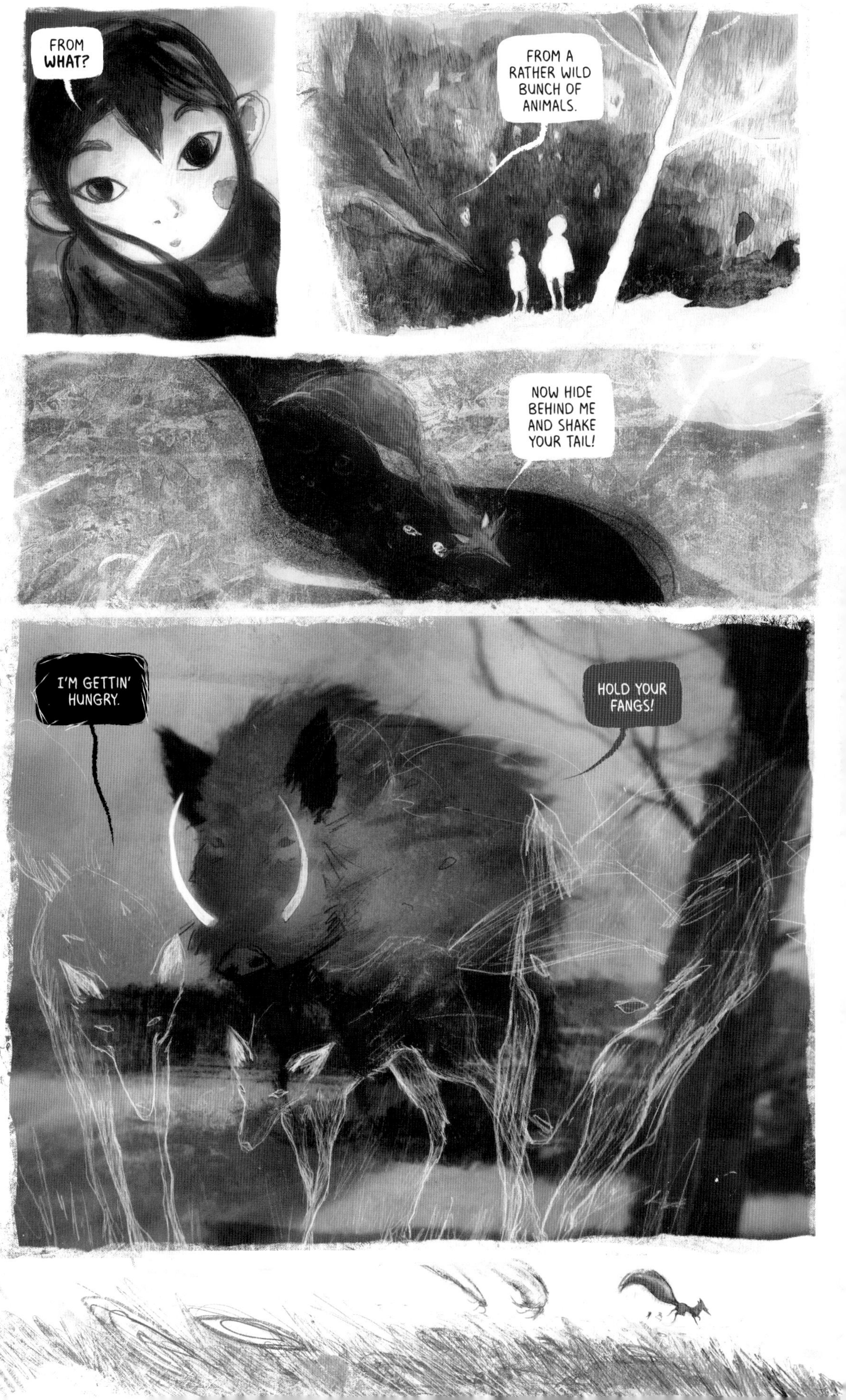
FROM WHAT?
FROM A RATHER WILD BUNCH OF ANIMALS.
NOW HIDE BEHIND ME AND SHAKE YOUR TAIL!
I'M GETTIN' HUNGRY.
HOLD YOUR FANGS!

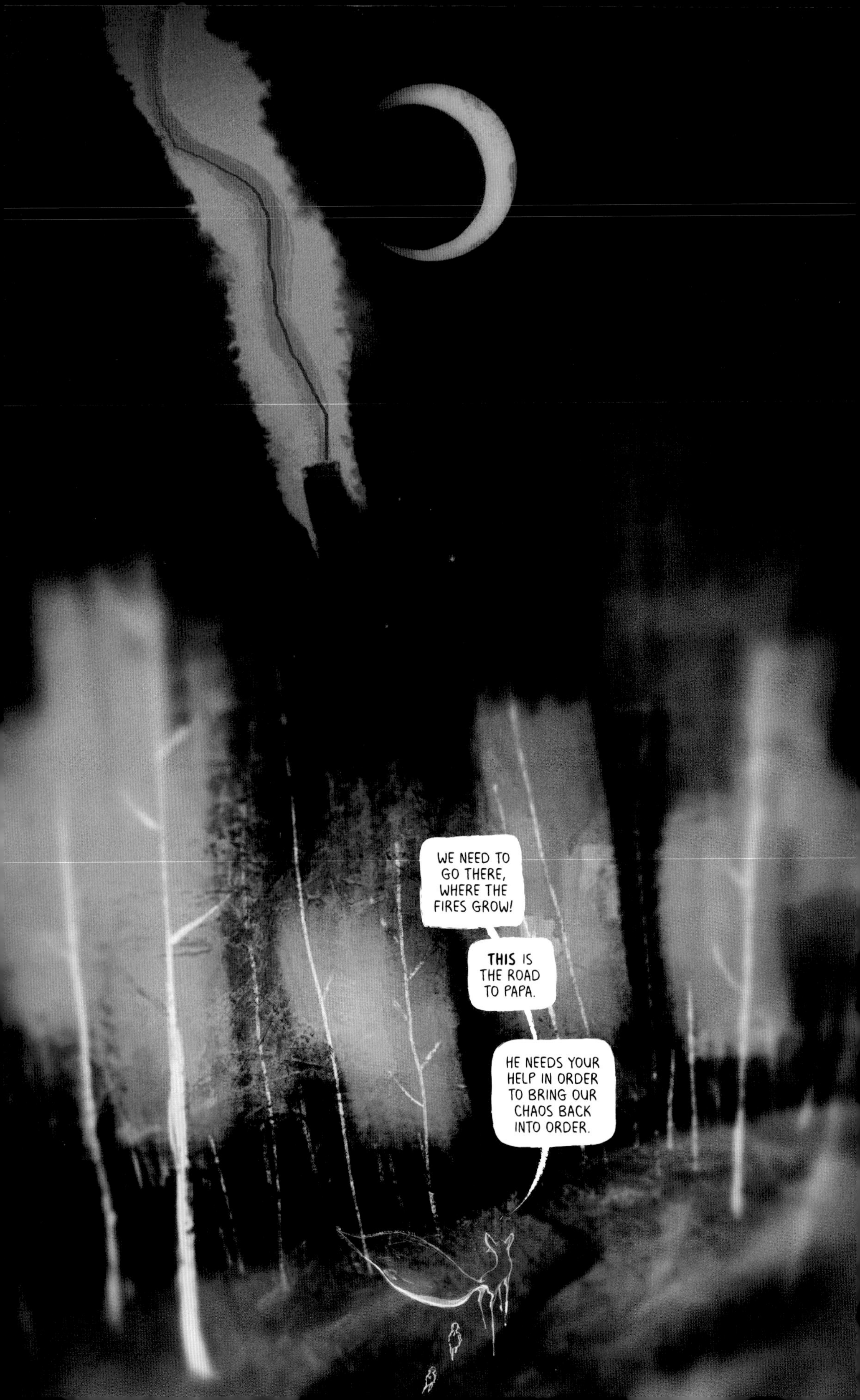
WE NEED TO GO THERE, WHERE THE FIRES GROW!
THIS IS THE ROAD TO PAPA.
HE NEEDS YOUR HELP IN ORDER TO BRING OUR CHAOS BACK INTO ORDER.

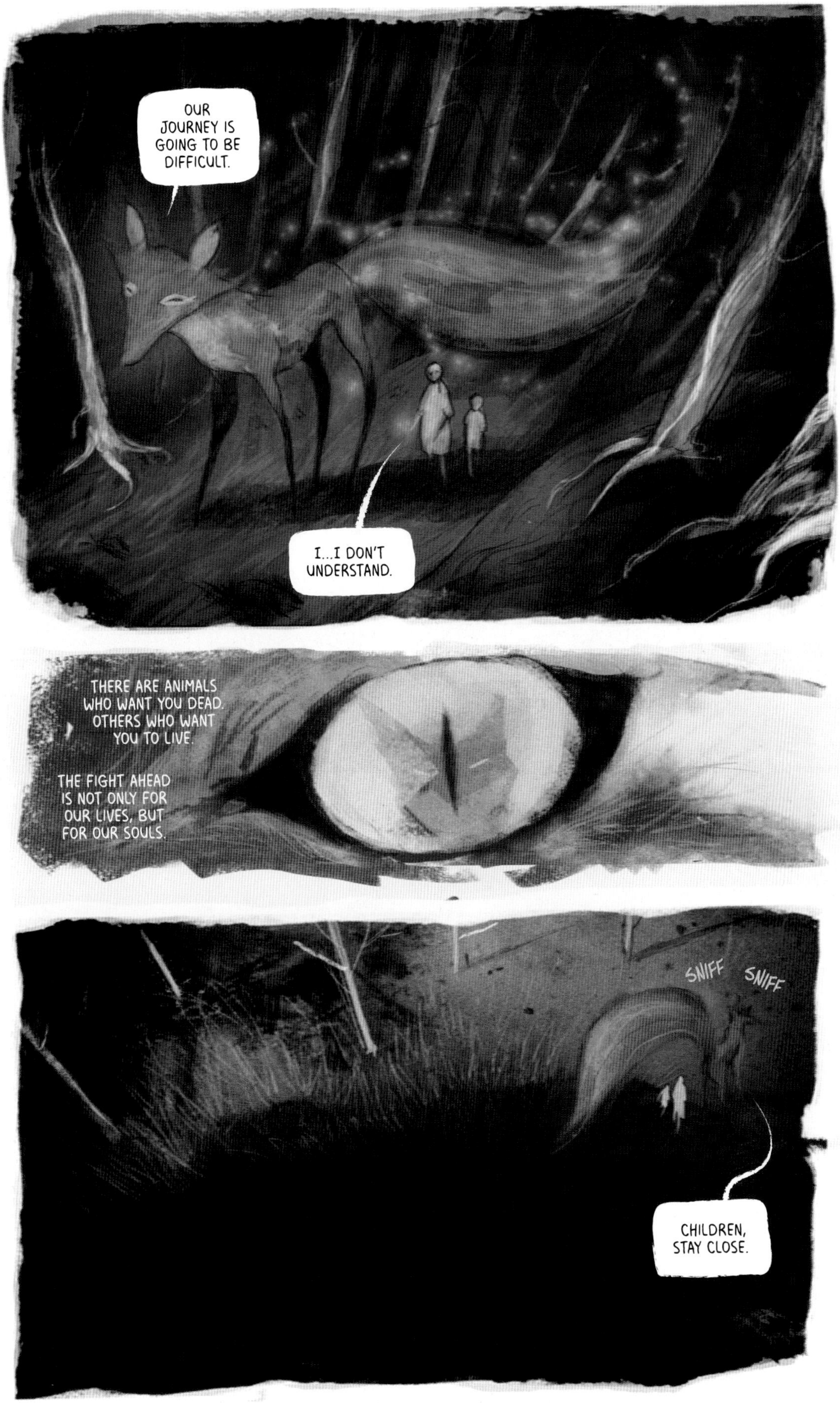
OUR JOURNEY IS GOING TO BE DIFFICULT.
I...I DON'T UNDERSTAND.
THERE ARE ANIMALS WHO WANT YOU DEAD. OTHERS WHO WANT YOU TO LIVE.
THE FIGHT AHEAD IS NOT ONLY FOR OUR LIVES, BUT FOR OUR SOULS.
SNIFF
SNIFF
CHILDREN, STAY CLOSE.

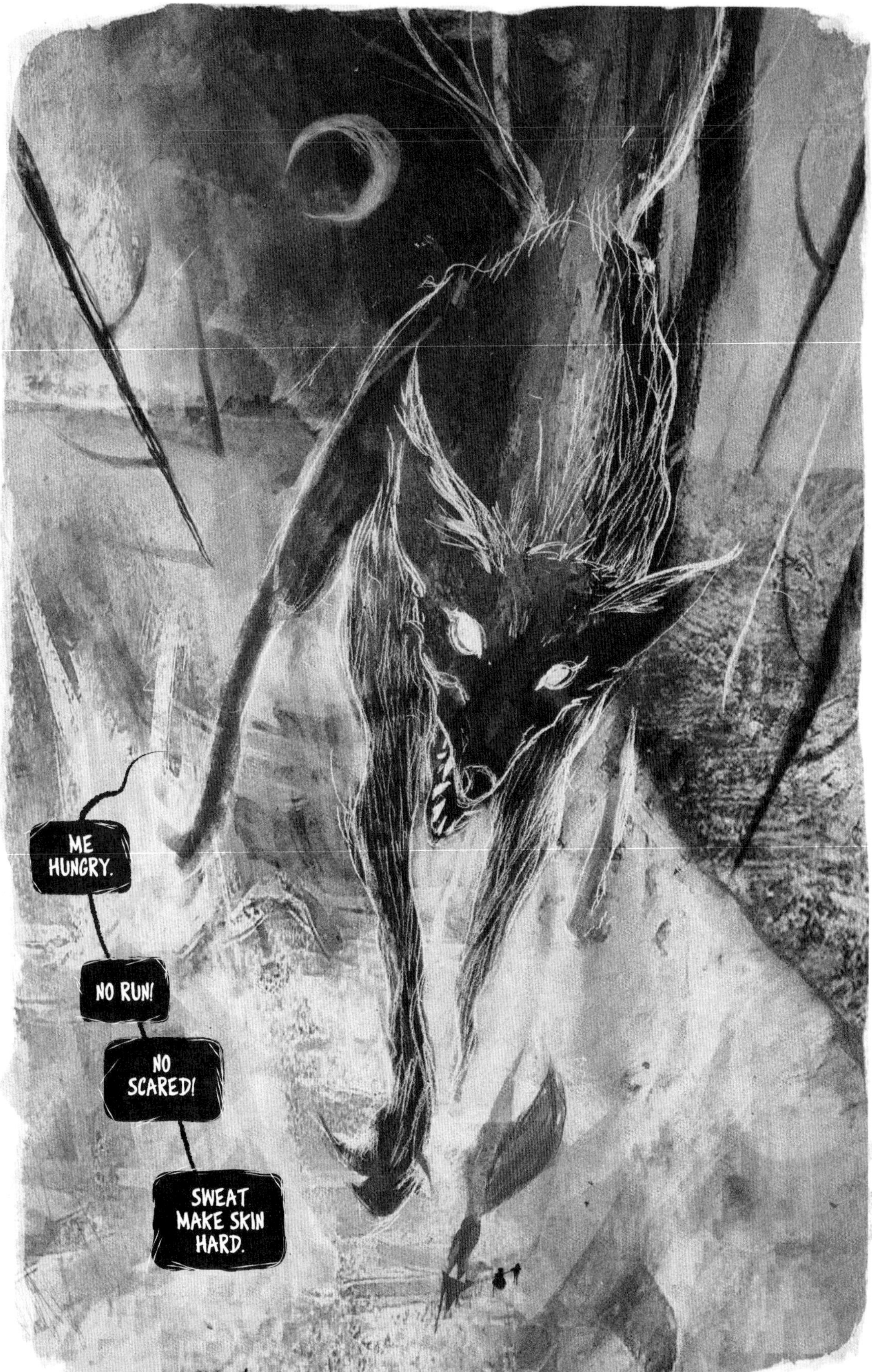
ME HUNGRY.
NO RUN!
NO SCARED!
SWEAT MAKE SKIN HARD.

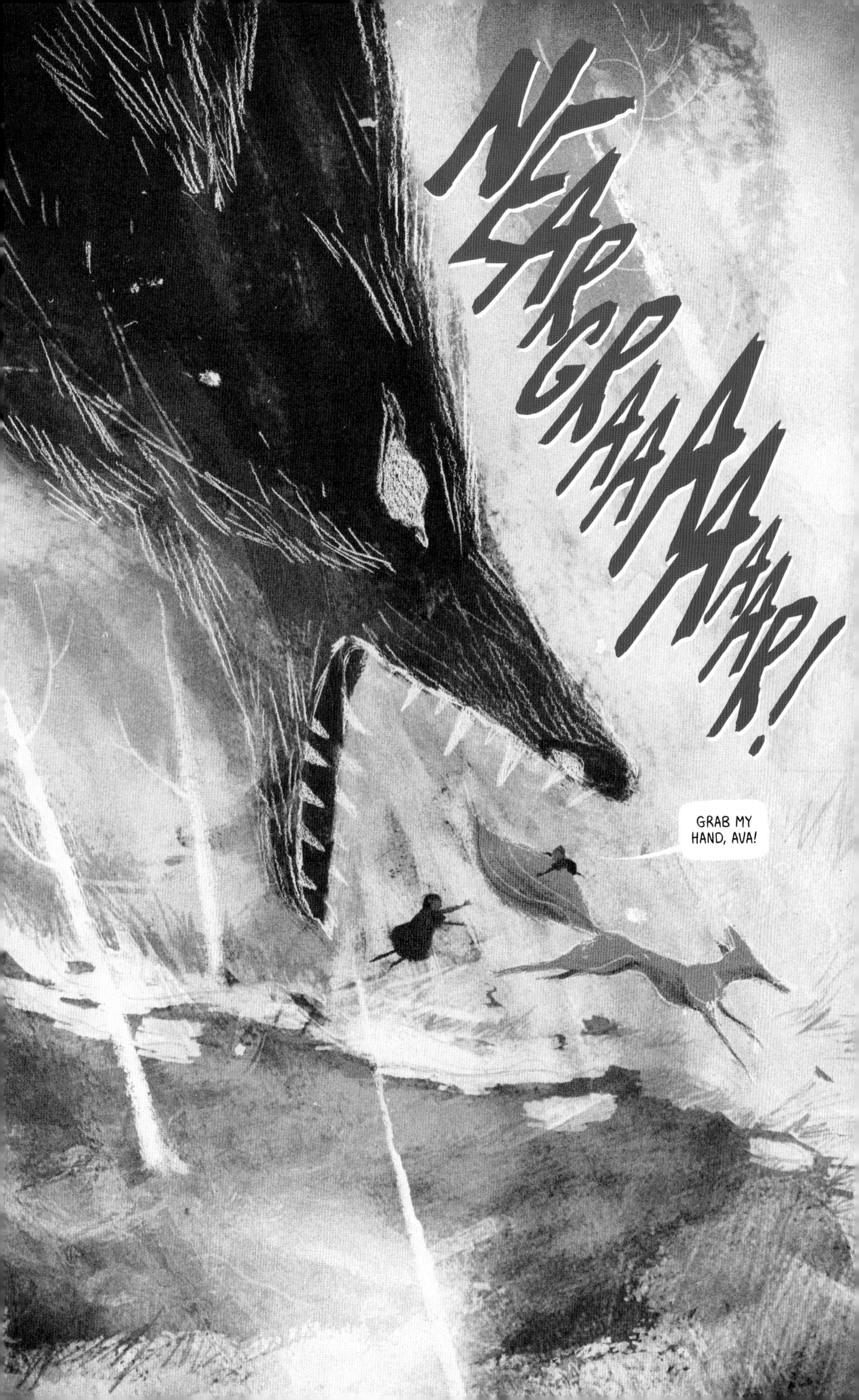
NYARGRAAAAAAR!
GRAB MY HAND, AVA!

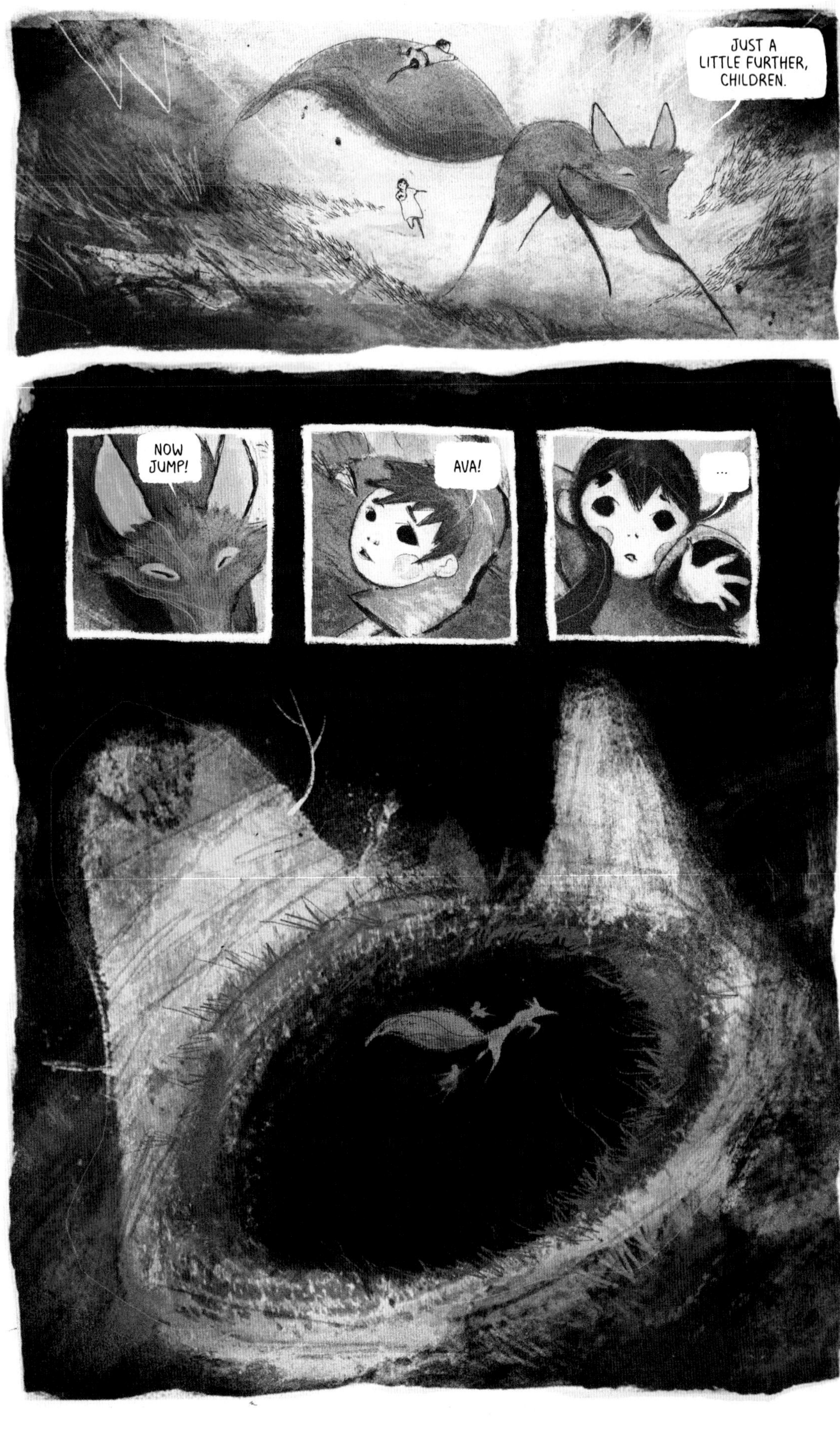
JUST A LITTLE FURTHER, CHILDREN.
NOW JUMP!
AVA!
...

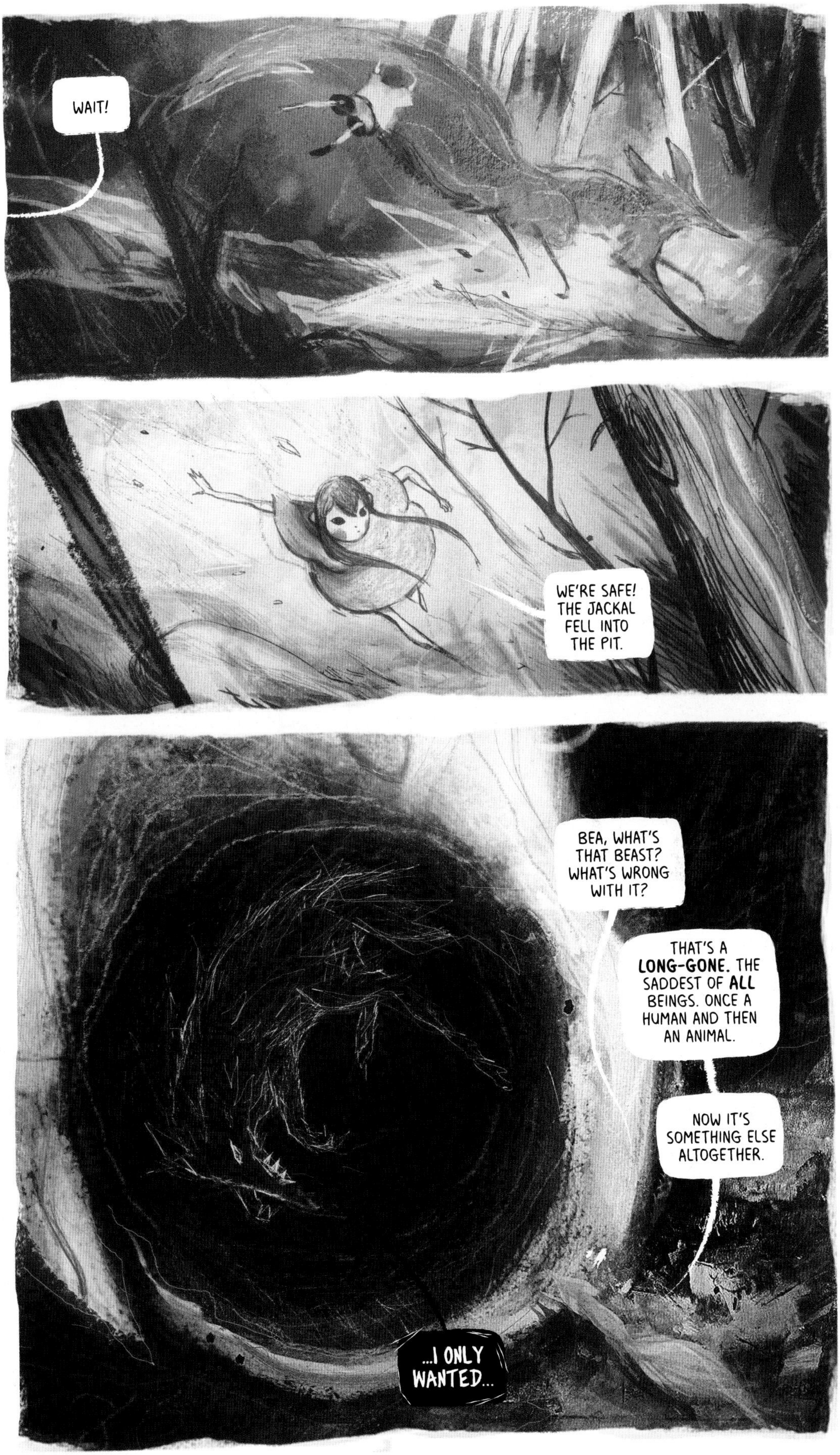
WAIT!
WE'RE SAFE! THE JACKAL FELL INTO THE PIT.
BEA, WHAT'S THAT BEAST? WHAT'S WRONG WITH IT?
THAT'S A **LONG-GONE.** THE SADDEST OF **ALL** BEINGS. ONCE A HUMAN AND THEN AN ANIMAL.
NOW IT'S SOMETHING ELSE ALTOGETHER.
...I ONLY WANTED...

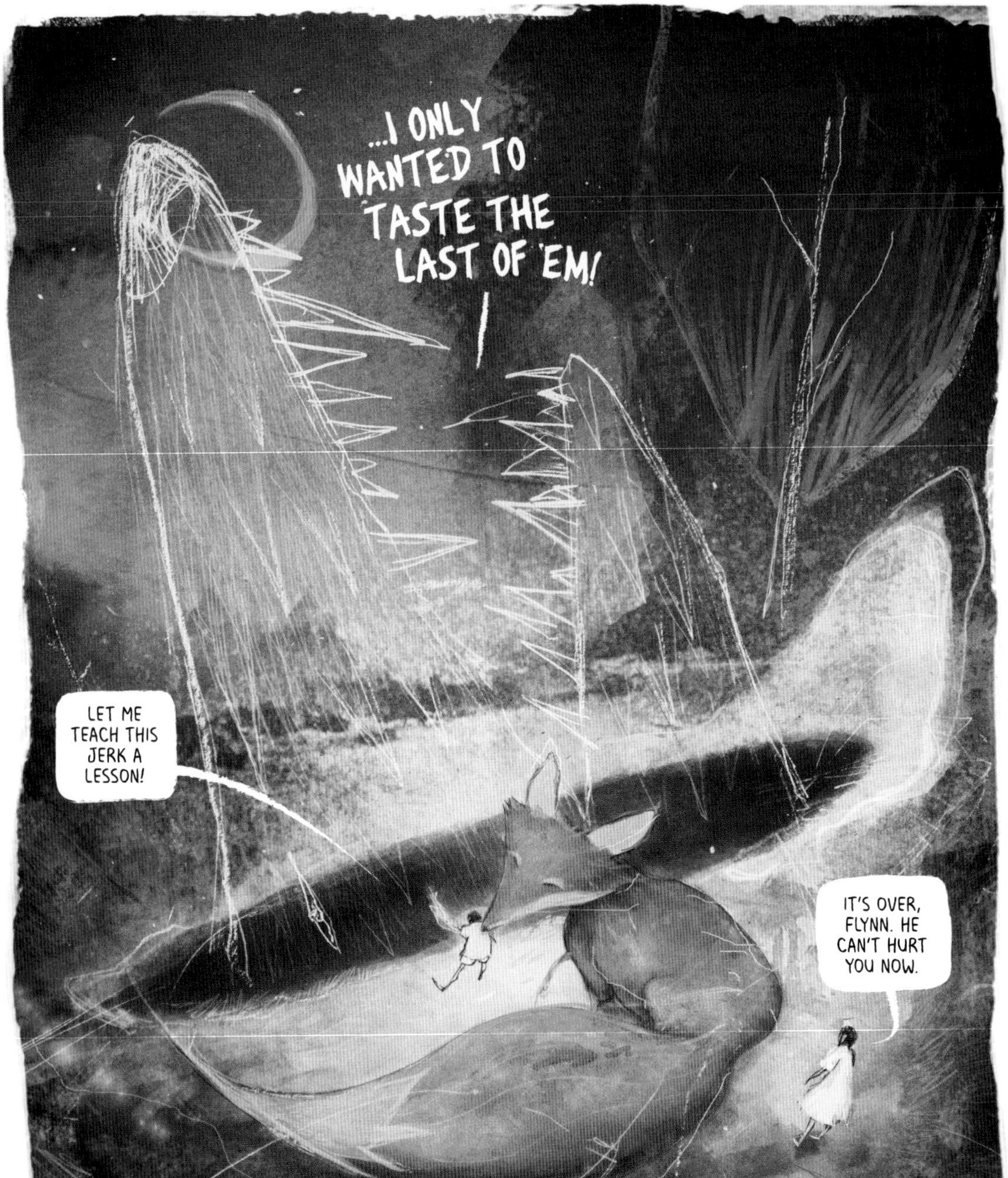
...I ONLY WANTED TO TASTE THE LAST OF 'EM!
LET ME TEACH THIS JERK A LESSON!
IT'S OVER, FLYNN. HE CAN'T HURT YOU NOW.

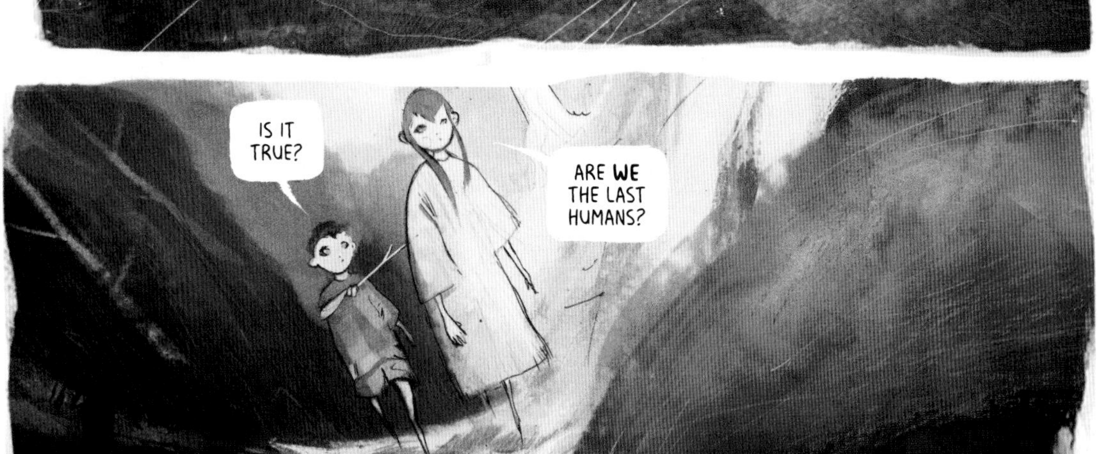
IS IT TRUE?
ARE **WE** THE LAST HUMANS?

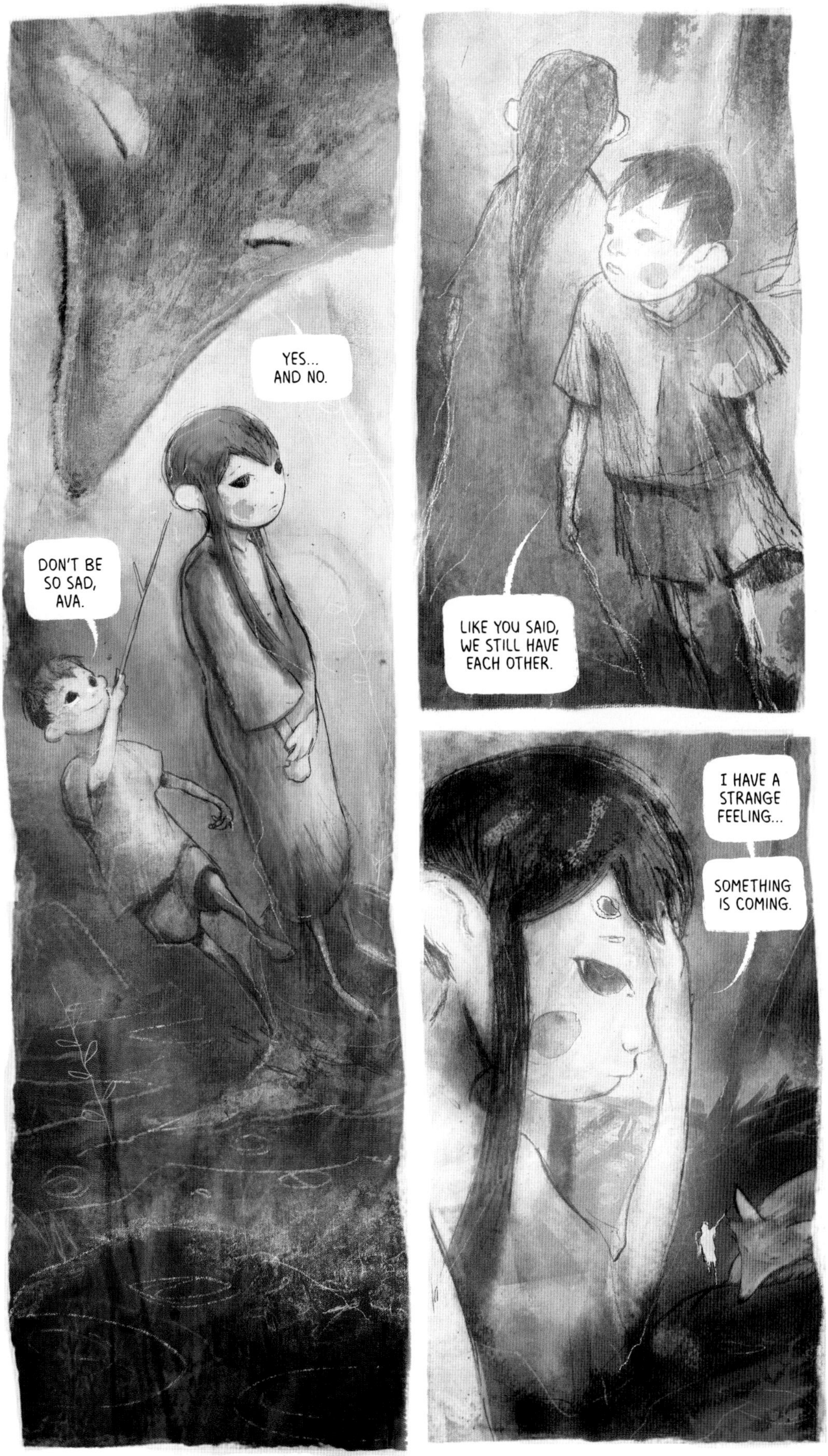
YES... AND NO.
DON'T BE SO SAD, AVA.
LIKE YOU SAID, WE STILL HAVE EACH OTHER.
I HAVE A STRANGE FEELING...
SOMETHING IS COMING.

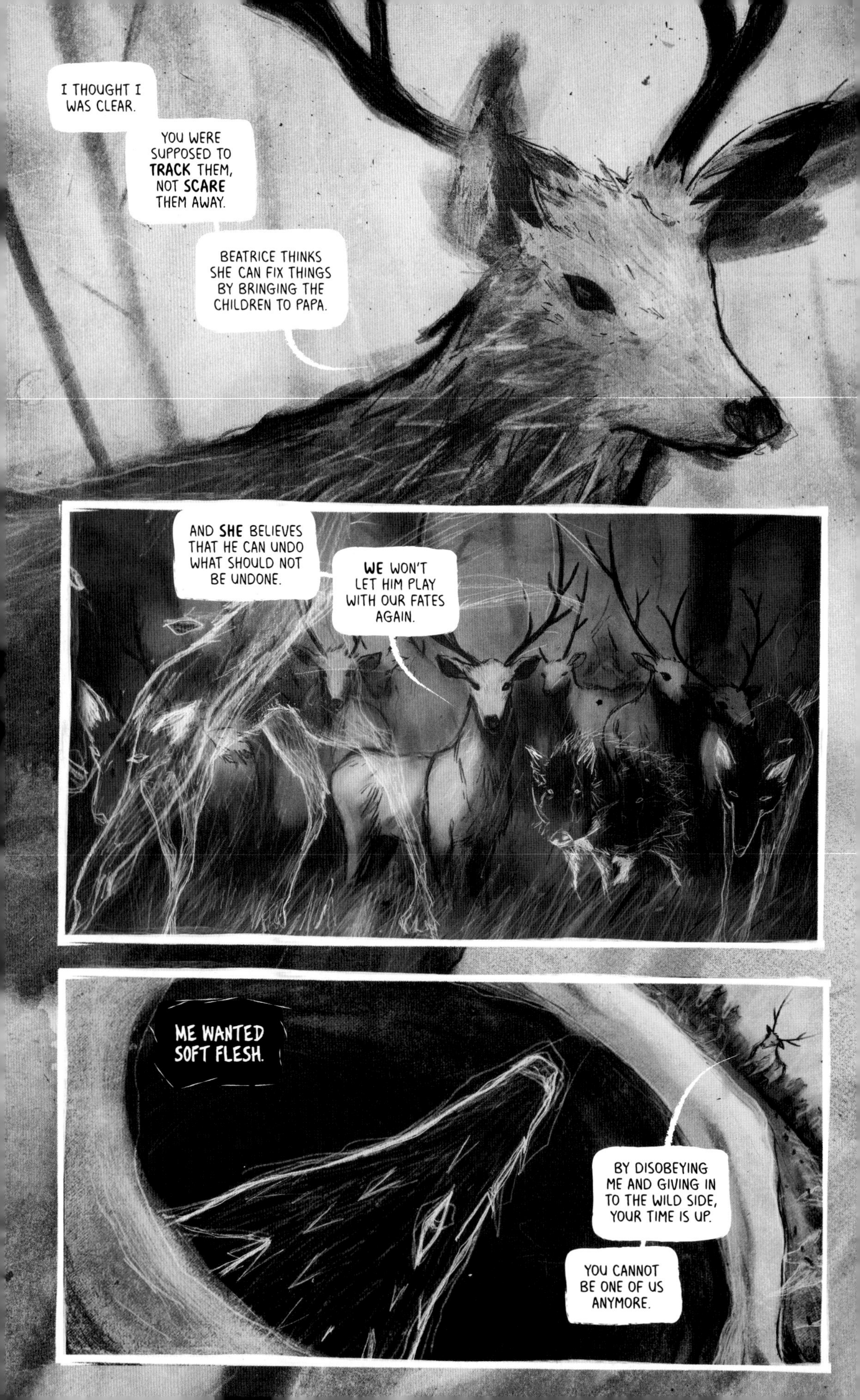
I THOUGHT I WAS CLEAR.
YOU WERE SUPPOSED TO **TRACK** THEM, NOT **SCARE** THEM AWAY.
BEATRICE THINKS SHE CAN FIX THINGS BY BRINGING THE CHILDREN TO PAPA.
AND **SHE** BELIEVES THAT HE CAN UNDO WHAT SHOULD NOT BE UNDONE.
WE WON'T LET HIM PLAY WITH OUR FATES AGAIN.
ME WANTED SOFT FLESH.
BY DISOBEYING ME AND GIVING IN TO THE WILD SIDE, YOUR TIME IS UP.
YOU CANNOT BE ONE OF US ANYMORE.

~WHINE~...
ME GOOD...

FOR NOW YOU'RE A LONG-GONE BUT SOON YOU WILL DISINTEGRATE AND BECOME ONE WITH THE EARTH.

DON'T YOU WANT TO BE USEFUL BEFORE YOU CEASE TO EXIST? DON'T YOU WANT TO NOURISH YOUR BROTHERS AND SISTERS?

IT'S ALL YOU'RE GOOD FOR NOW.

ME NO FOOD.

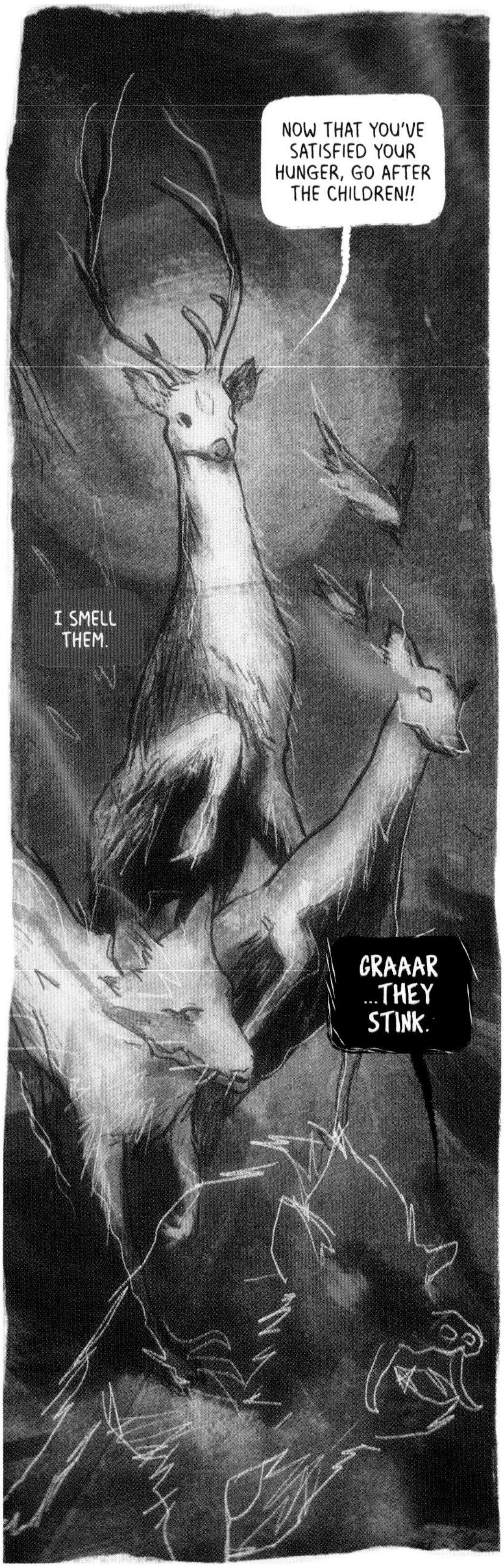
NOW THAT YOU'VE SATISFIED YOUR HUNGER, GO AFTER THE CHILDREN!!
I SMELL THEM.
GRAAAR ...THEY STINK.

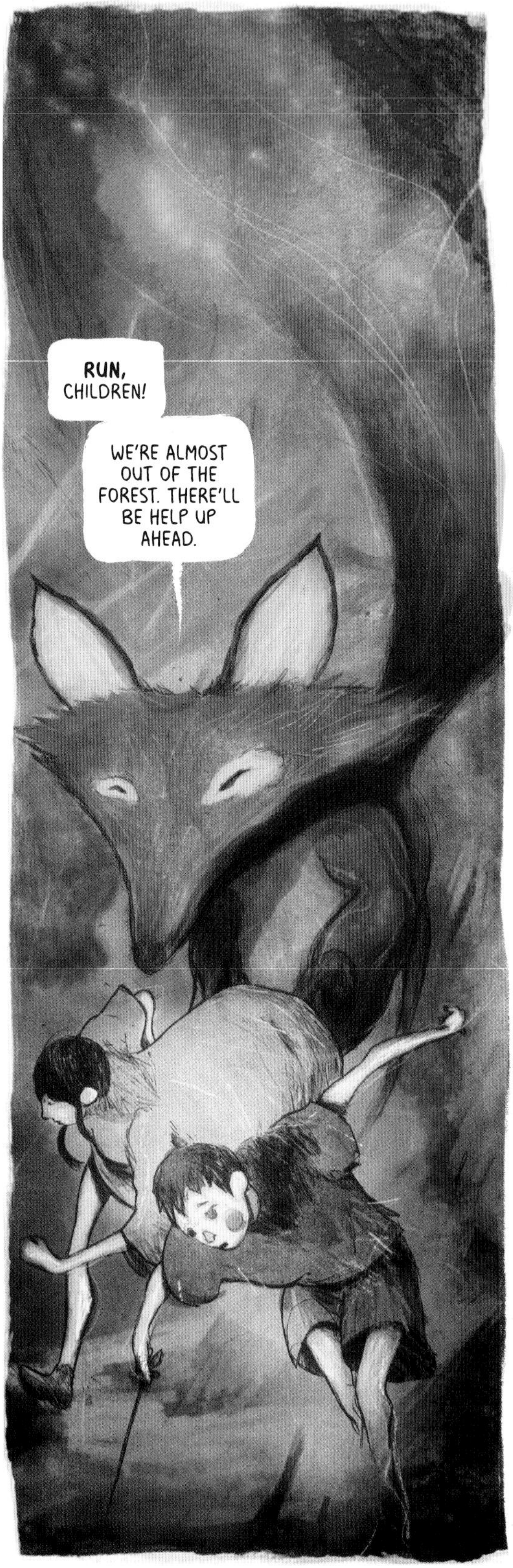
RUN, CHILDREN!
WE'RE ALMOST OUT OF THE FOREST. THERE'LL BE HELP UP AHEAD.

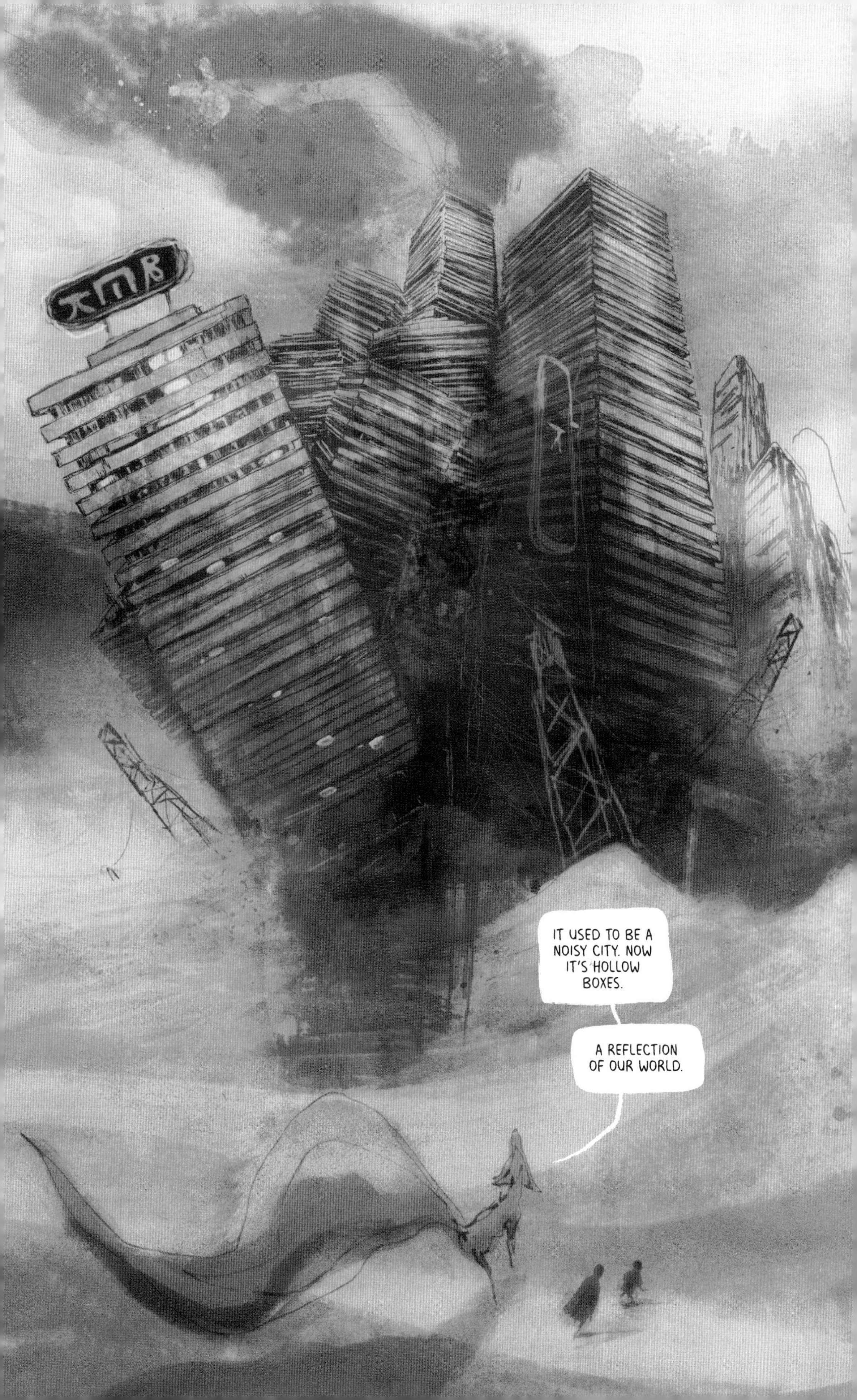
IT USED TO BE A NOISY CITY. NOW IT'S HOLLOW BOXES.
A REFLECTION OF OUR WORLD.

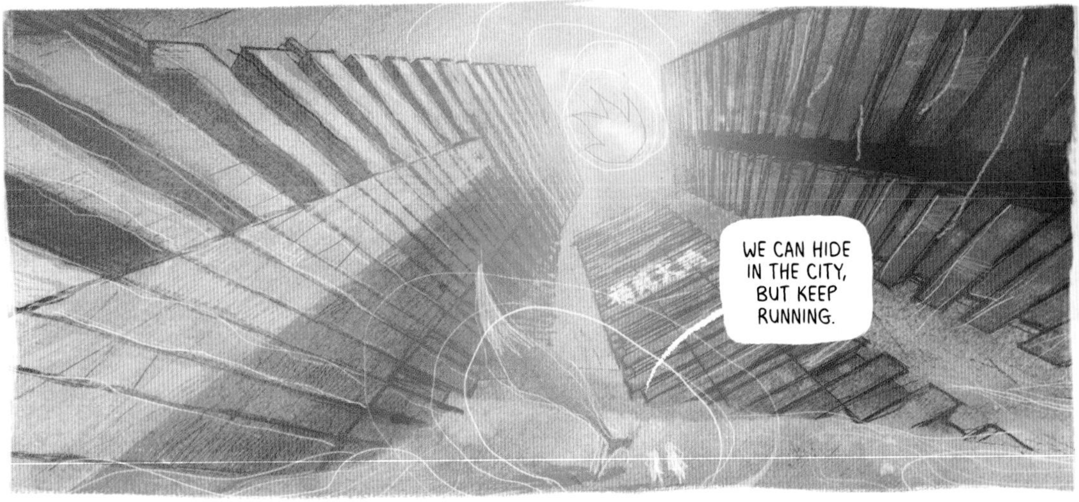
WE CAN HIDE IN THE CITY, BUT KEEP RUNNING.

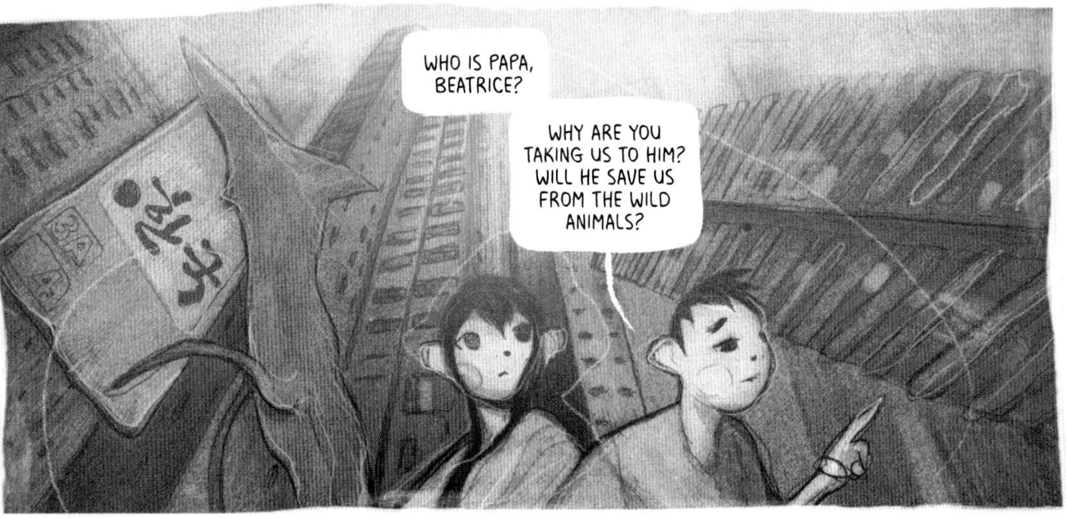
WHO IS PAPA, BEATRICE?
WHY ARE YOU TAKING US TO HIM? WILL HE SAVE US FROM THE WILD ANIMALS?

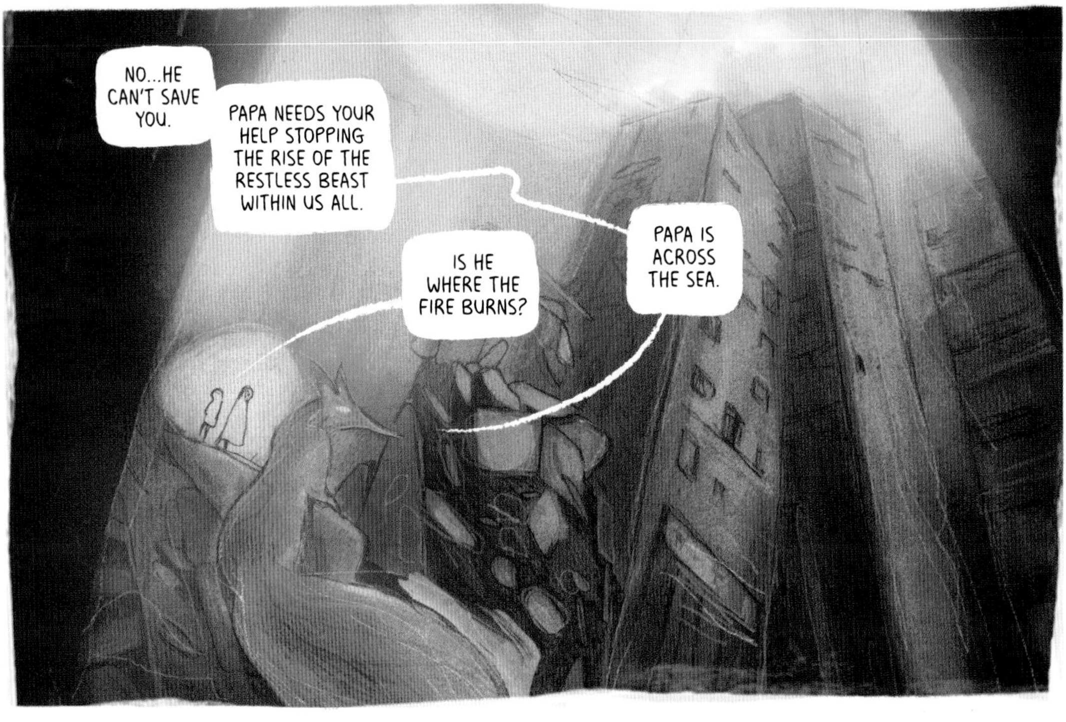
NO...HE CAN'T SAVE YOU.
PAPA NEEDS YOUR HELP STOPPING THE RISE OF THE RESTLESS BEAST WITHIN US ALL.
PAPA IS ACROSS THE SEA.
IS HE WHERE THE FIRE BURNS?

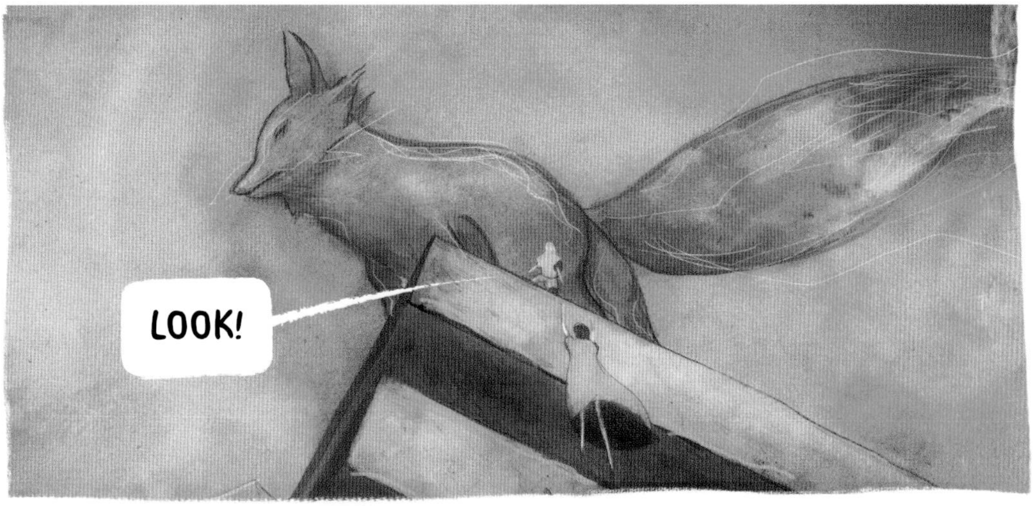
LOOK!

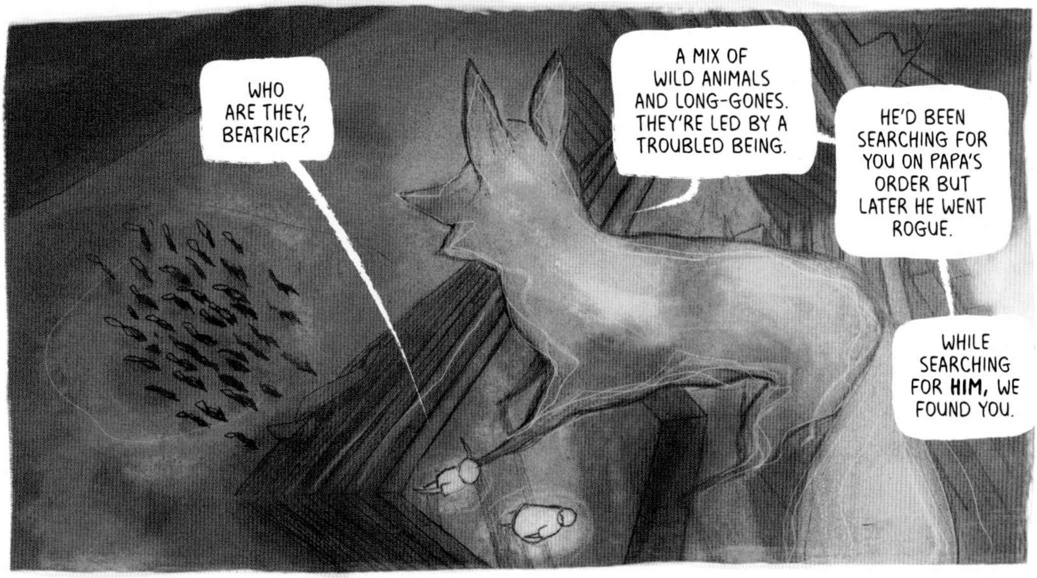
WHO ARE THEY, BEATRICE?
A MIX OF WILD ANIMALS AND LONG-GONES. THEY'RE LED BY A TROUBLED BEING.
HE'D BEEN SEARCHING FOR YOU ON PAPA'S ORDER BUT LATER HE WENT ROGUE.
WHILE SEARCHING FOR **HIM,** WE FOUND YOU.

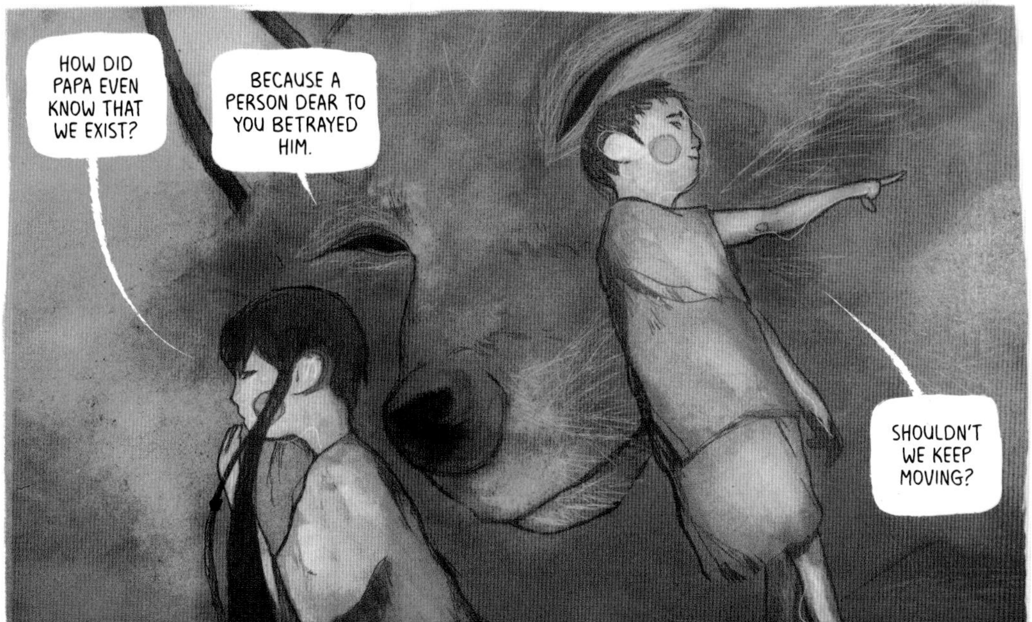
HOW DID PAPA EVEN KNOW THAT WE EXIST?
BECAUSE A PERSON DEAR TO YOU BETRAYED HIM.
SHOULDN'T WE KEEP MOVING?

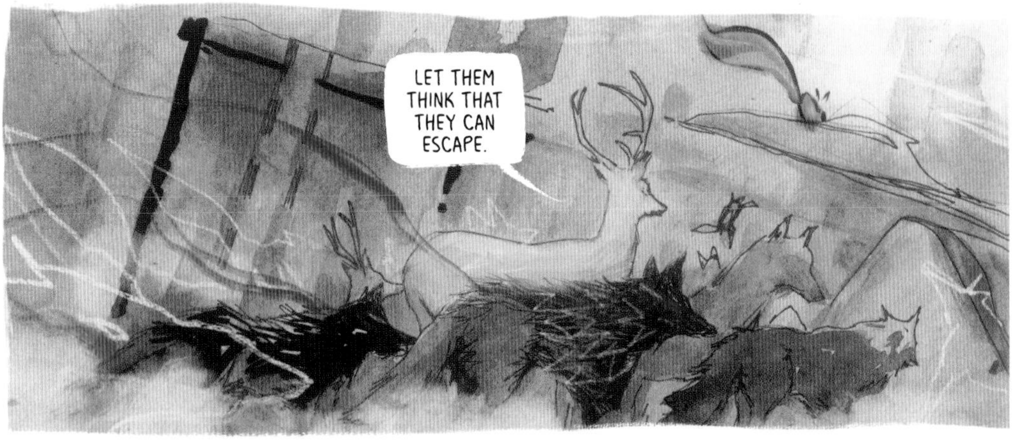
LET THEM THINK THAT THEY CAN ESCAPE.

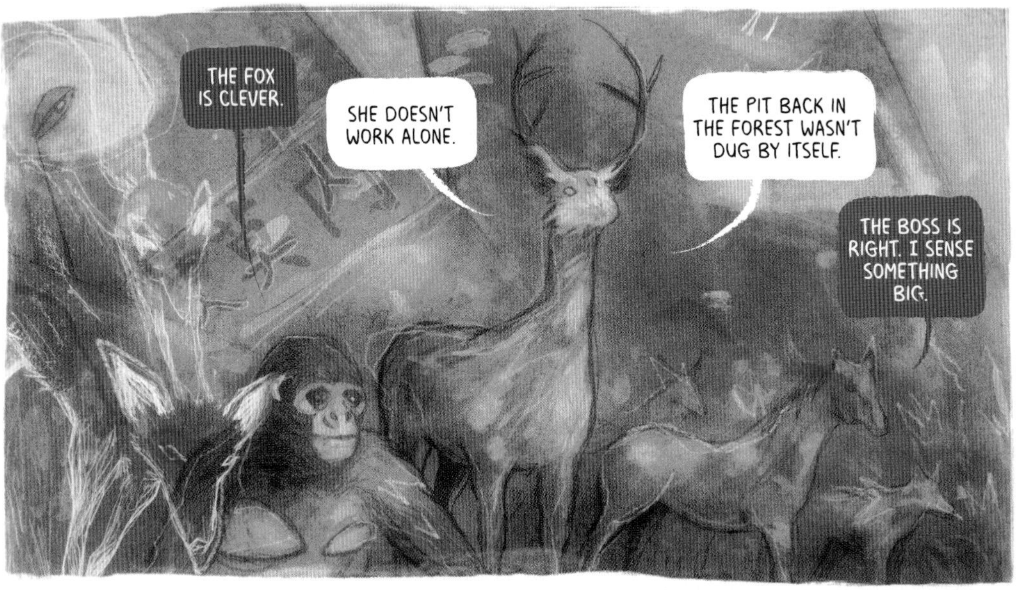
THE FOX IS CLEVER.
SHE DOESN'T WORK ALONE.
THE PIT BACK IN THE FOREST WASN'T DUG BY ITSELF.
THE BOSS IS RIGHT. I SENSE SOMETHING BIG.

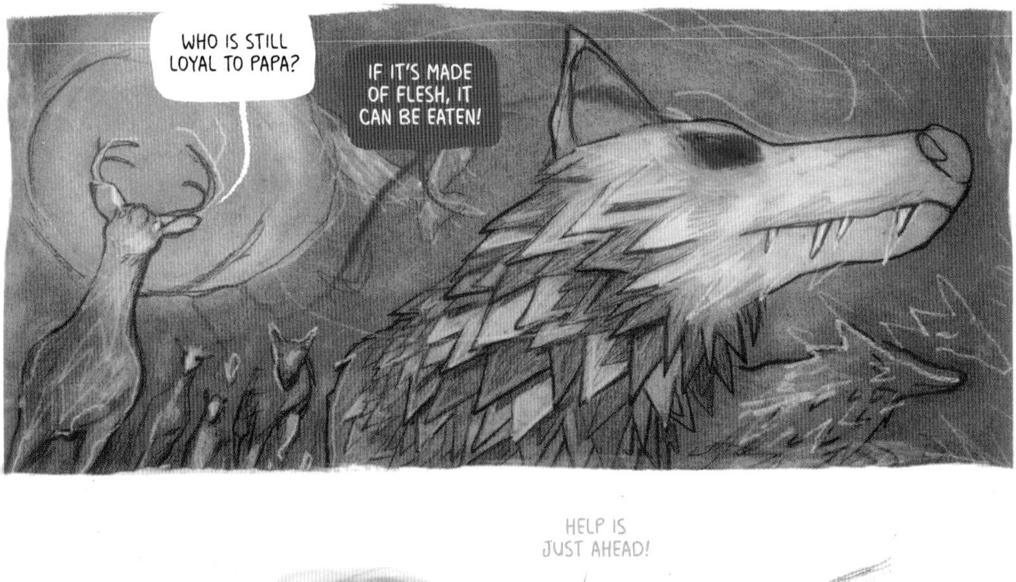
WHO IS STILL LOYAL TO PAPA?
IF IT'S MADE OF FLESH, IT CAN BE EATEN!

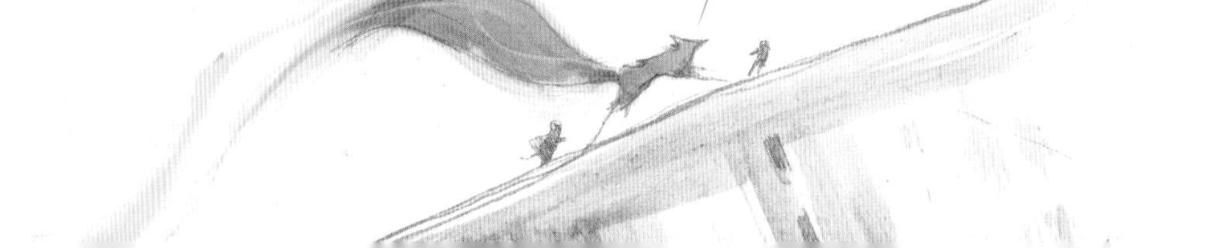
HELP IS JUST AHEAD!

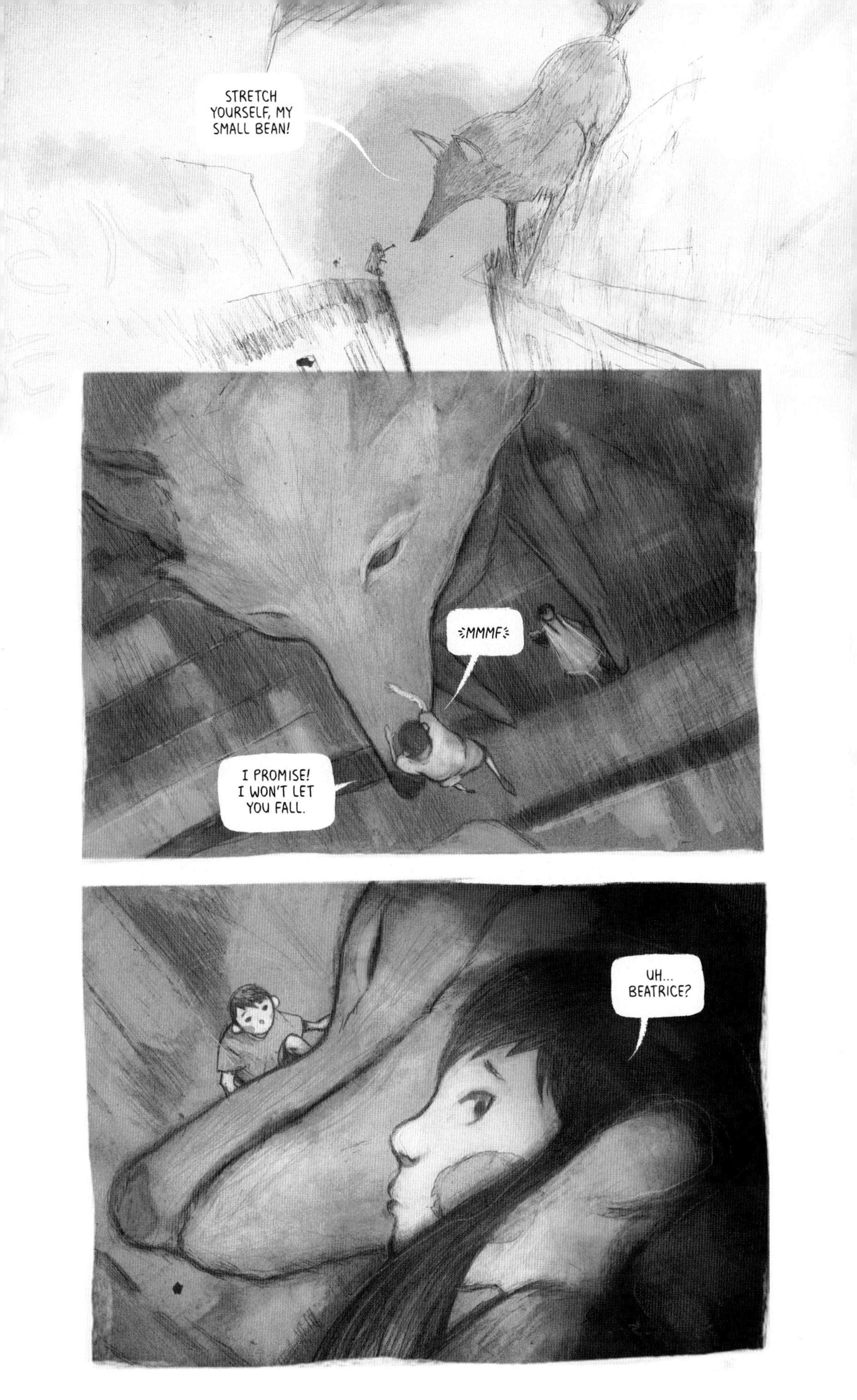
STRETCH YOURSELF, MY SMALL BEAN!
MMMF
I PROMISE! I WON'T LET YOU FALL.
UH... BEATRICE?

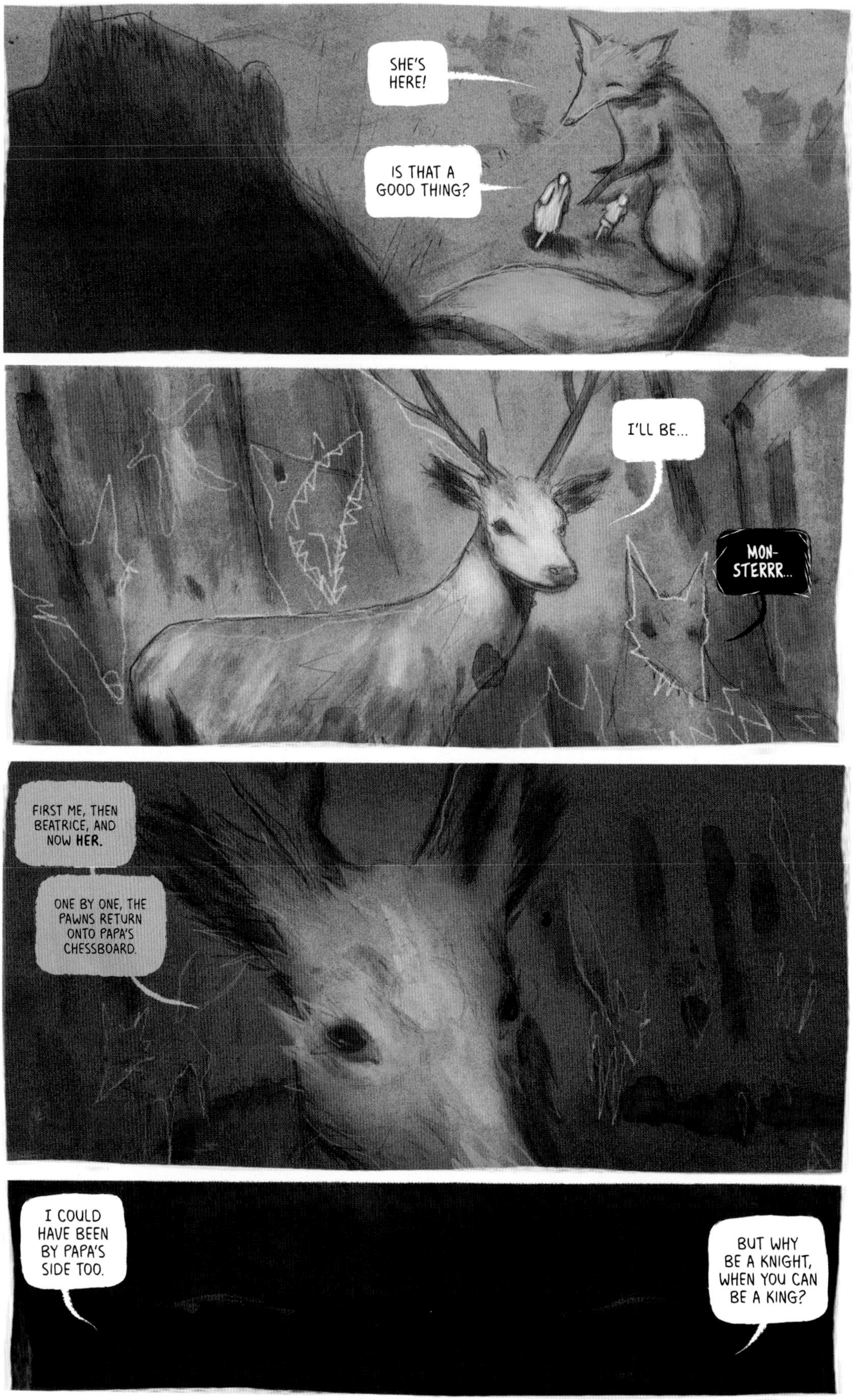
SHE'S HERE!
IS THAT A GOOD THING?
I'LL BE...
MON-STERRR...
FIRST ME, THEN BEATRICE, AND NOW **HER.**
ONE BY ONE, THE PAWNS RETURN ONTO PAPA'S CHESSBOARD.
I COULD HAVE BEEN BY PAPA'S SIDE TOO.
BUT WHY BE A KNIGHT, WHEN YOU CAN BE A KING?

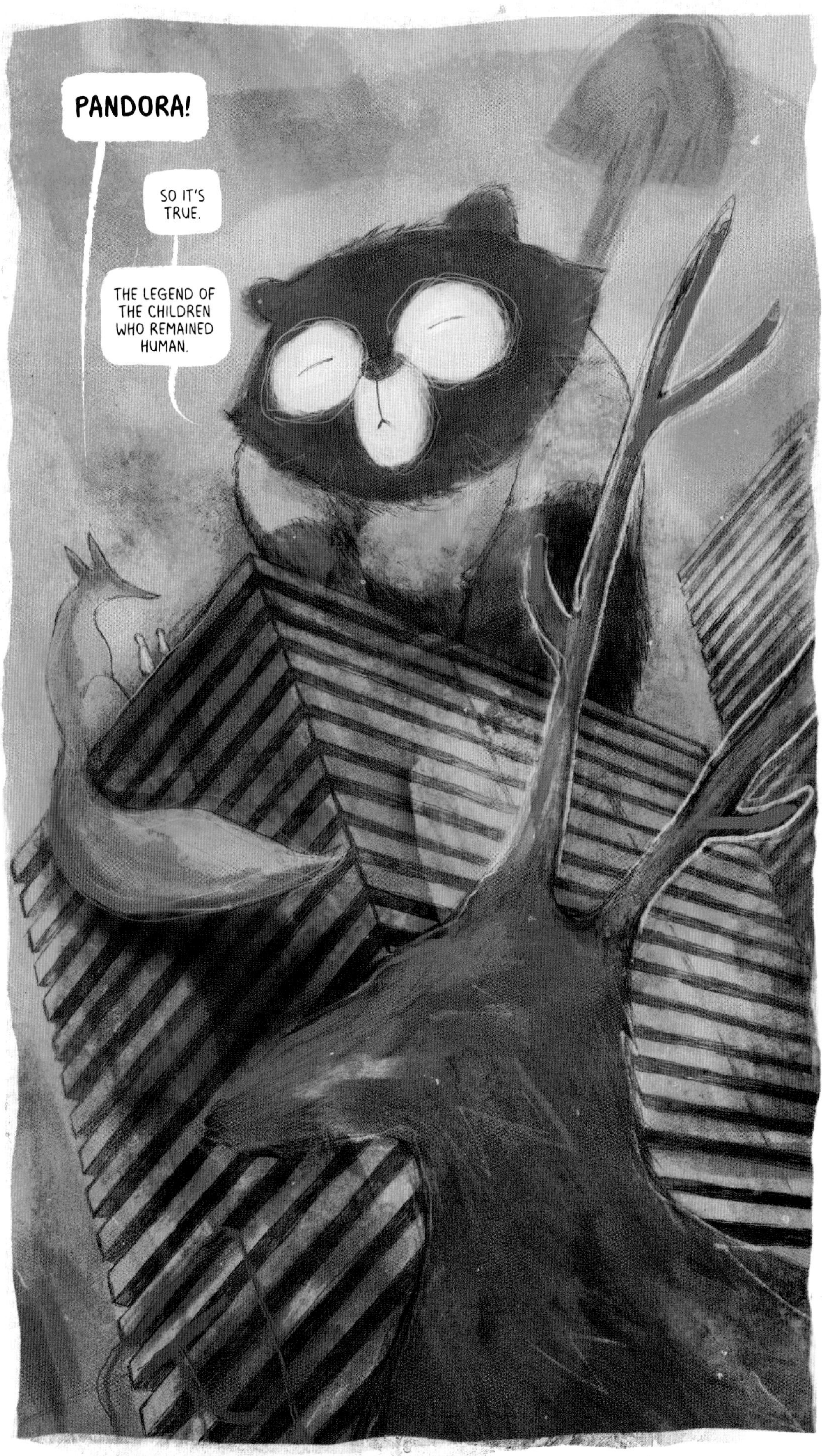
PANDORA!
SO IT'S TRUE.
THE LEGEND OF THE CHILDREN WHO REMAINED HUMAN.

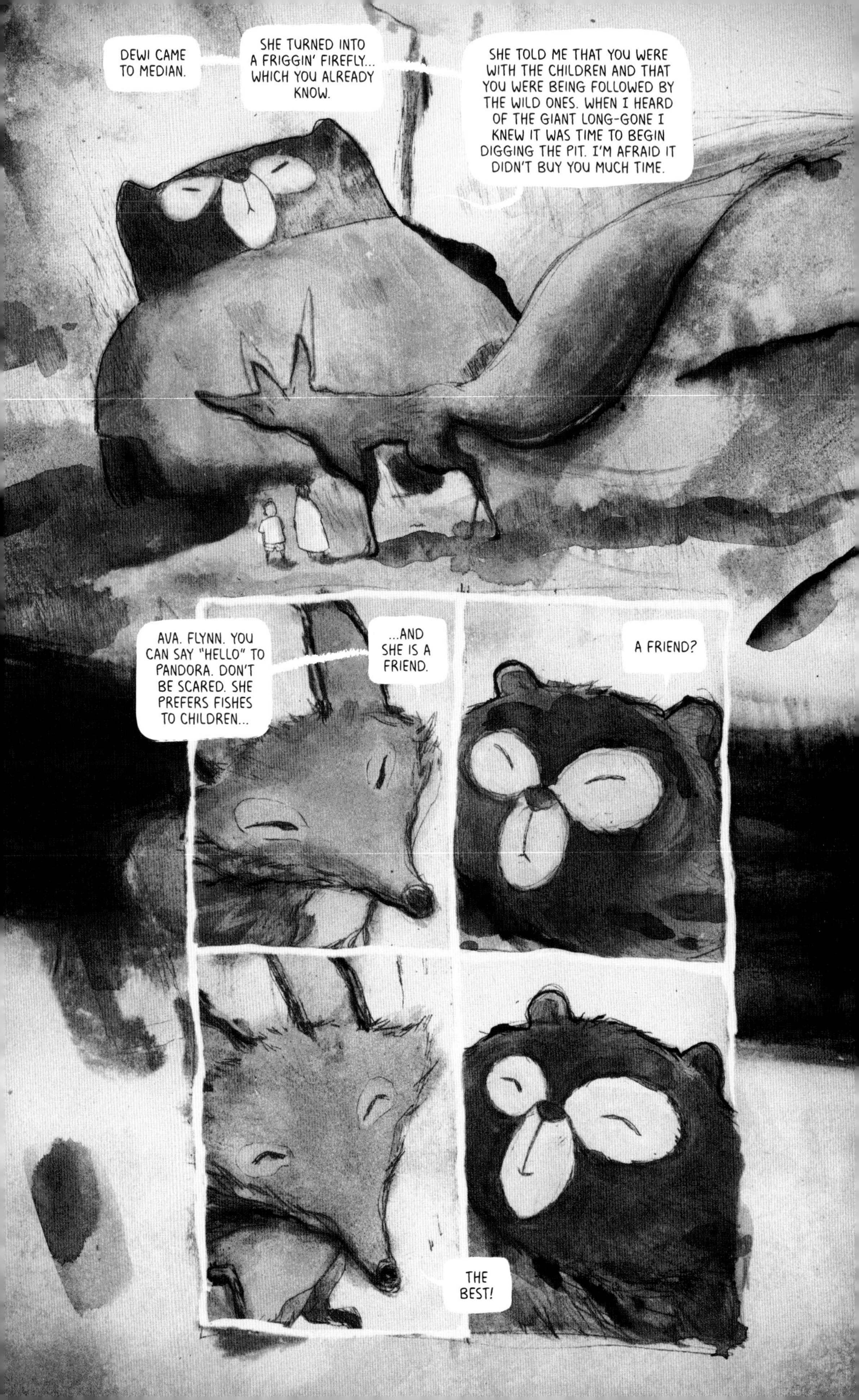
DEWI CAME TO MEDIAN.
SHE TURNED INTO A FRIGGIN' FIREFLY... WHICH YOU ALREADY KNOW.
SHE TOLD ME THAT YOU WERE WITH THE CHILDREN AND THAT YOU WERE BEING FOLLOWED BY THE WILD ONES. WHEN I HEARD OF THE GIANT LONG-GONE I KNEW IT WAS TIME TO BEGIN DIGGING THE PIT. I'M AFRAID IT DIDN'T BUY YOU MUCH TIME.
AVA. FLYNN. YOU CAN SAY "HELLO" TO PANDORA. DON'T BE SCARED. SHE PREFERS FISHES TO CHILDREN...
...AND SHE IS A FRIEND.
A FRIEND?
THE BEST!

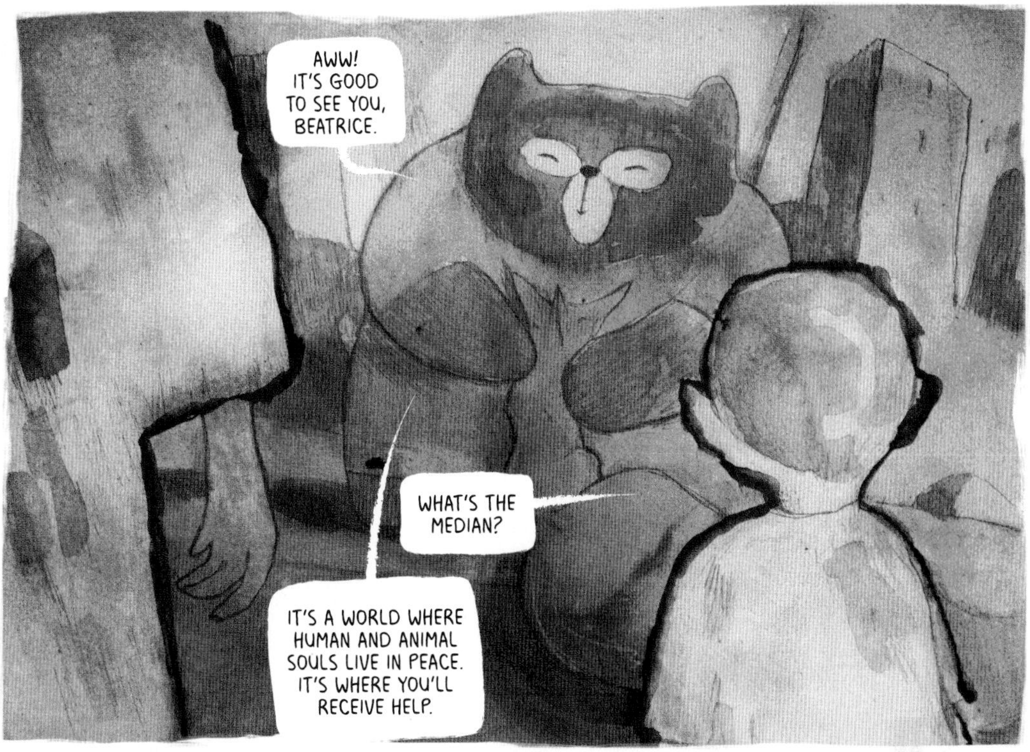
AWW! IT'S GOOD TO SEE YOU, BEATRICE.
WHAT'S THE MEDIAN?
IT'S A WORLD WHERE HUMAN AND ANIMAL SOULS LIVE IN PEACE. IT'S WHERE YOU'LL RECEIVE HELP.

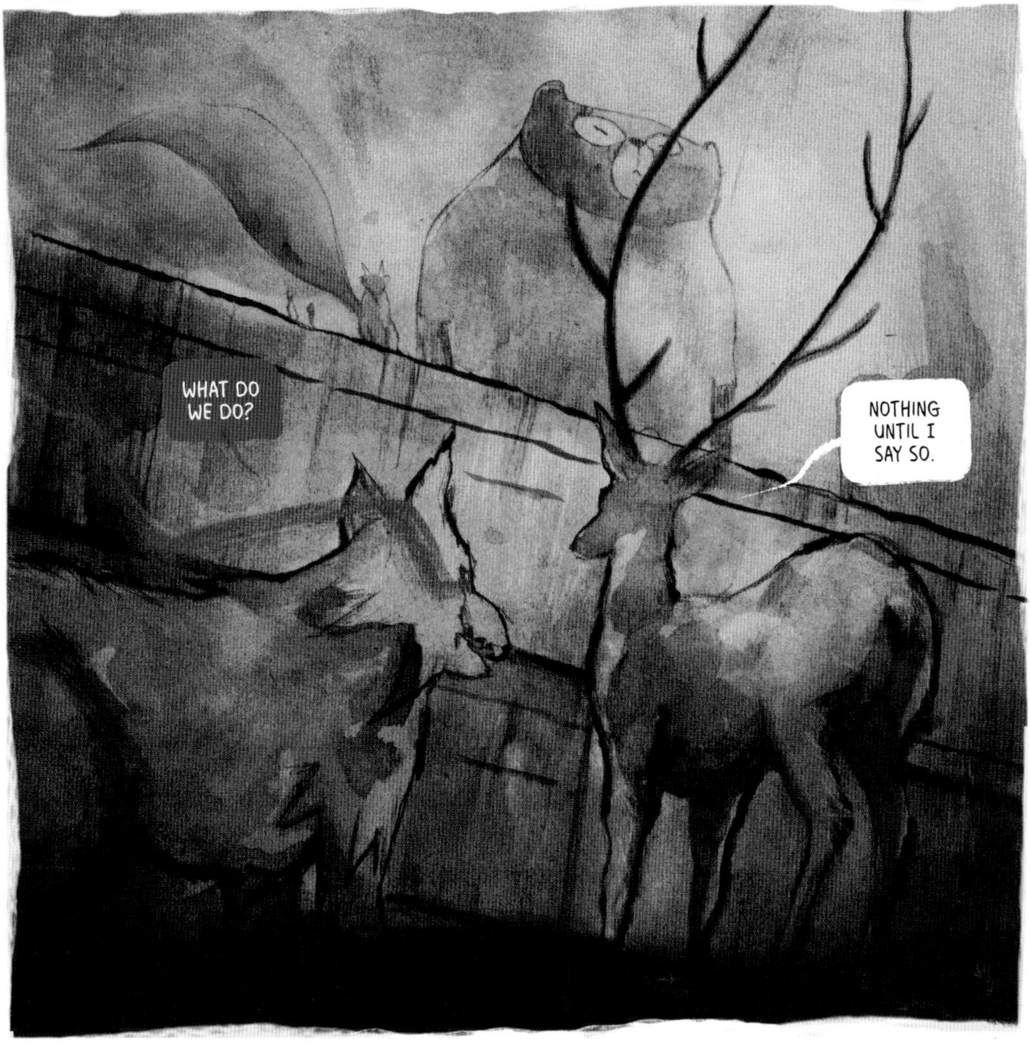
WHAT DO WE DO?
NOTHING UNTIL I SAY SO.

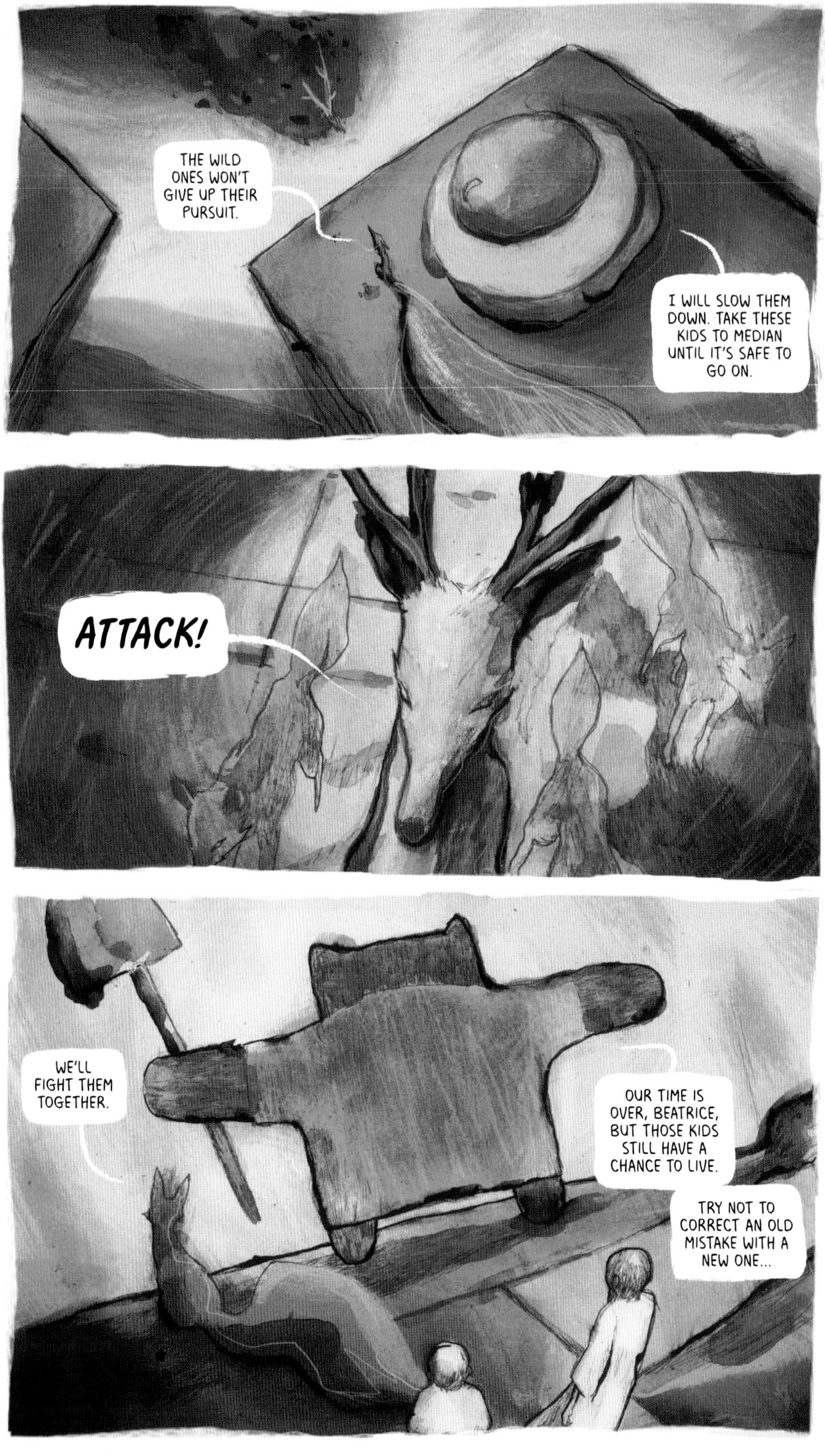
THE WILD ONES WON'T GIVE UP THEIR PURSUIT.
I WILL SLOW THEM DOWN. TAKE THESE KIDS TO MEDIAN UNTIL IT'S SAFE TO GO ON.
ATTACK!
WE'LL FIGHT THEM TOGETHER.
OUR TIME IS OVER, BEATRICE, BUT THOSE KIDS STILL HAVE A CHANCE TO LIVE.
TRY NOT TO CORRECT AN OLD MISTAKE WITH A NEW ONE...

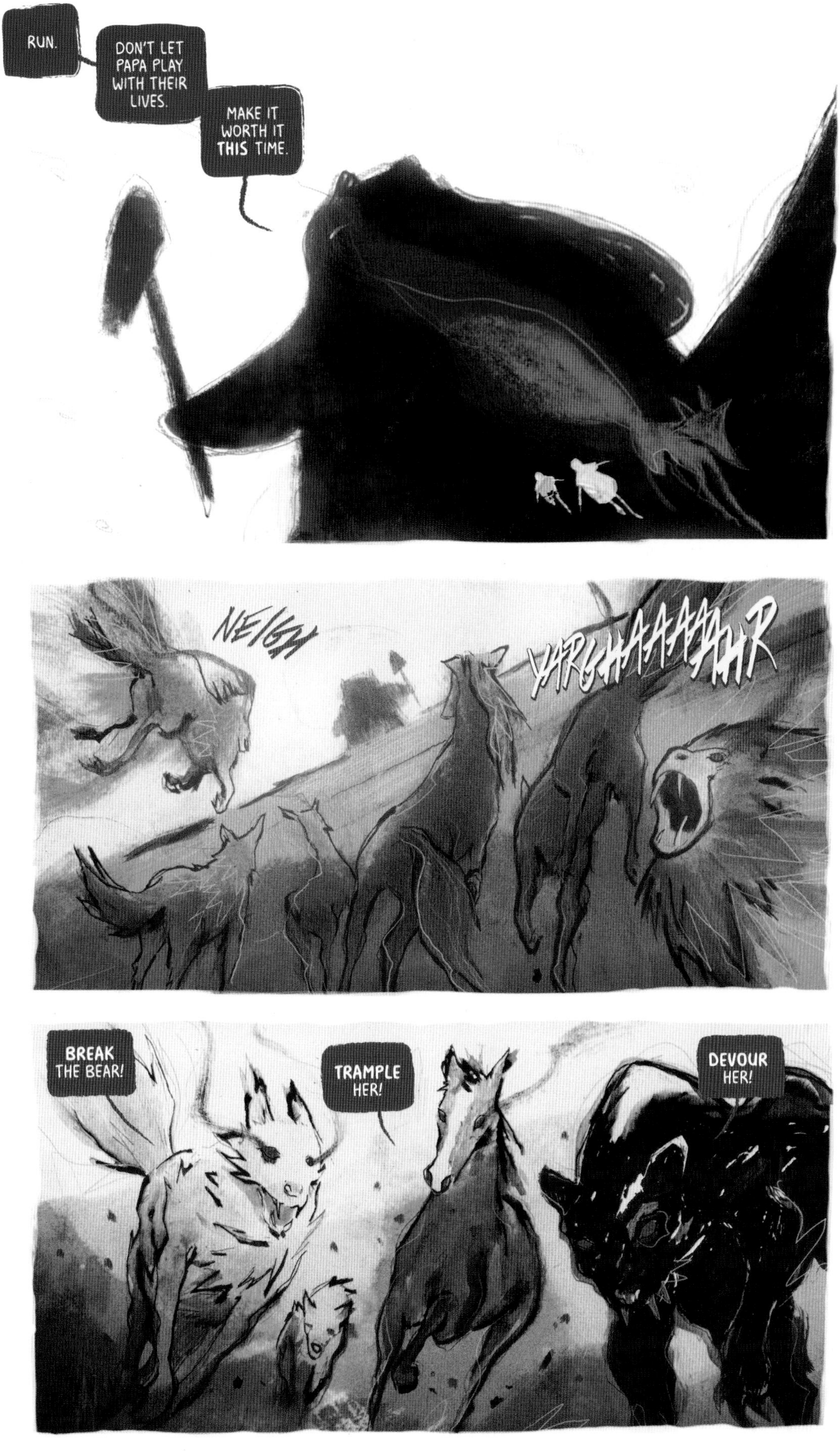
RUN.
DON'T LET PAPA PLAY WITH THEIR LIVES.
MAKE IT WORTH IT THIS TIME.
NEIGH
YARGHAAAAAAHR
BREAK THE BEAR!
TRAMPLE HER!
DEVOUR HER!

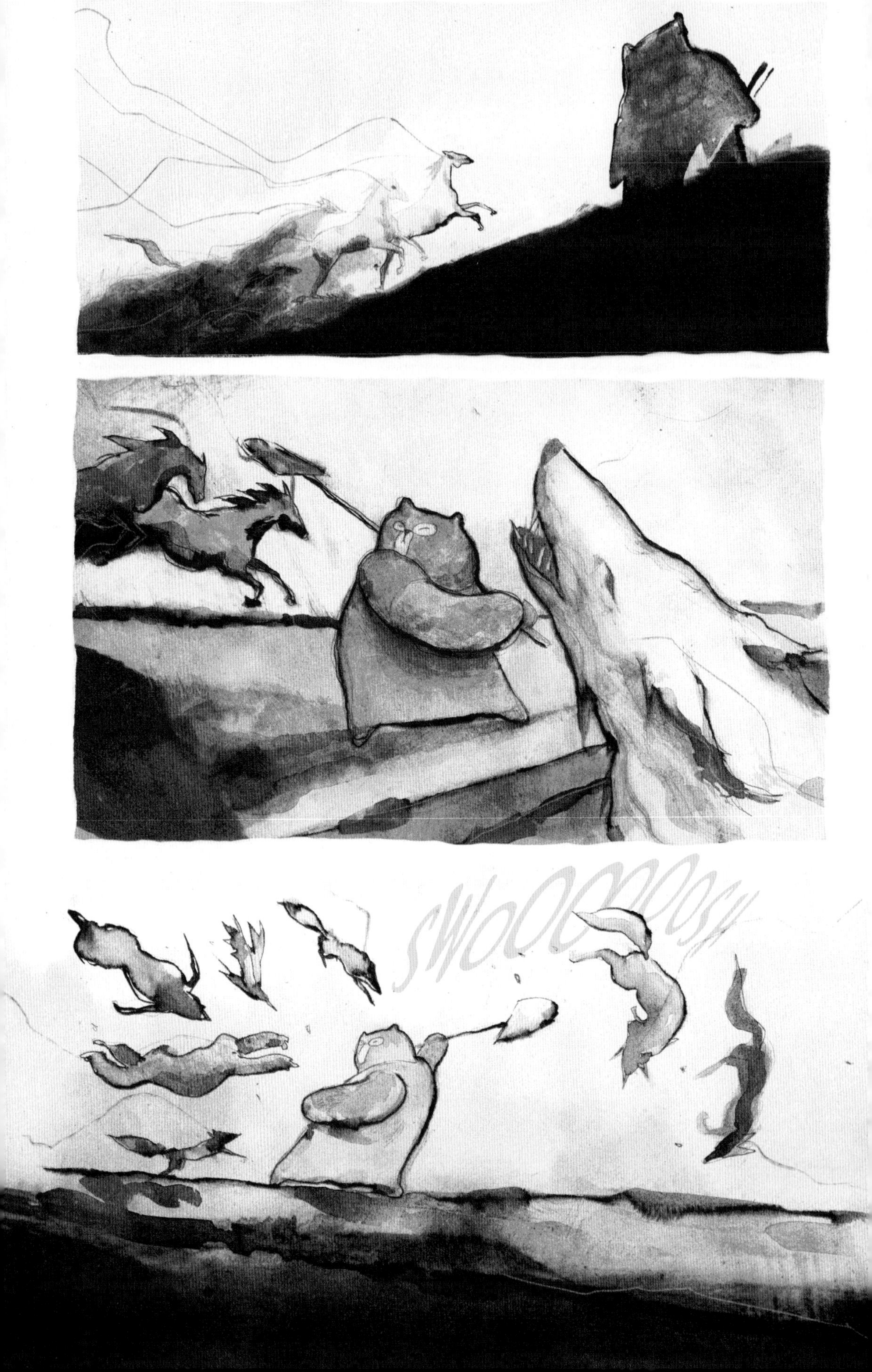
SWOOOOOSH

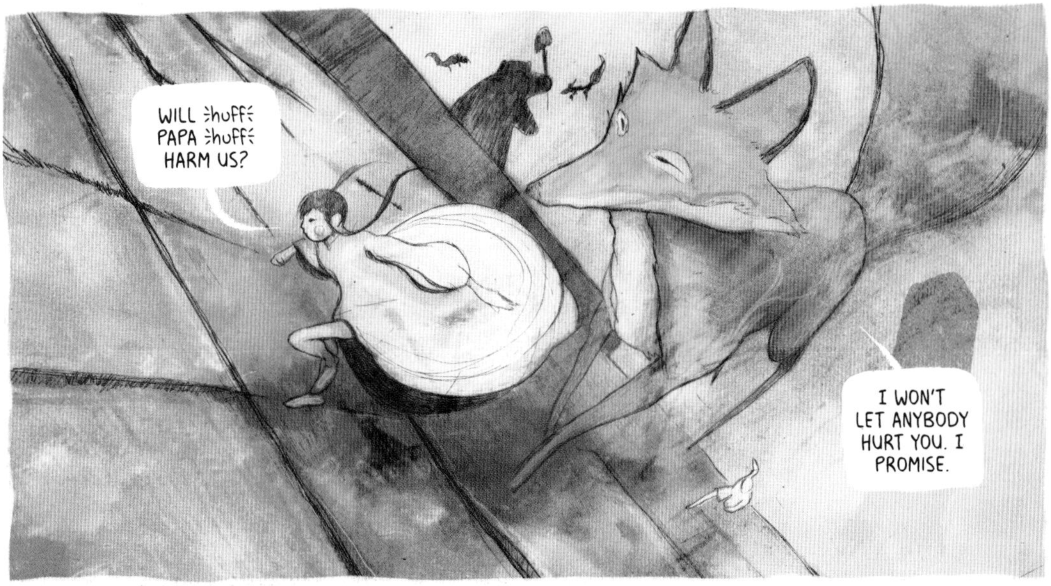
WILL huff PAPA huff HARM US?
I WON'T LET ANYBODY HURT YOU. I PROMISE.

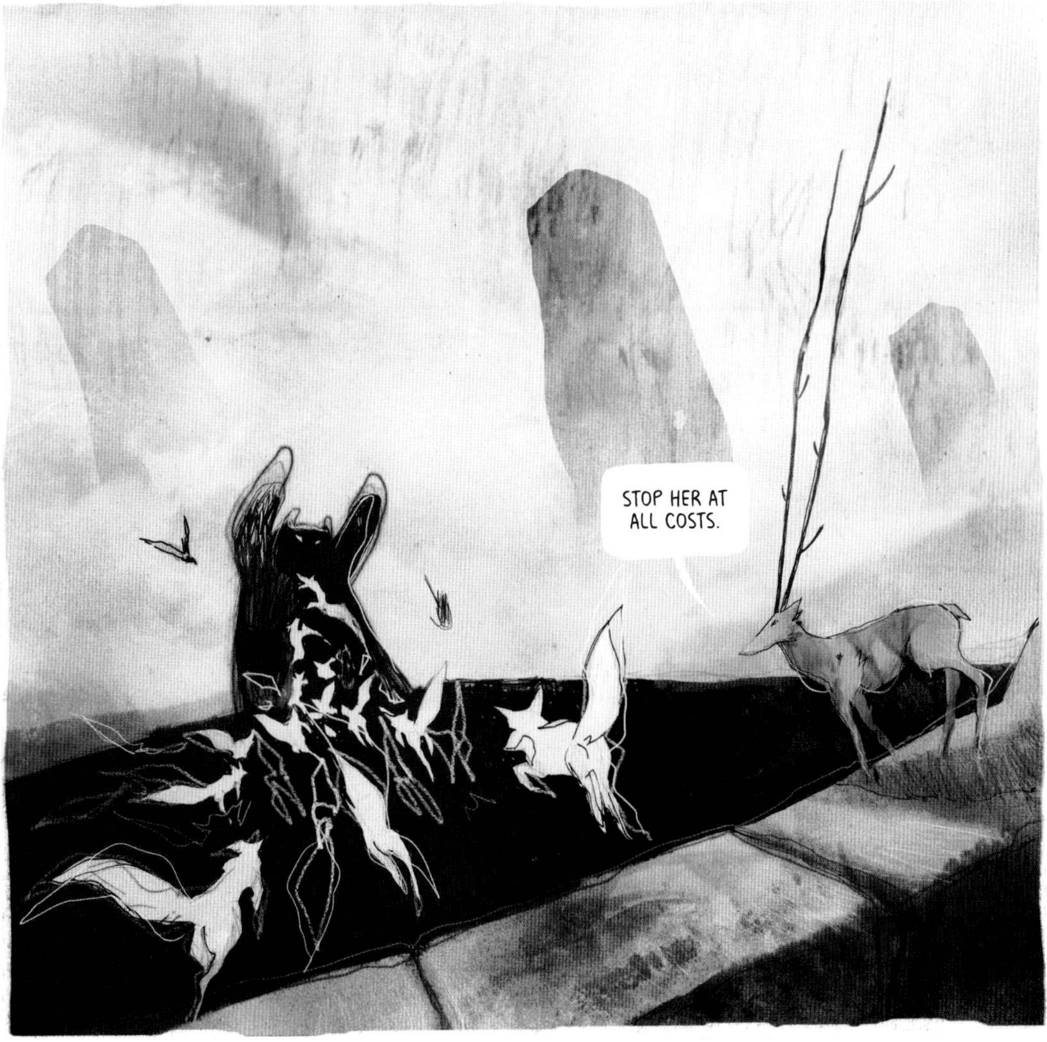
STOP HER AT ALL COSTS.

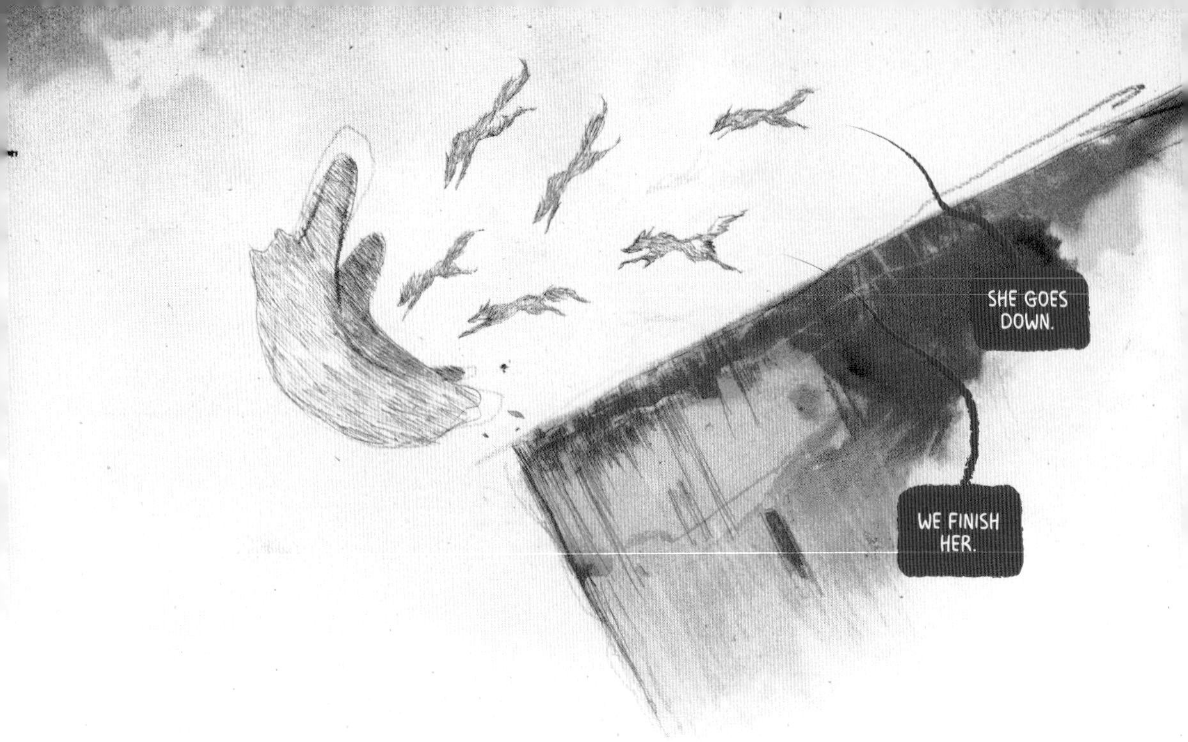
SHE GOES DOWN.
WE FINISH HER.

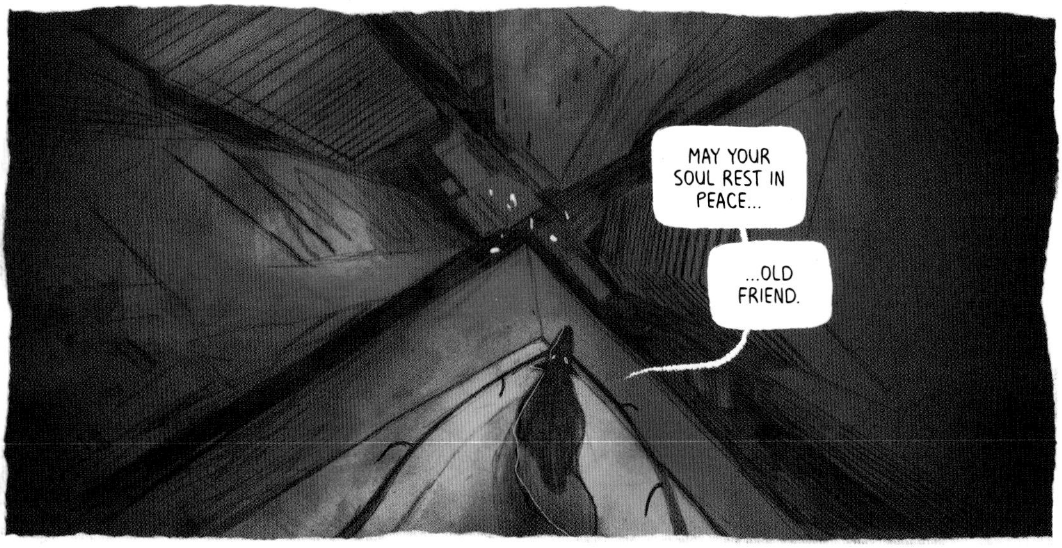
MAY YOUR SOUL REST IN PEACE...
...OLD FRIEND.

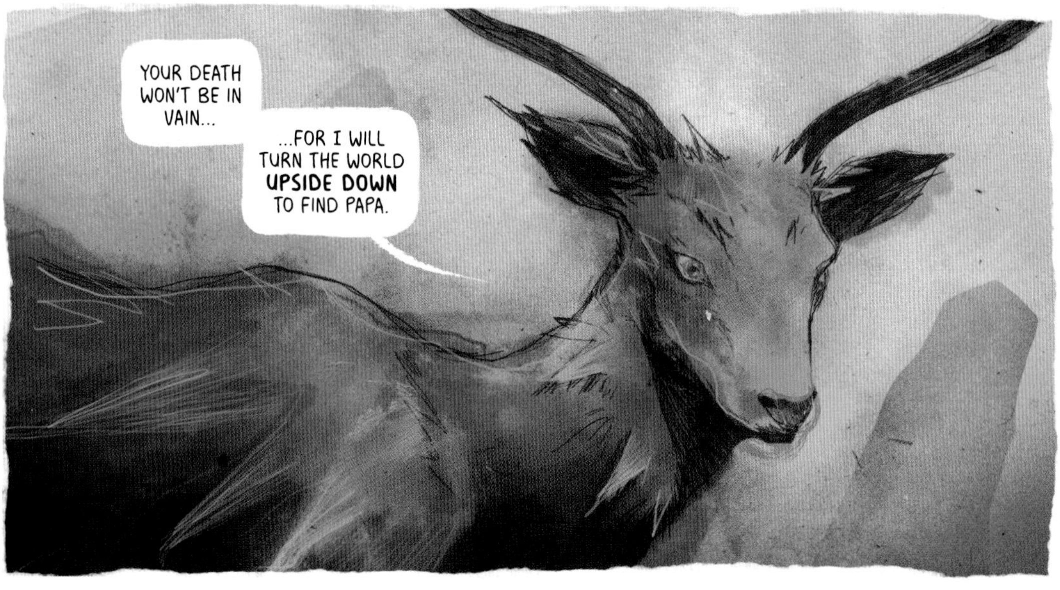
YOUR DEATH WON'T BE IN VAIN...
...FOR I WILL TURN THE WORLD **UPSIDE DOWN** TO FIND PAPA.

DON'T LOSE THEM.

ONLY BEATRICE KNOWS PAPA'S HIDEAWAY.

SHE WILL GO TO ANY LENGTHS TO DELIVER THE CHILDREN AND **HE** WILL BRING ABOUT A **SECOND APOCALYPSE.**

WE HAVE THEIR SMELL.

THEN FOLLOW IT, AND HELP ME KEEP MY PROMISE TO YOU.

"TO MAKE PAPA PAY FOR EVERYTHING HE DID."

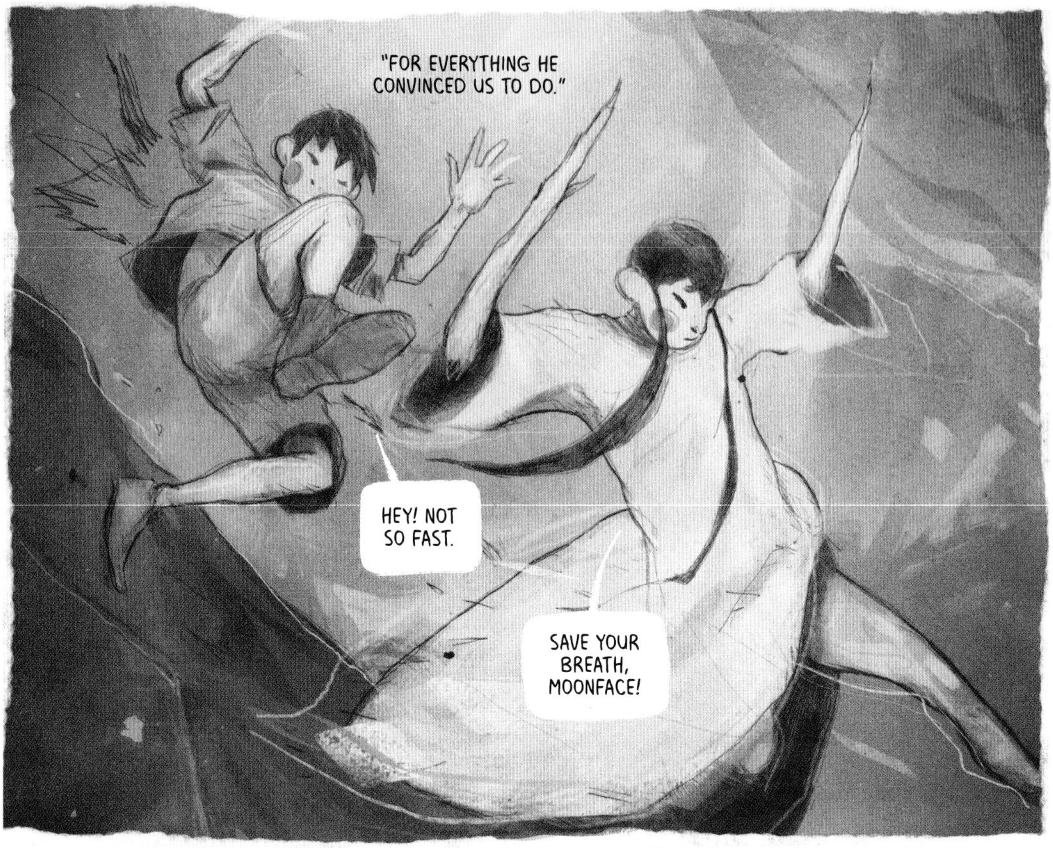
"FOR EVERYTHING HE CONVINCED US TO DO."
HEY! NOT SO FAST.
SAVE YOUR BREATH, MOONFACE!

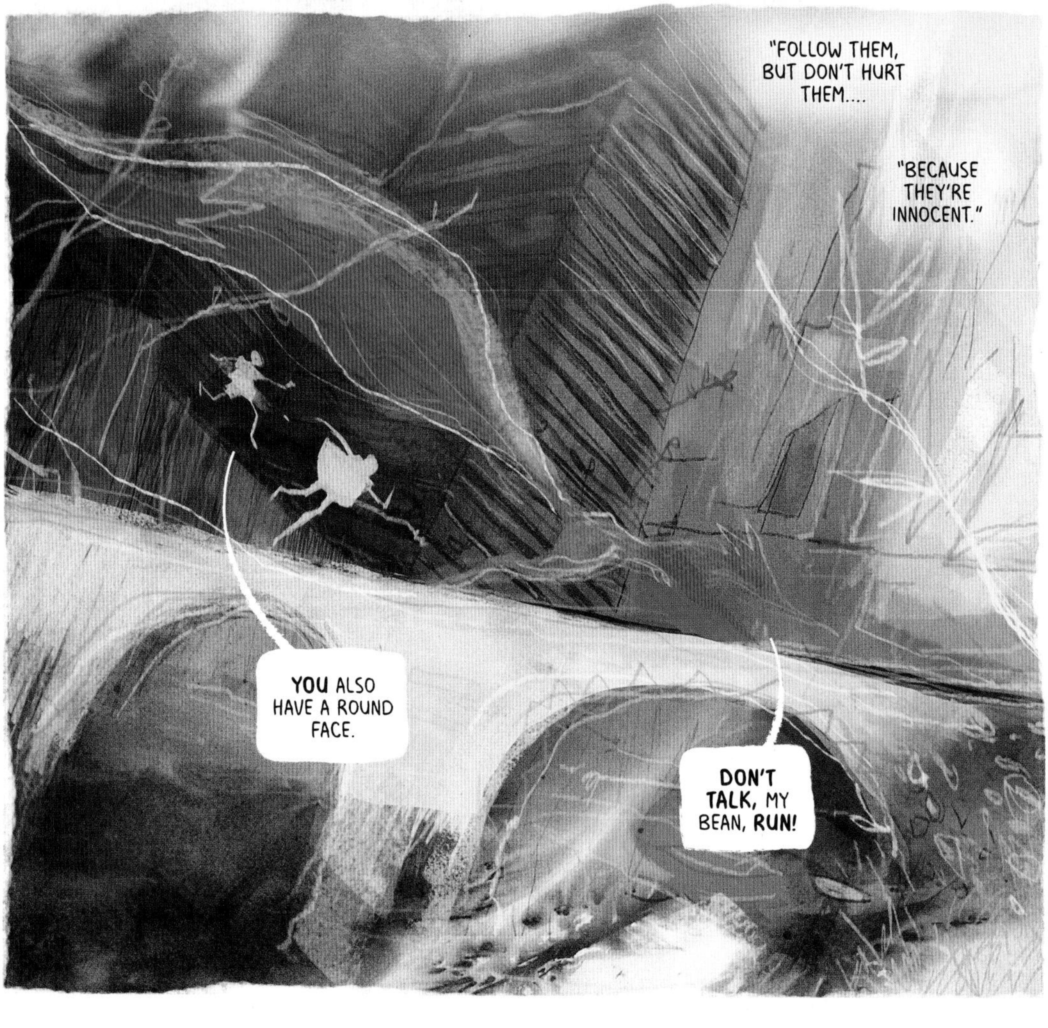
"FOLLOW THEM, BUT DON'T HURT THEM....
"BECAUSE THEY'RE INNOCENT."
YOU ALSO HAVE A ROUND FACE.
DON'T TALK, MY BEAN, **RUN!**

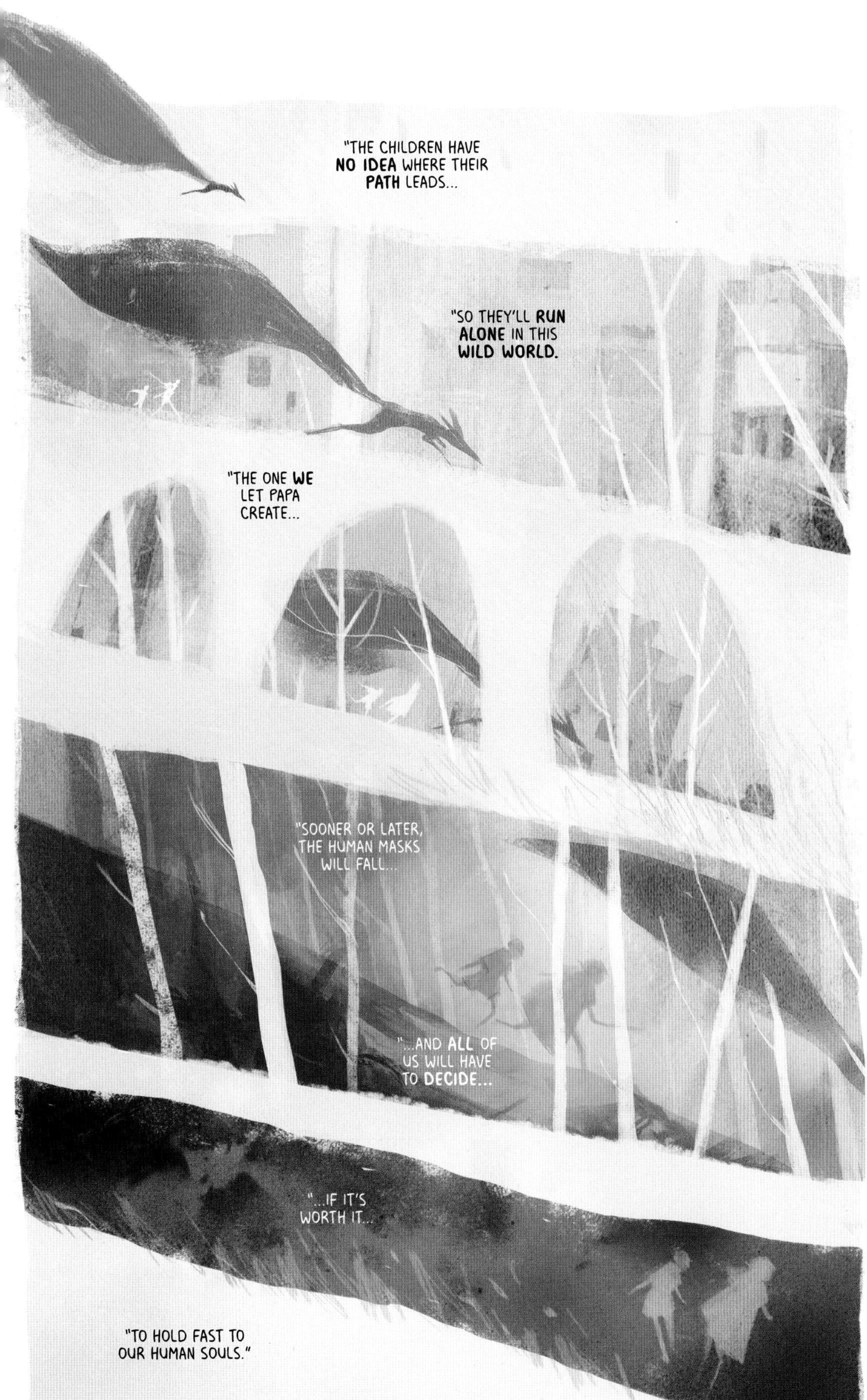
"THE CHILDREN HAVE NO IDEA WHERE THEIR PATH LEADS...
"SO THEY'LL RUN ALONE IN THIS WILD WORLD.
"THE ONE WE LET PAPA CREATE...
"SOONER OR LATER, THE HUMAN MASKS WILL FALL...
"...AND ALL OF US WILL HAVE TO DECIDE...
"...IF IT'S WORTH IT...
"TO HOLD FAST TO OUR HUMAN SOULS."

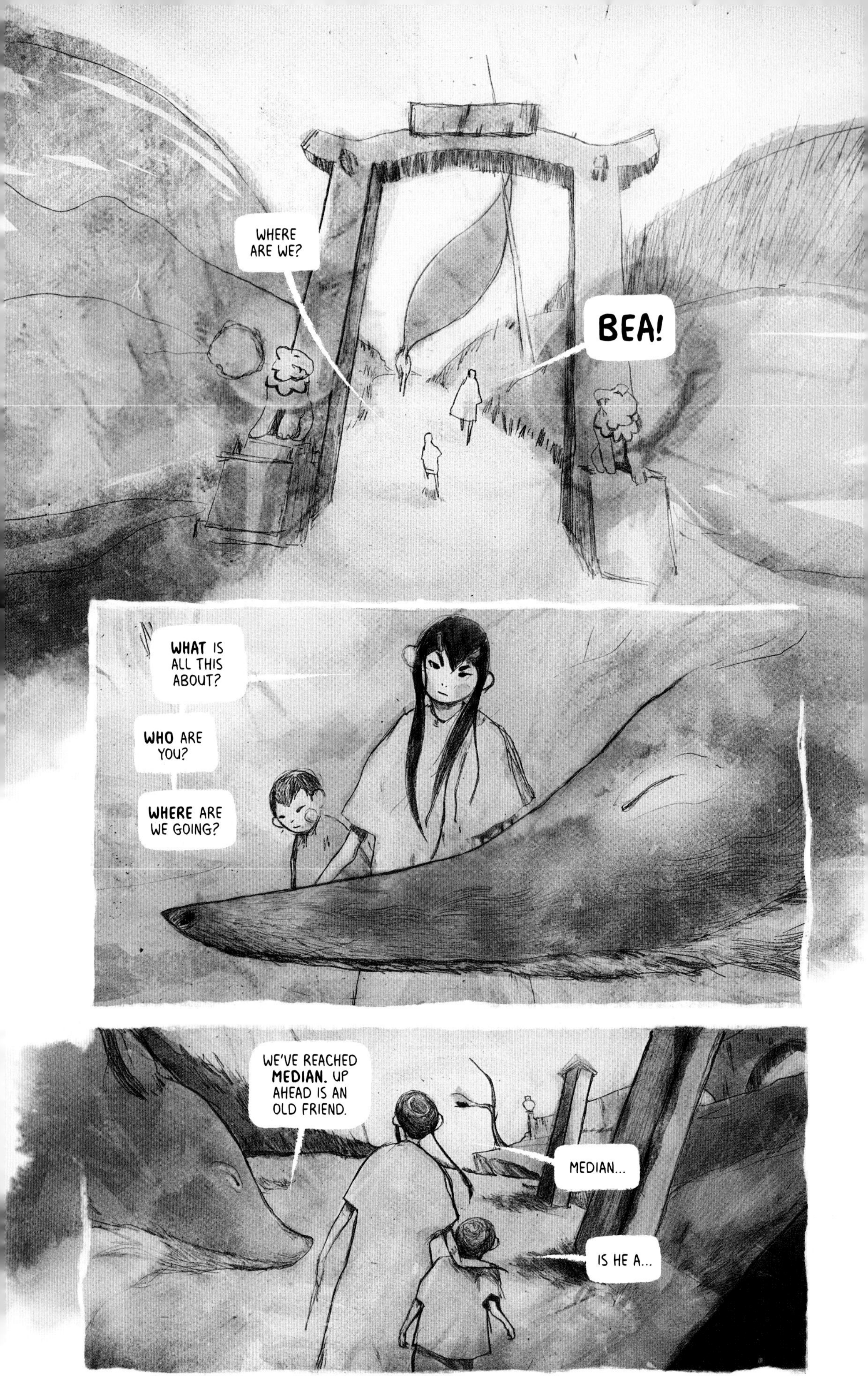
WHERE ARE WE?
BEA!
WHAT IS ALL THIS ABOUT?
WHO ARE YOU?
WHERE ARE WE GOING?
WE'VE REACHED MEDIAN. UP AHEAD IS AN OLD FRIEND.
MEDIAN...
IS HE A...

MY NAME IS ITSUKI.

I CHEW LEAVES AND TRY TO KEEP THIS PLACE SAFE.

WE NEED SHELTER. THE WILD ONES ARE AFTER US AND THEIR ARMY IS GETTING STRONGER BY THE MINUTE.

WE CAN'T OUTRUN THEM. WE NEED TO HIDE.

OF COURSE YOU DO.

DEWI WAS HERE, BUT NOW A FIREFLY! THEN PANDORA VANISHES, AND NOW YOU SHOW UP.

A MERRY REUNION OF OLD CLASSMATES, ORGANIZED BY HIS MAJESTY, PAPA HIMSELF.

WHAT A FINE SMALL HEAD!

RAP RAP

SINCE YOU'RE HERE, ALLOW ME TO GIVE YOU THE GRAND TOUR.

AND FOOD?

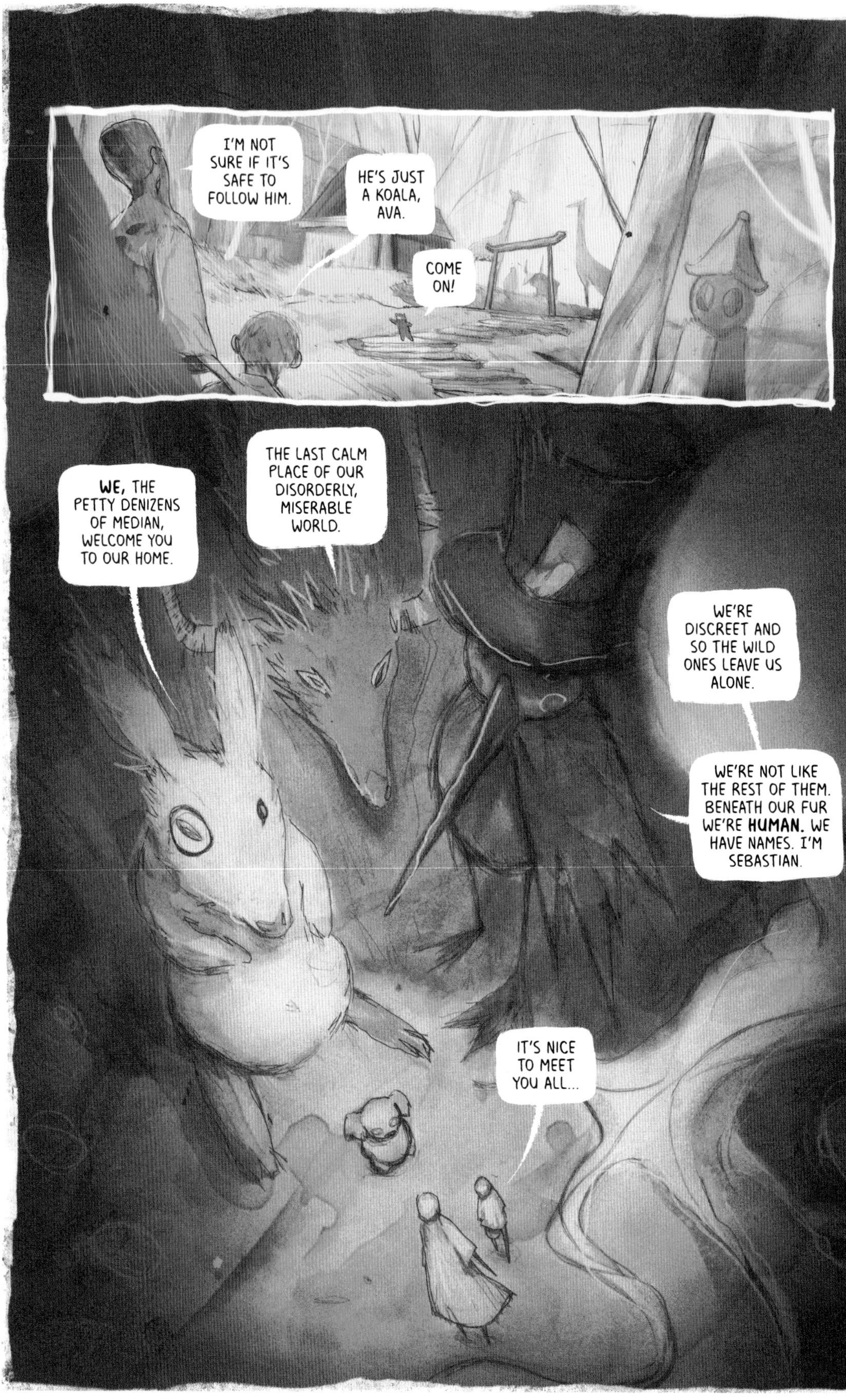
I'M NOT SURE IF IT'S SAFE TO FOLLOW HIM.
HE'S JUST A KOALA, AVA.
COME ON!
WE, THE PETTY DENIZENS OF MEDIAN, WELCOME YOU TO OUR HOME.
THE LAST CALM PLACE OF OUR DISORDERLY, MISERABLE WORLD.
WE'RE DISCREET AND SO THE WILD ONES LEAVE US ALONE.
WE'RE NOT LIKE THE REST OF THEM. BENEATH OUR FUR WE'RE **HUMAN.** WE HAVE NAMES. I'M SEBASTIAN.
IT'S NICE TO MEET YOU ALL...

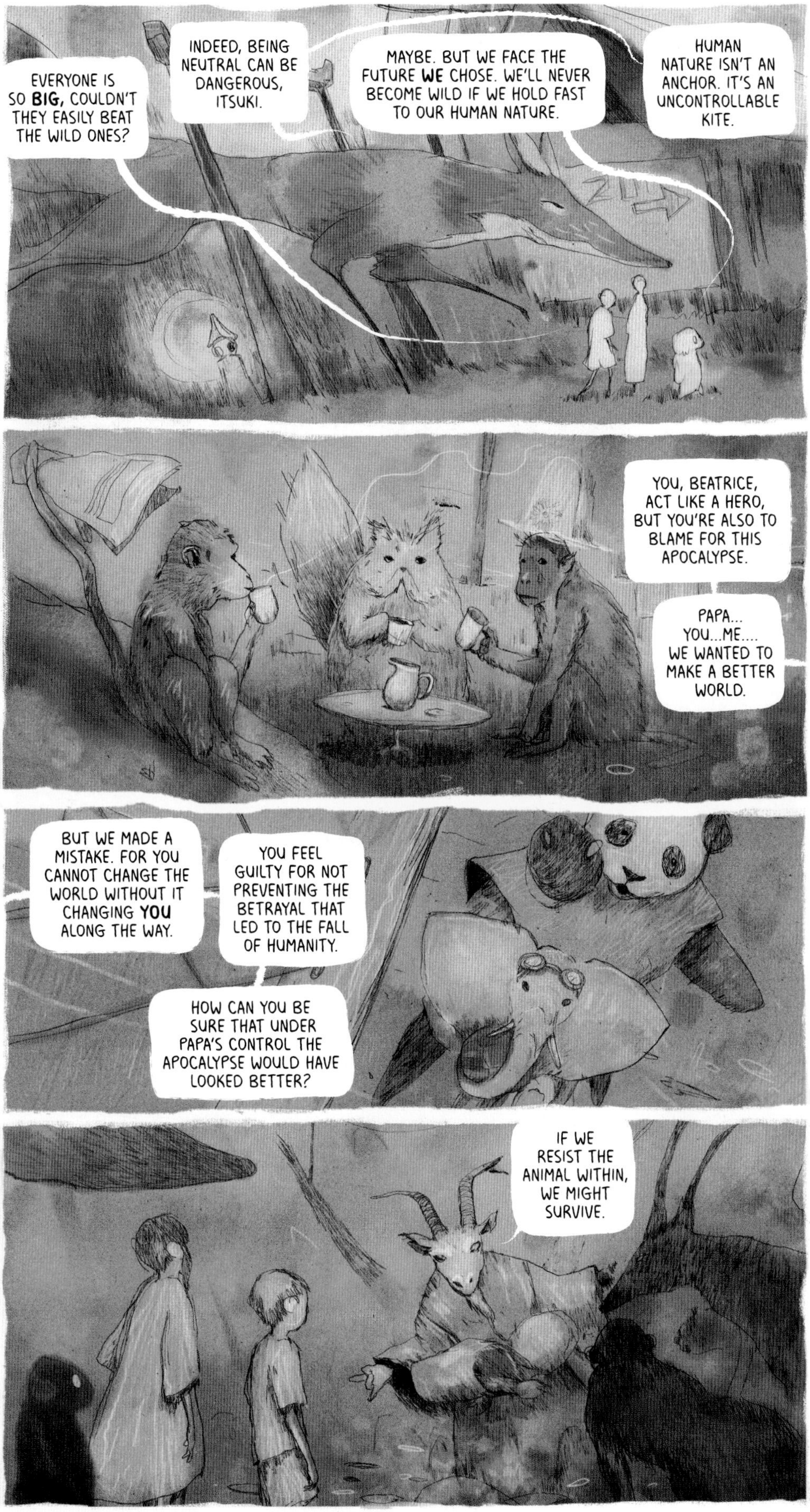
EVERYONE IS SO **BIG,** COULDN'T THEY EASILY BEAT THE WILD ONES?
INDEED, BEING NEUTRAL CAN BE DANGEROUS, ITSUKI.
MAYBE. BUT WE FACE THE FUTURE **WE** CHOSE. WE'LL NEVER BECOME WILD IF WE HOLD FAST TO OUR HUMAN NATURE.
HUMAN NATURE ISN'T AN ANCHOR. IT'S AN UNCONTROLLABLE KITE.
YOU, BEATRICE, ACT LIKE A HERO, BUT YOU'RE ALSO TO BLAME FOR THIS APOCALYPSE.
PAPA... YOU...ME.... WE WANTED TO MAKE A BETTER WORLD.
BUT WE MADE A MISTAKE. FOR YOU CANNOT CHANGE THE WORLD WITHOUT IT CHANGING **YOU** ALONG THE WAY.
YOU FEEL GUILTY FOR NOT PREVENTING THE BETRAYAL THAT LED TO THE FALL OF HUMANITY.
HOW CAN YOU BE SURE THAT UNDER PAPA'S CONTROL THE APOCALYPSE WOULD HAVE LOOKED BETTER?
IF WE RESIST THE ANIMAL WITHIN, WE MIGHT SURVIVE.

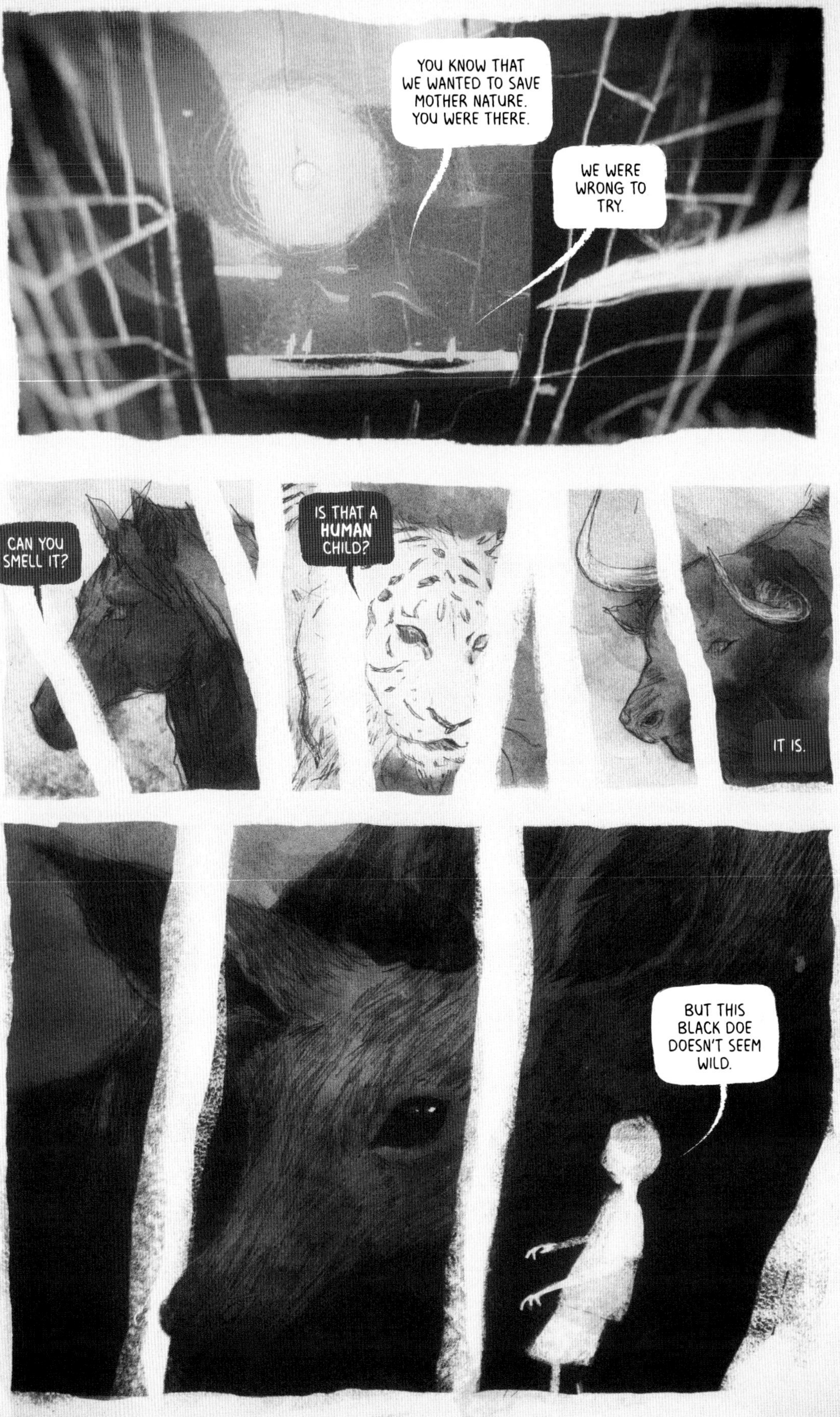
YOU KNOW THAT WE WANTED TO SAVE MOTHER NATURE. YOU WERE THERE.
WE WERE WRONG TO TRY.
CAN YOU SMELL IT?
IS THAT A **HUMAN** CHILD?
IT IS.
BUT THIS BLACK DOE DOESN'T SEEM WILD.

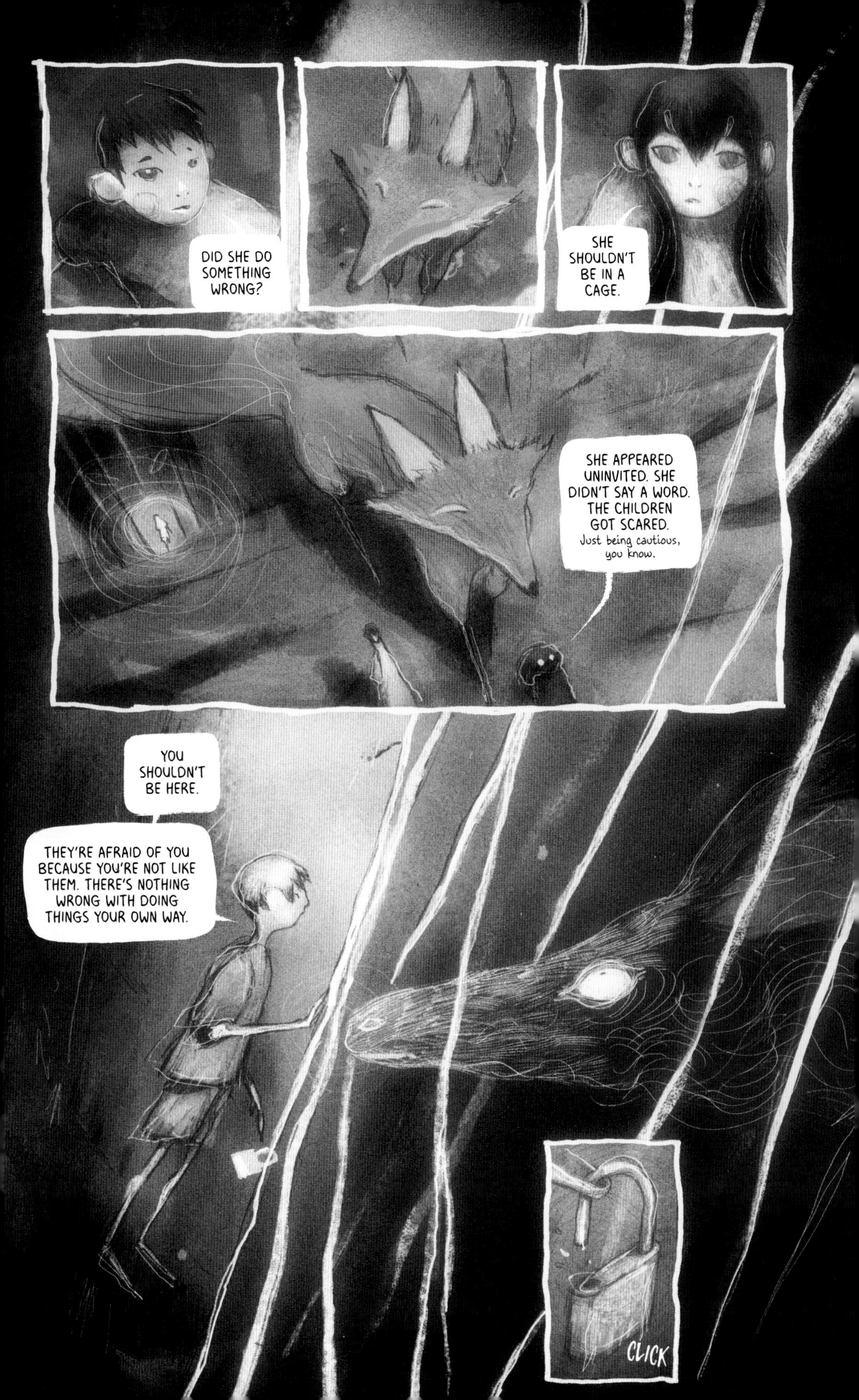
DID SHE DO SOMETHING WRONG?
SHE SHOULDN'T BE IN A CAGE.
SHE APPEARED UNINVITED. SHE DIDN'T SAY A WORD. THE CHILDREN GOT SCARED. Just being cautious, you know.
YOU SHOULDN'T BE HERE.
THEY'RE AFRAID OF YOU BECAUSE YOU'RE NOT LIKE THEM. THERE'S NOTHING WRONG WITH DOING THINGS YOUR OWN WAY.
CLICK

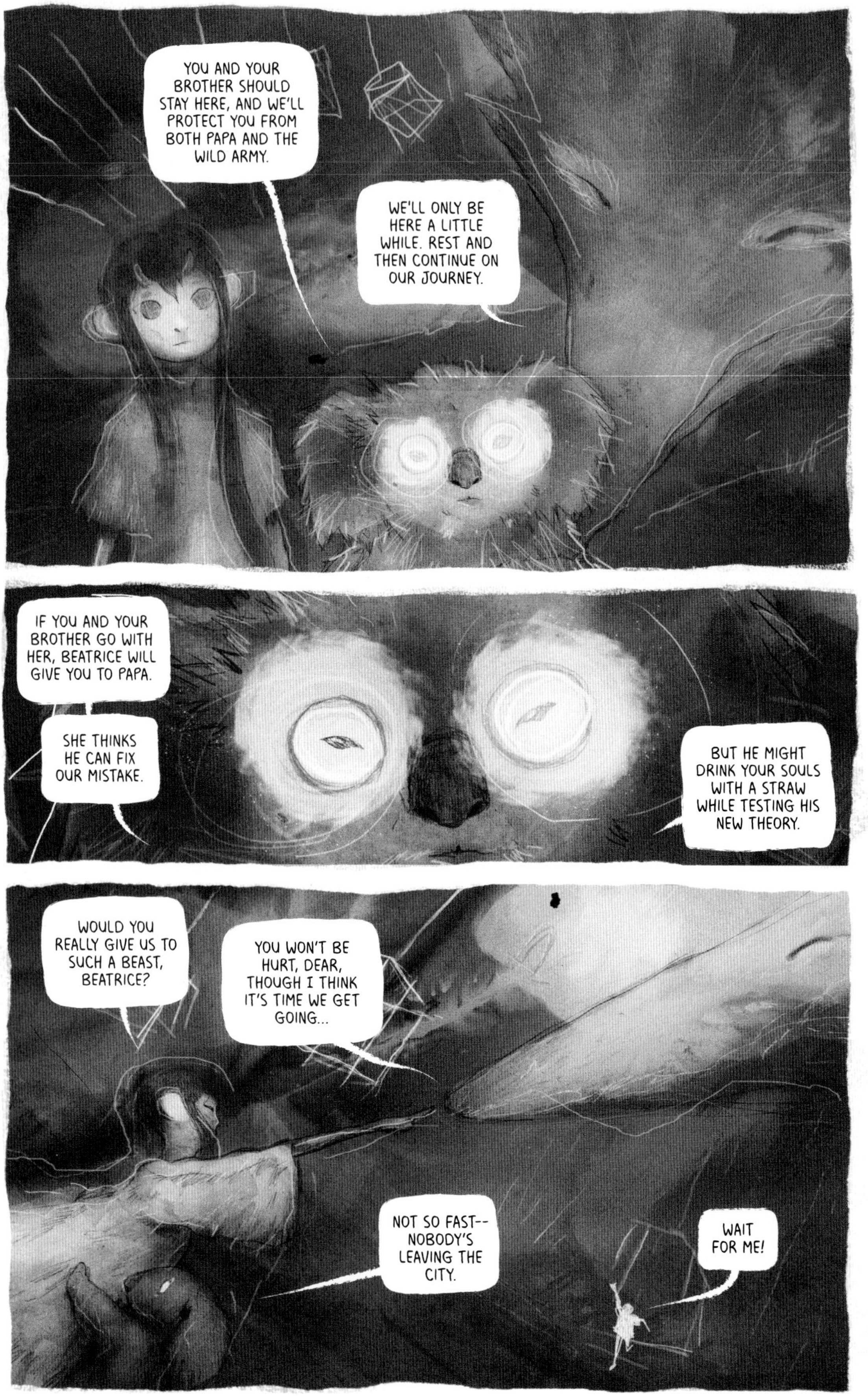
YOU AND YOUR BROTHER SHOULD STAY HERE, AND WE'LL PROTECT YOU FROM BOTH PAPA AND THE WILD ARMY.
WE'LL ONLY BE HERE A LITTLE WHILE. REST AND THEN CONTINUE ON OUR JOURNEY.
IF YOU AND YOUR BROTHER GO WITH HER, BEATRICE WILL GIVE YOU TO PAPA.
SHE THINKS HE CAN FIX OUR MISTAKE.
BUT HE MIGHT DRINK YOUR SOULS WITH A STRAW WHILE TESTING HIS NEW THEORY.
WOULD YOU REALLY GIVE US TO SUCH A BEAST, BEATRICE?
YOU WON'T BE HURT, DEAR, THOUGH I THINK IT'S TIME WE GET GOING...
NOT SO FAST-- NOBODY'S LEAVING THE CITY.
WAIT FOR ME!

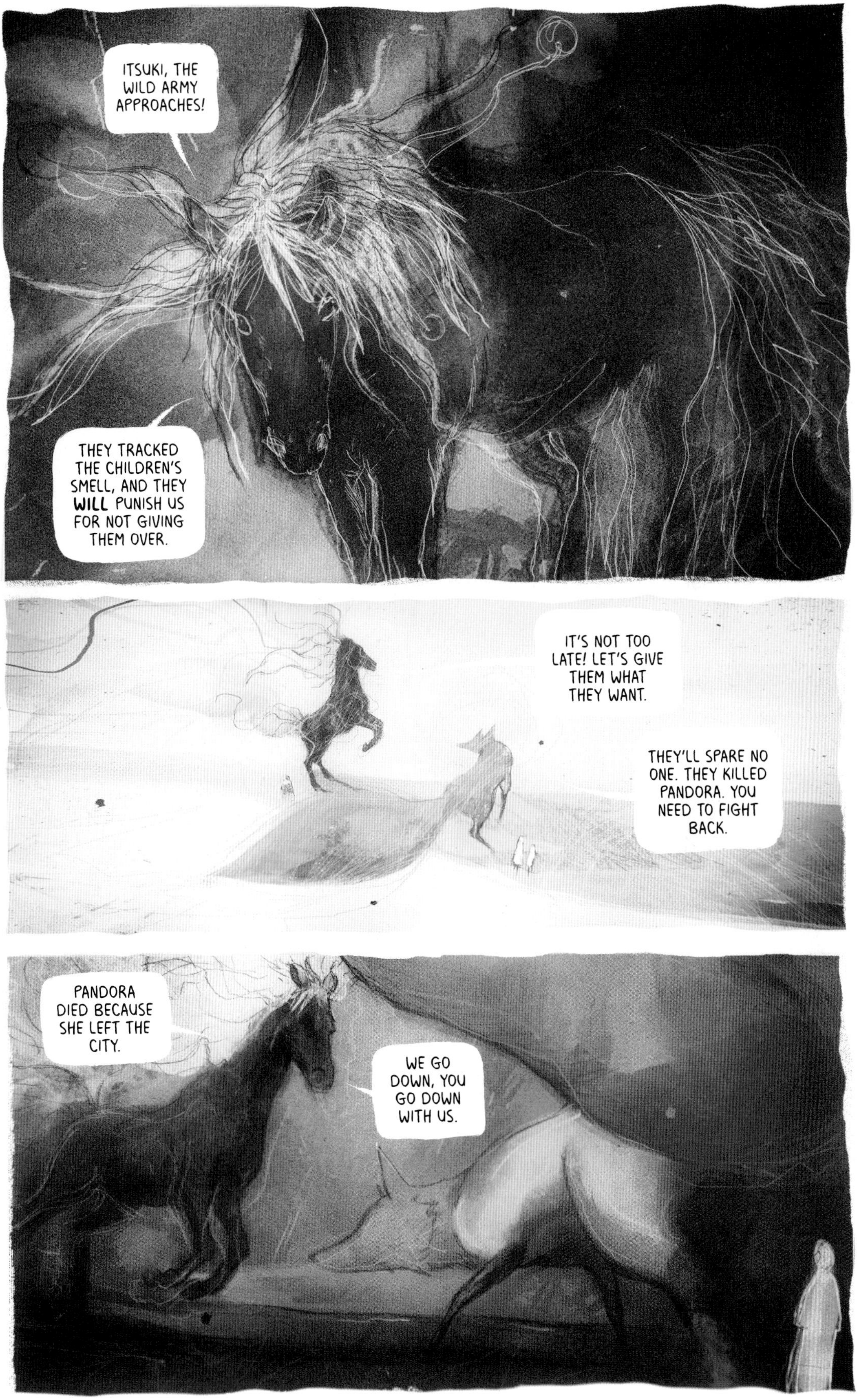
ITSUKI, THE WILD ARMY APPROACHES!
THEY TRACKED THE CHILDREN'S SMELL, AND THEY **WILL** PUNISH US FOR NOT GIVING THEM OVER.
IT'S NOT TOO LATE! LET'S GIVE THEM WHAT THEY WANT.
THEY'LL SPARE NO ONE. THEY KILLED PANDORA. YOU NEED TO FIGHT BACK.
PANDORA DIED BECAUSE SHE LEFT THE CITY.
WE GO DOWN, YOU GO DOWN WITH US.

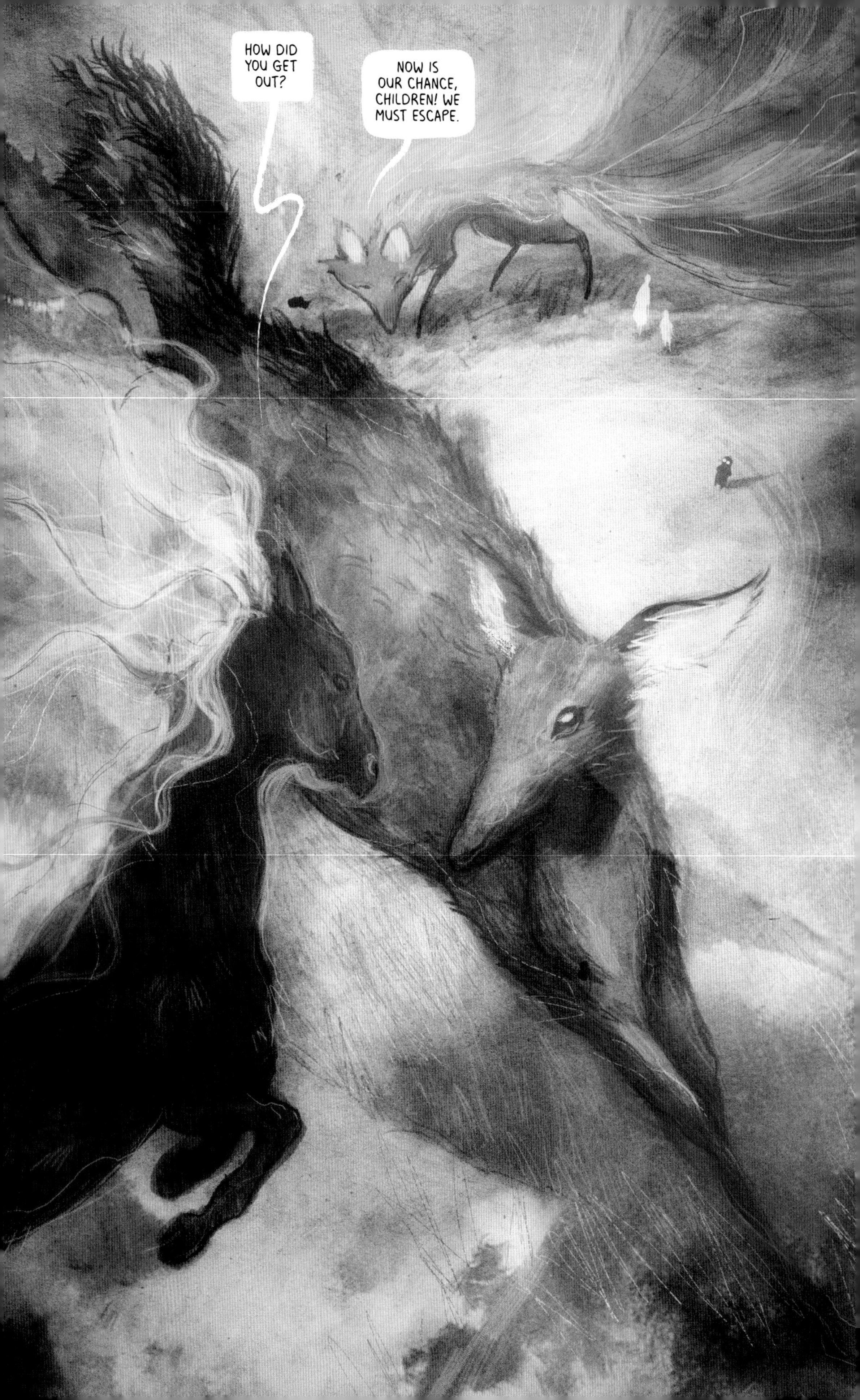
HOW DID YOU GET OUT?
NOW IS OUR CHANCE, CHILDREN! WE MUST ESCAPE.

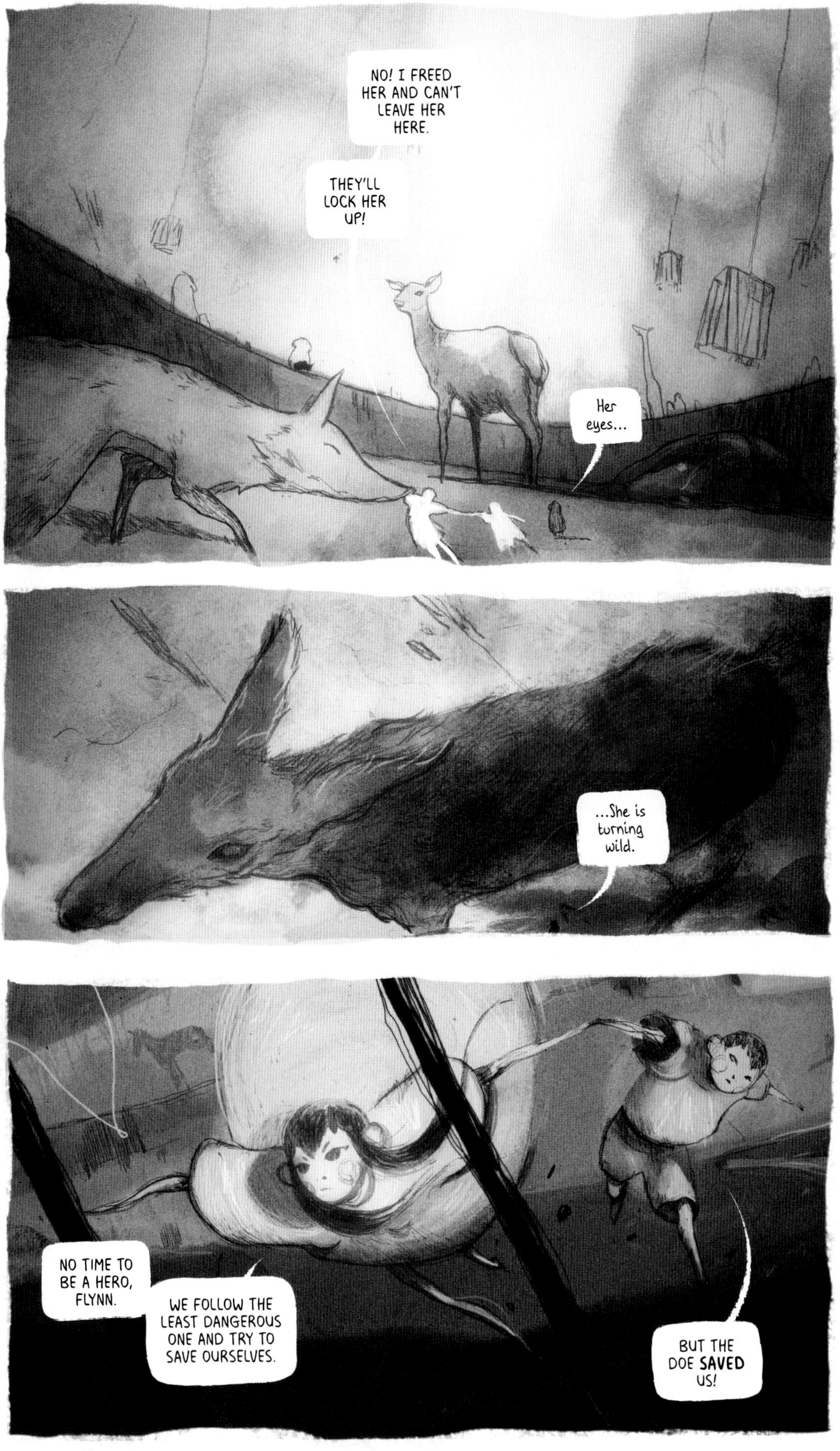
NO! I FREED HER AND CAN'T LEAVE HER HERE.
THEY'LL LOCK HER UP!
Her eyes...
...She is turning wild.
NO TIME TO BE A HERO, FLYNN.
WE FOLLOW THE LEAST DANGEROUS ONE AND TRY TO SAVE OURSELVES.
BUT THE DOE **SAVED** US!

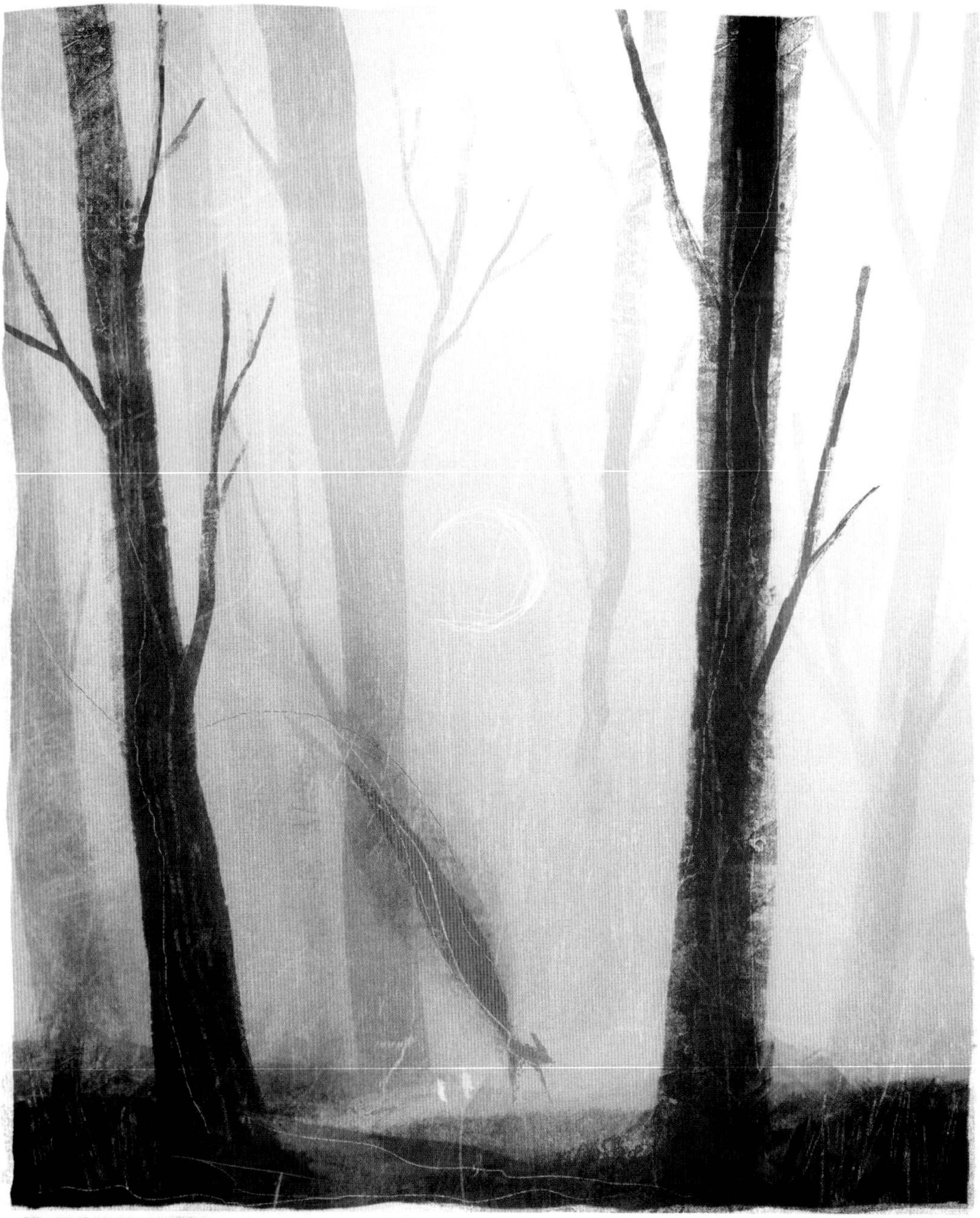

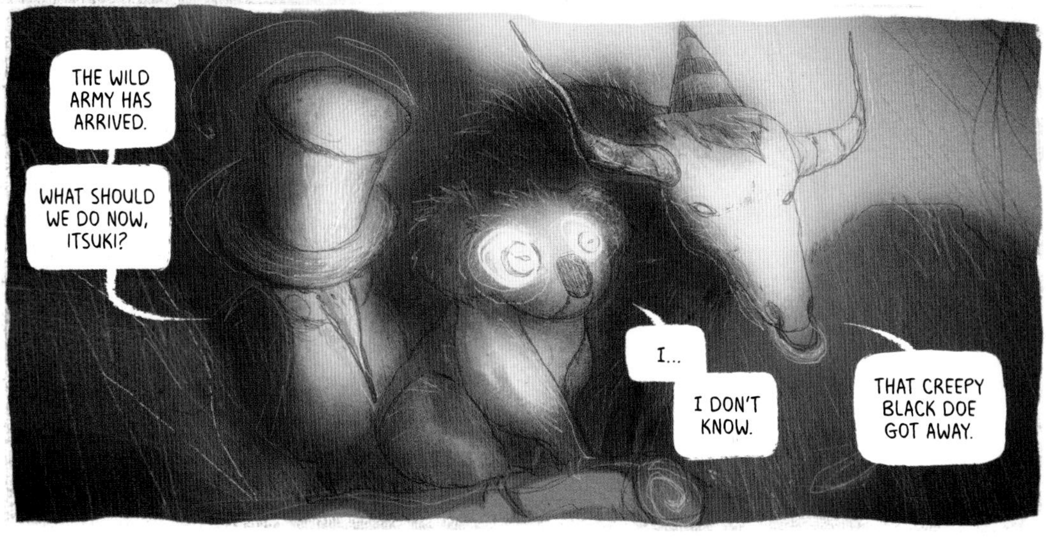
THE WILD ARMY HAS ARRIVED.
WHAT SHOULD WE DO NOW, ITSUKI?
I...
I DON'T KNOW.
THAT CREEPY BLACK DOE GOT AWAY.

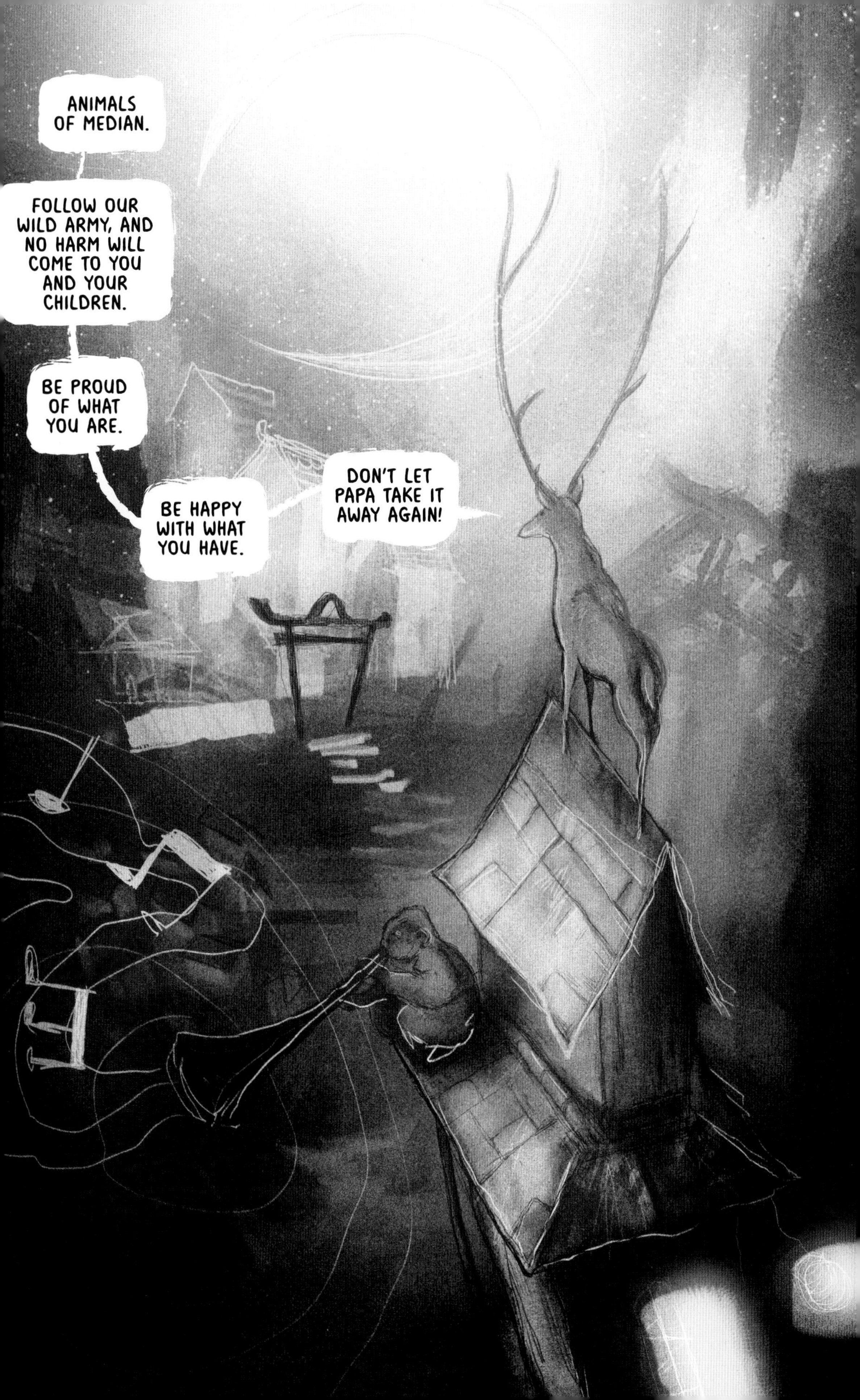
ANIMALS OF MEDIAN.
FOLLOW OUR WILD ARMY, AND NO HARM WILL COME TO YOU AND YOUR CHILDREN.
BE PROUD OF WHAT YOU ARE.
BE HAPPY WITH WHAT YOU HAVE.
DON'T LET PAPA TAKE IT AWAY AGAIN!

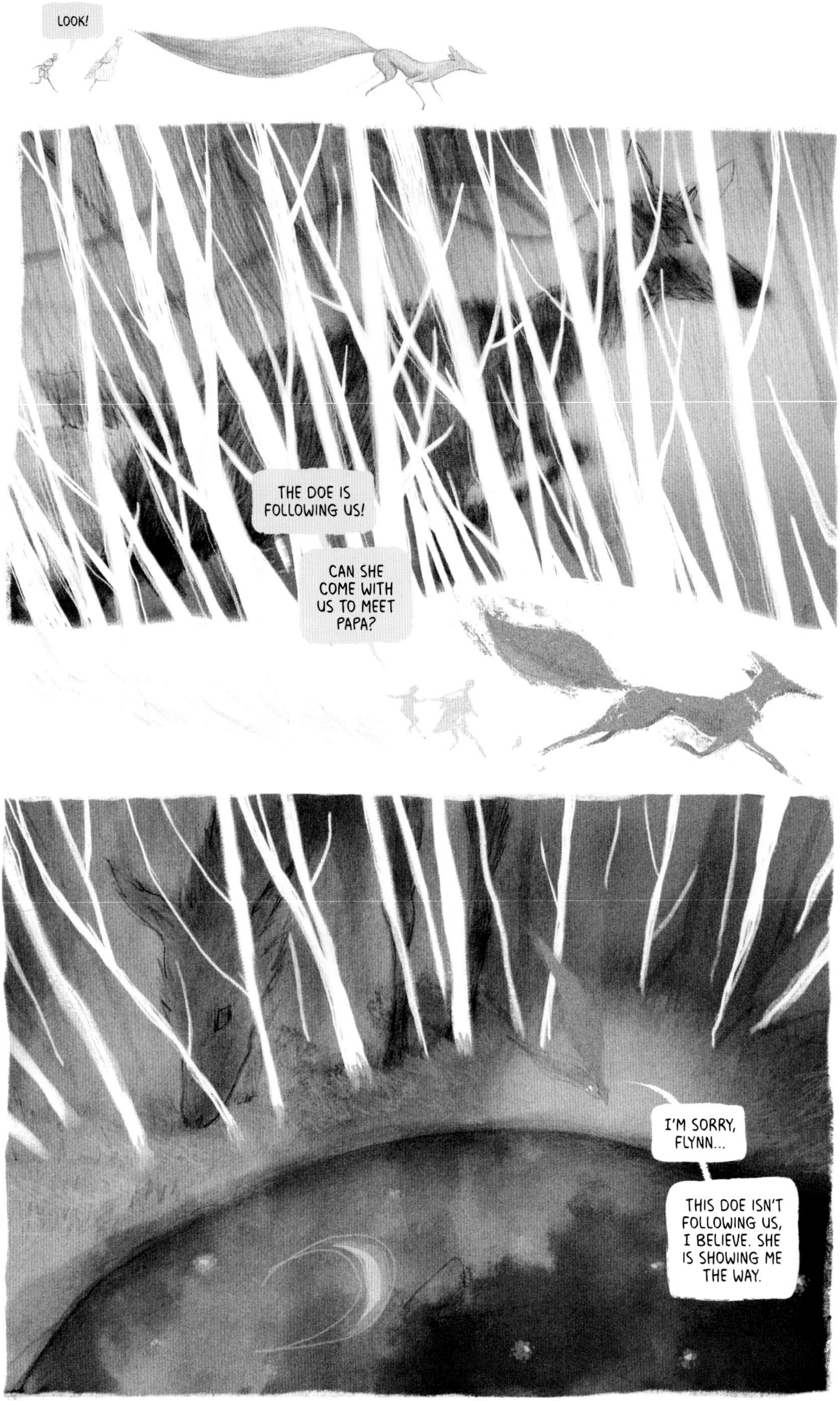
LOOK!
THE DOE IS FOLLOWING US!
CAN SHE COME WITH US TO MEET PAPA?
I'M SORRY, FLYNN...
THIS DOE ISN'T FOLLOWING US, I BELIEVE. SHE IS SHOWING ME THE WAY.

UP AHEAD WE
CAN HIDE AND
REST.

ARE YOU
OKAY, AVA?

SHE ONLY
NEEDS TIME
FOR HERSELF.

DON'T CRY, AVA.

EVERYTHING WILL BE ALL RIGHT.

BUT I'M TURNING.

WHO WILL TAKE CARE OF FLYNN?

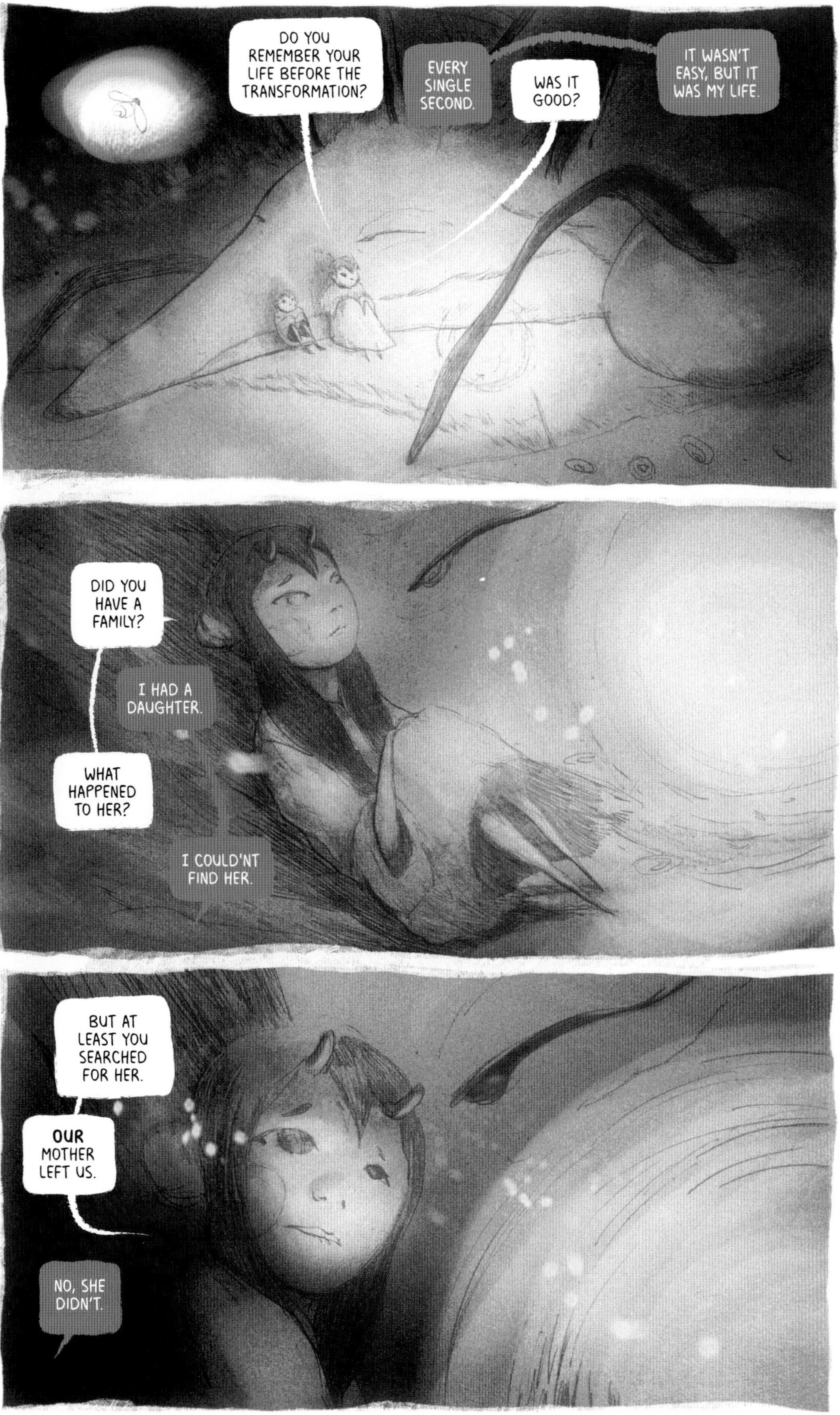
DO YOU REMEMBER YOUR LIFE BEFORE THE TRANSFORMATION?
EVERY SINGLE SECOND.
WAS IT GOOD?
IT WASN'T EASY, BUT IT WAS MY LIFE.
DID YOU HAVE A FAMILY?
I HAD A DAUGHTER.
WHAT HAPPENED TO HER?
I COULD'NT FIND HER.
BUT AT LEAST YOU SEARCHED FOR HER.
OUR MOTHER LEFT US.
NO, SHE DIDN'T.

HOW CAN YOU BE SO SURE?

BECAUSE A MOTHER WOULD TURN THE WHOLE WORLD UPSIDE DOWN, JUST TO SEE HER CHILDREN ONE LAST TIME.

NOW, GO TO SLEEP. YOUR BROTHER IS GOING TO NEED YOU TOMORROW.

THE WHOLE WORLD IS GOING TO NEED YOU TOMORROW.

I'LL MISS YOU BOTH, MY SMALL BEANS.

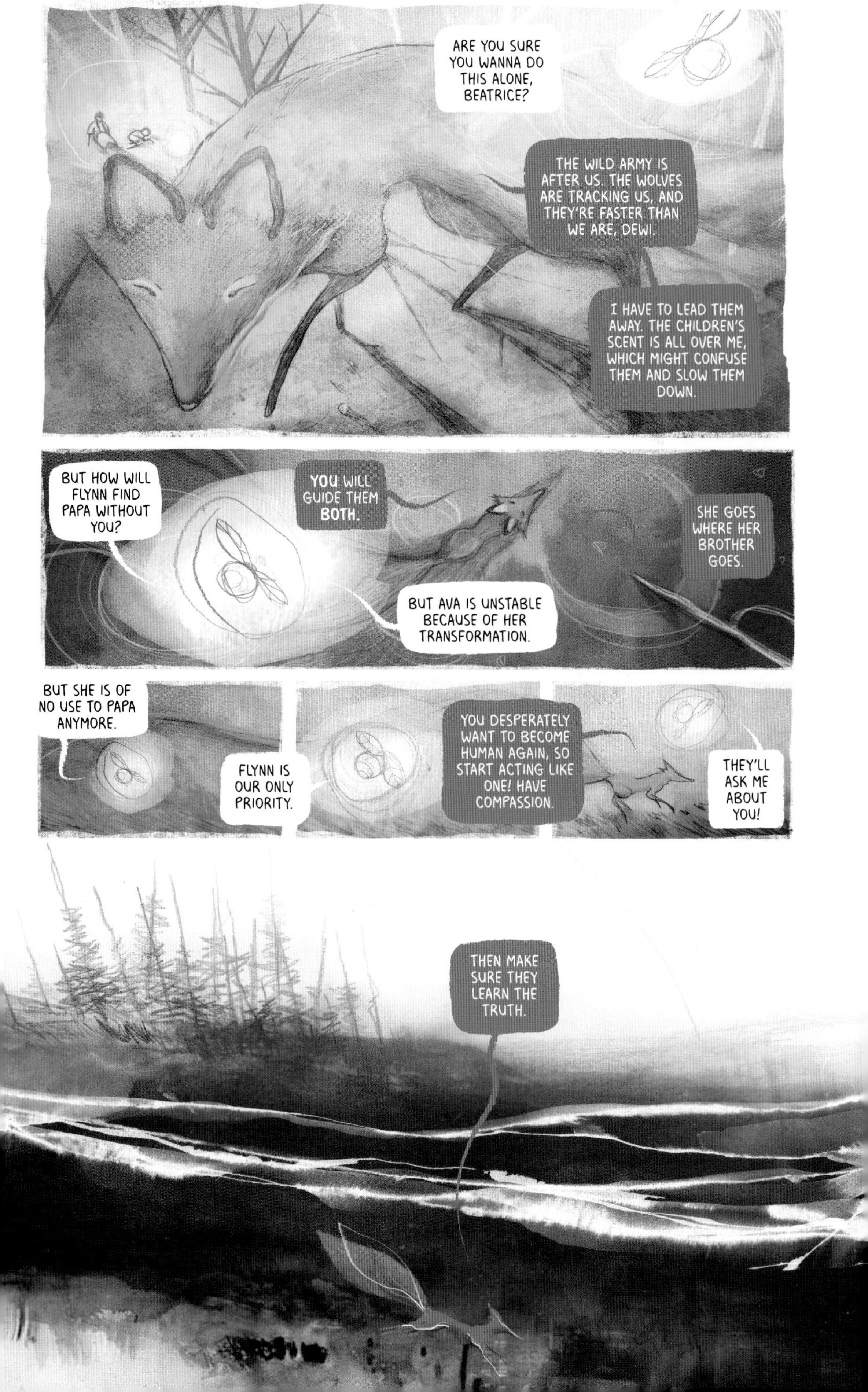
ARE YOU SURE YOU WANNA DO THIS ALONE, BEATRICE?
THE WILD ARMY IS AFTER US. THE WOLVES ARE TRACKING US, AND THEY'RE FASTER THAN WE ARE, DEWI.
I HAVE TO LEAD THEM AWAY. THE CHILDREN'S SCENT IS ALL OVER ME, WHICH MIGHT CONFUSE THEM AND SLOW THEM DOWN.
BUT HOW WILL FLYNN FIND PAPA WITHOUT YOU?
YOU WILL GUIDE THEM **BOTH**.
SHE GOES WHERE HER BROTHER GOES.
BUT AVA IS UNSTABLE BECAUSE OF HER TRANSFORMATION.
BUT SHE IS OF NO USE TO PAPA ANYMORE.
FLYNN IS OUR ONLY PRIORITY.
YOU DESPERATELY WANT TO BECOME HUMAN AGAIN, SO START ACTING LIKE ONE! HAVE COMPASSION.
THEY'LL ASK ME ABOUT YOU!
THEN MAKE SURE THEY LEARN THE TRUTH.

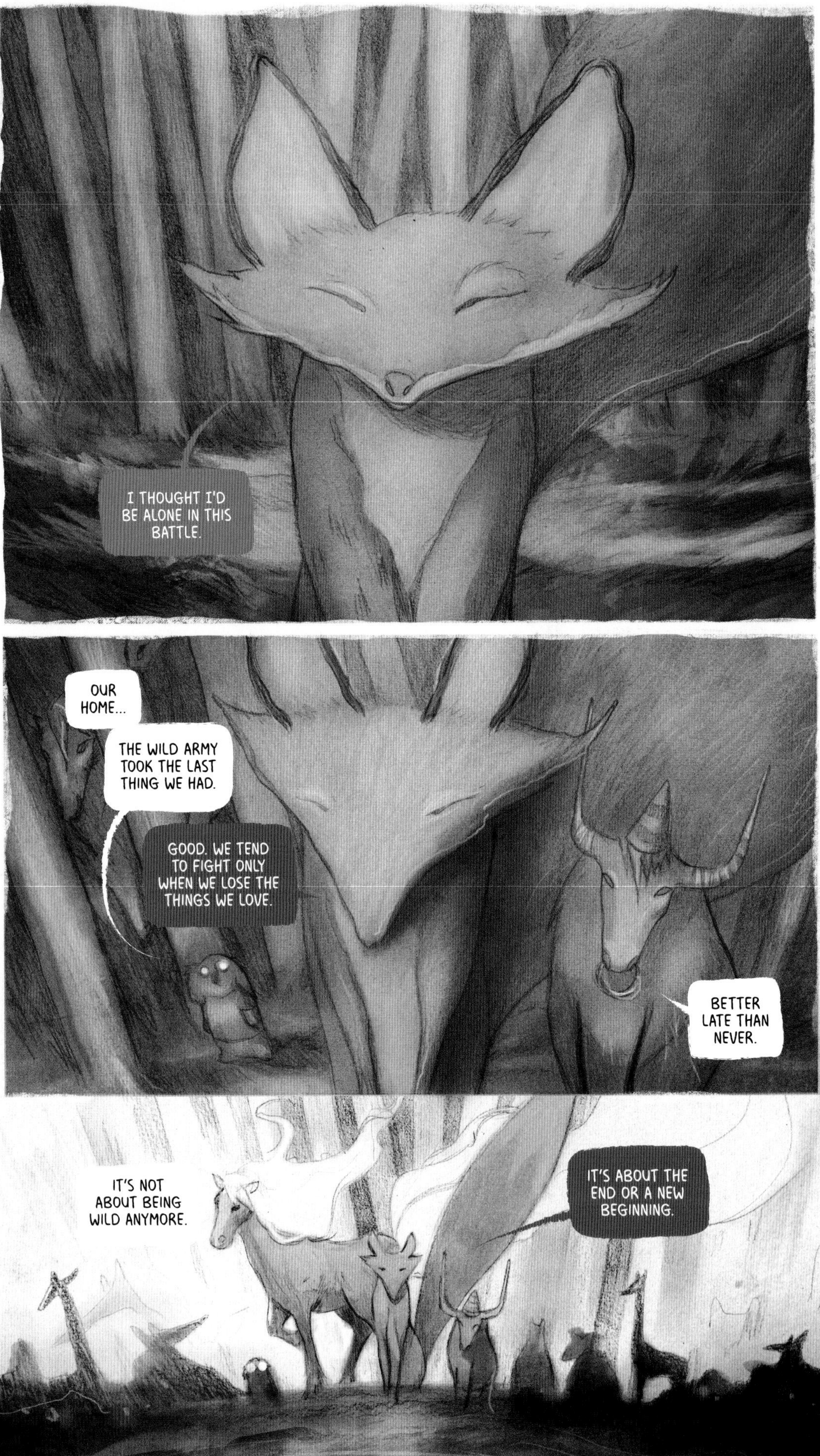
I THOUGHT I'D BE ALONE IN THIS BATTLE.
OUR HOME...
THE WILD ARMY TOOK THE LAST THING WE HAD.
GOOD. WE TEND TO FIGHT ONLY WHEN WE LOSE THE THINGS WE LOVE.
BETTER LATE THAN NEVER.
IT'S NOT ABOUT BEING WILD ANYMORE.
IT'S ABOUT THE END OR A NEW BEGINNING.

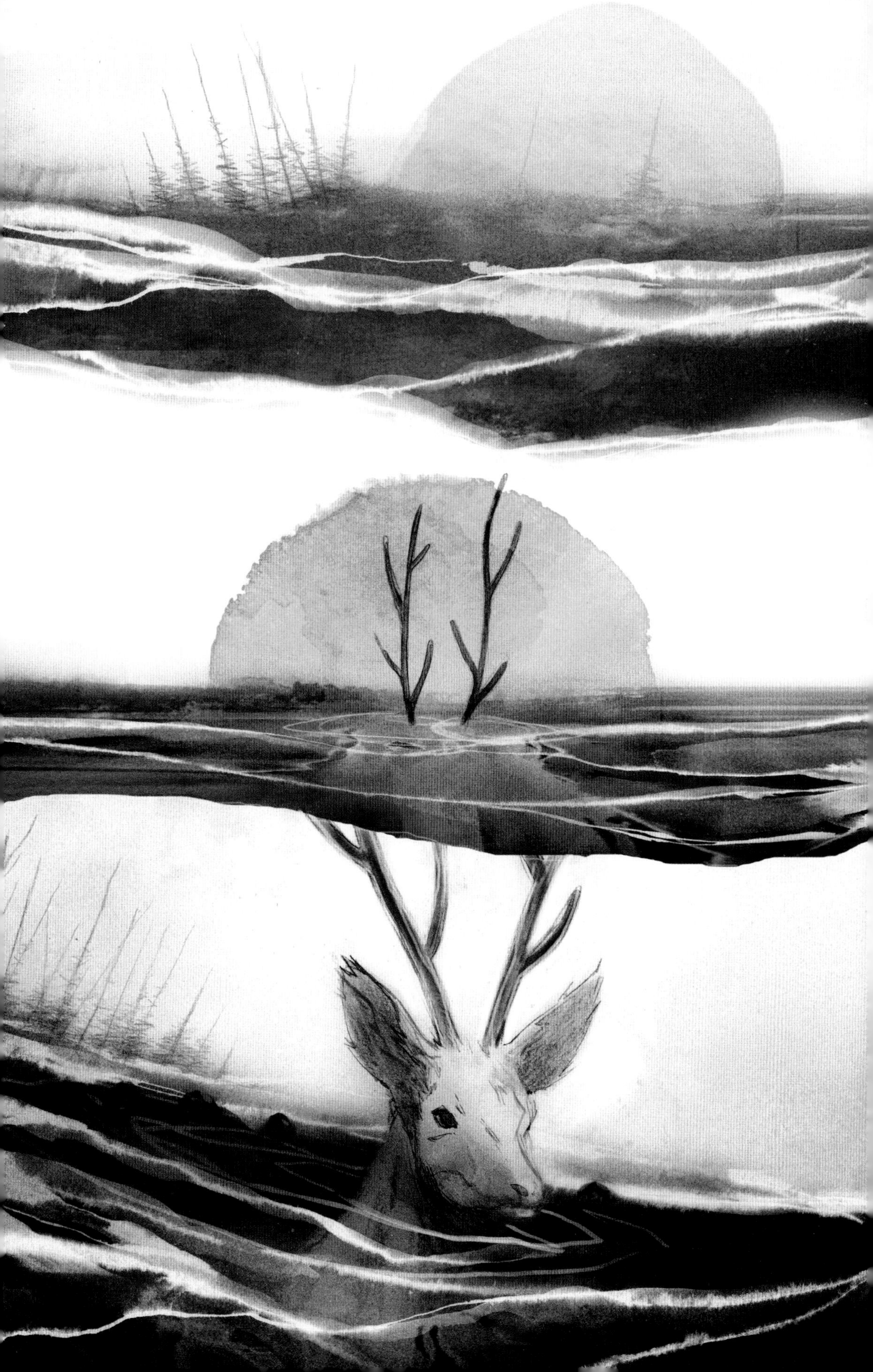

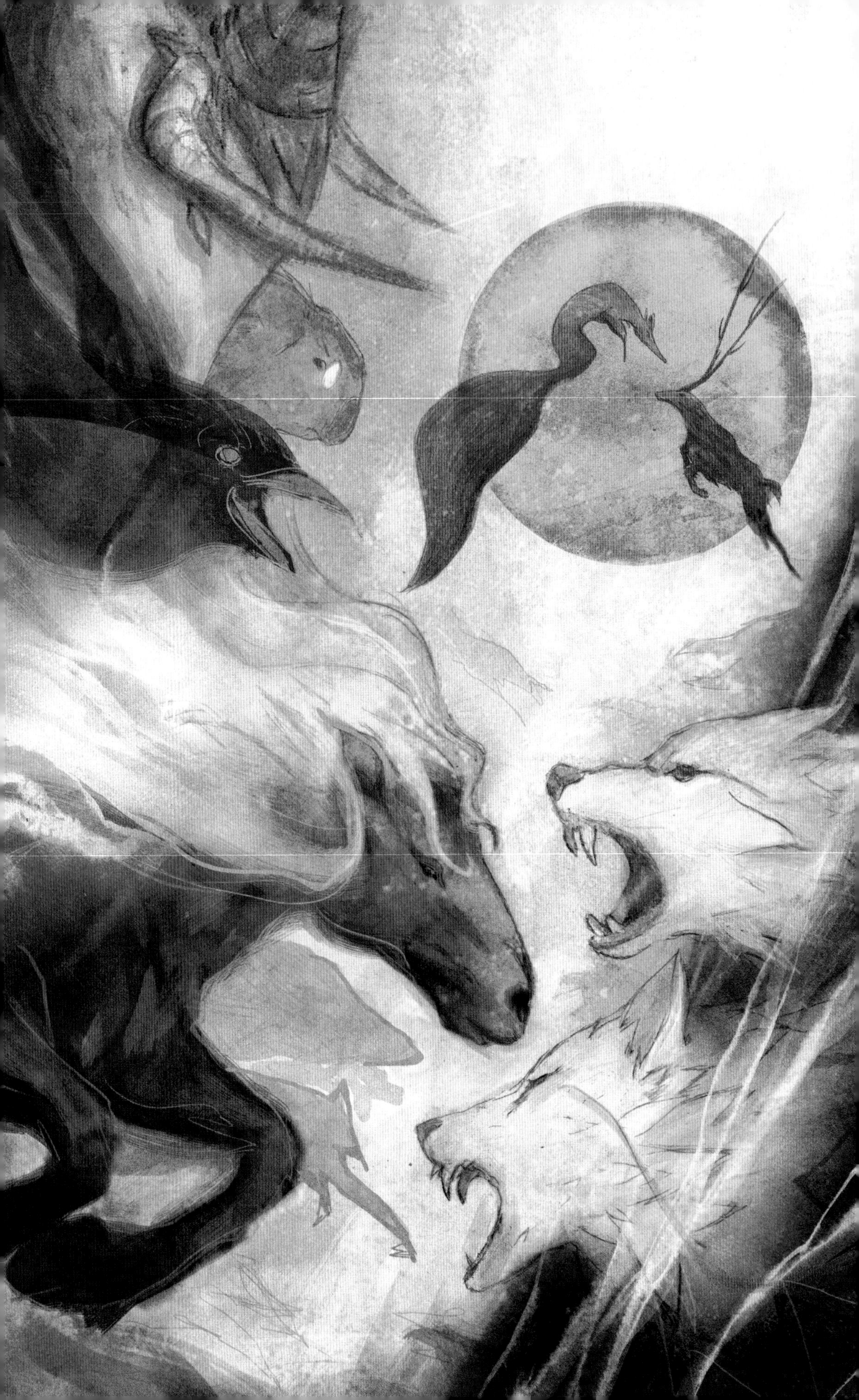

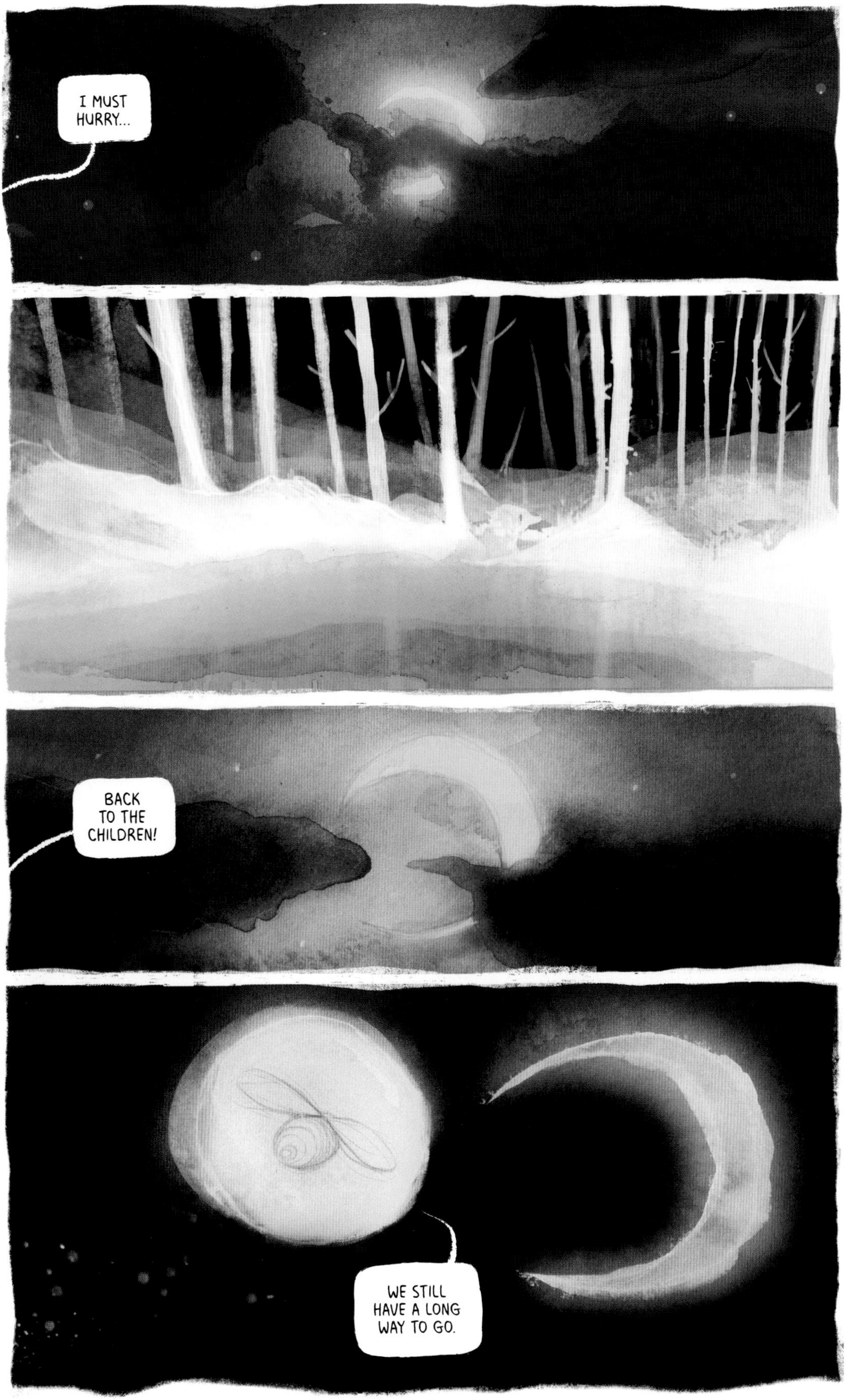
I MUST HURRY...
BACK TO THE CHILDREN!
WE STILL HAVE A LONG WAY TO GO.

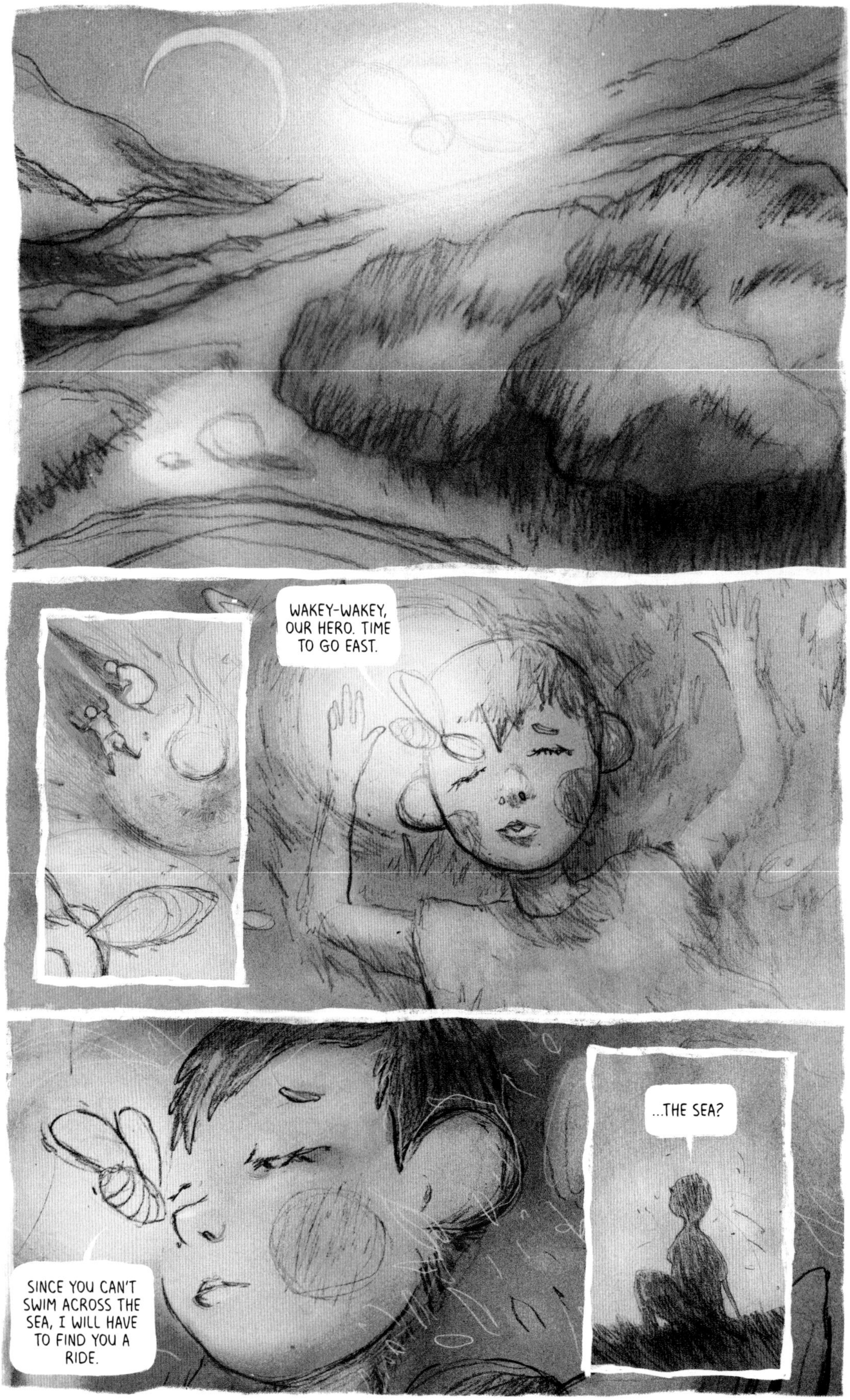
WAKEY-WAKEY, OUR HERO. TIME TO GO EAST.
...THE SEA?
SINCE YOU CAN'T SWIM ACROSS THE SEA, I WILL HAVE TO FIND YOU A RIDE.

AVA?

I HEARD A VOICE AND IT SAID THAT WE HAVE TO GO TO THE SEA. I THINK IT WILL LEAD US TO PAPA.

YOU LOOK DIFFERENT.

I'M TURNING, FLYNN.

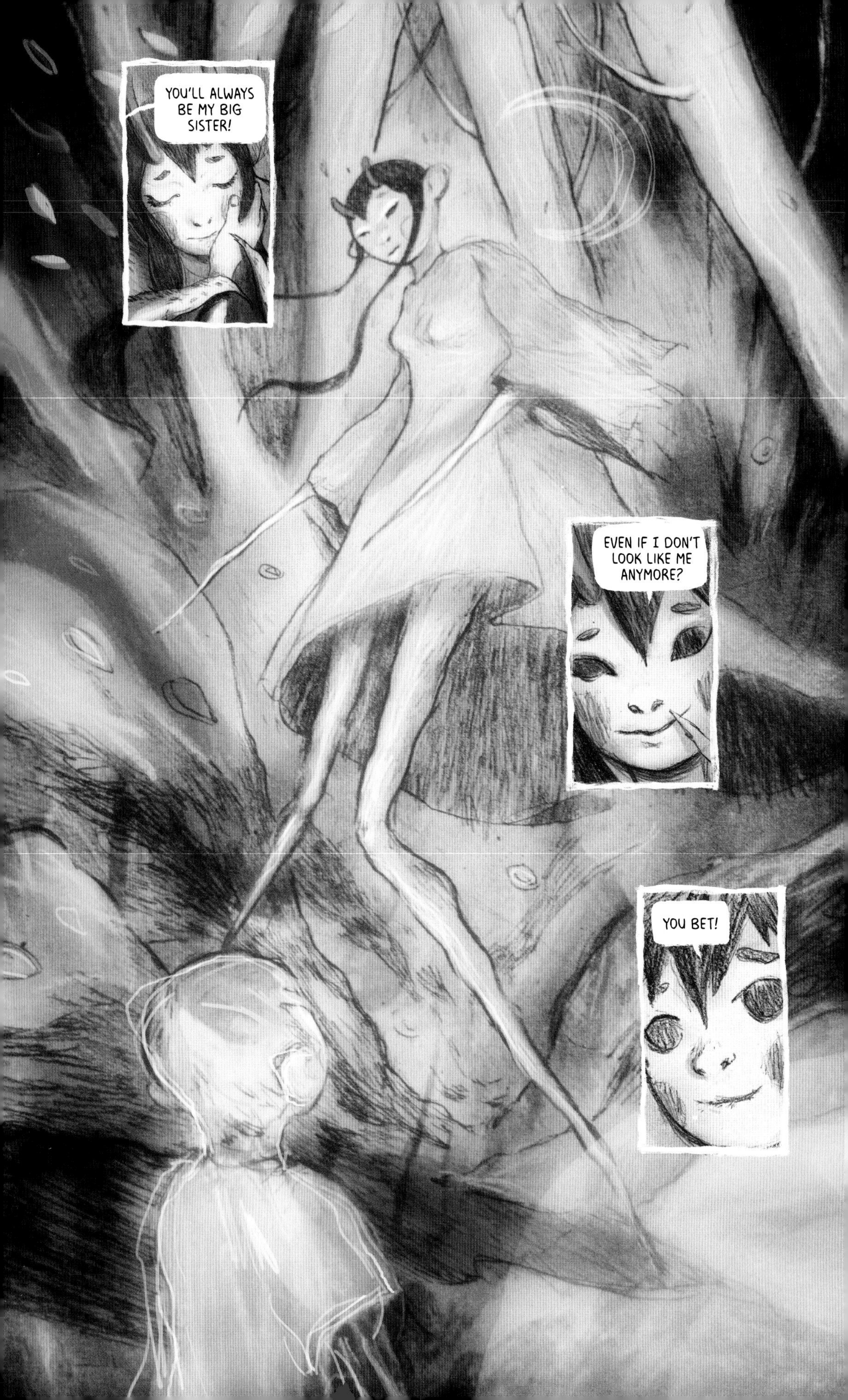

YOU'LL ALWAYS BE MY BIG SISTER!
EVEN IF I DON'T LOOK LIKE ME ANYMORE?
YOU BET!

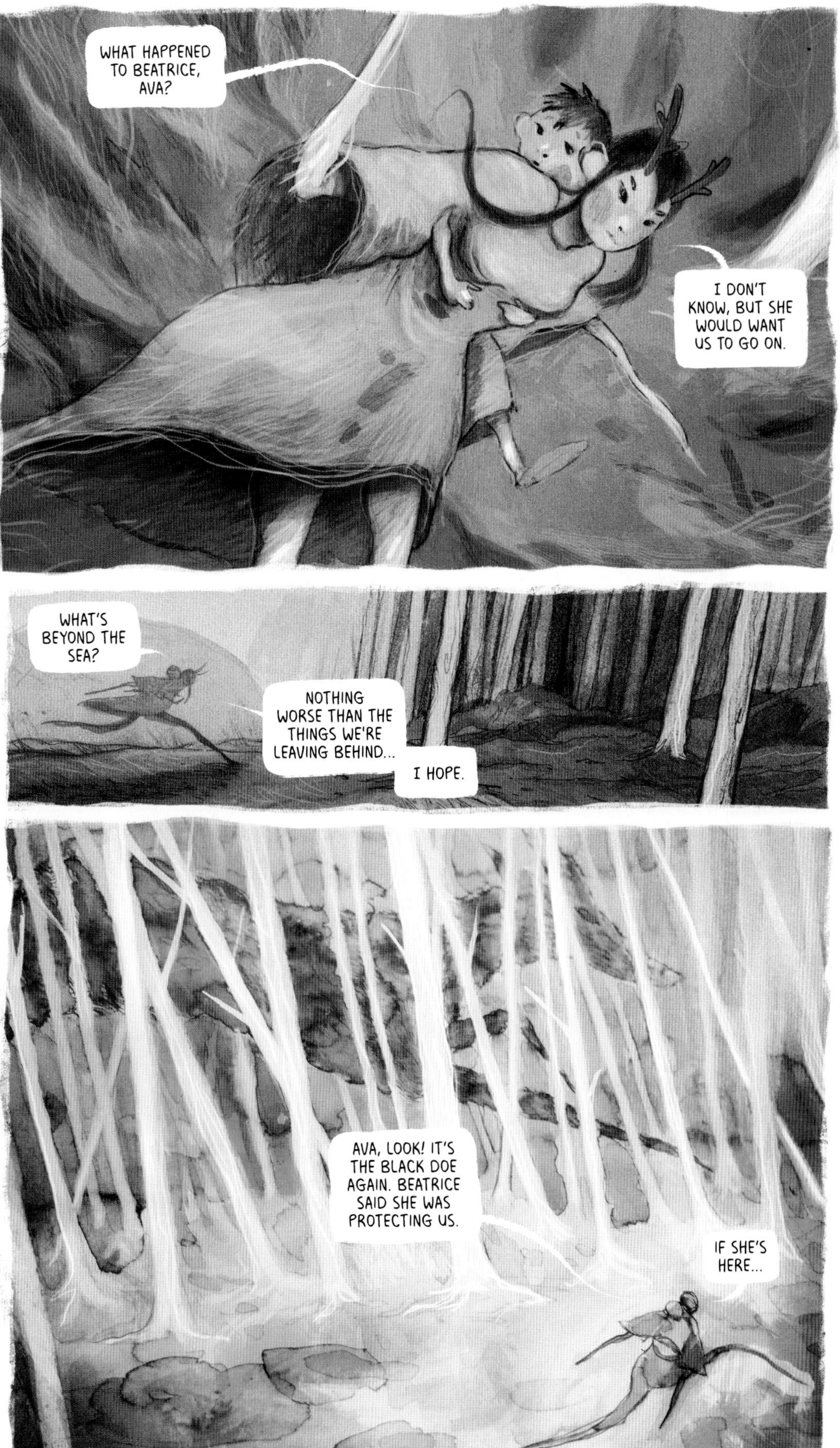
WHAT HAPPENED TO BEATRICE, AVA?
I DON'T KNOW, BUT SHE WOULD WANT US TO GO ON.
WHAT'S BEYOND THE SEA?
NOTHING WORSE THAN THE THINGS WE'RE LEAVING BEHIND...
I HOPE.
AVA, LOOK! IT'S THE BLACK DOE AGAIN. BEATRICE SAID SHE WAS PROTECTING US.
IF SHE'S HERE...

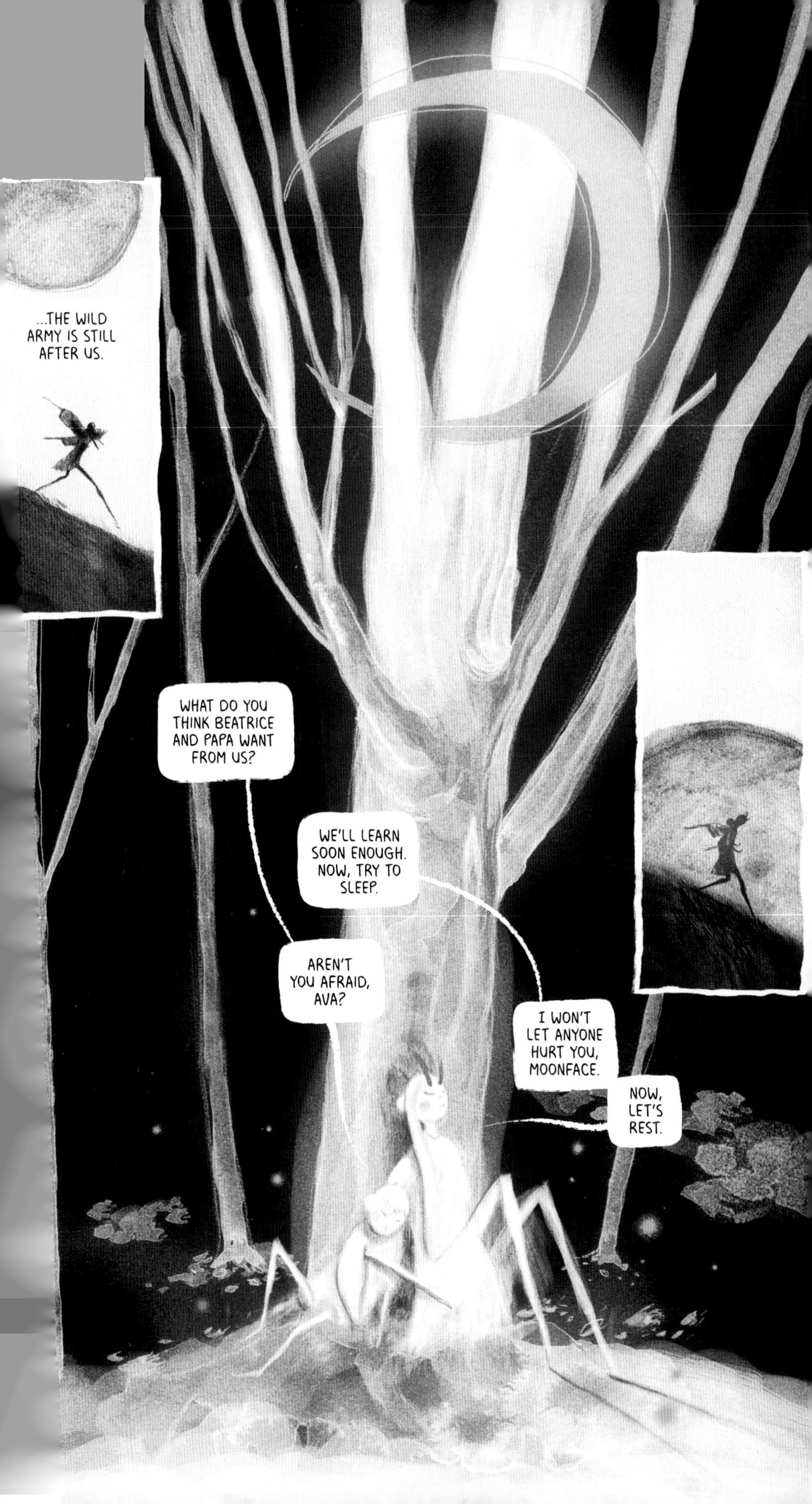
...THE WILD ARMY IS STILL AFTER US.
WHAT DO YOU THINK BEATRICE AND PAPA WANT FROM US?
WE'LL LEARN SOON ENOUGH. NOW, TRY TO SLEEP.
AREN'T YOU AFRAID, AVA?
I WON'T LET ANYONE HURT YOU, MOONFACE.
NOW, LET'S REST.

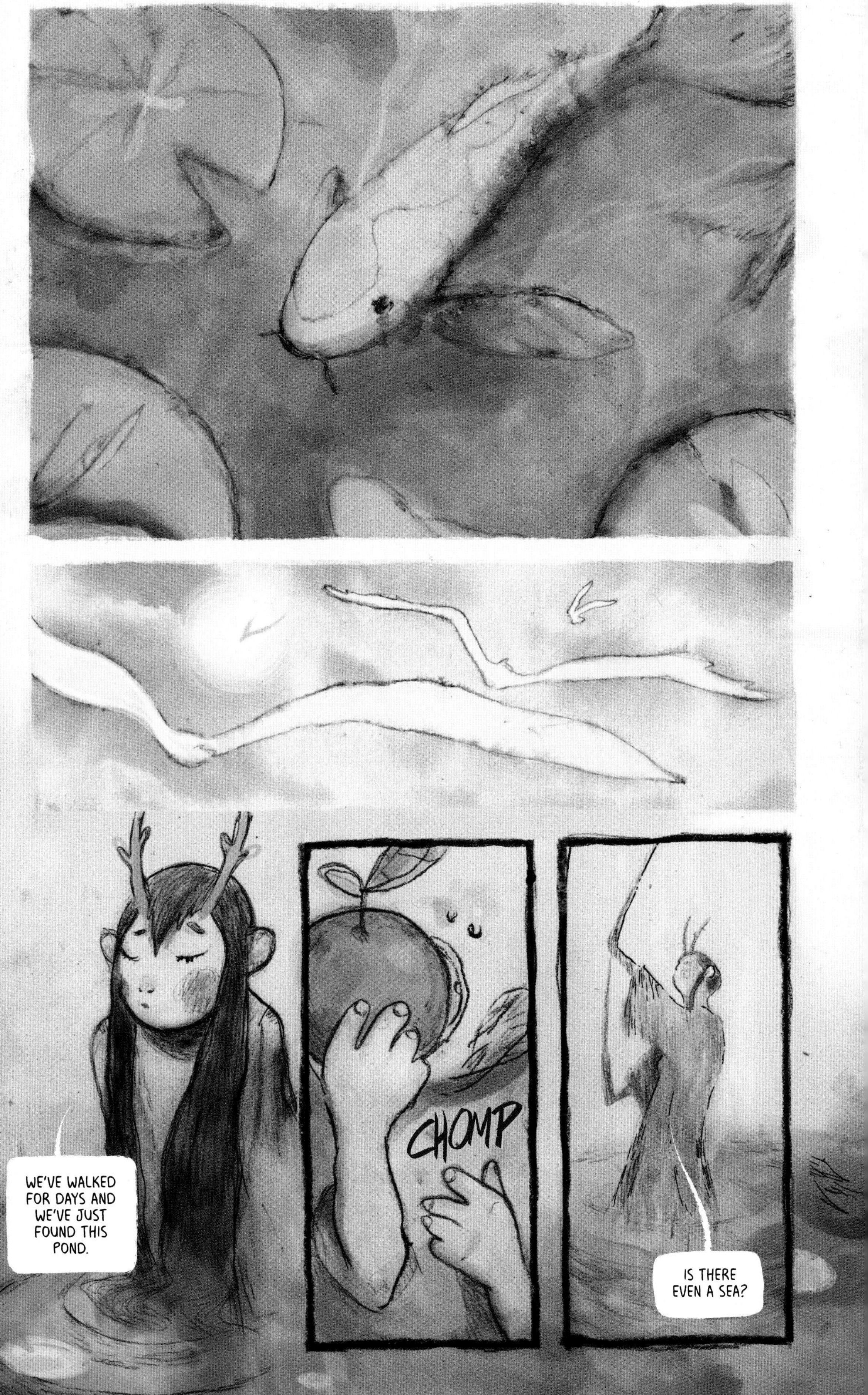
WE'VE WALKED FOR DAYS AND WE'VE JUST FOUND THIS POND.
CHOMP
IS THERE EVEN A SEA?

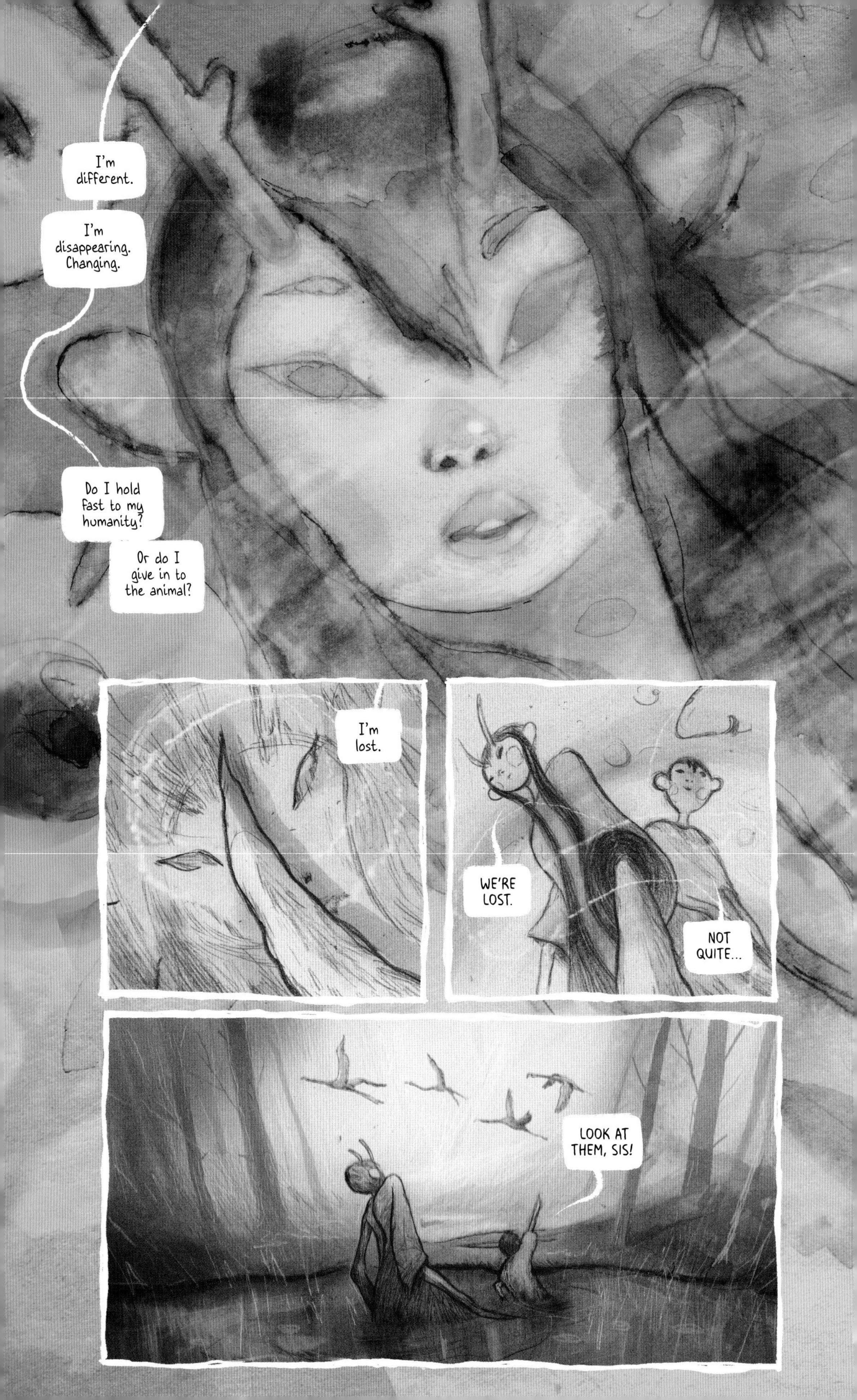
I'm different.
I'm disappearing. Changing.
Do I hold fast to my humanity?
Or do I give in to the animal?
I'm lost.
WE'RE LOST.
NOT QUITE...
LOOK AT THEM, SIS!

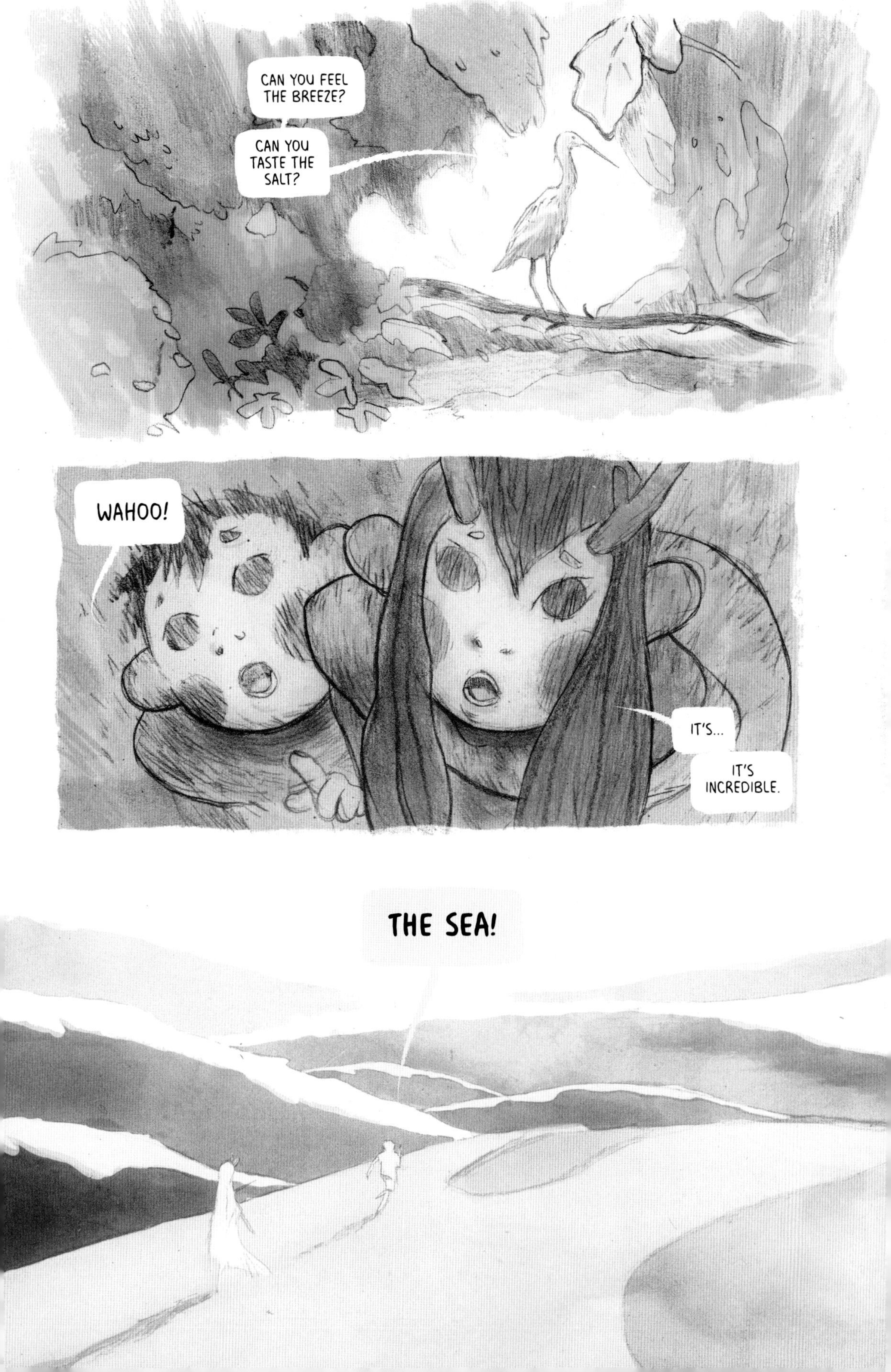
CAN YOU FEEL THE BREEZE?
CAN YOU TASTE THE SALT?
WAHOO!
IT'S...
IT'S INCREDIBLE.
THE SEA!

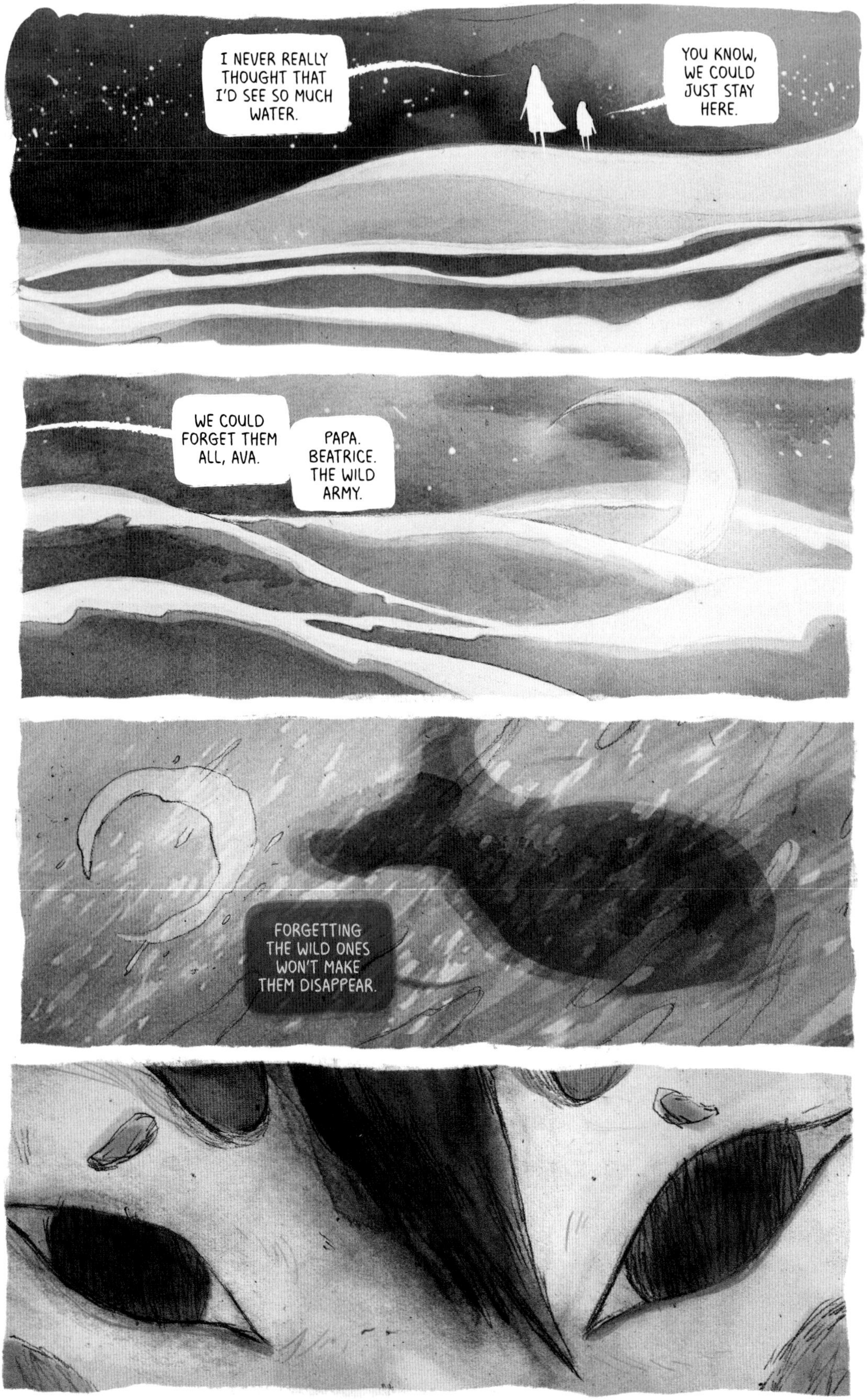
I NEVER REALLY THOUGHT THAT I'D SEE SO MUCH WATER.
YOU KNOW, WE COULD JUST STAY HERE.
WE COULD FORGET THEM ALL, AVA.
PAPA. BEATRICE. THE WILD ARMY.
FORGETTING THE WILD ONES WON'T MAKE THEM DISAPPEAR.

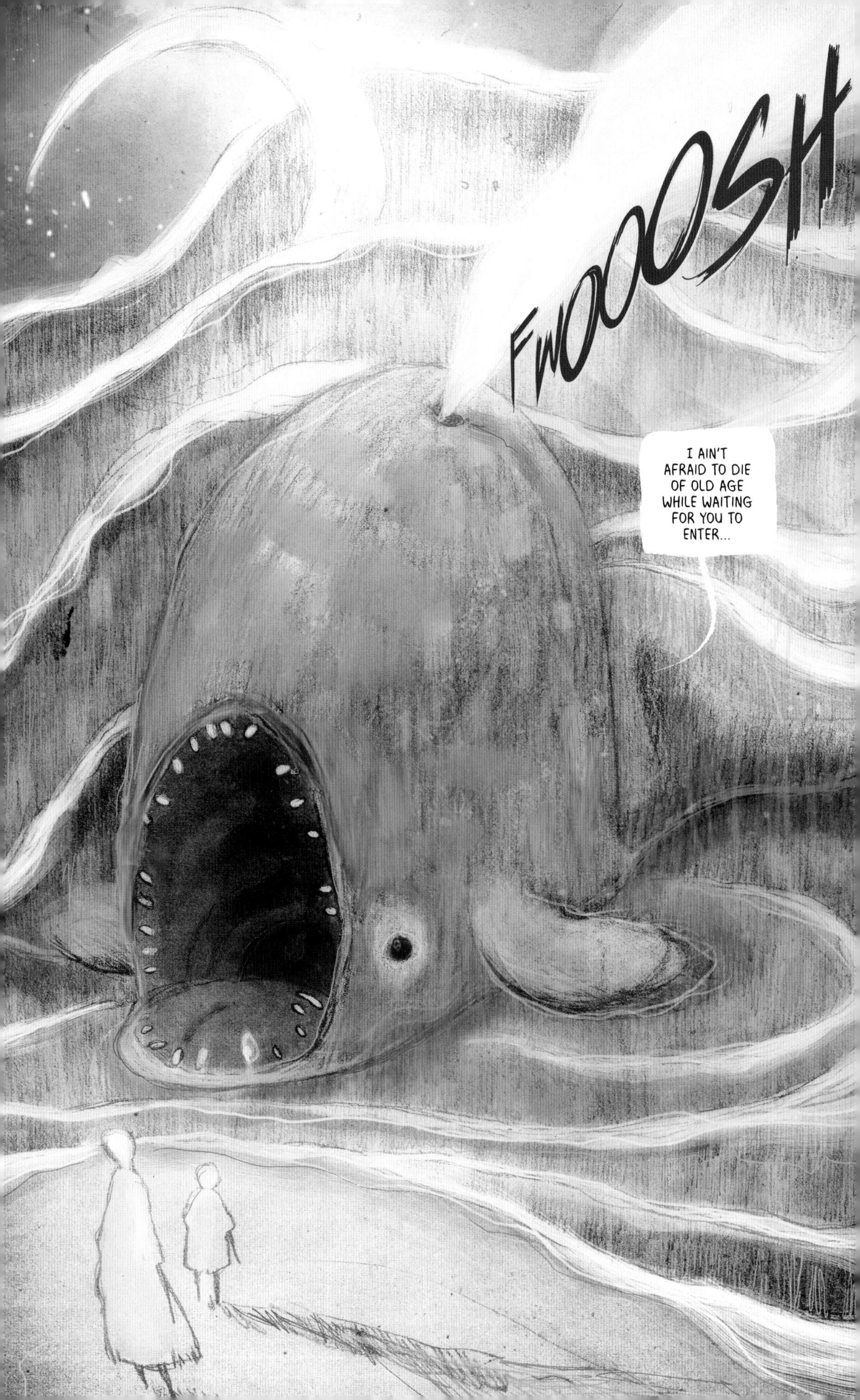
FWOOOSH
I AIN'T AFRAID TO DIE OF OLD AGE WHILE WAITING FOR YOU TO ENTER...

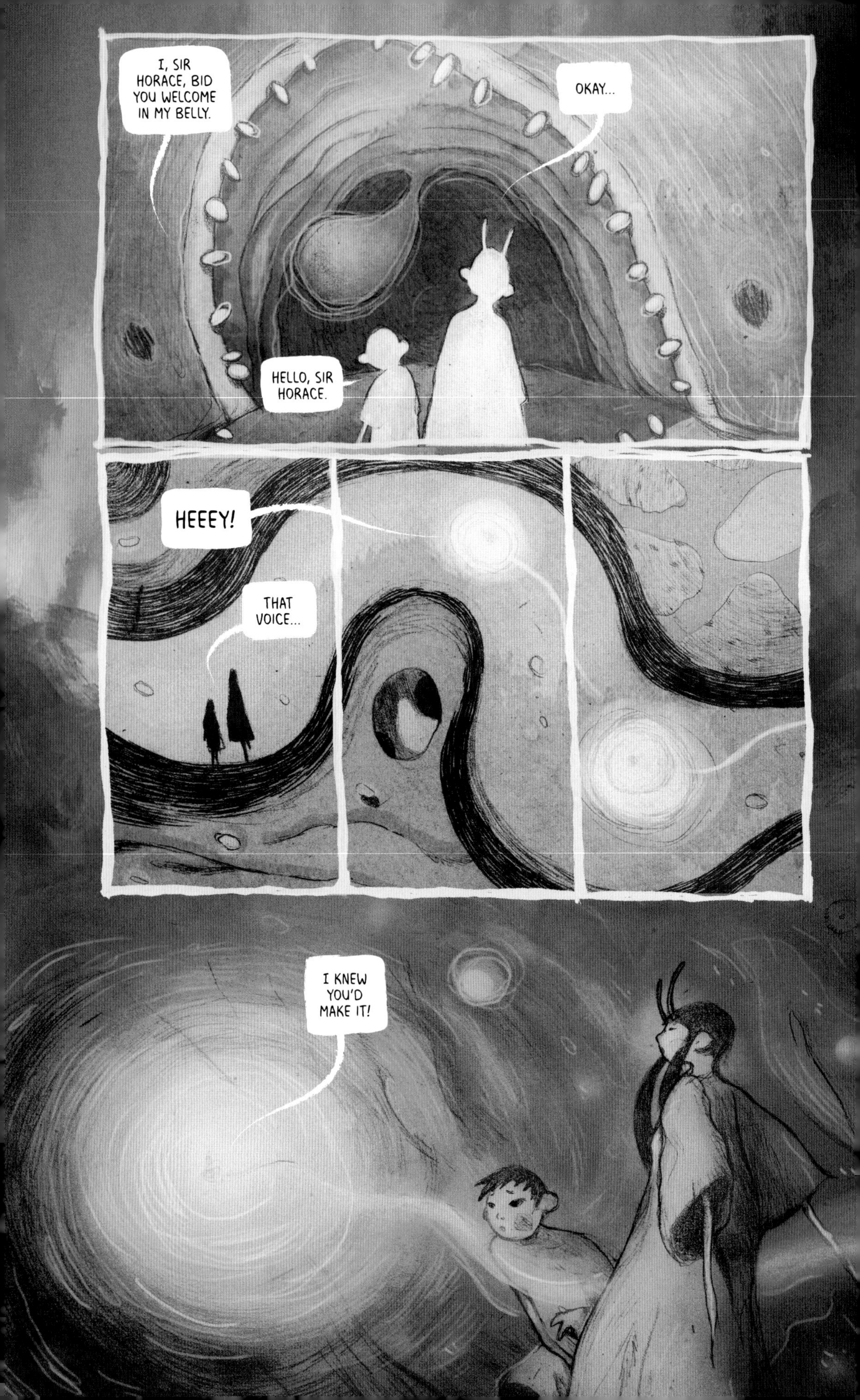
I, SIR HORACE, BID YOU WELCOME IN MY BELLY.
OKAY...
HELLO, SIR HORACE.
HEEEY!
THAT VOICE...
I KNEW YOU'D MAKE IT!

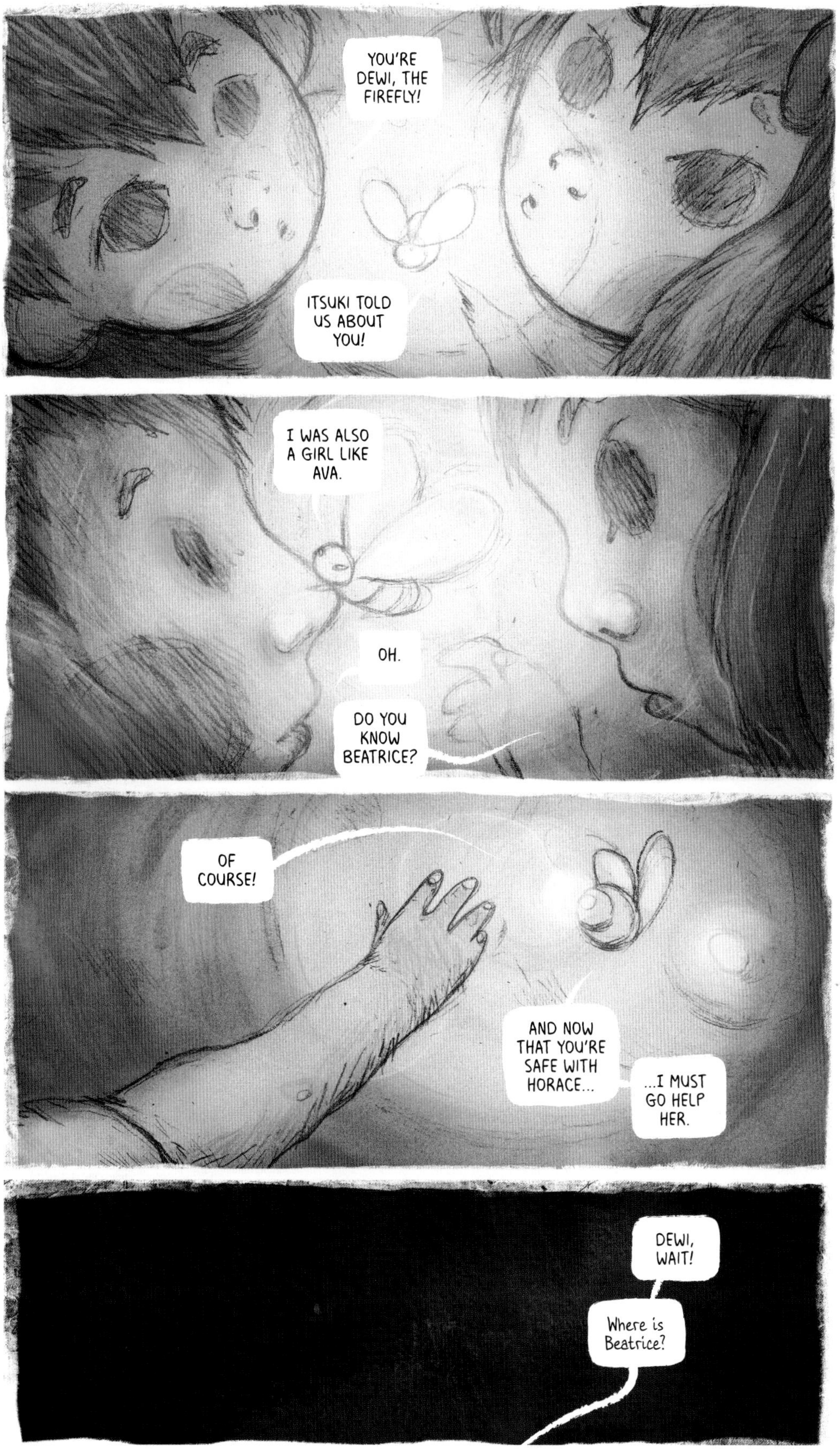
YOU'RE DEWI, THE FIREFLY!
ITSUKI TOLD US ABOUT YOU!
I WAS ALSO A GIRL LIKE AVA.
OH.
DO YOU KNOW BEATRICE?
OF COURSE!
AND NOW THAT YOU'RE SAFE WITH HORACE...
...I MUST GO HELP HER.
DEWI, WAIT!
Where is Beatrice?

DEWI, IT'S TOO LATE.
WE OWE IT TO BEA, HORACE.
IT CAN'T BE TOO LATE.
JUST HOLD ON A LITTLE LONGER, GIRL.

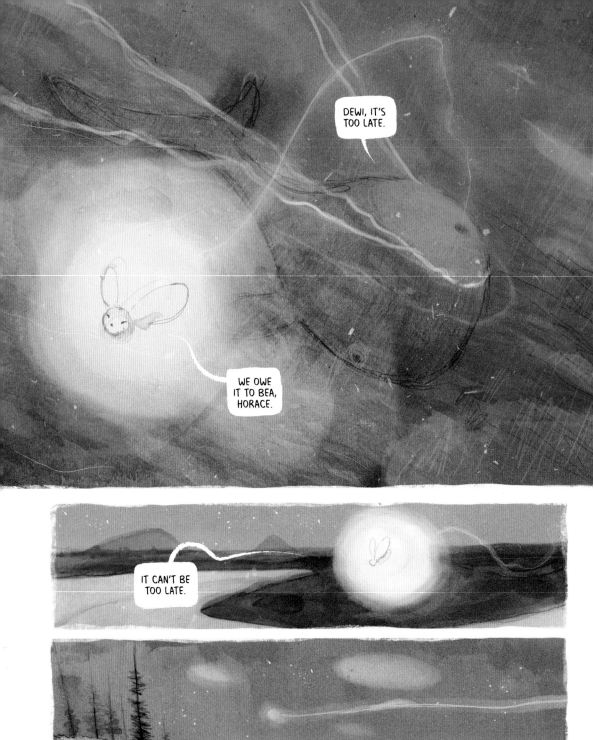

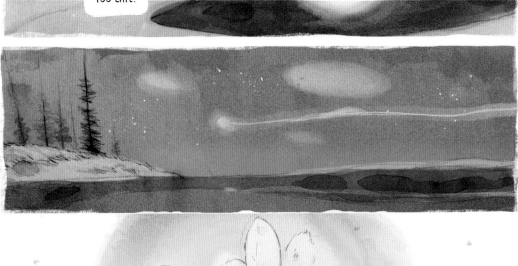

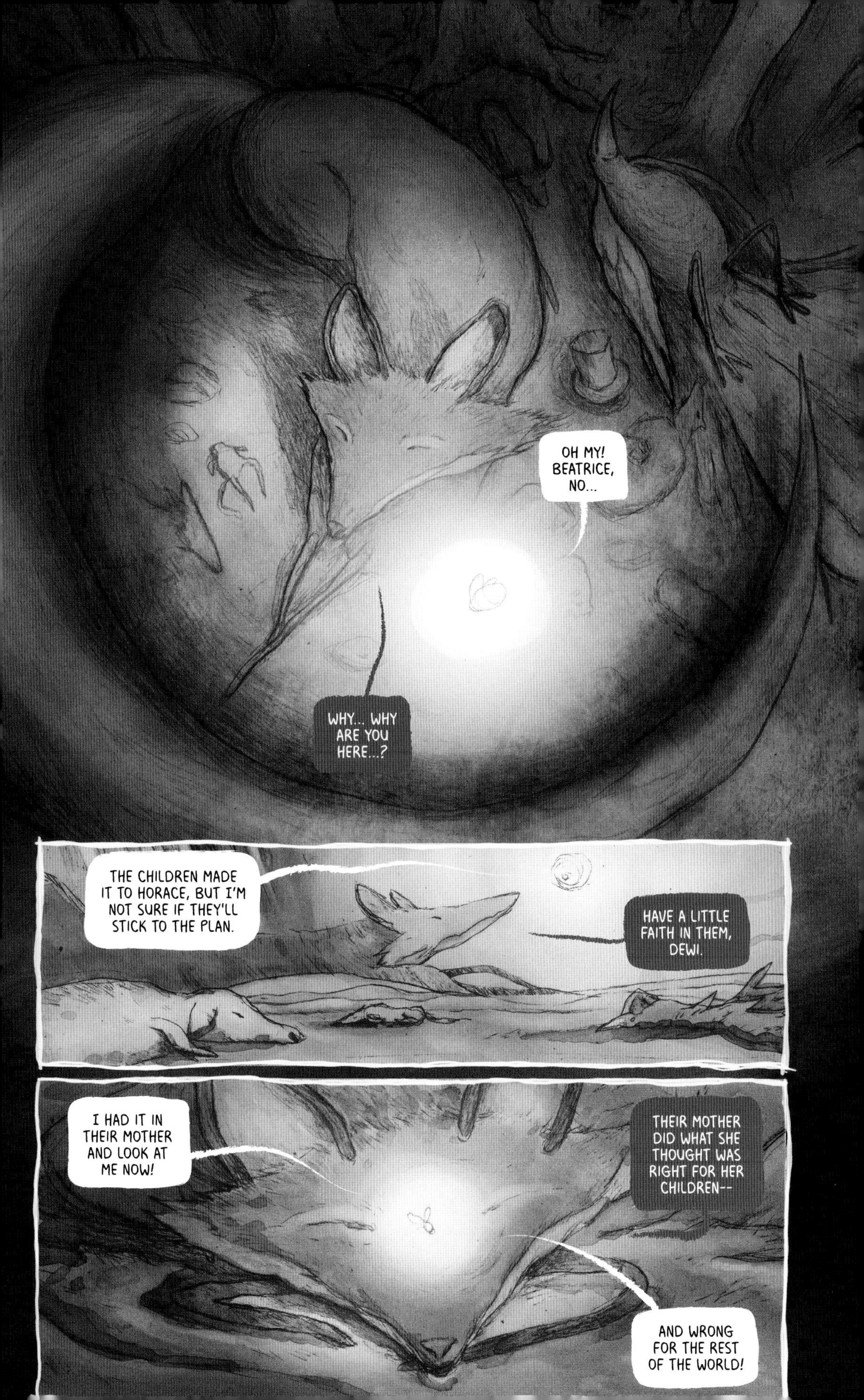
OH MY! BEATRICE, NO...
WHY... WHY ARE YOU HERE...?
THE CHILDREN MADE IT TO HORACE, BUT I'M NOT SURE IF THEY'LL STICK TO THE PLAN.
HAVE A LITTLE FAITH IN THEM, DEWI.
I HAD IT IN THEIR MOTHER AND LOOK AT ME NOW!
THEIR MOTHER DID WHAT SHE THOUGHT WAS RIGHT FOR HER CHILDREN--
AND WRONG FOR THE REST OF THE WORLD!

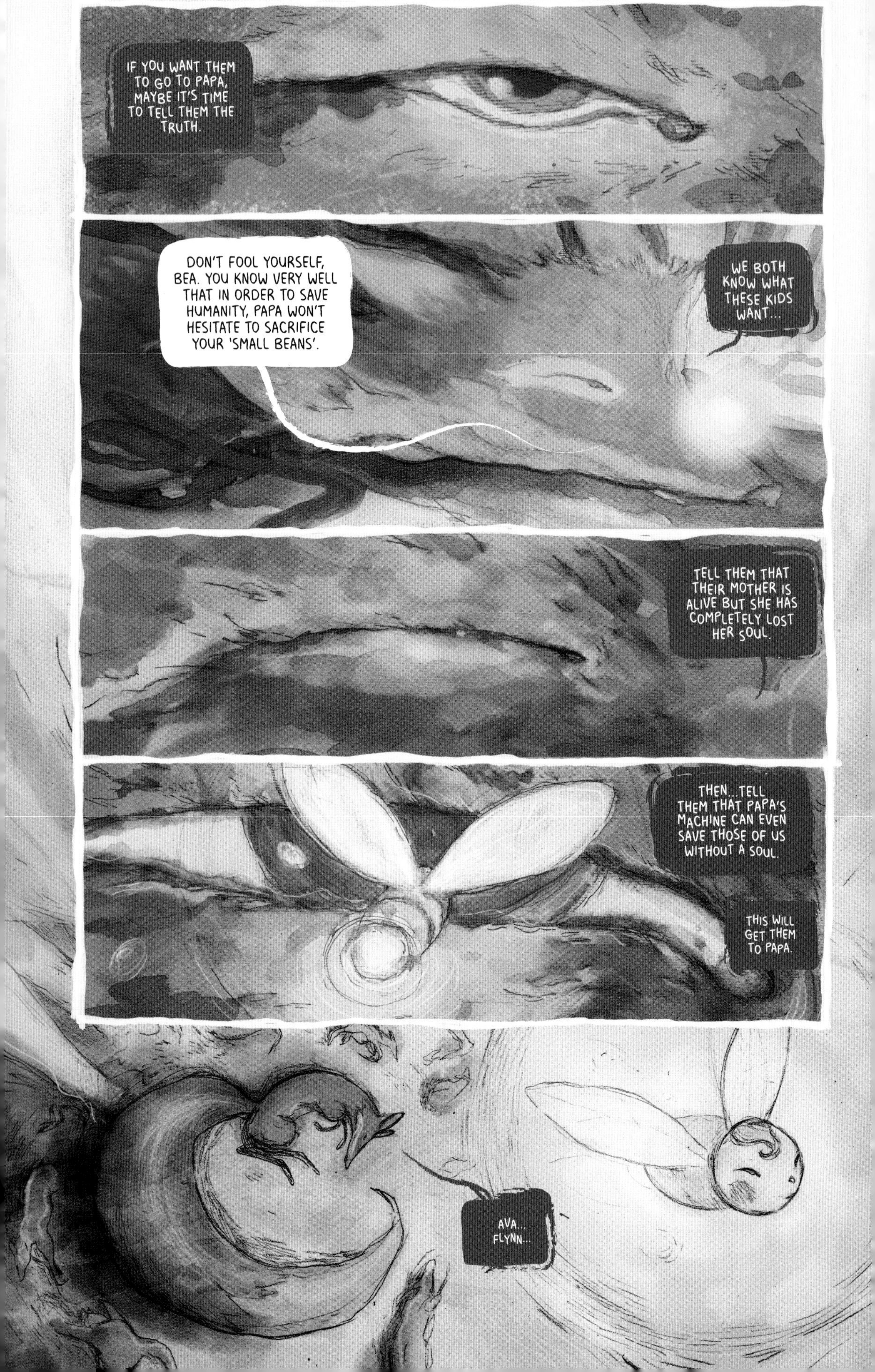
IF YOU WANT THEM TO GO TO PAPA, MAYBE IT'S TIME TO TELL THEM THE TRUTH.
DON'T FOOL YOURSELF, BEA. YOU KNOW VERY WELL THAT IN ORDER TO SAVE HUMANITY, PAPA WON'T HESITATE TO SACRIFICE YOUR 'SMALL BEANS'.
WE BOTH KNOW WHAT THESE KIDS WANT...
TELL THEM THAT THEIR MOTHER IS ALIVE BUT SHE HAS COMPLETELY LOST HER SOUL.
THEN...TELL THEM THAT PAPA'S MACHINE CAN EVEN SAVE THOSE OF US WITHOUT A SOUL.
THIS WILL GET THEM TO PAPA.
AVA... FLYNN...

I SEE LIGHT UP AHEAD.

WHERE IS IT FROM?

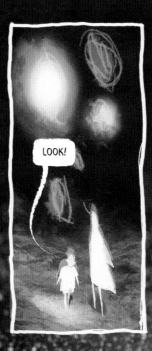

LOOK!

IT IS I, DENIZ...

...AND **YOU** MUST BE THE LAST HUMANS.

MY FRIENDS AND I WERE THE REVOLUTION AND NOW WE ARE THE PROOF OF ITS FAILURE...

...BUT YOU TWO CAN BECOME ITS SALVATION.

YOU BOTH LOOK LIKE YOUR MOTHER.
OUR MOTHER?
YOU HAVE HER ROUND CHEEKS.
AVA, LOOK!

"THERE USED TO BE NINE OF US.

"NINE TO SAVE THE WORLD."

"THE MISSING EIGHTH IS PAPA, THE FATHER OF OUR CAUSE, THE ONE WHO SACRIFICED HIMSELF IN ORDER TO ACHIEVE ENLIGHTENMENT THROUGH BRINGING THE SOULS OF HUMANS AND ANIMALS TOGETHER.

"THE NINTH IS YOUR MOTHER. A TRAITOR AND THE THIEF OF THE SPARK-- THE TRIGGER THAT WOULD SET THESE EVENTS ON THEIR COURSE."

THE SPARK?

THAT'S SEVEN.

"THE KEY TO THE MACHINE AND THE ONLY WAY TO MOVE A SOUL IN AND OUT OF A BODY, AND BRING HUMAN AND ANIMAL CONSCIOUSNESS TOGETHER."

"DEWI WAS THE YOUNGEST OF US ALL. A LIGHT IN OUR DARKNESS.

"THEN BEATRICE, WHO SAW HUMANITY AND NATURE AS ONE.

"ITSUKI WAS THE CURIOUS ONE--WOULD ANIMALS **HAVE** A SOUL?

"HORACE, WHO GREW TIRED OF DISSECTING FISH. AND NOW IS ONE.

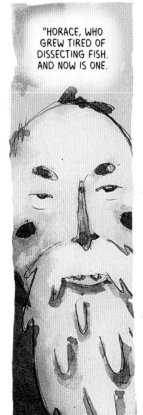

"PANDORA WANTED ANIMALS TO BE RESPECTED. WOULD A SHARED MOMENT OF CONSCIOUSNESS CREATE EMPATHY?

"I KNEW THAT EVERYTHING WOULD GO WRONG. WE WERE TOO AMBITIOUS. ARROGANT. I WASN'T ALONE IN THIS THINKING.

"THERE WAS OMAR. HE FOUND HIMSELF BETWEEN PAPA AND YOUR MOTHER.

"WHILE OUR SOULS MERGED WITH THE ANIMAL, HIS HUMAN SOUL BECAME A PASSENGER. HE GAVE INTO HIS BASER INSTINCTS.

"BECAUSE OF YOUR MOTHER, EVERYTHING WENT WRONG.

"SHE RAN AWAY WHILE BEATRICE STAYED WITH WHAT WAS LEFT OF PAPA. HE HAD SPLIT INTO SOMETHING NEW...SOMETHING BEYOND HUMAN OR ANIMAL.

"THE REST OF US WENT AFTER YOUR MOTHER.

"WE WALKED FOR WEEKS.

"ALL THE ANIMALS DIED...

"...AND THEN HUMANS BEGAN TO CHANGE. YOU SEE, THE SOULS DIDN'T PASS THROUGH. THEY MERGED."

"DEWI WAS THRILLED BECAUSE SHE GREW WINGS. HEH--SHE THOUGHT SHE'D BECOME A FAIRY.

"A WAR WAS BEING WAGED WITHIN US AND OUR HUMAN SOULS WERE LOSING.

"WE SAID GOODBYE TO ITSUKI AND PANDORA. THEY FELT HOPE WAS LOST AND HUMANITY WAS AT ITS END, SO THEY HID THEMSELVES IN AN OLD ZOO. AFTER ALL, THERE WERE NO OTHER ANIMALS LEFT TO LIVE IN THOSE RUSTY CAGES.

"HORACE AND I WERE DRAWN TO WATER.

"OMAR AND DEWI CONTINUED ON AFTER YOUR MOTHER...

"AND WE ALLOWED NATURE TO RULE OUR BODIES.

"WASN'T IT WHAT WE'D BEEN LONGING FOR?

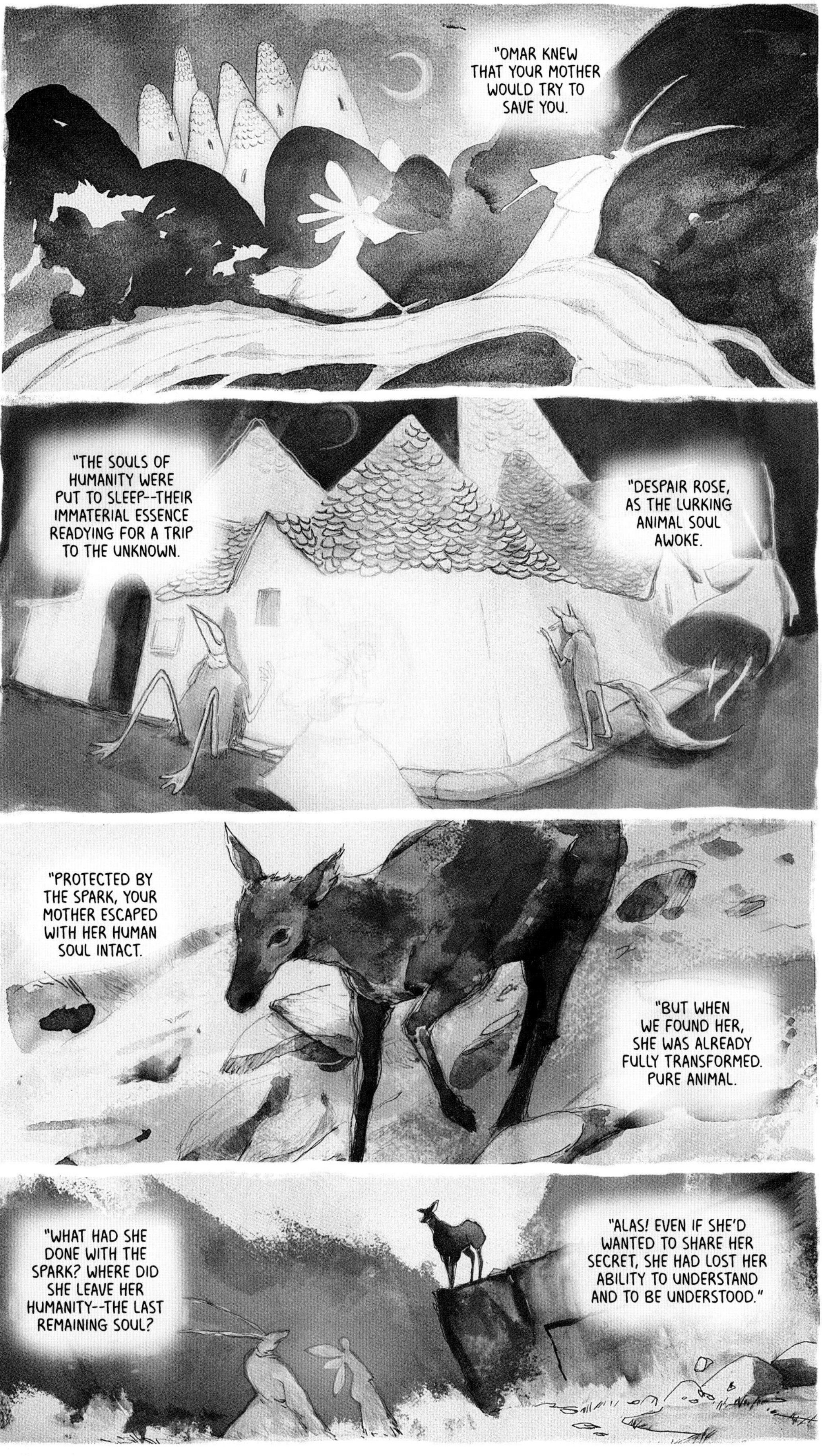
"OMAR KNEW THAT YOUR MOTHER WOULD TRY TO SAVE YOU.
"THE SOULS OF HUMANITY WERE PUT TO SLEEP--THEIR IMMATERIAL ESSENCE READYING FOR A TRIP TO THE UNKNOWN.
"DESPAIR ROSE, AS THE LURKING ANIMAL SOUL AWOKE.
"PROTECTED BY THE SPARK, YOUR MOTHER ESCAPED WITH HER HUMAN SOUL INTACT.
"BUT WHEN WE FOUND HER, SHE WAS ALREADY FULLY TRANSFORMED. PURE ANIMAL.
"WHAT HAD SHE DONE WITH THE SPARK? WHERE DID SHE LEAVE HER HUMANITY--THE LAST REMAINING SOUL?
"ALAS! EVEN IF SHE'D WANTED TO SHARE HER SECRET, SHE HAD LOST HER ABILITY TO UNDERSTAND AND TO BE UNDERSTOOD."

"DEWI WAS IN DESPAIR. SHE ASKED OMAR TO TRACK HER STEPS BACK TO YOUR MOTHER'S SHELTER AND FIND OUT THE FATE OF HER SOUL.

"HE DID IT, BUT THE ANIMAL IN HIM PROTECTED YOUR MOTHER'S SECRET--**YOU.**

"DEWI WANTED OMAR TO HELP HER CAPTURE YOUR MOTHER.

"HER PLEA FELL ON DEAF EARS.

"OMAR WASN'T THERE TO RETRIEVE YOUR MOTHER'S LOST SOUL.

"HE WAS THERE TO MAKE SURE THAT YOU CHILDREN NEVER FELL INTO PAPA'S HANDS.

"THE HUMAN IN OMAR HATED PAPA.

"THE ANIMAL IN HIM BEGAN TO HATE HUMANS TOO.

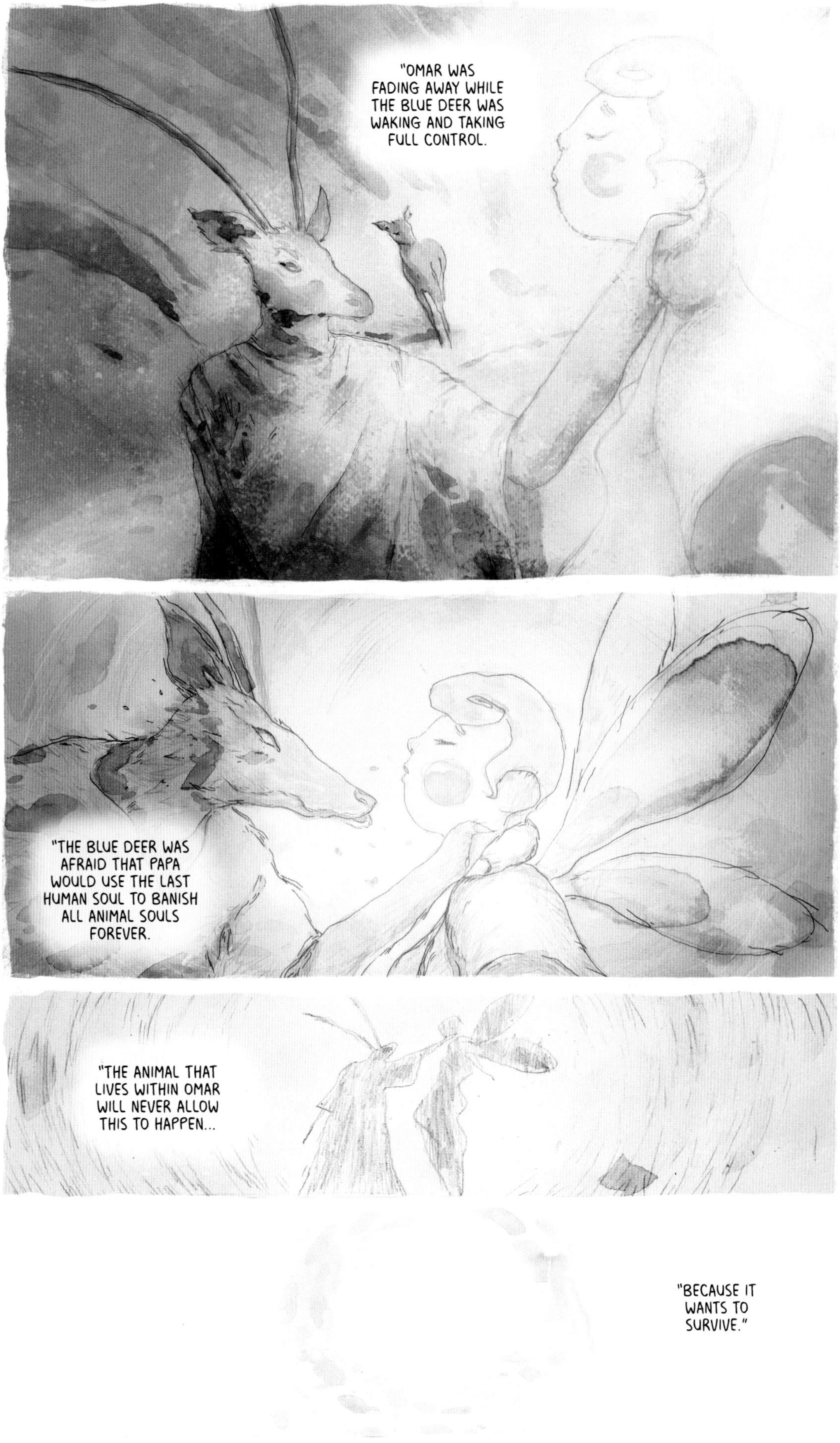
"OMAR WAS FADING AWAY WHILE THE BLUE DEER WAS WAKING AND TAKING FULL CONTROL.
"THE BLUE DEER WAS AFRAID THAT PAPA WOULD USE THE LAST HUMAN SOUL TO BANISH ALL ANIMAL SOULS FOREVER.
"THE ANIMAL THAT LIVES WITHIN OMAR WILL NEVER ALLOW THIS TO HAPPEN...
"BECAUSE IT WANTS TO SURVIVE."

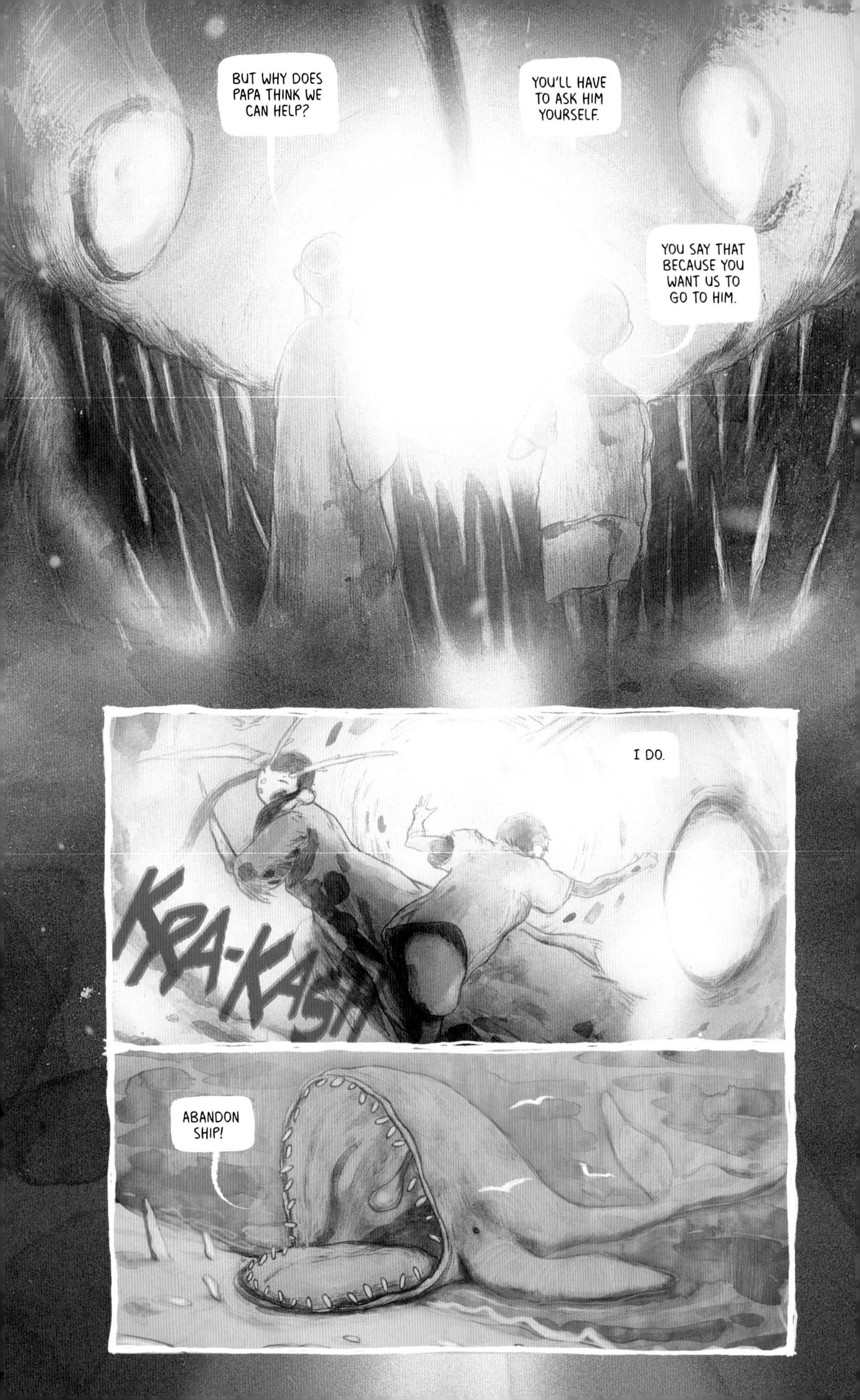
BUT WHY DOES PAPA THINK WE CAN HELP?
YOU'LL HAVE TO ASK HIM YOURSELF.
YOU SAY THAT BECAUSE YOU WANT US TO GO TO HIM.
I DO.
KRA-KASH
ABANDON SHIP!

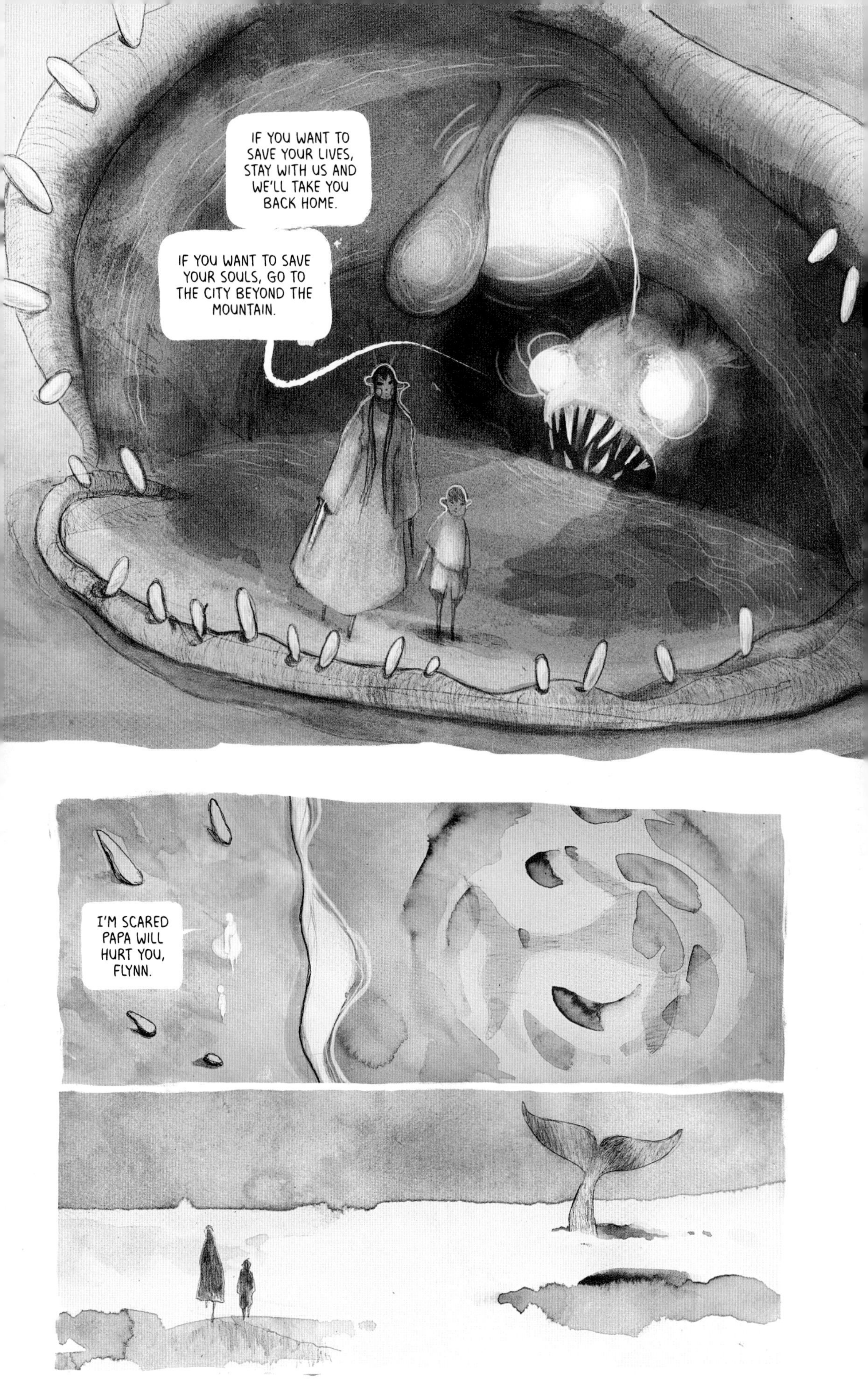
IF YOU WANT TO SAVE YOUR LIVES, STAY WITH US AND WE'LL TAKE YOU BACK HOME.
IF YOU WANT TO SAVE YOUR SOULS, GO TO THE CITY BEYOND THE MOUNTAIN.
I'M SCARED PAPA WILL HURT YOU, FLYNN.

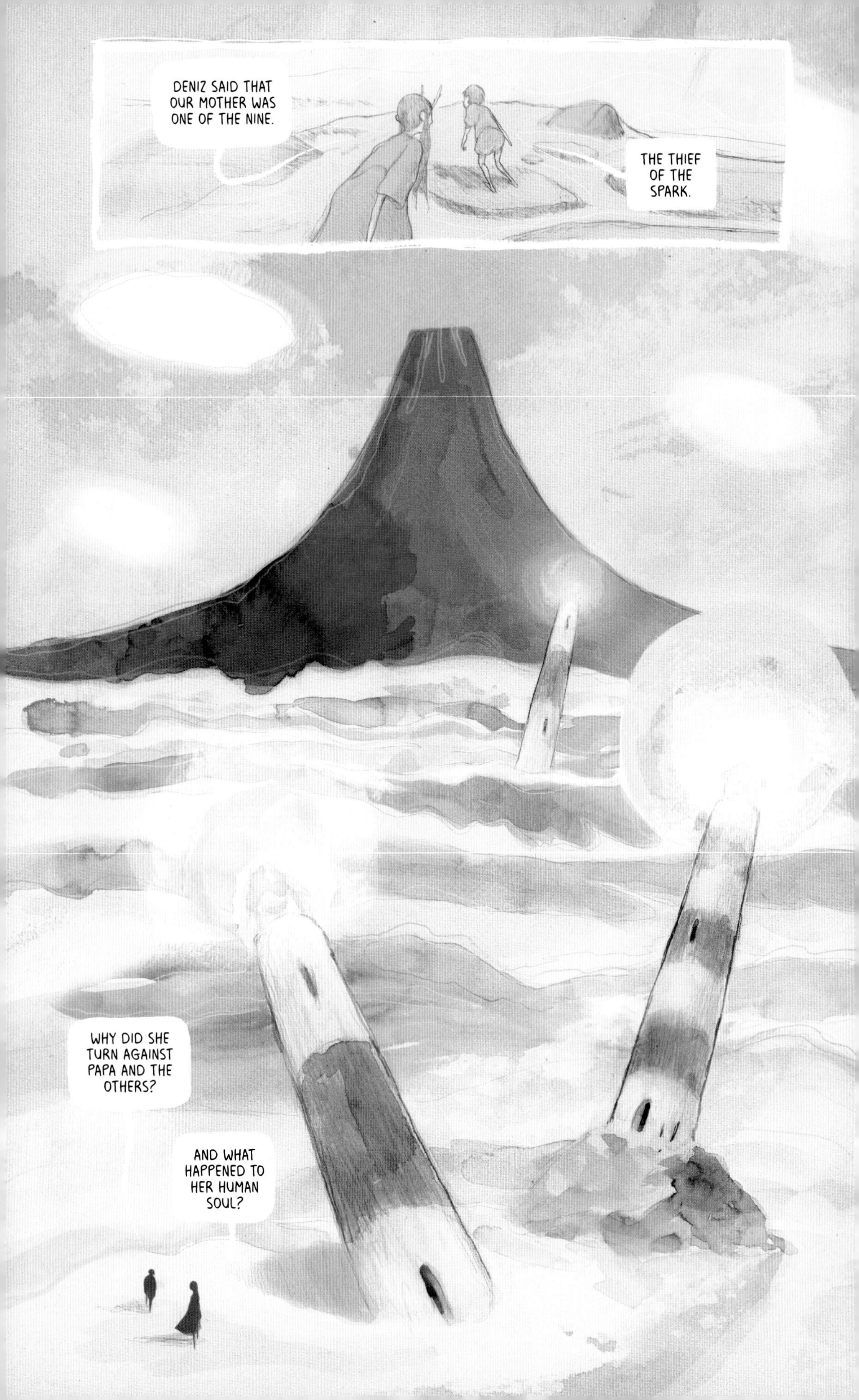
DENIZ SAID THAT OUR MOTHER WAS ONE OF THE NINE.
THE THIEF OF THE SPARK.
WHY DID SHE TURN AGAINST PAPA AND THE OTHERS?
AND WHAT HAPPENED TO HER HUMAN SOUL?

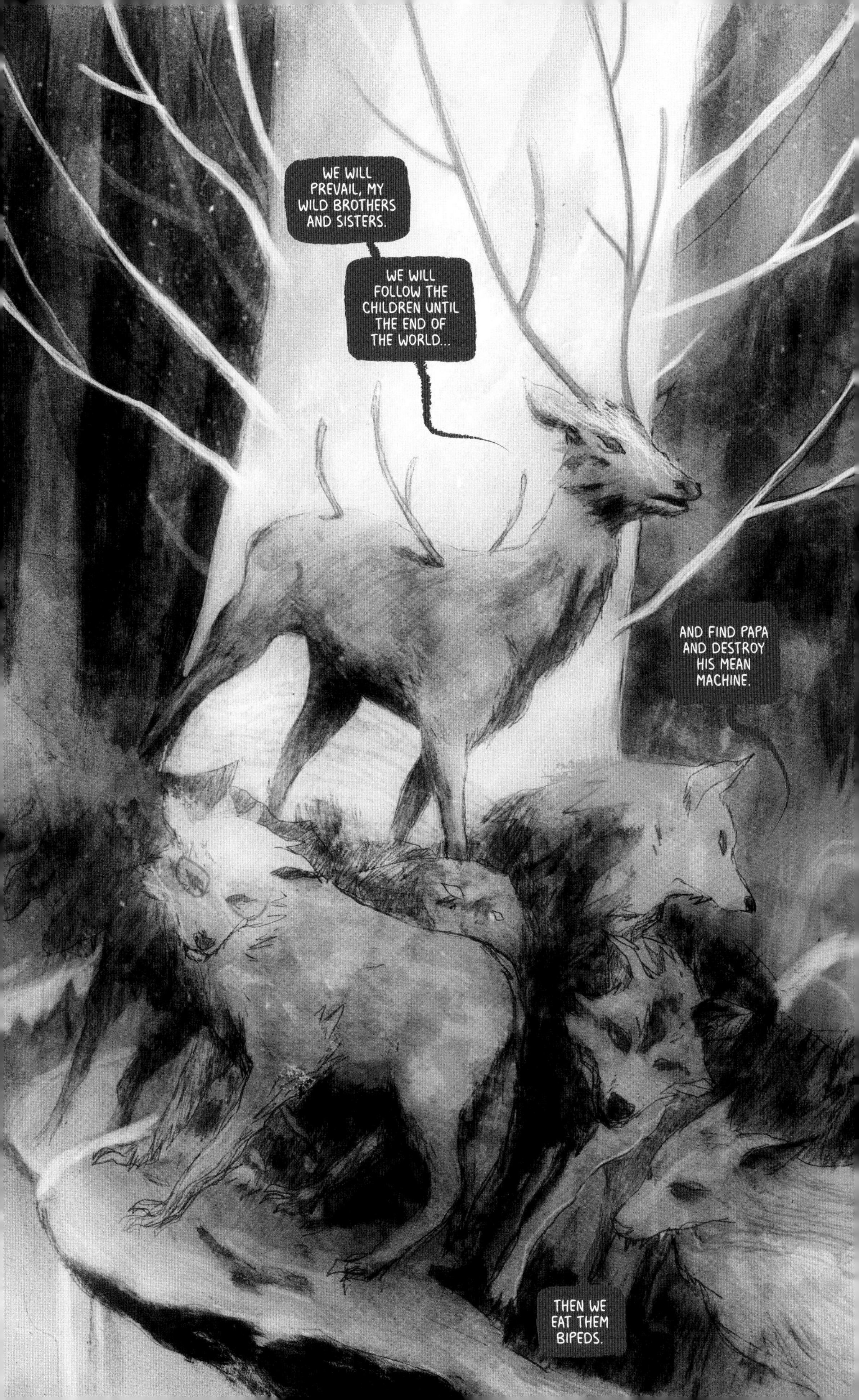
WE WILL PREVAIL, MY WILD BROTHERS AND SISTERS.
WE WILL FOLLOW THE CHILDREN UNTIL THE END OF THE WORLD...
AND FIND PAPA AND DESTROY HIS MEAN MACHINE.
THEN WE EAT THEM BIPEDS.

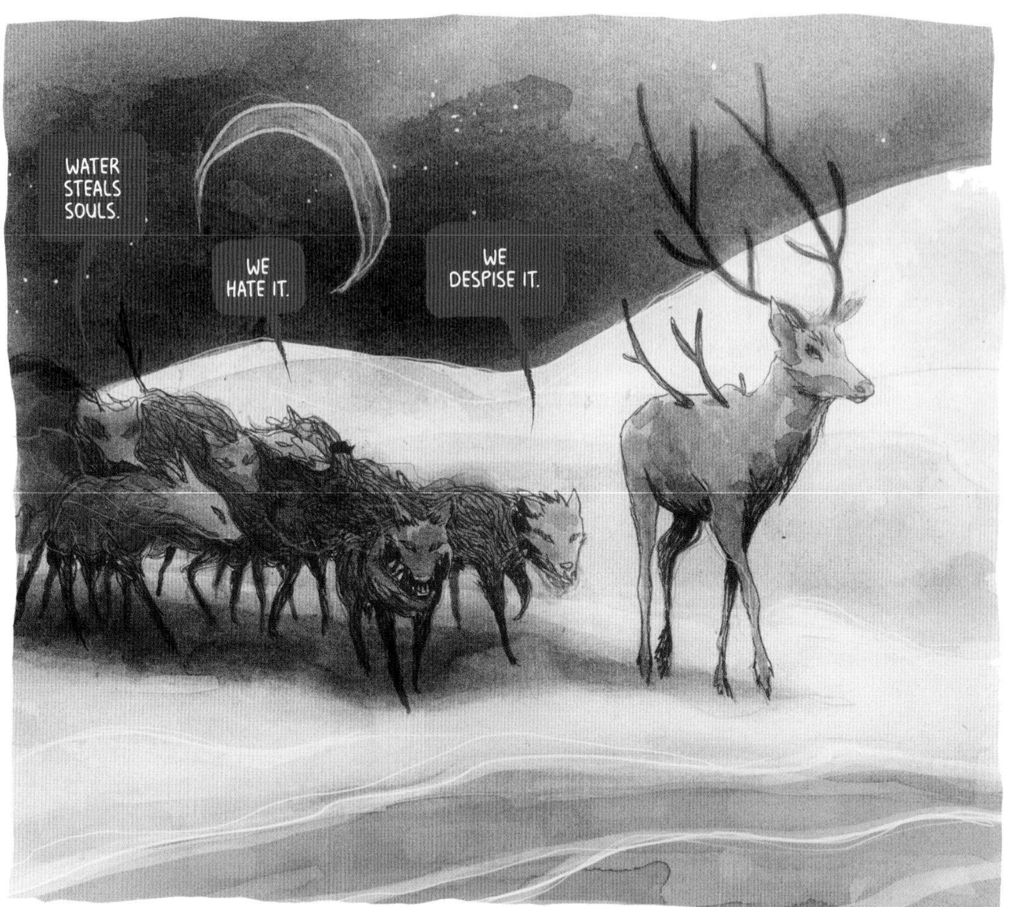
WATER STEALS SOULS.
WE HATE IT.
WE DESPISE IT.

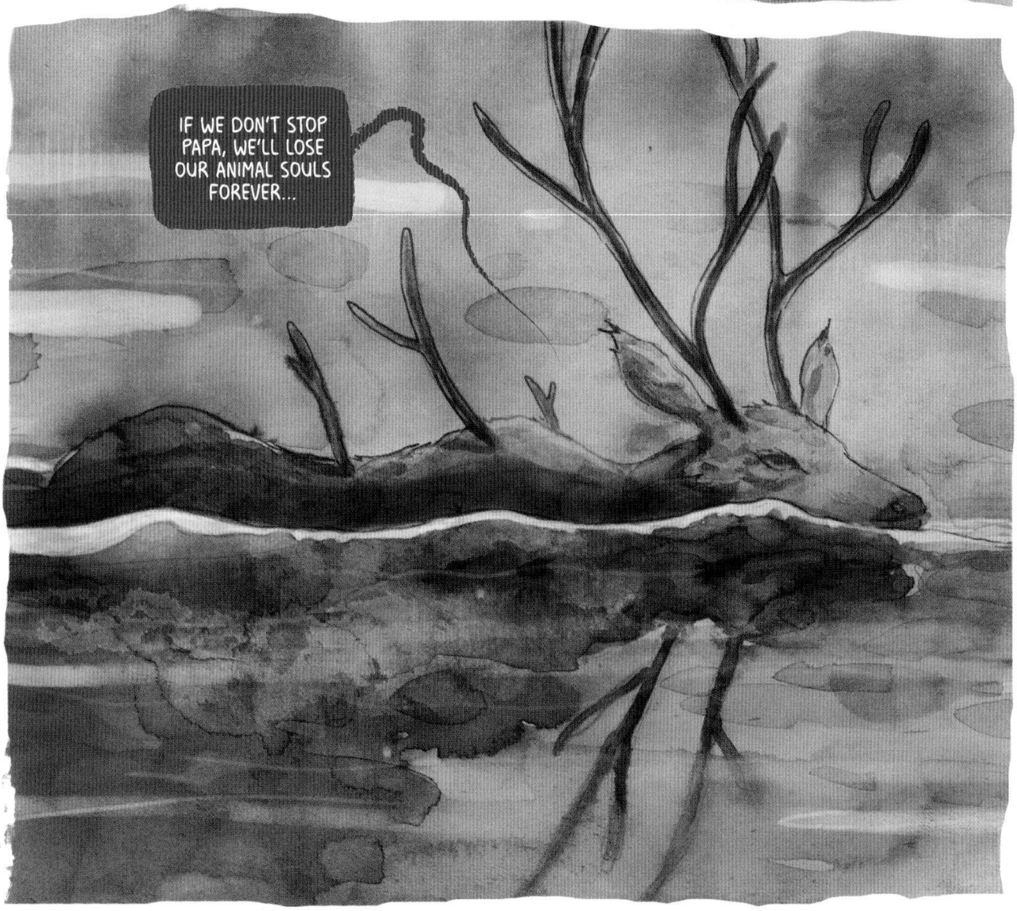
IF WE DON'T STOP PAPA, WE'LL LOSE OUR ANIMAL SOULS FOREVER...

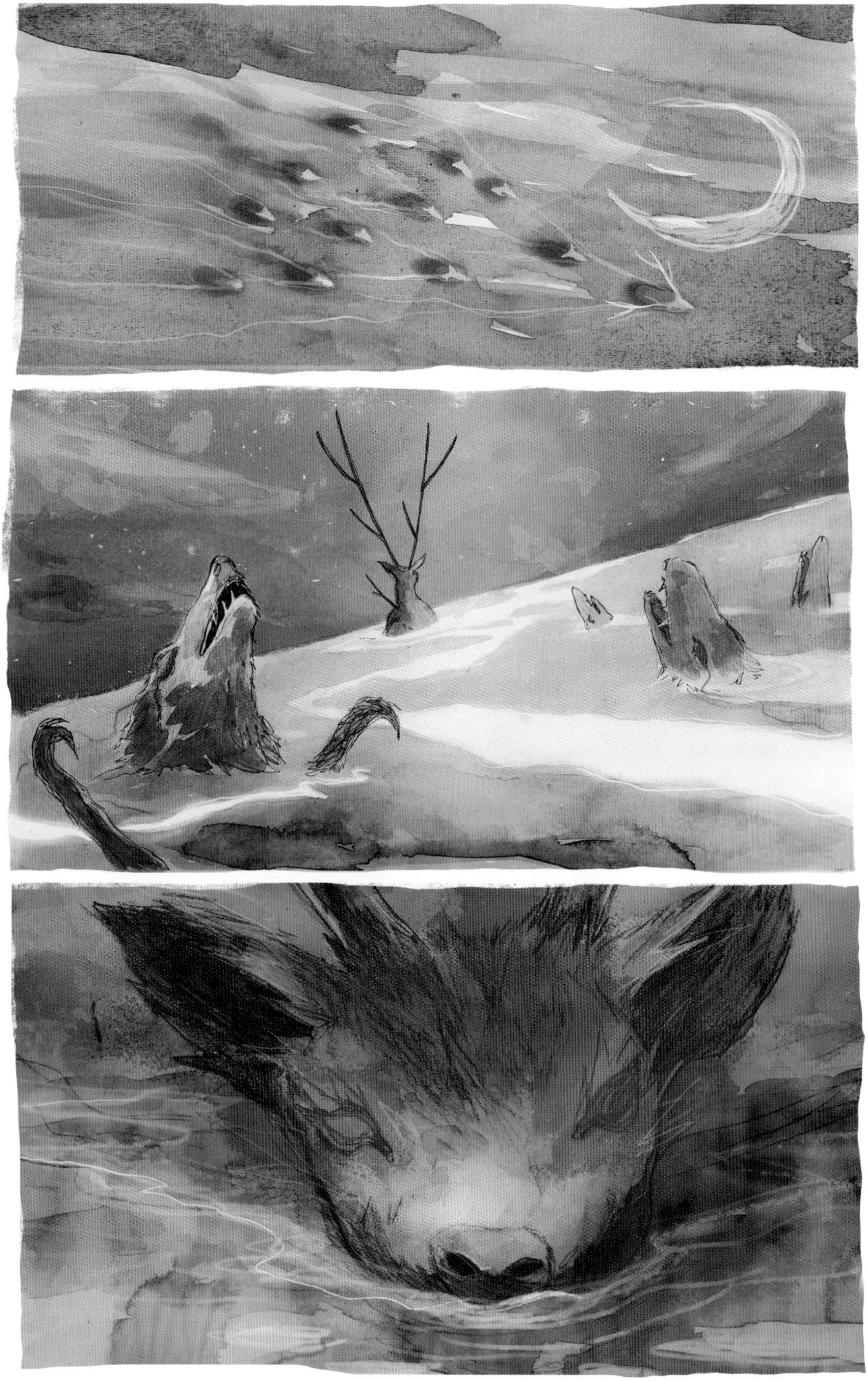

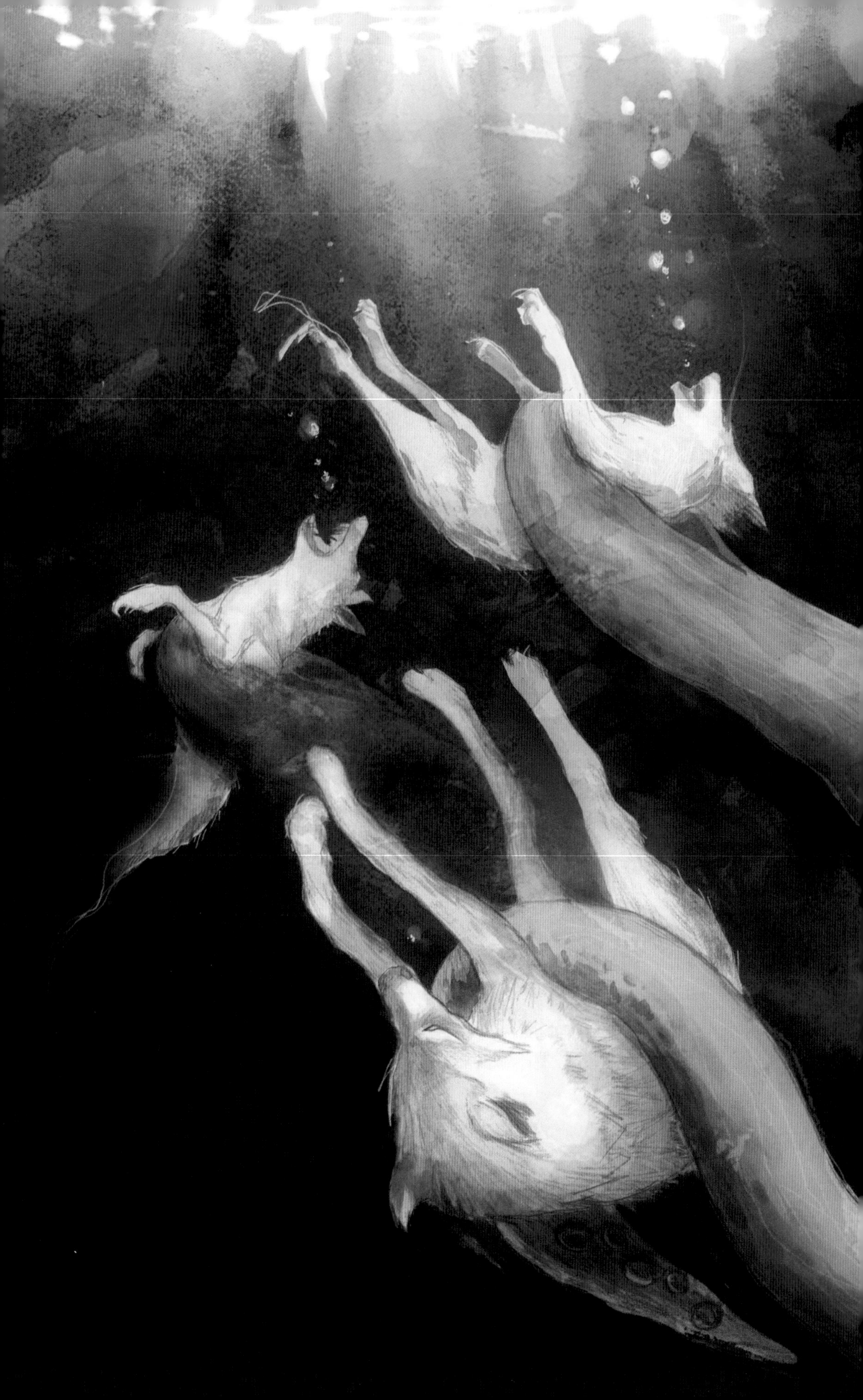

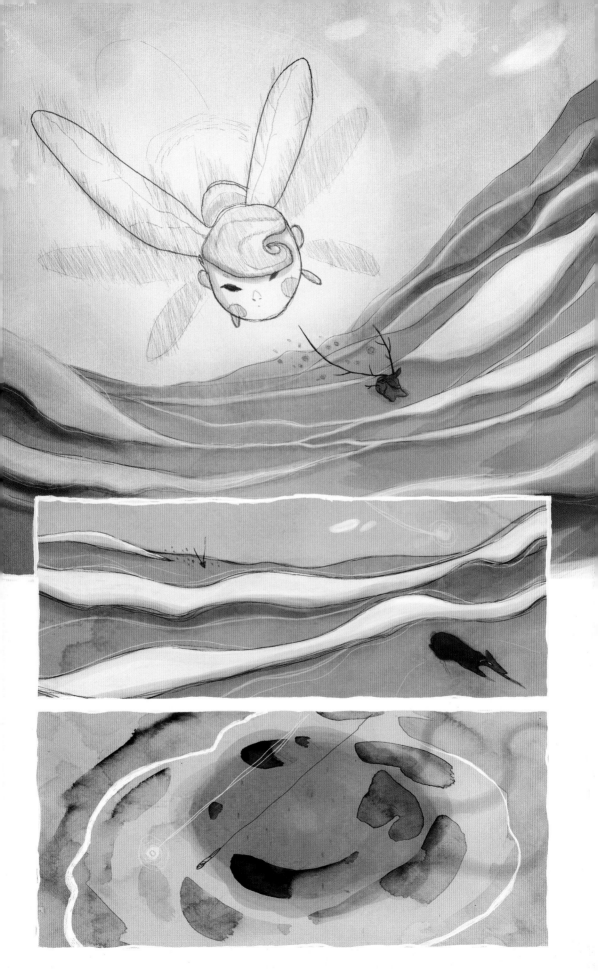

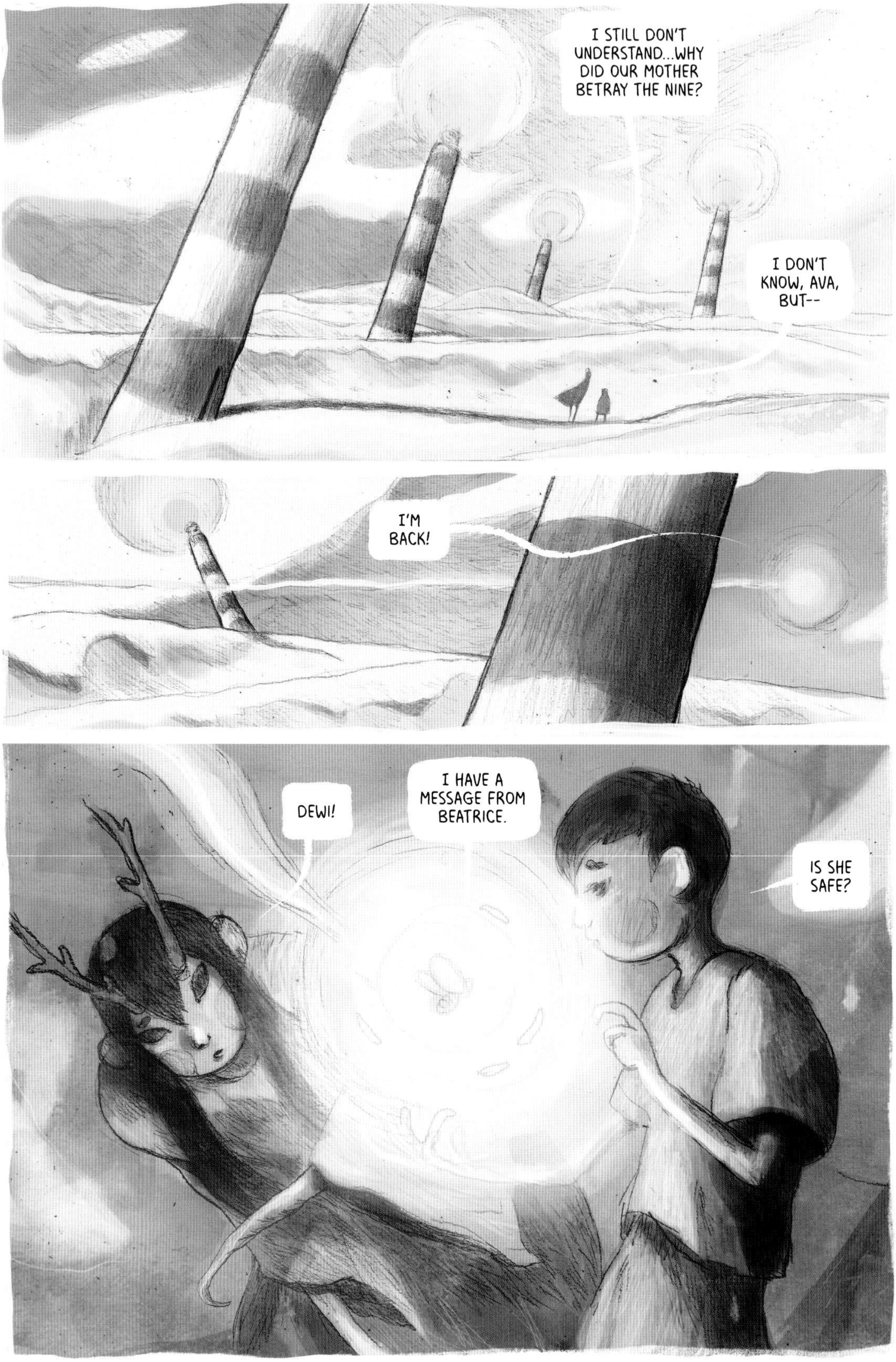
I STILL DON'T UNDERSTAND...WHY DID OUR MOTHER BETRAY THE NINE?
I DON'T KNOW, AVA, BUT--
I'M BACK!
DEWI!
I HAVE A MESSAGE FROM BEATRICE.
IS SHE SAFE?

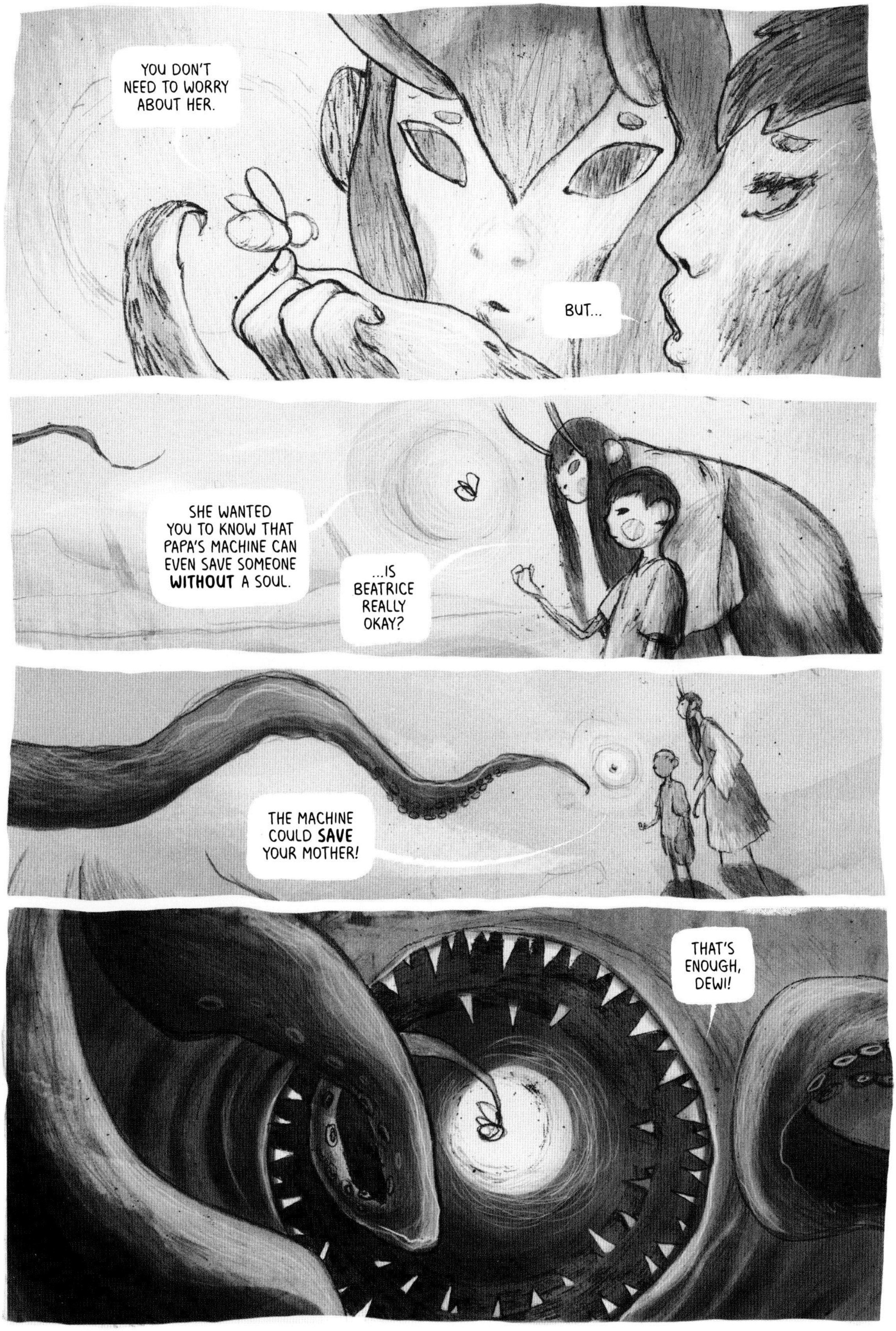
YOU DON'T NEED TO WORRY ABOUT HER.
BUT...
SHE WANTED YOU TO KNOW THAT PAPA'S MACHINE CAN EVEN SAVE SOMEONE **WITHOUT** A SOUL.
...IS BEATRICE REALLY OKAY?
THE MACHINE COULD **SAVE** YOUR MOTHER!
THAT'S ENOUGH, DEWI!

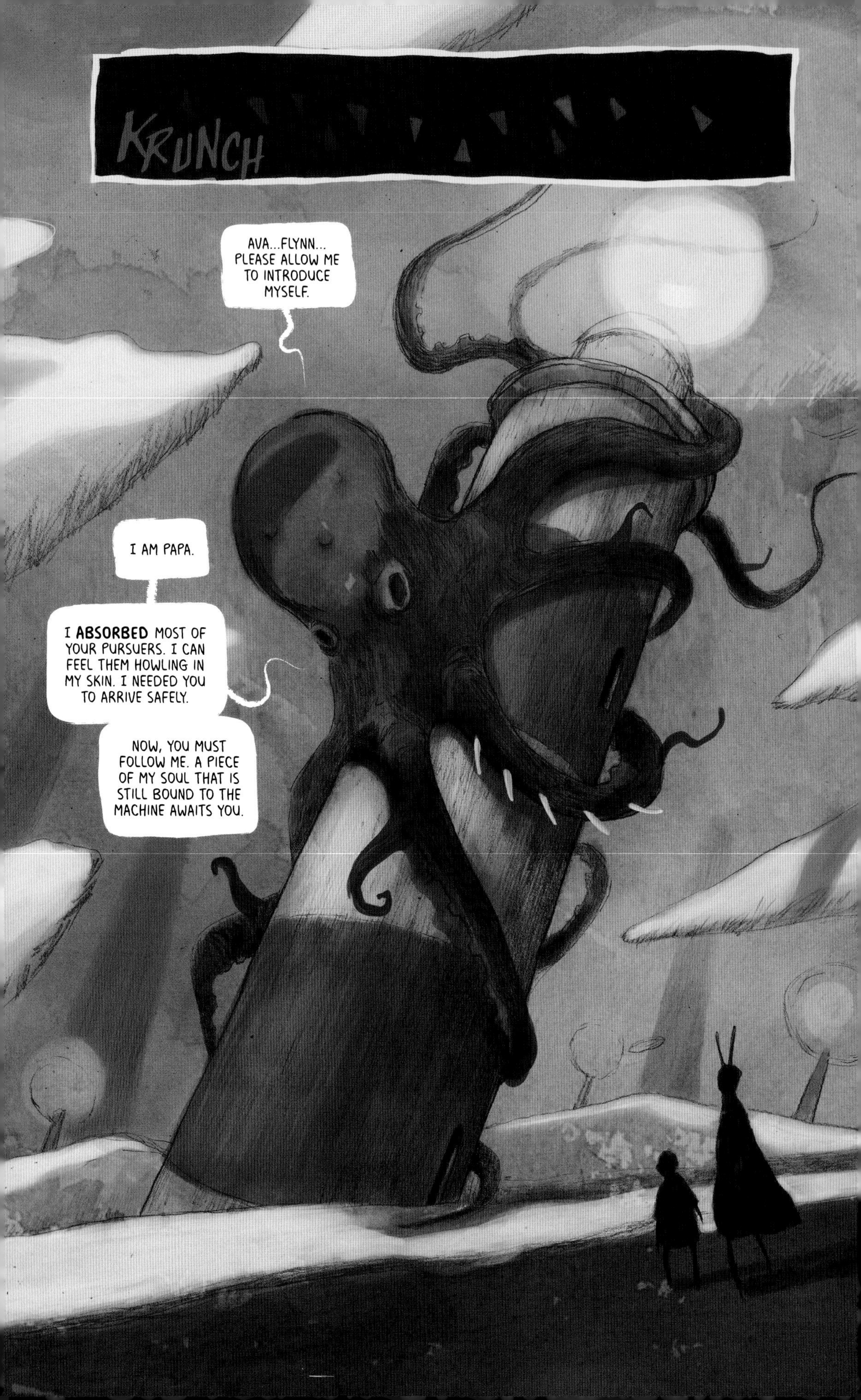
KRUNCH
AVA...FLYNN... PLEASE ALLOW ME TO INTRODUCE MYSELF.
I AM PAPA.
I **ABSORBED** MOST OF YOUR PURSUERS. I CAN FEEL THEM HOWLING IN MY SKIN. I NEEDED YOU TO ARRIVE SAFELY.
NOW, YOU MUST FOLLOW ME. A PIECE OF MY SOUL THAT IS STILL BOUND TO THE MACHINE AWAITS YOU.

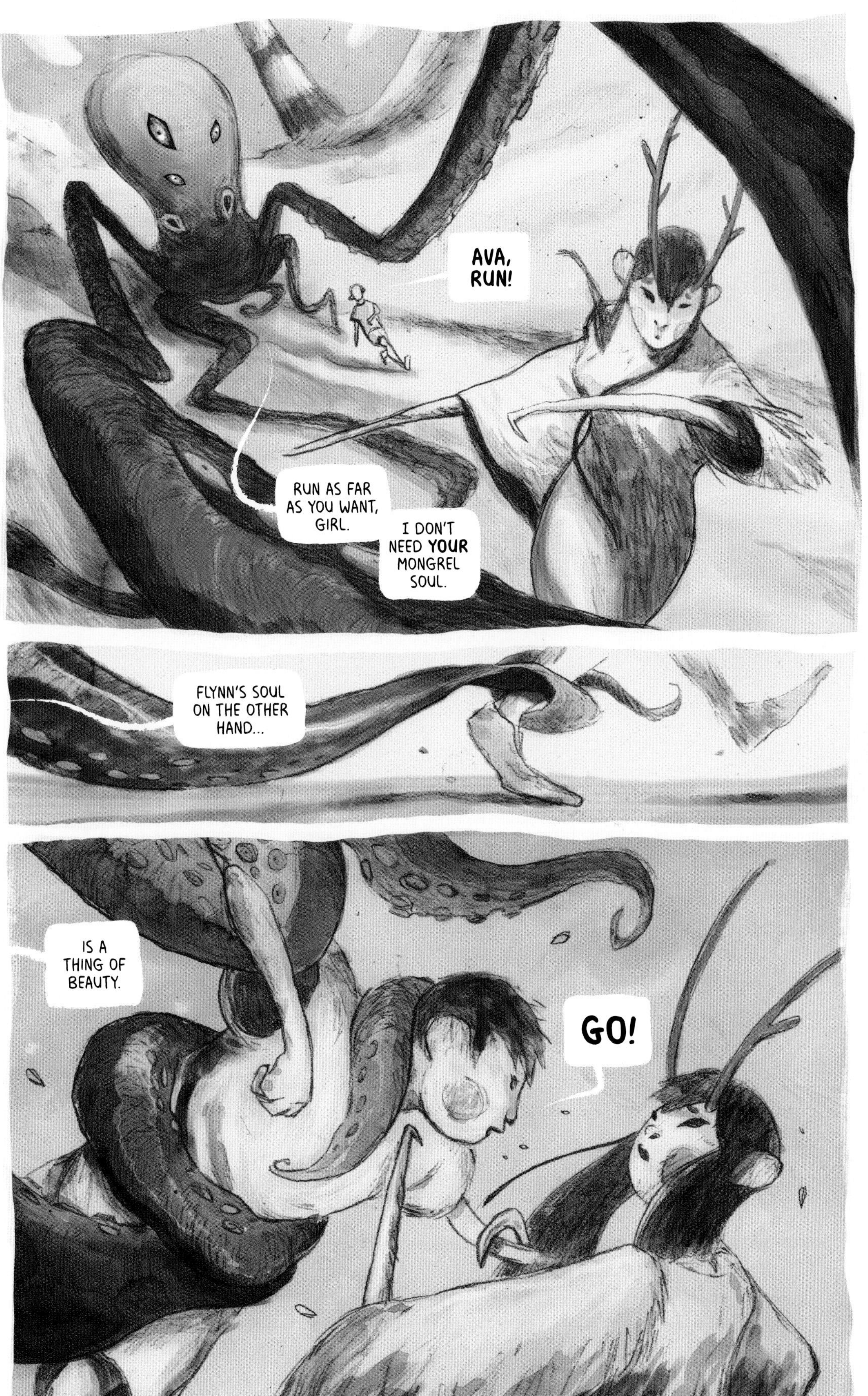
AVA, RUN!
RUN AS FAR AS YOU WANT, GIRL.
I DON'T NEED **YOUR** MONGREL SOUL.
FLYNN'S SOUL ON THE OTHER HAND...
IS A THING OF BEAUTY.
GO!

THE DOE!

SHE SAVED YOU.

IT IS HER...

OUR MOTHER, AVA. SHE'S CHANGING.

BECOMING A LONG-GONE.

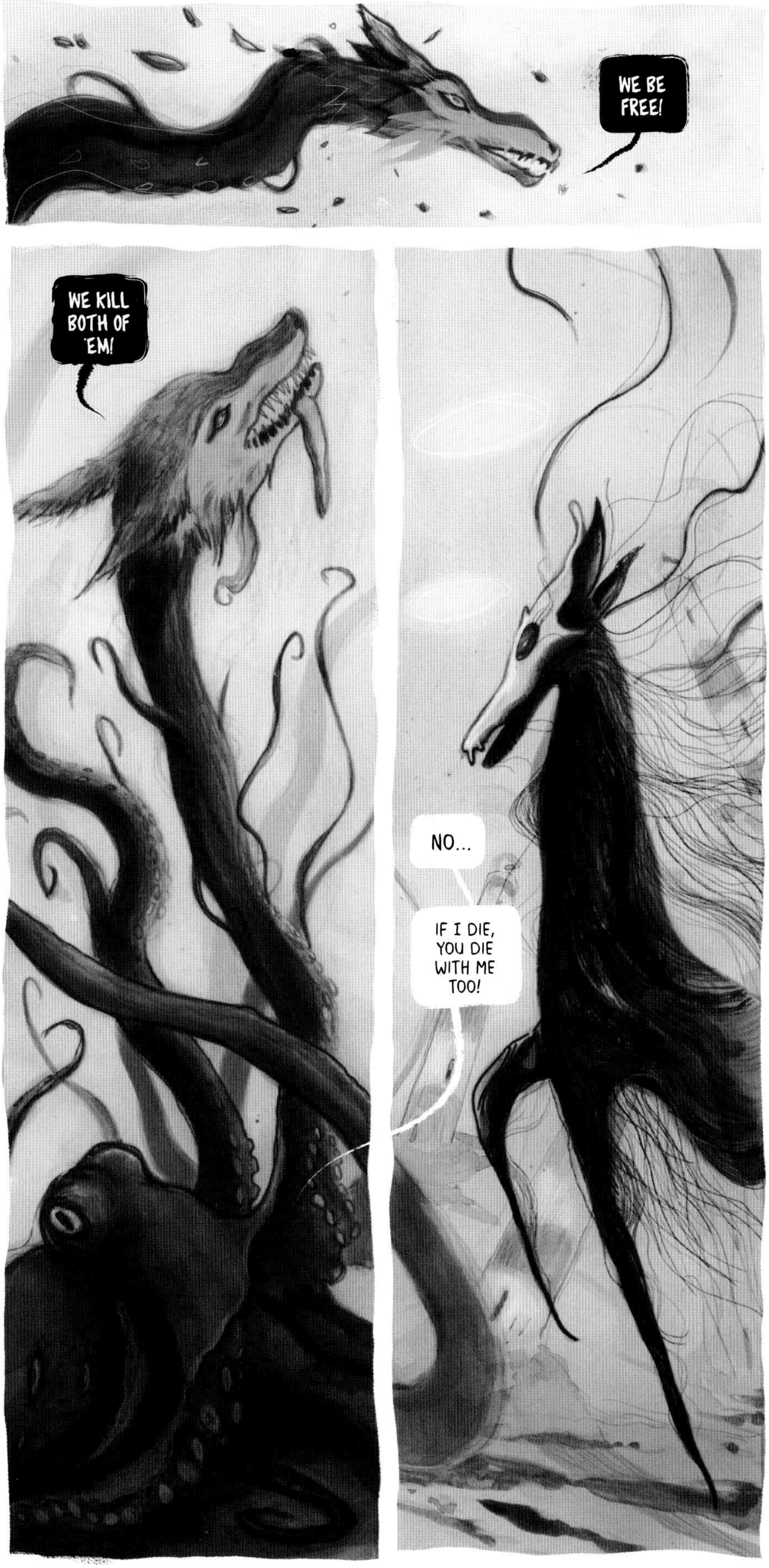
WE BE FREE!
WE KILL BOTH OF 'EM!
NO...
IF I DIE, YOU DIE WITH ME TOO!

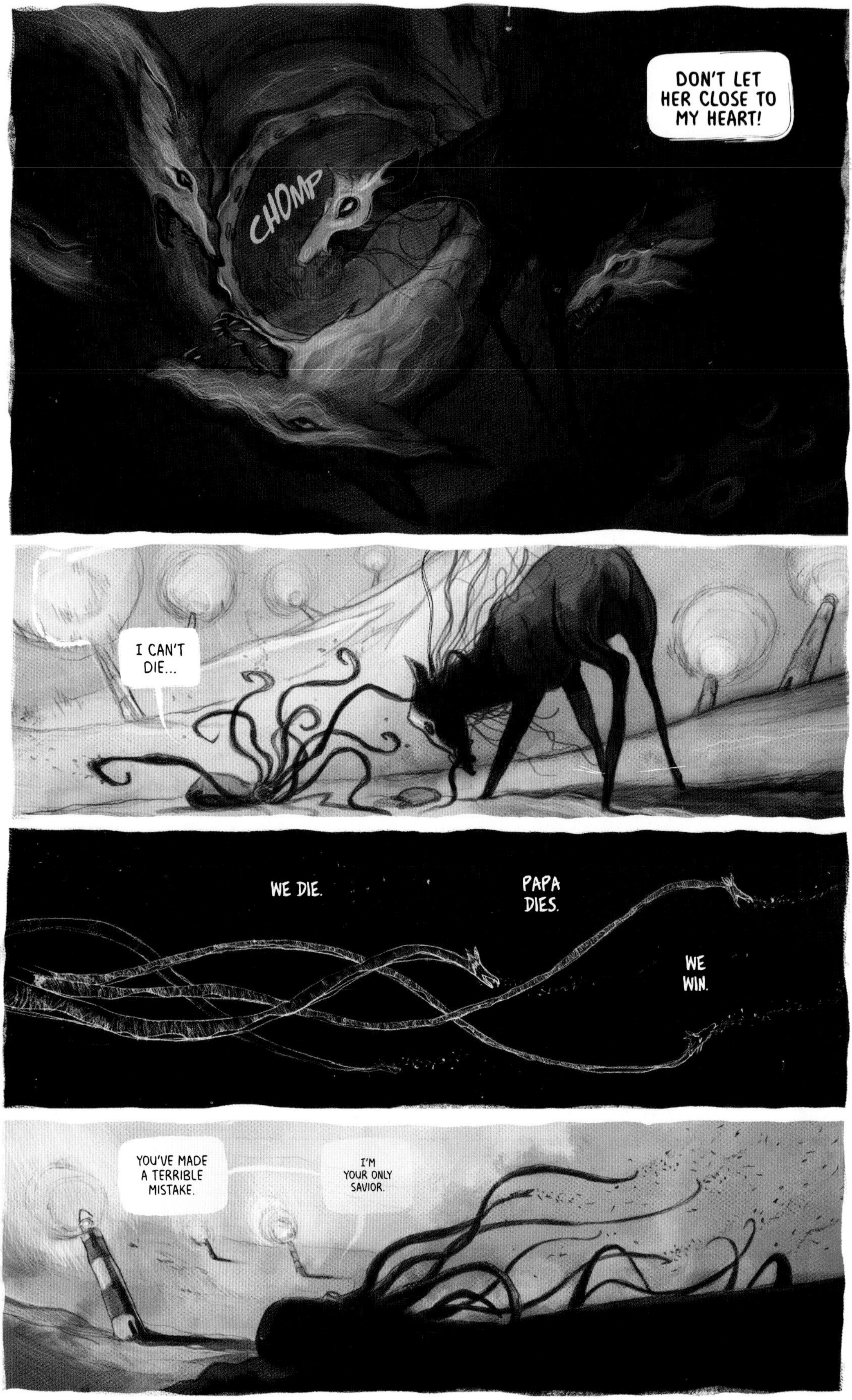
DON'T LET HER CLOSE TO MY HEART!
CHOMP
I CAN'T DIE...
WE DIE.
PAPA DIES.
WE WIN.
YOU'VE MADE A TERRIBLE MISTAKE.
I'M YOUR ONLY SAVIOR.

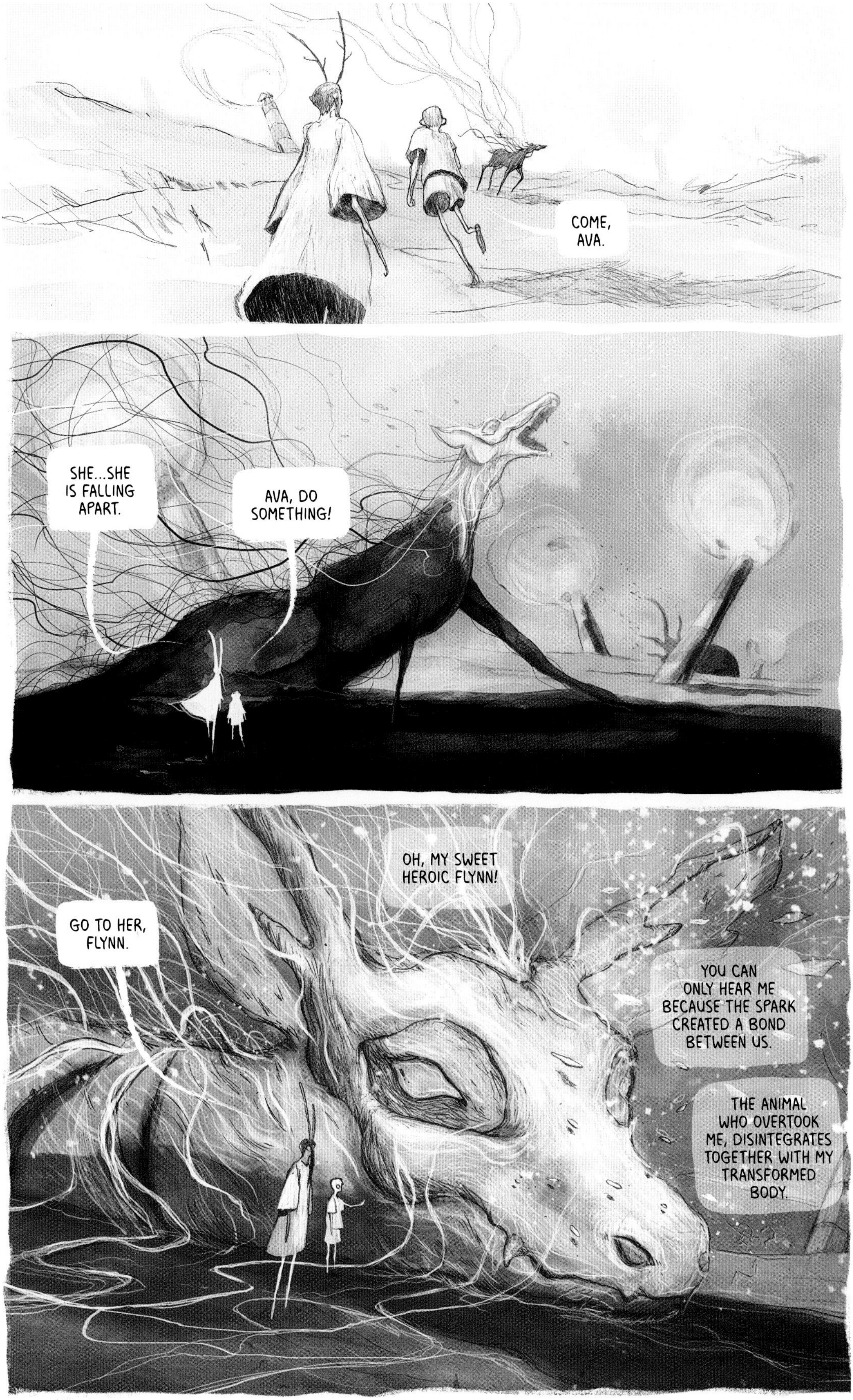
COME, AVA.
SHE...SHE IS FALLING APART.
AVA, DO SOMETHING!
OH, MY SWEET HEROIC FLYNN!
GO TO HER, FLYNN.
YOU CAN ONLY HEAR ME BECAUSE THE SPARK CREATED A BOND BETWEEN US.
THE ANIMAL WHO OVERTOOK ME, DISINTEGRATES TOGETHER WITH MY TRANSFORMED BODY.

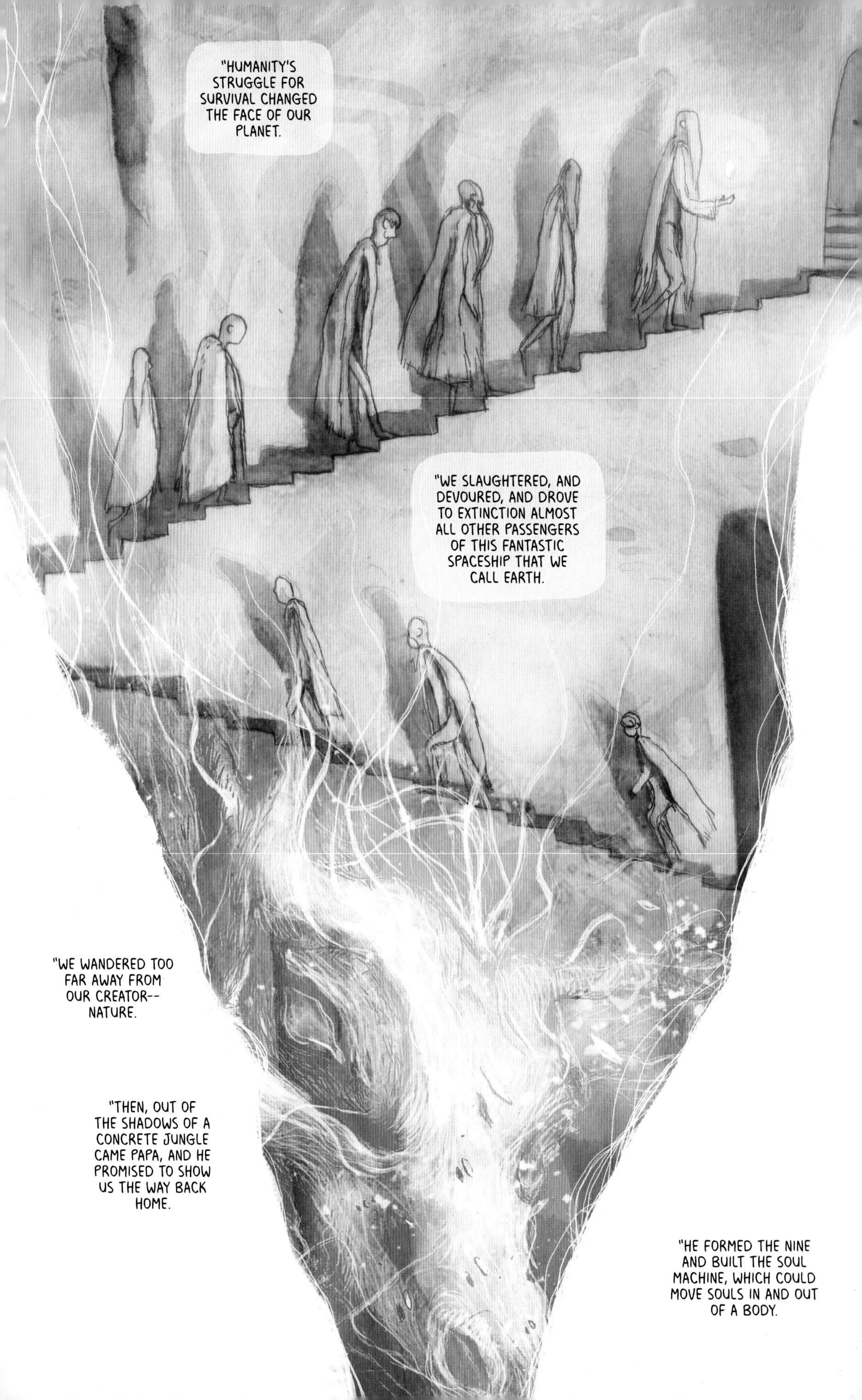
"HUMANITY'S STRUGGLE FOR SURVIVAL CHANGED THE FACE OF OUR PLANET.
"WE SLAUGHTERED, AND DEVOURED, AND DROVE TO EXTINCTION ALMOST ALL OTHER PASSENGERS OF THIS FANTASTIC SPACESHIP THAT WE CALL EARTH.
"WE WANDERED TOO FAR AWAY FROM OUR CREATOR--NATURE.
"THEN, OUT OF THE SHADOWS OF A CONCRETE JUNGLE CAME PAPA, AND HE PROMISED TO SHOW US THE WAY BACK HOME.
"HE FORMED THE NINE AND BUILT THE SOUL MACHINE, WHICH COULD MOVE SOULS IN AND OUT OF A BODY.

"PAPA CARRIED THE SPARK, THE KEY TO THE SOUL MACHINE.

"EIGHT IDEALISTS, A PREACHER OF THE APOCALYPSE, AND AN UNTESTED MACHINE.

"I WARNED OMAR THAT THINGS COULD GO WRONG.

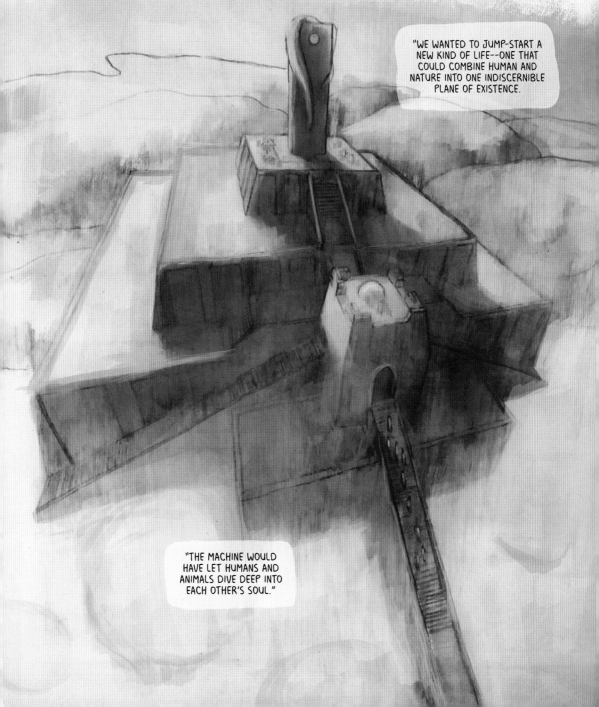

"WE WANTED TO JUMP-START A NEW KIND OF LIFE--ONE THAT COULD COMBINE HUMAN AND NATURE INTO ONE INDISCERNIBLE PLANE OF EXISTENCE.

"THE MACHINE WOULD HAVE LET HUMANS AND ANIMALS DIVE DEEP INTO EACH OTHER'S SOUL."

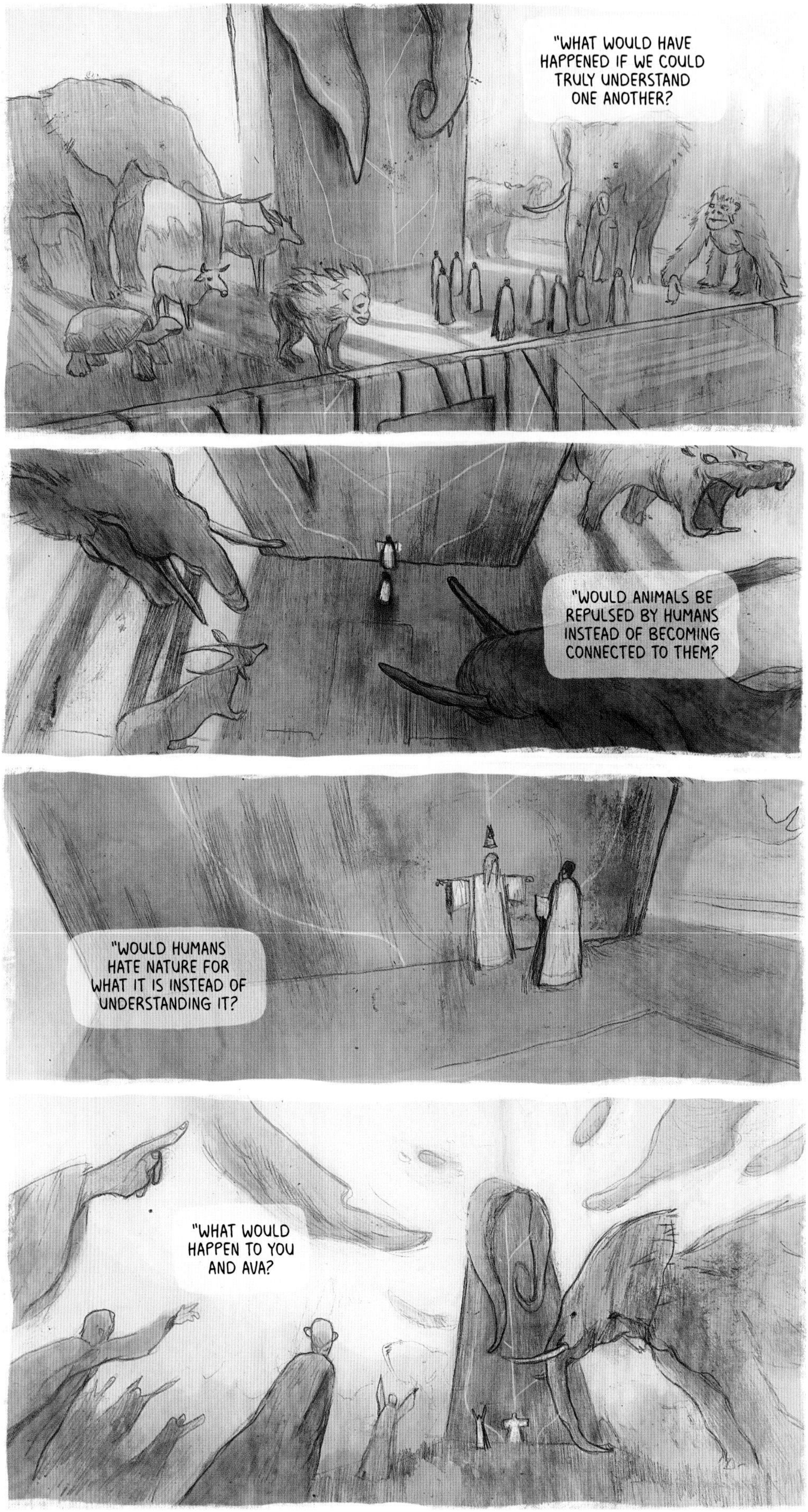
"WHAT WOULD HAVE HAPPENED IF WE COULD TRULY UNDERSTAND ONE ANOTHER?
"WOULD ANIMALS BE REPULSED BY HUMANS INSTEAD OF BECOMING CONNECTED TO THEM?
"WOULD HUMANS HATE NATURE FOR WHAT IT IS INSTEAD OF UNDERSTANDING IT?
"WHAT WOULD HAPPEN TO YOU AND AVA?

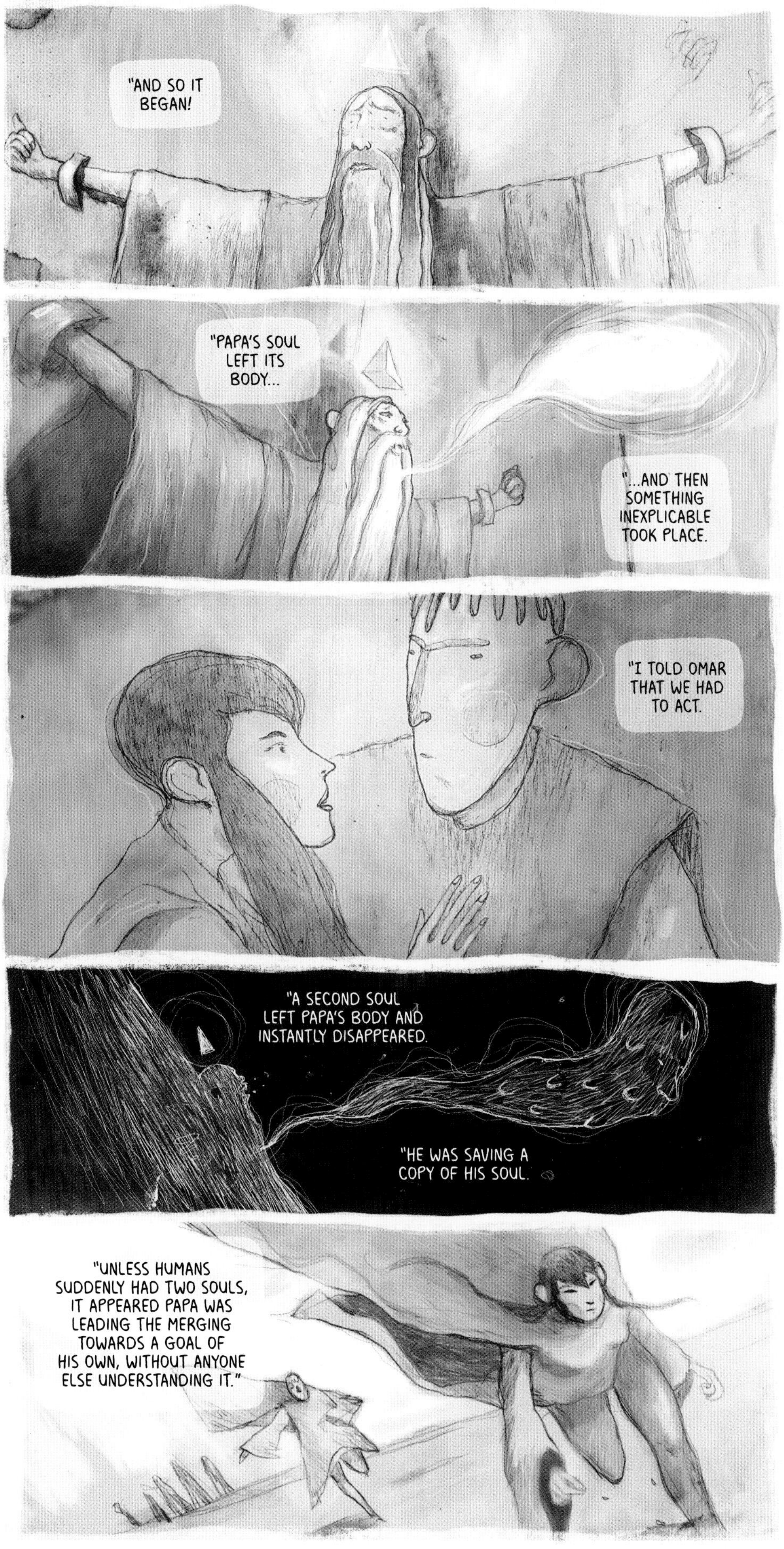
"AND SO IT BEGAN!
"PAPA'S SOUL LEFT ITS BODY...
"...AND THEN SOMETHING INEXPLICABLE TOOK PLACE.
"I TOLD OMAR THAT WE HAD TO ACT.
"A SECOND SOUL LEFT PAPA'S BODY AND INSTANTLY DISAPPEARED.
"HE WAS SAVING A COPY OF HIS SOUL.
"UNLESS HUMANS SUDDENLY HAD TWO SOULS, IT APPEARED PAPA WAS LEADING THE MERGING TOWARDS A GOAL OF HIS OWN, WITHOUT ANYONE ELSE UNDERSTANDING IT."

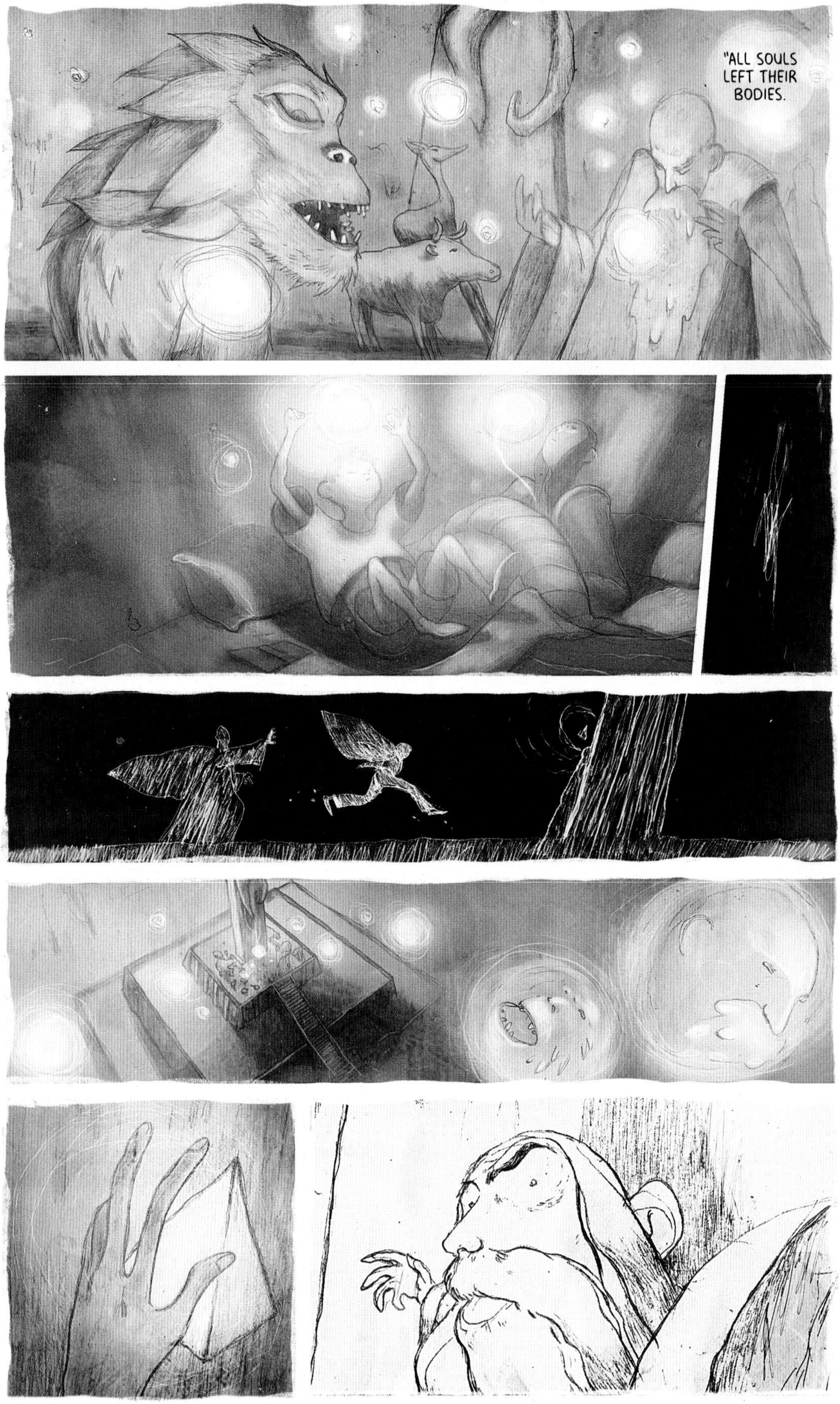
"ALL SOULS LEFT THEIR BODIES.

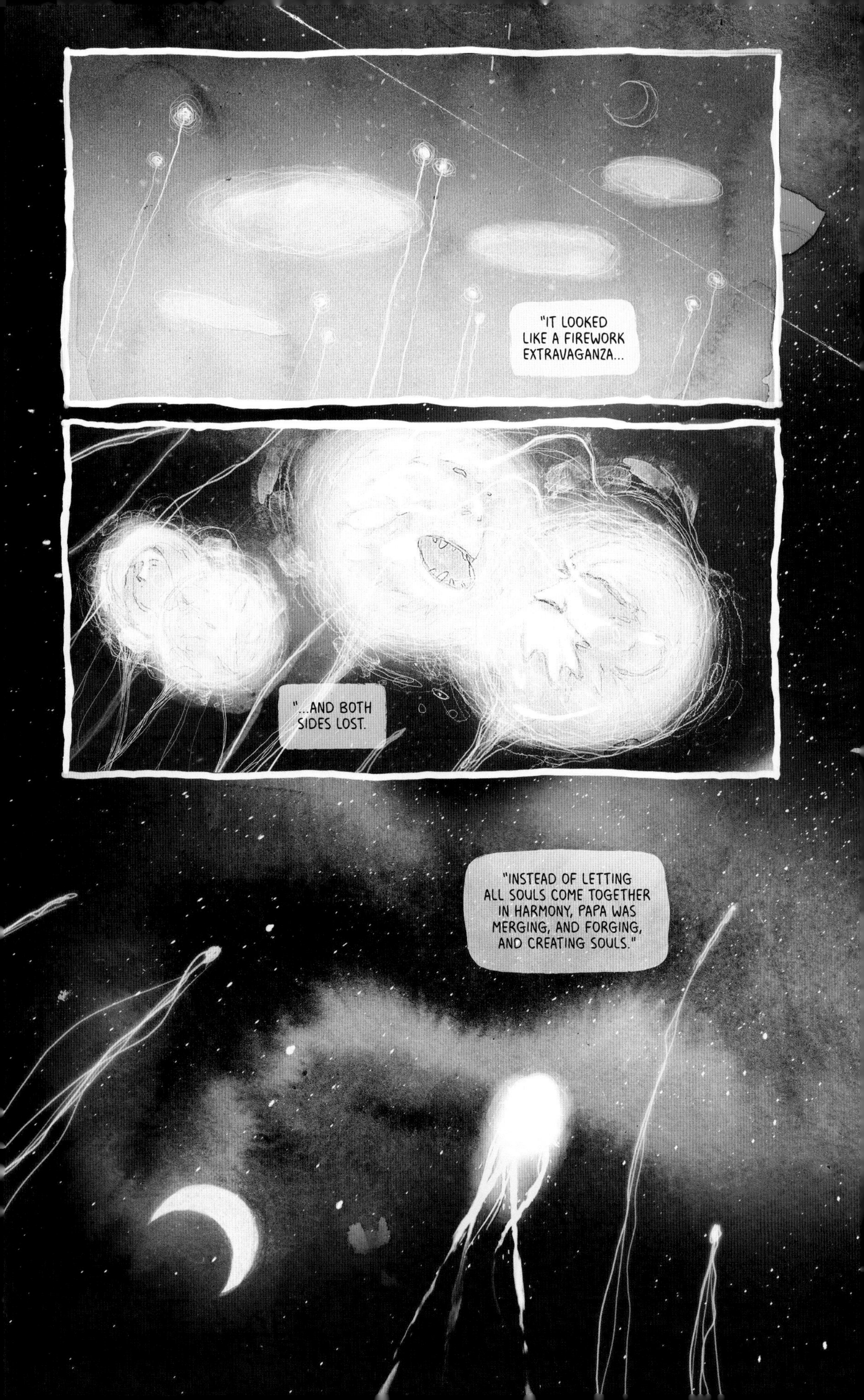
"IT LOOKED
LIKE A FIREWORK
EXTRAVAGANZA...
"...AND BOTH
SIDES LOST.
"INSTEAD OF LETTING
ALL SOULS COME TOGETHER
IN HARMONY, PAPA WAS
MERGING, AND FORGING,
AND CREATING SOULS."

"UNDER THE INFLUENCE OF THE SPARK, MY SOUL AND OMAR'S REMAINED UNTOUCHED BY THE MERGING...

"...BUT WITHOUT THE SPARK, PAPA COULDN'T HOLD THE SOULS AWAY FROM THEIR BODIES.

"SO, THE HYBRID SOULS FLEW BACK HOME.

"I DECIDED TO DO THE SAME.

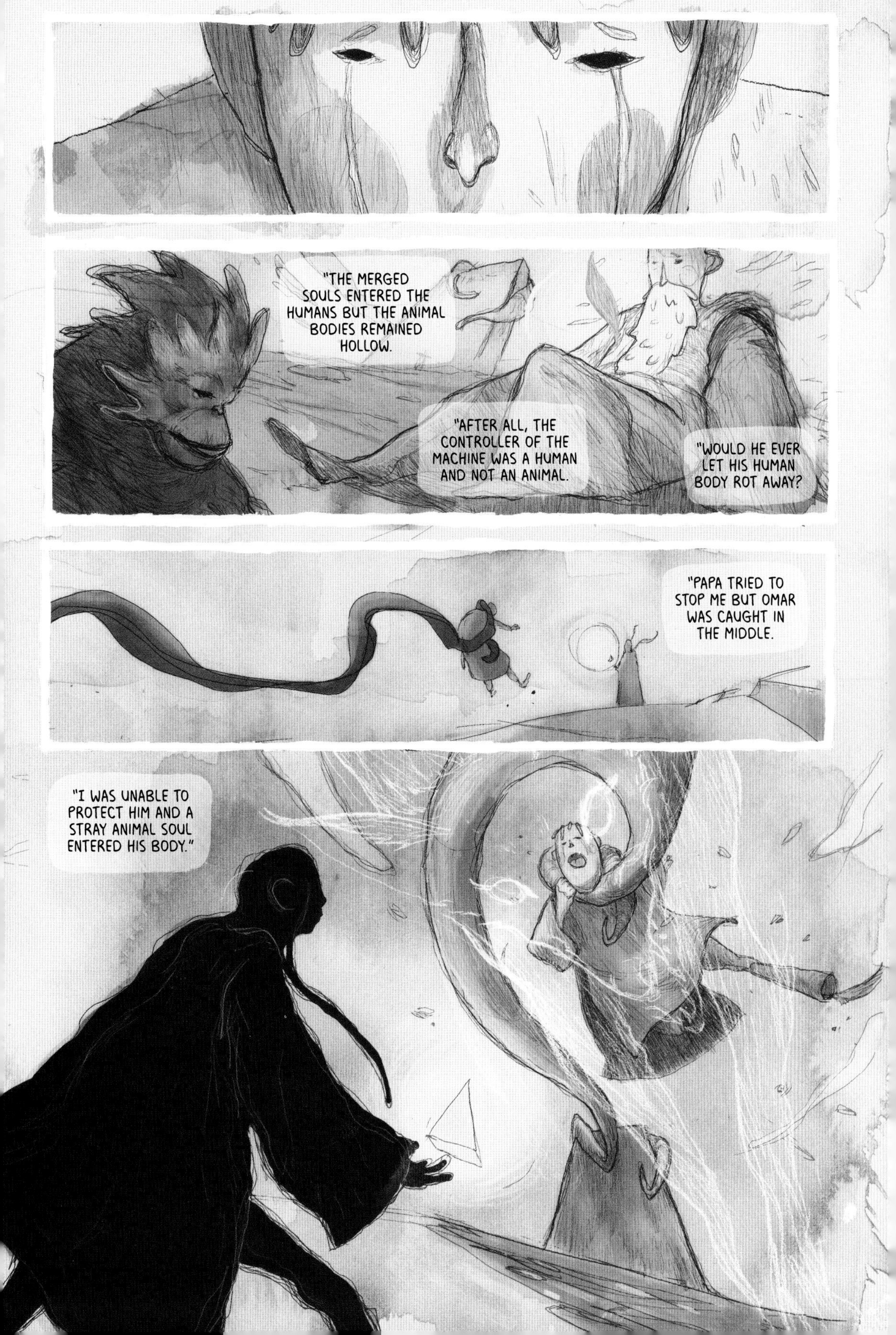
"THE MERGED SOULS ENTERED THE HUMANS BUT THE ANIMAL BODIES REMAINED HOLLOW.
"AFTER ALL, THE CONTROLLER OF THE MACHINE WAS A HUMAN AND NOT AN ANIMAL.
"WOULD HE EVER LET HIS HUMAN BODY ROT AWAY?
"PAPA TRIED TO STOP ME BUT OMAR WAS CAUGHT IN THE MIDDLE.
"I WAS UNABLE TO PROTECT HIM AND A STRAY ANIMAL SOUL ENTERED HIS BODY."

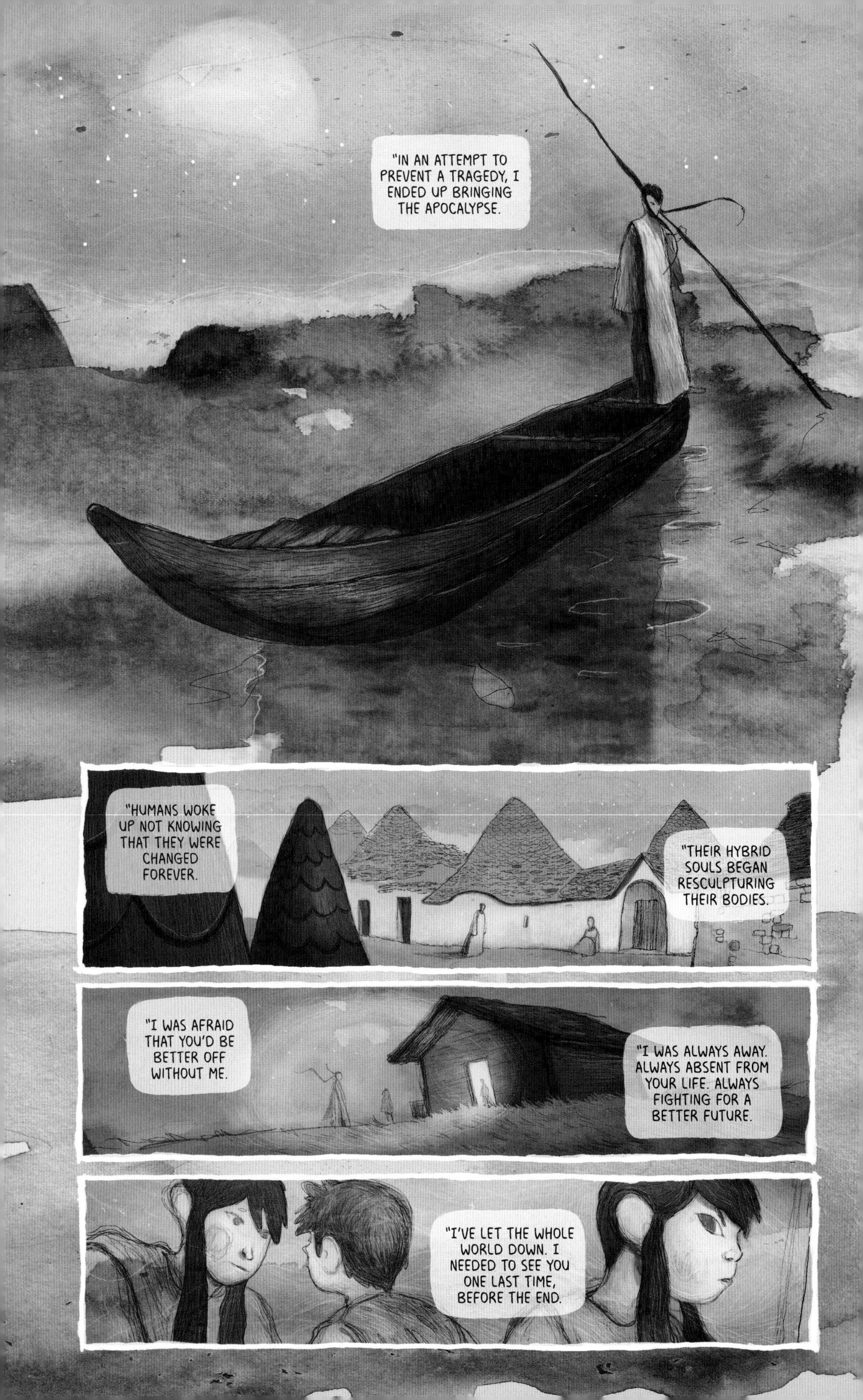
"IN AN ATTEMPT TO PREVENT A TRAGEDY, I ENDED UP BRINGING THE APOCALYPSE.
"HUMANS WOKE UP NOT KNOWING THAT THEY WERE CHANGED FOREVER.
"THEIR HYBRID SOULS BEGAN RESCULPTURING THEIR BODIES.
"I WAS AFRAID THAT YOU'D BE BETTER OFF WITHOUT ME.
"I WAS ALWAYS AWAY. ALWAYS ABSENT FROM YOUR LIFE. ALWAYS FIGHTING FOR A BETTER FUTURE.
"I'VE LET THE WHOLE WORLD DOWN. I NEEDED TO SEE YOU ONE LAST TIME, BEFORE THE END.

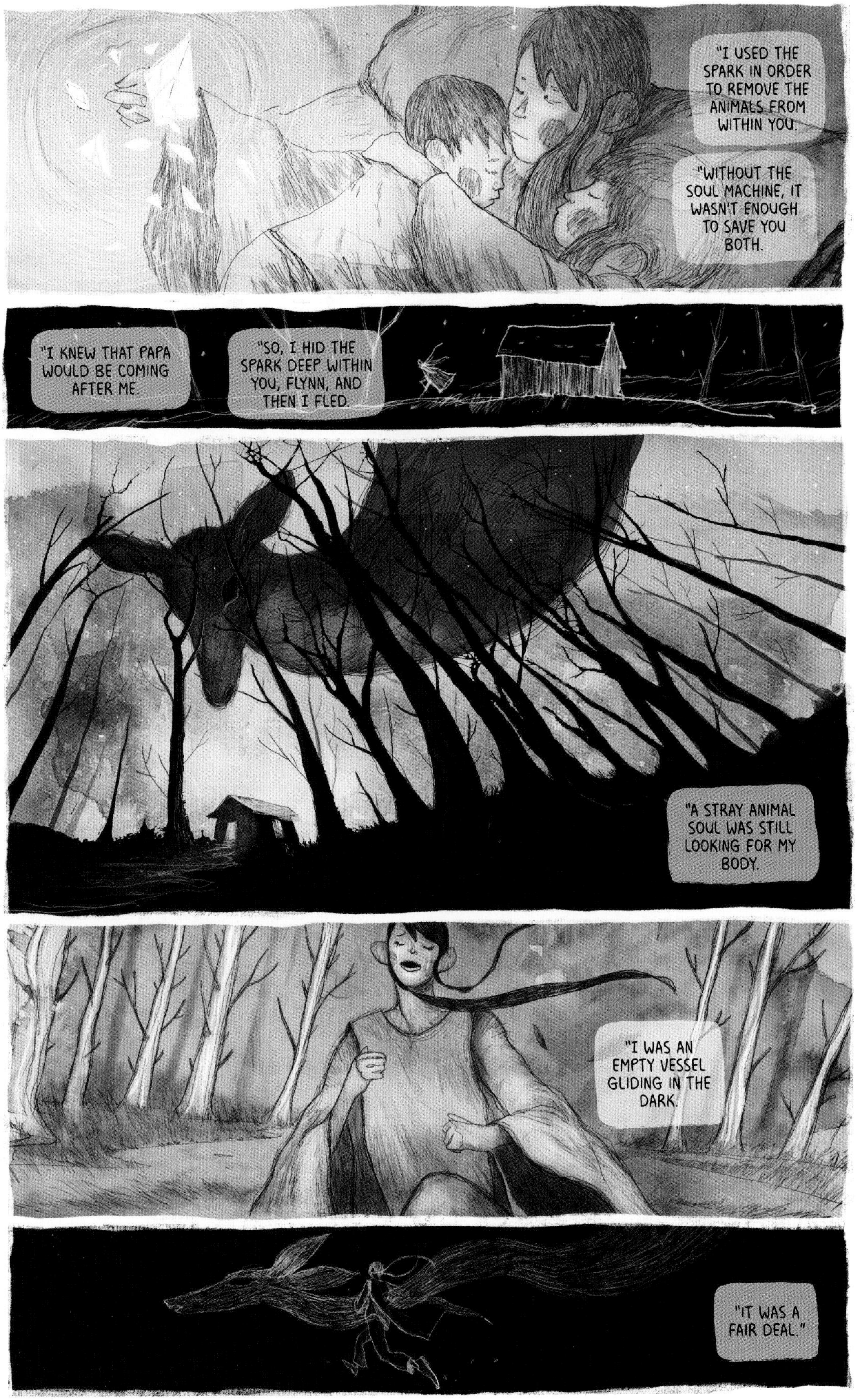
"I USED THE SPARK IN ORDER TO REMOVE THE ANIMALS FROM WITHIN YOU.
"WITHOUT THE SOUL MACHINE, IT WASN'T ENOUGH TO SAVE YOU BOTH.
"I KNEW THAT PAPA WOULD BE COMING AFTER ME.
"SO, I HID THE SPARK DEEP WITHIN YOU, FLYNN, AND THEN I FLED.
"A STRAY ANIMAL SOUL WAS STILL LOOKING FOR MY BODY.
"I WAS AN EMPTY VESSEL GLIDING IN THE DARK.
"IT WAS A FAIR DEAL."

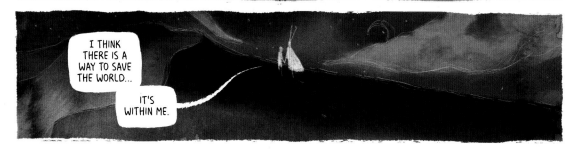

"HOW COULD
WE DO IT,
FLYNN?"

"FIRST, WE FIND
WHAT IS LEFT
OF PAPA."

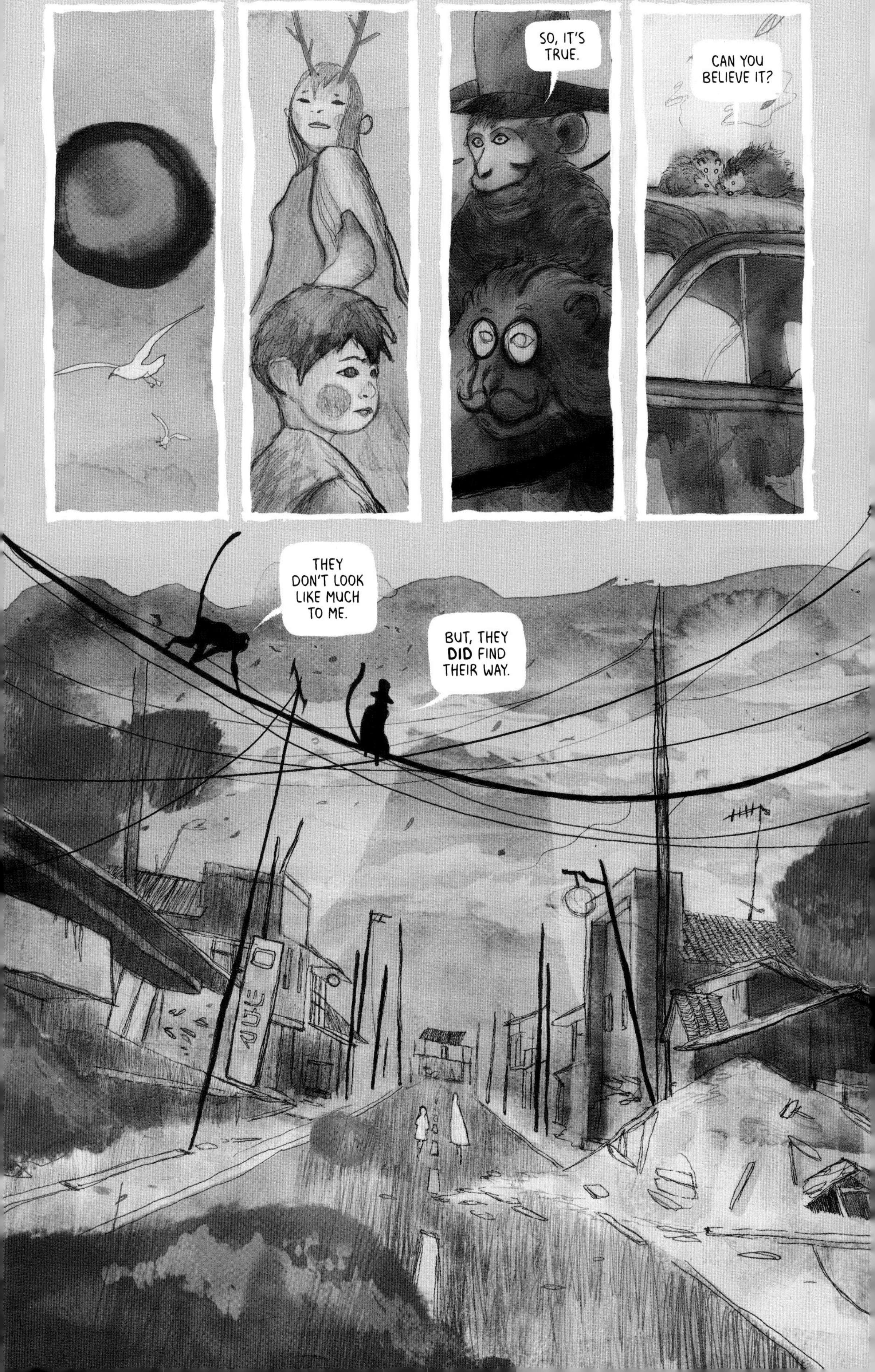
SO, IT'S TRUE.
CAN YOU BELIEVE IT?
THEY DON'T LOOK LIKE MUCH TO ME.
BUT, THEY **DID** FIND THEIR WAY.

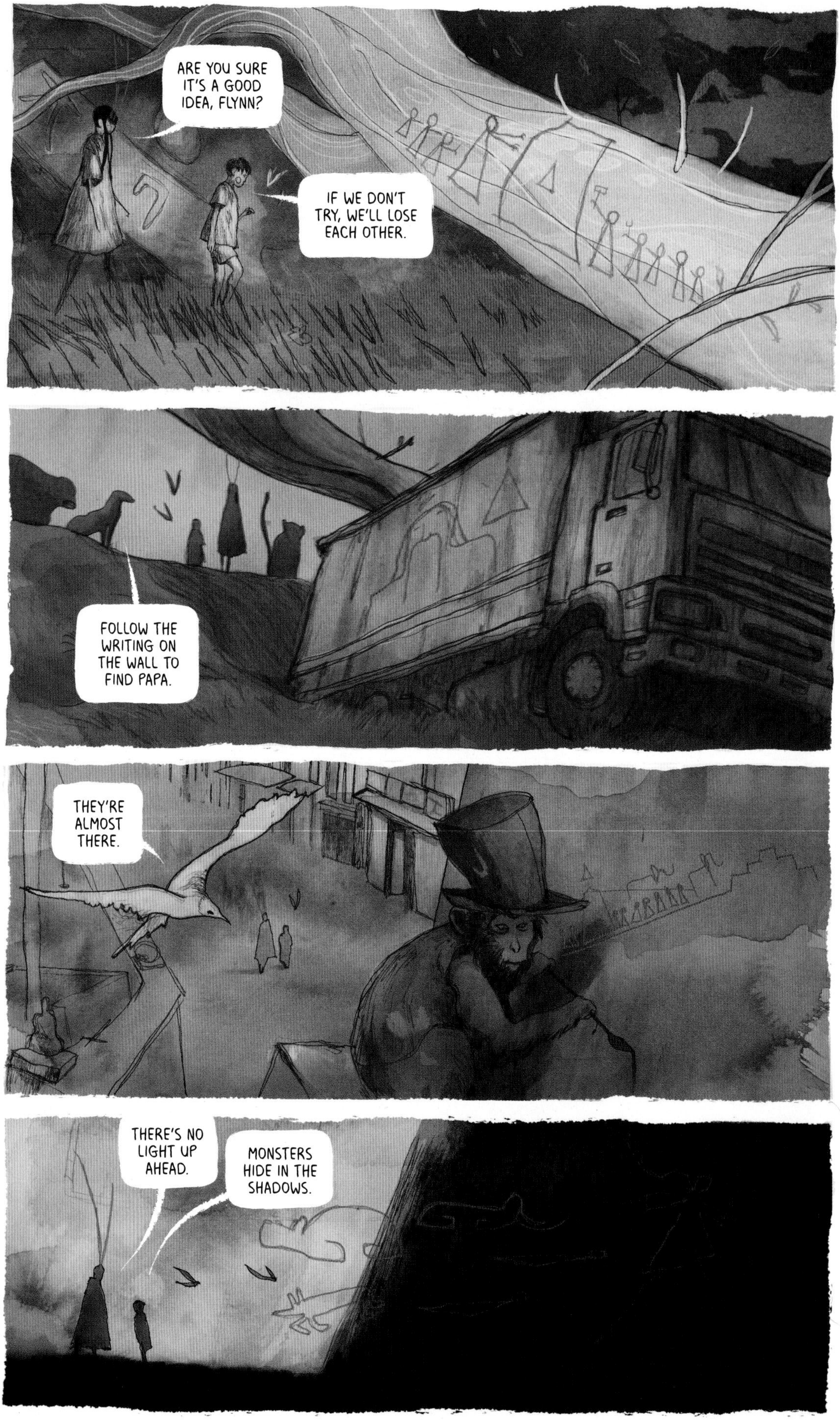
ARE YOU SURE IT'S A GOOD IDEA, FLYNN?
IF WE DON'T TRY, WE'LL LOSE EACH OTHER.
FOLLOW THE WRITING ON THE WALL TO FIND PAPA.
THEY'RE ALMOST THERE.
THERE'S NO LIGHT UP AHEAD.
MONSTERS HIDE IN THE SHADOWS.

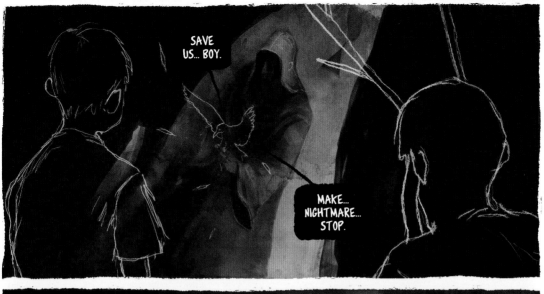

SAVE US... BOY.

MAKE... NIGHTMARE... STOP.

THE SOUL OF THE MACHINE USED TO BE PLACED HERE.

DON'T TOUCH IT!

WELCOME, FLYNN.

I SEE THAT YOU BRING ALONG A BIT MORE THAN YOUR SOUL.

LET OUR NEW APOCALYPSE BEGIN!

TAKE YOUR HANDS OFF HIM, MONSTER!

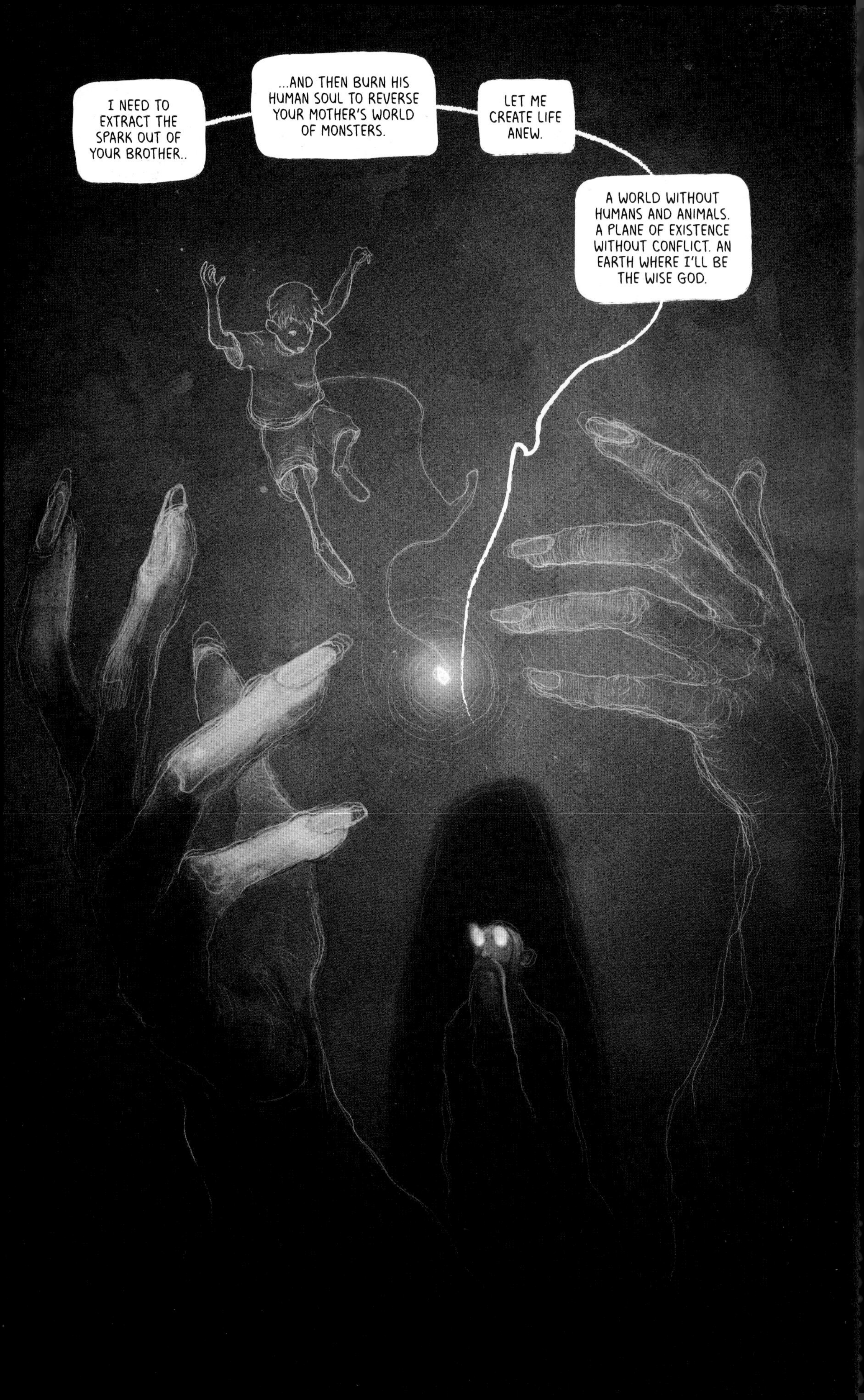
I NEED TO EXTRACT THE SPARK OUT OF YOUR BROTHER..
...AND THEN BURN HIS HUMAN SOUL TO REVERSE YOUR MOTHER'S WORLD OF MONSTERS.
LET ME CREATE LIFE ANEW.
A WORLD WITHOUT HUMANS AND ANIMALS. A PLANE OF EXISTENCE WITHOUT CONFLICT. AN EARTH WHERE I'LL BE THE WISE GOD.

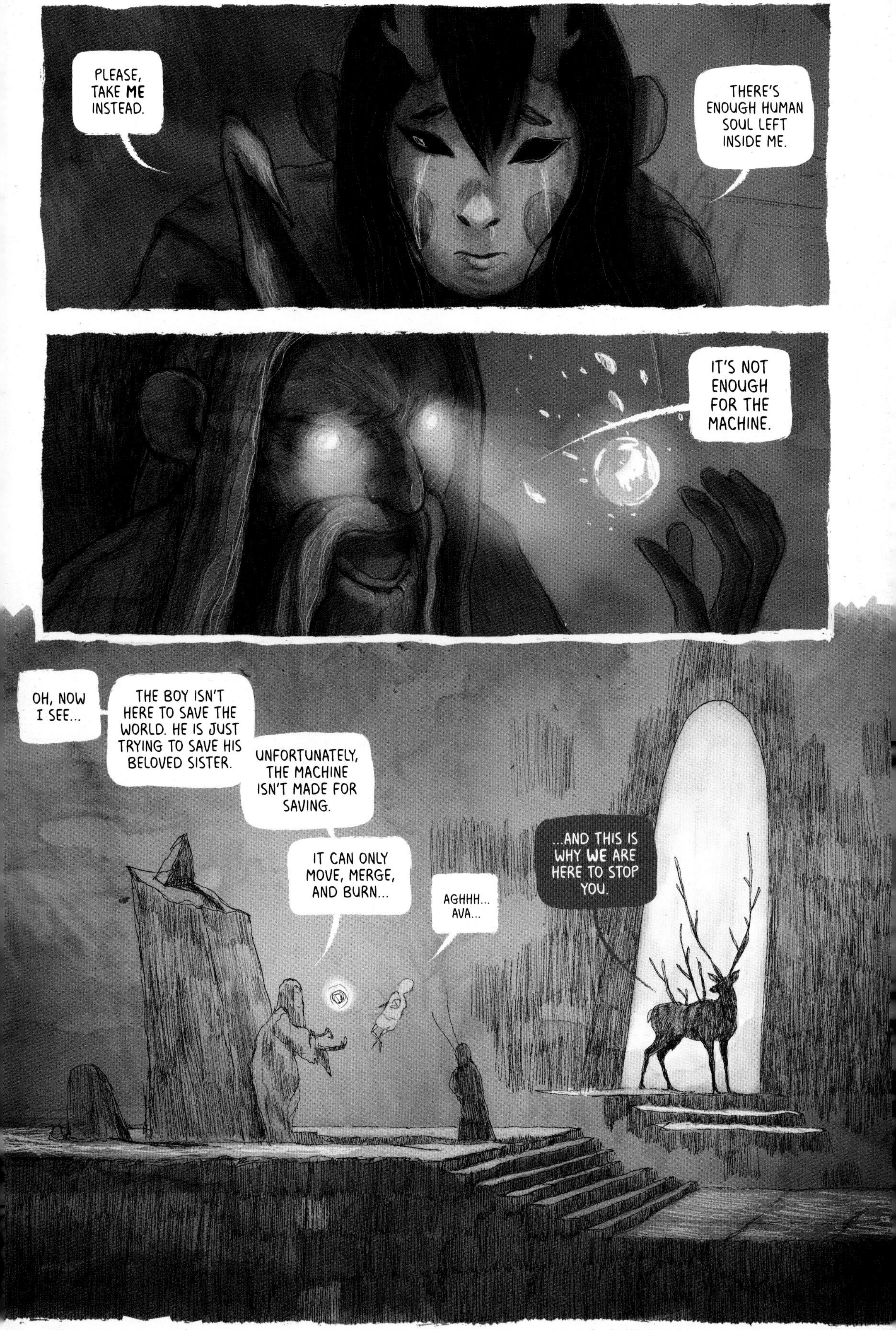
PLEASE, TAKE **ME** INSTEAD.
THERE'S ENOUGH HUMAN SOUL LEFT INSIDE ME.
IT'S NOT ENOUGH FOR THE MACHINE.
OH, NOW I SEE...
THE BOY ISN'T HERE TO SAVE THE WORLD. HE IS JUST TRYING TO SAVE HIS BELOVED SISTER.
UNFORTUNATELY, THE MACHINE ISN'T MADE FOR SAVING.
IT CAN ONLY MOVE, MERGE, AND BURN...
AGHHH... AVA...
...AND THIS IS WHY **WE** ARE HERE TO STOP YOU.

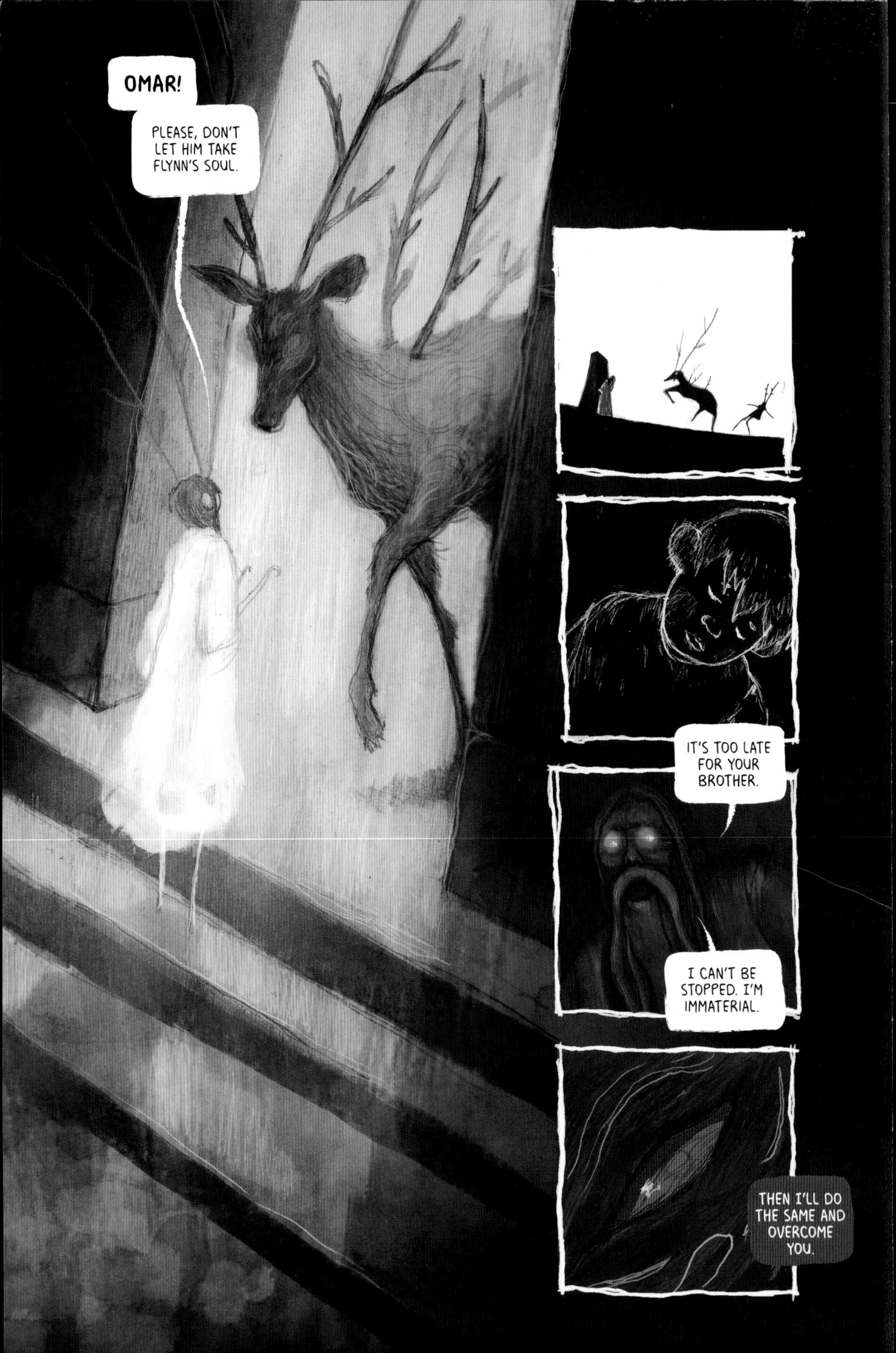
OMAR!
PLEASE, DON'T LET HIM TAKE FLYNN'S SOUL.
IT'S TOO LATE FOR YOUR BROTHER.
I CAN'T BE STOPPED. I'M IMMATERIAL.
THEN I'LL DO THE SAME AND OVERCOME YOU.

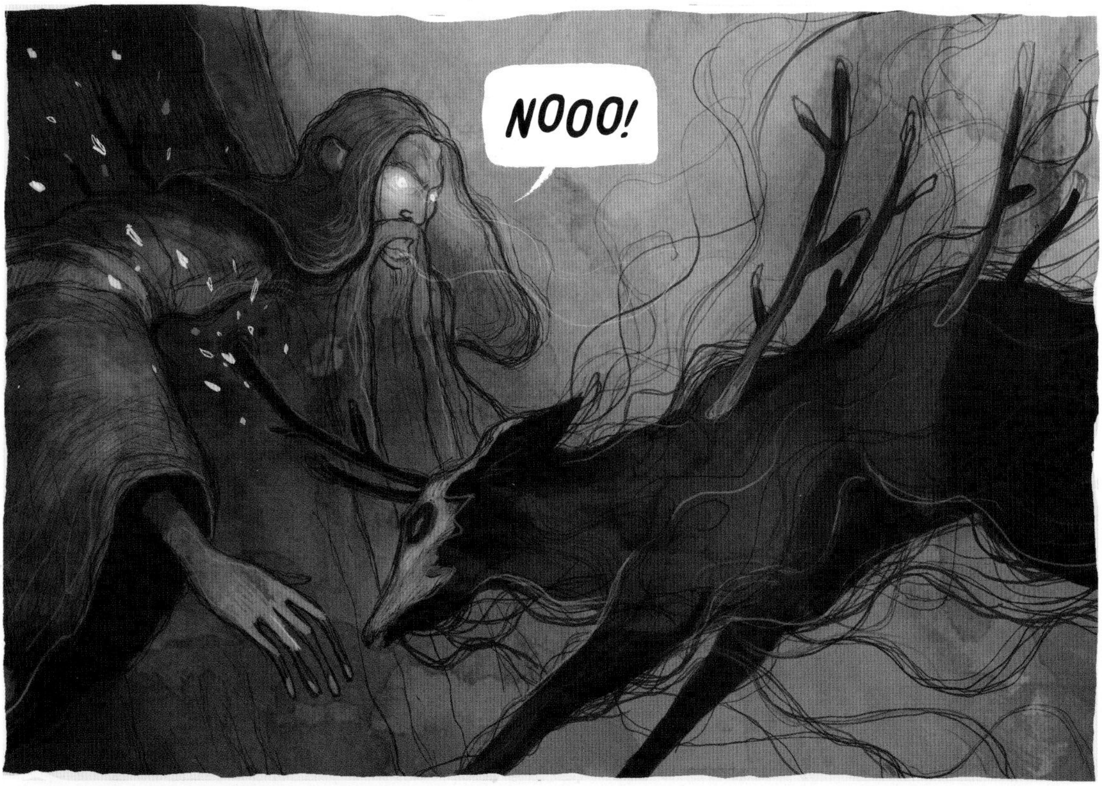
NOOO!

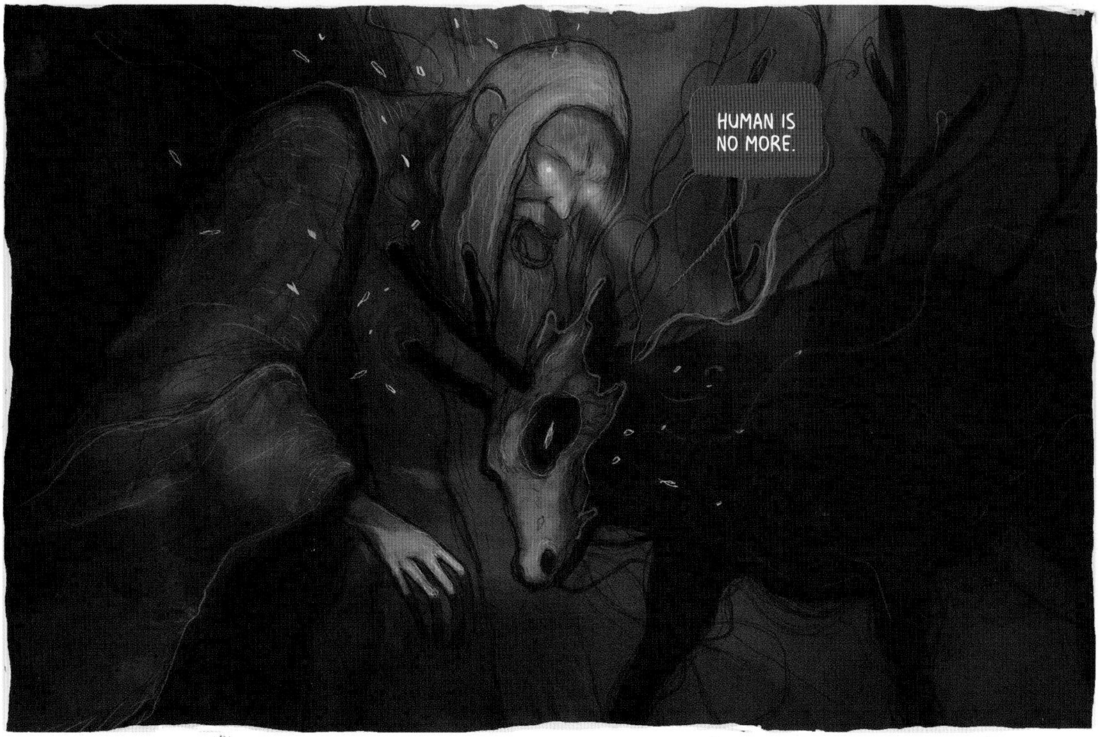
HUMAN IS
NO MORE.

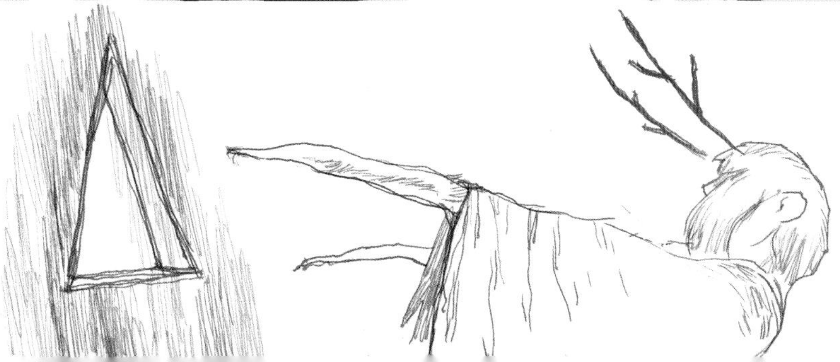
"MY LITTLE
BEAN..."

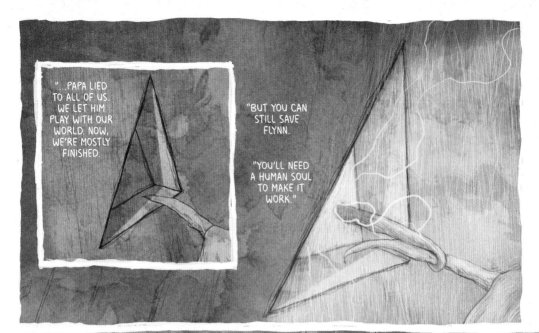

"...PAPA LIED TO ALL OF US. WE LET HIM PLAY WITH OUR WORLD. NOW, WE'RE MOSTLY FINISHED.

"BUT YOU CAN STILL SAVE FLYNN.

"YOU'LL NEED A HUMAN SOUL TO MAKE IT WORK."

IS IT YOU?

I'M YOUR MEMORY.

WHILE I HAVE PASSED ON, MY LOVE FOR YOU WILL LIVE INSIDE YOU.

ARE WE **IN** THE SOUL MACHINE?

SORT OF...THE MACHINE IS A GATEWAY TO YOUR SOUL.

THE CORE OF PAPA'S SOUL COULD MERGE, AND BREAK, AND BURN, BUT YOURS, JUST LIKE YOUR MOTHER'S, CAN ALSO SAVE.

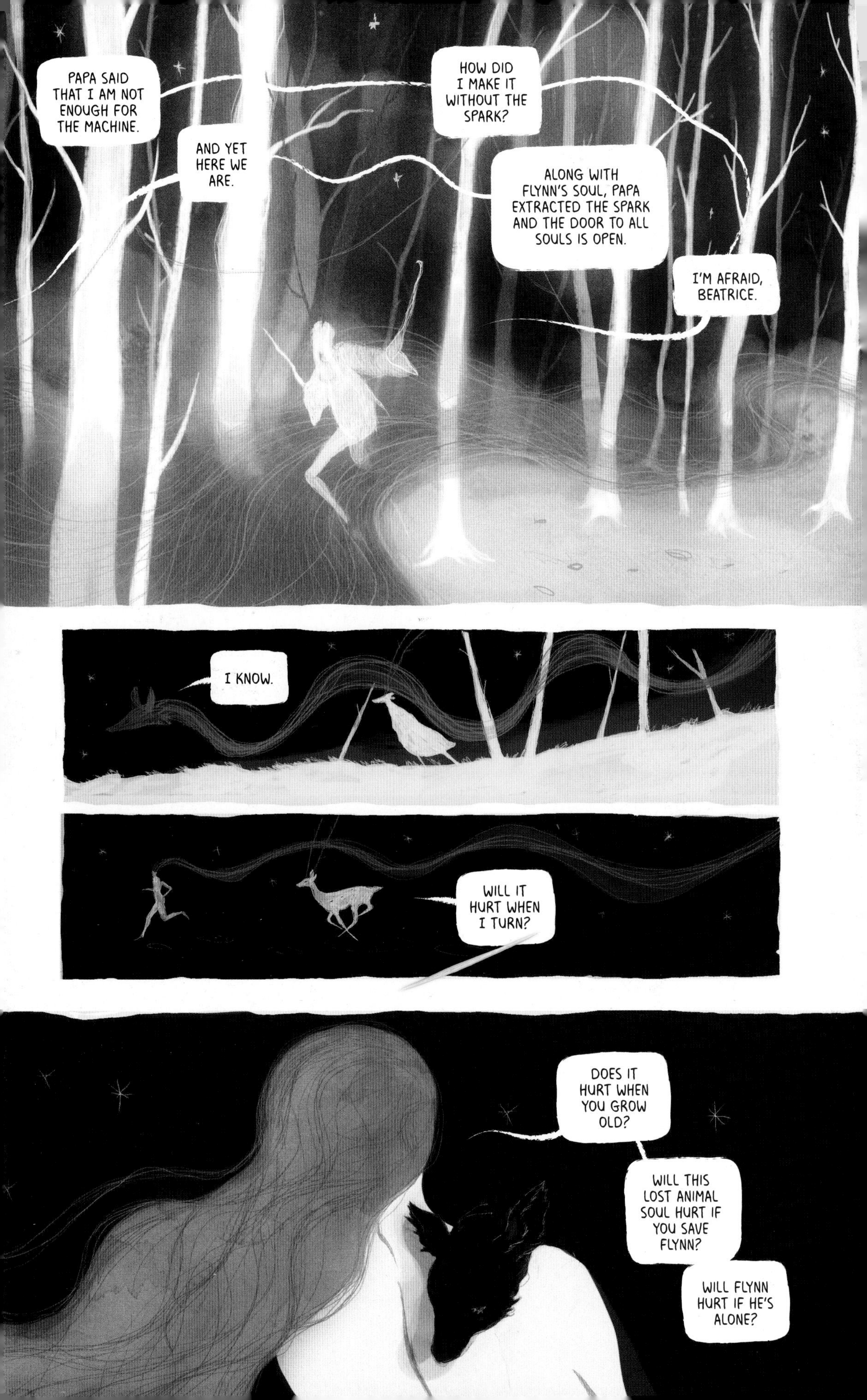
PAPA SAID THAT I AM NOT ENOUGH FOR THE MACHINE.
AND YET HERE WE ARE.
HOW DID I MAKE IT WITHOUT THE SPARK?
ALONG WITH FLYNN'S SOUL, PAPA EXTRACTED THE SPARK AND THE DOOR TO ALL SOULS IS OPEN.
I'M AFRAID, BEATRICE.
I KNOW.
WILL IT HURT WHEN I TURN?
DOES IT HURT WHEN YOU GROW OLD?
WILL THIS LOST ANIMAL SOUL HURT IF YOU SAVE FLYNN?
WILL FLYNN HURT IF HE'S ALONE?

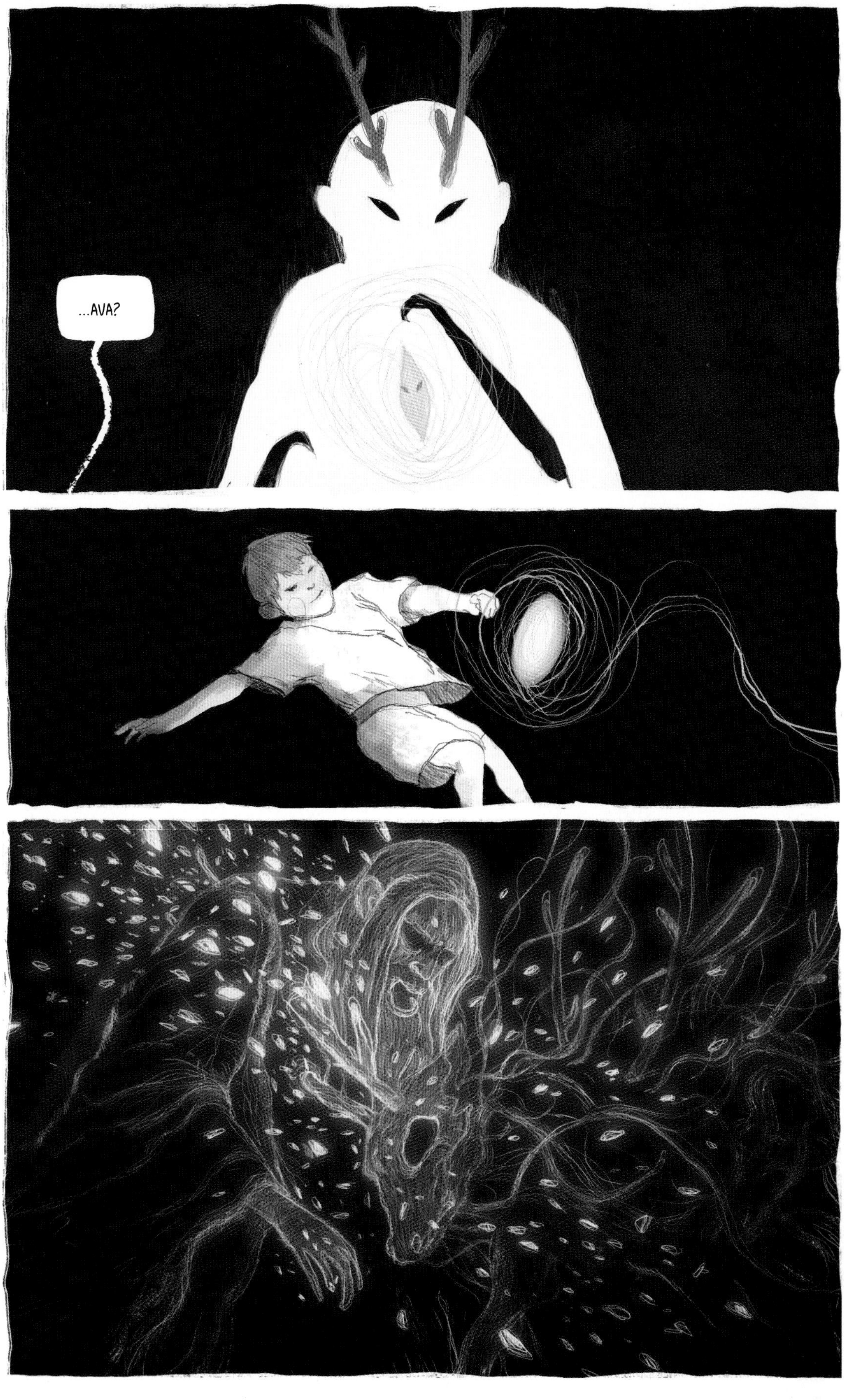
...AVA?

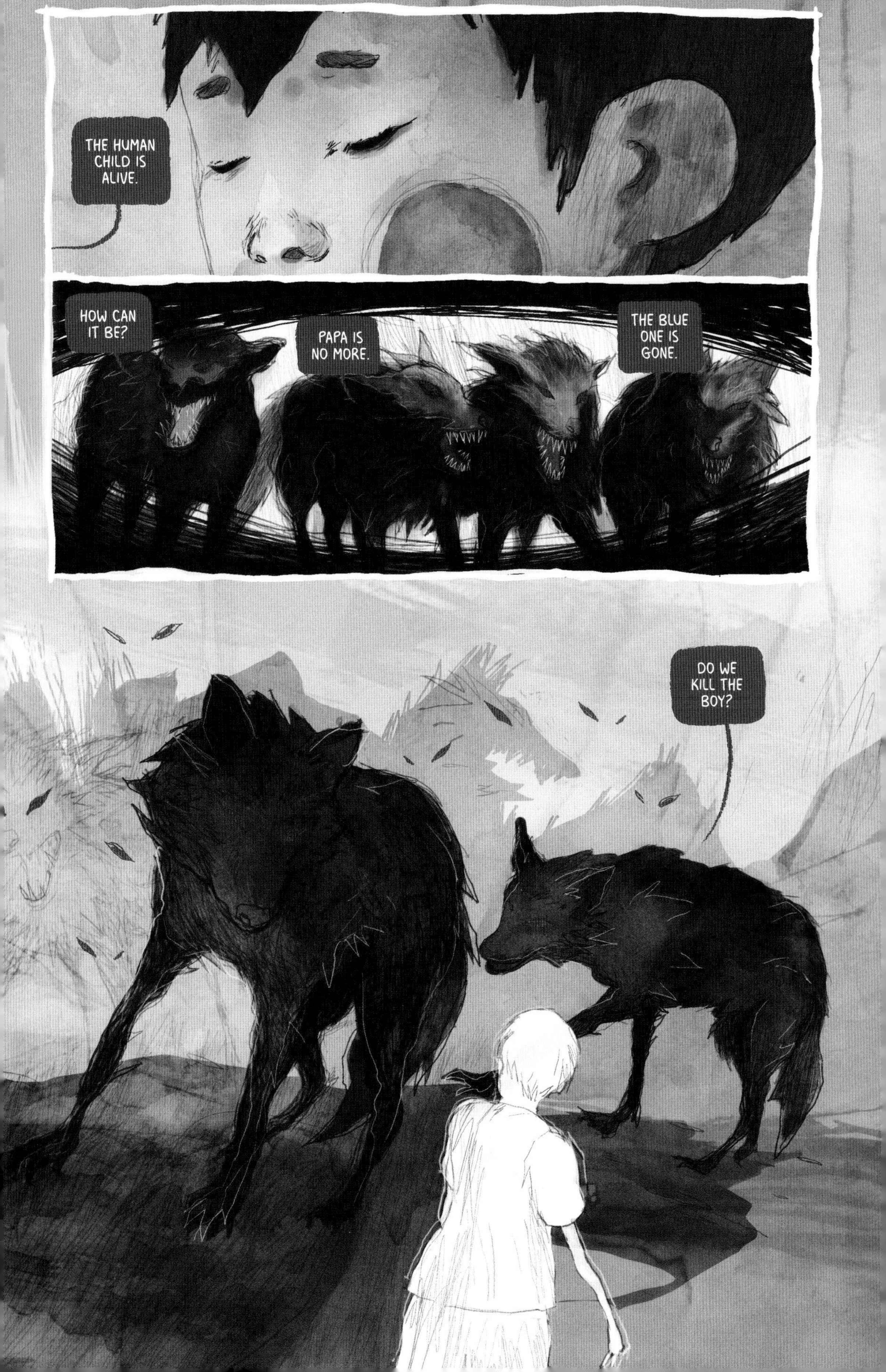
THE HUMAN CHILD IS ALIVE.
HOW CAN IT BE?
PAPA IS NO MORE.
THE BLUE ONE IS GONE.
DO WE KILL THE BOY?

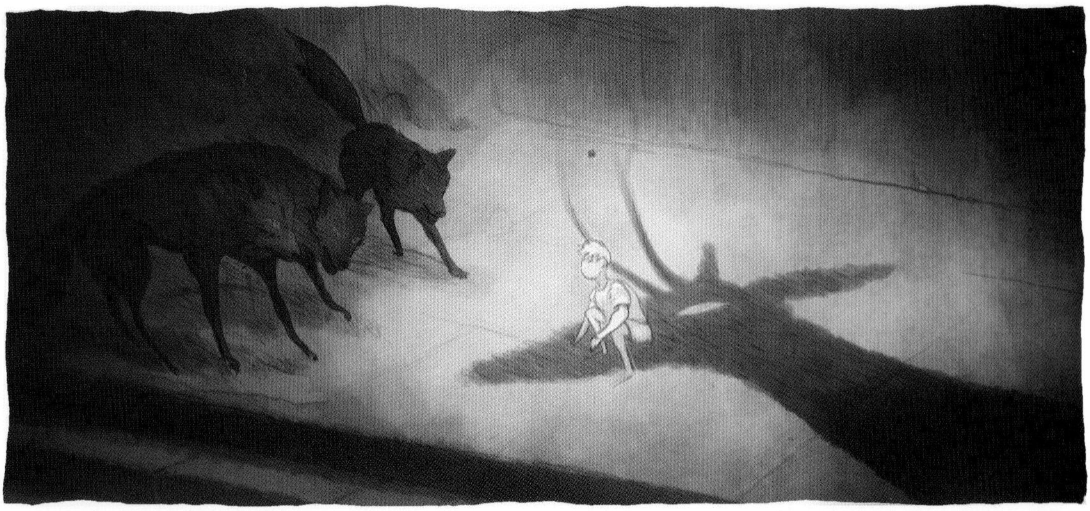

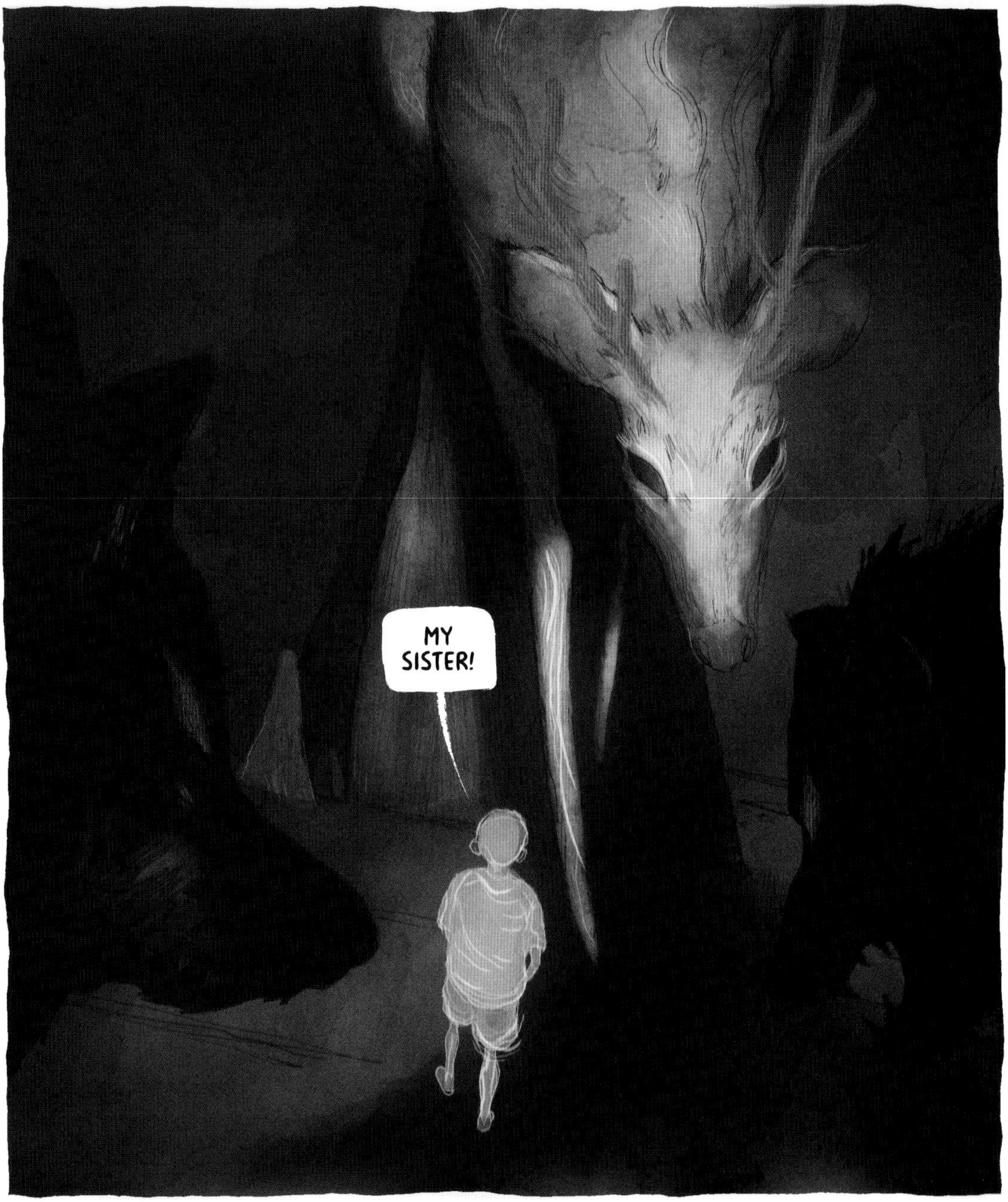
MY SISTER!

YOU...

YOU SACRIFICED YOUR SOUL FOR MY LIFE.

GRUNT

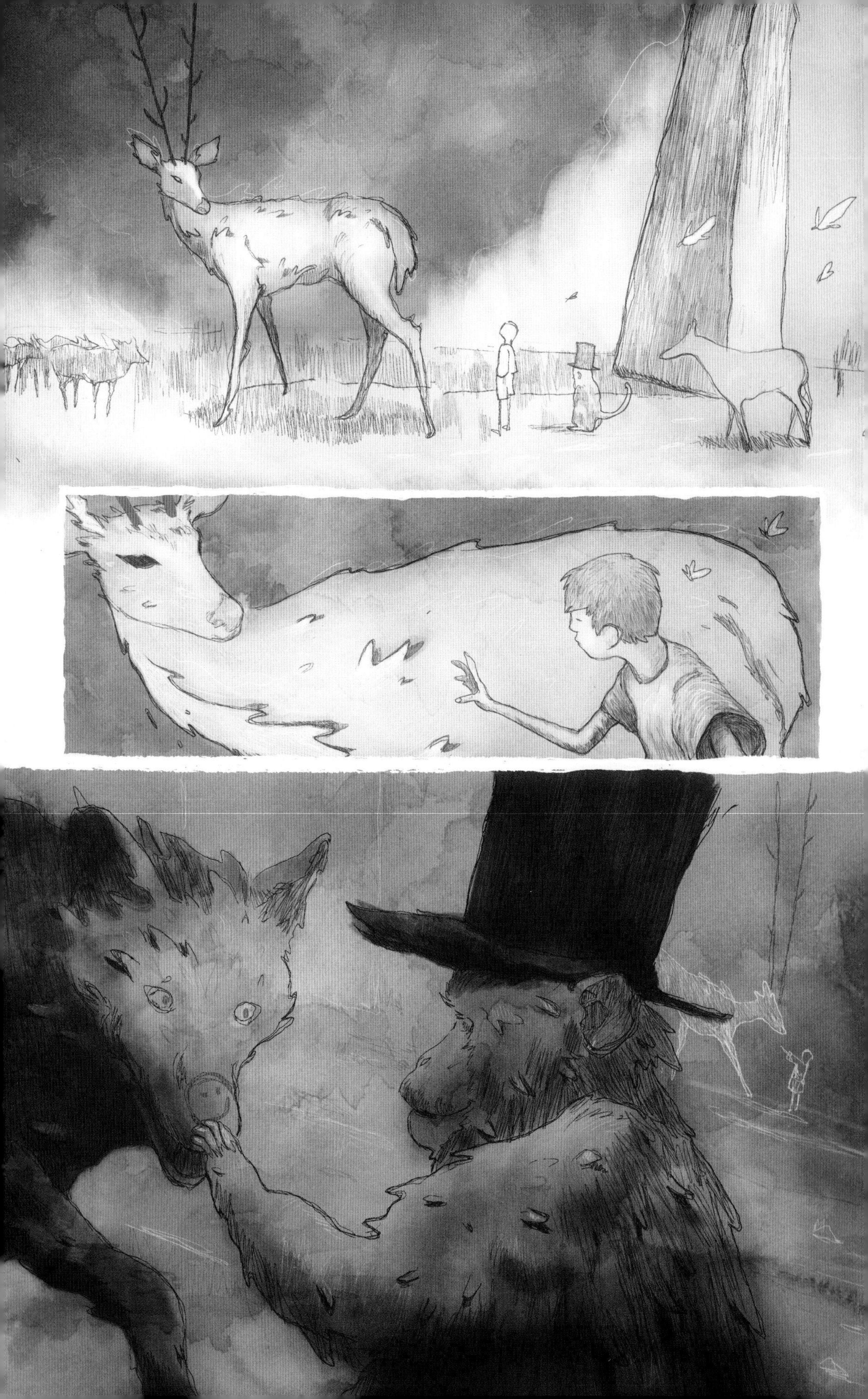

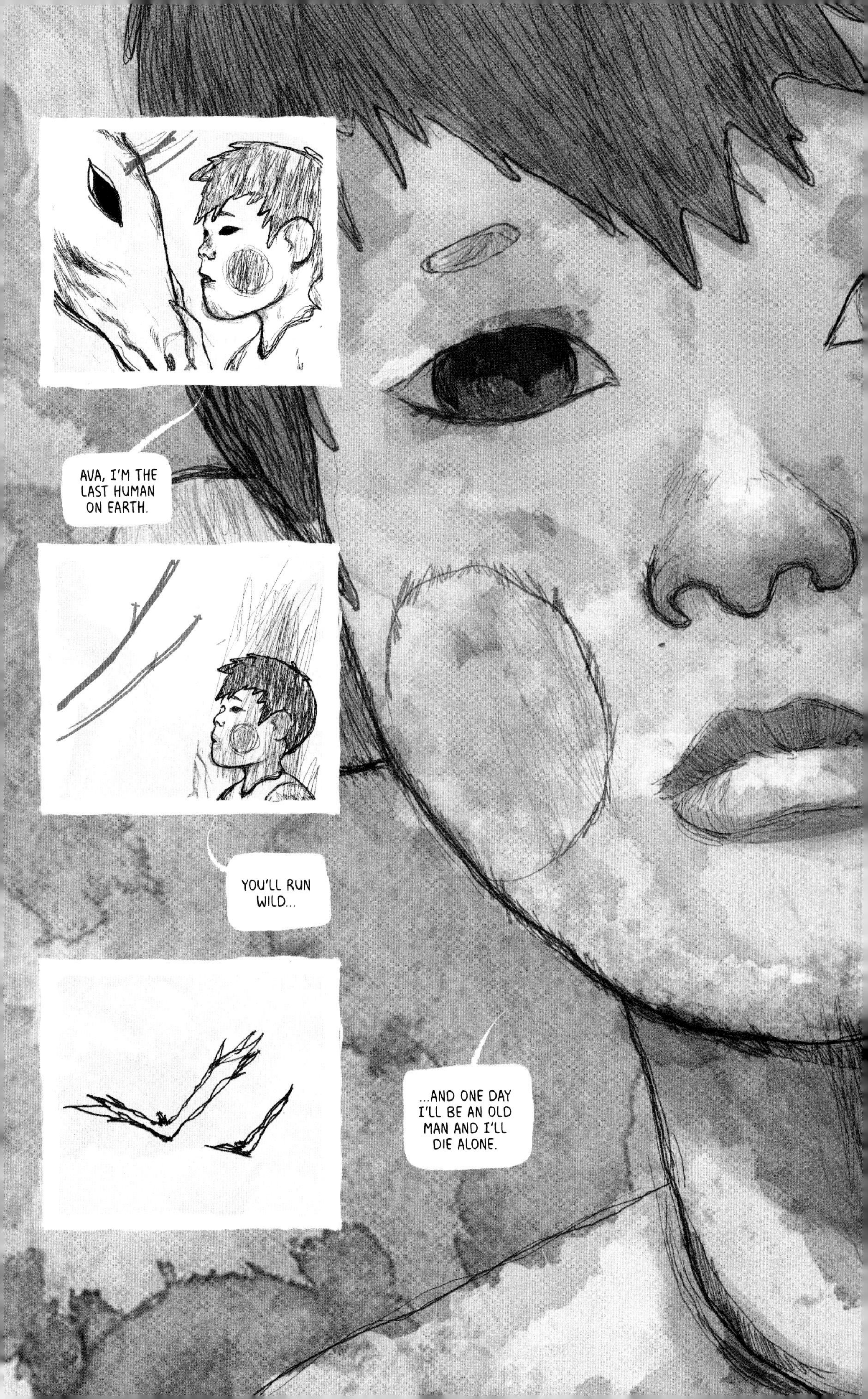
AVA, I'M THE LAST HUMAN ON EARTH.
YOU'LL RUN WILD...
...AND ONE DAY I'LL BE AN OLD MAN AND I'LL DIE ALONE.

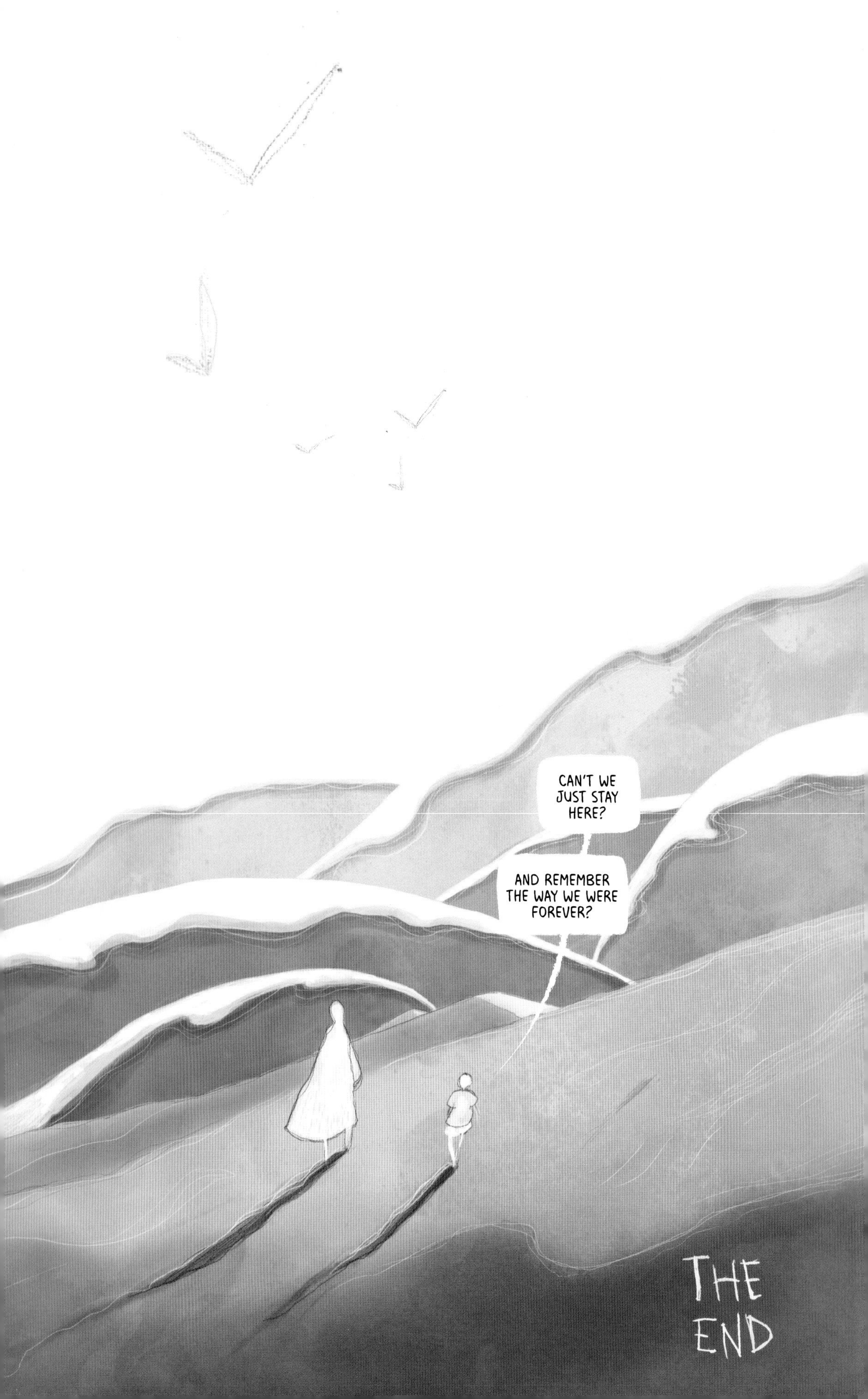
CAN'T WE JUST STAY HERE?
AND REMEMBER THE WAY WE WERE FOREVER?
THE END

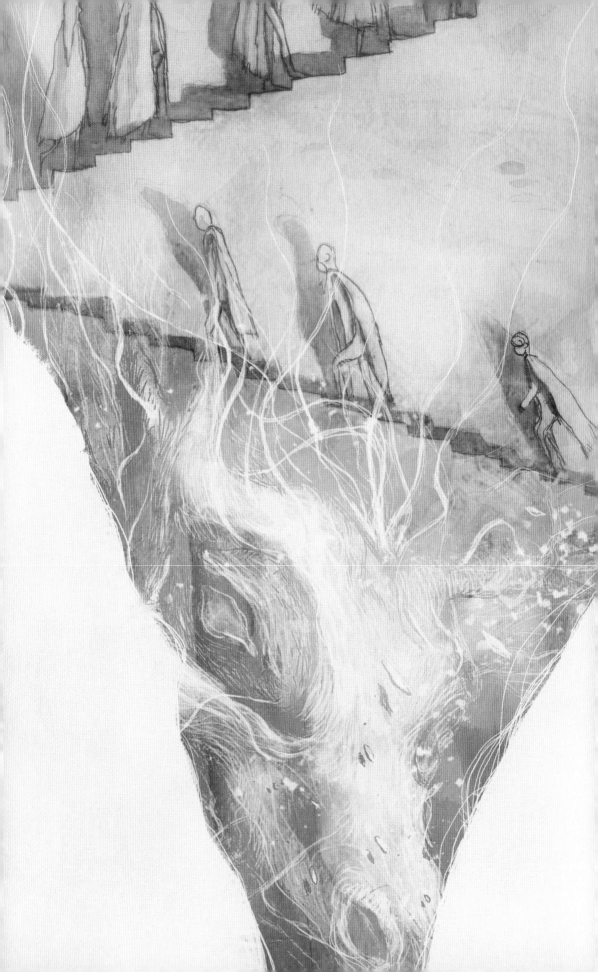

To Whitney and Sierra for showing me how to fly and reminding me how to walk. To Sophie for always being there. To Vincenzo for showing me that the deepest parts of every story come from the non-verbal language of art. To Lance, Filip, Ross, Jose, Mel, Sam, Stephanie, Matt, Irene, Kelsey, Jillian, Aaron, Scott, Eric, Amber, and Deron for your hard work, friendship, and trust. To Maria, Rainer, Dominic, Sina, Stefi, and Marco for being a family. To my sister and mother whom I everyday miss. To my late father who never hid his videotapes and comic books. To my wife Yvonne for sharing her life with me.

—K.I. Zachopoulos

I sincerely wish to thank all the people from BOOM! Studios/Archaia who helped me fully realize this book, my editors, and last, but not least my family and my Mary V. who has always been my support and inspiration.

—Vincenzo Balzano

K.I. Zachopoulos was born in Thessaloniki, Greece but he lives in the wonderful Esslingen, Germany. He participated in *Popgun*, the Eisner award-winning comics anthology published by Image Comics. He is the scriptwriter of "Mister Universe" published in *Popgun* Volume 4 and later as a one-shot comic book. He worked as a scriptwriter for the *Misery City* comic books by Markosia Enterprises and Jemma Press. After the end of *Misery City*, he created and scripted *The Fang*, which was also published in French by Wetta publishing and *The Cloud* with BOOM! Studios/Archaia.

Vincenzo Balzano was born in Torre del Greco in 1985. He studied at the Academy of Fine Arts in Naples majoring in graphic editorial. His first steps into the world of art came in collaboration with the artist Daniel Buren in various exhibitions that were held in Naples, Bologna, and Valencia. His works have been selected for the National Arts Award 2010 and in 2013 his graphic novel *Immortal* won the contest "ilmioesordio" receiving the award for best debut in 2013. In 2014, he illustrated the Marvel graphic novel *Revenge: The Secret Origin of Emily Thorne*, in 2016 he illustrated *Noumeno 4* and *The Cloud*.

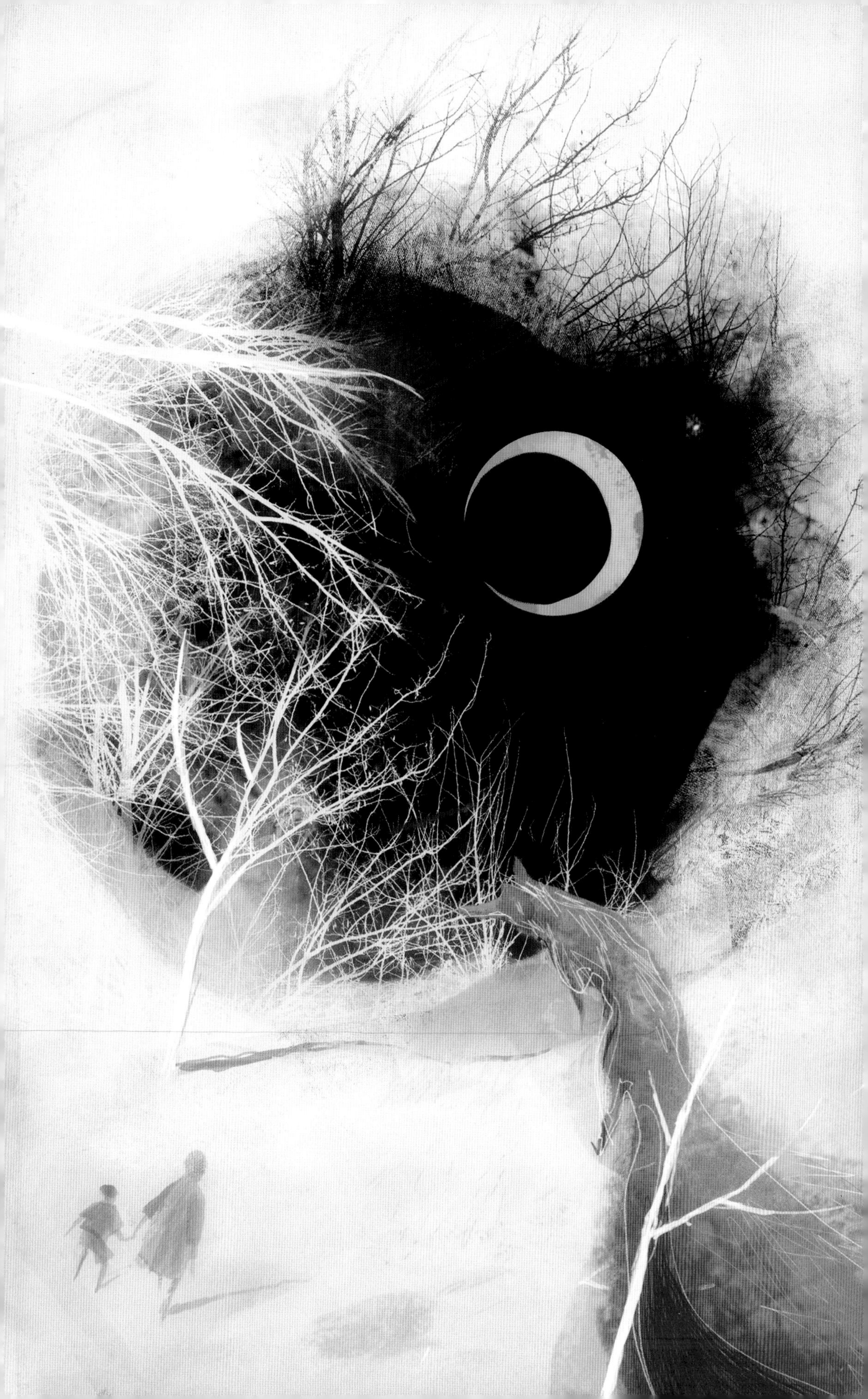

DISCOVER
GROUNDBREAKING TITLES

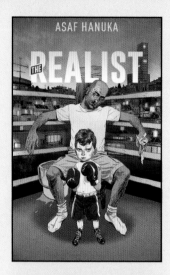

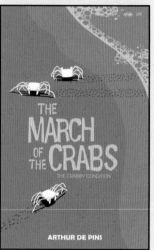

The Realist
Asaf Hanuka
ISBN: 978-1-60886-688-5 | $24.99 US

The Realist: Plug and Play
Asaf Hanuka
ISBN: 978-1-60886-953-4 | $24.99 US

Long Walk to Valhalla
Adam Smith, Matt Fox
ISBN: 978-1-60886-692-2 | $24.99 US

The March of The Crabs
Arthur De Pins
Volume 1: The Crabby Condition
ISBN: 978-1-60886-689-2 | $19.99 US
Volume 2: The Empire of the Crabs
ISBN: 978-1-68415-014-4 | $19.99 US

Jane
Aline Brosh McKenna, Ramón K. Pérez
ISBN: 978-1-60886-981-7 | $24.99 US

Rust
Royden Lepp
Volume 0: The Boy Soldier
ISBN: 978-1-60886-806-3 | $10.99 US
Volume 1: Visitor in the Field
ISBN: 978-1-60886-894-0 | $14.99 US
Volume 2: Secrets of the Cell
ISBN: 978-1-60886-895-7 | $14.99 US

Mouse Guard
David Petersen
Mouse Guard: Fall 1152
ISBN: 978-1-93238-657-8 | $24.95 US
Mouse Guard: Winter 1152
ISBN: 978-1-93238-674-5 | $24.95 US
Mouse Guard: The Black Axe
ISBN: 978-1-93639-306-0 | $24.95 US

The Cloud
K.I. Zachopoulos, Vincenzo Balzano
ISBN: 978-1-60886-725-7 | $24.99 US

Cursed Pirate Girl Coloring Book
Jeremy A. Bastian
ISBN: 978-1-60886-947-3 | $16.99 US

MOGULS, MONSTERS AND MADMEN

AN UNCENSORED LIFE
IN SHOW BUSINESS

BARRY AVRICH

FOREWORD BY PETER FONDA

Copyright © Barry Avrich, 2016

Published by ECW Press
665 Gerrard Street East
Toronto, Ontario, Canada, M4M 1Y2
416-694-3348 / info@ecwpress.com

Cover design: Alan Smithee
Author photo: Caitlin Cronenberg

LIBRARY AND ARCHIVES CANADA
CATALOGUING IN PUBLICATION

Avrich, Barry, 1963–, author
Moguls, monsters and madmen :
an uncensored life in show business
/ Barry Avrich.

Issued in print and electronic formats.
ISBN 978-1-77041-287-3
also issued as: 978-1-77090-851-2 (pdf);
978-1-77090-852-9 (epub)

1. Avrich, Barry, 1963–. 2. Motion picture producers and directors—Canada—Biography. 3. Advertising executives—Canada—Biography.

I. Title.

PN1998.3.A95A3 2016   791.4302'32092
C2015-907291-3   C2015-907292-1

The publication of *Moguls, Monsters and Madmen* has been generously supported by the Canada Council for the Arts, which last year invested $153 million to bring the arts to Canadians throughout the country, and by the Government of Canada through the Canada Book Fund. *Nous remercions le Conseil des arts du Canada de son soutien. L'an dernier, le Conseil a investi 153 millions de dollars pour mettre de l'art dans la vie des Canadiennes et des Canadiens de tout le pays. Ce livre est financé en partie par le gouvernement du Canada.* We also acknowledge the Ontario Arts Council (OAC), an agency of the Government of Ontario, which last year funded 1,709 individual artists and 1,078 organizations in 204 communities across Ontario, for a total of $52.1 million, and the contribution of the Government of Ontario through the Ontario Book Publishing Tax Credit and the Ontario Media Development Corporation.

PRINTED AND BOUND IN CANADA

PRINTING: FRIESENS   5   4   3   2   1

To my beloved Melissa and Sloan,
who are both support and compassion personified

Foreword by Peter Fonda . . . vii
Prologue . . . ix

PART ONE: The Warm-up Act
01. "Okay, Kid, You Can Tell Jokes" . . . 3
02. Printing Money . . . 14
03. Death of a Salesman . . . 20

PART TWO: My Life as a Mad Man
04. Birth of a Salesman . . . 27
05. This Isn't *Shoe* Business, It's *Show* Business . . . 37
06. Garth Drabinsky: Curtain Rising . . . 47
07. Garth Drabinsky: Curtain Falling . . . 61
08. Surrounded by Madmen and a Few Monsters . . . 75
09. Family, Mentors and other Invaluables . . . 87
10. Charity Begins with a Rolodex . . . 98
11. More Boldface: Name Dropping for the Love of It . . . 116
12. Hot Docs: All Dressed . . . 137
13. All Aboard the *Titanic* . . . 150
14. Public Mischief . . . 163

PART THREE: My Life in Film
15. Filling the Frame . . . 175
16. Guilty Pleasure: The Dominick Dunne Story . . . 192
17. The Last Mogul: The Life and Times of Lew Wasserman . . . 208
18. A Criminal Mind: The Life and Times of Eddie Greenspan . . . 230
19. Satisfaction: The Life and Times of Michael Cohl . . . 250
20. Unauthorized: The Harvey Weinstein Project . . . 270
21. Amerika Idol: A True Story . . . 292
22. An Unlikely Obsession: The Untold Story
    of Churchill and the Jews . . . 302
23. Show Stopper: The Theatrical Life of Garth Drabinsky . . . 313
24. Filthy Gorgeous: The Bob Guccione Story . . . 320
25. Quality Balls: The David Steinberg Story . . . 345
26. It's a Wrap! . . . 365

Acknowledgments . . . 367
Index . . . 369

FOREWORD

Reading Barry Avrich's book almost makes me envious. At nine years old, Barry Avrich knew exactly where he wanted to be: in show business. When I was nine years old, I was wondering what the hell was going on in life. I had little knowledge about the business and I was practically unaware of the siren song this industry wails out to the public. I was desperately trying to figure out what was going on in my family. Barry's father, Irving, and mother, Faye, were the best coaches a young performer could ever want. Irving was a performer with great practice. When he would display the fashion he was promoting, he made sure the ambience in the showroom was just right. He placed lights in such a manner to best display his new "collection" as part of his "staged production." In my mind, Barry's father was a working road show, and his son states that he "inherited" his "showmanship from my father." His mother was artistic with an elegant flair. This was a family that I could only dream about. This was Barry's true life beginnings and it was one hell of a start.

Many of the major players in the business, I know personally. I also know about their reputations in dealing with others. Barry went out into this world of moguls and encountered the power these major players use—from Dominick Dunne's heady, almost decadent, world to Lew Wasserman and his Spock demeanour. When Barry spoke to Lew about doing a documentary on him, Lew said, "Not while I'm alive . . . or dead, kid," while applying the Vulcan "pinch" on his neck. I first met Barry in January of 2010. I went on one of his fabulous Floating Film Festivals in the Caribbean. We became friends, immediately. His savvy and production abilities impressed me. His innate ability to seek out the perfect people to interview is right on target. Who else can put together the late great *New York Times* essayist David Carr, Hollywood power player Michael Ovitz and actress Suzanne Pleshette to speak about Lew Wasserman?

When I dealt with Lew, he was a perfect gentleman, as was Jules Stein. But they had both become the most powerful men in Hollywood in part because of acquiring agent Leland Hayward's client list, which included my father, Jimmy Stewart, and so many other top-tier actors. It is fascinating for me to read this book. It confirms so much about what I see in my industry, and it opens closets to some things I had never known. I like what I see in these hiding places Barry exposes to us all. He is an accomplished raconteur with a huge mental library of the business we both love so much. Dinners with Barry are always interesting and full of humour. I look forward to the fabulous stories, each time.

You, dear reader, will be dining on some of the great show-business stories in print today, brought to you through the eyes of someone who is so wonderfully entrenched in it, right up to his great smile and sparkling eyes.

Peter Fonda

PROLOGUE

Of course I was going to make a film about Garth Drabinsky. How could I not? We had worked together for nearly fifteen years. I had been with him through his biggest successes and his biggest failures. We had been close colleagues. I admired him for what he had achieved and was saddened by his perverse ambition and reckless implosion. I had warned him when we first met that someday I'd make this film and he was about as unenthusiastic as you would expect. He was unlikely to have warmed to the idea since his incarceration.

In March 2012, after Garth heard my documentary was actually in production, I received a note from his assistant, Adelaide Mitchell, stating, "Garth would like to see you. He'll put you on the list."

The list? This was an invitation to visit Garth in prison, but it was presented to me as if it were a privilege, like tickets to a Broadway opening. Of course, I accepted. I drove up to Beaver Creek Institution in Muskoka and, being a neurotic Jew, I arrived half an hour early for my 1:30 appointment. Because I was conscious that my car was somewhat fancy for a prison parking lot, I parked it about ninety-two blocks away from the gate, and then walked the rest of the way. I told the guard, "I'm here to see Garth Drabinsky."

"Who?"

"Garth Drabinsky."

She corrected me. "*Inmate* Drabinsky. What time is your appointment?"

"One thirty."

She became testy. "Then you can't be here until 1:30. Don't you realize you're on the property of a correctional institution?"

I hung out in nearby Gravenhurst, then returned at the appointed time.

The guards checked inside my car. They had dogs sniff me. They sent me through metal detectors.

"Okay, go in."

The institution was surrounded by forest. It was dated but quite beautiful. As a medium- and minimum-security facility, it had neither fences nor bars. The inmates bunked together in little cabins with kitchens where they could prepare their own meals. It was almost like a '70s commune, offering various activities; it was not so bad, perhaps, but it *was* a prison. Points of demarcation told the inmates where they couldn't go. Cross the line and it was back behind bars.

Once inside the main building, I was placed in a communal visiting room, like a Legion hall with faded signs, well-worn picnic tables and six antique vending machines. And there I waited. Family members visiting other inmates greeted one another in a scene that was scary and weird, like *The Shining* meets *Shawshank Redemption*.

Before he was at Beaver Creek, Garth had been sent to the maximum-security penitentiary in Kingston, where prisoners were assessed after they were sentenced. I had heard rumours to the effect that Garth had been treated roughly there. Normally, the assessment took thirty days; Garth had been held for 112. I had been told stories—second-hand—about his not having a proper bed, and about his being humiliated and tormented. The guards would announce, "Drabinsky," in a way that suggested he was about to be transferred when that wasn't the case. They knew who he was and they made his stay painful.

In walked Garth.

I hadn't seen him since 2012, when I was in the courtroom for his sentencing. It was a shock to see him a year later. He was wearing a Lionsgate sweatshirt, Ugg winter boots and jeans that hung loose because he'd lost at least thirty-five pounds. His hair was very long and grey. He told me he'd refused to let the prison barbers cut it. He was hoping to have his own guy in to style it, if only the authorities would allow it, whenever that might be.

We hugged, then sat down.

Garth said, "Can you get me something from the vending machines?"

I had been allowed to bring in only $3 in coins, which I had in a zip-lock bag. I bought popcorn (with fake butter), and a couple of chocolate bars, just as I would on each of my three visits. The irony of the man who reinvented the movie-going experience with "real butter," now shovelling microwave popcorn into his mouth was not lost on me.

Even now, Garth was curious about show-business gossip and Broadway casts. He even asked for suggestions about what his post-prison comeback might look like: *If I were to offer to buy the Mirvish empire, how much do you think that would cost?* Eventually, he got down to the reason why I made his shortlist. "I understand you're making a movie about my life?"

"I am."

"I know I can't stop you, but the story isn't over yet. I wish you'd wait."

"Garth, it's better for me to make the film than someone else. I'm proud of the work we did together. It's going to be a very honest film in which I'll give you a fair shake."

Garth baited his hook. "I wish I could somehow be involved in this film, I know you'd like to interview me, but they don't want me to have a high profile in here."

He was fishing for me to make him an offer, which I wasn't about to do. After we chatted back and forth, he came out with it: "I'd like to be your partner."

Translation: You, Barry, should raise the money and do all the work so I can control the film through final cut.

"That isn't going to happen, Garth."

It was a pleasant, emotional meeting. I felt torn. Part of me was witnessing the downfall of a valued mentor. Part of me was in research mode, trying to get inside Garth's headspace for my film: Did he have any remorse or would he express any culpability for what he had done? None that I could see. It was classic Garth. His defence mechanisms were in full operation—*poor me, trapped in this bad situation that isn't my fault.* Though it was hard to feel sympathy for him, I had to ask myself: was prison the best way to punish this man?

I was fascinated to see Myron Gottlieb—Garth's court-acknowledged partner in crime—with his family several tables over from us. The two prisoners had stopped talking to each other, which was Myron's decision. This informal prohibition was later made mandatory by a condition of their parole that forbade them from seeing each other. Unlike Garth, Myron had always been the quiet partner, content to play a backstage role. As a result he was always kind to me and to this day I still have affection for him and his lovely wife Bonnie.

Back in my car, on the long drive back to Toronto, I had much to brood about. No way did that involve dropping the film. Garth's story was compelling and I intended to tell it.

I didn't have to goad people into being interviewed about Garth, as I did with the other moguls I made films about. Far from it. Many of Garth's associates and acquaintances emailed me, volunteering to sit for the camera. Not that Garth cooperated. When he told Eddie Greenspan, the attorney who had defended him, that he was going to prevent anyone from speaking to me the same way he had stopped journalists from writing stories in the past, Eddie repeated to Garth what I'd already said: "Barry is the only guy who will be fair with you."

When I made my second visit to Beaver Creek, two months later, Garth had had his hair cut. Apparently, his prison roommate had styling skills. Garth told me his roommate was in for accidentally killing his wife. Three accidents, according to Garth—the guy's wife had been shot three times.

Garth's tone was more aggressive on this occasion. Now our conversation was all about the film, without any insider's gossip as foreplay. "Barry, to whom have you spoken?" he asked.

Since the interviews were in the can, I told him: Chita Rivera and Diahann Carrol, Tony- and Emmy-winner Elaine Stritch, and so on. "Some talked kindly about you, and a couple, like Christopher Plummer, wouldn't be interviewed out of loyalty."

Garth actually enjoyed hearing what had been said about him. I had the impression that he was proud to learn that Sid Sheinberg, who was Lew Wasserman's right-hand man at MCA Universal, had agreed to be interviewed. Garth's response surprised me, because Wasserman had eviscerated Garth in their Cineplex Odeon deal, and Sheinberg's comment was hardly flattering: "Lew and I woke up to realize we were in bed with a madman."

The warden walked by as we were talking and Garth broke off our conversation to call out, "Hi, Warden! Can I speak to you?"

The warden stopped. "Inmate Drabinsky, hello."

Garth turned anxious and supplicating. "Warden, I don't know if you received my request. I'd like to go home for Passover. It's a Jewish holiday."

"Yeah, I got your request."

Garth started to beg. "Let me explain the significance of this holiday in the Jewish tradition."

The warden cut him off. "Look, I'm a religious man. I know what Passover is. I've told you, Inmate Drabinsky. The Department of Corrections has asked that you receive no personal preference. I'll review your request and I'll get back to you."

It was clear the warden didn't give a shit about Garth and I found out later that Garth didn't receive his Passover leave. I felt badly to see him humiliated in that cringe-inducing way.

At length, Garth revealed why I had made his visitor's list for the second time, even though he knew the documentary was pretty much a done deal. "Barry, you have to promise that you won't release the film until I get out on parole. The attention it attracts might affect my parole situation."

"Garth, TIFF is in September. Your parole won't happen until later in the fall at best. If TIFF selects the film, I'm going to let them have it. If not, I'll make you that promise."

Even saying that much worried me. I knew Garth would use his strong relationship with TIFF to lobby, even from prison, to prevent the film's selection. I decided to do my own lobbying. When I submitted my rough cut to TIFF, I told them, "You may get a call from Garth Drabinsky wanting you to reject this. I'm asking you to judge the film on its merits."

For the pre-festival screening, TIFF called in more people than usual—programmers and board members—to make the right decision: Was the film salacious? Was it unfair? Was it going to be a problem for TIFF?

Show Stopper was accepted. I was elated. Garth . . . well, Garth was upset.

★

Some people are glad to be the subject of a documentary film. Bob Guccione, the man who as much as anyone took pornography mainstream, would have loved the attention. Others are aggressively hostile. There were times when I was working on my film about Lew Wasserman, who had close connections with seriously dangerous people, when I wondered if I really had gone too far. The subject's cooperation can be helpful but it's often not necessary, and I never let either their willingness or resistance get in my way. I just loved making films.

I got my love of culture from my mother, my showmanship and sense of style from my father. I loved the limelight and sought it from an early age—it never made me nervous to be the centre of attention. I would have been a singer if I could sing or an actor if I had the looks. But I couldn't sing or act so I told jokes instead. For a few weeks when I was nine years old I was the youngest member of a vaudeville-style show playing in Montreal. I wasn't born into money but my stage presence and sense of humour were the cards I played to get access, to hang out with the in-crowd. I wanted to be with the people who had the power to change the world, learn their secrets and possibly enjoy their kind of lifestyle.

I was bored at school but I had a knack for marketing—my father's influence again—and I soon understood that I could always make a living. I sold meat in a butcher shop for one uncle, worked in a printing plant for another. And then I discovered filmmaking. If I couldn't be on the stage myself then I would put others on the stage—or screen—and manage the production, the sets, the lights, the scripts. And the marketing! If marketing and promotion was my vocation, then film became my passion. It was Uncle Manny who told me to keep it that way, and while Manny had rather a sad life, he was wise and gentle and I still have a soft spot for him. As he suggested, I've been an ad man for most of my life and made documentary films simultaneously.

And through it all, I've hung out with people who had the power to change the world—who did change the world. Garth Drabinsky was one. Another was Dusty Cohl, the man who, more than anyone, was responsible for making Toronto a power in the world of film. His cousin, Michael Cohl, concert promoter for some of the greatest rock acts of all time, was another, as was the novelist and crime reporter, Dominick Dunne, who topped Truman Capote's capacity for celebrity access. I met and worked with A-list stars. And I was fortunate to have as a friend, mentor and father figure in Canada's foremost criminal lawyer, Eddie Greenspan.

It's been a fun ride. If there's a moral to it, it's that a kid from Montreal who was nothing extraordinary could have so many dreams come true.

PART ONE
THE WARM-UP ACT

* Chapter One *

"OKAY, KID, YOU CAN TELL JOKES"

By the time I was nine, I was already an entertainer. It's just that no one but my relatives knew it.

Like many aspiring middle-class people living in Montreal in the 1960s and '70s, my parents possessed a wonderful collection of recordings by such fabulous singers as Ella Fitzgerald, Eartha Kitt and Tony Bennett, along with the soundtrack of many Broadway shows. They also had albums by Jewish comedians like Lou Jacobi, Mel Brooks and Woody Allen. While other kids were playing baseball and hockey, I listened to these albums and memorized the jokes. Then, on weekends, my parents would take me to visit relatives and I would perform on top of coffee tables.

My father, Irving, knew this vaudeville guy, Sam Miller. Sam's wife, Sadie, looked like a flapper and had a wonderful smoky voice. She had turned down Broadway impresario, Florenz Ziegfeld, who wanted her for his famous Follies. Sam could have been a Ziegfeld himself if he hadn't had a family to support. Instead, every year he produced and directed a big show in Montreal. Somehow, he'd heard about me. He told my father, "I want to see your kid."

At our first meeting, Miller asked, "Do you want to sing or tell jokes?"

"I want to sing."

He gave me the sheet music for "What the World Needs Now" by Burt Bacharach. He said, "Come back in a week."

I worked every night with my mother, Faye, who has a musical ear. I learned that song backwards and forwards.

The following Saturday afternoon, I went to Sam Miller's house for my audition. Sam's son, Joey, who became a well-known composer, sat down at their upright piano in his underwear and began to play.

"Go!" ordered Sam.

I got as far as ". . . needs now . . ."

"Okay, kid," he said. "You can tell jokes." Somehow I was not insulted.

The Millers wrote an act for me in their show, *The Mamas and the Papas of the Next Generation*, about the disconnect between parents and grandparents and their kids, with me as the youngest member of the cast. I was listed in the playbill as The Interlocutor—a description I've never heard since. For four nights over two weeks, I wore makeup, a vaudeville jacket, a big bow tie and a straw hat. I would step into the spotlight and tell jokes, and everyone would laugh and applaud, and there would be flowers, and the other cast members would sign my playbill.

I got telegrams telling me, "You have a contract for life with NBC" and "We have a spot for you on *The Tonight Show*." They were sent to me by my father. It was his way of making something big seem even bigger.

How could I go back to a normal life after that?

A lot of entertainers will tell you they feel more comfortable on stage than off, and I'm like that. Though my friends have trouble

believing this, I feel shy and awkward in ordinary situations, but the moment I walk onto a stage my nervousness disappears.

Sam Miller made it clear to me that I was never going to be a singer. As a teenager, I was too insecure about my looks and my weight to believe I could be an actor. Still, I knew that someday I would be involved in show business.

I inherited my showmanship from my father. Armed with only a high-school education, he sold ladies' sportswear to the retail trade, but every day he was on the road, he demonstrated his sense of style in the way he staged his collections. He would rent a suite in the grandest hotel in town and display his goods, sorted by colour and designer, with the lighting exactly right. For his spring and fall collections, he would take a double suite in Montreal's legendary Mount Royal Hotel. When I was thirteen and fourteen, I would help him with his sample bags and the custom-made orange suitcase that opened up to become a portable bar. With so many people coming and going, and the excitement my father generated, I sometimes felt like I was in vaudeville myself.

My father wasn't the slimmest guy, but he always dressed well and he was charming. I could see that people loved him. I could see that Irving Avrich was somebody.

My father and his older brother, Sol, had cocreated Casual Togs, a ladies' sportswear company. Though my father could sketch, Uncle Sol became the lead designer, while my father handled sales. I don't know when, or why, but eventually Sol bought him out. This gave my father the opportunity to really focus on being the sales guy, which was his real passion. Since my uncle's designs were ultra-conservative, it wasn't until Irving had the guts to take on other designers that my father began to make significantly more money.

On Saturdays, when it was empty, I would go to the factory with my father to pick up the new collections. I have happy memories of playing with the sewing and adding machines, and using the intercom system to page fictitious people. "Mr. Smith, Mr. Smith, you're wanted in ladies' underwear." I liked the freight elevators that you pulled down with a big leather strap, then held on while the cage jerked up, *guh guh guh*. Uncle Sol's office, in contrast to that old-fashioned workspace, was quite swanky, decorated with art and sculpture. His desk was always pristine. On Mondays, my uncle used to complain to my father about my little weekend adventures, about the adding machines that were screwed up and the supplies that were askew.

My father and my uncle were avid fishermen, and sometimes I went on excursions with them. Of course, my uncle was *The River Runs Through It* kind of fly fisherman. Today, when I see him, I'm emotional, because he's the only genetic connection to my father.

★

Because my father was away from Monday to Thursday every week, my mother ran the household. Like my father, she did not have a university degree, but she was always elegantly turned out and extremely cultured—she still is today at eighty-seven. As well as music, my parents collected whatever art and antiques they fell in love with. There were no Old Masters hanging in our house, but make no mistake, every corner had something interesting to look at or talk about it. Like my father, my mother had artistic flair.

I believe my father enjoyed his time away from home, and I think my mother enjoyed having space to herself as well. He'd come back from his business trips at three or four o'clock on Thursday afternoons, exhausted. The door would fly open, we'd run to greet him, and that night we'd have a big dinner. Later in the evening, he would have his weekly gin rummy card game with his friends. I would beg him to invite them to our house because I wanted to see the guys he hung around with, and the kind of guy he was when he was with them. I would press my ear to my bedroom's central-heating grate, above the basement card game, so I could hear the friendly banter and smell the cigar smoke. At some point in those evenings, my mother's role was to carry in the dessert. I would plead with her, "Can I go? Can I go?"

Ironically, years later, when I was in high school and enjoyed my own floating poker game, my father hated it. I think he was afraid I'd get into serious gambling, but my gang always played for low stakes. When the game was at our house, my father would sometimes run in yelling, "It's a raid!"

On Friday or Saturday nights, my parents would often have people over for dinner. Partway through the evening, still exhausted from the workweek, my father would excuse himself. After that, I'd see this huge hulk of a man sprawled on the bed in the master bedroom, fast asleep. Irving was a larger-than-life character, in body and in spirit, a sweet guy, but you had to accept him on his own terms. He was never going to live the life of a quiet homebody, home from work every night at 5:30. He was eccentric. I remember all the strange things he used to buy on the road: the pot-bellied stove he stashed in the trunk of his car, then pretended to hook up in the basement; the old sepia portraits of strangers that he framed and hung on the wall and then claimed they were ancestors; the birch tree he found on a beach and shipped home.

Both my parents' families emigrated from Russia in the 1800s to escape the pogroms. My father's parents, who died before I was born, had owned a shoe store on the Main in Montreal. My mother's father,

Louis Garellek, was a kosher butcher. After he lost his wife in the 1950s, he married a simple but pleasant woman who was like a grandmother to us. We called her Aunt Minnie.

I had a fabulous relationship with Zadie Louis, as did everyone in our family, including my father. My mother, as his only daughter, looked after him following her mother's death. Zadie Louis was tall and handsome with a white moustache. Though traditional, he didn't object to my father driving to his place on the Sabbath because he wanted to see his grandchildren. Aunt Minnie often visited relatives in Israel or Vancouver for two or three weeks in the summer, and my grandfather would stay with us while she was gone. He was a playful, warm guy, interested in music, theatre and adventure. When he was around, our house overflowed with his generous spirit. Among my special memories are the Passover Seder dinners at his Montreal townhouse when thirty people sat around the table, as well as visits to his country place in the Laurentians. I also remember my parents driving him to Saratoga Springs. They used to spend a month in a modest little motel with a kitchen so they could keep kosher, while enjoying outings to the horse races and an annual Marx Brothers film festival.

Zadie Louis was our patriarch. When he died in 1980, our memorable days of huge extended family dinners, a celebration of our respect for him, came to an end.

My mother was always a doer. She had a strong network of friends, was very private and discreet and never complained. She worked so hard for others over the years that it was always difficult to give her a gift. She's also been good at keeping me grounded. If I'm going to the Academy Awards, or a newspaper article is written about me, she brings me down to earth with a casual, "That's nice," not overdoing it, and preventing me from getting too big a head.

Though she still keeps kosher, my father never did. When he cut into one of my grandfather's steaks, his invariable comment, which my mother hated, was, "The Jews are meant to suffer!" meaning that a kosher steak's flavour could never compare to those he ate on the road. At Passover, he'd toss out the lunch my mother had packed before he got to the end of the street. Faye occasionally tolerated us sneaking food into the house that wasn't kosher, but she wouldn't let us use her dishes. We joked that our family had three sets: for milk, meat and Chinese food. That last set was made of paper.

My mother was unquestionably our caregiver, but if ever my sister Cindy or I acted up during the week, she would warn us, "When your father gets home on Thursday, he'll deal with this." That never amounted to anything because Irving was too nice. He'd call us down to his den, which was hazy with cigarette smoke and untidy, with his briefcase, appointment book and fabric swatches strewn on the desk. He'd say, "Why did you do that? Be nice to your mother! Now, are we clear?"

There was a movie theatre in our neighbourhood shopping centre and my father often took me there on weekends. Of all the classics we saw, I was especially fascinated by those about show business: *Citizen Kane* with Orson Welles, *Sunset Boulevard* with Gloria Swanson, *Mame!* with Rosalind Russell. That movie experience, enhanced by being with my father, was so magical. And because of those memories, I still have a special fondness for working with older stars, such as Gena Rowlands, Kathleen Turner and Shirley MacLaine.

Most summers, my parents took Cindy and me to the Stratford Festival. Since it was a long drive from Montreal, we stayed overnight at a bed and breakfast, then saw two shows. That whole festival experience was beyond thrilling: the buzz, the fanfare, the playbills, the ushers, the anticipation. I especially remember *Taming of the Shrew* and *School for Scandal*. It was my introduction to Shakespeare and I loved it. Nothing compares to live theatre. To this day, I watch the audience as much as what's on stage. I watch as they laugh, I watch as they squirm, I watch as they clap—the audience reaction is a big part of my enjoyment.

It's also amazing to me how often my life has come full circle. When I chaired and produced a gala honouring Christopher Plummer, I told the audience, "This probably means nothing to you, but it means everything to me. I can remember, as a kid, going to Stratford, and seeing great actors like Plummer command the stage, and being completely spellbound. Now, I'm producing film adaptations of *The Tempest* and *Caesar and Cleopatra* with Plummer. And I can't think of anything more that I need in life."

My bedroom—the smallest—was next to our main bathroom, so even today I find the sound of whooshing water soothing. I turned that bedroom into a showbiz office, with a stereo and posters of my heroes, like Don Adams of *Get Smart* fame. Years later, I produced a series of commercials with Don, and we became close friends.

When I was eight years old, I discovered *Variety*, the bible of the entertainment business. The stories of moguls and kingmakers like Ed Sullivan and Johnny Carson attracted me even more than the biographies of stars. Poring over the pages of this magazine, I tracked the upper-echelon dealmaking and the box-office grosses of major productions. I'd tell my parents and friends about what I learned till their eyes glazed over. Even then, I was career-building. This was my real education.

I was twelve when my parents first took Cindy and me to New York with them. What a thrill that was. Times Square, the glittering marquees, the delis, the skyscrapers!

On our way to dinner on our first night there, my father proudly showed us our theatre tickets. "You know, kids, these cost twenty-five dollars each for orchestra seats—that's one hundred dollars for the four of us." Those tickets were for *A Chorus Line*. It was 1975, its opening year. For someone as stage-struck as I, that show was informational as well as mesmerizing. My parents also took us to see *Fiddler on the Roof* and *Carousel*, among other shows. I still remember watching transfixed as Pearl Bailey in *Hello, Dolly!* sashayed down a long staircase. These experiences created such a high that I promised myself I would go to Broadway every year for the rest of my life. In 2009, I took my daughter, Sloan, age five, to *The Lion King*, her first Broadway show. I made a point of telling her how lucky she was, just as my father had told me, though her ticket cost more than all four of my dad's tickets combined.

From grades one to eleven, I attended a private Jewish school. My marks were average in every subject except math, which were worse. Despite my fascination with movie grosses, I could never get numbers to add up. My parents hired a tutor, which made little difference to my marks but created a huge problem for my self-esteem. I didn't care about math but I *did* care about all that money they were spending for my education when all I was delivering was mediocrity.

I remember asking my father, with tears in my eyes, "Why are you bothering?"

He replied, "Just get the diploma and get out, you have what it takes."

After blowing that monkey off my back, he then spoke the magic words that told me I would always be the son he wanted: "Just make sure you never blend in."

My father never mentioned my marks again. I did get the diploma, and I have never blended in.

Chapter Two

PRINTING MONEY

My bar mitzvah was pure showbiz. Wearing the new suit. Standing up before an audience. Having that spotlight focused on me. Making a funny speech. Thanking my parents for dipping into their Swiss bank account to pay for the magnificent lunch. That was a joke: we kept the celebration modest so we could travel to Israel. I was cool with that, despite having attended extravagant affairs staged by the parents of some of my wealthier friends. Some of these had featured invitations printed on velvet, live camels in the garden and a bowl of real goldfish on every table. When she picked me up from one of these extravagant parties, my mother was horrified when the host said she was sorry to hear we were having trouble with our butler. This was of course a joke I had invented and mentioned in an aside. I never felt jealous of the people who lived in the big houses in Westmount and Hampstead. But it was something to aspire to later on.

After my bar mitzvah, it was left up to me to decide how often I would go to synagogue, so my attendance fluctuated a lot from then on.

As did my father's. On one occasion, he cut pages from his *Time* magazine to fit inside the prayer book so that, when my mother looked over the partition, she would see him engrossed in his devotions. He was particularly bad at keeping Yom Kippur, a day of fasting and prayer. As was I. I've always believed no religious service should last longer than a movie, which ideally is 102 minutes, our natural human attention span. Some Yom Kippur prayers droned on for hours, till I'd want to kill myself. Whenever I escaped home for a break, I would find my father there ahead of me, covered in cookie crumbs.

Even after years of attendance at synagogue, I still can't find an instant spiritual connection with my faith versus my heritage that I respect. I will never be overtly religious. I'm sure this bothers my mother, and it bothers me that it bothers her. Out of respect, I attend the famous repentance service on the eve of Yom Kippur, in which the rabbi lists every possible sin, so even if I haven't committed them, I'm covered.

Zadie Louis had four sons, the second eldest of whom inherited his kosher meat market. Starting when I was ten, I'd go bill collecting every Sunday with Uncle Jack or his son Steven. I'd knock on a door, and say, "Hello, I'm here from Garellek Kosher Meat Market. You owe fifty dollars." Because nobody ever paid in full—meat on the instalment plan!—I'd usually return with only $10.

My uncle would say something vulgar in Yiddish and we'd go on to the next house. In fact, my uncle, like my grandfather, was very forgiving. Both were known throughout the community for their support of poorer families. Uncle Jack was also generous with me. After our collections, he'd lay out the cash on the table and I'd get my percentage—$50 or $100, which was great money for a kid.

I had a couple of other jobs when I was growing up. One was

delivering the *Montreal Star* to three rundown apartment buildings. After I'd delivered a thousand papers, I'd return on the weekend to collect. As soon as I banged on a door, the television would be turned off, the lights would go out and you'd hear the sound of people scrambling from the living room.

I lasted a week.

My job with future impact arose out of my hatred of summer camp. When my father began making more money, he and my mother would go on trips to Europe while my sister and I were sent to camp. I couldn't stand it. I hated the organized physical activity. I hated the bunk beds. I hated the bugs. My camping exile began when I was nine. My parents sent me to B'nai Brith Camp, deep in the woods, and I cried for a month. When they wanted to send me back the following year, I protested, "Are you out of your mind? You got the letters. You got the phone calls. I don't ever want to go back."

My mother, who rarely became angry, would use one of two lines to convey her displeasure. She used the first one the day I slammed the vacuum cleaner into the pedestal holding her *Fiddler on the Roof*–inspired sculpture, smashing it to pieces.

She said, "Are you happy now?"

She used that line again when I brought a cake into the dining room for one of her dinner parties. I was holding it over my head like a singing waiter when I lost my balance, causing the cake to slide off the platter onto the floor.

"Are you happy now?"

For our impasse over camp, she used her other line: "You don't know what you like. It will be different this time."

So, yes, they packed me off to B'nai Brith Camp again, and this time it *was* different, because I developed a coping strategy. I talked my way out of doing anything physical, like going on a canoe trip, by using my well-worn gym excuse: "I don't know if you're aware of this—didn't my mother tell you?—I have a slipped disc." Then

I threw myself into the camp's theatrical production. Even though I did the whole month without shedding a tear, I spelled it out to my parents on their return: "I'm telling you now, I'm never going back. It was worse than awful."

When my parents went to Europe for the third summer, they enrolled me in the only day camp they could find and consigned me to the care of my sister. It was an orthodox camp, where they prayed a lot and potato chips were banned as not being kosher enough. I cut a deal with my sister not to tell my parents—I think I bribed her—then skipped out to look for a job.

One of my mother's four brothers, Uncle Manny, owned a printing company. He offered me work on the line, collating complex order pads that came in forty different colours—red, canary, green and so on—for which he paid me as a manual labourer. After a couple of days, I went into his office, which was as hazy with smoke as my father's den—and told him, "I can't do this."

"Then what do you want to do?"

"Let me be a sales guy."

I knew I could do it. I had watched the sales king, my father.

Next day, I showed up for work—an eleven-year-old salesman in a suit—and Manny gave me a briefcase. I took the bus downtown to visit Chinese restaurants, where I figured they always needed menus. I asked each owner, "Who does your printing?" Then I assured them, "My uncle's company can do it cheaper and better."

When I returned to the factory with ten orders, my uncle was astonished. That earned me a promotion to head of sales.

I knew my uncle was struggling to make his business work. He also had aspirations as a publisher: he was printing and distributing booklets on fitness and diet into drugstores and grocery store chains. Unfortunately, back in the 1970s, the health craze hadn't yet taken hold, and most of his publications were returned unsold. Even I could see that this business model was flawed. I began asking his printing clients to buy ads in his books to cover their cost before they were printed. That worked for a while, but it pained me that Manny wasn't making enough to pay for his Cadillac or to purchase a home for his family.

I liked working for Uncle Manny because he treated me like an adult. He was a dreamer, always looking for something better, but never quite making it. We'd sit in his office, where he drank at least fifty cups of coffee a day while leafing through magazines, discussing which ads worked and which ones didn't. He showed me ads by marketing pioneers like David Ogilvy, who invented the sophisticated eye-patched "Man in the Hathaway Shirt," and the elegantly bearded Commander Edward Whitehead, who personified Schweppervescence, a brand of tonic water. Uncle Manny taught me the selling power of the promise. Even today, I tell my clients, "If you don't arouse expectation in an ad, or offer a service, or make some kind of promise, it won't break out and be noticed."

While studying ads with Manny, I noticed many offered free samples: Life Savers, potato chips, bodybuilding manuals and hair-growing potions. Since this was before the Internet, I became a direct-mail maniac. Every day, about seventy packages would arrive for me, containing items I meticulously tucked away in a filing cabinet. More important to me than the products themselves was the thrill of seeing my name on all those envelopes and packages.

It was Manny who suggested that I set my professional sights on advertising instead of filmmaking. As he explained, "All you'll find in Canada is a film board producing documentaries about beavers. You've got the gift of the gab, and everyone always has a product to sell. Make advertising what you do, with filmmaking on the side."

And that's what I did.

Later in Manny's life, he lost his factory and became a salesman, like me in my suit with a briefcase. His wife left him and he ended up stories—second-hand—about his not having a proper bed, and about his being humiliated and tormented. The guards would announce, "Drabinsky," in a way that suggested he was about to be transferred when that wasn't the case. They knew who he was and they made his stay painful.

In walked Garth.

I hadn't seen him since 2012, when I was in the courtroom for his sentencing. It was a shock to see him a year later. He was wearing a Lionsgate sweatshirt, Ugg winter boots and jeans that hung loose because he'd lost at least thirty-five pounds. His hair was very long and grey. He told me he'd refused to let the prison barbers cut it. He was hoping to have his own guy in to style it, if only the authorities would allow it, whenever that might be.

We hugged, then sat down.

Garth said, "Can you get me something from the vending machines?"

I had been allowed to bring in only $3 in coins, which I had in a zip-lock bag. I bought popcorn (with fake butter), and a couple of chocolate bars, just as I would on each of my three visits. The irony of the man who reinvented the movie-going experience with "real butter," now shovelling microwave popcorn into his mouth was not lost on me.

Even now, Garth was curious about show-business gossip and Broadway casts. He even asked for suggestions about what his post-prison comeback might look like: *If I were to offer to buy the Mirvish empire, how much do you think that would cost?* Eventually, he got down to the reason why I made his shortlist. "I understand you're making a movie about my life?"

"I am."

"I know I can't stop you, but the story isn't over yet. I wish you'd wait."

"Garth, it's better for me to make the film than someone else. I'm proud of the work we did together. It's going to be a very honest film in which I'll give you a fair shake."

Garth baited his hook. "I wish I could somehow be involved in this film, I know you'd like to interview me, but they don't want me to have a high profile in here."

He was fishing for me to make him an offer, which I wasn't about to do. After we chatted back and forth, he came out with it: "I'd like to be your partner."

Translation: You, Barry, should raise the money and do all the work so I can control the film through final cut.

"That isn't going to happen, Garth."

It was a pleasant, emotional meeting. I felt torn. Part of me was witnessing the downfall of a valued mentor. Part of me was in research mode, trying to get inside Garth's headspace for my film: Did he have any remorse or would he express any culpability for what he had done? None that I could see. It was classic Garth. His defence mechanisms were in full operation—*poor me, trapped in this bad situation that isn't my fault.* Though it was hard to feel sympathy for him, I had to ask myself: was prison the best way to punish this man?

I was fascinated to see Myron Gottlieb—Garth's court-acknowledged partner in crime—with his family several tables over from us. The two prisoners had stopped talking to each other, which was Myron's decision. This informal prohibition was later made mandatory by a condition of their parole that forbade them from seeing each other. Unlike Garth, Myron had always been the quiet partner, content to play a backstage role. As a result he was always kind to me and to this day I still have affection for him and his lovely wife Bonnie.

Back in my car, on the long drive back to Toronto, I had much to brood about. No way did that involve dropping the film. Garth's story was compelling and I intended to tell it.

I didn't have to goad people into being interviewed about Garth, as I did with the other moguls I made films about. Far from it. Many of Garth's associates and acquaintances emailed me, volunteering to sit for the camera. Not that Garth cooperated. When he told Eddie Greenspan, the attorney who had defended him, that he was going to prevent anyone from speaking to me the same way he had stopped journalists from writing stories in the past, Eddie repeated to Garth what I'd already said: "Barry is the only guy who will be fair with you."

When I made my second visit to Beaver Creek, two months later, Garth had had his hair cut. Apparently, his prison roommate had styling skills. Garth told me his roommate was in for accidentally killing his wife. Three accidents, according to Garth—the guy's wife had been shot three times.

Garth's tone was more aggressive on this occasion. Now our conversation was all about the film, without any insider's gossip as foreplay. "Barry, to whom have you spoken?" he asked.

Since the interviews were in the can, I told him: Chita Rivera and Diahann Carrol, Tony- and Emmy-winner Elaine Stritch, and so on. "Some talked kindly about you, and a couple, like Christopher Plummer, wouldn't be interviewed out of loyalty."

Garth actually enjoyed hearing what had been said about him. I had the impression that he was proud to learn that Sid Sheinberg, who was Lew Wasserman's right-hand man at MCA Universal, had agreed to be interviewed. Garth's response surprised me, because Wasserman had eviscerated Garth in their Cineplex Odeon deal, and Sheinberg's comment was hardly flattering: "Lew and I woke up to realize we were in bed with a madman."

The warden walked by as we were talking and Garth broke off our conversation to call out, "Hi, Warden! Can I speak to you?"

The warden stopped. "Inmate Drabinsky, hello."

Garth turned anxious and supplicating. "Warden, I don't know if you received my request. I'd like to go home for Passover. It's a Jewish holiday."

"Yeah, I got your request."

Garth started to beg. "Let me explain the significance of this holiday in the Jewish tradition."

The warden cut him off. "Look, I'm a religious man. I know what Passover is. I've told you, Inmate Drabinsky. The Department of Corrections has asked that you receive no personal preference. I'll review your request and I'll get back to you."

It was clear the warden didn't give a shit about Garth and I found out later that Garth didn't receive his Passover leave. I felt badly to see him humiliated in that cringe-inducing way.

At length, Garth revealed why I had made his visitor's list for the second time, even though he knew the documentary was pretty much a done deal. "Barry, you have to promise that you won't release the film until I get out on parole. The attention it attracts might affect my parole situation."

"Garth, TIFF is in September. Your parole won't happen until later in the fall at best. If TIFF selects the film, I'm going to let them have it. If not, I'll make you that promise."

Even saying that much worried me. I knew Garth would use his strong relationship with TIFF to lobby, even from prison, to prevent the film's selection. I decided to do my own lobbying. When I submitted my rough cut to TIFF, I told them, "You may get a call from Garth Drabinsky wanting you to reject this. I'm asking you to judge the film on its merits."

For the pre-festival screening, TIFF called in more people than usual—programmers and board members—to make the right decision: Was the film salacious? Was it unfair? Was it going to be a problem for TIFF?

Show Stopper was accepted. I was elated. Garth . . . well, Garth was upset.

★

with a drinking problem. After I began earning money, I used to pay his way to Toronto once a year and treat him to dinner. Afterwards, I'd leave a bottle of Scotch out for him, and it would be empty by morning.

I always had a warm spot for Uncle Manny. Though his life fell apart, he pointed me in the right direction.

★ *Chapter Three* ★

DEATH OF A SALESMAN

At around three o'clock one morning in the winter of 1981, when I was eighteen, I was awakened by the sound of my mother's agitated voice. She was in the master bedroom, only five feet away, speaking on the phone. As I approached her half-closed door, I heard her repeat over and over, "I don't understand you. Please speak slower. I don't understand."

After my mother put down the phone, she said, "Something has happened to your father. Something medical. He's in Quebec City and the doctors are speaking in French. We must go there."

She was too upset to drive, and so was I, so we took the early morning bus. We were in agony the whole trip, fearful of what we would discover.

I've always been afraid of hospitals. My mother and father could whistle their way through a morgue, but not me. Years before, when I'd hurt my shoulder, and my father took me to emergency, I saw a gurney covered in a white sheet, bearing the sign, "Burn immediately."

I went into the bathroom, threw up and then announced, "My shoulder's fine." When my father protested, I insisted, "My shoulder's FINE!" I kept that up until he relented and we left.

I had never again entered a hospital until this moment when we walked into my father's room in the old Hôtel-Dieu Hospital in Quebec. He was connected to every possible tube, and though he was able to speak, his voice was very weak. We were told he'd had a brain aneurysm, but the doctors couldn't operate because his blood pressure was insanely high. Here was this Jackie Gleason of a man, lying in bed, holding my hand, saying, "Don't worry, don't worry." It was excruciating, but my mother was a rock. She held things together for both of us.

We wanted to take my father back to Montreal but we couldn't until his blood pressure came down. This meant keeping him in Hôtel-Dieu, which we soon discovered to be brutally anti-English, at least to us. The doctors were awful. I spoke French, but the situation was jagged and uncomfortable for everyone.

My mother and I checked into the Château Frontenac. My father had shown his collections there for years and somehow this made our circumstances all the more tragic. Relatives, including my sister, who was studying psychology at the University of Ottawa, began making pilgrimages to see him, perhaps to say their goodbyes. It was tough. Even though the brilliant doctors at the Montreal neurological institute were in communication with the Quebec medical staff, the days turned into weeks and we still waited to fly my father home. We celebrated Passover at Hôtel-Dieu as my father's condition worsened. He wasn't speaking anymore, and unless the escalating pressure on his brain could be relieved, blood vessels would burst, causing his death. It was heartbreaking and surreal. I went to the hospital every day, full of desperate hope, and attended synagogue every Saturday. One day, when the rabbi asked anyone who needed a prayer for the sick to come forward, I gave him Father's name and the rabbi prayed for him. At that very moment, religion truly comforted me. Then I walked back to the hospital. As soon as I entered my father's room, the doctors gave their permission to move him to Montreal.

At the Château Frontenac, I handed my mother's credit card to the woman at the front desk, knowing our bill would be astronomical. The woman rang her bell. Out came the manager. He said, "Your father has been coming here as our guest for twenty-five years. You don't have to pay anything."

I was speechless, not only because of the manager's generosity, but also because it showed that my father had been loved by people outside our family.

What I didn't realize, on our return to Montreal, was that the neurosurgeons would cut open Irving Avrich's head, and I would never again know the man who was my father. Even before I knew the results of this operation, I had to summon up the courage to visit him. It was worse than I expected. The part of his face that I could see looked ghastly, and the rest was swathed in bandages. Far worse, he couldn't communicate. I had my usual hospital reaction: I threw up.

My father was institutionalized for a year, first in rehab, then in a nursing home. It was the most intense, depressing rehabilitation I could imagine. He had to learn how to walk again. He had to learn how to talk. His sense of humour was gone. His free spirit was crushed by what had happened inside his head. He was like the walking dead, except he couldn't even walk, only shuffle.

One day in rehab, the old Irving returned, at least for a moment.

The woman in the next bed, who'd had a stroke, had been screaming, day and night, "Nurse! Nurse! Nurse!" My father gestured with his eyes for me to come to his bedside.

I leaned over him, "What is it?"

Though he could barely speak, he shifted his eyes toward the woman, then whispered, "Get a pillow, and kill her." He managed to deliver this message twice more through clenched teeth. "Kill her! Kill her!"

When my father was released from the hospital, he could no longer smoke, his big stomach was gone, and so was his thick bushy hair. He astonished us by demanding to go back on the road. He was like one of those old delivery horses that know only one route and stop at every door without being told. It was what he knew. His comeback was to be launched with a show at Montreal's Mount Royal Hotel. I set up the room for him and drove him there.

He looked extraordinarily slim in his new suit when he walked into the Mount Royal suite but he walked with a limp and his speech was somewhat slurred. People thought he was drunk. It was a bad, bad day and he returned home depressed and broken.

I kept driving Irving to the Mount Royal so he could finish out the week, and then he hired a driver to take him back on the road, but it was too much for him. I don't know for a fact that retailers and other associates were cruel to him. Probably it was just a case of business being business. The road trips came to an end for Irving when he had to sell his beautiful Chrysler New Yorker Fifth Avenue and watch a stranger drive it away.

The worst was yet to come. Uncle Sol suggested that Irving should run a weekend factory outlet out of his plant, where blouses with manufacturing imperfections could be sold at a discount. I was away at school, so my mother drove Irving to the factory with his lunch, and he'd stand behind the SALE sign in the window till the door opened and humanity came rushing in. My once-amiable dad despised the job so much that he became rude at times. When one woman came to him with a $10 blouse, saying, "This looks like a stain. Can I get it for five dollars?" he shouted at her, "Did you make that stain yourself? Ten dollars!"

Years later, I remember watching the world premiere of the film *Glengarry Glen Ross* at the Toronto Film Festival, which told the story of desperate real estate salesmen competing to make a living. I found it painful and depressing. Jack Lemmon portrayed a once-ace salesman who had slid tragically downhill and he reminded me of my father, sitting in that terrible factory outlet. My father had one more medical disaster to endure. After he went into a Montreal hospital to have a routine hernia operation, the medical staff misread his charts, so that he ended up having a stroke, forcing him to live another five years in even greater misery. When I consulted a Montreal lawyer, he said, "I know that hospital and I know that doctor. Let it go."

My father died on July 11, 1992, while I was visiting the Grand Canyon. It was about 110°F and I know it's a cliché, but I felt a sudden chill pass through me. Now, I don't believe in paranormal stuff, but that was what happened. This was before cellphones were ubiquitous. The next day, when I returned to Toronto, I found fourteen messages on my old telephone answering machine, all from my mother, and all saying the same thing, "Can you call?" "Can you call?" "Can you call?" Then I knew.

I wrote his eulogy on the plane from Toronto to Montreal. My sister and I went to the Paperman Funeral Home to pick out his coffin. Old Mr. Paperman was sitting among the caskets, eating a chopped-egg sandwich. He couldn't have been less interested. "You want redwood? You want oak?" My sister and I did the only thing possible: we laughed.

My father had a huge funeral. Despite those Job-like years when he was no longer himself, his friends and associates remembered how he had loved everyone, and how everyone had loved him. All of us in the family were both saddened and relieved by his death. I had to summon up all my courage to speak and say goodbye. I promised myself then that I would take my father's passion for life and run with it. I would never waste a minute through regret, sleep or missed opportunities. Most importantly, I would never blend in.

PART TWO
MY LIFE AS A MAD MAN

* *Chapter Four* *

BIRTH OF A
SALESMAN

From 1980 to 1982, instead of high school I attended Vanier College
in Montreal. At last the shackles were off: I didn't have to do math
or science! I didn't have to study Hebrew! I could take the courses
that interested me, like filmmaking, and concentrate on finding new
ways to earn cash. For a time, I worked as a drugstore clerk, shelving
heavy cartons of Pampers. I didn't care what I did if it meant that, in
the evening, I had money to spend.

Though I was accepted at McGill University when I graduated
from Vanier, I didn't want to go there. I didn't have the marks to
get into an Ivy League college in the United States, even if my parents could have afforded to send me there. With these options off
the table, it seemed inevitable that I was bound for Toronto. We had
visited the city once a year after my parents' closest friends moved
there in the 1970s, so we had dined at the only fine restaurant, La
Chaumière, with its little cart of French hors d'oeuvres, shopped at
the Eaton Centre and been served roast beef, frozen peas and mashed

potatoes at Ed's Warehouse. My father looked on Toronto as a cultural desert and described it acerbically as "dead from the neck up." And this is where my future lay.

I set my sights on the radio and television program at what was then Ryerson Polytechnical Institute. The name of the school worried my mother. I think she was alarmed at the idea that her son was going into an "institute." At that time, Ryerson's well-repected television program required a very high academic standard. I found this discriminatory given that it was an arts program; however, my average marks wouldn't get me into the program any more than they'd get me into Harvard, so I applied to their theatre production course. To qualify, I had to submit an essay describing my passion for the theatre and a set sketch. Okay, I knew how to write, but because I hadn't inherited my parents' drawing genes, I showed my Uncle Sol the photo of a period set I'd found in a book, and he sketched it for me brilliantly. I was accepted immediately.

My mother came to Toronto to help me find an apartment. Since we couldn't find anything in the Ryerson area, we branched out. A newspaper ad took us to a place at Church and Wellesley streets, a few blocks north of the school. We were greeted by a guy in a flowing, floral robe who showed me the bedroom we were to share. I declined. After that, my mother found a basement apartment at Bathurst and Eglinton, considerably farther from Ryerson and from downtown cosmopolitanism, where I could join the upstairs folk for Friday dinner. It was a strict Hasidic household: no female visitors were permitted at any time. Next!

My only other option—a temporary one—was to stay with my mother's cousin, Sylvia, an advertising executive at an electronics company, who had a magnificent condo at Granite Place on St. Clair Avenue West. Living there felt weird and awkward, especially when the doorman snickeringly referred to me as "Sylvia's boy." Still, being able to return from a rough day at Ryerson to a lavish condo with a swimming pool made the trade-off worth it.

Unfortunately, I soon realized Ryerson's theatre program was not for me. I was interested in directing, but much of what was taught was technical—how to hang lights, build sets and sew costumes. By trotting out my well-worn excuses for avoiding physical labour, I managed to be assigned jobs more suited to my abilities, such as selling ads for the playbill. Nevertheless, I found it exhilarating to see a big production come together. We put on *Spoils of War*, a dark play by Michael Weller about a teenager who tries to mend his parents' broken relationship. Years later, I would produce radio and television commercials for this play when it was revived by Ed and David Mirvish at the Royal Alexandra Theatre with actress Kate Nelligan. I still remember one brilliantly psychotic line, when the lead character exclaims, "Nothing exciting ever entered my life through the icebox, so I chose to pay the phone bill."

Partway through my first year at Ryerson, I found a bachelor apartment at St. Clair and Mount Pleasant for $289 a month. In the deal I had with my mother, she would look after my rent while I was responsible for everything else. In the matter of furnishing the place, I opted for a minimalist look: a single bed pushed against a wall; the desk from my childhood bedroom; a library table my mother found; a couple of Persian carpets that once belonged to my grandfather; a television set; and a director's chair to remind me of my dreams. Since I don't cook, my kitchen was a place to store my bike alongside the fridge, its freezer packed with food my mother had sent, and the cupboards repurposed as a filing cabinet. My closet, with its door removed, became a place for collectibles, mostly photos, since I like to frame memories. A thick glass door, which I had scavenged, was propped on cinder blocks to become a table. What turned my apartment into a classic bachelor pad was a giant Richard Avedon poster of German model Nastassja Kinski (the one with a snake wrapped around her), and a huge poster from the film *9½ Weeks*.

For the first six months, I was enormously homesick, so I took the train back to Montreal every weekend. Gradually, however, as I built up a network of friends and connections at TV stations and film companies, I threw myself into everything connected with entertainment. I volunteered for whatever was going: script assistant, labourer, even coffee boy. I had learned to make coffee from Uncle Manny—this was at a time when good coffee in Toronto was rare.

I didn't know any girls in Toronto but friends and relatives from Montreal were all too keen to set me up with cousins and nieces. I sometimes had three or four blind dates a week. This crash course in dating taught me how differently the Montreal and Toronto Jewish communities operated. In Montreal, you were either middle class, or iconically wealthy and untouchable, like the Bronfmans in Westmount. In Toronto, I encountered many *nouveau riche* Jews whose immigrant parents and grandparents had made big money, producing a generation of intolerable Jewish princes and princesses. In Montreal, I was not in the least self-conscious about living in a modest house in middle-class Côte Saint-Luc and driving my mother's Pontiac. In Toronto, however, my tiny apartment and bicycle felt woefully inadequate. I always felt judged by my pretentious dates.

I had an underhanded (and regrettably ruthless) way of fighting back. When unwanted blind dates were foisted on me, I sometimes made two reservations. If a girl was unappealing, I took her to Hunan Palace in Chinatown. If she was attractive, I took her to the decidedly upmarket (and more expensive) Pronto. In one night of folly, I had a six o'clock date and a nine o'clock date. As it turned out, the two girls knew each other—disaster!

This matchmaking system, remote-controlled from Montreal, yielded one bad date after another. On what was surely the worst, the door was opened by a plump girl who was extraordinarily short.

Circus short. When I asked for my date by name, this girl claimed the honour. When she replied, "Are you Barry?" I'm ashamed to say that I replied, "No, I'm selling subscriptions." Then, in an act of unparalleled insensitivity and immaturity, I fled.

Afterwards, when I challenged the guy who set me up, he protested, "But she comes from a very good family. You should have looked past merely physical attributes."

Look *past?* I looked over, under and around, and every glance told me to get out fast.

My active social life required money. By now, I knew I was born to sell. Though Ryerson students were forbidden to have jobs that might interfere with their scholarly focus, I took one with Sheplee's, a leather goods store in the Eaton Centre, which paid a salary plus commission. By working only Thursday and Friday evenings, then all day Saturday, I earned more than the full-time employees made in a month. My formula was simple: I gave people more than they expected. Leather was fashionable in the '80s, and the Eaton Centre attracted a lot of tourists. If someone came in to buy a sheepskin coat, leather pants or a jacket, I would offer to make a dinner reservation for them too, or get them theatre tickets, or I would simply give them a list of interesting places to visit. I had a lot of repeat business. At Christmas, it was not unheard of for a customer to spend $10,000. One guy purchased coats for his entire office staff.

Though people weren't keen to buy sheepskin in July, I'd say, "Have you read the *Farmer's Almanac?* It's calling for one of the coldest winters on record. Do you want me to save this coat for you till September, in case the price goes up?" I wasn't exactly selling refrigerators to Eskimos, but it came close. At first, the other salesmen resented my success, but I'd sometimes treat them to lunch, and they enjoyed my jokes, so they became okay with it.

I liked my job much better than school. At Ryerson, professors did the talking, while at Sheplee's I held the floor, and during my off-hours, the Eaton Centre became a wonderland for me. I especially liked hanging out at a store called "Models Only," though it proved to be a futile pursuit. Even the salesgirls turned me down.

A couple of decades later I was running the Floating Film Festival that took place on a cruise ship when I recognized an elderly man among the passengers. He was Irving Wortsman, who had owned Royal Leather, a family dynasty that included Sheplee's and Daniel among its brands. I told him, "My favourite jacket was your model 53870." He was so excited, he called his wife, "Sylvia! Sylvia! This man knows our 53870."

Two obstacles threatened to keep me from passing my first year at Ryerson. Obstacle One: For my final exam in stage management, I had to stand in front of the class and call stage cues from sheet music from a famous score. "Okay, stand by, fade down lights, fade up music and actors enter stage right!" Reading music was required to trigger certain cues and I didn't read music. In desperation, I checked out Gershwin's *Rhapsody in Blue* from the reference library. That score had many big moments, which I could recognize by all the ink on the page. I memorized them, and passed brilliantly. Obstacle Two: The challenge was to build a model set of my own design. I copied photographs of the set from an obscure old show, *The Sun Always Sets*, and then persuaded a friend of mine, who was becoming an amazing set dresser, to build it for me.

My professor commented, "It's very good. It reminds me of the set for *The Sun Always Sets* that played at the National in England in 1932. The staircase is very similar, even the furniture." I played innocent and he passed me.

In the remaining years of my university career, besides taking Ryerson's film course, I registered in classes at the University of Toronto in marketing, fine art and Marshall McLuhan, among others. Few professors interested me, though there were exceptions. John Crispo, a noted industrial relations expert was one; and Paul

Henderson, who taught business, was another. I continued to volunteer for everything and anything to do with film and commercial music videos, even marketing myself as an actor. I circulated my 8 x 10 glossies, auditioned for films and commercials, and landed one for the Shrimp Kitchen chain.

I also kept finding ways to keep cash in my pocket. My most successful money-making venture—and my greatest show-business enterprise to date—gave me my first taste of celebrity. It was my Rent A Fan Club, inspired by an article in a Los Angeles newspaper about a promotion company that used actors to create instant mobs for people at birthday parties. I pulled together a bunch of Ryerson actors and dancers, and supplied them with autograph books and cameras. For a fee, I made this ragtag troupe available to mob people and turn them into instant, faux celebrities. At the time, I was also doing a bit of freelance PR work for the Desrosiers Dance Theatre. A friend in the company, more savvy than I was, advised me to send out a press release for the Rent A Fan Club business. I had to tell him I didn't know what a press release was.

I soon found out. In no time at all, Rent A Fan Club was all over the news: I did fourteen interviews in a single day. The reporters wanted action so we gave it to them. We mobbed fashion journalist Jeanne Beker, which produced great publicity for her and us. We mobbed a national anchorman and North York Mayor Mel Lastman. It was the mayor's office staff who hired us as a joke to spoof Mel at his annual winter carnival and of course Mel, who was something of a ham, loved it. The phone number I had included in advertisements for Rent A Fan Club was my own. I had ninety messages to book us waiting for me on my answering machine when I returned home from classes one day.

The phone continued to ring for weeks. We always interviewed the person who wanted to hire us so we could customize our service to suit the occasion. It might be a woman who wanted to spoof her husband. "Tell me everything about Bob," I'd ask her. "What business is he in? What are his hobbies? Where and when do you want us to mob him?"

When Bob came out of a restaurant, or wherever, we'd shout like crazy, "Bob, Bob! Over here! Can I have your autograph? Hey, look this way!"

It was a great experience. It taught me a lot about marketing, branding and attracting publicity, and even though it was a joke, the person we mobbed usually felt good about the experience. We grew more creative about writing our lines, and all of us had fun. You could buy the Birthday Package, the Anniversary Package, the "It wasn't *you* who did it, it was *me!*" Pregnancy Package. For a thousand bucks extra, the customer received a videotape.

One of our most memorable events was when Ken McGowen, who started the convenience store chain, Mac's Milk, hired us to mob George Cohon, founder of McDonald's Canada, for a whole day. Cohon would come out of his house, and we were there. Cohon would come out of his office, and we were there. Cohon would come out of a restaurant, and we were there. At first, he was shocked but then he caught on: apparently, he and McGowen were always playing jokes on each other.

McGowen paid us $3,500 in cash—the most money I'd seen in my life. Then, a week later, Cohon hired us for a day to mob the head of McDonald's Japan. By then, our price had gone up to $5,000. He also mailed me a box of five hundred business cards, each with a free coupon, so that all of us at Rent A Fan Club ate Big Macs for years.

Thanks to Rent A Fan, I was able to pay part-time wages to a bunch of out-of-work actors and dancers, put myself through college and even do some travelling. When I was forty-eight years old, a friend said to me, "Ever since coming to Toronto as a student, you've always managed to have money and a comfortable lifestyle." That was true, but I worked my ass off for that bank balance. The same ethic I have today.

My initial investment in Rent A Fan Club was about $250 for fake cameras and autograph books. In 1982, I sold the business to a New York promotion company, which was a division of a major ad agency, for $42,000.

It was at Ryerson that I fell in love with Fran, a beautiful girl from a prominent Italian family, who was in the school's dance program. She lived in a big house, of the sort I'd never seen before, on a cul-de-sac in an exclusive part of Toronto. Fran introduced me to the dancers who became core members of Rent A Fan Club. We had one big issue that came between us: Fran's parents couldn't stand me. They disliked the flash of the fan club, and though I might be wrong about this, I felt a sense of veiled anti-Semitism when I was around them. I would go to Fran's for Friday-night dinner and we would sit silently around the table. It was very formal, quite unlike any other Italian occasion I had sat in on, and a world apart from the raucous Jewish family gatherings I was used to.

Fran's parents never softened and I ended our relationship after we'd dated for a couple of years. For some time afterward, Fran, who was heartbroken, would turn up at my apartment in the middle of the night and explain how much her parents really loved me. It was just awful, and so painful for both of us.

Many years later, I received an invitation to Fran's wedding. By then, I was also married. I wanted to take my wife, Melissa, but she refused. "Why would I want to see the girl my husband was in love with a hundred years ago?"

Nope.

Fran was marrying a German, who was severe and perfect. When I came to her Dad in the receiving line, I said, "Hi, it's Barry. Good to see you again. Mazel tov!" I thought he would throw up.

Despite the distraction created by my money-making schemes and my occasional forays in filmmaking (more on that later), I graduated from University of Toronto in 1985 after switching there full-time from Ryerson. I didn't bother to pick up the diploma but, without telling me, my mother collected it for me, had it framed and then presented it to me. I wasn't very gracious about that. I said, "Mom, I don't want it," and she was probably hurt. I should have thanked her and hung it on the wall, but all it meant to me was that I was now free to start my real career.

Chapter Five

THIS ISN'T *SHOE* BUSINESS, IT'S *SHOW* BUSINESS

As soon as I graduated from university in 1985, I began taking job interviews with Toronto's biggest advertising agencies. I was also interviewing with public relations firms because I didn't yet know where I wanted to work. I received offers from MacLaren McCann and J. Walter Thompson's, as a "suit" or more formally a junior account executive on automobile or a packaged goods account. Both seemed uninteresting to me because neither would allow me to be creative.

My mother's cousin, Sylvia, with whom I had stayed on my arrival in Toronto, said she knew a man, Ken Borden, who had an ad agency. His office was located far from downtown Toronto: to get there I had to first take the subway and then a bus. The trip was awful, but Borden was charming. He said, "I have eight people working for me. You want to write radio spots? Then write them. You want to direct a television commercial? Then do it. You're interested in entertainment? So, one of my clients is the Royal Alexandra Theatre."

I asked, "Is there any chance you'll be moving your office downtown?"

He said, "No."

I was to start that Monday with a salary of $18,500. Fine. I went home, broke the news to Sylvia and my mother, then showed up at the office at 8:30 a.m. on Monday.

I introduced myself to the receptionist, "I'm Barry Avrich."

"Yes?"

"I'm here to start my new job."

"I haven't heard anything about that."

"Where's Ken Borden?"

"He's off on a two-week cruise."

"Okay. What's my job?"

"I guess you're the new account guy."

The receptionist—whose name I discovered was Beverly Hills—directed me to a quiet, empty office. I took off my coat. The phone rang. It was Gino Empry, an entertainment impresario with public relations accounts for both the Royal York Hotel's Imperial Room and Ed Mirvish's Royal Alex Theatre. His first words were, "Who the fuck is this?" As I would later learn, that was Gino on a good day.

"Barry Avrich, the new account guy."

"Well, Barry Avrich, we have *A Chorus Line* coming into the Alex."

Amazing coincidence—that was the first show I'd seen on Broadway.

Empry continued, "I've got thirty-two thousand dollars for radio and television and I need a media plan by the end of the day."

What was a media plan?

I wandered around the office, introducing myself and asking for the media guy. *That would be me.* I asked for a radio or television producer. *That would be me.* I opened filing cabinets that were stuffed with old radio and television contracts. The first one I pulled out was with CFRB. The radio station rep was Laurie Graham. The contract listed her CFRB phone number. I dialled it and explained my problem to her. She said, "I'll be right there."

When Laurie arrived, her first question was, "How much money do you have?" I told her. She said, "You need to buy some time on CFRB," her station, but then she added other stations. "Here's how you do it." She was wonderfully honest for a salesperson.

We bought a bunch of radio and then I called Gino. He started yelling at me, which he continued to do for ten years. I soon understood this was a performance and I didn't take it personally with him, or later with Garth Drabinsky or with Victor Loewy. *Bring it on*, I thought, knowing that dealing with their bluster would be my best education.

By the time Ken Borden returned, tanned and relaxed, from his cruise, I had worked on six shows. They included every musical coming into the Royal Alex and the Imperial Room, featuring names like Peggy Lee, Donald O'Connor and Chita Rivera. Because I was young and Gino was a night crawler, our meetings were after the shows ended, at ten, eleven or even at two in the morning. If anyone tried to see him during the day, Gino would fall asleep. His office was something else. Every square inch was taken up by celebrity photos, all signed to him, but in handwriting that was remarkably similar. His suit for the night's premiere, fresh from the dry cleaner, would be piled on a chair, waiting for him. And he always wore a toupée—he was famous for them—that would have looked better on a leash.

I received a terrific education in the ad business at Borden's. As Ken had promised, I learned how to write radio copy, becoming familiar with recording studios, and directed well-known actors like Gordon Pinsent, and on-air gods like Wally Crouter, in voice-overs. I also designed film posters and created small promotions for Cineplex Odeon through my friend Jeff Sackman, who was working there. I loved all of it!

For one commercial, I had originally intended to cast actor Ken Welsh, whom I continue to book even today. At the last minute, I cast the brother-in-law of the girl I was dating instead. He was trying to get a start as an actor. My engineer complained, "Who is this guy? He's terrible!" After a few takes, I sent him home and called in Ken. I had learned my lesson: *No more using the job to get dates. Work only with talent.*

I had been attracted to Borden's mainly by their theatre accounts, but I also worked for some of their corporate clients. They had Towers Department Stores, which was okay, and smaller clients like Bausch + Lomb contact-lens solution, which I'd sooner kill myself than work on again.

It was great moment for me when I brought in an expanding fast food chain, Lick's Hamburgers. After tasting one of their hamburgers at their Beaches location, I contacted Denise Meehan, who had started the business. I told her, "I don't know your advertising plans, but this is the greatest hamburger, and you really need to tell the world."

She said, "We're opening a new restaurant downtown. You can come in and talk to me, but I should let you know, Jerry Goodis is pitching us, so why would we go with you instead of him?"

Jerry Goodis was an ad legend and the well-known agency for Harvey's, another hamburger chain. They claimed to have written the familiar jingle, "Harvey's makes your hamburger a beautiful thing!"

I replied, "Because I love your hamburgers."

I bought two hundred cases of Hamburger Helper, put Lick's labels on every box, then shipped them to Denise with a note, "You need only one Hamburger Helper and it's me."

She called me back. "You've got the business."

Another client was memorable because of the way he introduced himself. A guy walked into our office, opened his briefcase and showed us the $100,000 in cash he had inside. He said, "I'm distributing a drill-bit sharpener. I want it available for Father's Day, but the only way the stores will take it is if it's backed by a television campaign. Can you produce a television commercial and a media plan for us?" What the hell is a drill-bit sharpener? Does anyone sharpen drill bits?

Wait . . . did you say $100,000 in cash?

The guy had a ready-made commercial from Germany that needed a new voice-over. To save money, I said I'd do it, but I didn't realize until I was in the studio how much copy I had to read. It was like "The Minute Waltz," faster and faster, *click click click*, then came the list of stores in which it could be purchased *click click click*, like maybe eight thousand of them. I'm not sure how this worked out for the guy with his warehouse full of drill-bit sharpeners, but I've been incapable of uttering the words "drill-bit sharpener" ever since.

Ken also had a client who imported cheap kitchen products from Asia, for which we did the packaging and ran ads. For the food shoots, I hired the finest food photographer, bought incredible filet mignons, the freshest of red peppers—nothing but the best—and then styled them as lovingly as my father used to present the fashions he sold. I enjoyed that challenge for three years.

I also won a new account run by a couple of Portuguese brothers who had a shoe business. They wanted me to do packaging design and the usual, predictable marketing elements. But then they said, "There's a shoe convention in Los Angeles. We'd like you to design our booth."

Los Angeles! Hollywood! In my most solicitous voice, I said, "If you're going to Los Angeles, this isn't *shoe* business, it's *show* business."

I challenged a designer to create a booth so complicated that only I could set it up. He came up with an art deco marquee, flashing lights, a popcorn machine and a look based on the legendary Grauman's Chinese Theatre. I broke the news to the brothers. "I don't know how to tell you this, but I'm going to have to go to Los Angeles to set up the booth and to take it down at the end of the week."

They were cool with that. "We'll pay your air fare," they said, "and pick up the hotel tab."

Yes!

I flew into L.A. the day before the convention. I set up the booth—slot and slide, A into B, just like my father's garment racks. After that, I had Los Angeles to myself for a week. I hadn't realized how spread out the city was, and ours was a downtown hotel. I took the bus to Grauman's on Hollywood Boulevard. It was jam-packed with domestic servants en route to Beverly Hills. The mass of hot, sweaty humanity nearly suffocated me with their fragrant packed lunches on what seemed like an endless journey, so I rented a car. I booked a table at Spago's where I saw Fred Astaire and Jack Lemmon, whom I would meet a couple of years later in Toronto. I went to Beverly Hills—named for our receptionist at Borden's—and walked along Rodeo Drive, otherwise known as the Golden Mile.

In the neighbourhood around Hollywood Boulevard, I came across a bunch of stores selling vintage movie posters. I filled a suitcase with what I bought there. Then, walking along Melrose Avenue, just breathing the air, I came across a gallery that had a Herb Snitzer photograph of Louis Armstrong wearing a Star of David. When I asked the proprietor, Bill Goldberg, about it, he told me that Armstrong, who'd grown up in an orphanage, was close to a Jewish family, the Karnofskys. He wore the Star of David because he too had experienced discrimination. He knew everything there was to know about collecting photographs and shared that knowledge generously. Bill's still a close friend.

I had the greatest week of my life. I never went back to the shoe booth except to take it down. When I returned to Borden's, I said to myself, *If the closest I can get to* show *business is the* shoe *business, then I'm leaving this agency.*

I loved Ken. I received a magnificent education at his firm, but I knew it was time to leave. Ken had three children. Not one was interested in the business and he had no succession plan. I had become like a son to him and I was afraid one day he would say, "Time for me to leave. Now, you run the business." I wasn't ready to build a business, and certainly not this one. We'd moved several times since the strip plaza where I had first found him. We were now in a proper office building, but it was in another suburb, Don Mills, far from downtown. Along the way, I had asked for, and received, regular raises, but my salary of $27,000 was still ridiculously low for what I was doing.

Ken sensed that I was getting restless. One day he took me for lunch at Carrera's, one of his favourite Italian restaurants. Across the street was a Ford Topaz, tied with a big yellow ribbon. He handed me the keys. I gasped. But it wasn't excitement that took my breath away. I wanted something flashier than a conventional family sedan. Both my car and I had to be bigger than that. I couldn't expect Ken to know that.

The climax of my career at Borden's came while I was working on a campaign to promote the Canadian premiere of *Les Misérables*, a huge musical for the Royal Alex. I could see that Ed Mirvish was slowing down and ready to give the reins to his son David, and since Gino was Ed's guy, the writing was on the wall for Gino too. Since I was Gino's guy, it was obvious that I needed to run.

From time to time, I'd been taking meetings with Len Gill, who ran an entertainment ad agency called Echo, with star clients like Garth Drabinsky, founder of Cineplex Odeon, and Michael Cohl, the world's biggest concert producer. Our meetings hadn't gone well. Every time Gill had asked with whom I wanted to work, I always said the same thing, "Garth Drabinsky." His reply was always the same. "The only guy who works with Garth is me. Do you want to work on the First Choice pay-TV account?"

"No."

"Do you want to work on the Coca-Cola Entertainment account?"

"No. I want to work with Garth Drabinsky."

Deadlock.

This was no passing whim on my part. I'd been tracking Garth Drabinsky's career ever since I'd arrived in Toronto. I'd met him in person on two occasions.

Famous Players owned half of the Imperial Six, a downtown movie theatre with six screens. They leased the other half from an elderly woman in Michigan. When they played hardball with her to lower the rent on her half, she offered the lease to their rival, Cineplex Odeon. As Cineplex's cofounder, Drabinsky picked it up in a heartbeat. Without the lease, the only access Famous Players had to their half of the theatre was through a narrow passageway, now controlled by Drabinsky. At the crack of dawn on the day the deal was finalized, he led a procession of vehicles—bearing security guards, German shepherds, locksmiths, workmen and drywall—through Toronto's core. Within twenty minutes, the entrance to Famous Players' half of the theatre was boarded up, making their property useless to them.

Drabinsky bought the rest of the Imperial Six, which he restored to what it had once been, a single-screen auditorium called Pantages Cinema. He opened the new theatre in 1987 with the feature film *Wall Street*. I was there, of course, and I recognized Drabinsky sitting on the marble steps leading to the stage. He was listening for imperfections in the newly installed Dolby sound system. I introduced myself, complimented him on the theatre's stunning renovation and we chatted amiably.

Wall Street opened to the tune of "Fly Me to the Moon," a favourite of mine. I've used the song in some of my own films.

The second time I met Drabinsky I was having dinner at Fred's Not Here in Toronto with Jeff Sackman, a friend from Montreal with whom I had made a couple of films. Drabinsky walked in with Lynda

Friendly, his head of communications. Since Jeff worked for him at Cineplex, he came over to our table. I noticed for the first time that he limped, a legacy of childhood polio.

Drabinsky was once again spending millions of dollars to painstakingly restore the Imperial Six/Pantages Cinema, this time to its full 1920s glory as the 2,200-seat Pantages Theatre. This was partly in preparation for the Canadian premiere of *The Phantom of the Opera*.

We chatted briefly and then Drabinsky surprised us by asking, "Would you like to see my new theatre?"

Garth was warm and charming on our private tour. He showed us the grand staircase, the murals, the faux-marble walls, the gold-leaf plasterwork and stained glass. We saw the orchestra pit, the technologically reconfigured stage with its 190 trap doors and the big chandelier, which played such a dramatic role in *Phantom*. It was awe-inspiring.

In September 1989, Garth Drabinksy opened Andrew Lloyd Webber's *The Phantom of the Opera* at the Pantages Theatre, with a world-record box-office advance of $23.8 million. Everything about the production was as dazzling as its gorgeously restored theatre.

Two months later, Drabinsky was unceremoniously dumped from Cineplex Odeon by his partners. The reason? Over-expansion had caused Drabinsky to sell 50 per cent of his company for $150 million to MCA Universal, chaired by Lew Wasserman, the most powerful person in the entertainment industry. Drabinsky had then taken on other partners, leaving him with only 7 per cent ownership and an enormous escalating debt. This was bothering MCA and they wanted him out. With little control left, Garth tried a fast move to force MCA out through a leveraged buyout with his partners, the Montreal-based Bronfmans who had backed him nearly fifteen years earlier. He lost the battle and was shown the door. On his departure, Garth paid $88 million for a package that included the company's live entertainment division (Livent, Inc.), the Pantages Theatre and the rights to *Phantom*.

As soon as the deal became public, Len Gill initiated another meeting with me. I knew that Drabinsky was a major client and that this change would impact Gill's agency. I also knew that Gill had little interest in live theatre.

I told him upfront that my script had not changed. "I want to work with Garth Drabinsky."

This time Gill replied, "You want Garth? You've got him."

I pushed my advantage, "Okay, but I have to come in as an account director, and I have to make forty-two thousand dollars a year."

"Done. You can start at the first of the year."

It remained for me to break this news to Ken Borden. We met, as so often before, at Giorgio's, over the Italian food that he loved. I told him as gently as I could, "It's time for me to leave, Ken."

It was the saddest breakup you could imagine. I was never disappointed in Ken. He was—and is—a really lovely man, a sweetheart. He wept at the same time as he understood.

Birds gotta fly.

Chapter Six

GARTH DRABINSKY: CURTAIN RISING

When I arrived at Echo in January 1990, I was greeted with about as much enthusiasm as when I had arrived at Borden's four and a half years earlier. I'd had some furniture and personal items shipped to the Echo offices while I took a holiday between jobs. Now I found it sitting in the hall.

I introduced myself to Darlene, the receptionist. "Hi, I'm starting here today. Where's my office?"

She pointed to a cubicle.

I went to see Len Gill. He was sitting in his office, behind a smokescreen created by what looked like a dozen cigarettes burning at once.

"What's with the cubicle? It's awfully cramped in there."

He exploded. "You want *my* space? Only two people at Echo have offices, that's me and my partner."

Whoa!

As I was leaving, Len shouted once more. "What did we agree on for your salary?"

"Fifty thousand dollars."

He nodded. "Okay."

The $8,000 raise on my first day encouraged me to swallow the insult.

My cubicle was stuffed with files left by the person who'd been fired before me. I told myself that this was going to be my new life in a big agency. Even on my first day, with my grandfather's Persian rug still tied up in the hallway, I could feel Echo humming.

I went to meet Garth in his now-humble little Livent office in an office block on Yonge Street, across from the shiny headquarters of Cineplex Odeon, which he had once ruled. At the top of our agenda was *The Phantom of the Opera*'s Canadian tour to Montreal, Winnipeg, Calgary, Edmonton and Vancouver. Garth listed every theatre on the tour, its seating capacity and ticket prices section by section, mentally calculating the gross for every city.

Given my math-challenged brain, I could only stare.

"Avrich," he informed me, "all it takes is focus."

Since I was now Livent's account director, it was up to me to plan the ad campaign for all their shows. I attended *Phantom* every night, filming hours of Colm Wilkinson singing the lead. I cut twelve commercials from the footage, then had actor Graeme Campbell intone, "At the stroke of dawn, *The Phantom of the Op-er-ah!*" Graeme had starred in *Les Misérables*, which had been produced by David Mirvish, Livent's main theatre rival. Mirvish was incensed when he discovered we had poached him.

I showed the commercials to Garth. He said, "We'll run them."

As I would learn, that was Garth-speak for, "They're great."

Garth was brilliant at marketing. He could sell emotion more inventively than anyone I've ever met. At night, giant billboards featuring the iconic *Phantom* mask and broken-glass lettering glowed eerily all over Toronto. A year earlier, on a chilly January evening, in a campaign called Midnight Madness, Garth put *Phantom* tickets on sale at the stroke of midnight. He partnered with CBC-TV to produce an hour-long documentary, *Behind the Mask*, timed for opening night. A Canadian cast album sold close to 700,000 units.

Garth was a genius at finding ways to maximize sales. With Cineplex Odeon, he had championed two-dollar Tuesdays and putting real butter on popcorn. To keep *Phantom* running, he sold tens of thousands of tickets for The Phantom Express, a bus package to Toronto from London, Ontario, and from a variety of cities in the United States, including Syracuse, Cleveland, Buffalo, Detroit,

Pittsburgh and Rochester. Every junket allowed visitors plenty of time in the gift shop, where they could purchase papier-mâché masks, gummy masks, chandelier earrings, musical dolls, pop-up books and black mugs painted in heat-sensitive ink so that the *Phantom* mask appeared when filled with coffee.

Livent's *Phantom* production—a fascinating, somewhat garish and hugely theatrical affair—hung around in Toronto for a decade, becoming the highest-grossing theatre production in the world for a continuous run. Then, thanks to the success of our Canadian tour, Livent acquired the rights for productions in Honolulu, Anchorage, Singapore and Hong Kong.

I spent as much time as I could with Garth. I wanted to learn as much as I could from him. That had a downside.

Garth was a control freak with a savage temper. His marketing meetings began every Tuesday morning at eight and ran for hours. He employed three competing agencies to create print advertising and pitted them against each other in a publicly humiliating way.

One agency was from Toronto and led by a pretentious and sour graphic designer. The other firm, located in New York, was run by a flamboyant character with a Napoleon complex. He would attend the meetings in tight red pants and so much black hair dye that I was afraid if the sprinkler system went off we would drown in the Black Sea.

If someone made a mistake, or failed to answer a question, Garth took that person down ruthlessly, not just for that one error, but for every stumble and misdeed in his victim's employment history, not just at Livent but anywhere. Then, for the rest of the meeting, he would upbraid that person again and again.

Anyone employed by Garth was supposed to assume the position and take it. We would ask each other, "Who's going to get it today?" On the other hand, if Garth was wrong about something, you had to go for his throat. Then he respected you. I never took his viciousness personally, so he never wounded me, but some people left Garth's employ damaged for life.

In order to establish a close relationship with Garth, I made myself available on Sundays. That's when I showed him the commercials for our productions—*Phantom* in Honolulu, *Phantom* in Hong Kong, and so on—and we went over the footage. He was never effusive in his praise. He never said, "Fantastic work!" But once he had approved them on Sunday, he dismissed any criticism that was levelled against them at the Tuesday meetings. Whenever circumstances forced me to bring a commercial to the marketing session that Garth hadn't approved, thirty suffering employees, who'd been yelled at and beaten, would attack it as ferociously as Garth had ever done, just to show they had opinions too.

I cherished our Sundays together. One-on-one, Garth could be charming. I was seduced by the liking he expressed for me, even though I knew our relationship was mutually self-serving. Because I was the only person creating his radio and TV commercials, an ad agency rival would occasionally attempt to horn in by turning up with a script or storyboard. That's when Garth demonstrated his loyalty to me, along with his appreciation for our shared cinematic approach, by allowing me to blow out the interloper, fast. He had a different persona in a group. Even on our Sundays together, the minute more people were added to the mix, Garth was transformed, becoming one of the great tyrants of show business.

Garth kept bringing in new shows while *Phantom* was playing. Andrew Lloyd Webber's *Aspects of Love*, a three-generation love-and-jealousy saga wrapped in chamber music had lost its $8 million investment on Broadway. The *New York Times* described it as "perhaps the greatest flop in Broadway history." Garth nevertheless agreed to bring it to Canada out of eagerness to nurture his artistic partnership with Webber. He also wished to showcase the brilliant director Robin Phillips.

I flew out to see it when it opened in 1991 at Edmonton's Citadel Theatre. Although Phillips had entirely restaged it, the production seemed sparse, antiseptic and dull. I heard a group of theatregoers singing its big song, "Love Changes Everything," in the intermission. That seemed promising, until I moved close enough to discover that they had changed the lyrics to, "It's boring, it is so bo-rrring."

I told Garth I thought *Aspects* was a loser. He remained noncommittal. As I learned, he would ride a dead horse till its skin fell off in a futile attempt to turn a dud into a winner. Bad reviews didn't matter. When *Phantom* had opened in Toronto, the *Globe and Mail* had given it a zero rating. In Garth's mind, this proved that critics were often wrong while he was always right.

He opened *Aspects* in Toronto at the Elgin Theatre. Everyone who attended the Tuesday meetings was praying that he would shut it down. Nope. There was always another place to send it. And another. As long as a show was running, Garth didn't have to declare it as a loss, which helped when it came to making Livent's books look good.

Since Garth was hungry for the next big one, he was constantly flying to other cities in Livent's ten-seat jet, scouting productions. Though Garth's company shared it with a major bank, I doubt they ever saw it. Garth would yell at the pilot, "Go faster! Faster!"

I need only four hours sleep a night. When I was on the plane on Livent business, everyone else would doze off except for Garth, who checked grosses hourly. This gave me another chance to talk with him, to study his style of showmanship, marvel at his keen attention to detail and be impressed by his dizzying mathematical skills. I learned that there are at least ninety-two ways to market something, and that you can never rest on your laurels.

I remember flying to La Jolla, California, where the rock opera *Tommy* was being workshopped by director Des McAnuff with Pete Townshend and The Who. As a child of the '60s, at least in my own mind, I thought it was incredible. Garth proclaimed it a great load of horse manure.

As fate would have it, *The Who's Tommy* became Garth's chief competitor for Broadway's highest-stakes' game: the Tony Awards. Livent's entry in 1993 would be *Kiss of the Spider Woman*, a gutsy choice for a musical, involving prison, torture, homosexuality and a fantasy diva whose kiss meant death. At director Hal Prince's urging, Garth had agreed to produce it in order to keep alive their grand collaboration that began with *Phantom*.

For his Spider Woman, Garth cast Chita Rivera, who'd had her Broadway breakthrough in the mid-'50s as the firebrand Anita in *West Side Story*, but whose career had faded with time. It was fantastic casting, creating another star vehicle for Chita.

Since Garth was eager to get the buzz going, I had to produce *Kiss* commercials before we had sets or costumes. We built a jail cell for Chita. As the camera moved in, the cell doors opened and Chita raised her arms to reveal her web-like wings. Juan Chioran, a Spanish actor from Stratford, doing the voice-over, intoned, "The *Kisssssss of the Spider Woman* is coming to the St. Lawrence Centre." It was stunning.

Kiss opened in Toronto in the summer of 1992, in London's West End that fall and on Broadway in the spring of 1993, where it received a standing ovation and enthusiastic reviews.

Kiss and *Tommy* were nominated for a dozen Tonys each. Garth attended the awards ceremony at the Gershwin Theatre in New York, while I watched a simulcast with a gang of friends and family at the Pantages in Toronto. *Kiss* won three Tonys in quick succession, then it was *Tommy*'s turn for a run, then *Kiss* again with some big ones: Best Actress for Chita Rivera, Best Actor for Brent Carver, Best Book for Terrence McNally. So far, so good, but then Hal Prince, who'd already won nineteen Tonys, was passed over for the director's prize, and that seemed to lessen our chances for Best Musical. It was a nail-biting evening, electric with suspense, but *Kiss* won Best Musical too, bringing the number of the show's Tonys up to seven.

It was an exhilarating moment for Garth. *Kiss* was his greatest critical success, and yet it would also prove to be one of his biggest disappointments. The show did some business after its win, but no matter how hard Garth struggled, he couldn't turn it into a block-buster. The story was too deep, too complex, too sophisticated and too controversial to find a significant audience outside of New York and London. When Chita left the cast, Garth replaced her with Vanessa Williams.

While filming TV commercials with Vanessa, she and I became friendly to the point where she recommended a herbalist to help me sleep. As I said, I don't need a lot, but I do need some, and working with Garth was making the sleep I got fitful. Vanessa's herbalist turned out to be a tiny Chinese man who looked like the Dalai Lama. He wore a giant $25,000 Rolex watch and wanted to charge me thousands of dollars for his herbs.

He also offered me advice. "Let me tell why you not sleep," he said. He put his thumb on my pulse and announced, "You not sleep because you masturbate too often."

I asked, "What's too often?"

Garth hoped Vanessa Williams would draw in the black audience to *Kiss*, and it worked. Next, he cast María Conchita Alonso, a Latino star best known to North American audiences for *Moscow on the Hudson*. He flew in Robert Enrico, PepsiCo's former head of marketing, and also a Latino, for advice on how to promote her. Enrico told Garth, "Mr. Drabinsky, Latin people don't go to Broadway," and Garth had him ushered out the door. That was the end of the magical *Kiss*.

Garth's popular success after *Phantom*—the crowd-pleaser he so desperately needed—was *Joseph and the Amazing Technicolor Dreamcoat*, also with music by Andrew Lloyd Webber. Inspired by the book of Genesis, it told the story of the betrayal of Joseph by his eleven brothers, his deliverance into slavery and his subsequent triumph at the Pharaoh's court through his ability to interpret dreams. Garth's choice for the lead was yet another example of his casting genius: Donny Osmond. As a former teenage idol and TV star who was struggling to reinvent himself as an adult performer, Osmond currently was, in show-business terms, a loser.

It was my job to market this dynamic, born-again performer for his breakthrough role. What *Dreamcoat* demanded, apart from a terrific voice, was an equally terrific ad campaign. For our photo shoot, we hired top-of-the-line photographer Bert Bell, with the hope of producing a full-page ad of Donny looking cool in jeans and a white shirt. Donny had stage fright. He was especially anxious about a scene in which he had to perform shirtless, meaning that he had to be buff. In his nervousness, he became forgetful.

When he arrived for the photo shoot, he said, "I forgot my belt. Can I borrow yours?"

"Sure."

"I didn't bring the right shoes. Can I borrow yours?"

"Sure."

After the shoot, I received a call from Lynda Friendly, head of Livent's communications, who was anything but friendly. Because she was Garth's long-time employee and reputed mistress, she had some of his power, which she enjoyed abusing. She was clearly angry when she said, "Look, Donny says he wants to have dinner with you tonight."

I was caught off guard. "Who?"

"Donny Osmond."

Apparently, this request had not gone down well with Garth. Much as he liked me, I was just his ad agency.

Lynda laid down the ground rules. "Here's the deal. You're going to pick up Donny at seven at the Intercontinental Hotel. You're going to go to Joe Allen's for dinner, but you're not going to talk about

Livent. You're not going to talk about grosses. You're not going to talk about marketing. Nothing. Do you understand me?"

I said, "Okay."

She said, "Call me afterwards with your report. Here's my personal number."

I was on my way to pick up Donny when I received a call from my wannabe actor and lawyer friend, Jerry Levitan. Jerry asked, "What are you doing tonight, Barry?"

"I'm having dinner with Donny Osmond."

"Wow! Can I come?"

"No. He made a whole big deal about wanting to relax alone with me over a hamburger."

"What restaurant? I'll drop by and say hello."

I couldn't resist the rush of having someone I knew see me with Donny Osmond.

"Okay. It's Joe Allen's. I'm picking him up at seven. Arrive an hour later and come to our table. I'll introduce you, then you can leave."

I picked up Donny—a really nice guy who was beyond squeaky clean. Right off he said, "I'm looking forward to spending time with you without having to worry about anyone else."

I didn't reply. I was already sweating because of Jerry. I told myself that his arrival would just be a blip.

We walked into Joe Allen's. Jerry was sitting at our table.

"Who's that?" asked Donny.

I had no choice but to introduce them.

Fortunately, Jerry is funny, and Donny enjoyed his blunt sense of humour. When Jerry said, "My wife is the greatest Donny Osmond fan in the world," Donny replied, "Let's go and ring your doorbell."

Jerry's wife all but fainted.

It was a great evening. Donny and I kept in touch for a long time afterwards.

Joseph and the Amazing Technicolor Dreamcoat opened in the spring of 1992 at Toronto's Elgin Theatre, where it played for five years. At first it attracted Donny's old teen fans, then word of mouth brought in thousands more. Donny also toured the show throughout North America. Garth had the mega, post-*Phantom* hit he had been looking for. The show spun money in every city, serviced by the multiple touring companies Garth mounted.

Garth's next assault on Broadway was with a lavish recreation of the American classic, *Show Boat*. It was set in 1887 in Natchez, Mississippi, and dramatized the plight of the country's newly emancipated blacks in a poignant love story. After Garth had seen what he considered a lacklustre 1990 London production of this Jerome Kern and Oscar Hammerstein II masterpiece, he dreamed of transforming it into a dynamic extravaganza. He considered it ideal for opening the newly constructed 3,000-seat North York Performing Arts Centre, then under Livent's exclusive management. Once again, Hal Prince would be Garth's director.

Before I met him during *Kiss of the Spiderwoman*, I knew Prince only from his picture on the cast album of *Fiddler on the Roof*. Twenty-five years had passed, but he still looked exactly as he had in that picture, with his glasses pushed back on his head, except now his hair was white. It was phenomenal to watch him direct. When he raised his hands like a conductor, you could see he had the entire show in his head—the actors, the choreography, the set, the lighting—much like Garth with his numbers. He was amazing. Garth and I flew in Livent's private jet to Natchez, Mississippi, before the production began. Garth wanted to experience first-hand the angst of the black cotton pickers. The temperature felt like 900 degrees as we went from plantation to plantation. It was especially hard on Garth, still suffering the residual effects of childhood polio.

I knew exactly the voice I wanted for the commercials. I called CNN in Atlanta. "Who does your voice-overs?"

"James Earl Jones."

The voice of Darth Vader!

I contacted Jan Eckman, Jones's New York agent. She told me, "Sorry, Barry, but James is completely locked up. CNN has given him a million dollar buy-out fee to use his 'This is CNN' clip for the life of the network."

"But, Jan," I protested. "What I'm requesting is in a different category."

Eventually she agreed. We signed up Jones, with his magnificent *basso profundo*, and I spent the next three years writing *Show Boat* commercials, then flying down to Los Angeles to direct him.

Garth had an unfortunate habit of adding more scripts—hundreds of them—to the list waiting to be recorded. Now James had conquered a childhood stutter on his way to becoming an actor, but if you gave him too much to read at once, he'd say, "We're moving on." His breaking point came when I handed him another Garth commercial that required James to say, "If you order your *Show Boat* double CD cast album now, you get a *Show Boat* recipe brochure."

James said, "Barry, I'm not doing this."

I replied, "I don't blame you."

When I got back to Toronto, I had to pretend to Garth that James couldn't do the commercial because he had a cold.

Show Boat's gala premiere at the North York Performing Arts Centre was marred by scurrilous publicity.

The original 1927 production had opened with a black chorus singing, "Niggers all work on de Mississippi . . ." This had later been changed to "Coloured folk work . . ." Garth had consulted widely in the black community, both in Canada and in the States, to eliminate potentially offensive phrasing, without sanitizing black history. Nevertheless, a Jamaican North York school trustee denounced the production, sight unseen, as "hate literature" posing as entertainment. Her protest turned even nastier when she attributed anti-black racism "especially [to] the Jews." Anonymous flyers denounced *Show Boat* as "a cultural holocaust" and the North York Centre as a potential "gas chamber" for black culture.

Shocked that his good intentions had been inverted, Garth asked the distinguished black historian, Henry Louis Gates Jr. from Harvard, to critique *Show Boat*'s script. In a lecture at the North York Centre's Recital Hall, which attracted extensive media coverage, Gates described the Livent production as a "victory for tolerance and sensitivity." This shut down the protesters. Though a few turned up at the 1993 premiere, they were vastly outnumbered by approximately 250 North American theatre critics, who came to see the production for themselves, and applauded it.

Garth had made one miscalculation. He thought that theatregoers in North York, a suburban community to the north of Toronto, would be glad to skip the commute to downtown. As he later discovered, for many people, making that trip was part of the evening's excitement.

Show Boat opened on Broadway in the fall of 1994 at the Gershwin Theatre. As a $10 million production that cost an additional $600,000 a week to run, it was described by the *New York Times* as "probably Broadway's most expensive show." Garth couldn't stand fake extravagance, even on the stage. If the set design called for a Persian rug, it had to be a real one. To raise the money, he and his partner and financial officer, Myron Gottlieb, had taken Livent public the year before. A number of Broadway savants doubted the show's viability. When he was questioned by a reporter for the *New York Times*, Garth replied with his usual arrogant aplomb, "You have to apply an innovative vision to the restoration of these shows. They have to be made larger than life and brought up to audience expectations. If I'm going to do something, I'm going to do it so it has implications for years."

I sat behind Garth at *Show Boat*'s Broadway opening, celebrated afterwards with a no-expenses-spared party at the Plaza Hotel that was chockablock with stars. The reviews were marvellous and ticket sales were on their way to breaking records. I also attended the 1995 Tony Awards at the Minskoff Theatre. *Show Boat* had ten nominations and won five, including Best Director for Hal Prince and Best Revival of a Musical. The show played Broadway for more than 900 performances. After *Show Boat* went on the road, along with *Phantom*, *Joseph* and *Kiss*, Garth was boasting that by the end of 1995, Livent would generate 25 per cent of the North American box-office receipts in commercial live theatre, estimated at a quarter of a billion dollars.

The World According to Garth seemed to be unfolding as it should, and I was thrilled to be a part of it.

Chapter Seven

GARTH DRABINSKY:
CURTAIN FALLING

If Garth had financial worries about Livent, now a publicly traded company with responsibilities to its shareholders, he never telegraphed them to me.

He had critics, both in Toronto and in New York, who saw Livent as a house of cards on the verge of collapse. I defended him from them in good faith. Garth was paying our ad agency millions of dollars every year, and though payments were sometimes late, we had no reason to believe Livent was in dire straits. For every Garth doubter, you could find an admirer who saw him as the saviour of musical theatre, not only for the opulence of his productions, but also for the seriousness of their themes. The prevailing view was that Garth Drabinsky was on a roll.

Meanwhile, I continued to fly all over the world, shooting and recording commercials for which Garth insisted on nothing but the best. I attended the premiere of the Lloyd Webber musical, *Sunset Boulevard*, for which Garth held the Canadian rights. I thought it was awful. The only thing going for it was Glenn Close, who played a manic Norma Desmond, the silent film star trapped inside her world of delusion. At the after-party, I asked Billy Wilder, who had written and directed the classic film on which the musical was based, what he thought of the production. He replied drily, "I thought it was a great movie."

As his Norma Desmond, Garth cast Diahann Carroll, with former rock star Rex Smith as the struggling screenwriter. He played up his genius of breaking the colour barrier by casting Diahann but she wasn't right for the role and her co-star Rex Smith, a '70s teen idol, was past it. They had no chemistry. They didn't even like each other.

For the trailer's voice-over, I booked Malcolm McDowell, best known as the delinquent in Stanley Kubrick's *Clockwork Orange*. He was supposed to say, "*Sunset Boulevard* with Diahann Carroll and Rex Smith at the Ford Centre for the Performing Arts." Instead, to piss me off, he'd say, "at the *Chrysler* Centre," and then, "the *Toyota* Centre." He did this all day, in his mischievous voice, but we had a good time, and he was a hit in the commercial.

Sunset opened in North York in 1995. Reviews were mixed and the show struggled.

Garth's next venture—*Candide*, an operetta based on a novella by Voltaire—was undertaken as a vanity project for director Hal Prince. It opened in 1997 at Broadway's Gershwin Theatre. It was a big overblown musical with a ridiculously complicated plot. For my voice-over, I chose John Forsythe, familiar to fans of TV's *Dynasty* and *Charlie's Angels*. We signed a contract with him for $50,000, and I flew to Los Angeles for the recording.

I thought Forsythe would be brilliant, but he soon had me worried. Age had caught up to him. He could neither read properly nor muster the strength to blow out the words. It was a nightmare. I managed to get Livent out of the contract but I didn't know what to tell Garth.

Back in Toronto, I persuaded my friend, Henry Ramer, famous for his voice-overs, to record the *Candide* commercial on spec. When

Henry came to the studio, he brought out this little zip-lock bag, as he always did, and he showed me the same photo that he always showed me, presumably a souvenir from the 1983 film, *Between Friends*, in which he appeared with Elizabeth Taylor. The photo was of Henry with Taylor in bed.

When I explained to Garth about Forsythe at our Sunday session, then played for him Ramer's recording, he simply nodded, and I walked out unscathed. It reminded me that when I worry about something, it's usually okay, but if I'm cocky, it's likely to be a disaster. Paranoia has served me well.

Echo was growing, and so was my role within the company. My relationship with Len Gill could be tempestuous at times, and it had started to deteriorate through the years as Len became increasingly resentful of my profile as a filmmaker. Len also didn't like the fact that Garth would defer to me instead of him around the marble table, even though Len and Garth had a long friendship that included private sailing trips. Despite the tension, I admired Len's business skills and worked hard. He made me an Echo partner in 1995.

By then, the Livent account had grown exponentially. Garth had long since taken over the top floor of 165 Avenue Road as his office, turning it into a palatial sanctuary with whitewashed wood floors and gorgeous furniture, motorized drapes and state-of-the-art screening equipment, a lavish boardroom and a fabulous collection of contemporary Canadian art. As the operation had grown, Livent took over floor after floor until it claimed nearly the entire six-storey building. Now, instead of dealing directly with Garth, I was forced to deal with Garth's people, all of whom were suffering from Stockholm Syndrome. Having been beaten and pissed on by Garth, they were eager to beat and piss on everyone else beneath them.

One morning I said to myself, *Enough!* If I was going to be pissed on, it had to come directly from the top, not from the minions. I decided I would work only on Livent's radio and TV commercials, for which I still reported directly to Garth. This decision did not go down well with Len and the other Echo partner, because it meant they would have to figure out how to handle the rest of the account.

In fact, Garth was such a seductive and relentless psychopath that Len and I occasionally fantasized dropping him altogether. Our relationship came close to spontaneous combustion in 1996. We were simultaneously promoting Garth's *Show Boat* and the Ed Mirvish production of *Tommy*, both on Canadian tour. We usually considered working for Mirvish a conflict of interest, but Len and I rationalized that in this instance we were actually employed by Michael Cohl's CPI Theatre, which was coproducing the *Tommy* tour with Mirvish.

Garth and his partner Myron Gottlieb didn't agree. To them, Mirvish was the enemy. They summoned Len and me to the Livent office and tortured us for hours, threatening not only to fire us, but also to sue us unless we resigned the Cohl account. The question then became, *Do we dump Garth, who paid our agency tens of millions every year, and who put a swimming pool in Len's backyard, or do we call his bluff?*

We lawyered up for the battle, which took place in a suite at the Four Seasons Hotel in New York, and we called Garth's bluff. That proved to be the right tactic. We retained Livent as a client, while agreeing to restrict our competitive work to producers with short-run engagements. As always with Garth, every upside had a downside. His friendship with Len was damaged forever, and while Livent's relationship with Echo continued to evolve, Len and I would soon have good reason to ask ourselves, How do you stop when racing in a Ferrari at 150 mph?

You don't. You crash.

★

The musical *Ragtime,* based on E.L. Doctorow's bestseller about class struggle in early-twentieth-century America, was a stupendous production. *Ragtime*'s logo was the Statue of Liberty with upthrust torch, wrapped in the star-spangled banner: brilliant iconography for a musical about the American dream. For the jazzy voice-over, I chose blues singer Lou Rawls, and for the uptown voice, Oscar winner Jack Palance—a wonderful old cowboy who lived on an ostrich farm outside of Los Angeles.

Garth tried out *Ragtime* in Toronto and L.A., where it received raves. Then, to mark his return to Broadway, he built a new theatre on 42nd Street incorporating elements from the ruins of the Apollo and Lyric theatres. The 1,800-seat Ford Center for the Performing Arts featured the façade of the Lyric Theatre, curving staircases and a giant marble mosaic of the masks of comedy and tragedy. One of *Ragtime*'s most conspicuous props was a Ford Model T: Garth was ahead of his time in soliciting product placements from sponsors too.

The musical enraptured its opening-night audience. From my perspective, the Toronto show had been grittier and purer, but Garth kept tweaking and fixing and changing things until the story became too self-important.

As my girlfriend, Melissa, and I were leaving the Ford Center, I suggested to Jack Palance that he share our limousine. As soon as we stepped onto the street, the press went crazy over Jack. When a photographer shouted, "Who's the girl?" Jack grabbed Melissa by the waist, and announced, "This is my daughter." The next day, the *Daily News* published a full-page photo of Jack with Melissa along with my severed arm. I still get kidded about that.

Ragtime was nominated for thirteen Tonys—one more than *Kiss.* Its chief competitor in the musical category was *The Lion King,* up for ten. The Disney production was playing directly across the street from *Ragtime* at the Amsterdam Theatre, also newly renovated. Its golden marquee lit up Garth's office window.

The awards were held in June at the Radio City Music Hall, with Nathan Lane as host. *Ragtime* won a couple, and it looked like the evening might be going our way. *Ragtime* was the thinking man's choice, a phenomenal pastiche of America in the '20s. *The Lion King* had all the charm of Disney at its best, with the emotional backing of a blockbuster film. I knew how urgently Garth—seated a couple of rows ahead of me—needed the Tony for Best Musical. Broadway runs on a potent combination of word of mouth and critical acclaim, and he had to have that top accolade to keep his expensive production afloat through the winter months.

"And the winner of Best Musical is . . ."

Garth stood, face ashen, and stumbled past me up the aisle to the washroom, where he threw up. Then he left the theatre.

He was still pasty when we met at his New York agency that same night. We were seated around a table loaded with bagels and cream cheese, planning the next day's ads. His shirt was sweat-soaked. *Ragtime* had been what you call a "come bet" in craps. Garth had put everything on the pass line and he'd lost, and now he knew there wasn't going to be a payday. He also must have realized that he should have brought *Ragtime* to Broadway a year earlier, when the competition would not have been as stiff, but he had wanted it to open in his glorious new theatre.

Ragtime had won four awards, one of which was for Best Score, so I suggested we run a headline, "Winner! Best Music." That wasn't very ethical—a salvage operation—but Garth thought it brilliant, and that's what we did. But the headlines in the next day's newspapers all were variations on *Lion King Rules!*

Garth relentlessly toured *Ragtime*. If musicals historically did well for two or three weeks in a particular market, he'd run the production there for twelve. Predictably, it would make a profit for two or three, then lose for nine or ten.

★

Livent was on the verge of collapse, but the only ones who knew were Garth and his accountants—until June 1998. That's when the news broke that Hollywood power broker Michael Ovitz had purchased Livent for $20 million. *$20 million?* This was staggering news. If Garth would give up control for such a paltry sum he must be frantic.

The new management kept Garth on as Livent's chief creative officer with no financial responsibility. Though I didn't see how that could last, I became excited all over again when we began working on his next musical about legendary choreographer Bob Fosse. My parents had taken me to see Fosse's work on Broadway, and his auto-biographical film, *All That Jazz*, was one of my all-time favourites. I was sixteen when I saw it in 1979, and I was thrilled by the scene in which Roy Scheider, as Fosse, throws back a slew of pills, slaps cold water on his face, then tells his bathroom mirror, "It's showtime!"

I still say that to myself every morning.

Garth's production was based on Fosse's life: it was just two acts of singing and dancing. This was disappointing, but I figured it still had to be marvelous: Fosse was still Fosse. With Garth's approval, I hired Crescenzo Notarile, the world's best concert cinematographer, who filmed Madonna and Pink Floyd concerts. We shot some sensational footage of the dancers for the commercials, and I showed them to Garth the next Friday. This was in August, two months after Ovitz had taken over Livent. Aside from the fact that Garth was often screaming mad at being second-guessed by the new team, everything seemed normal as Garth and I cut footage in a downtown Toronto post-production house.

Garth's phone rang. Ovitz's henchmen wanted to see him the next day, Monday, at the Livent office.

We continued to cut commercials all night. It was vintage Garth and Barry, with Garth as the king of the world, and me giving his creative mojo a boost. If he had any foreboding that the curtain was falling on his life, he never gave the slightest hint.

★

On Monday morning, August 13, 1998, Garth Drabinksy was fired from Livent. He and his partner, Myron Gottlieb, were escorted from the building by guards.

I went to see Garth that evening. He was now divorced and living in a beautiful apartment in the Sutton Place Hotel with his girl-friend Karen. He was distraught. I put my arms around him as he broke down, revealing his tender, vulnerable side to me for the first time. My sympathy was unclouded. I knew nothing about Livent's cooked books and fudged numbers. Those details didn't emerge until November, when Livent sought bankruptcy protection in the United States. Apparently, Garth's accountants went to Ovitz and confessed that they had been keeping a second set of books. "We can't handle the pressure anymore," they told Ovitz. "The published numbers are fake. Here are the real ones."

Security regulators in Canada and the U.S. began their investi-gations.

I continued to feel sorry for Garth, but the fallout from his crum-bling world sent Echo into a dangerous and daunting period. A gov-ernment lawyer phoned to give notice that the RCMP would be visiting our offices. Investigators had uncovered kickback schemes involving other Livent suppliers, and they simply assumed that they would find irregularities in our arrangements too.

Len gathered the staff to assure them that our agency had nothing to hide. He told them to stay calm and be cooperative. When the RCMP arrived, they told us, "We're going through your offices and seizing computers. If anyone wants to leave, that's fine, but if you do, you can't come back today. If you want to stay, that's fine too."

I stayed, for sure. I also asked Len outright, "Is there anything I should know?"

He said, "We're fine."

Despite our cranky relationship, I trusted him. I felt obliged to ask because, if a client who's paying you $30 million a year, wants you to put $100,000 into a privately held account, that could be tempting to anyone. But Garth never made any attempt to manipulate Len. The only request he ever made was to delay payment. Nothing illegal about that.

The RCMP went through all our accounting files with the forensic equivalent of a fine-tooth comb. It felt surreal. They were in uniform, and at least I had the presence of mind to ask them to stand *inside* our building instead of outside, so we wouldn't make next day's news. They ransacked Len's office but left mine alone. They didn't interview me. As the lead guy on the Livent account, I felt rather insulted—until Len was called by the Crown to testify at Garth's trial. Not being called is an insult I can live with.

I always thought it bizarre that Garth's defence team claimed he didn't know anything about the day-to-day running of Livent. If the RCMP had examined my office with the same zeal as Len's, they would have found ironclad evidence that Garth was a control freak. I had memos from him telling me what food to order on the set. He didn't only tell me what words to use in a print ad, but also the font and type size. My favourite piece of micro-management concerned a commercial featuring a pair of hands on an old typewriter, spelling out the words, "SUNSET BOULEVARD, 1950." According to Garth's memo the hands were "too feminine."

Echo was innocent of any wrongdoing but we did not step away unmarked from under Garth's dark shadow. Livent left us on the hook for $11 million. This was money we owed to media outlets and suppliers for work contracted on Livent's behalf. While we partners were figuring out what to do, a New York financier contacted Len, offering a kind of deal I'd never heard of before. He ran a vulture fund that bought debt at, say, thirty cents on the dollar, allowing a company to settle with its creditors, while the vulture fund gambled that, when the smoke cleared, it would collect, say, seventy cents on the dollar, thereby profiting from the spread. This deal was a godsend for Echo. Many of our creditors either accepted our low offer, or wrote off our debt, so we rode into the sunset relatively unscathed.

★

In 1999, Garth and Myron Gottlieb were indicted for fraud in a New York court. They became fugitives from justice when they failed to appear for their indictment.

Garth continued to enjoy little comebacks. Though Len wisely wanted nothing more to do with his former friend, I still felt connected to Garth because of the camaraderie we had once shared. He had given me wonderful opportunities to develop my creativity with the world's best. He had taught me about the importance of elegance in design and striving for perfection. I had been at his side in his days of triumph and during his darkest hour.

I helped Garth market a CBC-TV reality talent show called *Triple Sensation*. I helped him run a Colm Wilkinson concert tour. I helped him market the African prison play, *The Island*. In fact, after he'd been dumped from Livent, I helped him with all but one of his many projects—and got burned just about every time. He would renegotiate terms, or fail to pay, or borrow money from me that he never returned—$1,000 here, $2,000 there—claiming to be desperate to make his office rent. At the same time, he was living the life: the multimillion-dollar house in Forest Hill, the Muskoka property, the Range Rover, the remarkable collection of Canadian art.

What really bothered me was Garth's betrayal of my loyalty and friendship. He used me when it suited him. If he was producing something he knew might actually interest me, he became secretive and deceptive. Because I'd set a cinematic benchmark when I filmed the Stratford productions of *Caesar and Cleopatra* and *The Tempest* with Christopher Plummer, he came to me for advice about filming the theatrical production of *Barrymore*, also with Plummer. Then, after he'd sucked my brain for information on how I'd raised the money and to whom I'd sold the film, he went to the same people behind my back, without involving me. That really bugged me, and ended our collaborations forever.

In October 2002, both Garth and Myron Gottlieb were charged in the Ontario Superior Court with nineteen counts of fraud over $5,000, and in March 2009, they were found guilty on some of those charges.

I phoned Garth the night before his trial to wish him well. He had called me when I was sitting shiva for my father, and spent half an hour sharing the grief he felt at my loss. I appreciated that gesture, though it was one of the few times Garth showed any interest in my life. I also went to court for the sentencing. I sat beside his brother, Cyril. It was awful. The trial judge, Justice Mary Lou Benotto, noted that Garth had medical issues from childhood polio, and credited him for his spectacular success within the community. Then she made it clear that he was not above the law, and that the evidence showed conclusively that he had systematically manipulated Livent's books. She sentenced him to seven years, and Gottlieb to six. Both made bail, and remained free until September 13, 2011, when their appeal was scheduled to be heard.

I saw Garth on Saturday, September 10, forty-eight hours before he had to present himself to the court. We were both attending the annual luncheon hosted by George Christy, legendary former columnist for the *Hollywood Reporter*. The event was part of the festivities associated with the 2011 Toronto International Film Festival. The Christy lunch was always a hard ticket. Only eighty people were invited, mostly celebrities and Toronto notables. Garth sat with

George at the VIP table as usual, along with media mogul Ivan Fecan, movie magnate Robert Lantos and Christopher Plummer. He didn't appear to have a care in the world. The champagne and the accolades flowed. Life was good if you were Garth Drabinsky.

George Christy, our host, was noted for separating spouses at these luncheons, so Garth's second wife, Elizabeth Winford, was at my table, along with actor Geoffrey Rush. Elizabeth was glamorous and seemed happy. You'd never know the Drabinsky household was facing a crisis. That was the thing about Garth. You never knew. The only tiny sign of his loss of status in this elite gathering was in the naming of George's main course—the one he'd served for thirty years. Once known as Chicken Pot Pie à la Drabinsky, it was now described on the menu as simply Chicken Pot Pie.

At some point in the luncheon, Garth waved to me, and I waved back—in guilt and sympathy and some residual anger for taking advantage of my generosity one too many times. Afterwards, he screened *Barrymore* as part of TIFF, and then hosted a dinner at the downtown restaurant, Bymark, to which I wasn't invited.

The next day, on September 13, Garth and Myron Gottlieb lost their appeal in the Ontario Superior Court, on the grounds that the evidence against them was "overwhelming." They did, however, have their sentences reduced by two years, to five and four, respectively. They were denied bail, both then, and later on appeal. Garth was led away in handcuffs.

I had been a close associate of Garth for ten years, but he remained a paradox to me. He produced exceptional art. He created an entertainment factory that employed thousands of talented people and attracted billions of tourist dollars. He revolutionized the movie business with his Cineplex chain, and then dramatically revitalized live theatre, not only through the depth, scope and splendour of his productions, but also by refurbishing theatres in Toronto, Vancouver, Chicago and New York.

His toughest critics consider these accomplishments irrelevant because they were based on deception. They point to the evidence amassed against him in his prolonged march through the justice system, the carnage he left in his wake, and his refusal to take responsibility for any of it. To them, jail was what Garth Drabinsky deserved, and the longer his sentence the better.

Did greed motivate Garth to build his fabulous empire on quicksand? Not in my opinion, though he revelled in the luxuries his privileged life afforded.

Was he driven by a desire for glory? Absolutely.

What role did childhood polio play in his hunger for recognition? Certainly, his pronounced limp would have set him apart from his peers from a young age. Physical deformity drove the Phantom in Garth's greatest theatrical success. He was self-conscious enough about it to instruct cameramen at award shows to wait until he arrived on stage before framing him. Garth's talent far eclipsed his handicap. He would have been a high achiever under any circumstances. Without it, perhaps he would have been a more balanced one.

Another recurrent motif in Garth's theatre work was imprisonment. The characters in some of his plays chose confinement: the Phantom chose his underworld and Norma Desmond disappeared into her decaying mansion. Some had no choice, as in *Kiss of the Spider Woman*, his prison drama *The Island* and *Dreamcoat* after Joseph had been sold into slavery.

These works now seemed prophetic, as did the title of his 1995 autobiography, *Closer to the Sun*. In the Greek myth that Garth invoked, Daedalus warned his son, Icarus, not to fly too close to the sun. When Icarus ignored the warning, his feather-and-wax wings melted and he plunged to his death.

In his memoir's Prologue, Garth inverted this tragic example of hubris with the vainglorious words, "Never be afraid to fly closer to the sun. Not just escape. But escape into something greater."

Garth remains to my mind an enigma, a flawed genius. He was a certified bastard and betrayer, but I missed him.

Chapter Eight

SURROUNDED BY MADMEN AND A FEW MONSTERS

My career within advertising brought me into contact—and sometimes into a fruitful continuing relationship—with a number of brilliant, creative and enterprising people, some of whom changed the world in meaningful ways. Some were on the rise of a meteoric career; others on a downward slide. My lust for their wisdom and success drove me to stay close and learn their secrets, emulate their style in some cases and hopefully avoid their mistakes.

AN ENDURING ALLIANCE

Though Garth had sucked up much of my energy at Echo, I also had other stimulating clients.

One was Alliance, a film distribution/production company owned by Robert Lantos and Victor Loewy. Victor was an ill-tempered Romanian who preferred to stay out of the limelight while Lantos was a charming, dashing Hungarian romantic, and a very successful producer. It was Lantos who saw the big picture: he eventually took Alliance into the home-video field, and then created specialty television channels including Showcase and History.

Loewy and Lantos began their partnership in 1972 in Montreal when they formed Viva Films. They then purchased the rights to the best of the NY Erotic Film Festival to show at McGill University. Lantos also produced successful Canadian films, such as *In Praise of Older Women* (1978) and *Joshua Then and Now* (1985). After the partners moved their company to Toronto, they approached Echo for film-marketing expertise. My media director, Marilyn Sherman, and I went to see what they had to promote. The answer was not very much, just a few horror films, such as *Friday the 13th*, and a film about a teenager who ran a pirate radio station, *Pump Up the Volume*, whose main virtue, when it was released in 1990, was that it launched the career of Christian Slater.

Alliance did have one prestigious property: *Black Robe*, scripted by Irish-Canadian Brian Moore from his novel. Set in 1634, and shot entirely in Quebec, it told the tragic story of a young Jesuit priest's attempts to convert Native American tribes to Christianity. For this and the other Alliance properties, our main job at Echo was to cut radio and television commercials and a trailer for the film. My Alliance contact was Mary Pat Gleeson, a veteran marketer, who saw me as a protege. This was happening simultaneously with my early work with Garth and I still had much to learn.

I remember taking my *Black Robe* trailers to the Alliance offices. Lantos had visions of the film as a potential Oscar winner, so from his point of view, there was a lot riding on it. To keep expectations in perspective, we underlings jokingly called it *Black Bathrobe*.

Lantos was famous for making people wait and I sat in reception for two and a half hours. This was before the age of the BlackBerry so there was nothing to distract me. Occasionally, Lantos's long-suffering assistant, Cherri Campbell, would appear to apologize, "I'm really very sorry. Robert will be with you in a minute." Meaning another half hour.

Finally, I was ushered into Lantos's office, which was in the grand Hollywood tradition—spacious, elegant and comfortable. I showed him several *Black Robe* trailers and then waited for his verdict. In his slightly accented, deep basso, he said, "I hate to be the voice of gloom and doom, but I hate these trailers."

I was mortified. "Tell me what you hate about them."

Fortunately, everything Lantos disliked could be easily fixed. Though he and I never became close friends, we developed a respectful working relationship, and he remained loyal to me as he built his film and television empire. Since I had caught Alliance's coattails at the right time, this translated into a massive account for Echo.

At Alliance, we had the opportunity to work on hundreds of film releases as they grew steadily, picking up output deals with mega U.S. studios like Harvey Weinstein's Miramax and New Line Cinema. One of my favourite films to work on was David Cronenberg's creepy film *Crash* in 1996. Frank Mendicino, one of Gleeson's young proteges, gave us free rein to design the key art (the poster), trailers and TV spots. The film, starring James Spader and Holly Hunter, was Cronenberg at his best and my young and talented account executive Steph Sebbag had a ball developing iconic creative for the film. Steph was a fellow Montrealer who was filled with the same kind of passion for show business that I had. Years later, he moved to Hollywood and opened up his own ad agency and I hired him to work on the campaign for *The Last Mogul*.

To Victor Loewy, I remained an ad-agency commodity. He was constantly applying pressure. "Maybe it's time to get someone new to do something new."

Mary Pat Gleeson always countered, "No. Barry and Echo are great."

When she left Alliance, I figured my days were numbered but we stayed onside until 1998. That's when Lantos sold his share of Alliance to Michael MacMillan, who turned it into Alliance Atlantis. Ultimately the great brand and company that Lantos had built was split and sold several times and finally folded into eOne Entertainment. After that, Lantos founded Serendipity Point Films, for which I created the branding and the logo. Although Lantos and Loewy had started out together, it was Robert's vision that created an empire and I believe Loewy resented the breakup of their partnership.

With Robert gone, the upside for Loewy was in getting rid of me.

CREDIT WHERE IT'S DUE

One lesson I had learned early on was that there were endless ways to make a dollar. For me, this often meant bringing together my entertainment and corporate clients for their mutual benefit. Seeing that both American Express and Livent were among my Echo accounts, we worked out a Front of the Line program that gave Amex card members an opportunity to buy advance tickets for his productions. To add sizzle to our 1990 launch, I contracted Céline Dion to host our press conference. She was already a rising Canadian star at the time, but had not yet attained international celebrity. That would happen the following year with the release of Disney's *Beauty and the Beast*, for which Céline sang the title song.

For the backdrop to the Toronto press conference, we manufactured the world's largest American Express Card. At the last minute, some of us grew apprehensive: *Would Céline think this too crass for her burgeoning reputation?*

As Céline walked on stage, she glanced at the card, smiled and ad libbed, "Now that's the card I'd like to take shopping with me. It looks like it has no limit!"

Céline was 100 per cent sincere: she was then and remained the unspoiled little girl from Quebec—genuinely appreciative of her fans and of her success. My colleagues used to joke that any time we went hunting for music for a commercial, I would bring up her hit, "My Heart Will Go On." Their reply was just as predictable, "Oh my God, not that song again!" I'm still a fan.

I had an opportunity to confirm my first impression of Céline nearly a decade later when as a founding board member of Canada's Walk of Fame, we presented Céline, now indisputably an international celebrity, with an inaugural star.

CROONERS

While earning my Ph.D. in Show Business, I occasionally worked on events for Michael Cohl, Echo's other big client. That's how I came to be backstage at Maple Leaf Gardens for Frank Sinatra's November 1991, sold-out final tour. Steve Lawrence and Eydie Gorme were his warm-up act, and it was terrible for them. Even while they were singing, the audience was yelling, "Frank! Frank!"

My contact with Sinatra was sad rather than cool. When we shook hands backstage after I was introduced by Michael's cousin, Dusty Cohl, he stared at me with those famous ice-blue eyes, looking as if he would just as soon snap my neck. He smelled strongly of old guy cologne. He was obviously wearing a toupée but his self-assurance—or was it arrogance?—remained intact. When I asked him for something about himself that few people knew, he replied, "I do the crossword in pen." Then he barked, "I'm thirsty."

"What are you drinking?"

"Chivas Regal." He pronounced the first word *Shivas*.

I got him the drink and that's how he went on stage, in his tux, holding his glass high. "Ladies and gentlemen, I'd like to introduce you to my friends, Mr. Shivas and Mr. Regal." *Ha ha.*

His singing voice was no longer great. The drinking and smoking had taken a toll. Because the stage was circular, some of the audience could see the teleprompters carrying his lyrics and script. I was witnessing the decline of a great star. It was depressing.

By contrast, Tony Bennett, whom I've booked many times, continues to astonish me as the classiest, most elegant octogenarian I've ever met. Tony's instrument has remained perfect, because he protects his throat as the vital organ that it is. He has preserved his style too: the Brioni suit, coiffed hair, tortoiseshell glasses, gleaming cufflinks and the pocket puff. He's the last of his generation. He doesn't want to step out of the spotlight, and he doesn't have to.

I booked Tony when he was eighty-seven for a private Italian function for one thousand people. When we walked him backstage through the kitchen, all the chefs and dishwashers stopped to watch as he passed by. The floor had been taped to indicate the route, but he didn't want anyone to help him. He did all the meeting and greeting that could be expected of him. Once he was on stage, however, he skipped the chit-chat to give more of what everyone really wanted: his incomparable voice. In mid-performance, he paused and said, "Okay, let's turn off all the microphones." He sang, *a capella*, without amplification, and he was fantastic. Tony has survived. Frank lost it.

Still on the subject of stars who do (or do not) age well, I can't forget Barry Manilow.

At the end of the '90s, I was approached by a group of New York producers who wanted to make a musical based on "Copacabana," Barry Manilow's nauseating song. It would star Gavin MacLeod from *The Love Boat*, so you knew right away this would be a winner. I was asked to film the show, with the footage to be used to cut commercials for the tour and for a possible television special media use.

Mr. Manilow didn't know it but we already had history. My parents used to take me to Saratoga Springs, which meant passing Latham, New York. One summer, we bought tickets for a concert

there featuring a then-unknown singer, who performed "I Write the Songs" and "Mandy," and all those sugary songs that give me a cavity. My mother, unlike me, thought Manilow was a sensational talent. When I told her, so many years later, that I was working with him, she couldn't have been prouder.

I flew to New York to meet Manilow and the team involved in *Copacabana*. It was being coproduced by a theatre in Pittsburgh and the head of the Pittsburgh contingent was Van Kaplan, who turned out to be a very nervous impresario. Who could blame him? How do you build a whole musical on one wretched song?

Manilow's face was so waxy and stretched, perhaps from plastic surgery, that he looked like the guy in that Edvard Munch painting, *The Scream*. What he was screaming was, *Too Much Work*. Though his clothes were custom-made, they were anything but current: shirt collars too big, pants all wrong, everything and anything to recall his glory days.

He took an immediate dislike to me without knowing that I had beaten him to that by several decades. As I described my approach to the filming, he said, "I don't think you understand my music."

I replied, "My responsibility is to film the show, not to love your music. We aren't making a Fellini or a Godard here."

To my surprise, Manilow's team supported me and I was hired.

I flew to Pittsburgh to shoot *Copacabana*, where it was premiering. I would be directing from inside a truck, using multiple cameras. Manilow kept sticking in his nose, until the crew finally put up a sign, "THERE IS ROOM IN THIS TRUCK FOR ONE BARRY ONLY." When I wasn't there, he returned to complain, "Barry doesn't like me."

We filmed the show professionally and it went on tour in 2000 as intended. The show itself was awful.

AN ANTHEM FOR AIDS

In 1993 I had the most sublime working experience with Liza Minnelli.

Garth Drabinsky's critically acclaimed Broadway production of *Kiss of the Spider Woman* was based on Argentine novelist Manuel Puig's 1976 book that told the story of the intimate bond between two cellmates, a window dresser and a political activist. Long before the novel became a musical, Puig's book was also turned into a beautiful film starring William Hurt, Raúl Juliá and Sonia Braga, that Garth distributed in Canada in 1985.

Kander and Ebb, the famed composer-and-lyricist team responsible for musicals such as *Chicago* and *Cabaret*, wrote the score for *Kiss*, and included a powerful anthem called "The Day After That." The song was one of those tingle-inducing Broadway showstoppers and Liza Minnelli was instantly transfixed by its message of hope.

Minnelli, like many Broadway artists, had lost many friends to AIDS and she wanted the song to become a signature track for the cause.

When she approached Garth through Hal Prince, he came up with a grander plan. Not only would Garth record the track with Liza, he would also shoot a lavish music video featuring a choir holding dozens of candles. My job was to film Minnelli during the recording session to get footage for the video. Now, being the daughter of the great director Vincente Minnelli and the iconic Judy Garland, Liza was a perfectionist and wanted to meet me and discuss details like camera framing and the overall approach to the shoot.

Armed with the usual militant instructions from Garth and his commandant Lynda Friendly on what I could and could not say, my cinematographer John Holosko and I went to visit Minnelli in the presidential suite at The King Edward Hotel. What happened next was disconcerting. I knocked on her door and a woman answered. She was wearing a colourful caftan, a matching turban and not a stitch of makeup. I told her that we were there to meet Ms. Minnelli. She told us to have a seat in the living room, and that Ms. Minnelli would be with us shortly. I assumed this rather eccentric woman was Liza's assistant or maid.

The living room was old-school massive with a baby grand piano and a half-dozen glasses filled with cigarettes. After about 45 minutes, Minnelli made her entrance looking radiant and quite glamorous. I then realized that the woman who answered the door was actually Liza. It was odd, but somewhat charming in a faded Mae West kind of a way. We had a very technical conversation on process and camera angles. She was impressively knowledgeable about filmmaking.

The shoot the next day was at a recording studio in Toronto and you could feel the excitement in the air. We set up our camera equipment among the dozens of musicians. Garth had assembled the orchestra, choir and sound engineers and it was thrilling to be in the middle of it. The door to the mixing booth swung open and

Charles Aznavour walked in as if he was a natural thing to be in a recording studio in Toronto. He and Minnelli were touring together and appearing at the O'Keefe Centre and he wanted to watch her record the song.

Watching Liza was like watching an architect design a house. After each take, she would rush into the booth and suggest changes to the instrumentation and her own interpretation of a lyric. She would then watch the playback with me and suggest camera angles by holding up a compact mirror to check lighting. She was a one-woman tour de force.

At the end of a long day, Michael Cooper, a photographer we hired to document the session climbed up on the roof to take a photograph of the giant cast that had taken part in what felt like a historic day.

GOING PUBLIC

My most unexpected Echo client was the Toronto Stock Exchange. The opportunity came about in 2001 through a friend, Robert Pattillo, a corporate communications guru who had previously worked at Alliance, CBC and Scotiabank.

On the recommendation of my Alliance mentor, Mary Pat Gleeson, Pattillo called me into a meeting to discuss a couple of Alliance TV series that weren't doing well: *Once a Thief* and *Bordertown*. People had warned me, "Be careful. This guy has a horrible temper. He loves his dogs more than he loves people."

Robert was tough. He was cold and direct. He was acerbic. Right away, we loved each other. Lucky are the people who have angels in their lives, and Robert was one of mine. We worked together on ad campaigns for the two struggling television series and managed to push them through several more seasons. Our relationship outlasted our collaboration. To this day, we love finishing off a couple of bottles of expensive French wine at a single sitting.

After Robert left Alliance for Sun Life Financial Canada, he had called me to work on another ad campaign. When he moved to the Toronto Stock Exchange, he called me again. "The TSE is about to celebrate its one hundredth anniversary. We're looking for an agency of record, but we have to do a search. What do you know about us?"

Not much. I had done some work on Dynamic Mutual Funds, but financial services had never been my core interest. I did know that Barbara Stymiest was the first woman in North America to chair a stock exchange. I also remembered an effective ad campaign Scotiabank had run when Robert was there. It featured Mary the Bank Teller, whose job was to put a human face on the institution. I felt the TSE also needed to personalize its operation. Unlike the New York Stock Exchange, the TSE had no trading floor of the kind that is so often featured in movies, with people shouting and waving their hands and papers fluttering to the floor. Everything in Toronto was automated. Our audience was not the one Mary's was aimed at. Unlike her, we weren't trying to attract customers to use our services to pay bills or take out a mortgage. We were trying to encourage corporate executives and entrepreneurs to see the TSE as the place where they could build their companies then take them public.

I called the public relations department of the New York Stock Exchange and asked for a tour. This was just after 9/11: they didn't do tours anymore. I called back. This time I told them I was thinking of listing my company on the NYSE and that I wanted to meet some of the people with whom I would be dealing. Different story. A meeting was arranged.

The security was insane. Barricades blocked off the building so no one could pull up in a vehicle in order to bomb it. For clearance, I needed my passport and a NYSE sticker, which I still have. But after putting me through all that, they gave me a royal tour, which included the private dining room where NYSE customers have permanent seats. They gave me a NYSE forest-green, linen bound book as a souvenir, along with some videos—in short, all the tools I needed to create my own vision of the Toronto Stock Exchange as a place of flesh and blood, rather than as a place where rows of machines hummed at one another.

My Echo account director, Tori Laurence, and I pitched our ideas, and we won the contract, no doubt sending shockwaves through the advertising community. Suddenly, our entertainment-based agency would be cutting multimillion-dollar corporate TV and cinema commercials. As so often with my ad career, there was never a dull moment and I loved every minute of it. If someone could have predicted that a math idiot like myself would one day be working on a stock exchange account, I would have bought land in Kabul.

Chapter Nine

FAMILY, MENTORS AND OTHER INVALUABLES

IF YOU LOVED DUSTY, YOU FLOATED

A year after my dad, Irving, died in 1991, I found a second father.

I was working in the Echo office when a tall guy with a white beard strode in. He was wearing a black cowboy hat and a Rolling Stones jacket, and carrying a bag labeled *Outrageous*, from the film starring female impersonator Craig Russell.

I asked Len Gill, "Who's that?"

"It's Dusty Cohl—Michael Cohl's cousin. He was one of the founders of the Toronto International Film Festival. Stay away from him. He'll ask you to do jobs for him, then suck you into his life."

Len was right on both counts. No sooner had I introduced myself to Dusty than he said, "I need a poster for the Floating Film Festival. Can you get that done?"

"Sure." And so I made the poster. And in 1996 I attended my first Floating Film Festival. Dusty founded the festival in 1992 when he got bored of wintering in Florida and decided to invite two hundred of his closest friends to cruise for ten days in the Caribbean, watching movies. If you were Dusty's friend, you floated. Attorney Eddie Greenspan used to complain for the entire ten days, "The festival is a wonderful thing, if you like the extreme heat of the Caribbean, and I don't. The festival is a wonderful thing, if you like the ocean moving under you making you feel seasick twenty-four hours a day, and I don't." Nevertheless, Eddie attended every year to smoke cigars and laugh with Dusty, surrounded by friends and film lovers.

In 2002 Dusty persuaded me to take over the festival for him. I agreed as long as I could do it my way. That meant booking a better cruise line and honouring celebrities. I also ended the custom of inviting critics, who chose obscure films that no one liked and declined to socialize with our guests. I brought in more accessible films instead.

Through the years, the festival provided me with some wonderful theatrical moments. When l visited Gena Rowlands in her Beverly Hills home along with friend and long-time festival programmer George Anthony to discuss her participation, I felt like I was meeting Norma Desmond on the set of *Sunset Boulevard*. All around me were the faded film posters, the Golden Globes, the Oscars from *Faces* (1968), *A Woman Under the Influence* (1974) and *Gloria* (1980), all starring Gena and directed by her husband, John Cassavetes. On the bar were cigarette burns from those bygone days when the Cassavetes entertained the greats of Hollywood: Peter Falk, Ben Gazzara, Judy Garland, Robert Taylor, Burt Lancaster.

Gena is still an elegant woman and a fabulous actress, as she proved in 2004 in *The Notebook*, directed by her son Nick Cassavetes. At the Floating Film Festival, she told wonderful stories, as long as she didn't find the bar before we needed her to perform.

In 2015, we honoured Dick Cavett—the cerebral version of Johnny Carson. Cavett had interviewed giants on his show: Katharine Hepburn, Salvador Dalí, Marlon Brando, Alec Guinness, Groucho

Marx, Jack Benny, Muhammad Ali, Orson Welles, Bette Davis, Fred Astaire, Frank Capra, and then, of course, Richard Nixon.

Dick was a machine. You'd press a button with a celebrity's name, and he'd produce a story or some pithy commentary. On Groucho Marx: "We were sneaking out of a snobby Beverly Hills party when the hostess stopped us. 'Why are you leaving?' she asked. Groucho replied, 'I've had a wonderful evening. This wasn't it.'" On Richard Nixon: "He was a foul-mouthed son of a bitch. His obsession with his manhood was material for a psychiatrist." After Cavett's Watergate interview, another journalist asked Cavett, "Does any part of you feel sorry for Nixon?" Cavett replied, "After examining all my parts, I'd say, Yes. That poor man died without knowing the answer to his question, 'Is Cavett a Jew?'"

Through the years, Dusty became a close and much-loved mentor to me. His office above Echo reeked of smoke, just as my father's office had done. We gravitated toward each other as if drawn by some cosmic force. He introduced me to everyone in Toronto show business. If a photographer came to take his picture, Dusty would call to me, "Hey, kid. Come over here." He'd introduce me, "This is Barry, watch this one." Then he'd pull me into the photograph.

It was because of Dusty that I became involved in the Toronto International Film Festival, which he cofounded with Bill Marshall in 1976 as the Festival of Festivals. As that story goes, Dusty and his wife, Joan, found a parking spot in front of the famed Carlton Hotel during the Cannes Film Festival. He loved it. From that time forward, year after year, he returned to network, schmooze, hold court and buttonhole every Canadian there about the need to kickstart the Canadian film industry with a festival of our own in Toronto.

Dusty's father, a house painter, was a self-declared Communist; his mother was a salesperson for Eaton's. Dusty trained as a lawyer. He married his high-school sweetheart, Joan Carin, with whom he had three children. He was rumoured to have made a lot of money in real estate, but apparently retired to work full-time building friend-ships and instigating bold projects, for which he preferred the title "accomplice."

Dusty was more than a role model to me—though he was that too. He involved me in many of his projects, including Canada's Walk of Fame, which he also cofounded. He brought me onto the board. And on and on. Much later, when Dusty began to slow down, and the pendulum began to swing the other way, I pulled Dusty in by taking him to Los Angeles to introduce him to younger celebrities. I also nominated him for the Order of Canada that he received in 2003.

THE WEDDING PLANNER(S)

Most of my friends and relatives thought I would never marry. I was too independent, too hedonistic, too footloose, too driven. I was a perennial dater.

In 1996, when I was thirty-three, I met the woman who walked into my life and would change it forever. Her name was Melissa Manly and she was a knockout.

It was a blind date, sort of. Rey Tabarrok, who worked for me, said, "I'd like to set you up with a good friend who's just moved back from France."

I protested, "But I'm dating someone else."

"I know. You always are, but it's always the same kind of girl."

That came as a surprise. I had no answer.

Rey continued, "What I told my friend was, 'Barry knows everyone. He'll help find you a job.'"

I protested again. "If this is a date, then I'm not going."

"Relax. Melissa has a boyfriend in Provence. You're not in his league."

I remember the exact date of our first meeting: November 8, 1996.

We hooked up at a jazz club called the Black and Blue above the Prego restaurant in Yorkville. Melissa walked in wearing a camel coat with a pair of zebra gloves. My heart stopped. I told myself, *Okay. Don't mess this up.*

It went well: Melissa laughed at my jokes. When I lit a cigar—you could do that in restaurants in those days—Melissa shared it with me. We talked till three in the morning.

Next day, I called Rey. "Have you spoken to Melissa?"

"Yes."

Don't make me beg. "What did she say?"

"She said she had a good time, and that she was looking for some furniture."

I suggested a place where Melissa could find cool furniture, then phoned her to invite her to dinner that night. Over drinks, she said,

"We both know there's chemistry here, but my guy's coming in from France, so nothing can happen between us."

I told her, "I'm going to Hawaii with a friend, but until then, I'd like to get together with you for dinner as often as you want."

We had dinner every night till December 22. I called Melissa when I was still in Hawaii. "How's it going?"

"I can't stand the guy. How's it going with you?"

"Hawaii's pretty good."

By the time I returned to Toronto, Melissa had broken up with her French boyfriend, who had returned to France. That's when we began dating with intent. Though everything felt great, I was nervous because I knew Melissa was The One, but I was afraid to commit.

We had one issue—in my mind, anyway. When I pressed her about rebooting her career, Melissa stormed out of my house. "I can't do this any longer."

That winter, while I was visiting Dusty in Florida, he asked me, "How's it going with you and Melissa?"

"I'm concerned we aren't a match," I replied dolefully. "I'm an entrepreneur, and I don't understand why she isn't looking for some kind of career."

"Are you crazy?" snapped Dusty. "Do you want to be married to yourself?"

The horror of that struck home. The fog cleared from my head.

Melissa and I were married on May 16, 1999.

We had two wedding planners at the start. In this corner, Melissa's mother, Doreen; in the other, Barry the producer. The referee: Melissa, the bride, practising the diplomatic skills she'd learned as youngest child.

I didn't want to be married in a synagogue, because that was too much of a cliché, and they lacked great spaces. I wanted the Four Seasons Hotel ballroom, where I'd been booking gala events. Doreen—a force of nature, tough and opinionated—had different ideas. She was marrying off her only daughter about whom she cared deeply. I love Doreen and also Melissa's father, Sheldon. I would have been afraid to marry Melissa if I hadn't, because I've witnessed too much fallout among friends with bad in-law relationships.

Probably Melissa would have enjoyed being more involved in wedding details, but we'd been together long enough for her to trust my taste. More to the point, Melissa, like her father, was wise enough to know some battles aren't worth fighting.

Doreen and I sat down in the Manly kitchen to divide up the territory. I told her, "You can have catering and floral, but I want venue and entertainment."

Though Doreen agreed, she would continue to manoeuvre around me. One day she announced, "The food tasting for the catering will be on Thursday."

"Okay."

"You have to come."

"Why? That's your domain. Who eats at a wedding anyway? Certainly not the groom."

Doreen was insistent and I went to the synagogue basement where the caterer had set up his food, which was kosher, out of respect for both sets of religiously observant parents. Everything I was given to taste, I said, "That's fantastic."

Doreen said, "You have to make a choice."

"I love it all."

"You just want to get out of here, don't you?"

I said my first, "I do."

Unexpectedly, Doreen announced that she wanted a wedding planner.

What, with two Type A's already in the ring?

I said, "I don't need some *yenta* to tell me how to walk down the aisle or how the tables should be set up."

When I sensed I was losing this battle, I went for compromise.

"Okay, if you want the peace of mind of having some 'expert' make recommendations, to which I won't listen, then fine, but I don't ever want to see her."

Doreen said, "I'd like the whole wedding filmed."

"I don't want a camera and a microphone in front of people's faces, including mine. I live and breathe that stuff daily."

Doreen was heartbroken. She wanted her memento.

"Okay, here's the compromise. I'll bring my own film crew. They're not going to go around the tables interviewing people. They're going to shoot it and I'll edit it."

We ended up with about three hundred guests. Doreen wanted the tables mixed so the two sides of the family could get to know each other, whereas I insisted on keeping them separate. Who wants to make chit-chat with someone you'll never see again? I also didn't want a head table. Instead, Melissa and I would sit together at a table for two.

"We're not holding a Hadassah meeting. This is a party."

Doreen proved skilled in keeping her wedding planner out of my sight until the day of the wedding. That's when we learned that this genius had lost the guests' place cards. After a panicked search, they were found, probably under her car's spare tire.

I had insisted on inviting Garth, even though he'd become a pariah since his fraud indictment. Turned out he was obsessed about where he'd be sitting: I had to call a prominent friend to ask if Garth could sit with him. Garth didn't bring a gift—classic Garth—and left early. Which was fine. A couple of years later when Garth remarried, I attended the affair, also at the Four Seasons Hotel. I didn't bring a gift and left early.

Our wedding video was sixteen minutes long, just the high-lights: walking down the aisle, the vows, the best of the speeches and some of the dancing. We also shot that lovely Jewish ritual where the bride's father puts his hand over his daughter's head, after the wedding contracts have been signed, and says a blessing. When I presented Doreen with the video, she asked for all the outtakes. I don't know what she did with them, but she has them.

After sixteen years, Melissa and I still enjoy each other's company. We laugh a lot and have fun travelling together. Melissa knows how to give me space. She knows my artistic nuances and my eccentricities. She just knows. She can sense by my voice if I'm stuck in a creative rut, and she'll say hopefully, "When are you going out of town again?"

That's her punchline because space for me also means space for her. I had seen how well that had worked for my parents. At the same time I miss Melissa when I travel. We speak over and over during the course of a day, and when I'm involved in something terrific, I want her to share it. Meeting celebrities, attending award ceremonies, going to great concerts used to be my selfish prerogative. Since I married Melissa, I don't enjoy anything quite as much unless she's present.

MY GREATEST PRODUCTION

On February 11, 2004, Melissa gave birth to our daughter, Sloan. Since it was by C-section, it was a scheduled event, which meant no labour—a big relief for me (and, I hope, for Melissa). It's still the case that the more time I spend in hospitals, the more nauseated I become.

Dr. Jackie Thomas, at Mount Sinai Hospital, told me, "Okay, we'll be doing this in an hour. What role do you want to play?"

I didn't answer. I was staring at her surgical shoes, which were covered with blood, "Was it an autopsy, or a car accident?" I asked.

She said, "Don't look down." Then she calmly repeated, "What role are you planning to play?"

I knew Dr. Thomas was asking where, in the operating room, I wanted to stand. While some curious people might want to watch the birth, I knew where my place was. "At Melissa's head," I said. I knew I would be safe there, with a sheet in place to screen off all that southern exposure. To this day, I don't really know what a C-section is. I have zero interest in Googling to find out.

At some point near the end, as our daughter was being delivered, Dr. Thomas asked from the other side, "Do you want to cut the umbilical cord?"

I replied, "Get her out, clean her up, hand her over. I've already played my role."

Dr. Thomas laughed.

When the nurses did "hand over" Sloan, wrapped in a pink blanket, she had a head of blonde peach fuzz, which grew in later as red. It was a great moment when I carried her out to show Melissa's parents, and later to my mother, who arrived from Montreal the next day.

So far, my relationship with Sloan is like my relationship with my wife. She understands me, even the fact that it's necessary for me to travel. Both she and Melissa know that it's quality time that matters, not quantity. I am not an accountant who comes home for dinner and reads to her before she goes to sleep. I don't help her with her math. Fortunately.

Sloan often makes Melissa and me laugh, and not always intentionally. When she was five years old, her teacher called to tell us, "When I asked my class today to name the four seasons, your daughter put her hand up and said, 'There's one in New York and there's one in Toronto.'"

Recently, I hung up a piece of art I'd bought in London. When Sloan came home from school, she visited me in my home office. "Did you see that painting someone hung in our house?"

"Yes."

"Don't I have a role to play?"

"What are you talking about?"

"That piece of art—it's horrible, and I wasn't consulted. I don't like it."

"Sloan, you don't have to like it."

"Well, you have to move it to the basement. It's an embarrassment."

"Why is that?"

"I have friends who come here."

"Since when did you become an art collector?"

She grew indignant. "I just want you to know that when you're dead, I'm going to sell it."

In point of fact, my daughter, the critic, hasn't liked any art that Melissa and I have purchased, so maybe she has some insight that still escapes us. My mother used to call me a *macher*, meaning "the little expert." So I guess she got it from me.

Chapter Ten

CHARITY BEGINS WITH A ROLODEX

My work in showbiz marketing and film production has given me access to celebrities. Because of this access, organizations in Canada and the United States that can use a bit of star power ask me to produce their fundraising events. I have always made it a practice to honour a celebrity, to treat him or her as if this were a Hollywood premiere; to make sure the ballroom looked as fabulous as for the Golden Globes, to have great music and to do a press junket. My aim is to catapult a nondescript, well-intentioned gala into a prominent place in the host city's social calendar.

From 2004 to 2012, I was involved with Best Buddies, an organization started by the Kennedy Shriver family with a mandate to create friendships for people with intellectual disabilities by pairing them with high school and university students. Typically, their annual fundraiser would consist of a film showing and dinner, and attract only marginal local coverage. I changed things up by putting my

Rolodex to work and timing the event to coincide with the Toronto International Film Festival, so we could bring in the stars.

Sometimes our honourees were personal friends. Sometimes I approached them through their agents, in which case I stressed that this was a major charitable occasion at which their client would receive a beautifully designed Lifetime Achievement Award. With this reinvention, Best Buddies galas attracted national coverage and almost doubled their fundraising, to a high of over $1.5 million the year my friend James Earl Jones was honoured.

Every year the event produced memorable moments. These were some of them.

"IT'S FORTUNATE YOU'RE GOOD-LOOKING, YOUNG MAN"

Lauren Bacall, whom I had met at one of Garth Drabinsky's opulent Broadway openings, was my most delightfully outspoken honouree. When I asked her to accept a Lifetime Achievement Award, her response was a vigorous, "Why the hell not? I love Toronto."

During the seventy-two hours we spent together, I was prepared for bouts of her infamous temper. Bacall, according to one agent, had fired a chauffeur for not parking close enough to the curb.

When I picked her up at Pearson Airport in a Rolls-Royce Silver Ghost, she expressed her disdain at such pretension. Then she told me she wanted to go to a Danier factory outlet that, according to the newspaper ad clutched in her hand, offered great deals in leather. I called the owner of the outlet to ask, "Do you want to meet Lauren Bacall? I'm going to be taking her to your outlet."

I had expected enthusiasm. Instead, he said, "Oh no, she's going to want everything for free."

Sure enough, Bacall picked out a half-dozen items. For free.

I'd planned a gourmet lunch in Bacall's King Edward Hotel suite, but she wanted a hot dog from a stand she had patronized on other visits. She insisted that I buy a hot dog for myself. I told her, "Ms. Bacall, my grandfather was a butcher, and he made me promise never to eat one of those things."

"Kid, you'll be eating these dogs with Bacall in her suite. It doesn't get any better than that."

Before the gala, a well-known entertainment TV host interviewed Bacall. He asked, "What was it like to stand with Bogart, saying goodbye in that famous airport scene in *Casablanca*?"

It was Ingrid Bergman, not Bacall, who stood on that tarmac. "It's fortunate you're good-looking, young man," Bacall told the reporter, "because there's not much going on inside that head."

In the evening, when I escorted Bacall to the gala, she was greeted by a standing ovation from the awestruck guests. On discovering the same reporter would be the evening's host, she did not mince words: "Not that fucking idiot!"

I was not immune to her barbs. When we ran her tribute reel, she sat beside me, questioning my edits and occasionally offering praise of her own performance.

Most importantly, when Lauren Bacall stepped up to the microphone, she was everything anyone could hope for. She demonstrated a genuine admiration for the charity, and after hugging one of the intellectually challenged adults on stage, exclaimed, "Now I have a buddy for life!" She was a pro. She got it. Some of our other guest stars did not.

Offstage, Bacall continued to be her tart, unpredictable self. When a man shyly said to her, "I met you at George V Hotel in Paris in 1972," she responded with a throaty, "Yes, yes, I do remember." Then, as he walked away, she muttered, sotto voce, "What an asshole."

My favourite Bacall line was uttered after the entire staff of the King Edward Hotel lined up to bid her farewell. When I asked her if she would like to say something to them, she glanced disapprovingly around the hotel lobby, then snapped, "Decorate!"

ENCHANTED BY CHANTAL

In 2007, we honoured Burt Reynolds, who was memorable in all the wrong ways. Though he was no longer the No. 1 box-office star as he'd been in the '70s and '80s, he had supported young actors in his native Florida, qualifying him for a Lifetime Achievement Award.

He was suffering from bronchitis when he arrived and he made it obvious that he didn't want to be there. He had also fallen into that awful Hollywood trap: he had undergone so much plastic surgery that his face was stiff.

Reynolds cancelled a long lineup of interviews, making it instantly clear that he planned to step onto the stage, do his job, grab his trophy, then get the hell out. Ah, but that was before he discovered his dinner mate, Chantal Kreviazuk, the beautiful Canadian singer we had hired for the evening. Reynolds was so smitten by Chantal that he wouldn't talk to anyone else. When she began to sing, he stood up as if mesmerized, and started crying. The audience stared at him in complete bafflement.

Afterwards, Reynolds told Chantal he loved her. She kept protesting, "But I'm married."

Director Norman Jewison, who was our go-to guy for these events, presented Reynolds with his award. As expected, Reynolds gave a short dismissive speech. He had exhausted all his passion on Chantal.

MR. ANN-MARGRET NEEDS A SUIT

In 2009, I invited Swedish singer-actor Ann-Margret to be an honouree. I did this through her agent, Alan Margulies, whom I knew. She was famous as a '60s whip-cracking "sex kitten," but in reality, Ann-Margret was shy. She lived a quiet, private life with Roger Smith, her husband of forty-two years, who was probably best known for the TV series *77 Sunset Strip*, *Hawaiian Eye* and *Mister Roberts*. Smith was no longer the debonair leading man he had once been, however, having contracted a neuromuscular disease that caused him to retire from acting to become his wife's manager and producer.

It took a great deal of persuasion to get Ann-Margret to accept our invitation. The clincher was the prospect of receiving her award from Norman Jewison, who had directed her in *The Cincinnati Kid* with Steve McQueen. Despite her initial hesitation, however, when still-glamorous Ann-Margret did get to Toronto with Roger Smith, she proved to be a trooper, doing all the press interviews with warmth and charm.

I showed her the banquet room at the Four Seasons Hotel, where we had put up massive, black-and-white blowups of film stills from her career: *Pocketful of Miracles*, *Bye Bye Birdie*, *Viva Las Vegas*, *Kitten with a Whip*, *Bus Riley's Back in Town*, *Carnal Knowledge*, *The Cincinnati Kid*, *The Who's Tommy*. She was excited, but there was something else on her mind. She said, "Roger needs a suit."

"What?"

"He didn't bring one."

I took Roger Smith to a menswear store on Bloor Street, Harry Rosen, hoping he had mediocre taste. Of course, he didn't. He picked out a $3,800 Canali suit.

Although the charity founder was annoyed with the bill for the suit, all was forgiven when Ann-Margret made a wonderful speech. She is a true star.

EASY RIDER

Both Peter Fonda and James Earl Jones, who were personal friends, also did a fabulous job. Jones's charities included the children's Make-A-Wish Foundation, while Peter was an active supporter of those with autism and the Special Olympics. His acceptance speech in the Regency Ballroom of the Four Seasons Hotel had many of our guests—including Peter himself—in tears.

"We should be embracing everybody because we all need a hug sometimes. I was in lots of boarding schools, and I got picked on because I was this skinny kid. I befriended this other skinny kid with polio, who also got picked on."

That night, we auctioned off a Harley-Davidson motorcycle, which Peter had signed, for $35,000, along with signed photographs of Peter with their purchasers.

Whenever I take Sloan and Melissa to Los Angeles, we hang out with Peter and his wife Parky. Sloan and Peter have a special chemistry, like some kind of soul connection that's interesting to watch.

STRAIGHT ARROW

In 2011, we honoured Kathleen Turner, a passionate spokesperson for women's health, Planned Parenthood and the Red Cross. I was familiar with Turner's husky voice from my youth, when she did commercials for Arrow shirts. My father and my uncle were so enamoured of her voice that they had tried unsuccessfully to have her do commercials for the women's brand, Arrow Pour Elle, which they marketed. I had met her a couple times at New York parties, where I amused her with my Arrow story, and when I invited her to be an honouree, she replied, "Absolutely." Afterwards, she came to me with a request. "I know this is stupid, and I'm sure you'll say no, but my daughter is an aspiring singer. Would it be okay for her to perform at this gala?"

"Certainly."

Though Turner was delighted by my response, the charity's organizers were furious. "How do you know if she's any good?"

"I don't."

In 1981, Turner had sizzled on the screen in *Body Heat*, and later on the Broadway stage in *Cat on a Hot Tin Roof*. Then, in the 1990s, she had become crippled with rheumatoid arthritis. The medication altered her looks and caused her to gain weight. That, in turn, led to a bout of alcoholism as she sought to deaden her physical and psychological pain.

I always sat in when our celebrities were interviewed by the press. I wanted to make sure the reporters understood why our stars were being honoured, to see they were treated properly and to protect our charity. One crass female reporter asked Turner, "When you remember how you looked in *Body Heat*, and you see yourself in the mirror now, how do you feel?"

Turner replied, "The same way you feel when you look at yourself in the mirror."

That ended that interview. Afterwards, I asked Turner, "Do you want to cancel the rest?"

"Nah, that's just one bad one."

She was such a class act.

At the gala, we showed a compilation of scenes I had made from Turner's movies: *Romancing the Stone*, *Prizzi's Honor*, *The Accidental Tourist*, *Peggy Sue Got Married*. These tributes were always a labour of love. Kathleen Turner was a joy but I was still nervous about the performance of her daughter, Rachel Ann Weiss. The young woman was nervous too—so anxious, in fact, that I half-anticipated disaster. Rachel took her place at the microphone, and I held my breath. She announced, "This is for my mommy." Then she blew the room away with an original composition. Rachel Ann Weiss has since released her first album, *Dear Love*, to positive reviews.

ALIEN INVASION

I had been introduced to Shirley MacLaine when she starred in Garth Drabinsky's solo show *Out There* in 1994. To persuade her to be our 2008 honouree, I met her in Santa Monica's charming Shutters Hotel. MacLaine was frank about her reasons for wanting to do the event: with TIFF going on at the same time, she felt it might give her the opportunity to green-light an obscure film she was having trouble getting produced. As she put it, "I've researched you, and you seem well-connected."

I read the script, and it was one of those alien stories, with which I couldn't help, but at least that possibility had brought her to Toronto.

It soon became clear that MacLaine preferred the company of men to women. I happen to like having women around me, but she regarded them as irrelevant. She was very demanding, and she took a special dislike to my assistant. She didn't want to meet any of the people involved in the charity. She didn't want to be told when to speak. MacLaine was not going to be one of our honourees who made a real connection to the charity and their developmentally challenged clients. She talked mostly about her career, and that was it.

MAGIC CARPET

In 2005, Joey Adler, the head of Diesel Canada located in Montreal, and Samantha Brickman, asked for my help with the founding of their organization and subsequent gala to help distressed children.

Their philosophy was, *Every life is precious, and every individual can make a difference.* I branded their organization ONEXONE, and we launched that fall during the Toronto International Film Festival. The event was hosted by Kate Hudson, who was a friend of Samantha's. Bono attended, as did supermodel Elle Macpherson and singer Chantal Kreviazuk, our performer.

Thanks to Samantha, I became better acquainted with Kate Hudson, while collaborating on her script for the evening. She was very sweet, super-bright, incredibly talented and well aware of her brand. More than that, she had an alchemy that was a mixture of innocence, sexuality and Hollywood glamour. She glowed.

Despite a successful launch, I soon became aware that Samantha and Joey had differing agendas and were at war. There was a falling out, Samantha left the charity she cofounded and I was torn. Samantha was my friend who introduced me to the project but I believed in the cause, and I liked producing the show. I stayed on with Joey. I lost Sam as a friend temporarily and I missed her enthusiasm, but theirs had been a partnership made in hell.

In 2006, the event grew bigger when Matt Damon agreed to host and invited Brad Pitt to attend. Brad was every inch a gracious star, not at all aloof, and willing to pose with anyone who wanted a photo. One of the live auction items was an opportunity to walk the red carpet with Brad and Matt at an *Ocean's Eleven* screening. After that sold for about $100,000, Brad said, "You know what? I can walk the red carpet twice, so let's have another auction for this." He was fun.

To change ONEXONE from a small concert with guest stars into a major celebration of philanthropy, I suggested we should honour celebrities for their charitable work in 2007. Joey agreed.

I had already talked about her charity, the Happy Hearts Fund, with supermodel Petra Nemcova during a New York fashion week. Petra had been caught in the tsunami that struck Thailand in 2004. She had saved herself by clinging to a tree even though her pelvis was broken and she'd suffered severe internal injuries. Tragically, her fiancé, Simon Atlee, a renowned British photographer, had been swept out to sea. She told herself, *I can mourn for the rest of my life, or I can pick myself up and give back.* Petra then used her beauty and her fame to create the Happy Hearts Fund, dedicated to rebuilding safe schools in areas struck by natural disasters.

Petra accepted my invitation to receive an Award of Distinction. Though my friends made sly jokes about my spending so much time with this stunning *Sports Illustrated* model, I adored Petra as a lovely person.

THE HUG

I'd been a fan of Richard Gere ever since I saw him playing a guy who makes a lucrative living as an escort to older women in *American Gigolo.* I admired his style and swagger, the way he dressed and the way he looked. I also knew that he had built a second career as an activist for human rights, for ecological causes and especially for HIV/AIDS awareness. He was also a practising Buddhist. All these things made him a great ONEXONE candidate.

I got the chance to invite him when we were at the Dubai Film Festival in 2006. I took him aside at one of the festival parties and asked if he would be an honouree. Gere introduced me to his assistant and suggested that she set up a meeting for us in New York. Meanwhile, there was still a film festival going on where director Oliver Stone was receiving a lifetime achievement award.

For the award presentation, Gere and Stone, along with other VIPs and members of the jury (which included me) were driven from Dubai into the desert. En route to our venue, I saw buses filled with migrant workers who had been flown in to build Dubai's palaces and hotels. This was disturbing: I knew how little they were paid and the terrible conditions they endured. It amounted almost to a form of slavery, and here I was in my luxury limousine.

Our destination was a stadium in the middle of which a stage floated on a man-made lake. Everything about the stadium was luxurious—even the stadium chairs were upholstered in leather. After a sumptuous dinner we were treated to a spectacular show featuring flame-throwers and galloping white Arabian horses. I was sitting next to Oliver Stone, and we both had the same reaction: "This is over-the-top crazy."

Oliver was called down onto the floating stage to accept his award. After he hauled it back to his seat, we both stared at it, marvelling. It was a massive crystal horse's head, conjuring up the same thought, which we expressed aloud: *"The Godfather!"*

Soon after I returned from Dubai, I met Gere in his New York office, as he had suggested. He was welcoming in every way, even giving me a signed copy of his book of Tibetan photographs. We talked about ONEXONE and he agreed to accept our award. He had one condition.

I held my breath: *A private jet?*

"I want the award to be presented to me by Shilpa Shetty."

Who is Shilpa Shetty? I had the feeling Gere thought his request would be controversial, but I replied, "Absolutely, I love that idea."

On my return to Toronto, everyone at ONEXONE asked the same question: *Who is Shilpa Shetty?*

As I would learn, she was a Bollywood star who had joined with Gere in his HIV/AIDS awareness work. Their cooperation led to an India-wide scandal. Gere is a hugger. While on stage in New Delhi, where he and Shilpa were teaching safe sex to truckers, Gere had given her a bend-over-backward hug topped off by a kiss. This public display had caused a firestorm—literally. Indian fundamentalists had burned Shilpa's posters.

After ONEXONE flew Shilpa Shetty and her mother to Toronto,

I dropped by the Royal York Hotel to give her the script. Even wearing UGGs and sweatpants, Shilpa was ravishing. Later that evening, when she presented Gere's award, they hugged and kissed again. This time, the audience cheered with approval.

For the 2007 ONEXONE gala, Matt Damon again invited a buddy, Ben Affleck this time, to cohost. This time I wanted to take the event to another level: I sold a network on the idea of airing a 90-minute special to be shot at Toronto's newly opened opera house, the Four Seasons Centre for the Performing Arts. As I envisioned it, we would have a glamorous dinner on stage, followed by speeches and a concert, which I would direct from a camera truck. Thanks to Matt Damon's drawing power, we were able to attract Venezuelan bombshell Shakira and Haitian rapper Wyclef Jean.

The Four Seasons Centre, designed by Jack Diamond, was a magnificent, modern, musical palace. The opera's first artistic director, Richard Bradshaw (who tragically died not long after it opened), had spent months with acousticians fine-tuning the hall so that if, say, Ben Heppner were singing on stage, he wouldn't need a mike.

For our gala, Wyclef moved in his huge orchestra. When my wife and a couple of friends joined me for a rehearsal, the music was so loud we were sure the lighting fixtures would fall, chairs would explode, eardrums would bleed. I could imagine Bradshaw in his grave with his hands over his ears, as Shakira and Wyclef rocked his palace. I was concerned. Those running the opera house were concerned too. "Oh my God, this will not do!"

I could barely understand Wyclef's heavy Haitian patois. I tried to tell him, "You don't need to have the volume up that loud in this place."

He would agree, then run through a sound check with Shakira that was just as loud as before. Wyclef told me his Haitian version of "You know what you need to do, so let me do what I need to do."

On the night of the concert, Wyclef and Shakira performed "Hips

Don't Lie," in which Shakira, a tiny bundle of energy, moved her body as if it were connected by elastic bands. Wyclef did one song that lasted almost an hour, which threatened to tear the place apart, but he had the audience on its feet, dancing. My crew and I were in the camera truck: even with the volume turned down the sound was still off the dial. I guess having 1,200 people inside, sucking up vibrations, must have helped, because Wyclef provided a great show, and we weren't sued for damages.

Once again, behind the scenes, there was a battle brewing unknown to me. Things were going too well. After the enormously successful gala concluded, things boiled over. Joey, who was obsessive about control, became extraordinarily concerned about the ownership of the television special, which I had produced. The terms had been spelled out in a contract she approved: the television show was owned, title and copyright, by the ONEXONE Foundation. Joey couldn't understand that. Nor could she understand that the TV show was a one-shot deal, with no marketability outside of Canada.

By the night of the show, Joey wasn't talking to me, without my knowing why. She'd gone silent, while I was busy with practicalities. Days later, she accused me of stealing it, as if this were something I would own and could sell for millions. Lawyers were involved, and Joey insisted, "I want final cut." Her minions, with whom she surrounded herself, were like a Greek chorus supporting her. Who steals a television show? Did they think I was planning to sell DVDs from my trunk? Oy.

I had no quarrel with her wanting to see the final cut. The show was about the foundation, and when I wrote it, I made sure Joey had a starring role. Visually, it looked glamorous and beautiful. All our stars had praised her charity. The TV special was her fabulous vehicle that would take ONEXONE from a tent to the big time. She just didn't realize it. I was now thinking I should have exited stage left with Samantha Brickman two years earlier.

Joey was tight-lipped when she came to the editing room. I ran the show for her and she managed to say, "Fine." It was ready to air, but by this time Joey had caused so much friction that the network was nervous about running it without her signed approval and was holding back the last production payment. This was so ironic. During our three-year relationship, Joey had talked endlessly about integrity, how important it was and how some people had none. Now this.

While all this was going on, my mentor, Dusty Cohl, had been in failing health. One day, I brought him to the camera truck while we were shooting. He met Joey and afterwards he warned me, with his usual acuity, "Be careful, kid. That woman's desire for glory will collide with her desire to give back, and you'll be caught in the middle."

Months later, just before Christmas, I went to see Dusty at the Princess Margaret Hospital, where he was being treated for colon cancer. As we chatted, I told him the whole story, along with my concern about whether the show would air. Dusty said, "Okay, kid," and then he did this Dusty thing. He called Ivan Fecan, head of the network, whom he knew very well, and he said, "This is a dying man's request. Please make sure that Barry's protected here."

It was Dusty to the rescue once again, with almost his last breath. Though I had been sitting beside him when he made the call, I still didn't know if I would get paid.

I was in bed at 11:30 on Christmas Eve when the phone rang. My wife said, "It's Dusty."

He asked, "Did you get the cheque, kid?"

"Yes I did."

"Come down and show me."

"Dusty, it's 11:30 p.m."

"Come and talk to me."

I put my coat on over my pyjamas. I drove to the hospital, and I managed to slip past the security guard.

Dusty said, "Show me the cheque."

I showed him.

He nodded. "Good."

I resigned from ONEXONE. In my letter to the board, I said, in effect, "I wish you success. I'm proud of the work we did together. I need to go."

Matt Damon also left eventually. Though ONEXONE still carries on in some quieter form, in my view, it went from being the star attraction gala at the film festival to one last glorious climax with the Four Seasons show. It never had a gala on that same scale again.

DUSTY: EXIT STAGE LEFT

Dusty Cohl died on January 11, 2008. He was seventy-eight. One of my first phone calls was to Ivan Fecan. In reply, he told me, "You and I will always be friends." And we are.

In his gentle, dynamic, outrageous way, Dusty had changed the face of entertainment in Toronto, which meant he had reinvented the city itself.

Tributes poured in.

Movie director Ted Kotcheff, who first met Dusty when they were kids at Camp Naivelt, recalled that Dusty had been expelled from this mostly Jewish Communist summer camp for allegedly being a Trotskyite: "He was amusing and totally adorable, the most lovable man I'd ever met. And he was exactly like that decades later when we reconnected."

Wayne Clarkson, a former TIFF director, said, "Quite simply, Dusty put Toronto on the showbiz map."

Helga Stephenson, another former TIFF director, remarked,

"Dusty took the boring out of being Canadian. And he took care of a lot of people."

Attorney Edward Greenspan, a great friend of Dusty's, added, "He was an original—unorthodox, free-thinking, genuine, creative, eccentric."

Piers Handling, a TIFF festival CEO recalled, "The key point about Dusty was that he set a tone for this festival that set it apart from all the others. If European festivals were stuffy black-tie affairs, Toronto was going to be the opposite—irreverent. With his cowboy hat and T-shirts, he made a fashion statement, announcing who and what we were—rebels."

Bill Marshall, a festival founder with Dusty, said, "There would be no festival without Dusty. Going to Cannes with Dusty was like going with Princess Diana."

Toronto Star movie critic Ron Base, also speaking of Cannes, remembered, "Dusty would plunk himself down, and before you knew it, the most amazing assortment of people joined him—movie stars, directors, journalists, starlets, a movable feast."

Movie critic Roger Ebert, recalled, "One day in 1977, when I was a stranger at the Cannes Film Festival, I was crossing the famous terrace of the Carlton Hotel, when I was summoned by name to the table of a man with a black beard, wearing blue jeans, a Dudley Do-Right T-shirt and a black cowboy hat studded with stars and pins. How did he know who I was? He knew who everybody was. One way you knew you were a friend was when Dusty honoured you with a Dusty Pin, a silver hat with a star on it. Rule was, wear it at film festivals. At Cannes and Sundance, even on years Dusty wasn't there, I spotted them on studio heads Michael Barker and Harvey Weinstein and half the members of the North American press corps. When Dusty took a year off from Cannes, the Carlton Hotel purchased a full-page ad in a festival daily, showing only a cowboy hat and a cigar, with the caption, 'We miss you.'"

On February 15, 2008, Eddie Greenspan and I coproduced a memorial for Dusty at the Elgin Theatre. It was awash in Schwartz's smoked meat and Crown Royal, Dusty's sustenance, along with music and speeches. In my video tribute, friends and admirers shared their memories.

"Dusty could speak to street-sweepers and kings."

"He gave out more cigars and poured more Crown Royal than the Bronfmans."

"He told it as it was, and as it should be."

"He defined 'come as you are.'"

"We all participated in the magic he created."

"Everything was first-rate with Dusty, including Dusty."

Together, Eddie and I tearfully wrote the main eulogy entitled, DUSTY COHL: EXIT STAGE LEFT, which I delivered.

In vintage Hollywood style, Dusty didn't go to see you, you went to see him. You never needed an elevator to find him. The unassuming impresario took his meetings on park benches, in diners, and occasionally perched like a Dalai Lama on that huge rock in Yorkville. Many wondered what he did for a living and some even accused him of being a socialist. If that was true, he was the only socialist I knew that asked me for upgrade coupons on Air Canada . . .

I once asked Dusty if he ever imagined that the Toronto International Film Festival he helped create would grow to be the world's biggest, and his response was classic: 'No. Let's go get lunch.'

In the last decade of his life, Dusty declared that he had played out his role of the creator. He would dedicate every minute of his time to helping those he loved to succeed . . . In between those 'projects' as he

called them, he meticulously scheduled time with his friends during the week and his granddaughters on the weekend. His ability to power breakfast, lunch and dinner was simply unmatched by even Hollywood standards . . . You kind of wish people like Dusty would live forever and then when you replay the memories, you realize they do.

It's been eight years since Dusty's death, and I still haven't accepted the fact that this fantastic guy is no longer with us. With me.

Chapter Eleven

MORE BOLDFACE: NAME DROPPING FOR THE LOVE OF IT

I WILL LICK YOUR SHOE

My friendship with Samantha Brickman had gone into hiatus after she was essentialy pushed out of ONEXONE and I had stayed on. I wanted to repair the damage. In 2008, I invited her for a drink, during which I told her, "Samantha, I know you're upset with me, but I have a special drink to serve you. It's called Redemption."

"What do you mean?"

"I've been hired to produce a major fundraiser next year for Richard Branson's charity foundation, Virgin Unite. Why don't you coproduce with me?"

So that's what we did. Samantha's friend Kate Hudson came in. Petra Nemcova came in, and, of course, we had Richard Branson. He was sensational and unforgettable.

The president of American Express was eager to meet him. I said,

"Richard, would you do me a favour and say hello to the president of American Express?"

"She's one of our sponsors?"

"Right."

Branson walked over to Denise, got down on his hands and knees, then licked her shoe. Literally. She loved it.

He and I worked together on another event, in which he was once again everything you would expect of Richard Branson—rebel, pioneer, reckless genius and completely unpredictable. At a press conference, an enterprising guy asked him, "With all the media here, what's the best way for me to get noticed?"

Branson picked up a pitcher of water and poured it on the guy's head. "Tomorrow morning you'll be in the newspapers with Richard Branson pouring water on your head."

Sure enough, this picture made the papers the next day.

"HELLO, PUSSY. IT'S HELEN"

Malcolm Forbes's son, Chris (Skip), used to borrow his father's vintage yacht and take guests sailing in New York Harbour every July 4. It was on one of these excursions that I met Helen Gurley Brown and her husband, David Brown, in 2002.

Shortly after I boarded, I saw Helen and David sitting by themselves, which seemed odd for a couple belonging to both New York and Hollywood royalty. In 1962, Helen had became a household name with her non-fiction bestseller, *Sex and the Single Girl*, in which she told a shocked world that it was okay for unmarried women to have a sex life. She parlayed her notoriety into the job of international editor of *Cosmopolitan* magazine. I recognized David as the producer of blockbusters like *The Sting* and *Jaws*.

After I introduced myself, I mentioned somewhere in our chatter that I had written a book on entertainment marketing called *Selling the Sizzle*. This caught Helen's interest. "I'm supposed to give a lecture about that for my alma mater, Brown University. Can you help me?"

We exchanged letters and emails. Helen would also leave voice-mails on my home phone, "Hello, Pussy. It's Helen, I want to thank you for your last email." I assured Melissa that "Pussy" was for Helen a casually friendly form of address. Melissa nevertheless adopted a certain tone when she told me, "Pussy, Helen called again."

The Browns' marriage was remarkable. Here were these super-wealthy people, living at the epicentre of the New York and Hollywood firmaments, who adored each other. Helen worked in the Revlon building; David worked in an office tower around the corner on Broadway. At the end of each day, she would meet him at his office, they would walk home together, and she would make dinner.

I visited Helen's office for the first time to interview her for a film I was making on *Vanity Fair* writer Dominick Dunne. She stood in the doorway of her reception room, wearing a see-through negligee and called out to me, "Barry, I'm just finishing my yoga. I'll be one minute."

Helen's office was entirely decorated in leopard. Thankfully, by the time I was ushered inside, she had changed into a gorgeous Chanel suit. As I would learn, by this time her role as *Cosmopolitan*'s international editor was essentially as a figurehead. Listening to her editorial rundown was hilarious. She would sit at her desk, with various *Cosmo* editions fanned around her, and dictate comments into a tape recorder: "Serbian edition, page seventy-eight: If you're going to show a man's ass, show his whole ass. British edition, page forty-two: If you're going to write about oral sex, make sure you know how to do it."

Helen was over-the-top outrageous. David Brown, in contrast, was a kind and thoughtful gentleman in an entertainment world that was full of rogues. Both have now passed away: David, age ninety-three, in 2010; Helen, age ninety, in 2012.

KID NOTORIOUS

Robert Evans is one those extraordinary Hollywood producers who is one of a kind.

He arrived in Hollywood with the dream of escaping his New York ragtrade roots by becoming an actor. His looks were pure Hollywood, tanned and stylish in a Cary Grant meets Clark Gable kind of way. His rise to prominence was a Hollywood cliché. The legendary actress Norma Shearer discovered him and the Paramount mogul Charles Bluhdorn made him. He went onto become an uber-producer and studio head responsible for epic films like *Love Story* and *The Godfather*. Years later, he would be the subject of one of the greatest biographical documentaries ever made, *The Kid Stays in the Picture*.

When I asked him to be in my film, *The Last Mogul*, he invited me to his home behind the Beverly Hills Hotel. The house, once owned by Greta Garbo, was simply amazing: it came complete with staggering art and a butler named English.

Evans took all of his meetings in a mink-lined bed overshadowed by a massive photograph of two women performing oral sex on each other. The photograph was personally dedicated, "Bob, I always love dining with you, Helmut Newton." Wild!

My shoot with him lasted nine hours. He was full of stories and I adored him. While I was flying home, I hatched a plan to produce a one-man show on Broadway, by, with and about Evans. It couldn't miss. With enthusiastic support from Evans himself, I subsequently flew to New York to pitch it to Broadway producer Scott Zeiger. He loved the idea and tentatively approved the budget, but he first wanted his production executive, Hailey Lustig, to meet with Evans at his home.

Before that happened, Evans leaked news of the impending production to the *New York Times* and they ran a story. I now had to
make this work. I warned the often outrageous romantic that he had
to be on his best behaviour with Hailey.

The meeting was pure Fellini. Of course, he was in bed in his
pajamas sipping his customized house drink (a souped-up Cosmo).
At first he could not have been more charming and elegant, but
of course the conversation gradually took an outrageous turn. At
one point he showed us the collection of Polaroids of anonymous
vaginas, all of which he claimed to have "known." *Oy.*

At dinner later at the Palm, Hailey thanked me for the meeting
of her life and said, "You know we aren't doing this show." *Onwards.*

I brought Evans to Toronto during the film festival as part of
my work with the Best Buddies charity. Like Reynolds before him,

he became enamoured of one of the guests, a glamorous blonde socialite, and insisted that I seat them together.

Evans, as it turned out, was a practical joker. Without my knowing it, he hatched a plan with the socialite to tease her husband. They took off in the middle of the dinner, climbed into her Porsche (with difficulty, as she later reported, because Evans was well into his seventies) then went for a drive. When they returned, they expected there to be some buzz about their disappearance. In fact, the socialite's husband hadn't noticed (or cared) that they went missing.

Later that night, I again found myself in his bed at The Four Seasons Hotel taking a picture of him with Liam Neeson. He had an affectionate nickname for the Irish actor, in appreciation of the Irish actor's alleged physical attributes. He called him "The Cock."

THE LADY IS A DAME

On September 10, 2012, The Stratford Festival honoured Dame Maggie Smith with its annual Legacy Award. Smith had graced the stages of Stratford during four seasons, where she gave some of the most memorable performances in the Festival's history, including Cleopatra in *Antony and Cleopatra*, Rosalind in *As You Like It*, Beatrice in *Much Ado About Nothing*, Mistress Overdone in *Measure for Measure*, Queen Elizabeth in *Richard III*, Titania/Hippolyta in *A Midsummer Night's Dream* and Lady Macbeth.

The glamorous evening was held at The Royal York Hotel—which seemed like a good fit, given its long history serving the royals—and was elegantly hosted by *Q* personality Jian Ghomeshi, just two years prior to his fall from grace. Everything about this evening was going to be great. As producer and cochair of the gala, I was thrilled when Christopher Plummer, who had been honoured with the award the year before, agreed to present the award to Dame Maggie.

Now, here is where the Downton Abbey crumbles. Given that the gala was being held at The Royal York Hotel, it made infinite sense to book a suite for Dame Maggie at the hotel so that her gala was only an elevator passage away from her room. Good thinking, right? No.

The dame checked in to the hotel, had a one look at her room, and had a royal meltdown. Now, I can't blame her. The Royal York, although grand fifty years ago and perhaps has been renovated in the last decade or so, is old, damp and vast. You can bowl in the hallways and you have to plug your iPhone into the gas lamps. I once stayed there and at 3 a.m. that morning, there was a knock at my door and it was Louis Riel.

Back to the story. Stratford's lovely Rachel Smith-Spencer, who was handling Dame Maggie, reached me in panic as I was sipping a Scotch at the bar at Nota Bene following the TIFF film screening. Yes, this was during TIFF, and the entire city and every hotel was booked solid. Rachel was apoplectic: "Barry, I beg of you, find a room. She will kill me and will not unpack her bags."

I called David Mounteer, the great manager of the Hazelton Hotel and a client, to save me. He said Madonna was coming in and had all the suites. That was until I mentioned who my client was. He went to the Royal York himself to get her.

On the evening of the gala, I was introduced to Dame Maggie as the man who saved her life. Her response: "Barry, my dear boy, that hotel is like checking into *The Shining*. Permanently."

PORTRAIT OF A LADY AND HER LORD

Barbara Amiel and Conrad Black—now Lord Black of Crossharbour and Lady Black—have turned up at intervals through my life in minor ways.

I remember Dusty Cohl regaling me about the strange eccentricity Barbara had contracted after she moved to England. According to Dusty, within a week, she had developed an upper-crust English accent and had become quite dismissive of him. Dusty got a taste of this when she accompanied him to New York in 1977 for a story about the film *Outrageous*, which he had produced.

I, too, number myself among the dismissed. When Melissa and I shared a table with Barbara, Robert Lantos, TV executive Moses Znaimer and TV personality Seamus O'Regan, among others, at the Giller Prize, a literary awards dinner, Barbara ignored everyone except Moses, to whom she passed notes like a schoolgirl. Lord Black, by the way, having been incarcerated at the Coleman Federal Correctional Complex in Florida, was absent.

When Conrad and I were on better terms, we used to have lunch once or twice a year at Auberge du Pommier, an upscale French restaurant. Our conversations, sometimes heated, dealt with politics and the media. Conrad is a smart man but fatally self-absorbed. Perhaps he needed that kind of dermis to survive what he refers to as the time he spent as "a guest of the United States Government." Somehow, he made the best of it by becoming a model prisoner and, on his release, carefully rebuiding his brand.

Before he started his prison sentence, on the advice of Eddie Greenspan, he generously donated to a project that involved me building a cinema at Sick Kids. Humourously, he made sure I knew he was not happy with the architect whom he called an "arriviste." I did admire his vocabulary.

Our lunches were consistent in two ways. I always had to wait for the Lord to arrive, and he never reached for the cheque. I decided, okay, maybe it's worth the price as a piece of theatre or perhaps one day I would make a film about him.

I've interviewed Conrad for two of my documentaries, one on Eddie Greenspan, who was his defence attorney, and one for a film based on the book *Churchill and the Jews: A Lifelong Friendship* by Sir Martin Gilbert. Conrad is an astute historian. For the Churchill film, which I called *An Unlikely Obsession*, I had to fly to Conrad's Palm Beach home, then still in his possession. He had already completed one stint in prison, and had been released on bail, pending an appeal of his sentence.

When I arrived at the estate, a housekeeper was walking Barbara Amiel's dogs around the grand circular driveway leading to their sprawling contemporary home. They were big ferocious-looking Stormtrooper dogs, not your standard poodles. As the gates opened, they came toward me, looking ferocious.

I had the opportunity to take in the inside décor as I waited for Conrad to make his entrance. The house was classic Palm Beach: white furniture, white carpets and elegant dashes of floral fabric, along with sensational artwork. There were hundreds of history books in the library, including many first editions. In the hallway outside the living room was an American flag from FDR's Oval Office, purchased at auction, and other memorabilia. A tunnel that Conrad had constructed gave him direct access under a road from the house to the beach. Meanwhile, the dogs that had shown their distaste for me outside were now prowling around inside, having caught my scent.

I had actually visited the house once before to discuss another film project. On that occasion, the gates to the estate wouldn't open when my wife dropped me off. Conrad himself came down in the pouring rain to let me in. He was soaked but gracious, telling Melissa at the wheel of the jeep, "You may not have the grandest carriage in Palm Beach, but you are the most beautiful chauffeur."

Later, when I was sitting in Conrad's living room, I admired the enigmatic painting of a woman, standing in front of a building, probably in New York. It was raining, and her face was turned away as if she didn't want to be recognized. When he finally got off a long call with Brian Mulroney and I asked him about it, he told me it was by the Canadian artist, Tony Scherman. Then, he had laid down a challenge. "Barry, if you can identify the woman in the painting, you can have it."

After a period of amused anticipation, Conrad delivered his big reveal, "It's Greta Garbo."

During this visit, while my crew and I were waiting for Conrad— and waiting and waiting—my director of photography also noticed the Scherman portrait. "What a beautiful painting!"

I told him. "Here's what we're going to do. When Lord Black comes in, I want you to point to the picture and repeat what you just said. He's going to reply, 'If you can tell me who it is, I'll give it to you.' You're going to ponder for a while, and then you're going to say, 'It's Greta Garbo.'"

Eventually, Lord Black made his appearance, thinner since his stint in prison, but well-tailored in a blazer with the shiny brass buttons, pinstriped shirt and good shoes with no socks, to indicate this was casual.

He welcomed the crew and we settled in for the interview when my director of photography exclaimed on cue, "Lord Black, excuse me, but that's a wonderful painting you have there."

"Thank you,"said Conrad. "It's a Tony Scherman."

"It's fascinating."

A pause, and then, "Do you know who the woman is?"

I waited anxiously for the rest.

Pleased once again to be a man of taste and knowledge, Conrad prompted, "If you can tell me who the woman is, you can have the painting."

Yes!

My cameraman appeared to consider the matter. "Let's see, that's New York, perhaps in the sixties or maybe the seventies? That building . . . hmm . . . looks to me like the Upper West Side. Uh, let's see . . . could that be Greta Garbo?"

Conrad turned white and began to stutter. He was so clearly anguished that finally I confessed. To Conrad's credit, he laughed, and then he gave me a provocative interview about Churchill, as I knew he would.

CUE TO Q

Petra Nemcova introduced me to legendary humanitarian Quincy Jones. Now eighty-two, Quincy has received a record seventy-nine Grammy nominations and won twenty-seven, including a 1991 Grammy Legend Award.

Quincy lives in Bel Air, the old money part of L.A., high up in a gated compound, reached by a drive under a canopy of beautiful trees, decorated with multicoloured lanterns. Once inside, you find your-self in a Shangri-La of music and luxury. The scale is immense with full-grown indoor trees and glass walls that showcase a billion-dollar view that overlooks everything and everyone, including the property owned by his neighbour, Zsa Zsa Gabor.

Quincy's cream-coloured living room with its immense fireplace is filled with overstuffed furniture, an ebony baby grand, silver-framed portraits of Michael Jackson, Oprah Winfrey, Bill Clinton, Frank Sinatra. Quincy-composed music plays in a loop in the background, and his staff always has fresh tropical juice and a platter of guacamole and crispy tortilla chips ready for his guests.

The screenroom is old Hollywood. The curtain across the screen is a poster from *The Color Purple* and the seating includes a few leather directors' chairs from movies Quincy has scored. Down the grand staircase to the lower level are private guest rooms, a well-stocked wine cellar, and walls covered in gold and platinum records from albums Quincy has produced, including Michael Jackson's epic *Off the Wall*. You meet Quincy for breakfast when he wakes up at two or three in afternoon.

Quincy taught me one of life's great lessons. Putting his hand affectionately on my knee, he told me, "Listen, laugh, love and give back." After that, he took me to a marathon birthday party for the founder of the *Girls Gone Wild* video franchise. Go figure.

On one of my visits with Quincy, he introduced me to a young Cuban prodigy, Alfredo Rodriguez. Quincy was really astute when it comes to discovering talent and he had a winner in Alfredo. He had him play on the baby grand in his breathtaking great room and I was blown away. Quincy then told me he had a treat for me. We were going to go to the famed Capitol Records recording studio in Los Angeles to record eight tracks with Alfredo. I was going to watch Quincy direct Alfredo in a studio where everyone from Frank Sinatra, Neil Diamond and Elton John to the Beatles and the Beastie Boys had laid down their work. Off we went late at night in a limousine packed with snacks that included an assortment of Italian tuna salads and dry seaweed chips. Quincy's diet was meticulously monitored by health-care professionals under instruction to ensure his longevity. He liked to brag that a team of doctors in Switzerland had a plan to keep him alive well beyond a hundred.

As we entered the studio, I asked Alfredo what he was feeling at that moment, given that he was about to record his compositions under the direction of Quincy Jones. Alfredo was giddy. Just six months earlier Quincy had discovered him as a virtual unknown at the Montreux Jazz Festival and now he was going to make Alfredo famous.

For the next three hours, I watched in awe as Alfredo recorded track after track with passion. After each track, Quincy gave him notes and then he would skilfully direct the sound engineers on the final mix. I was witnessing the work of a man who had brilliantly produced albums for Michael Jackson and Frank Sinatra among others. It was a thrilling experience. At the end of the session Quincy handed me a CD of the tracks and said, "Something to groove to."

Alfredo is now a sought-after Grammy-nominated artist who recorded with Chick Corea and has played jazz festivals around the world and Carnegie Hall.

I am now collaborating with Q on a docu-concert about Marvin Gaye. There is no better partner than Quincy as he has the incomparable skills to identify a stunning new generation of talent to cover Marvin's music for the film. When we meet to discuss the film, he loves showing me clips of his latest protegees and they are all staggering. One of his discoveries is a young British vocalist named Jacob Collier who layers his own vocals with astonishing result. And another ingenue is Grace, an Aussie that will give Adele a run for her money. At eighty-two, this man is so extraordinarily inspiring, I am fortunate for every minute of his time. On a recent visit, he enquired as to how my mother was doing knowing that she had been ill. The one thing to know about Q is how fiercely proud and protective he is of his family. I was in tears as I explained how my mom was fighting to stay strong and independent. He hugged me and said, "Son, if you want to see God laugh, tell him your plans. You can't produce your mother's life like a film. Love her. Protect her. Honour her. As long as possible." My plan exactly.

THE CHRISTIANS, THE JEWS AND HARRY BELAFONTE

The Canadian Council of Christians and Jews is a post–World War II group founded to combat anti-Semitism. Its members believe that prejudice in a multicultural world is about more than Christians and Jews. For their sixtieth anniversary in 2008, they decided to change their name to the Canadian Centre for Diversity (CCD), and to celebrate the change with a fundraising dinner at which they would present an inaugural International Diversity Award. As the event's hired producer, I suggested honouring Harry Belafonte. Though some board members considered Belafonte to be too political, the head of the organization, Amanda Sherrington, endorsed my argument that diversity really meant diversity.

I brought in Harry Belafonte through Michael Cohl, who was making a film about his life. And just as the newly minted CCD was nervous about Belafonte, so it turned out, was Belafonte nervous about the CCD. His people told me, "Harry will do this for you, and he'll give some interviews, but he doesn't want to be approached by people at the dinner."

That was a problem, because at a non-profit gala, people think they own the celebrity—*Hi, Mr. Belafonte, may I take a picture with you? Will you sign my program?*

Still, I acceded to his request and positioned security in front and behind Belafonte at the head table. This was uncomfortable, given that he was representing diversity, but Belafonte was so elegant, and then so eloquent with one of those "I Have a Dream" speeches about his life, that the evening was a true game-changer for the organization.

The following year, I suggested honouring the three kids who starred in the Academy Award–winner *Slumdog Millionaire*. Everyone thought this a great idea until two weeks before the gala when a scandal broke out. Although all kinds of money supposedly had been going into these kids' education, it turned out that they were not attending school. Had something happened to the money, or were the kids skipping? Under the circumstances, Amanda was unhappy about presenting them with the Emerging Leadership Award, which had already been announced. I argued, "I'm hearing different versions of this story. No one seems to know what is actually happening."

I hired an Indian film crew, none of whom could speak much English. Because the kids were not fully bilingual either, I had to hire a translator as well. I was directing from Toronto, which meant getting up at 3 a.m. because of the time difference. I directed operations from my bathroom, using my cell on speakerphone, in order not to wake up Melissa and Sloan. I would tell them, "Okay, kids, I want you to say, 'Thank you, Centre for Diversity.' No, that's not quite right. Say it again."

We ended up with a nice warm tribute, so everything worked out yet again.

Another year, we honoured filmmaker Deepa Mehta for her work in telling the story of India. It was an easy evening for me as her friend and the gala's producer, and the CCD was happy as well.

Deepa hated *Slumdog Millionaire*, by the way. She described it as exploitative bullshit.

MASTER FRESH PRINCE:
TEACHING PRINCE CHARLES TO SPIN

I have met different members of the Royal Family, and some of those connected to them, over the years. Sarah, Duchess of York, was an honouree at one of the charity galas I produced. She had weathered some bad press—an unfortunate television venture and then the so-called "cash for access" scandal—and there was worse to come. But she had also served as fundraiser and patron for many charities, especially those involving children and cancer. She was a wonderful recipient: open, glamorous and with no royal airs.

The British tabloids' relentless focus on the royals' personal lives distracts attention from their good work. Too few people know the full extent of Prince Charles's public service. Under the Prince of Wales' Charitable Foundation, he directly and indirectly assists in raising around $200 million each year in the UK for his core interests, which include disadvantaged youth, the arts, responsible business, improving the built environment, heritage regeneration and environmental sustainability.

In 2014, Prince Charles founded The Prince's Charities Canada (PCC), patterned on his existing UK organization. Its aim was to use business resources to tackle barriers to youth employment in at-risk neighbourhoods.

Galen Weston, who had played polo with Prince Charles, agreed to assume responsibility for setting up the Canadian branch of the charity. Its president and CEO was Amanda Sherrington, with whom I'd worked at the Canadian Centre for Diversity. It was because of her that I was invited to become a founding PCC board member.

I met Prince Charles for the first time during his 2012 official visit to Toronto, when he toured neighbourhoods at risk. It was my role to join a few selected executives showing him the wonderful Regent Park neighbourhood organization, UforChange, which provided

youths from ages sixteen to twenty-nine with free professional mentoring and counselling to develop their creative talents as actors, play-
wrights, filmmakers, photographers and fashion designers. During
the tour, I taught the prince how to spin records in order to be a competent disc jockey. He was warm and enthusiastic and we ended up
with a photo of me in headphones while he mixed and spun his way
to becoming Grandmaster Prince Charles. Since he had been briefed,
he knew my name, and since I had been briefed, I knew the protocol,
which meant not touching the prince or putting out my hand unless
he offered his first.

I met Prince Charles for the second time in 2013 at his official
London residence, Clarence House. There were a dozen of us, all
business people and PCC board members, there to present ideas
about moving his charitable work forward. He greeted me with an

amused, "You're the man who taught me how to be a DJ. How's that
going for you?"

We sat in his dining room, which had been visited by royals as
far back as George III, eating shortbread and drinking tea, while
Prince Charles questioned each of us about creating opportunities
for Canada's troubled youth. What would a "second chance" mean to
them? What kind of support and mentoring would bring this about?
Prince Charles's UK charities provided an admirable model, having
created hundreds of thousands of jobs for homeless kids, poor kids
and even women with criminal records.

I met Prince Charles for the third time in Winnipeg in 2014. He
shook my hand, then apologized for having a horrible cold.

I asked, "Then, why did you shake my hand?"

We both laughed.

I tell everyone that Prince Charles is a warmer and more complex person than the press would have you believe. Too many still judge him in light of the troubled years with Princess Diana, or as the fanatic who talks to trees, or as the monarch's progeny perpetually in waiting to be king. I now see him as a smart and well-educated person with a keen knowledge of political affairs and a strong sense of purpose.

Two years before meeting Prince Charles, I had met Queen Elizabeth at a lunch at Toronto's Pinewood Studios. She was terrific, as everyone says, but now I would ask her, "Why are you still holding onto that crown? Beyond being charming and competent, your son has proven that he deserves to be king."

"YOUR TENT HAS A HURRICANE IN IT"

I'm sure my parents made charitable donations, but we did not have the means to make it a central preoccupation. My own good fortune has made me want to give back. I'm a hands-on action guy. I didn't want to involve myself in good works that would take forever, or sit on do-nothing committees and boards, or sell tables, or simply sign cheques. Instead, I wanted to create a project of my own, to have some control, and to make a big difference right away. I also liked to connect philanthropy to my passion, which is entertainment.

In the summer of 2006, I was visiting a friend in the hospital when I passed a kid in a room who was fumbling with a DVD player so he could watch a movie. That had me thinking: Why should a kid trapped in a hospital be prevented from escaping into the world of film? Why should that kid have to squint into a small screen? Surely, when a kid is ill and separated from friends and family, that's exactly when escape is most needed.

I called Mary Jo Haddad, then president and CEO of the Toronto Hospital for Sick Children, and I told her, "I have a forty-eight-hour offer for you. I've never been to Sick Kids. I won't even drive by it because I'm afraid of hospitals. I'm betting the hospital doesn't have a movie theatre, so if you give me the green light within forty-eight hours, I'll build you one. You don't know me, but if you did, you'd know that if you say yes, I will get this done."

She was understandably surprised. "I'll have to get back to you. Why forty-eight hours?"

"I don't want any red tape, and I don't want any yellow tape. I don't want to have to deal with a bureaucracy or to report to anyone. I'll raise every dollar, and I'll work within the rules laid down by the administration. You'll have your theatre by next spring, and we'll open with *Shrek the Third*, but I'm serious about the forty-eight hours. After that, this idea is dead."

Ms. Haddad did return my call within forty-eight hours. "We have the space for you."

It was a lecture hall on the second floor of Sick Kids. I checked it out and we decided it was a go.

On September 12, we held a news conference attended by director Norman Jewison and theatre builder Daniel Greenglass. We unveiled our plans, and singer Chantal Kreviazuk performed. We promised to build a 230-seat, $1 million theatre with both a digital and 35mm projection system and Dolby surround sound. It would feature new releases from major Hollywood studios, with free admission for patients and their families. Movies would also be broadcast via closed-circuit TV to kids who couldn't leave their beds. The press conference was attended by kids who were patients in the hospital, many in wheelchairs or hooked up to breathing machines, making even the announcement a moving experience.

Now all I had to do was raise the $1 million. I told ten friends, "I want one hundred thousand dollars from each of you."

Five were a snap, but raising the second $500,000 was tough. It also involved me with the bureaucratic crap that I had tried to avoid.

The administrators of the foundation who raised money for the hospital and the administrators who ran the hospital, didn't like a donor who would control every aspect of the project. I hadn't anticipated this, nor had I anticipated that this wonderful endeavour would be so difficult to execute. The foundation people were angry that I was not hiring their costly "approved" suppliers. At one point, the foundation's head phoned me to say, "Barry, we'd like to be in your tent, but your tent has a hurricane in it."

I said, "Then get the hell out of my tent. I'm getting the job done." And I did.

On May 18, 2007, I experienced one of the great moments of my life: walking this very special red carpet, cutting the ribbon to the theatre, then seeing the faces of the children light up as they escaped momentarily from the misery of their illness into the movie magic of *Shrek the Third*, given to us by Ellis Jacob at Cineplex and Jeffrey Katzenberg of DreamWorks. Petra Nemcova, who adores children, came to Toronto to cut the ribbon with me. Eddie Greenspan, who was one of the donors and attended the opening, took me aside. "I know you're thrilled because you built this theatre and you've given these kids a beautiful fantasy, but the only thought in the minds of the adults here is, *What's going on between Barry and Petra?*"

A year later, our close friends and philanthropists Myrna and John Daniels gave us a wonderful gift and named the theatre the Daniels Hollywood Theatre.

Chapter Twelve

HOT DOCS:
ALL DRESSED

KIDNAPPED IN NEWARK

I was intrigued by comedian Jackie Mason, rebel son of a rabbi, who became a '60s household name as a frequent guest on the *The Ed Sullivan Show*. Sullivan, like Johnny Carson decades later, had the power to catapult relatively unknown entertainers into mainstream superstardom, as he proved with both Elvis Presley and the Beatles.

Mason, by the way, described the Beatles as, "Four kids in search of a voice, who need haircuts." His style—ridicule, much like that of Don Rickles—often provoked controversy. In 1964, during one of his appearances on *The Ed Sullivan Show*, Sullivan gave Mason a two-finger signal, indicating that he had only two minutes left. The comic allegedly gave his host a one-finger response and Sullivan banned him from ever appearing on the show again. After Mason won a retaliatory libel suit, maintaining that he had just jabbed the air with his finger the way he often did in his act, he did one comeback on the show, in which he reintroduced himself with the line, "It is a great thrill to see me in person again."

Mason's career went into something of a decline as the years passed. Then, in the '80s, he made a comeback with his one-man production, *Politically Incorrect*, in which he hit the audience with his brilliant, rapid-fire one-liners:

"Eighty per cent of married men cheat in America. The rest cheat in Europe."

"People rave about their Caribbean holidays. 'The water's so blue.' I stay home and open my toilet. The water's so blue."

"I have enough money to last me the rest of my life, unless I buy something."

"My grandfather always said, 'Don't watch your money; watch your health.' So one day while I was watching my health, someone stole my money. It was my grandfather."

In 2005, I was asked to be the ad agency for Mason and his producer, Jyll Rosenfeld, a tough dynamo of a woman whom he later married. This resulted in a visit to their NY apartment in the Metropolitan Tower between Carnegie Hall and the Russian Tea Room. Jackie and Jyll had a great comedic rapport, and it was fun being with them. They also served terrific food.

We worked together on a Broadway show called *Freshly Squeezed*, which I named, and which was a big success. After that, they asked me to market the world's first and last Jackie Mason musical called *Laughing Room Only*, a horrible vaudevillian show with music, skits and Jackie doing standup. The musical *Chicago* was a big hit at the time and I suggested a *Chicago* parody for a TV spot promoting the show. We would open with a chorus line of gorgeous Bob Fosse–style dancers, then Jackie would walk through the line saying, "Who were you expecting, Catherine Zeta-Jones? Come and see me in . . ."

We shot the commercial in Windsor, the only place where we

could find the right theatre. Our TV spot was a success, but the show was a disaster. I was sitting among the critics and investors on opening night and listened as they described the reviews that would kill the show the next day.

I figured that would be the end of my relationship with Jackie and Jyll, but they asked me to make a film about Jackie doing his final Broadway show. It was called *The Ultimate Jew*. I agreed to be executive producer and director. "I'll finance it, but I want to keep Canadian rights, and we can split the other world rights." That, I felt, would cover my risk.

Between filming the Broadway show, Jackie, Jyll and I went to have dinner at the famed Joe Allen Restaurant on 46th Street. Joe Allen is famous for having its wall lined with posters of Broadway flops including *Laughing Room Only*. While we made our way to the table, we passed an older couple having dinner. The late Anne Meara, the acerbic actress and comedian and her husband, *Seinfeld* alumnus Jerry Stiller, looked up.

Anne barked, "Sure, Jackie, walk by and don't say hello! Shmuck!"

Jackie responded, "Hello and fuck you!"

The other guests thought it was part of a routine. I asked Jackie what gives and he explained that forty years earlier, Stiller and Meara were a comedy team on Broadway and he went backstage to visit them and they were apparently rude to him.

Now we have to leave to shoot the show and the exit is just as dramatic as the entrance.

Anne: "So long, asshole!"

Jackie: "Goodbye and fuck you!"

And he mutters under his breath, "Irish drunk" and we exit. I said to Jackie, "You've been holding a grudge for over forty years?" He responded, "Why not? It's fun."

My crew shot the show, and every month I'd fly to the Masons' apartment to show them some of our editing. They loved the film, and *The Ultimate Jew* played in festivals all over the world. That was in 2008. So far so good.

The next chapter in our relationship was more chaotic. Jackie had cowritten a screenplay called *One Angry Man*. It was a parody of *Twelve Angry Men*, which was an intense, inside look at the jury of a homicide trial. Jackie and Raoul Felder, the well-known divorce lawyer, were to be on the jury of *One Angry Man*. It would debate the guilt or innocence of an Arab accused of murder, with Jackie as the only one who believed in his innocence. Jackie wanted me to direct the film, to which I agreed, until I read the script. Then it was a flat no as I felt the script was not reflective of Jackie's wonderful comedic talent. I also turned down the role of producer, but finally agreed to be executive producer. For the director, they hired Steve Moskovic, who owned a film equipment company and had filmed a few documentaries, but this was his first feature. He has never forgiven me. Fights erupted constantly over the script. Jackie improvised all the time, confusing the other actors. It was chaotic.

When it came time to shoot a big scene in the Newark courthouse, Jyll asked me to fly in to watch it. A cab picked me up from the Premier Hotel in Times Square. As I climbed in, I asked the driver, "Do you know where the Martin Luther King Court House is in Newark?"

"Yes, of course."

After a while, I could see we were lost, but the cab driver denied it. Finally, I exploded, "Do me a favour and take me to Newark airport."

He refused. "You won't pay me the fee."

"I *will* pay you the fee. I need to get out of this cab."

The driver was from the Middle East and this was just post–9/11. I was uncharacteristically nervous for no good reason. While he driving me all over the map, he was also on the phone using his headset, listening to music and talking in a language I didn't understand. Whenever I complained, he told me not to worry because his brother had a GPS system.

"Your brother's not in this fucking taxi. I need to get out."

By now I was panicking. l called the taxi commission, which is the 311 number posted in the cab, but they shrugged me off. "We can't help you."

Finally, I told the driver, "Unless you take me to Newark airport, I'm calling 911."

When Melissa phoned, I told her, "I can't talk to you now. I've been kidnapped in a taxi cab." Then I hung up, leaving her in a panic.

I called 911.

The responder asked, "Where are you now?"

"I see a sign that says Hoboken." I told them everything else I could read.

"We'll be there in one minute."

One minute later, the police cars showed up. They circled the taxi, they rescued me then drove me to the courthouse.

When I told Jackie and Raoul the story, Raoul said, "Let's sue."

"No, I don't want to."

I watched the filming of the courthouse scene in *One Angry Man* as requested. Jackie had cast a *Sopranos* actor, an anchorwoman and a character actor, whose names I won't reveal to protect the innocent. I did a poster for them for free and I arranged a sale in Canada.

Ever the comedian in search of a hit, Jackie worked a joke about my cab experience into his routine, which is too racist to repeat. This, of course, was rather ironic, given that Jackie was supposed to be the *One Angry Man* on the jury who wanted to acquit the Arab of murder.

One Angry Man was released in 2009, and, in my opinion, my taxi ride was a metaphor for the whole experience.

Aside from working on a few films with Jackie Mason, I would occasionally book him for personal appearances and charity fundraisers. Jackie is always entertaining and his observations on life are hysterical. But not always. Ned Goodman, a Toronto-based mogul was chairing a gala for Maccabi, a national, non-profit, athletic organization and asked me to book Jackie to headline. Goodman loved him and thought he would be a great draw.

I booked Jackie and briefed him on the demographics of the older and very liberal crowd. In recent years, Jackie had become very right-wing and political in terms of his material. He hated that Barack Obama had recently been elected as president and his material was very hardline and negative towards Obama. I told him that would not play well in Canada and that he should stay away from politics and focus on his own greatest hits. He nodded and ignored me.

What followed was a caustic set that was so mean-spirited and anti-Obama that he failed to capture the crowd. He did have a few good lines on Obama: "We elected a President who has absolutely zero experience in running a country. If American Airlines called you and said we are looking to hire a few pilots who have never flown a plane before, would you fly that airline?"

The crowd sat on their hands and hated his material. As people started to leave prematurely, I knew I had to get him off. I signaled him with a flashing light to wind up and get off. He ignored me as he was looking for a big laugh to end on. No luck. He finally wrapped up by saying, "What a crowd! May the people at your work tomorrow do to you what you did to me tonight!"

In his dressing room, Jackie was apoplectic. "What a fucking crowd! Who are these people?" At a private meet and greet after the show, Ned Goodman humorously suggested to Jackie that he refund his fee. Jackie was not laughing. Years later, backstage at his show in Miami, Jackie admitted to me that he made a mistake and used the wrong material. He wasn't offering a refund, but there was some mea culpa.

ONE THING THAT WILL CURE SHYNESS

In 1997, Anita Gaffney, then head of marketing for the Stratford Festival, rejected me as a candidate to be their advertising agency. My friend, Jonas Prince, a festival board member, later told me, "Anita concluded from your interview that you didn't understand entertainment marketing."

What? I'd worked for the Mirvishes, I'd worked for Drabinsky, how could I not understand the business?

After interviewing other agencies, Gaffney came back to me. "Okay, I've made a mistake. How would you like to have the festival's ad account?"

I also served on the board for six glorious years before joining the Stratford Festival Senate (retired board members).

I still love working for Stratford because it's where my parents took me to see my very first plays, but the festival is a demanding client. It's driven by passion, drama and a particular point of view when it comes to marketing.

Richard Monette, the festival's artistic director from 1994 to 2007, encouraged my agency team to be unorthodox and bold. During our first season, Stratford staged *A Midsummer Night's Dream*, *West Side Story* and *Dracula*. I suggested the headline, "Fairies, Gang Members and Blood Suckers. What the hell is going on at Stratford?"

Though Richard loved it, he cautioned me, "Barry, you'll have to sell it to the board."

The meeting in Toronto was chaired by Jonas Prince, head of the festival's marketing committee. After a few moments of silence, Joan Chalmers, the great art philanthropist, pronounced, "If we don't run that ad campaign, I'm quitting."

In 2003, I made a TV documentary for Bravo about Richard Monette called *The Madness of King Richard*.

Born in 1944 in Montreal to working-class French-Italian parents, Richard never dreamed his imagination would fuel his destiny. Both parents were alcoholics who paid little attention to him or his younger brother, Mark. "We weren't beaten or molested, but it was dramatic because we were always ducking the crockery and there were a number of horrible incidents."

Richard's father, Maurice, made one bold move that set the course for Richard's life. "He felt his sons would have a better future if we were educated in an English school. When I was rejected because our family was French, he wrote the cardinal to say, "If I can't send my son to Loyola College, then I'm taking my wife and sixteen children out of the church."

That threatened soul drain had its impact. Richard was welcomed into Loyola.

Richard first visited Stratford in 1959 when he was fifteen. William Hutt and Irene Worth were playing in *As You Like It*. "I don't know what came over me, but when the usher took me to my seat, I spontaneously genuflected. I was embarrassed by my behaviour, but at the end of the performance, I knew I wanted to be an actor, to do Shakespeare and to work on the Stratford stage. This was my church."

Richard began his professional acting career while still in college. When his acting coach asked him what he wanted out of life, he replied, "I would like to be as great an actor as Laurence Olivier and John Gielgud."

"Mr. Monette, we have a great deal of work to do."

At nineteen, Richard became history's youngest Hamlet in a production staged by Toronto's Crest Theatre. Though Richard Burton was playing the same role down the street at the O'Keefe Centre, actor William Hutt was more impressed by Monette's interpretation. "It was extraordinary for a man so young."

In 1967, at age twenty-nine, Richard appeared at Stratford in

Antony and Cleopatra. He was Eros, the slave to Antony, who was played by Christopher Plummer. As Plummer later recalled, "I always liked to keep Richard in mind as my slave, no matter how successful he became. The last thing I expected was that he would turn from Eros into Stratford's Caesar, and run the damn place."

"I had a lot of scenes with Plummer, including dying in his arms, and he was terrifying," said Monette. "He became nice later in life, but wow! What a lot of temperament."

In 1970, Monette appeared in the original London production of *Oh! Calcutta!*, an avant-garde British revue in which the actors played in the nude. "I was too shy to expose myself on the inside," said Monette, "but if there's one thing that will cure shyness, it's doing a nude revue."

Monette added to his professional notoriety when he played a drag queen in Michel Tremblay's *Hosanna*, which travelled to Broadway in 1974.

"Richard's Hosanna was the first star-making performance I had seen on the stage in this country," said William Hutt. "He was shockingly good."

It was after *Hosanna* that Monette permanently established himself at Stratford. "I thought this should be Richard's home, from what I had seen of the young man," said Hutt. "While he was rehearsing, I walked across the stage to him and said, 'Welcome home, Richard.'"

"I was learning from the best, like a blotter sucking it all up," said Monette. "I found later that I could remember the gestures and bits of business that those who did them on stage had forgotten."

Monette eventually chose to direct rather than act. "I always found it hard to think of real-life incidents on stage that would make me laugh," he said, "but thanks to my family, I had much unhappiness to draw upon." In 1988, when he directed Stratford's *The Taming of the Shrew*, he told his actors, "When you throw the crockery, make it funny because it was never funny for me."

His style as a director was sometimes fierce, but spiced with humour. As actor Dan Chameroy recalled, "He liked us to discover our characters on our own, but when he wanted your attention, he would shout loud enough for anyone in the theatre to hear, 'You look like a fool walking on the stage that way. Do you want to look like a fool?' You didn't do that a second time."

Cynthia Dale remembers a gentler Monette. "Richard taught me how to work the Stratford stage. He showed me its magic and its sweet spot."

When Monette became artistic director in 1994, no one seemed more surprised than he was. "The board president knocked on my door Saturday morning to say, 'What would you think if I told you that you would be Stratford's next artistic director?' I said, 'What would you think if you opened your mail Monday morning and received the notice I sent to you on Friday telling you that I've withdrawn my name?'"

Despite that momentary failure of nerve, Monette became the Stratford Festival's first Canadian artistic director, a job he held till 2007. "You never dream as a kid that you want to be an artistic director. Maybe a firemen, yes, and there's no school to teach you how to be an artistic director."

In Monette's first year, he turned the festival's accumulated deficit into a surplus of $800,000, an instance of financial alchemy that he continued for thirteen years as he built a broader audience, established an endowment, created an acting conservatory and introduced new Canadian plays.

He also made musicals a regular festival feature, an innovation for which he was often severely criticized as a populist in the tradition of P.T. Barnum. Though Plummer played in the deep end of the festival pool, he defended Monette's vision. "The job of Stratford's artistic director is only second in its demands to being prime minister. You take all the blame and you're the butt of all the jealous intrigues. When

Richard went home each night, he didn't know whether he was loved or hated. It's a job for a masochist. Richard is actually a loveable guy. I admire him immensely."

Monette's talent for business came as a surprise even to himself. As for the negative reviews, "I stopped reading the tabloid terrorists. Bad reviews stick like burrs inside of you. I remember one that began, 'If you happen to be Richard Monette stop reading this dot dot dot.' No one else remembers that review, but it remained a billboard in my mind."

Monette found it lonely at the top, without family or a partner. "There would be a full house, and I'd go home alone without even a cat to kick. I'd like to be remembered as a man of the theatre who loved the Stratford Festival more than myself. It's a public service. It's very hard but not many people have this chance."

Richard Monette died not long after he retired in 2008, at age sixty-four. Making the film about Monette was a personal pleasure for me. He was so exciting and loyal to me that I wanted to honour him. He was also a nervous and insecure individual: when I showed him the film privately in his home, he cried and thanked me. Although he died from cancer, I always felt he died of loneliness and the loss of his leading role in running the theatre he saved and so loved.

Des McAnuff, director of such Broadway musicals as *The Who's Tommy* and *Jersey Boys*, became Stratford's next artistic director in a power-sharing arrangement with Don Shipley and Marti Maraden. There could only be one star on the door and Des soon took over from the other two, who left.

I always felt that Antoni Cimolino, Monette's protege, should have been his heir. Though Des was sometimes theatrically daring and thrilling, my loyalty was with Antoni. I was thrilled when Antoni finally became artistic director in 2013. Though I was no longer on the board, I coached him when he asked and I lobbied for him, and I was delighted when the boy who would be king actually became king. Antoni is extraordinary, with a good understanding of the festival's business side as well as its artistic side. Since Anita Gaffney had by then been promoted to executive director, I have now been working with her and the festival for eighteen years.

"I AM NOT A JUKEBOX"

I filmed nine Stratford stage productions including *King Lear*, *Hamlet*, *King John*, *Antony and Cleopatra*, *Caesar and Cleopatra* and *The Tempest*. Those last two productions starred Christopher Plummer.

I had met Plummer—in the sense of being in the same room— when I moved to Toronto in 1982. Over time, I gravitated to Alexandra's, a piano bar at what was then the Sutton Place Hotel. Plummer was often there. After a while, I'd say hello, and he'd nod, though he had no interest in me, or anything else beyond his drink, and perhaps the music.

In 1996, Plummer portrayed the silent star John Barrymore during his slide into alcoholism. *Barrymore*, a two-actor play, pre-miered at Stratford, then went to Broadway the following year. I was hired to direct Plummer in commercials for the production, which, as it turned out, metaphorically cast me in the role of the slave Eros. As Richard Monette had exclaimed when similarly cast, "Wow! What a lot of temperament."

Plummer kicked the shit out of me. He roared at me, "I'm not just a jukebox that spits out lines when you stick in coins. If you want another take, tell me *exactly* what you want."

In 2009, I again worked with Plummer, when I produced *Caesar and Cleopatra* from stage to screen, and then the following year, when

I filmed Shakespeare's *The Tempest*. Though Plummer was skeptical at first about this transformation, he warmed up to the idea. For *The Tempest*, we had ten cameras on dollies and cranes to make it a real cinematic production. Plummer looked at rough cuts and gave us notes. He was a fantastic resource, and often pushed to give his cast members more screen time.

As Richard Monette had also observed, Plummer did mellow with age. Even in his milder incarnation, however, he would often tease or torment me as if I were still the invisible kid who used to hang out at Alexandra's bar. Years earlier, before we shot the films, when I attended Garth Drabinsky's second wedding, Plummer called out to me as I was passing his table, "Hey, boy, will you see if they can lower the music?" He didn't recognize me. It didn't bother me.

In 2011, I attended a sold-out screening of *The Tempest* in New York, then served as moderator for the post-screening discussion. It was only after I had appeared on stage in front of nine hundred people that I came to exist in the eyes of Christopher Plummer and we developed a warm relationship. He is the last of the great actors. I was thrilled when he finally won an Oscar in 2012—it was long overdue.

Chapter Thirteen

ALL ABOARD
THE *TITANIC*

I met my future business partner through the Young Presidents Organization, an exclusive group with chapters around the world. Since YPO membership is restricted to individuals under fifty who are president of qualifying companies, it would seem to be the best— or most deceptive—place to meet someone with whom to build a career. All the faces around you reflect your collective success. What could possibly go wrong?

Despite some noisy clashes with my boss, Len Gill, we had forged something of a father-son relationship while he grew Echo, with my help, into a fantastic agency with more than one hundred employees. I admired the way he skilfully captained Echo through the Livent tsunami. We had blended our entertainment and corporate marketing to create an enviable model. In the process, I had gone from being an account guy to become president and chief operating officer. However, after more than twenty-five years at the helm, Len wanted to cash out.

Echo was an attractive property to various marketing conglomerates that were then on a buying spree. In 2002, Len negotiated the sale of the firm to CSS Stellar, a publicly traded company located in the UK. Though I was aware of the deal as it went through, I had no power as a minority shareholder to play a role in it. What Len and CSS Stellar decided became a fait accompli.

CSS Stellar was a sports and literary management company with famous directors, authors and race-car drivers as clients. Since they also owned U.S. and UK ad agencies, Echo seemed a perfect fit. Because we handled the Rolling Stones account and they handled Ray-Ban sunglasses, they imagined that the world would look brighter for everyone if Mick Jagger wore Ray-Bans.

Len negotiated a lucrative deal with the majority of the cash on signing. This was unprecedented in the ad industry, where long earnouts are used to retain the key staff, an agency's chief asset. We both had three-year contracts, leading to another much smaller payout.

When the gold dust settled it appeared that Len might have had seller's remorse. It's textbook that you shouldn't remain at your company after you've given up control. Len stayed on, even though he didn't need the money and he had already assigned his Echo clients to other account managers. Without these relationships, he had lost his leverage inside the company, which left him with time on his hands. He used the time to launch a campaign to run CSS Stellar's North American operation with its offices in New York and Atlanta. When this failed, he became angry. It began to taint our relationship.

I wrote Len an affectionate letter in which I said, "Len, you built an unbelievable agency. You trained and grew me so that I could run this agency. Take a step back. Enjoy your life."

But he couldn't.

CSS Stellar decided to pay out Len's contract and sever ties. When he cleared out his office, we all gathered round to wish him good luck. Sadly, that was the end of Len's and my personal relationship.

When the press announced that I had been made CEO, Len sent me a rude email accusing me of orchestrating a coup to assume his leadership. That absolutely was not true. The last thing I wanted was responsibility for a ship I suspected was on a dead-end course.

Len subsequently set up a small agency, essentially to service his good friend, Michael Cohl, the former Rolling Stones' promoter. We never spoke again. It's too bad. We had fun travelling the world together.

Meanwhile, I was left with the running of Echo under British rule. Though we had great clients, our British owners did not understand our financial models, especially the fact that the bulk of our billings, such as work for Christmas movies, occurred at the back end of the year. I found myself having to report to London on a monthly basis in meetings that compromised my daily work, and they brought absolutely nothing to the table. After I had run through two years of my three-year contract, I was ready to admit to myself, This isn't working. I own the client relationships. Why am I explaining everything, over and over, to the Brits who don't want to understand?

In 2004, I attended what proved to be a fateful retreat with the Young Presidents Organization in Washington. By then, our YPO group included Larry Latowsky, a retail pharmaceutical executive who had recently left his job with a very rich package. When I told him I was thinking of starting a new ad agency, he said, "Why don't I finance you? We'd be partners. I'd run finance, as well as bring in lots of clients through my connections in retail and pharmacy."

I drew up a business plan, which included both the staff and the clients I thought might follow me out of Echo. In return, I expected a seven-figure investment from Larry, along with his alleged twenty-five years of accounting expertise. When I showed this plan to Larry, he was enthusiastic.

By the end of the summer, I was ready to resign from Echo, but first I needed a formal agreement with Larry about the terms of our partnership. He was still enthusiastic: no problem. With the deal in hand, I flew to England to see my British bosses. I admit that I was scared, because I was leaving a wonderful job in which I had invested fifteen years of creative enterprise. Sean Kelly, my British contact, turned out to be a pleasant gentleman. I told him, "It's time for me to go. I'd like you to waive my non-competes and my non-solicits so I can do whatever I need to do."

To my surprise and relief, he readily agreed. "All I ask in return is that you hold off announcing this until after Christmas. We don't want to affect the stock price and I don't want to have a bad Christmas."

We shook hands. Deal.

By February, I was looking for office space for Endeavour, which would be Larry's and my new agency. Rob Hain, who had been hired by CSS Stellar to take Echo through my exit, told me with great confidence and ignorance, "We're going to let the clients fight this out to see where they want to go."

I replied, "Since they don't know you, there won't be any fight, but I promise I won't solicit, so it really will be their choice."

My exit in May 2005 was civil. Hain gathered the Echo staff, then said, "Barry Avrich has done great things for this company. We celebrate him, and we congratulate him, and we wish him well." Everyone applauded, and out I walked, along with the five staff members who were coming with me, including Tori Laurence as a junior partner.

Many key clients followed me immediately, others came later, in spite of generous offers from Echo intended to persuade them to stay. By October—six months later—Echo was no more. Len Gill probably blames me for the destruction of his baby, but he had already sold his baby and I was long gone.

Though Endeavour was a small company in a temporary office with rented furniture, we had a heady first year. Our expenses were relatively low, and we were bold and feisty. A local casino said to me, "Okay, Barry, Endeavour sounds good, but before we sign on, we need to assure ourselves that you have the infrastructure to service our business."

Inspired by my Rent A Fan Club days, we filled the office with a bunch of people to sit in hastily furnished offices to be present for the client's walkabout. Casino Niagara signed on, and our agency gave them everything we promised.

Endeavour was doing so well that Larry, our majority partner, made his money back in our first year. My big mistake was in not ending our partnership then and there. Instead, I let him hang around for seven more years, acting as our chief executive officer and chairman. Endeavour grew into a big agency with both entertainment and blue-chip clients with little help from Larry, who had promised to bring in new business from his pharmaceutical connections.

I had had great lifestyle mentors, I had had great show-business mentors, but I had had no great business mentors. Larry was CEO and chairman, and he controlled the accounting department. When I asked to look at statements, he always had some reason why this couldn't happen. I have no explanation for how I could have let this situation get so far out of hand. I was busy working with our clients and I felt we were doing exceptionally well. I'd become fed up making reports to Echo's British owners every month for two years. I trusted Larry or . . . maybe I just didn't want to know? I certainly should have paid attention. There were warning signs, such as the number of accounting staff we kept losing. I looked the other way.

What Larry developed under my nose was an elaborate and flawed plan in which he used Endeavour profits to buy businesses that had nothing to do with Endeavour's core mandate. He bought businesses that dealt in beverages, coupon publishing, pharmaceutical promotions, energy bars. He later justified these purchases as fast-profit opportunities, but he had an uncanny knack for finding companies on life support that never materialized into anything. Six years into what would turn out to be the eight years of Endeavour's life, I told Larry,

"This is a hard meeting, but let's face it. You're not bringing any value to this company. You need to look for something else to do; you can't take a salary any longer. It's time you moved out of this office. You're still an owner, but I can't see you here day to day."

Larry agreed. He probably was relieved that I hadn't yet discovered the dire state of our accounting and how he had funded the purchase of so many failed companies. I personally hired a truck to haul away his furniture. To the best of my knowledge, a year later the business was still flourishing—that is, until Christmas 2012. Endeavour experienced a sudden cash crunch that I couldn't understand. On the face of it, we were having the year of years. In reality, I was on the *Titanic* and we had just hit the iceberg.

At first, I was flabbergasted, and then I was sick. I'd been through difficult negotiations before, but nothing like this. I was not a controlling shareholder. The company that my staff and I had built on our backs belonged to Larry. Len Gill and I could fight like cats and dogs, but Larry and I had never fought. He was a passive person who I believed had a dark side. I felt violated. I felt frightened, but I also knew that I had a responsibility to forty-five staff members and clients who trusted me.

I also had my family to support and protect. Christmas was approaching, along with the holiday we had planned. Suddenly, I had business expenses that had to be paid immediately and it amounted to a lot of money. Hindsight is 20/20. Why had I gone into business with Larry Latowsky? Why hadn't I believed in myself enough to borrow the start-up money so that I owned my own firm?

A friend of mine had recently sold his company for billions. Through the years, he had often asked, "How's everything going? Can I help?"

I went to see him, which was very difficult for me, and I told him, "I need a small loan for ten days, then I'll be fine. Could you help me with that?"

My friend turned me down, though the amount I needed was equivalent to lint in his pocket. Then he added, "Let me tell you why."

"No, I don't need to know."

"Well, I'm going to talk to my father tonight about this."

His father? What an odd statement, given that he was so affected his whole life by having lived in the shadow of his uber-successful father. He carried a chip the size of a lumberyard on his shoulder. He often confessed the pain he felt about not being recognized for his own accomplishments, but it was tough to have sympathy for someone who had the resources to strike out on his own but stayed in the warm cocoon and suffered. I found it boring.

"No, that's fine."

He called me the next day to say, "I found a company in Vancouver. I know them, and they're going to help you. You'll get a phone call in ten minutes."

I received the call, during which I was told, "We'll give you the money, short term. It's not a lot for us, and we'll have to charge you a significant service fee."

I accepted their offer. It was a complex arrangement that required me to involve my wife in signing papers, which I found humiliating. I received the money. I used it and then I paid it back as I said that I would. A company representative called to thank me on behalf of his lending company and my friend, who'd brokered the deal and had turned me down.

I asked, "Why is he thanking me?"

"Because he owns our company."

Great. This friend, who wouldn't loan me the money, "found" his own company to make the loan in order to charge me interest. It was another hard lesson in the scarcity of loyalty.

That night, when I was still trying to hold my world together, I had dinner at the House of Chan with my friend, Eddie Greenspan.

Eddie, who knew of my troubles, told me, "I want to give you the money you need."

I broke down at the table. "Thanks, but I've figured it out already."

I also figured out that I had one true friend.

That was Act I.

I still hadn't decided how I was going to handle Act II, in which I would have to deal with Larry. No one in the advertising world knew his name. He was unknown to our clients. If I simply abandoned Endeavour, what would happen to the company and the staff I left behind?

I made my junior partner, Tori Laurence, our COO, in the hope that we could take control and eventually buy out Larry. Thank God for her bloodless approach to managing issues! We spent many days behind closed doors, plotting, weeping and sometimes laughing out of desperation. I also created a legal team, composed of Eddie Greenspan and Ken Rosenstein from the law firm Aird & Berlis LLP, to advise me on how best to take control of the situation. It was during these investigations that Endeavour's comptroller, who had been under Larry's control, finally broke down and showed us a complicated, handwritten schematic organization chart with Company A, Company B, Company C, Company D, which was where all our cash had been going. There was also some plan involving the German stock exchange. As we uncovered Larry's intricate move of cash around the various companies, attempts at asset-based loans and a failed merger, it became apparent that in spite of Endeavour's stock of goodwill, its massive success and blue-chip clients, the agency was unsalable and could not be saved.

Eddie was not happy with what he saw and advised that I should take serious legal action against my partner, but I knew that any suggestion of a scandal might ruin my career in advertising. Was it reckless business moves of a fool or something worse? It was not an accusation or headline I was prepared to risk. Instead, Aird & Berlis came up with a plan of attack that had me set up a breakfast meeting with Larry at the Intercontinental Hotel. He was still unaware we had uncovered his schematic organizational chart and, as far as I could tell, suspected nothing. I told him, "I want to buy Endeavour. How much do you want for it?"

Larry was thrilled. "Wow, do you have the money?"

"Yep."

He gave me the figure he wanted for the company. I said, "Thank you," then stood up to leave.

"Aren't we having breakfast?"

"Nope."

I walked out of there, feeling like Charlie Sheen wearing a wire in *Wall Street* after meeting Gordon Gekko in the park. I didn't have a wire. I felt like I did, because my goal had been accomplished: I had left Larry feeling secure, perhaps even hopeful and enthusiastic, giving us time to plan our exit with clients and staff, so that he would not, in a panic, seize funds—which he had the power to do as the controlling shareholder—for a midnight run.

I went directly to Aird & Berlis to tell Ken Rosenstein the figure that Larry wanted for Endeavour. Three weeks later, I called Larry, "Come to Endeavour and we'll present you with our proposal for the business."

On a cold day in February 2013, Larry arrived for what he thought would be a great occasion. Ken told him, "We've uncovered the true nature of the accounting problems at Endeavour so this is your choice. We will conduct a forensic audit that will potentially expose you to potential liability.

"The second choice will be an orderly windup of the agency. Barry will walk away from Endeavour with his team intact, with the exception of the accounting department, which we obviously don't want, and with the company's client list. There'll be no non-competes, no non-solicits, and what's left of Endeavour will be cleaned up by a professional accounting firm that will collect receivables and settle with the creditors."

Larry chose to let me go. My exit happened on March 1, 2013. I walked out of Endeavour to create my own agency and begin anew. It was the biggest decision of my life. I had had to ask myself, Do you really want to start all over again? Why not just make films? But I had clients that I loved. I had a staff I loved, some of whom had been with me for seventeen years.

When I decided on the new agency, I made Tori Laurence— who had faithfully been at my side for fifteen years—my partner at BT/A, which accounts for the "T" in our agency's name. I promised her a great life if she would embark on this adventure with me, then we locked and loaded for battle. We were walking into a hell of uncertainty, which brings me to Act III.

While still at Endeavour, Tori and I had gathered together the staff to tell them, "Whether you were aware of it or not, we had a majority partner in this agency. You might have seen him come and go from this office, or maybe you didn't. That partnership has dissolved. It's time for us to start our own agency. You won't see any decrease in your pay. We're all leaving this place on Friday, and we're starting up in our new place on Monday. We'll probably hit some bumps on the road, but we want to make this as seamless as possible. If you believe in us, then come with us."

And they did.

I also had to manage our clients, along with everyone else who was asking, "What happened to Endeavour?" While flying on a wing and a prayer, all I could tell them was, "Trust me, go with me."

And most did.

Tori and I had fourteen days to find office space, then forty-eight hours to move everyone in. Before we finished packing up, the real estate agent called to say, "Sorry, you've lost the space."

I asked, "Who owns the building?"

The agent replied, "You'll never get to them."

"I get to everybody."

I made three phone calls. I found the building's owner through real-estate mogul David Kosoy. He fixed the problem, and we moved in. The space Tori had found for us was completely furnished, including the phones and the computers lines, so it was literally plug in and play. We were up and running within twenty-four hours.

I still had to face collateral damage from Endeavour. It still existed. No one was there, but it existed as a legal entity. What the hell was happening with Larry in full charge? I was sure creditors' meetings must be taking place, with people demanding to be paid, and with my name the only one publicly associated with the firm. Larry hired BDO, a professional accounting firm led by Ken Pearl as a trustee, and they successfully settled with creditors. Ken was compassionate and clearly saw what had occurred to me. Endeavour didn't go bankrupt, but this was not a painless exercise, and I lost a few clients who continued to blame me.

A few trade magazines began to print garbled accounts about Endeavour's demise. Eddie Greenspan brokered a meeting for me with Dale Lastman, a former mayor's son and an influential lawyer in his own right. Dale, whom I didn't know, sat at his power desk, listening to me, before advising, "Pack away your pride, suck it up, and tell your story."

"But it's embarrassing. I lost my business at the hands of another."

"Tell the story. Don't be afraid to say you were a victim. You won't find any nobility in silence."

That's what I did, while being careful not to name names or to incriminate anyone. I thought the worst was over. Then, on the way to a downtown business meeting, I received a call from a friendly publicist. She said, "Barry, I want you to know that a Toronto newspaper is doing a major story on you for Saturday. It's called 'The Rise and Fall of Barry Avrich.'" I walked into the King Edward Hotel and I threw up in the washroom. Then I called the newspaper's editor. I said, "I've just been through this fucking nightmare. My own mother is calling me every day, worrying that I'll have a heart attack. I'm starting a new business. I'm moving forward. I don't know if I'll succeed, but whoever does, and I don't have time to fight these false rumours."

I threw up again, then called the newspaper's section editor. "What are you doing to me? There's no 'Barry's fall.' I'm okay. I still have my major clients."

The editor said, "You're a good story. You're an influential guy with high-profile clients."

"It's all wrong, and I don't want it done."

"Well, we're doing it. If you've got something to say, I recommend that you call the journalist and tell her."

I called my friend, Robert Pattillo, one of this country's best spin doctors, and asked him what to do.

"Get on the ship and steer it. If you don't participate, you've got a problem."

I knew the journalist. She'd written about me in the past. We'd also had our outs, including the time I'd angered her by setting up difficult terms for an interview with Matt Damon. By the time I called her, I knew she'd been interviewing all around me. Her first words were, "So, Barry, I was going to call you."

We talked for about five hours as I explained: I wasn't the majority shareholder. We had a falling-out over running the company. Marriages end.

This was mid-week and the journalist was planning to file for Saturday. I hung up feeling anxious and confused. Should I warn clients about the story?

On Saturday morning, I told my wife and daughter, "Don't turn on your electronic devices. Don't go online. Don't read the paper. We're leaving town."

We drove to Niagara Falls, New York, did some shopping, went for pizza, then came home Saturday night. That's when I told myself, Time to face the music. I turned on my BlackBerry. Instead of the three hundred emails I had expected, I found only a few, none of which mentioned the article. That's when I noticed a Friday evening email that I'd missed. It was from the journalist: "I just wanted to let you know that the story was killed."

I emailed back, "What happened?"

"It was a good story, and that's why we killed it. No dirt to report."

When I made my documentaries profiling famous people, I was often criticized for not including enough dirt. It was good to know this dubious journalistic principle could also work in my favour. I felt a wave of both gratitude and relief. By its nature, the fast-paced ad industry produces disgruntled competitors, disgruntled staff, disgruntled partners and disgruntled suppliers. I sometimes expect to read quotes that say, "Barry Avrich is a colossal asshole" along with "Barry Avery is a smart, philanthropic guy." One headline I didn't ever want to see was "The Rise and Fall of Barry Avrich."

In creating BT/A with Tori Laurence, I tried to draw inspiration from the failure of Endeavour. The big difference was that BT/A represented a clear choice. I liked the idea of leading a double life—ad man by vocation, filmmaker by avocation—with one side creatively feeding the other.

Business at BT/A is very good indeed, and I feel amazingly relaxed. I owe much of that to Tori, who runs the operation with her husband, Craig Laurence, who is our chief financial officer. I trust Tori and Craig from long experience, and they also have a vested interest in taking care of our business. Together we make it work.

★ Chapter Fourteen ★

PUBLIC MISCHIEF

THE SHOW STARTS ON THE SIDEWALK

In 2008, Toronto was holding strong to its reputation as a world-class sports fail. Our professional teams hadn't won a championship or title in years; in some cases, in decades. We hadn't hosted an international athletic event in living memory, and we had recently lost our second Olympic bid. Our sports brand was Toronto the Loser.

In July 2008, David Peterson—former Ontario premier with many other notches in his belt—came to see me. "Barry, I have a dream. I want to win the 2015 Pan Am Games for Toronto."

I didn't know Peterson well, but I found it easy to share his dream. The Pan Am/Parapan Am Games, held every four years, was one of the world's largest multi-sport events. My partner Tori and I were thrilled to be asked by Peterson, chairman of Toronto's bid, to look after their branding. Our agency would be working with media guru Bob Richardson, representing the Ontario government.

Peterson was like General George S. Patton: he wanted to know everything about everything. *Who are we competing against?* Bogotá, Colombia; Lima, Peru; and Caracas, Venezuela. *How many votes does Toronto need to win?* Twenty-seven out of fifty-four, representing forty-two countries. *Where and when will the judging take place?* Guadalajara, Mexico, November 2009. *What jackets and ties will our delegation be wearing? How will our cocktail-party napkins be branded?* While that level of attention might drive some people crazy, I liked the fact that someone was on top of everything, leading the way. For David's personal ground war, he had a binder with pictures of all the voting delegates, carefully profiled regarding their taste in food, where they travelled, and so on. Before we were finished, each would have been schmoozed and entertained as part of the Peterson charm offensive. Every hand would have been shaken, every baby kissed, twice.

For the bid itself, David gave Tori Laurence and me a blank canvas on which to paint our creative vision. I knew we would need plenty of theatre. Toronto the cold, the boring, the sports loser would be competing against Venezuela, Columbia and Peru with their Latin charisma, their beautiful scenery, their sexy dancing, and, yes, their better coffee. We wanted the delegates to understand that Toronto was a city with plenty of sizzle. For that, we needed Hollywood-style videos and trailers, utilizing the international language of sports and show business.

While in Mexico, our team watched 2016 Olympic bids by Tokyo, Chicago and Rio to see what had worked and what hadn't. Chicago had flown in Michelle Obama, who did a good job for them, but the filmmakers had made the mistake of presenting the city as a series of parks—pretty but dull. We had to take our bid to the next level. That meant creating an incredible film about the facilities Toronto would build for the Games. We would eschew the usual "Here's a stadium" slideshow stuff and would instead go virtual, with divers actually shooting as they jumped off diving boards. We also had to show the delegates all the exciting things they could expect while visiting Toronto in July 2015. Our philosophy was to showcase a city of festivals—Caribana, the Dragon Boat races, TIFF, Luminato, the ROM, the AGO, the ballet and opera. Our videos made Toronto look like one big party, 24/7/365.

Along with film, we needed a theatrically perfect show. Since we were prevented from using Cirque de Soleil because they had a sponsor conflict, I began to speculate: *surely, there must be people who once worked for Cirque de Soleil?* We found a troupe of Cirque de Soleil alumni. We also engaged the Canadian Tenors.

Caracas dropped out, leaving Bogota and Lima. Toronto would have four days in Guadalajara to entertain delegates, leading up to a forty-minute presentation. While huddled in our Toronto office, our team laid out its strategy, day by day, hour by hour, minute by minute. Our plan was simple: razzle-dazzle the delegates from the moment we set foot in Guadalajara, and never stop. Our high-tech booth would project images of our athletes' village, as well as offering imported Timbits and frozen gelato. Our hospitality suite would be party central, with the best swag (including the latest BlackBerry for every delegate) and Canadian maple syrup. Our luncheon would feature trapeze artists flying overhead. We knew that all this would just be popcorn if we didn't knock out the judges with our presentation. It had to be flawless.

Technically, our show would feature 750 carefully cued images, seven videos, plus a highly emotional piece of cinema, entitled *Share the Dream*, as our finale. If we could make the delegates cry, we could beat the Latin Americans at their own game of passion.

The problem with our ambitious presentation, for which we would be allowed only a brief setup, was this; in Guadalajara, we would be up against third-world technology. I told David, "You must give me some latitude here. I need to bring in my own equipment."

He agreed, without my having to confess how anxious I was about potential technical problems. Instead, I smiled bravely, promised the moon and never slept.

My team flew into Guadalajara six months early to check out the hotel, to study the ballroom where the presentations would be shown and to consult with the local technicians who would be working for us. We pre-installed our own lighting, and imported our own computer mainframe to run the show. I had already witnessed the horrific problems other countries had experienced when trying to run their multimillion-dollar Olympic bids from laptops that froze or broke down. We had to invest in the right equipment, the right technical crew. My secret weapon was Alex Olegnowicz, a Spanish-speaking tech wiz from Toronto.

The great vaudeville impresario Florenz Ziegfeld always said, "The show begins on the sidewalk." In Guadalajara, Bob Richardson hired a satellite truck to do live daily updates to be viewed around the world. Though Bob was supposed to be the face of our campaign, to his selfless credit, he invited me to sit next to him. The morning of our presentation, I referred to the Pan Am Games as the Academy Awards of sport, and that buzzword stuck.

For our presentation, "beginning on the sidewalk" meant choreographing how our delegation entered the ballroom to face the judges. As we waited outside the room's big double doors, Tori lined up everybody in their uniforms—a group of seventy including, in order, two RCMP officers, our circus performers, our delegates, our speakers and our athletes.

At the sound of Toronto's starting bell, which would be rung by Mario Vázquez Raña, head of the Pan American Games, my first cue would be "house to black," meaning you douse the lights. In the ensuing few moments of darkness, your audience prepares itself for the shift from ordinary reality to the world of their imagination. After that, I'd cue the lights and our parade would begin.

We heard the starting bell.

I cued, "House to black."

Boom! The lights went out in the ballroom.

Alex, my wiz technician, exclaimed, "Barry, we have no sound!"

After two flawless rehearsals a few sound cables had come loose.

The seconds ticked by as our technicians scrambled around looking for the fix amongst thousands of cables.

The bell rang again. Mario Vázquez Raña called out, "Toronto, we are waiting!"

David Peterson came to me. "When are you going to cue us?"

I faked it. "Anticipation, David, anticipation."

In this kind of situation, three minutes can feel like thirty. The audience started to chant, "Toronto, Toronto."

Now Bob Richardson asked, "What's the problem?"

"We only have sound for half the room."

He ordered, "Run the show. We can't wait any longer."

Alex exclaimed, "It's back, we have it."

I cued, "Hit it."

Lights! Music! Videos! Our delegation marched, our circus troupe tumbled and our tenors sang "Your Moment Is Now," in Spanish, English and French. The audience cheered, venting their pent-up excitement, and from then on, everything was flawless. Our eleven speakers, who included Chairman David Peterson, Premier Dalton McGuinty and Mayor David Miller, were clear and persuasive. Our theatrics were spectacular. Our cinematic finale, *Share the Dream*, produced by Tori, had everyone crying on cue. It showed the journey of three children—one from South America, one from the Caribbean, one from Toronto—who dreamed of competing in the Pan Am Games in 2015. As a school bus drove through the streets, the kid who dreamed of being a runner raced after it. The soccer-playing kid playfully kicked a ball around the house while still in pyjamas. The swimmer eagerly woke up her mother, "Mommy, I have to go to practice!" Then, five years later, the three kids triumphantly arrived in Toronto to compete in the Pan Ams. Cue the fireworks!

After our presentation, the Toronto delegation returned to our hotel suite to await the verdict. Since our show had been last, we would have only three hours until six o'clock, when the results were to be announced. Some of our people were handicapping the outcome—"I know we have St. Kitts, but I don't know if we have Mexico."

I never admitted to David or the others the problem I'd had with the sound, which I suspected was due to sabotage—a deliberately pulled cable. The Bogota team was always complaining that we were bending the rules with a bigger display booth, more lights, better signage. So, we believed they played games with our sound.

By six o'clock, the votes had been counted and the teams reassembled in the ballroom. Mario Vázquez Raña announced, "The 2015 Games have been awarded to Toronto, Canada."

Our city had won spectacularly on the first ballot: Toronto with 33 votes, Lima 11, Bogota 7.

The hosts played our theme music, we turned on our pre-installed ballroom lights and had a fantastic party. Toronto the sports loser no more!

I had assumed that our team, which had so skilfully won the bid, would carry through to the 2015 Games. Instead, we were disbanded. There would be a new competition for the ad account for the hosting city. Nineteen agencies entered the first phase of this new competition. From these, Endeavour and two others were selected to present detailed proposals. We brought in experienced branding strategists, Peter Francey and Jeanette Hana, to perfect our pitch. In June 2010, Endeavour was unanimously selected. Our theme was "United We Play." These three simple words that I wrote on a napkin for Tori inspired a sensational presentation to the board. Our team pulled out all the stops when we made our pitch and won the account.

At first, we found ourselves working under different leadership. That is, until David Peterson was brought back as chair, which was immensely satisfying to both Tori and me. In July 2015, both Tori and I were torchbearers, which meant *sharing the dream* in a very personal way.

JUST CALL ME MR. MAYOR

I had some some previous, peripheral brushes with political power and its machinations in putting a candidate into office but nothing like working on one of the most heated and publicly followed mayoral elections in recent Canadian history.

I knew John Tory—our social circles overlapped—and I liked him immensely. Bob Richardson, one of Canada's top political whisperers, had sat me down with Tory in 2009 to help convince him to run against the unlikely Rob Ford, a fairly anonymous city councillor. Tory, who had failed at several previous attempts to enter the political arena, declined, and Rob Ford became our next mayor.

By fall 2014, Tory was ready to fight what was now called Ford Nation and a mayor who was being called a global disaster by the media. Richardson asked me to join the team as lead marketing strategist and it was a beyond-exciting ride. I had seen and loved the George Clooney–directed film *The Ides of March*, and I saw myself catching a ride on this express.

John Tory's 2014 mayoral campaign was not the first on which I had worked. In 2010, I was hired to market George Smitherman for his mayoral bid. That election, as all Torontonians and global comedy fans know, culminated in the horrendous loss to Ford. Smitherman had a lot of baggage and his whole campaign was a mess. Nobody could make a decision. Nobody seemed to be in charge. I pushed for

Smitherman to run with the Angry Man line from the movie *Network*: "I'm not going to take it anymore!" When Rob Ford became the Angry Man while Smitherman dithered, I knew we were finished.

John Tory, like David Peterson, was a man who thrived on detail and numbers. *How many boroughs do I need to win? What steps must I take to get to the finish line?*

I branded Tory as the honest guy, a straight-talker who didn't over-promise, which he was and is. We needed to stay away from wealth and privilege, except to say that John didn't need the job, but that he cared enough about the city to apply for it. His record as a civic activist spoke for itself. So did his civility—a necessity if Toronto was to overcome the embarrassing Ford years. We knew from all our polling and research that the big election issue would be transit, and John was clear about having a plan to fix it. When he presented it to his strategists, I said, "Your plan needs to be branded. The public and the media need a sound bite."

Someone asked, "What are you suggesting?"

"Let's call it SmartTrack."

Both John Tory and Bob Richardson were enthusiastic. "We love it!"

I was amazed. This was the first time in two mayoral campaigns that one of my ideas had been accepted instantly. Almost immediately, we had signs that said "John Tory SmartTrack," which, to the best of my knowledge, was the first time in a mayoral campaign that policy had been posted on people's lawns. Nobody called it "DumbTrack," which had been one of my worries, and SmartTrack became John Tory's signature.

Our campaign hit a road bump when Rob Ford's brother, Doug, entered the mayoral race to replace Rob, who was suddenly ailing from cancer. We had discovered early on that Olivia Chow, a well-known former city councillor whom we initially regarded as our

chief competition, had a serious problem in public debate because of her inability to communicate effectively. She was smart and experienced, but she performed poorly when she had to speak off the cuff. We knew that if we kept her talking, we were in good shape. We also knew that John could easily out-debate Rob Ford.

When Doug stepped in, we faced a more serious set of problems. Doug wasn't a nice guy, but he enjoyed public sympathy because of Rob's cancer and continuing popularity. During the first debate, Doug ate John for lunch by seeming to show the audience that John didn't know how City Hall worked. In fact, John did, but Doug made John look like a fool, which is hard to do.

We knew we had a formidable foe. John worked it. He went to everything, he spoke at everything. I filmed him at a Caribana costume factory, which was Doug's territory. He talked about how important the Caribbean community was to him. He was tireless. He was spectacular.

We still had a problem when John met Doug in face-to-face encounters. John was a gentleman. Ford was not. Immediately, he started hitting below the belt: "John you're an election loser. *You're a loser, you're a loser.*" After this went on for while, John unexpectedly hit back. "Well, Mr. Ford, you're going to experience that feeling pretty soon, aren't you?" Those of us who knew John cheered—*whoa!*— when we heard those words. From then on, John was on his game, not fighting dirty, but standing like Teflon Man against all Ford's crap.

Election night was still a nail-biter. I watched with John and his family and the other insiders as the results came in. Number crunching is a science. From the outset, the statisticians were saying, "If you drop below twenty-one points, we have to watch it. If below eighteen, hmm." I was hoping for a landslide, but the Ford name had a lock on certain suburban neighbourhoods where John remained personally unknown.

In the end, John won handily. I was present for his private swearing in and for the celebratory dinner. Because John Tory was a client who let me do what instinct and experience had taught me, I felt that I had been a real part of the team, and not just hired help. In the ad business, that's a rarity.

Shortly after John was installed as mayor, I drove into downtown Toronto. The traffic was moving, because he had already cleared the streets of illegally parked FedEx trucks, idling cars and intersection hogs. John knew he would have rough days, because Toronto isn't easy to run, but he wasn't afraid to take the driver's seat.

As far as I'm concerned, John Tory is the closest Toronto will ever have to a JFK. They even look a little alike.

PART THREE

MY LIFE IN FILM

★ *Chapter Fifteen* ★

FILLING THE FRAME

My love of film began innocently. Like many other filmmakers I discovered great performances at an early age. I loved the power of storytelling on such a mass and impressive scale. From the films I watched with my father to the wonderful classics a college professor introduced me to, there was no question that I too wanted to tell stories by making movies. As I began my life in advertising, I kept my promise to myself by starting off with short films and then graduating to modest documentaries and eventually a filmography of high-profile and sometimes very provocative projects.

While I love advertising—bumps, bruises and all—filmmaking allowed me a vast freedom to shape a story and captivate an audience without any interference or opinion beyond my own imagination. This is a wonderful pleasure. So, from a rarely seen amateur short film designed to help me meet women that was produced some thirty-five years ago, to a short film produced by my daughter that had a world premiere at TIFF thirty-five years later, my life in film has been nothing short of beautiful.

CANADIAN IDOL

I wasn't good-looking, athletic, tall or rich enough to be one of the cool kids at Herzliah High School, but I used my other talents—storytelling, joking and generally being the entertainer—to work my way into the A group. Some of my less popular friends resented the fact that I played to the in-crowd, especially after I bought a Lacoste T-shirt—a hot new fashion item—and started The Lacoste Club. I have a picture of a bunch of us, wearing our little alligator T-shirts, looking ridiculous.

My big high-school coup—Grade 9, 1978—was producing, directing and hosting an ambitious talent show, which I called *The Gong Show*, after the hit TV show with Chuck Barris. I raised the money, brought together a terrific Gong Show Orchestra, printed playbills, created a set with a giant gold lamé starburst, then had one of those Voices of God announcers saying, "Live from Montreal!" at the start of the show. It was the precursor of *American Idol*, with teachers as judges. The whole production was a big thrill—I loved it.

We had our casualties. One girl, who'd rehearsed for months, sang only one note of Billy Joel's "Honesty," before a teacher gonged her. At intermission, she attacked me. "How could you let this happen?" I was pretty shocked too. The gong was supposed to be a joke for kids who were just horsing around. I remembered how I felt, auditioning "What the World Needs Now" and being cut off before I could get out the first line, and I sympathized with her.

The Gong Show played to a packed house. It was a triumph. I was the king—I couldn't have asked for a better launch to my high-school career.

I continued to look for ways to earn money in order to finance the kind of lifestyle to which I was determined to become accustomed. Another of my gigs was as a wedding videographer. I didn't last long, simply because my standards were too high. If a speech was boring—and most were—I cut it out. Of course, what my clients really wanted was a complete play-by-play record of the event. I remember one rabbi's shock when I presented him with a ten-minute video of his daughter's wedding. He had expected it to go on for hours.

"I'M A DIRECTOR"

I should have known that a substance made to stick to skin would be hard to remove from glass, but I had no clue.

At Vanier College, being relieved of the necessity of taking courses I hated, I gravitated naturally toward anything useful for a life in entertainment, such as debating, public relations, business and filmmaking, for which Bob Del Tredici was the school's guru. He introduced me to serious movies like *Battleship Potemkin* or Kurosawa's *Seven Samurai*, along with film technique and theory. It was rivetting, an eye-opener. Now, all the Hollywood stuff I'd seen with my family seemed frivolous.

For Bob's class, I was required to make Super-8 films, which would be my second awakening at Vanier. My first was my discovery that I'd stepped out of my insular Jewish shtetl into a world of spectacular blondes and other exotic women, like none I'd seen before. Since I was a nobody, the only way to attract these women was to put my two passions together: girls and films. I wrote a screenplay called *Models*, in which two women fought over a photographer, as in a Woody Allen fantasy. Then, I approached Heidi Kaplan and Bridget Scullion, the two best-looking girls in the school, and uttered the magic words, "I'm a director."

In the opening sequence, the letters spelling *MODELS* appeared, one by one, in red lipstick, on a bedroom mirror. It was my parents' bedroom mirror and my mother's red lipstick. When she walked in during the filming, she was horrified.

"What's this?"

I said, "I'll clean it up."

I did, but it wasn't easy.

My high-school friend, Jeremy Stern, had a magnificent home in Westmount, with a spectacular staircase, where I was going to have jealous Heidi stab to death her rival, Bridget. It was inspired by that famous, much copied and parodied scene I had been mesmorized by in Sergei Eisenstein's *Battleship Potemkin*, in which a baby carriage slowly bumps down the Odessa steps. My version took me a couple of days to shoot.

When I presented *Models* to my film teacher, Bob Del Tredici, he said, "Very twisted, but I love it."

I replied, "Yes, but now I have a date with one of those models."

I was referring—with more hope that truth—to Heidi, on whom I had a mad crush. She was The Unattainable, like Ali MacGraw in *Goodbye, Columbus*—the princess whose family had travelled the world, had been on safari and had a fantastic country house. I was Neil Klugman, the guy who arrives in New York with a suitcase packed by his mother and a salami sandwich. I plied her with funny notes in film class and finally she agreed to a mercy date.

I took Heidi to this fancy restaurant, La Diligence, which I couldn't afford. When I whipped out my wallet to pay the valet to park my mother's car, I realized I'd forgotten most of my money. I didn't have a credit card. La Diligence was a high-end steak place with a salad bar. After some quick calculating I decided I could afford a trip to the salad bar for $7.95 and pleaded "not hungry" so Heidi could have steak. So I was good until the waiter came with the dessert menu and Heidi ordered a crème brûlée. A crème brûlée? I was ruined!

Perhaps guessing my dilemma, Heidi insisted on paying for the dessert. I muttered a very relieved, "Fine," and got through it.

But wait! On our way home, Heidi said, "Let's go downtown and have some drinks."

Normally, I would have been thrilled. Instead, I said sadly and reluctantly, "Do you really want to do that?"

She replied, "Then why don't you come to my place so we can watch TV?"

Yes!

Heidi remains a good friend. When her mother died, I went to the funeral. Sharing Heidi's grief at the loss of a parent later helped me through the loss of my father. She was my first, albeit one-sided, love. Though we didn't date again, we had fantastic chemistry. Years later I think we both regretted that we hadn't explored our chemistry further, though by then, I was happily married.

I made one more film before I left Vanier. The story was framed as a family dinner in which someone was going to be poisoned to the music of "Moondance" by Van Morrison. My mother was flabbergasted: how is this preparing you for university? My parents probably wished I would become a lawyer, but they knew by now that I was a kooky, creative guy who knew how to take care of myself.

HOMAGE TO RICHARD GERE

I made two films while I was attending Ryerson: *The King of Yorkville* in 1984, and *The Ladies' Room* in 1985. My producing partner was Jeff Sackman, whom I knew from Montreal. When Jeff arrived in Toronto in the '80s, with his MBA from Syracuse University, he asked me how he could get into film. I told him the only going concerns were Garth Drabinsky, who was running Cineplex, and David Cronenberg, the filmmaker.

Jeff said, "Do you think you can get me a job interview?"

I was still in school and hanging around the fringes of the entertainment industry, but I had a contact in Garth's office. I also found what I thought to be Cronenberg's phone number and business address. When Jeff landed that interview as well, he asked if I wanted to accompany him. We were waiting in the lobby when I noticed an Academy Award in one of the showcases. I read the inscription: "Bob Crone." Apparently, he had invented something called the Steadicam, a device that made it possible to walk around shooting film while keeping the camera steady.

I had mixed up the names.

Jeff ultimately landed a job in Drabinsky's film-booking department, and we kept in touch, with the idea of making films together.

I wrote the script for *The King of Yorkville*, based on my experience in Toronto's Yorkville district of the '80s, with its big cars, nightclubs and beautiful women. I used to sit in the bar of the Bellair Café—Action Central on Saturday nights—and attempt pickups without success. For the film script, I wrote not about a student, but an aluminum salesman out of his league, looking for love in ritzy Yorkville. He kept getting kicked to the curb until he met Ellen, a Mary Kay cosmetics saleswoman and another loser. They found love at the Bellair Café.

Of course, the plan was to shoot at the Bellair. When the owner asked to see the script, I doctored it up to say how great the Bellair was, when we were actually satirizing the superficial Yorkville scene. He gave us permission to shoot in the restaurant for free and we did a location scout, during which the cameraman accidentally left behind our real shooting script. The owner of the Bellair called a couple of hours later. "I read your script," he said. "You're out!"

That was on Friday, and we had to shoot the next day. I walked into Pete & Marty's, a nightclub restaurant at College and Bay, and met the owner, Marty Soltys, who was also an aspiring filmmaker.

He said, "Okay, you can have it from midnight Saturday till midnight Sunday, and here are the keys."

I didn't as yet have enough confidence to direct so I hired Hans Friedrich from Ryerson's theatre program. He was gay and had a very soft voice. When he said, "Action! Action!" no one could hear him. I told him, "You've got to butch it up a bit." He tried, but we still had to help him.

I had a cameo as the bartender, but couldn't hit my mark. I'd walk in, say, "What are you having?" and get it wrong every time.

I stole my favourite scene—let's call it an homage—from *American Gigolo*. Our lead actor opened his closet to pick out a suit, just as Richard Gere had done, then he laid it out on his bed and went into the bathroom to shave and put on cologne. "Call Me" by Blondie was playing in the background—the same music from the opening track of *American Gigolo*. This was the first time I applied for a licence to use copyrighted music. I sent the screenplay to Chrysalis Records in New York, and they let me have it for free—I couldn't believe it!

Jeff and I invited hundreds of friends to the premiere at the Bloor Cinema. It was actually reviewed on television by critic Richard Crouse, who loved it. He called it one of the slickest films he'd ever seen and urged everyone to keep a close eye on the lighting. That was a joke because the lighting was awful. He and I still laugh about it.

Jeff's and my costs for making the film were close to zero—let's say $1,000 max for food and renting some gear. The actors donated their time for the experience; I borrowed a Bolex camera from a friend, which I returned broken; and the film was processed for free. We sold *The King of Yorkville* in 1985 to City-TV for a small profit.

Our second film venture, a year later in 1985, was *The Ladies' Room*. It came out of a drunken conversation about what we thought women said about men when in the washroom. That was to be the premise: what men think women say, not necessarily what women actually did say.

For research and casting, we invited dozens of women to Jeff's apartment, which was bigger than mine, and interviewed them about men, sex and dating. We recorded some really good dialogue. Whether it was my idea or Jeff's, I don't remember, but since I was the director, I'll take the bullet: Instead of using women in the film, we decided to cast men dressed as women—not gay men, just male actors in drag. We chose five, then shot them over two days at a dinner party and around a fireplace at my sister and brother-in-law's suburban house. I hired a product placement firm that gave us free food and booze, like Tia Maria and Pringles, which our guests passed around being sure to show their brand names. In that way, we were ahead of our time, but the cross-dressing idea was just so bad that the film was truly awful. Jeff and I soldiered through with another screening at the Bloor Cinema: our friendly audience couldn't decide whether to laugh or cry. Let's just say this isn't a film I've ever bragged about on my resume.

"SURE, I CAN GET YOU CHARLTON HESTON"

Jeff and I joined forces to make another film when my day job was as an account guy at Borden's. *Let's Kill All the Lawyers* focused on two lawyers who get mixed up with the mob. It was very funny in a Seth Rogenesque, black humour kind of way. We cast two actual lawyers who wanted to be actors, shot a trailer and created a poster. That was about as far as we could take it on our own. We wanted it to be a feature, but we had no money, so we sold the screenplay to an L.A. studio for $20,000.

I was looking forward to returning to Los Angeles as a promising screenwriter instead of as a shoe salesman. Jeff couldn't make the trip, but I flew down with one of our actors, Jerry Levitan, to meet with the studio head at the storied Beverly Hills Hotel. To take full advantage of our time, I also set up appointments with actors and other movie people. This included the great casting director, Lynn Stalmaster, who cast *Ben-Hur*. That was relevant, because in a court scene in our script, Moses testifies. After we made our request, Stalmaster told us, "Sure, I can get you Charlton Heston for the day."

We sailed out of that meeting on top of the world.

I phoned the studio head, who had bought our script, to confirm our appointment.

He replied, "Sorry, but I have an opportunity to go on a yacht today."

"Tomorrow?"

"Nah, we don't need to meet."

His name was Colin Huron, or something like that, but we called him Colon Urine after that. We never did meet and his studio never made our movie.

THE GUN IS/IS NOT IN THE DRAWER

From Borden's I moved on to Echo, where the day-to-day pressure—with Garth among my clients—was relentless, but I still felt driven to make films of my own. Influenced by the theatrical world of Drabinsky, I wrote a short, dark screenplay called *The Madness of Method*, in which I satirized method acting as taught by Lee Strasberg. It was about an unsuccessful actor who could never land a role. Partly, this was the result of his terrible judgment. He would go to a Chekhov audition and sing something from *Fiddler on the Roof*.

After spotting an ad for Thorndyke's *Ultimate Method*, the actor makes an appointment and meets the coach who explains that the Thorndyke Method taps the actor's deepest, most authentic emotions by taking him through his entire life cycle from birth and childhood to marriage and death. The actor signs up. However, after experiencing most of these life stages under the coach's direction, he begins to wonder: Why are all the actors' photos on my coach's wall of unknowns? Where are the stars produced by the Thorndyke Method?

When he dares to ask, the coach grows angry. "Don't insult me! Actors aren't famous for who they are, but for the roles they play. These are my Hamlets."

For his final lesson, the coach takes his student through the ultimate life scene: his own death. This is not faked, but real.

I had a script. Now all I needed was a name actor to star in it. I had been impressed by M. Emmet Walsh, who played a private detective in the Coen brothers' film, *Blood Simple*, in which a man hires a killer to eliminate his wife. My producer sent my screenplay to Walsh's agent. Amazingly, the agent called me back to say, "Emmet loved the screenplay. He's willing to come to Toronto for three days to shoot it for free." He had only one condition. "Emmet wants the acting student in the film to be played by his friend Richard Kind."

Wow! Kind was an up-and-coming actor from the hit television series, *Mad About You*. Suddenly, I had two Hollywood actors flying to Toronto to be in my film. For free.

I asked Garth if he would appear in a cameo, playing the off-camera casting director who rejects the actor, triggering his search for a coach. Garth agreed. When I pre-recorded his scene, he improvised by using his own kiss-off line, one he often used when he knew he wouldn't be casting someone: "We'll be in touch."

Walsh, Kind, my crew and I shot *The Madness of Method* in black and white, over three days, twenty-four hours a day, in winter. Our set was an unheated abandoned warehouse that I rented for $200 from a slum landlord. It turned out that Emmet had agreed to do the film because he would be a lead instead of a character actor, and now that he was the lead, he had turned into a full-blown diva. When he was unhappy, he would storm off the set into what we called a dressing room. Our relationship went from bad to worse. At lunch, he liked to sign a rare issue of a $2 American bill for the crew. On mine—and I still have it—he wrote, "What is it that you do?"

In the film's final scene, Kind was to lie on the floor in the fetal position. Emmet would draw a gun from his desk, say "Embrace death!" and then shoot.

Emmet called me into the dressing room. "Barry"—he rarely used my name—"if I go to the desk to get the gun, that will telegraph the move. It's a bad idea. The coach should have the gun on him."

I replied, "Emmet, why would he have the gun on him? You're wrong, absolutely wrong."

"No, I'm right."

"Do it as written."

"I won't do it that way."

I'd had enough. "Then do me a favour and go home."

"How will you do this scene without me?"

"I'll work around it somehow. I have enough footage."

He relented. "All right, I'll do the scene your way, but I'm going to tell the crew that you're wrong."

I was so mad, I shouted, "Get the fuck out!"

"Nope, we'll do it your way, but it won't work. I'll walk around the desk and look like an idiot."

I strode out, slamming the door.

Minutes later, the director of photography approached me. "Barry, it's about the last scene." Though I was quite sure he hadn't heard the argument, he continued, "We don't have enough shooting time for Emmet to go around the desk. I'd have to move the camera. That's not going to work. He'll have to have the gun on him."

Oh God. Must I reverse myself and be humiliated?

I returned to the dressing room. "Emmet, I've blocked the scene, and I've decided that you'll have the gun on you."

"Oh no, I won't. We're doing it your way."

We argued back and forth, wasting the little time we had left. Finally, Emmet agreed. We shot the scene his way, with the gun on him, and it was really good.

I was proud of *The Madness of Method*. I convinced Deluxe, which was owned by Garth, to process the film for free. I rented a theatre, hired a publicist and gave it a premiere. Major articles were written about me, which ticked off Len Gill. Our relationship was already strained, and while Len couldn't fault my work, he hated my growing public profile. By contrast, Garth was supportive. I showed him the film in his home and received his stamp of approval.

I sold *The Madness of Method* to ten different TV networks, probably quadrupling my investment of $6,000. It also won first prize at the 1995 Bilbao Film Festival. One amazing day, a cheque for $5,000 and a statuette of a Golden Bear arrived by FedEx from Spain. I had won awards for commercials, but these were my first for a film.

SPOKEN HISTORY

"I don't even buy green bananas."

In 1999, I filmed *Unforgettable: 100 Years Remembered*, for CBC-TV in anticipation of the millennium. I interviewed dozens of people who had lived through most of the twentieth century, and even a couple who'd lived a few years longer than that. Among them, they had witnessed the evolution of transportation from horse-and-buggy to automobile; from double-winged "flying machines" to jets and spaceships. The magic of radio had given way to the magic of television. Black-and-white silent movies had acquired voice and colour. And then computers changed everything.

This generation had experienced two World Wars and the Great Depression, the Holocaust, the dropping of the atom bomb, the rise of feminism and of Black Power.

Sister Maria Cordis, age eighty-five, spoke of the Depression bread lines: "Mother Superior told us, 'Make sure you give everyone a lunch because he may be St. Joseph.' When one man turned up drunk, she said, 'Give him a lunch anyway. He may be St. Patrick.'"

Legendary broadcasting pioneer Johnny Lombardi, age eighty-two, had this to say about war: "We were told it was a war to end all wars, then a few years later, we had another war. When I asked my father, 'Why do people fight?' he replied, 'Why do you fight with your brothers and sisters?' Now I'm a man of peace because I know the folly of war, of being envious."

Retail mogul Ed Mirvish, age eighty-four, shared his secret to longevity: "Don't stop breathing! At my age, I don't even buy green bananas. Because I had little formal training, I had a basic philosophy, 'Keep it simple.' I also decided, 'Go against the trend,' even put 'Honest' in front of your name because it makes everyone suspicious."

Composer John Weinzweig, age eighty-six, ruminated on life's purpose: "My only regret is that I never created a perfect composition, but as William Faulkner said, 'If you've created the perfect work, you have no more reason to live.'"

I asked my interviewees for words of wisdom as we entered the twenty-first century:

"Some people live only twenty years, but pack in one hundred. Others live one hundred years, but only really live twenty."

"If we had a quart of milk, we drank a quart. If we had three, we drank three. Kids today want five quarts, and that's just for starters."

"You have to figure things out for yourself whether it's the twentieth century or the twenty-first."

"If you've made a friend or done some good in a day, then you've justified that day, but no one is entitled to death until they've justified their life."

"When you turn ninety, you have to watch out because people

are going to start opening doors for you and helping you across the street, and then you lose your confidence. Push back."

"I'd like to live to be ninety-nine and then be shot by a jealous husband."

"Why am I living so long? Because I'm not finished the job I was given to do."

"I have severe arthritis. I'm blind in one eye, and I don't give a damn!"

"If you put back the cap on a bottle of Coke, you keep in some of the bubbles. Always keep in some of your bubbles."

I was nervous about meeting Canadian-born John Kenneth Galbraith, age ninety, once the world's most famous economist. Tori's family knew him, so that was our entree. He lived in Massachusetts, where he had been a Harvard professor for half a century. Deep in the woods, as it turned out. Tori and I drove around and around for hours, completely lost; it was like *The Blair Witch Project*. Finally, we came to a hut. I climbed out of the car. A guy approached me.

"We're lost."

"What are you looking for?"

"John Kenneth Galbraith."

"He's my father." The son gave us no-fail instructions, "Turn here, make a left, then go straight."

Dr. Galbraith was six-foot-eight. Because of his height and age, he was often in pain from spinal arthritis, but his intellect was intact. He escorted us to a coach house, which he referred to as his writing pavilion. It was a simple white wood structure, classically New England, sparsely but tastefully furnished. Everything was arranged around a massive writing desk, meticulously neat, yet laden with mementos from the Democratic presidents whom he had served—Roosevelt, Truman, Kennedy, Johnson, Clinton. Among the memorabilia were letters from FDR, some White House writing paper and a paperweight, a 1946 Medal of Freedom from President Harry Truman, a 2000 Medal of Freedom from President Bill Clinton. Occupying pride of place was the weathered typewriter on which Galbraith had written some four dozen books, including *American Capitalism* (1952), *The Affluent Society* (1958) and *The New Industrial State* (1967).

Once we were seated in well-worn club chairs, Dr. Galbraith talked about crafting the New Deal with FDR, and his work as Kennedy's ambassador to India, where he became a trusted adviser to Prime Minister Jawaharlal Nehru. About two minutes in, I realized I was in way over my head, intellectually as well as physically. I might as well have been discussing the universe with Stephen Hawking. The man was such a genius! To bring the conversation down to my own level, I finally asked, "What do you do for fun?"

"Occasionally I go to a movie. Just the other day, my wife took me to see *Titanic*, but after five minutes, I was praying the boat would sink."

I asked him how he chose his career. He said, "My father was a livestock producer, so as a young man, I faced the choice between all the hard work that an Ontario farmer must do, and the leisurely life of a college professor. I had no difficulty with that decision." On his view of his profession: "Economists are most economical about ideas. They make the ones they learned in graduate school last a lifetime." On war and depression: "I could never persuade anyone, including myself, that World War II was justified in economic terms, but there's no question that it put an end to the terrible menace of joblessness and mass poverty in Canada and the United States." On social reform: "One of the great achievements of this century is that we began with women not having the right to vote, but now they play a strong and, in some cases, a dominant role." And on the human spirit: "Optimism verging on insanity is normal."

★

My skill as a filmmaker was becoming more polished and had come a long way from that first wedding video. I was beginning to find my voice, learn how to shape a story and fill a frame with characters. I was also ready to take on bigger subjects and rattle a few cages.

MY DAUGHTER'S DEBUT

My daughter, Sloan, who was then ten, was looking at all the film posters in my office. "Why don't you make something I would like?" she asked.

I told her, "Go find what you want to do and we'll film it together."

Sloan discovered that only 1 per cent of the world's population has red hair like hers, and that scientists predict that redheads will be extinct in a hundred years. We worked out a script, called *Red Alert*, with Sloan in the starring role, in which she would get "to the bottom of this nightmare."

I was surprised at how brave and confident she was on camera. She had fun but she gave me a hard time if she thought something was amiss. She also learned that filmmaking was hard work, that it required organization and discipline.

We were slated to talk about the film before its premiere at TIFF. The two of us were backstage, listening as we were introduced to the audience, when the applause hit and I felt Sloan's legs buckle. She held my hand tightly, then asked, "You're coming out there with me, aren't you?" We walked onto the stage together, and the minute Sloan stepped into the spotlight, she relaxed, just as I used to at her age when doing theatre.

We had two screenings that day; the second was a private showing for about two hundred guests. For that, Sloan stayed with the audience, and when she heard the applause all around her, she didn't know how to deal with it. She said, "I have to get out of here," then ran for cover. Again, I understood that feeling, though I don't know where it comes from. I, too, both crave praise and am uncomfortable with it.

From Sloan's distinctive red hair to her stage presence, I knew she had already absorbed the lesson my father had taught me to never blend in.

Chapter Sixteen

GUILTY PLEASURE: THE DOMINICK DUNNE STORY

Melissa and I loved reading *Vanity Fair.* One day in 2001, we were fighting as usual over who would read it first when Melissa exclaimed, "Wow, I'd like to meet this Dominick Dunne." Dunne was a regular contributor to the magazine.

On impulse, I replied, "I'm going to make a film about him. Then we'll both meet him."

As soon as I said these words, I knew it would happen. I also knew that a film on Dominick Dunne would be highly saleable. His reportage on the trial of O.J. Simpson for killing his wife, Nicole Brown Simpson, had jump-started his career as a hugely popular chronicler of the rich and famous gone horribly wrong. As it turned out, I was right about his market appeal. He was the only subject I've ever approached for a documentary without first having secured the financing; however, as soon as I mentioned his name, I easily sold the project to Bravo, TMN and Court TV USA.

Dunne and I had a mutual friend in Brian Linehan, renowned for his meticulously researched celebrity interviews on his popular City-TV show, *City Lights*. After Brian made the connection for me, Dunne not only agreed to be filmed, but he also sounded excited. And he didn't lay down any conditions, such as the right to make the final cut.

He agreed to three interviews. The first took me to his Connecticut home, which was as rich and magnificently eccentric as a setting for one his novels. Dunne had purchased the place with the proceeds from the sale of *An Inconvenient Woman*, which had been made into a TV miniseries. He named it *Cloud* after the mansion in that novel. Its huge rooms were comfortably luxurious and littered with upscale objects reprising Dunne's career. Two English footstools were from Palm Beach, where he had covered the 1991 William Kennedy Smith rape trial. The painting of a turn-of-the-century Parisian scene had been purchased in Italy when he was writing about socialite Roberto Polo, who had been arrested for misappropriating $110 million. A wonderful woven rug came from an antique shop in Jordan, where he had been travelling in 1991 with Queen Noor of Jordan. Two red-lacquered Chinese tables were souvenirs from Dallas, where he had interviewed Angelina Jolie in 2006 as she was filming *A Mighty Heart*. A pair of elaborately carved wood console tables came from Bolivia, a beautiful Kilim runner from Turkey, and so on. Dunne had surrounded himself with meaningful and beautiful objects that imbued every day with memories.

Dunne himself was the sort of dandy that made me think of David Niven or Noel Coward. Everything about him was elegant, from his Savile Row suits and perfectly styled grey hair to his over-sized, tortoiseshell glasses. Dunne even smelled great, as I noted when he greeted me with a big hug. "You're Barry?"

He was such a class act, always so effortlessly at one with his surroundings, whether in a Connecticut estate or, as I would later discover, his East 49th Street New York apartment. The one-bedroom apartment was a tightly packed jewel box, with its celadon-coloured living-room opening through French doors to a wraparound terrace, a small study and a minuscule kitchen jammed with the best art and crockery. Both apartment and estate featured silver-framed pictures, leather-bound *Vanity Fair* magazines, the *Architectural Digest* and refrigerator reminders: "Call Lauren Bacall." Or Diane von Furstenberg. Or Joanne Carson.

Dunne and I spent two days together in Connecticut. I knew I would have to hone my interview skills for this man, who routinely interrogated celebrities and dined with Barbara Walters. I reminded myself to maintain eye contact with him, to persuade him to trust me and be passionate. I stayed up late, memorizing everything about his life so I could work without notes, and throw unexpected details his way to intrigue him, appeal to his ego, provoke him into being candid and establish some positive chemistry between us. We became so comfortable together that after one interview, Dunne said to me, "I want to show you something. Leave your camera crew."

He took me into the coach house, opened a filing cabinet and showed me unpublished crime-scene photos from the O.J. Simpson trial so graphic and gruesome they will remain in my head till the day I die. I'm talking about Nicole Brown Simpson's decapitated head barely attached to her torso. I wondered: *Why is he showing me these? Is he testing me?* I decided, no, he was proud to demonstrate the access he had attained when he occupied a front-row seat at the O.J. trial. I stared, mesmerized, as he flipped through these bloody photos as if through pages of a *Town & Country* magazine. He'd seen it all.

Dominick showed me another set of photos, which I believe were a test. They were from the trial of Lyle and Erik Menendez, who killed their mother and father, then went on a binge with their parents' money. The brothers had admitted their responsibility for the murders, but claimed their father had sexually abused them—a defence that failed to sway the jury. The photo Dominick lingered over was of Lyle Menendez, sitting on a rock, modelling white Calvin Klein underwear.

Dominick commented, "Would you look at Lyle's body. Isn't that marvellous? He could have been a successful model, couldn't he, Barry?"

Dominick had a feminine way about him, and though he didn't come out as gay while we were filming, he did five years later, during the making of a documentary by an Australian team, to which he also agreed because he was so hungry to be immortalized. I was invited by the *New York Times* to a private screening of that film, which Dominick was, by then, too ill to attend. After Dominick's death, two weeks later, his son, Griffin, confirmed that his father was bisexual, though he had been celibate for twenty years, perhaps to keep his secret.

Dominick Dunne was born on October 29, 1925, into a privileged, close-knit, Hartford, Irish-Catholic family, the second of six siblings. His father was a prominent heart surgeon, his mother an heiress. It was what Dunne called a "Big Deal family."

During a Hollywood sightseeing trip, nine-year-old Dominick stared out the window of a bus that toured the neighbourhoods where the stars lived, soaking in the glamour, and decided that's where he belonged. Years later, while he was building his career as a moderately successful Hollywood studio executive, he had a whirlwind love affair with heiress Ellen Griffin. They were married in 1954, and had three children: actor-director Griffin; Alex, a teacher; actress Dominique.

Hollywood was a fast-paced ride in which Dominick described his role as that of "a B-level producer on an A-level social list." They packed their chic parties with the who's who of Hollywood: Natalie Wood and Robert Wagner, Ronald and Nancy Reagan, Kirk Douglas, David Niven, Liz Taylor, Gore Vidal, Paul Newman, Loretta Young,

Audrey Hepburn, David O. Selznick. As the '60s drew to a close, Dunne found himself in a losing battle with his addiction to star-studded parties, cocaine and alcohol. He hit bottom in 1973, while in Italy producing *Ash Wednesday*, starring Elizabeth Taylor and Henry Fonda, with Richard Burton also on location.

"You couldn't get any more glamorous than that," he said. "All sorts of intrigues were going on, and we were all drunks except for Fonda. It was over for me after that movie."

Dunne's consuming addictions cost him his career, his marriage, his social status and his glamorous life. "I left Hollywood like a whipped dog. I was drinking, snorting, doing anything anyone could think of that I wasn't supposed to do."

Dunne decided to go cold turkey. "For six months, I lived alone in a one-room cabin in Oregon. I had been the kind of guy who went to a party every night, along with a party on my way to the party, and another on my way home from the party. Now, there I was, living in silence. All the Hollywood crapola had ended. I came to terms with who I was, and why my career was destroyed. It wasn't the fault of all those people I used to blame. I had created my own downfall."

By 1982, Dunne had reinvented himself as a successful novelist, writing about the high society that had snubbed him. Life was good again. And then, a phone call delivered horrific news. His twenty-three-year-old daughter, Dominique, had been strangled to death by her boyfriend, a celebrity chef at Ma Maison, an A-list L.A. restaurant.

Dunne was devastated. "I was very close to her, truly close. The last word she ever said to me the night before her death, on my birthday, was, 'I love you, Daddy.' She had been making a movie in Hollywood, while I was in New York, and she knew I always wanted to know what was happening on set. The hospital kept Dominique on life support, and we went as a family to say goodbye—my former wife, with whom I'd remained close, my two sons and myself. We talked to her, and if you've had a child murdered, you have thoughts of revenge. I even went through moments of thinking I would hire an assassin, though I knew I never would. Instead, I kissed her head, and I asked, 'Give me your talent.'"

He was battling despair in the aftermath of his daughter's death when he received an invitation from Tina Brown, then editor of *Vanity Fair*, to write about his daughter's murderer's trial. That struck Dunne as exactly right. His power—his revenge—lay in his ability to expose evil to public gaze. "Through the lowest point in my life, came this whole new career as a columnist for *Vanity Fair*. I came to think of Dominique as my guardian angel, so that any time I was in trouble, I'd say, 'Honey, help,' and I would feel that she was there."

The Los Angeles trial shocked Dunne anew. "What I realized was that the rights of the victims do not equate with the rights of the killer. The man who killed my daughter had a history of violence against women, but that was kept from the jury. It was the most unfair, unjust trial. Every day, for nine weeks, I sat in the front row of the courtroom keeping notes . . . four feet away from my daughter's killer."

The killer who, when convicted, would serve only three years in prison.

Dunne's first article for *Vanity Fair* was called "Justice." It was passionate and gripping and it caused a sensation. His obsession with the rich and famous was now driven by a purpose beyond envy. Dominick Dunne was, at last, in step with his destiny.

Dunne signed an exclusive contract with the magazine and channeled his rage into stories about privileged and wealthy people who cheat, steal and sometimes kill. His subjects included the trials of O.J. Simpson, the Menendez brothers and Claus von Bülow, who was accused of attempting to kill his wealthy wife. He also published eleven novels that explored the kinds of lives his articles reported on, including the bestsellers *The Two Mrs. Grenvilles* and *People Like Us*.

"I became a victim's advocate," he told me. "The O.J. Simpson verdict shocked America. After a trial that lasted a year, the jury arrived at its not-guilty [verdict] in a couple of hours—there was something shameful about that. The defence had a jury consultant whose sole job was to watch the jurors, day by day, for signs anyone might be leaning towards a conviction, and then they would find a way to get rid of that person. Only rich people can do that. To win an acquittal, it came down to lawyers sitting around a table, and thinking up falsehoods to fool the jury. When I left the courtroom the day of the verdict, a CNN guy said, 'Dominick you gotta go on TV.' I should never have agreed. I was too upset. When legal analyst Greta Van Susteren said, 'Well, the jury has given its opinion,' she made me so crazy that I took off my microphone and threw it at the cameras. I mean, I went nuts. I knew O.J. was guilty before the freeway chase, just as I knew that Lyle Menendez was responsible, though not necessarily Erik, for his parents' murder, six months before he was arrested. It was his cockiness as he walked out of his parents' memorial service. I had a feeling about that, and I go with my feelings. So far, I've been right every time."

Given Dunne's unshakeable righteous anger, I was surprised when Johnnie Cochran, Simpson's lead defence lawyer, agreed to be interviewed for my documentary. I knew Cochran had a big ego, but his relationship with Dunne was so combative during the trial that I thought he might have had enough. Dunne made faces whenever the defence scored a point during the trial, then stepped out of the courtroom and up to his pulpit each evening on *Larry King Live* to expound his views to over one million viewers. After that, he would pour more scorn on the O.J. defence team in his *Vanity Fair* articles.

I interviewed Cochran in Toronto, where he arrived impeccably dressed and smoking a cigar. To my surprise, he was generous in his appraisal of Dunne. "Every trial needs a Dominick Dunne to cover events. I thought he was very entertaining."

He continued in the same vein. "If you've already figured out a trial's result, how you report the facts in between gets a little muddled. When Dominick Dunne wrote about 'justice,' it was justice as he saw it. He is who he is—a strong personality with strong, strong views coloured by the incomprehensible loss of his loved one. He felt his daughter's trial produced an outrageous result, which pretty much coloured everything he did afterwards. In this country, if you think about victims' advocates, you think about Dunne, and if you're on the defence, you know any article he might write would be an attack against you. That's what he lived for."

As for the trial itself, Cochran continued: "Clearly money plays a role in any trial, celebrity also plays a role. The prosecution kicked off nine out of ten black jurors. They just kept doing it, so we had to deal with whoever was left. We started out with twenty-four jurors, including twelve alternates, and we ended up with only fourteen. It wasn't black and white, as Dunne would have it. There were shades of grey, but he believed in what he was doing, even when misguided. He carved out his own niche, catering to the rich and famous, and interpreting justice for them."

Long before I did the Dominick film, Eddie Greenspan used to rant to me about Dunne being a shill for the prosecution. The fact that this completely biased individual had direct access to the media made Eddie's resentment boil over. When Eddie heard about my documentary, he told me he wanted to be in it.

While Cochran was conciliatory, Eddie was furious. "Mr. Dunne proved both mean-spirited and dangerous in his lack of respect for the judicial system. 'I, Dominick Dunne, will decide who is guilty, who is lying, who's telling the truth.' No matter how rich and powerful a defendant may be, the state is richer. The state has more people, more money to throw at the rich and powerful, than the rich and powerful can possibly throw against the state. A trial is not a play where people at the end stand up and applaud. In court, if the jury doesn't 'applaud,' your client may go to jail for life, or even lose his or her life. It's real."

Hollywood producer David Brown felt that Dunne's lack of legal training gave him an advantage as a reporter. "Dominick didn't have to hide behind legal niceties. He was fascinated with power, the corruption of power in particular and the ability of power to get away with things. That became his signature. Dominick was above gossip. He was a diarist. He was able to capture the essence of people. His own story was also one of great regeneration."

Larry King's response to my request for an interview was as surprising as Johnnie Cochran's, but in the opposite way. He was dismissive and quite cold. We met in L.A.'s famous Nate 'n Al's Deli, where King regularly held court. He looked like a caricature of himself: very gaunt, in shirt and jeans with his signature suspenders and bad hair-dye job. Equal to his reputation for having been married a hundred times was his reputation for never preparing for *Larry King Live*. It was always, "Okay, so who's on tonight?"

When he defended Dunne, he seemed to offer a defence of his own style of reporting as well. "We live in an age of spit it out! Learn it now! Fast! Cover it tomorrow! Go here! Go there! Dominick Dunne put his audience right into the courtroom. He knew justice from the perspective of a wounded man. He was not an expert on justice, and he was the first to admit to his bias. If the evidence in the O.J. trial had been presented differently, that jury might have voted differently. However, a lot of people told me that if they had been on that jury, they would have voted 'not guilty' based on the prosecution's presentation. Remember, the audience saw a lot of stuff the jury never saw. The DNA witnesses were all thrown out, and the judge lost control of the trial."

Graydon Carter, who became editor-in-chief of *Vanity Fair* after Tina Brown, valued Dominick Dunne as one of America's most popular feature writers. "The age range of people reading him went from young to old. Nick peppered his stories with social and Hollywood tidbits like candy drops along a path through the forest, but he was always taking you somewhere, because at the core of everything was his fight for the rights of people who had lost their rights. People would come up to me at parties, imagining they could be the next Dominick Dunne, because they knew about society, but Nick brought something much more complex, and much more soulful—a large part of which, unfortunately, stemmed from the murder of his daughter. He found a voice, and he stuck with it, full-time—I mean, he never let up. That was his life."

Another key to Dunne's success was his access, not only to those in high social circles, but in every walk of life. As he told me, "A lot of people think I am this great investigative reporter, but the fact is, people seek me out. I have these incredible coincidental meetings happening almost daily."

Dominick's son Griffith verified the claim. "My father was like an Alacrity spy. People would contact him, and he would get so excited about that. He was a great listener, and he'd talk to a complete nut, giving him the benefit of a doubt."

The late *New York Times* writer David Carr described Dunne as a cat who sat quietly, licking his paws and waiting. "Over time, you would feel compelled to tell him things. With his combination of fluff and substance, he mirrored perfectly what *Vanity Fair* is about. Dunne left the gravitational pull of journalism, and moved into another business, which was the business of being famous, and he did a really good job of it. He was a black belt in dropping names, and as shallow and as silly as that seems, it gave him adjacency to either brilliant or dark people whom we all found fascinating."

Dunne's sartorial flare, his A-list connections and his writings about violent crime sometimes drew comparison to the critically acclaimed, openly gay novelist Truman Capote. Capote too, was the darling of New York high society. That is, until he wrote too cruelly, scandalously and invasively about his famous friends, especially Barbara "Babe" Paley, married to CBS founder William S. Paley. Their humiliating rejection of him led to his steep decline into drugs, alcoholism and isolation.

As David Carr continued, "Capote stepped over the line and got clobbered, banished from a society which he loved and which provided him with his living. When Dominick wrote his novel *People Like Us*, he wasn't actually writing about 'us.' He always maintained an outsider's stance so that when he sat down at his computer, he served as the messenger from a party to which most of us commoners would not be invited. Unlike Capote, he did a good job of revealing just enough to sell books, but not so much that he wouldn't be invited back. If Capote was the skunk at the garden party, Dominick Dunne was the perfumed skunk."

Dunne's own take on Capote echoed Carr's. "Let me tell you exactly what I think of Truman. He became too much a part of the world he aspired to. Instead of keeping some distance, he did a very stupid thing. His ticket to New York's inner sanctum was Babe Paley, and after he embarrassed her, she never spoke to him again."

During our post-interview conversations, Dunne taught me his secret for being a sought-after party guest: "Always come armed with the best stories to entertain the other guests." Of course, that was simple for him because of his access. He called it the Dominick Dunne Roadshow. "You prepare your stories for a party the same way as you select your wardrobe," he explained. "You know your audience, you rehearse and then you tap dance for your host and the other guests."

This backfired once at a dinner party where Dunne enraptured his audience with details of the ongoing O.J. trial. Only afterwards did he learn that one of the catering staff, hired for the evening, was one of O.J.'s sons. To Nick's credit, he felt awful about that incident.

As a victim's rights advocate, Dunne was at the top of his game when pursuing justice on behalf of the Moxley family after the partially nude, bludgeoned body of their fifteen-year-old daughter, Martha, was found in their backyard, on October 30, 1975. Suspicion fell upon the Moxleys' neighbours, the Skakel brothers, Thomas and Michael. The murder attracted worldwide attention when the media reported that the two boys were the nephews of Ethel Skakel Kennedy, widow of Robert Kennedy.

In 1993, after almost two decades with no arrest in that case, Dunne wrote a roman à clef, *A Season in Purgatory*. With the certitude he always brought to the cases he wrote about, he was convinced that he knew the identity of Martha Moxley's killer: he was sure it Michael Skakel. More significantly, he became the driving force in having the case reopened in January 2000, resulting in the arrest, trial and conviction of Michael Skakel.

As David Carr confirmed, "Whatever side Dunne picked, you couldn't write him off as a dilettante. He was like a dog on a meat bone, and he stayed with it. The Moxley story is a testament to his durability."

This is an accolade Dunne accepted. "I worked so hard on that case for so many years, and put so much of myself into it. Martha Moxley and my daughter Dominique were only a year apart in age, and both were murdered on October 30, though in different years. In 1991, I sought out Dorthy Moxley, mother of Martha Moxley, who was so media shy that she wouldn't let me go to her house. When I met her in a coffee shop at the Baltimore/Washington Airport, I asked her, 'Why did you leave Greenwich? Now there's nobody fighting for you.' She said, 'Every time I looked out the window into the Skakel house, I was sure someone in that house knew who did it.'"

When I interviewed Dorthy Moxley for the Dunne film, she told me how blunt and sure Dominick had been in his approach. "One morning, he called to say, 'Dorthy, I know who killed Martha. It was Michael.' Dominick gave me a feeling of hope. All of a sudden he came to me, and my prayers were answered. People like him are truly angels."

Michael's father, Rushton Skakel, had hired the Sutton Agency, made up of retired detectives and NYPD cops, to dissolve the dark cloud hanging over his family. When the agency came up with damning evidence against Michael, the elder Skakel was so horrified he paid the agency's $750,000 bill, then suppressed the report.

Dunne acquired that report and it provided the evidence that was decisive in the case. As he explained, "The agency had hired a young guy out of the University of Virginia to put all the reports together for Rush Skakel. When the student learned the report had been quashed, he stole it. It's as simple as that. The Skakels were able to ward off justice for twenty-seven years, ruining everybody's life. If they had dealt with the murder when it happened, everyone would have been happier."

Michael Skakel's guilty verdict took Dorthy Moxley by surprise. "I never dreamed the jury would convict. I was all set to talk about an acquittal, and I didn't know what to say. Then it occurred to me that this was Martha's day—what so many people had worked so hard and so long for."

After I finished filming *Guilty Pleasure*, Dominick received a cut of the film, against my wishes, before it was ready. Should I have been surprised? Wasn't he the man who had access to everything? The result was a sudden voicemail from Dominick on my answering machine, "I've got to talk to you!"

When I called back, he told me, "Look, I loved the film except for two things: First, I don't like the title, I don't understand it."

After I explained that "guilty pleasure" was what readers felt when reading his *Vanity Fair* columns, he said, "Okay. You're the marketing guy. I'll leave that with you."

His second complaint: "I don't know who Eddie fucking Greenspan is, but I want him out of the film. Cut him. I want him out."

I replied, "Look, Dominick, this is not a bar mitzvah film. Eddie is a well-respected lawyer."

"To whom? I don't know who he is."

The film—with Eddie Greenspan still in it—was given a

private screening in a New York screening room, attended by all of Dominick's friends. It was a glittery event, definitely A-list. Afterwards, Dominick wrote in his *Vanity Fair* column, "I just attended the screening of a film about my life, and it was thrilling, except for the presence of a Canadian lawyer, to whom I will not give any publicity by mentioning his name."

Three years later, when I did a documentary on Eddie for CBC-TV's *Life and Times*, I made sure to tell Dominick when he would be able to watch my film about "the lawyer you love to hate which was sold to Court TV in the U.S." Dominick replied, "Thanks for giving me advance notice to throw my television out the window."

Eddie loved that email, which he framed and hung on his wall. He said it was almost as good as being in *Vanity Fair*.

After *Guilty Pleasure* was released, Larry King invited Dominick and me to appear on *Larry King Live*, which would have been terrific publicity. Dominick agreed. Unfortunately, around this same time, the Gary Condit/Chandra Ann Levy scandal went into high gear. Levy, an intern at the Federal Bureau of Prisons, disappeared in May 2001. Investigators later discovered she was having an affair with a married congressman, Gary Condit. Dominick, with his usual self-assurance, was convinced of Condit's guilt. Why? Because he had heard it from a horse whisperer in Dubai. As it turned out, the horse whisperer was wrong. When Condit was cleared, he sued Dominick and *Vanity Fair*. Dominick, caught in mid-scandal, was mortified, because he'd always had the best information. When he told me he wasn't going to appear on *Larry King Live*, I tried to persuade him, "We'll insist that the Gary Condit case is off-topic."

Dominick was adamant. "Larry would not be doing his job if he didn't ask about the Condit case."

He was right of course, proving that even if you are at the centre of the media, you can't control it. I lost my chance for *Larry King Live* just as Eddie Greenspan lost his for *Vanity Fair*.

I was gratified when our collaboration over the filming of *Guilty Pleasure* turned into a friendship. During the five years before Dominick's death, he tutored me on networking and event planning, how best to use information and to build up my Rolodex. His lesson in power was simple: if you don't have it, get close to those who do. Dunne taught me that we are all three degrees away from access.

My ultimate story about celebrity, Dominick-style, occurred the last time we lunched together. I knew his favourite restaurant was the Four Seasons in New York's Seagram Building. Everything about it spelled power, from the scale of the walls to the sculpture and other famous artworks that hung on the walls. I had made the reservation, even though I knew this lunch would cost a fortune, because I wanted to have the ultimate power lunch with the ultimate power player. I also had a Cartier pen with Dominick's name inscribed on it, because he collected pens, he wasn't well, and I wanted to thank him for his friendship. When I arrived at the Four Seasons, I identified myself to the snooty owner, Julian Niccolini.

"Avrich?" He snapped his fingers, then directed someone else to take me to a table. I knew Dominick would be late, because that's the way it is with famous people. Meanwhile, legends were walking by my table—Clive Davis, Edgar Bronfman, Henry Kissinger, Mike Nichols, Barbara Walters—making it clear from each placement that I was on the D-level of this cruise ship. After about forty-five minutes, Niccolini walked by, paused, then returned. "Who are you waiting for?"

"Dominick Dunne."

He banged his fist on my table. "Why didn't you tell me you were dining with Mr. Dunne?"

"You didn't ask. You didn't even look up."

"Follow me for God's sake!" Suddenly, he stopped. "Wait here."

I watched as he removed a couple from what I would learn was Dunne's table, at the centre of the Four Season's universe. I received

their table, and they got mine. Dunne would have loved the news that Niccolini was arrested for sexual harassment in 2015.

Eventually, Dominick made his appearance. "Sorry, Barry. Long call with Nancy." I assumed he meant Nancy Reagan. Once he was seated, everyone who had whisked by me came over to say hello.

It was an intimate lunch, and very poignant. Dominick told me he was dying of bladder cancer, which was shocking news. Dominick craved exposure and publicity but this was a headline he'd planned to avoid till his last breath. Long before this moment his life had been all talk and all action, and that was the way he wanted it. Celebrity for breakfast, lunch and dinner. Celebrity all the time.

Chapter Seventeen

THE LAST MOGUL: THE LIFE AND TIMES OF LEW WASSERMAN

As soon as I met Lew Wasserman at an L.A. screening in the early '90s, I knew that I was going to make a film about him, and that's what I told him. At six-foot-two, he towered over me, gaunt and craggy-faced. He stared down at me through his oversized, black-rimmed glasses, put his hand on my shoulder, and with his thumb dug deep into my neck said, "Not while I'm alive or dead, kid."

He was half right. I started researching Wasserman that day, then began filming on June 3, 2002, the day of his death. Lew Wasserman was easily the most powerful and imposing figure Hollywood has ever known. George Orwell wrote, "Absolute power corrupts absolutely." He must have just had a meeting with Lew Wasserman.

Isaac and Minnie Weiserman arrived in America from Russia in 1907 with empty pockets and dreams of a better life. They settled in the east side of Cleveland, then a hotbed of prostitution, gambling and racketeering. They changed their name to Wasserman, and in 1913 Minnie gave birth to Louis, their third and last child.

When he was twelve, Lew took a job selling candy at Keith's, a raunchy burlesque house. He became doorman for one of the mob-controlled speakeasies on Vincent Avenue when he was still a gangly kid. In high school, he hired bands for dances from the same talent agency that booked for Al Capone's mob-controlled Chicago nightclubs. That agency was the Chicago-based Music Corporation of America, or MCA, founded by Jules C. Stein. After he graduated from high school, Wasserman became publicity director for the Hippodrome Movie House. One night after his shift, he watched *The Jazz Singer*. That movie changed his life. Like Al Jolson's character, he was the son of a devout immigrant Jew who had craved a career in show business. Lew's own dream began to take shape.

In 1935, when Kingpin Moe Dalitz, head of the Jewish Mafia known as the Silent Syndicate, opened the Mayfair Casino, he hired Wasserman to run promotions. After countless raids by prohibition investigator Eliot Ness, the real-life inspiration for the TV series *The Untouchables*, Dalitz sold the casino to a New York crime outfit known as Murder Incorporated. Jules Stein offered the unemployed twenty-two-year-old a $60-a-week job as a publicist for MCA, provided that he move to Chicago. Lew was eager to leave Cleveland behind. So was his new wife, Edie Beckerman, daughter of a prominent family caught up in scandal. Her father, Henry Beckerman, who'd made a fortune doing business with Moe Dalitz, was charged with embezzling from the city. He was later acquitted, but not before the Beckermans lost their wealth and social standing.

Stein was making big money booking bands into clubs for Big Jim Colosimo and his protege, Al Capone. He had persuaded James Caesar Petrillo, head of the American Federation of Musicians, to give MCA a waiver to not only represent big bands but also to produce radio shows. Petrillo then helped keep the money rolling in by blocking costly musician salary increases or strikes that might hurt the agency. By 1938, MCA was managing 90 per cent of America's dance bands. For Sophie Tucker, Tony Martin, Benny Goodman, Tommy Dorsey and a host of others, MCA was the only game in town. MCA also controlled comedy writers, producers and film stars.

Inspired by Stein, Wasserman created the radio show *Kay Kyser and His College of Musical Knowledge*, which regularly attracted an audience of twenty million per episode. Stein was impressed and made Wasserman his New York agent. The move would prove to be temporary: Wasserman had his eye on Hollywood. In 1939, when he moved to the grand, white-pillared office in Beverly Hills to head up MCA's movie division, Hattie McDaniel and Ronald Reagan were MCA's only Hollywood clients. Wasserman dug into MCA's deep pockets and bought up talent agencies rich with stars such as Greta Garbo, Ginger Rogers, Fred Astaire, Henry Fonda, and writers including Billy Wilder, Dorothy Parker and Ben Hecht. Almost overnight, MCA became the largest talent agency in the world, shifting clout away from the movie studios. MCA represented seven hundred movie stars and three hundred Broadway actors. Its booking team controlled radio programming, big-band bookings and most nightclubs. Stein rewarded Wasserman by making him president of MCA. At thirty-three, he was the most powerful person in Hollywood.

In 1951, at a time when the new medium of television was hurting movie business, MCA created Revue Productions to produce TV shows. This, despite the fact that the Screen Actors Guild (SAG) prohibited talent agencies from also being producers. No problem. Meet the new president of SAG—former MCA client Ronald Reagan. What a happy coincidence! Reagan's first order of business was to oversee the granting of an exclusive waiver for MCA to produce. Wasserman was using the same strategy with the actors' union that Stein had used to persuade music union chief James Petrillo to allow MCA to represent big bands while also producing radio shows.

Reagan had good reason to be grateful to Wasserman. After Reagan starred in *Kings Row* (1942), Wasserman negotiated an unprecedented seven-year $1 million contract for him as host of *General Electric Theater*. He bailed Reagan out of financial troubles by brokering a deal to sell 236 acres of Reagan's Malibu ranch, appraised at $115,000, to 20th Century Fox for $2 million. He helped Reagan became governor of California. He would go on to help Reagan become president of the United States but first he had to deal with another president's brother.

MCA's growing power had set in motion a counterforce. As early as 1946, the *Saturday Evening Post* had carried a feature story, *MCA: Star-Spangled Octopus*, detailing MCA's grip on the entertainment industry. In 1962, President John F. Kennedy's brother, Attorney General Robert Kennedy, convened a Grand Jury Investigation to look for evidence of corruption and abuse of power at MCA. With the threat of criminal and civil penalties for alleged antitrust violations hanging over it, MCA divested itself of its talent agency. As producer David Brown, who was on that grand jury, told me in an interview, "I remember quite well that when we put together *The Young Lions* with Dean Martin, Marlon Brando, Montgomery Clift and Maximilian Schell, every actor was an MCA client. If you wanted one, you had to take all the others. The U.S. government overnight upset Lew's applecart, and MCA the talent agency was no more, cutting adrift some of his closest associates."

Even as it stopped representing performers, MCA expanded its operations in other areas by buying then-struggling Universal Pictures and Decca Records and creating the largest entertainment assembly line in Hollywood. Building on its Revue library of detective shows, westerns, situation comedies and specials, MCA and Wasserman transformed moribund Universal Pictures into Universal Studios, the largest and busiest lot in Hollywood.

With profits from MCA-produced TV hits such as *Dragnet*, *Alfred Hitchcock Presents* and the groundbreaking miniseries, *Roots*, Wasserman paid $11.25 million for Universal's property and facilities. He turned the four hundred acres into Universal City, which offered studio tours to the public and attracted five million guests a year. He added a 1,800-room hotel and a live concert amphitheatre that opened with the Grateful Dead. The long lineup of hippies horrified Wasserman, but those concerts became the fastest-growing outdoor attraction in California.

As a monument to his own success, Wasserman hired architect Mies van der Rohe to duplicate the New York tower that he had built for Bronfman's Seagram Company. This became MCA's new office and impressive evidence of his mainstream power. Nevertheless, Wasserman's reputation was tainted by the company he still kept. This included Sidney Korshak, known as his fixer and an attorney to the mob. Though Korshak was a polished and sophisticated lawyer, a mobster once testified under oath that "a message from Korshak is a message from us."

Dominick Dunne of *Vanity Fair*, who knew Korshak well, told me, "Sidney's was the first house I ever went to for a party where they had a guy at the door with a gun."

Korshak negotiated contracts for people like Robert Evans for free. He forced MGM's Kirk Kerkorian to release Al Pacino for Evans' production of *The Godfather*. It has been said that the character of the consigliere played by Robert Duvall was based on Korshak.

Larry King shed light on some of the dark corners of the entertainment industry when he told me, "Wasserman, who called himself a pencil-pusher, would never talk about the Mafia. He was as sharp as they come—a legit [Meyer] Lansky! As Frank Sinatra once told me, 'You work for certain clubs that are owned by certain people that are backed by certain people, so are you going to say, I will not work that club? I will not do that deed?'"

When Jules Stein took MCA public, he gave Wasserman 20 per cent of the stock. After opening at $17.50, the shares flew up to $78 in three years.

As undisputed Hollywood royalty, Edie and Lew moved into a

custom-designed, modern home in Beverly Hills, complete with a state-of-the-art screening room. The house became the setting for many high-powered political parties, and Edie's equally influential Hollywood Wives Club. Stars such as Janet Leigh, Polly Bergen and Rosemary Clooney, as well as wives hidden behind their famous husband's shadows, shared gossip that Edie passed on to Lew.

By the time he was forty-six, Lew Wasserman was godfather of an entertainment empire that had never been seen before and would never be seen again. This was the man whose life I wanted to chronicle. No biography of him existed, either in film or book form. He was famous for having a clean desk. No notes. No files. Though he had experienced a dramatic fall from grace before his death at eighty-nine, his grip on his life remained as firm as the Vulcan pinch he had applied to my neck on our first meeting.

How was I going to capture the career of this man who strode the entertainment world like a colossus but left no footprints? Everything about making the film was difficult, from financing it to persuading Wasserman's associates and even his critics to be interviewed, and then getting them to actually show up. Everything about marketing, premiering and showing the film was also fraught. Why? The Wasserman family was always one step ahead of me, blocking my way, preventing access and threatening me if I persisted. I felt his presence and power every day that I worked on the project.

My interest in Lew Wasserman had been piqued by my interest in Garth Drabinsky. Even before I worked with Garth, I had followed his fatal relationship with Wasserman.

Fortunately I had backing. When I pitched the film to Robin Mirsky, who heads up the funding arm at Rogers Communications, she was spellbound by his story and instantly agreed to provide financing. Robin is a national treasure: she has consistently supported independent filmmakers and has invested in most of my films since 1998. Having the money in place, however, did not guarantee access.

★

Wasserman had the look of a powerful man. He had the Palm Springs tan, the silver hair, the black-framed glasses, the extraordinarily tall, lean body encased in a designer black suit with crisp white shirts and a black-silk tie. Everyone who worked for him was required to wear a suit.

His handshake was his contract, but given his connection to Sidney Korshak, you knew it came with mob enforcement. When honouring Lew at Universal Studio's fiftieth-anniversary celebration, Johnny Carson had quipped, "We're here tonight for one reason only: fear." That got a big laugh, as dangerous truths wrapped in a smile always do. Lew ran Hollywood on fear. You didn't fuck with Lew Wasserman. Even though I trod softly and tried to keep my interviews clandestine, his friends and colleagues soon alerted his family. "This guy Avrich is trying to make a film about Lew."

Once word was out, I wrote to Casey Wasserman, Lew's grandson, requesting an interview. He replied, also by letter. "I am going to respect the wishes of my grandfather, who never gave interviews. I will not participate, and I'm going to ask you not to make this film." I took an ad in the *Hollywood Reporter* and in *Variety* by way of answer: "Dear Casey, I loved your grandfather and his immeasurable contribution to Hollywood. You'll love the film."

There was no response.

Instead, Casey sent out word that no one was to participate in the making of the film. I knew I was being watched. When I pulled up to L.A.'s Sunset Marquis Hotel, where I usually stay, the same car would be there, as if waiting. I felt lucky to have a few significant interviews already in the can. One was with Jack Valenti.

After Bobby Kennedy hit MCA with the civil antitrust suit, Wasserman understood that he needed to develop clout in Washington. What better way than to become a serious political fundraiser? He hosted a hugely successful $1,000-a-plate dinner for President John F. Kennedy at the Beverly Hilton in June 1963. Later, Wasserman raised money for the new president, Lyndon Johnson. As Johnson's press chief, Jack Valenti was such an important Washington player that he was on Air Force One, standing over JFK's bloody corpse, when Lyndon Johnson was sworn into office. Later, Wasserman convinced Johnson to make Valenti head of the Motion Picture Association of America, where he could function as Wasserman's Washington puppet. Valenti kept MCA rolling in billions of TV syndication dollars by keeping a restrictive Federal Communications Commission (FCC) rule in place that prevented networks from producing TV shows.

My Valenti interview was a killer. "If Hollywood was Mount Olympus," he told me, "then Wasserman was Zeus. As an agent, he knew that it was the client who should get the publicity. You could call it the Greta Garbo Syndrome, which was part of his mystique. Some people used the word 'questionable' when talking about Lew's friendship with Sidney Korshak, who was the attorney for the mob, but Korshak was never charged, and in this country you're innocent until proven guilty. Lew had what Mr. Churchill called 'the seeing eye,' which is the ability to see beneath the surface and through walls into what for others is a vapoury future. While other movie moguls tried to exile TV, Lew saw it correctly as the most pervasive force ever. I think he paid about fifty million dollars for Paramount Pictures' pre-1950s library, then sold it to content-hungry TV stations for about a billion dollars in revenue."

Valenti confirmed that Wasserman had unusual clout with a succession of presidents. "Ronald Reagan was never a class-A star, but he had a good career. When that faded, Lew got him the host job on *General Electric Theater*. That not only gave Reagan a mass audience, it also allowed him to go around the country giving speeches at GE plants, making his views known. Without Lew, who knew where his career would have gone?"

As for Lyndon Johnson, "When he was elected president, he was indebted to Wasserman for the money Lew had raised. When Johnson asked me for a list of people he might want to bring into his administration, Lew's name was on it, and the president thought that a jolly good idea. When Lyndon made Lew an offer, Lew said he was flattered, but that he had recently bought Universal so he couldn't accept."

Reagan always understood his debt to Wasserman. "Everyone knew I was a comrade-in-arms with Lew," said Valenti, "and anyone who attacked Lew was attacking me. When Reagan was president, I gathered lobbyists and lawyers and we were able to put in place the FCC restrictive ruling that prevented networks from producing TV shows. After that, we managed to keep it in place until 1995, when it was overturned."

Though I tried for an interview with Ronald Reagan, he was suffering from Alzheimer's and Nancy declined to be in my film. Bill Clinton, who was also deeply indebted to Wasserman as a fundraiser, agreed to an interview, but then suffered heart problems leading to bypass surgery. He had to cancel.

When I wrote to the Carter Center, I was told that Jimmy Carter would love to talk to me about Lew Wasserman, so I flew my crew to Atlanta.

The Carter Center, a compound on the University of Georgia campus, looked like a horrible gift shop in a third-world airport. Displayed here was all the stuff given to Carter as president—plates, cups, paintings, local artisan-made souvenirs. When I walked in, I expected to see a sign saying, "Everything Must Go."

Someone took me through the protocol. *What do I call him?* Mr. President. I had been nervous about meeting John Kenneth Galbraith, but not Jimmy Carter. I hadn't respected him as president because of his stance on Israel. I knew him as the peanut president, with a drinking brother named Billy. True, Carter was better at foreign relations after he retired.

My crew and I entered a room decorated with the presidential seal and flags and all the paraphernalia one might expect. After introductions, I launched my conversation about power and Hollywood. "Mr. President, if you were still in office and Lew Wasserman was phoning you at the same time as some major head of state, which call would you take first?"

"Oh, Lew Wasserman's."

When I asked him to elaborate, he continued. "I was more removed from the Hollywood scene than some of my compatriots who served in the White House. No doubt, Ronald Reagan was intimately involved, and Bill Clinton deliberately cast his political life with movie stars. I looked on Lew as an entree for me into that mysterious realm of very famous, very influential and very wealthy people. If he had accepted the invitation to join Johnson's administration it would have been a step down for him. I can perfectly understand why Johnson made that offer, and why Lew refused it."

I was so involved in the frankness of our discussion that I leaned in and said, "Jimmy, did you think that . . ." I stopped myself. "Oh, Mr. President, I just called you Jimmy."

He was reassuring. "That's alright. Where are you from again?"

"Canada."

As soon as I made that reply, Carter lost interest. I was reminded of a roundtable discussion in which I had participated years ago with Henry Kissinger. Someone at the table had asked, "Dr. Kissinger, where does Canada sit on the stage of international politics?" He replied, "I don't want to embarrass and offend you with my answer."

"No, tell us where." He replied, "Irrelevant."

When Jimmy Carter heard I was from Canada, I became irrelevant. He didn't have much to say after that. Fade to black.

Having Suzanne Pleshette, best known as the co-star on *The Bob Newhart Show*, agree to be interviewed was a tremendous coup: she was Lew and Edie Wasserman's closest friend. She too was a tough broad, who hung out with a few rounders. Why did Suzanne agree? Probably as an Edie plant sent to kick the tires and find out what questions I was asking. Suzanne was particularly keen on seeing that Edie received credit for all she had contributed to her husband's success.

Suzanne insisted that I fly her makeup people in from New York and that I supply her with a driver and a limousine. The joke was this: The chauffeur ushered Suzanne into the limousine at her West Hollywood condo, drove about three feet, then let her out at the Sunset Marquis Hotel where I was filming.

When she walked into the room, she exclaimed, "You're looking at my fucking hair, aren't you, Barry?"

I denied it, though I probably was. She had been transformed from a sultry brunette to a platinum blonde.

"I know my hair is fucked up but it is what it is."

Whatever Suzanne's reasons for turning up, she was astonishingly frank and forthright. "Before Lew, agents were subhuman guys in plaid jackets. They were scum. Lew thought it was a respectable business so he insisted on dressing up in a suit and tie. He had an incredible temper. Anyone who behaved stupidly or jeopardized a deal would get violently ill before facing Lew. If Lew was pissed off with someone it was often Edie who cut them off. She would take the flak and the person would never know it was Lew. Edie also had her own wars, to which she was entitled, if people didn't pay her the proper respect."

Suzanne confirmed what others had told me: Unlike so many lascivious Hollywood power brokers, Lew was asexual. He slept alone so he could get up early to call England and Japan to hear the movie grosses. Suzanne said that if she wanted to freak him out when they were driving somewhere together, all she had to say was, "You know, Lew, I just got my period." He would tell the chauffeur to stop the car, then get out and walk.

I'm indebted to Suzanne for one of the all-time great lines about show business. When I asked her how she had survived so long in the industry, she said, "I don't have a gag reflex."

When Suzanne talked about Lew's funeral, she had me crying right along with her. "I think Lew would have been pleased with the choice of people, both those who were important to him and the movers and shakers of today. I wanted the world to understand that, with all of the triumphs credited to Lew, Edie had his back, and how much theirs was really a love story. Since I still have Edie, that's like still having Lew, because we talk about him, and he's always there in the house. When I lose Edie, I will have lost both of them."

A year after *The Last Mogul* came out, I walked passed Suzanne's table in L.A.'s famous Palm Steakhouse. She yelled to me, "Hey, Barry, where's the fucking DVD you promised me?"

I confess that I was flattered. I sent her the DVD that evening. Suzanne died on January 19, 2008, twelve days before her seventy-first birthday. Edie Wasserman survived her by three years, dying at a ripe ninety-five.

Janet de Cordova, a former starlet and wife of Fred de Cordova, Johnny Carson's sparring partner and producer of *The Tonight Show*, was another member of Edie Wasserman's Hollywood Wives Club. She was also a high-spending, party-giving A-lister in her own right. After Fred died in 2001, leaving her bankrupt, she moved in with her devoted maid—not such a bad life, since her maid, who was far better at handling money than the De Cordovas, had built a duplicate of their Beverly Hills mansion in New Mexico, complete with high ceilings, a grand staircase and glass walls.

Janet de Cordova was classic Hollywood. She showed up for her interview at 10 a.m., looking wonderful in a Chanel suit but dead drunk. She handed her pricey crocodile purse to one of my cameramen and said, "Can I trust you with this?" He was Black. I was offended. He wasn't.

After she had shakily taken her seat, I asked, "May we get you a coffee?"

She replied, "I'll have a double vodka."

She made two memorable remarks. On Wasserman's connection with Sidney Korshak: "Lew was a big friend of Sidney's, but not the only one in town." About Lew's fall from power, in which she could have been talking about herself: "Strange how the minute something changes, everything changes."

Signs that Wasserman might be losing his golden touch began appearing in the late '60s. By then, the bombs produced by MCA's movie division, Universal Pictures, had chalked up a debt of $90 million, resulting in the incredible rumour that Jules Stein might fire Lew Wasserman. Smaller pictures, like *Easy Rider* and *The Graduate*, were then in vogue, attracting more publicity, more prestige and more money. Wasserman had the box-office hit he needed in 1970 with *Airport*, the first of the disaster movies, which cost $10 million to make, then grossed $50 million. It also earned ten Oscar nominations. He followed that with *American Graffiti* and *The Sting*, which won seven Oscars.

You win some, you lose some. Universal Pictures was riding high with revenues of $62 million, but Wasserman turned down both *Star Wars* and *Raiders of the Lost Ark* after producer George Lucas asked for 50 per cent of the profits. Another costly mistake was keeping MCA out of cable TV, which let Time Inc. reap billions from HBO, which they created in 1976 for only $7.5 million.

It took the combined efforts of producers David Brown and Richard Zanuck, who had recently been turfed from 20th Century Fox, to prevent Wasserman from making yet another major blunder. As Brown explained, "Wasserman invited us to MCA mere seconds after Richard and I knew we were no longer wanted at 20th Century. When we offered him *Jaws*, Lew felt Steven Spielberg was too young and inexperienced to direct, but we prevailed. I think the only time

Lew ever had an orgasm was at the *Jaws* opening, when he saw the audience's reaction. After that, he would tell us what the movie was doing in every theatre in the U.S. and Canada, and everywhere in the world. He knew how many seats were in each theatre, and how *Jaws* compared with other films. He was a human computer."

Jaws cost $7 million to make and grossed more than $470 million.

Brown added, "Lew's authority was unbelievable, like Genghis Khan. If he was angry, he could foam at the mouth—literally, I've seen that—even though he was otherwise courteous. He didn't want anything on paper."

Jules Stein passed away in 1981. His funeral was scored by Henry Mancini, and featured seventy-six pallbearers, including Cary Grant, Sam Goldwyn and alleged mobbed-up union chief James Petrillo. Bearing in mind how close Stein had come to firing her husband, Edie Wasserman was rumoured to have said at the funeral, "It's about time."

By 1983, both the media and federal agencies were investigating MCA because of its rumoured mob connections. Wasserman allegedly pulled in a big favour from a former actor who, since 1981, had been living at Washington's most prestigious address. In record time, an apparently solid FBI case against MCA was dropped. It was the third federal investigation the company had survived in sixty years. As Jack Valenti told me, "I'm sure there had to have been some conversation between Lew and President Reagan, but I never asked about it."

The stock market crash in 1987 sent MCA stock spiralling downwards, leaving MCA vulnerable. Enter Michael Ovitz, the cofounder with Ron Meyer of Creative Artists Agency (CAA), representing such actors as Tom Cruise, Dustin Hoffman, Michael Douglas, Barbra Streisand and directors like Steven Spielberg. As a corporate consultant, Ovitz also negotiated international business mergers, which is how he came to play a key role in the Lew Wasserman story.

In 1989, Ovitz brokered a deal that at first appeared to rescue MCA with an infusion of capital. With Ovitz acting as intermediary, Wasserman sold MCA to Matsushita of Japan for $6.6 billion. Wasserman's personal payday was in excess of $350 million, but his new Japanese bosses didn't know who he was, and they didn't care. Wasserman lost his power.

In 1995, Ovitz brokered a second deal. This time, Edgar Bronfman Jr. of the Seagram dynasty purchased controlling interest in MCA from the Japanese for $5.7 billion. Though Wasserman might have hoped this would restore him to his rightful position, Edgar Bronfman—who *did* know who Wasserman was and *did* care—had a different idea. Bronfman sold off MCA assets, changed the company's name to Universal and invited Wasserman to leave the board.

I was excited when Michael Ovitz, the power broker who had sold Wasserman twice, agreed to an interview, but it came with conditions: I had to sign a forty-page agreement detailing what I could and couldn't ask. I then had to spend hours with Ovitz's art curator while she decided which painting from Ovitz's world-class contemporary collection should hang behind him while he was on camera. Should it be Picasso, Jasper Johns or Willem de Kooning? I would have happily shot Ovitz in front of a fridge. Curiously, after she had judged painting after painting from different angles, the final selection turned out to be photographs by Gregory Crewdson, who had shot stills for the hit HBO series, *Six Feet Under*. Was this perhaps a comment on Lew Wasserman's current whereabouts? In any event, the shots of Ovitz in the film are so tight you can't see the backdrop.

When Ovitz finally showed up, he was wearing a black suit and tie. He said, "This is what Lew would want me to wear."

His first comment, once he had settled in, was a surprise: "You're from Toronto? I'm not going to talk about Garth Drabinsky." This was a reference to the negative fallout from Ovitz's investment in

Livent, with its fraudulant bookkeeping. Though always of interest to me, it wasn't currently on my mind.

Ovitz and I talked for three hours in an interview that treated Wasserman reverently. "Lew was tough as nails, but he was a gentleman when you got to know him, unless of course you crossed him. He earned his MBA working from the bottom up, making bookings and learning the nitty-gritty of the business. He knew how to start something, and, most of all, he knew how to close it. He worked to get the best from his client, always coming up with new strategies that would benefit them, and, of course, he got a percentage of the profit."

Ovitz first had business dealings with the Wasserman empire early in his career. "When I was seventeen years old and a senior in high school, I found that Universal City was starting studio tours. I applied, and was lucky enough to be one of the first ten guides hired."

By the time Ovitz had brokered the MCA deal with the Japanese, he probably knew Lew's time was up. "The Japanese hired me to recommend to them companies in which they might invest. I recommended two. Both Lew and I knew he had a weakening stock, and the Japanese brought a solution that allowed MCA and Lew to stay in control for five years. If Lew had had a vision for MCA, and could have pumped money into the stock and taken it forward, then maybe he shouldn't have merged. I love the Asian culture, but they do things differently than we do, and I spent quite a bit of time explaining this to Lew. Since he had spent so long as a sole controlling proprietor, I don't think it crossed his mind to deal with these people as partners. The reality was that he had sold the company."

When Wasserman flew to Osaka to speak to his new owners, he was kept waiting hours before they would see him, and when the Japanese sold the company, he was not the first to be informed. "I received a call from Japan asking me to come to Osaka immediately," continued Ovitz. "Everything the Japanese said about selling was put in the conditional. 'If we should do this, if we should do that . . .' They never knew how to deal with Lew. He embarrassed them, and they left him waiting because they didn't want to get into a confrontation."

Michael Ovitz was a dealmaker, just like Wasserman, and if their roles had been reversed, Lew Wasserman would probably have done the same to Ovitz. However, I couldn't ignore the feeling that the student had destroyed his teacher. Anytime I questioned Ovitz about his motives and if he was potentially hurting his mentor, he would change the topic or ask me to move on.

Though stripped of his power, Wasserman continued to turn up every day at his office, with no one to talk to but his secretary, and then to eat his tuna sandwich in the commissary. As Jack Valenti observed, "After Lyndon Johnson, the thirty-sixth president of the United States, went back to his ranch, he was dead in four years at age sixty-four. I saw Lew as this great lion in winter and it wasn't a pleasant sight."

Given the mob connections so often associated with Lew Wasserman, I wanted to see if I could get at least one of these tough guys to talk. A name I uncovered was Salvatore Pisello, a reputed NY mafioso, whose high living was partly financed by a six-figure executive's salary from MCA. As a record distributor, Pisello was rumoured to have forced retailers to buy records no one wanted in order to purchase the ones they did want. Sal Pisello—also known as Big Sal—did not take no for an answer. He was jailed for two years in the mid-'80s for evading tax on his mostly unreported $600,000 MCA income.

When I asked a friend, with New York connections, for Pisello's phone number, he exclaimed, "Barry, stay away from that."

I said, "No, I want to speak to him. I'm a documentary filmmaker."

My friend insisted, "I'm telling you, don't get mixed up in that." Then he gave me the number.

When I dialed the number from a pay phone, a woman with a harsh New York accent replied, "Hello."

"Hi, this is Barry Avrich . . ."

"Who? What do you want?"

"I'm making a film about Lew Wasserman."

"Well, what the fuck do you want from me?"

"I'm trying to get a hold of Sal Pisello."

"I'm his wife. He has the cancer. He's in the hospital."

"I'm sorry to hear that, but is there any way I can visit him for an interview for . . . "

"Yeah, and you can go fuck yourself!"

I figured, if the wife was this tough, how about Big Sal and his friends? I was a father. I was a husband. I liked my life. I let Sal Pisello—Big Sal—go.

★

Despite all the ups and downs, I knew *The Last Mogul* was good. I think I captured a great era in Hollywood. I commissioned Jim McGrath, a wonderful composer, to score the music with a huge orchestra. To my knowledge, this had never been done before for a documentary, but Lew's story was about six decades of music, from Kay Kyser's 1940s swing band through to the '90s. I watched the session go down. It was thrilling.

When I tried to enter *Mogul* into the Sundance Film Festival, Darryl Macdonald, who ran Sundance, told me, "The film is fantastic but you should take it to the Palm Springs Festival."

"Palm Springs—what's that?"

Macdonald persisted, "You're a Canadian filmmaker, which means you'll be put into a different category and your doc will get lost. Trust me, you'll do well with this at Palm Springs."

I became arrogant. "No, I want this at Sundance."

"Okay, but I'm telling you that everyone from Hollywood goes to Palm Springs. Let me call them and they should take it."

I agreed reluctantly. I was not yet aware that Palm Springs was a great festival and exactly right for a Hollywood 101 film. Palm Springs took it automatically, and this turned out to be life-changing for me. The *New York Times* gave me a rave review, then sent a reporter and a photographer to Toronto to interview me. I had my picture taken holding up a caricature of Lew Wasserman as I sat in movie theatre seats.

After the *NY Times* story appeared, my assistant told me, "I have Ron Meyer on the line for you."

Ron Meyer? The cofounder with Michael Ovitz of Creative Artists Agency, then president of Universal Studios? That Ron Meyer?

He said, "Barry, I've read a review of *The Last Mogul* and I just have to see your film."

I replied, "Mr. Meyer, when I was researching the Universal archives for material on Lew, an old-time archivist informed Edie Wasserman, and she had me thrown off the lot. Why would I show you the film if you're going to prevent it from being distributed?"

He replied, "I'm a good guy, Barry. Let me show you that. I'll fly you to L.A., we'll screen the film and we will discuss it."

By then, I was so nervous from all I'd gone through that I replied, "I'll fly to L.A. on my own nickel. I'll book a screening room, and you and I can watch the film together. Alone."

He agreed. "But on one condition. That you let me take you to dinner afterwards."

Wow! Now I was really impressed with myself! I, the schmuck from Toronto, was laying down terms to the chair of Universal Studios.

I did fly to L.A., and Ron and I—first names now—watched the film, then went to the Palm steakhouse for dinner. He said, "Let's turn off our phones and have a great dinner."

Ron Meyer told me some great Hollywood stories over that dinner. And then he asked me, "What can I do for you? Though I run a studio, it's not my role to green-light movies, so don't pitch me those or bring me scripts. Anything else?"

"I need an agent."

"Fine."

He arranged for me to meet with the five most powerful agents in Hollywood, and I ended up with one at William Morris. Ron then said to me, "Next time you're in L.A., let me know, and I'll show you Lew Wasserman's office, which we haven't touched. You can stand in it, and then we'll have lunch at Lew's table at the commissary." And that's what Ron Meyer did for me. I drove into Universal one day, and I was given a private parking spot. I was shown Lew's office and the desk that never had any papers on it. I had lunch at Lew's table, where he ate tuna loaf until he died. Even now, any time I make a film, I send it to Ron. Though I consider him a friend, I've never asked him for anything more than for the agent, which he delivered.

When *Mogul* opened in Los Angeles, *Vanity Fair* threw an opening night party at The Silent Movie Theater on Fairfax, with its marquee announcing, "*Vanity Fair* presents *The Last Mogul.*" This would be the big time for me—the red carpet of all red carpets.

We had unbelievable RSVPs—the crème de la crème of Hollywood—until suddenly the cancellations began pouring in. The incompetent publicist hired by ThinkFilm, our distributor, had sent one of our beautifully designed invitations to Edie Wasserman. Still sharp at ninety, this behind-the-scene power broker took out her little black book and started calling anybody she guessed had been invited, and issued the order: "Don't go."

Edie, working on dead power, had snatched my *Vanity Fair* moment. The people who showed up for the most part were not people who had been close to Wasserman, but it didn't matter. We had a full house, a big party and *Mogul* had fantastic box office on its first weekend.

★

If the Ron Meyer story was about the making of a friendship, this next story is about the dismantling of one.

The lead financier of *Mogul* was a U.S.–Canadian distributor called ThinkFilm, controlled by Jeff Sackman. Jeff and I were close boyhood friends. I had named his company and created his branding. Though the publicists had told me my film had Oscar buzz for best documentary, and *Hollywood Reporter* called it Oscar-worthy, Jeff told me, "We're going with *Murderball* for the Oscar."

I was upset. "I have a Hollywood film everybody says is Oscar-worthy and you're not going to submit it?"

"That's right. We're pushing *Murderball*."

"Can't you support both?"

"Nope. Our Academy strategist says it's best to go with one."

Complete bullshit, as Harvey Weinstein had invented the multi-Oscar campaign. Jeff knew this well, given that he worked for Harvey.

Now I was furious. "Okay, but I want to buy back my movie."

Though *Mogul*'s budget was modest, ThinkFilm came back with an astronomical price that, typical of Hollywood, included hidden and inflated costs, including trips to Cannes and marketing costs. This was truly Hollywood accounting, but who cares when you are friends? Even Robert Lantos tried to convince Jeff to give the film back. Eddie Greenspan and his partner, Todd White, succeeded in negotiating better terms and purchasing the film, but not in time for the Oscars.

Murderball, a documentary about wheelchair rugby, was nominated but didn't win, which, I have to admit, gave me momentary satisfaction. I didn't speak to Jeff for eight years. Though ThinkFilm was eventually dissolved, Jeff's hardball taught me a lesson I would not forget. We have since buried the hatchet but I will not soon forget the nasty treatment from his team of lawyers and an episode that could have been avoided.

I subsequently released the film myself, believing it was a strong insider show-business doc. I booked it into art houses with a finite audience in New York, Chicago and various other cities, where it received strong reviews, including one in the *New York Times*. I felt vindicated after the nasty episode with ThinkFilm, but more than that, I was proud of the film.

About five years after *Mogul*'s debut, friends of mine were at the Peninsula Hotel in Beverly Hills when they found themselves sitting next to an elderly woman. She asked them, "Where are you from?"

They replied, "Toronto."

She told them, "A fine young man from Toronto made a wonderful film about my late husband."

Could this have been Edie Wasserman? Could this even be true?

Another example of the influence of Wasserman and my film was on fashion. Designer Michael Bastian told the *Los Angeles Times* that his Menswear 2016 summer collection was influenced by *The Last Mogul*. He told the reporter, "The seed for the collection was planted after I watched the 2005 film biography of Hollywood agent and executive Lew Wasserman titled *The Last Mogul*. Edie and Lew Wasserman were chic as hell. He was the first agent to dress like a businessman in a black suit and a black tie every day . . . and that movie got me going about this kind of Los Angeles glamour." I love that. Now, send me a few suits please.

Chapter Eighteen

A CRIMINAL MIND: THE LIFE AND TIMES OF EDDIE GREENSPAN

One day in 1990, Dusty Cohl phoned to ask, "Do you know who Eddie Greenspan is?"

"Sure. The legendary criminal lawyer."

"Eddie is trying to find a copy of a rare film—*The Leopard* by Luchino Visconti. If you could help him that would be great."

I found the film, then I asked Dusty, "Do you want me to send it?"

"No, kid, you take the film to Eddie."

That was Dusty's way with me, and anyone else he could commandeer as his concierge.

When I walked into Greenspan's downtown office, all leather and dark polished wood, the air was thick with cigar smoke, with both Dusty and Eddie on couches happily puffing away. I gave Eddie the film and he began his cross-examination: Who are you? What do you do? Where do you come from?

As we settled down into a three-sided conversation, I experienced Eddie's warmth, his powerful intelligence, his incredible sense of humour. He could talk about art and literature, the finest Parisian restaurants and Jean-Paul Sartre, but he also liked to discuss pastrami. I thought of the Bob Dylan song about dining with kings and being offered wings, and being unimpressed by both.

Eddie was that guy.

So, Eddie and I became friends through Dusty, but it wasn't until after Dusty died in 2008 that our friendship deepened. We gravitated toward each other because we both missed Dusty. Now, all that remained of Dusty in Eddie's office was an indentation in Eddie's leather couch. Dusty had used Eddie's office as his own, and if Eddie wasn't at his desk, Dusty would usurp it to take calls. Eddie paid Dusty a dollar as a retainer, should he happen to refer a case. He did the same with me. It was Eddie's joke. "If you're going to sit in here, you're going to be part of the firm. Otherwise, you're not allowed to hear what goes on."

After Eddie and I coproduced Dusty's memorial, we became inseparable. We had lunch every Saturday, either at a restaurant before returning to Eddie's office, or I'd bring food to the office and we'd eat there. The office always meant cigars and good talk about life, our families, films and theatre, politics—everything. Eddie was my version of *Tuesdays with Morrie*. Ever since I started reading *Variety* when I was eight, I had been on a tear to make myself successful. Eddie said to me, "You're on the path, just take your time and make it great."

Eddie became my third father, after Dusty, and in fact, he reminded me of my biological father. Just as Irving Avrich could appreciate the niceties of sportswear design with cookie crumbs dribbled down his sweater, so Eddie could admire the beauty of a Lalique vase with mustard drippings on his Charvet tie.

In 2006, Eddie was the host of a TV show called *Reel Justice*, in which he and a guest would watch a film involving the law, then debate its merits in terms of real justice. During its single season,

Eddie invited many famous guests, including Canadian Lieutenant-General Roméo Dallaire and movie director Norman Jewison. Then he invited me.

Our film was *The Star Chamber*, a 1983 thriller with Michael Douglas and Hal Holbrook. Frustrated by a legal system that allowed violent criminals to escape justice on technicalities, they were part of a group of judges who secretly hired assassins to do the job the courts were unwilling or unable to do.

I loved the film. Eddie saw it as a vigilante movie like *Death Wish* with Charles Bronson. What Eddie hadn't counted on was that I would spend a week at the University of Toronto and Osgoode Hall doing research. I had all these statistics on how the death penalty affected the crime rate, where it worked and where it hadn't. Eddie was expecting an amiable push-and-shove exchange of opinion. Instead, I started hitting him with my data for which he was uncharacteristically unprepared. He grew so angry that when the director called for a commercial, Eddie announced, "We'll take a break, then we'll come back with my former friend Barry Avrich."

While the lights were off, Eddie lit into me, "What the fuck are you doing? Your statistics are bullshit!"

"No, they aren't. I have research papers from Harvard, Yale and Brown."

Eddie remained in a state of shock for the rest of the show. With good reason. In 1987, Eddie had closed his law practice for six months to tour the country in a one-man crusade against the reinstatement of the death penalty. He had fought the Mulroney government, and he had won, but that was almost ten years earlier, and he was no longer up to date. After he finished the show in a rage, he gave my notes to his students to check. Typically, he then calmed down sufficiently to invite me on a lecture circuit to universities and related venues to continue the debate.

Eddie and I also fought when he crossed into my territory. He was excited that I was making a film about Garth Drabinsky, but he was torn as to whether he should appear in it. American lawyers often go public about their cases, but in Canada it's not done. Because Eddie was a criminal rather than an appellate lawyer, he had worked for Garth only until Garth went to prison. He told me, "I'll do this because we're friends, but some things I won't talk about."

Eddie also drew the line at attending the 2012 premiere of my documentary, *Show Stopper: The Theatrical Life of Garth Drabinsky*, at the Toronto International Film Festival because he didn't want viewers and the media asking him uncomfortable questions. Instead, I screened a rough cut for him in his office. After the first eight minutes, he said, "This is your best film ever. I love this. It's fantastic."

I appreciated the praise, but I knew there could be turbulent waters ahead. As a metaphor for Garth's troubles, I inserted clips from Mel Brooks's *The Producers*, a 1968 cult classic, in which a failed theatre producer, played by Zero Mostel, persuades his guileless accountant to cook the books to cover up his investor fraud. When Eddie saw the cut, he went ballistic. While I was partially prepared for his wrath, I was taken aback by his argument, "You know this is anti-Semitism, don't you?"

I was dumbfounded.

He would not back down.

A couple of days went by without my hearing from him. Knowing Eddie, I figured the only way to mollify him was by presenting research that supported my position. I read every review of the original 1968 movie that I could find. I read every review of the 2001 Broadway musical, the revival of the Broadway production and the 2005 film based on the musical. No critic ever suggested that *The Producers* was anti-Semitic. I bound these reviews together in a thick file, which I delivered to Eddie at his office. "Here's everything on *The Producers* from the *Wall Street Journal* to *Film Comment* to the Film Society of Lincoln Center. Nobody said it was anti-Semitic, so fuck you."

Eddie laughed, and that ended our dispute.

Eddie and I shared the same sense of humour. While Eddie was a passionate and brilliant orator, especially about the law, he sometimes asked me to help add humour to his speeches. He provided the wit. I added the zaniness.

When Eddie agreed to host a benefit for a Jewish theatre company, he said, "Find out whom they're honouring."

I told him, "It's Ucal Powell."

"Who's he?"

"Head of the carpenters' union."

Eddie was bemused. "What's his connection to a Jewish theatre company? I'm tied up in a trial, so I'm afraid you'll have to write my opening speech."

I wrote the speech, which I read to Eddie while he puffed on his cigar, the day before the event. I began by explaining satirically that Ucal Powell was being honoured "because Ucal Powell's mother in Kingston, Jamaica, told him forty-eight years ago, if you want to be someone, you have to move to Toronto, become head of a carpenter's union and be honoured by the Jews."

Eddie laughed throughout my reading and then delivered his surprise verdict. "Okay, it's funny, but it won't work. It's too ridiculous."

"Eddie, the event's tomorrow. If you want to rewrite it, then do it yourself. I'm not going to."

This brought us to an impasse. All Eddie's speeches were in binders, with marginal notes and references, as befits a meticulous man of letters. He didn't do hasty and he didn't do ridiculous, so he was stuck. All the way to the event—a two-hour limousine ride to the Paramount Theatre in Woodbridge—Eddie was angry, and he let me know it. Worse, we found he would be addressing a sold-out crowd—1,200 people were pouring into the theatre.

Eddie asked, "Do you know anyone here?"

"No. It's Woodbridge."

"They're all union people come to honour this Yuckel Powell guy." I corrected him. "It's Ucal."

By now, he was so testy he insisted, "Well, I'm going to call him Yuckel."

Once inside, we took our places at the head table. Next to me was Louise Pitre, the star of Broadway's *Mamma Mia!*, whom I knew from her *Les Misérables* days. Louise was the evening's main entertainment. Meanwhile, Eddie had his briefcase on the table and was reading his notes, sweating profusely. He wouldn't look at me. More seriously, he wouldn't look at the food on his plate. That's how upset he was.

Finally, it was Eddie's turn at the mike. He took his place, still without making eye contact with me, then started my speech. When he got a couple of big laughs, he began to relax. As the laughs built, Eddie came alive. Now, he was loving *his* speech. Eddie Greenspan, it seemed, could do ridiculous after all. He was killing it.

After the applause died down, I introduced Eddie to Louise Pitre, citing her accomplishments. Louise whispered to me, "Eddie just screwed me with that speech. How can I top that?"

The benefit turned into a great evening. Ucal Powell received the Order of Ontario in 2014. It seemed Mama was right: "Move to Toronto, become head of a carpenter's union and be honoured by the Jews."

I subsequently helped Eddie with many of his hosting events. In one, he addressed the criminal attorneys of Canada at a huge conference in Toronto's Ritz-Carlton Hotel. This organization had come a long way since the days when they used to meet at one of the seedier downtown hotels, a fact Eddie used as his lead: "In the hotel where we used to meet, the hookers rented rooms by the hour. Here, they can walk right through the classy lobby."

On another occasion, I hosted an event at which Eddie was receiving a lifetime achievement award from ORT, an organization that provides educational training for recent immigrants. I secretly flew up F. Lee Bailey, one of America's most powerful criminal defence attorneys, from Boston to join us. Bailey was a hero of Eddie's, though he would later be disbarred for financial irregularities.

Because Eddie was quite heavy, once he was seated, people had to come to him at his table. He wouldn't even turn his neck, which made it easy to hide Bailey at the back of the room. I showed a video tribute, based on the hilarious Dos Equis, "Most Interesting Man in the World" beer commercials. With Eddie visually inserted into the video, a voice-over said, "People hang on his every word, even his prepositions, because he's the Most Interesting Man in the World. He can speak French in Russian because he's the Most Interesting Man in the World. He has been known to cure narcolepsy just by walking into a room. Dolphins line up to swim with him because he's the Most Interesting Man in the World."

I then announced, "And now, let's bring up a legend to honour The Most Interesting Man in the World. Ladies and gentlemen, the great F. Lee Bailey."

Eddie's jaw dropped. He was in such shock that he wept. F. Lee Bailey was brilliant, and it felt great to honour a man I loved so much in a way that he loved so much.

Eddie was a Toronto puzzle in that neither he nor his wife, Suzy, wanted social prominence, but Eddie, the defence lawyer, actively courted the press. He probably had five hundred scrapbooks in his basement, stuffed with photocopied articles about himself, meticulously curated by his staff. I shouldn't have been surprised when, a few years into our friendship, Eddie began to ask, "When are you going to make a film about me?" When I pitched the idea to CBC-TV for their *Life and Times* series, they went for it immediately.

Eddie was born in 1944 in Niagara Falls, Ontario, to Joseph and Emma Greenspan. He was the first of three children in a close-knit Jewish family that would spawn a Canadian legal dynasty.

"We had no money," said Eddie, "but I don't remember being deprived. Niagara Falls was a great place, near a world wonder. I spent many hours beside the falls reading about life. High school was a melting pot. We were mixed together, rich and poor, of every ethnic background. Niagara was a border town, and many of my friends got into trouble and went to jail. I was so glad that I didn't live on the side of the street where you were more easily drawn to crime, and that I had a family that wouldn't let me go there."

In 1957, just thirty days after celebrating Eddie's bar mitzvah, his father suffered a fatal heart attack. The family was devastated, but this event also pointed Eddie toward his destiny.

"I went into my father's library, which wasn't very extensive, and I picked up his book about famed American lawyer, Clarence Darrow. At age thirteen, I decided that's what I wanted to do. I knew that being a criminal lawyer was what my father had wanted, so I guess I was living out his dream. I would have settled for being a born singer, but I ended up as a born lawyer."

In 1966, after moving to Toronto to study law, Eddie met an attractive recent immigrant named Suzy Dahan. "I'd just arrived from Morocco," she told me, "and we met at a party. I didn't know any English so I don't know how we communicated. Most everyone was dancing, but there was a table full of food, and the only person eating was Eddie. He weighed about three hundred pounds."

Eddie protested, "She exaggerates. I was two hundred and ninety. I think we fell in love when we first looked at each other. She arrived in this country without anything, and she managed to find someone who also didn't have a nickel."

"We danced," said Suzy. "Eddie was so light on his feet for a big man. I was surprised. And then we never danced again."

After Eddie graduated from Osgoode Hall, he asked Suzy to marry him, while stipulating a few conditions. "He told me that he loved me very much, but that the law would always come first, and that I would be a close second. He brought the criminal code with him on our honeymoon as bedside reading, and every night he insisted in reading to me a few of the clauses. The law was always Eddie's mistress, but he loved me enough."

The Greenspans had two daughters, Julianna and Samantha. Eddie was not the kind of father who attended school plays or helped with their homework. "We spent most of our family time in downtown restaurants because that's where Eddie was," said Suzy. "I insisted he spend at least half an hour or an hour with his daughters every day."

In 1970, Eddie joined the Pomerant & Pomerant law firm. His brother, Brian, who was three years younger, followed him several years later. After only a week at the firm, Eddie argued his first case before the Supreme Court. As he remembered that event, "The judge called me Mr. Greenburg, then Mr. Greenspoon, so I corrected him, 'It's Greenspan, my lord.' He replied, 'I don't care what your name is. Sit down!' It was a case I deserved to win, and I did."

Eddie was now ready for prime time. In 1973, Peter Demeter, a wealthy real estate developer, was charged with the brutal slaying of his wife Christine, a former model, in what appeared to be a crime of passion. "In real life it's almost always the husband or the wife who commits this kind of crime, though not on TV," said Eddie. "If not him or her, then who else could it be? That's what a defence lawyer has to fight against every time."

Demeter was convicted and sent to prison, where subsequent convictions kept him for the rest of his life.

Eddie insisted, "Mr. Demeter always told me, 'I did not kill my wife.' On the evidence, I believe he should have been acquitted.

When a client tells me he's not guilty and I lose, I always fear that an innocent man has been wrongly convicted."

I wrote to Demeter where he was being held in Bath Institution, a minimum-security facility near Kingston, asking for an interview. He replied, "You don't need anyone's permission but mine. Come ahead."

It was my first visit to a prison and it was frightening. My coproducer, Tori Laurence, and I were led to a private room and Demeter shuffled in, pushing a walker. He had shrunk to about a third of his former size. The door was locked, leaving the three of us alone. Demeter kept picking up on Tori's scent like Hannibal Lecter in *Silence of the Lambs.*

When I asked him about Eddie, he couldn't have been more flattering, despite the outcome of the trial. Though Eddie was the junior on his case, Demeter had insisted on relying on him in preference to senior counsel, Joe Pomerant. He even kept in touch with Eddie, sending him cards on his birthday.

There were two chilling moments. The first was when I asked Demeter, "What did you think when you walked into your garage and saw your wife with her head cracked open, lying in a pool of blood?"

He became angry. "This interview is supposed to be about Eddie Greenspan, why ask me about that?"

I replied, "I'm just building up the background."

Demeter snapped back, "You want to know what I thought? I said to myself, 'I've ruined a good set of tires.'"

He was referring to the fact that his wife's blood was pooling around his Cadillac. Nice.

I had been wearing a Harrods black cashmere scarf. When I got back to my car, I realized I had left it in the prison. I returned to retrieve it and the warden confronted me: "What are you doing back here?"

"I forgot my scarf."

The warden pointed to a monitor, where I could see Demeter

shuffling down a hallway with my scarf hung around his neck. He asked, "Do you want to go and get it?"

Another chill. I declined. During all the time I had spent with Demeter, I felt that I could have been interviewing Charles Manson.

The Demeter case had the effect of jump-starting Eddie's career; it also soured his relationship with his senior partner, Joe Pomerant. "I thought the defence was being mishandled," said Eddie. "We also disagreed on a lot of very important principles."

With the relationship damaged beyond repair, both Eddie and his brother Brian left to form their own practice, which turned out to be a wise move. In 1992, Joe Pomerant was found guilty of forgery and theft, for which he was disbarred and sent to prison—yet another case of a criminal lawyer crossing over to the dark side.

"I had never imagined he was involved in illegal activity," said Eddie.

I also wanted to interview F. Lee Bailey. The club made up of criminal defence lawyers who take on front-page crime is an exclusive one, and Bailey had noticed the freshman lawyer making headlines north of the border. He even flew to Toronto to watch the rising superstar at work. I reversed that flight by taking my crew to Boston.

Bailey's high-profile cases included, most famously, O.J. Simpson, but he also defended Dr. Sam Sheppard, found guilty of murdering his wife, but whom Bailey got off in a retrial; U.S. Army Captain Ernest Medina, who was tried for his responsibility in the My Lai massacre during the Vietnam War; and Patty Hearst, a newspaper heiress who participated in armed bank robberies with her kidnappers.

Bailey told me, "The Demeter case was the O.J. Simpson case of its day. Since Eddie, the junior, was getting all the attention, I knew he must be doing something right. While it's true that the poor have to make do with a public defender who doesn't have much time for them, the rich like Demeter have more trouble getting a sympathetic public hearing."

After Demeter, Eddie seemed to be everywhere, often making front-page news, which sometimes made life difficult for his children. During one sensational Toronto case, in which Eddie was representing a man charged with sexual assault and homicide, Eddie's six-year-old daughter, Julianna, told him that the kids at school were saying that her father was a horrible person who defended horrible people. When Eddie explained to her that everyone deserved a defence, Julianna understood, young as she was. Much later, Julianna would practise law with her father, partly because she, too, felt the calling, and partly to spend more time with him. She eventually took over his firm after Eddie passed away.

In 1984, Helmuth Buxbaum, a multimillionaire from London, Ontario, was charged with paying $10,000 to a hit man to stop his wife, Hanna, on the highway and put bullets in her head. Eddie lost that case, despite an impassioned three-day summation without notes. "It was an exceedingly difficult trial with a lot of witnesses," said Eddie. "We'd make headway with one witness, then another would cut us off."

Buxbaum died in prison in 2007 at age sixty-eight.

In 1995, Eddie defended former Nova Scotia Premier Gerald Regan, facing seventeen counts of related rape charges, creating yet another storm of headlines. This time, Eddie won a controversial acquittal that critics denounced as a case of wealth buying a verdict.

"What bothered me was how quick people were to conclude that Mr. Regan was guilty without a trial," said Eddie. "The jury acquitted him. That's what trial by jury is about. Sometimes I feel I'm the only one in the country who believes in innocence until proved guilty. Even my mother sometimes thinks that when a person is arrested, they must have done the crime."

In the '90s, Eddie and writer and CBC producer George Jonas coproduced the TV show *Scales of Justice*, which recreated some of Canada's most famous criminal cases. It was yet another of Eddie's attempts to educate the public on how he felt the legal system should work. By then, Eddie was receiving backlash for his flamboyant, headline-grabbing style. "I don't make people Page One stories," he protested. "I'm retained by people who already are on the front pages."

Partners and articling students who watched Eddie up close were more impressed by the painstaking work he put into his cross-examinations, which he loved. To them, he was the Wayne Gretzky of the courtroom. One police officer, who covered the Mafia in Toronto, told me that Eddie's cross-examinations had made him a better cop by teaching him how carefully he had to conduct his investigations and how specific he had to make his notes.

Both Eddie and I had lost our fathers. When I asked him, "Do you regret that your father did not live to see the success you achieved as a lawyer?" he teared up, and then became upset with me. "Why did you do this to me?"

Suzy, who was in the kitchen, heard Eddie weeping. She strode into the room, gave me a stern look and said, "Stop filming." Then she took Eddie away for about half an hour until he settled down.

When he returned for filming, he said, "I'm so angry that you asked that question. You made me cry. You had no right to do that." He was also somewhat impressed that I had found his weak spot. Eddie was so conscious of his brand that he wasn't going to let me, or anyone else, expose him in that way.

Having composed himself, Eddie faced the cameras, "When my father died of a heart attack," he said, "it was totally unexpected. I was shattered. He knew nothing of whom I would become. I was always aware of that, knowing that being a criminal lawyer was his dream."

After the documentary was finished, Eddie threw a wonderful screening party at Toronto's Albany Club. He loved the film. Every time he read an article about me that didn't mention his film, he complained about the oversight.

★

I also interviewed Conrad Black for the Greenspan documentary. He agreed to see me provided I came to his Park Avenue office in New York. Once there, I had more than enough time to admire his Franklin Delano Roosevelt memorabilia and other framed historical artefacts while he kept me waiting. On this occasion, Lord Black had reason to be late: Rome was burning. He was being investigated for irregular activity inside his corporation, Hollinger Inc.

When he did turn up, he was distracted. He had not yet hired Eddie as his lawyer, but perhaps he was signalling his intention when he described Eddie as "possessing that kind of brilliant mind you'd want on your side if you were in trouble." He continued in that same vein. "Eddie fearlessly and tirelessly defends, even if someone doesn't have the means. He loves the intricacies of the law. He's a professional genius with great sensitivity."

I said that Eddie sometimes is accused of manipulating the media. Conrad replied, "You've got to do whatever you can for your client."

In November 2004, the U.S. Securities and Exchange Commission (SEC) filed civil fraud lawsuits against Conrad Black and others involved with Hollinger, alleging that they had cheated shareholders through deceptive schemes and misstatements. A year later, the Chicago U.S. attorney filed eight criminal fraud charges against Black and three former Hollinger executives. On December 15, 2005, four new charges were laid against him, alleging racketeering, obstruction of justice, money laundering, mail fraud, wire fraud and tax evasion. On March 14, 2007, the criminal fraud trial against Hollinger executives began in Chicago, with Eddie Greenspan acting for Conrad Black, and with well-known criminal attorney Edward Genson of Chicago as cocounsel.

Eddie, as usual, excelled at cross-examination. After a particularly spectacular day, in which he questioned coaccused Hollinger executive David Radler, the *Toronto Sun* ran an Andy Donato cartoon showing a puddle on a seat next to the judge's desk, with the caption, "Mr. Radler you may be excused."

Despite Eddie's brilliant performance, Eddie told me that Conrad was allegedly referring to him behind his back as "the defence that I could afford." Conrad reportedly had first approached the famous New York law firm of Sullivan & Cromwell, which had quoted a massive fee. Eddie told me that both Conrad and his wife, Barbara Amiel, were giving him a rough time. Barbara, in particular, kept second-guessing his defence strategy. Dominick Dunne told me that Barbara Amiel was sending him notes critiquing Eddie. As a *Vanity Fair* journalist, Dominick made it a habit of knowing the wives of powerful men, and Barbara had made herself conspicuous through an infamous 2002 *Vanity Fair* article in which she showed off her fur closet, her sweater closet and her evening-gown closet, while confiding that it was necessary to have jets both in the UK and in the U.S. to support her "extravagance that knows no bounds." This article was accompanied by a much-mocked photo of Barbara posing with her head on the knee of Lord Black as he sat enthroned outside their Palm Beach mansion, which in turn led to the gleeful reprinting of a more infamous photo of Barbara and Conrad, dressed for a costume ball at Kensington Palace. He was draped in scarlet robes topped with a scarlet hat as Cardinal Richelieu, the ruthless chief minister to Louis XIII of France. She, with fake white hair piled high, was the self-indulgent Marie Antoinette.

The Chicago trial was sufficiently within Dominick's beat that he attended it from time to time, writing several columns in which he lauded Eddie's cross-examination skills, finally giving Eddie the *Vanity Fair* exposure that he had previously denied him.

On July 13, 2007, the verdict was delivered to Judge Amy J. St. Eve. After twelve days of deliberation, the jury acquitted Black of

nine charges, while finding him guilty on three counts of mail and wire fraud, and one count of obstruction of justice. On December 10, 2007, he was sentenced to seventy-eight months in prison, to be served at the Coleman Federal Correctional Complex near Orlando, Florida, beginning on March 3, 2008.

Conrad had been facing twenty-five years in prison, if not one hundred years, till Eddie succeeded in having almost every charge thrown out. The stickiest one was for obstruction of justice. Conrad was caught by his own security cameras carrying boxes from his Toronto office in the middle of the investigation. In that video clip, he was seen looking up at the cameras with an expression of simultaneous scorn, disdain and disrespect. No lawyer could fight that. It was like the scene in *Scarface*, when Pacino's character is caught on camera laundering money and his lawyer says, "Honey baby, when you are looking into a camera, there's no money in the world that can help."

After lengthy appeals and partial re-trials, Conrad's sentence was reduced, leading to his release on May 4, 2012. He then returned to Canada, the country he had renounced in order to accept a British peerage as Lord Crossharbour.

Eddie was sensitive about Conrad's comments. If you were a student of the law, as I somewhat became under Eddie's tutelage, you could see that Eddie had wrung all possible advantage from the case. The Blacks' low-key criticism of Eddie came to nasty fruition in Conrad's self-justifying memoir, *A Matter of Principle*. Eddie and I sat in his office when the book came out, using a highlighter to mark the sentences that portrayed Eddie negatively. He was especially upset by Conrad's reference to him as "a slumbering buffalo," for his frail health or for allegedly falling asleep in court. The insulting charge that Eddie Greenspan was "the best defence that I could afford" was implied.

Knowing how wounded Eddie felt, I asked John Stackhouse, an editor of the *Globe and Mail*, if the *Globe* would publish a feature by Eddie about Conrad Black's book. When he said yes, I broached the idea to Eddie. Eddie was interested, but he then did what Eddie always does, which meant getting six opinions. While he vacillated, I kept pressing the issue. "You have three granddaughters who've entered the digital age, and the only record they'll see is the one by Conrad Black insulting you. You have to write a rebuttal, and you know you're smart enough to figure out how to do it without crossing any legal lines."

Eddie wrote the rebuttal. He wrote that any client who doesn't get what he or she wants will always blame the lawyer. It was a powerful punch-back, which garnered letters of praise from judges and lawyers across North America.

★

I was vacationing with my family in Florida over Christmas 2014 when I awoke to one of those horrific emails you hope never to receive. It was from Eddie's daughter, Julianna, who was with her family at their home in Arizona. It read, "My father just died."

When I called Julianna in Arizona at 6 a.m., she was in shock. Eddie had passed away quietly in his sleep at 3 a.m. on Christmas Eve. It was the worst day of my life, even more poignant than when I lost my own father, because when my father died, he had already been lost to me through years of illness. Eddie was woven through every aspect of my life. He had helped me with family issues and business problems. His counsel was always wise. I was grateful that he had become part of my family, as I had become part of his. My wife adored Eddie. My daughter adored Eddie. It was tough for all of us.

His health had been tenuous for years. By the previous fall, Eddie was on his second pacemaker. He had diabetes. He was losing weight, and he looked gaunt. He was on a cocktail of pills of all kinds, plus insulin shots, by which his doctor had likely already extended Eddie's life by ten years. His beloved cigars were forbidden, and he was miserably unhappy with his salt-free diet, which he described as also taste-free. Because I sensed Eddie was running out of time, I added dinner every Tuesday or Wednesday to our Saturday lunches with Ralph Lean. When we went to a restaurant, the debate with the waiter over dessert was always about what *not* to order. Eddie used to joke, "There's a new restaurant called Boiled and Bland, let's go there."

All of us around Eddie loved him so much that we all, at one time or another, were his enablers. Sure, have the smoked meat, have the cigar. His family told me that forty-eight hours before he died, they had given in to his wish to enjoy all the foods that made him happy— lobster and mac and cheese.

In my documentary, Eddie had said his ideal way to die would be to hear a judge say "not guilty" about one of his clients, just before he keeled over. We couldn't give him that, but he would have a grand and good-humoured goodbye.

I was asked to be a pallbearer, and my wife and I had to make the decision as to whether or not ten-year-old Sloan should attend the funeral. I explained to her that a funeral has two parts. The first would be in the synagogue, where she would hear great and funny things said about Big Eddie. The second would be in the cemetery, where we would say goodbye. After listening to my explanation, Sloan said she wanted to go with me, and she did, and she was strong.

Since Dusty Cohl had been cremated, the last person for whom I had been a pallbearer was my father. After the service, all eight of us lined up, each chosen for a reason. As I put my hand on Eddie's casket with the rest, then walked it in sync out of the synagogue, we were assaulted by the click and whir of the cameras, and I thought, *Another press conference for Eddie. How he loved his media scrums.*

I helped lift Eddie's casket from the hearse when we got to the cemetery, and then walked it to the grave. Everything after that is a blur, until I remember Julianna putting her notes for the eulogy onto the casket. All of us were crying as it was lowered into the ground. But wait. Julianna had a second brilliant thought. She added a blank sheet of paper and a pen, in case Eddie wanted to make changes.

So, that was that, and I still haven't found a way to fill the void.

A few days after Eddie's funeral, my wife and I met friends for dinner at an uptown restaurant. I arrived late, having come from evening prayers at Eddie's shiva. While I was in no mood to be sociable, I needed the distraction. My wife noticed Conrad Black in a nearby booth, but I had no time for him, given that the only quote the Lord could spare for the press on Eddie's death was, "We haven't spoken in years."

After dinner, when my wife and I were leaving the restaurant, Conrad stopped me, resulting in the following exchange, which I quote verbatim.

"Barry, did you go to the Greenspan funeral?"

"Yes." That question from the one-time media mogul who claimed to read multiple papers every day seemed disingenuous, given that all those from Toronto, including the one he used to own, had published photos of me helping to carry the casket.

"How many attended?"

"About nine hundred." This too had been reported.

"Who were the speakers?" Also covered.

"His daughter, Julianna, delivered the main eulogy."

"Yes, I heard she can be amusing."

Ah, just the right amount of limp pretension from the Lord, who then delivered his final spiteful *coup de grâce*, "Eddie has not been Eddie Greenspan for the last ten years."

"Oh?" I said. "And what have you been doing for the last ten years?"

I wrote an essay in a national newspaper chronicling my relationship and colourful history with the larger-than-life lawyer. The essay was candid and at times raw. I included Eddie's battle with Conrad Black.

A day after the story ran, I received a caustic and defamatory email from Conrad Black. He was again as dismissive of Eddie's handling of his trial in Chicago as he had been in his book. Black told me that our friendship was now over. When I reminded him that our "friendship" consisted of an annual lunch I paid for, he responded by calling me a "cunt." I was disappointed that a man famous for his multi-syllabic vocabulary chose that word.

* *Chapter Nineteen* *

SATISFACTION:
THE LIFE AND TIMES
OF MICHAEL COHL

The Rolling Stones won't make a move without asking him first. The roster of stars and former stars that he has worked with includes Frank Sinatra, Michael Jackson, Prince, Stevie Wonder, Barbra Streisand, Pink Floyd and U2. Among concert promoters he occupies a position of unrivalled eminence. His name is Michael Cohl.

In 1989, when I joined Echo advertising, the company had two major clients I wanted to work with. The first was Garth Drabinsky, of whom I'd had my fill. The second was Cohl.

Michael was Dusty's cousin and it was Dusty who wanted me to make a film about him. Dusty, the great self-promoter with the big cowboy hat and cigar, thought Michael should be celebrated on the cover of *Forbes*. By contrast, Michael was an aloof, quiet guy, lurking behind a dark, full beard, long hair and round glasses. He enjoyed his status as the most famous man you've never heard of. *Fortune* magazine had called him the Howard Hughes of rock and roll.

My relationship with Michael was tentative at best. My partner worked on his concert account and I was called when needed to cut a commercial or shoot a video, which actually included working on a slick video that was used by Michael to pitch a slew of sponsors for the iconic and global Stones Steel Wheels Tour. Convincing him to sit for a film was difficult. After he'd changed his mind a few times, he finally agreed—sort of. He told me, "I'll give you forty minutes, but you'll have to come to Miami while we set up a Stones concert." He ended up giving me three hours, during which he delivered an oral history of the business of rock and roll. Afterwards, he surprised me by adding, "Come to the concert arena tonight, and you can have Mick Jagger and Keith Richards."

It was a fabulous start to what would be an emotional—sometimes painful—journey.

Michael was born in Toronto in 1948, one of the generation that believed they invented everything from sex to rock and roll. He was the eldest son in a middle-class family, with a father who worked in the garment trade manufacturing lingerie. "The great thing about my upbringing was that my dad absolutely didn't care what I did," said Cohl. "He just wanted me to be successful, and to make lots of money. My father's life was cards, the track, gambling. He wasn't around much, but he was great. My mom was the most disciplined, strong-willed, organized person I've ever met, so during my early years, when I suffered through Woodstock Syndrome and some miserable failures, the discipline all came from her. I think I lived a rather parochial life. Hebrew school every night, while skipping my homework because I was bored to death. The one thing I'd learned—I don't know where it came from—was that whatever I did, I had to win. There was a school debating tournament for which you needed seventy-five in English to enter. I was getting about thirty. I decided to do what it took to win, and I did."

"Michael and his young partner won the Ontario Debating Championship," said Dusty. "They came to me with their trophy. Michael was an extraordinary debater."

Mick Jagger would later express his agreement. "There's one thing you can't do with Michael," he said, "because you'll always lose, and that's to have a debate. Every time we had a discussion that turned into some sort of logical argument, I would lose."

Unlike the rest of his Beatles-loving, pot-smoking demographic, Cohl favoured folk music—the Weavers, Pete Seeger, Woody Guthrie and Lead Belly. One day, during a visit to Columbia University, he encountered the Grateful Dead and Jefferson Airplane. "I'd never before heard rock bands live. It was a mind-blowing event."

When it came to making a buck, Cohl was not the shaggy-haired hippy he appeared to be. At eighteen, he and a friend opened a sordid little Ottawa strip joint, appropriately named Pandora's Box. "We were arrested thirty-four times, and ended up in the Supreme Court," said Cohl. "The day after we won, we ditched the club because it didn't seem the right path to follow."

Cohl learned from a friend, who promoted the Guess Who, about the profits to be made from concerts. "My mind exploded. I marvelled, 'You made five thousand dollars in one day? Tell your people I'm going to be promoting shows in Toronto.'"

And that's what he did. Or tried to do.

"I was borrowing money from everybody. I was the family member, friend, cousin you didn't want to see, because I left with three grand here and five grand there, and for a whole year I signed up zero groups. My office was my girlfriend's father's apartment. He would leave about six thirty in the morning, I'd arrive with all my stuff at eight, then disappear before he came home at six thirty or seven."

Though it looked unlikely at this early stage of his career, Cohl had found his calling as a rock concert promoter.

With remarkable chutzpah, he booked the biggest joint in town,

Maple Leaf Gardens, and then filled it with a popular country act. "Buck Owens and the Buckaroos had the number one TV show, *Hee Haw*," explained Cohl. "After I bought the show, Buck wouldn't go on unless I paid him the second half of his fee, which I didn't have."

Cohl's nervy idea was to ask the arena's owner, Harold Ballard, whom he'd never met, for $20,000. Ballard replied, "I don't know why I'm doing this. I give people money all the time. Nobody ever pays me back."

Cohl gave the $20,000 to Buck Owens. Now what could possibly go wrong? "The fricking band didn't turn up, and they didn't tell us until the day of the show. At least, it was before we'd opened the doors, so it wasn't like we had five thousand people trashing the arena with me still paying for it."

In fact, they hadn't sold enough tickets to cover the floor of the arena. "I lost all the money I had in the world, but it was a mistake I'd never make again, right?"

In 1973, the mercurial Harold Ballard decided that he was going to deal with only one concert promoter for Maple Leaf Gardens. Whoever landed that gig would be The Man in Toronto. Ballard's team interviewed every promoter in North America before he told Cohl, "You're it. You will basically be our exclusive promoter. You're a pretty responsible guy. I like your discipline. I like the way you approach things." Then Ballard added what seemed like a strange condition: "I have this son in law school who has no idea what he wants to be. He's going to be your partner, and you have to look after him."

That forced marriage turned out to be amazingly durable. "Billy Ballard is still one of my best friends," said Cohl. "We're spiritual partners forever and a day. He's good luck. I'm very superstitious."

Bill Ballard was equally satisfied. "I kind of liked Cohl, and it helped that our fathers were friends. The two of us were just out of school, with similar histories. I wasn't into the hair thing—he used to wear his down to his ankles—but Michael's a quick read and I've always found him straight up. To understand him, you have to know something of his family. Fifty years ago, some were ardent members of the Communist party, but his dad could have been a member of the world's Capitalist party. Michael is between these two. As much as you think he's a capitalist, there's a good socialist in him as well."

One of Cohl's first concerts at the Gardens featured the rock group Rush. To open the concert Cohl hired Bob Saget, an emerging standup comedian. Saget would go on to make a fortune on two major U.S. television series: *Full House* and *America's Funniest Videos*. Most of the world perceived Saget as "America's dad" from those shows, but his standup act was beyond filthy. When he showed up at the Sunset Marquis Hotel to shoot the interview, he was in a very dirty mood. His comedic recollection of Cohl was so obscene I could not use any of the footage. He just sat down and began spinning. "Cohl? Yes, I remember

him. When I arrived at the Gardens, he took me down to the basement where all of those sexual abuses happened and fucked me over and over. The detectives from *CSI* had to put that yellow crime tape on my ass." This was not going into the film.

Having learned the value of controlling the Toronto entertainment business through his lock on Maple Leaf Gardens, King Cohl, as some now called him, added the CNE and later the Skydome to his collection of venues. However, before he could expand the Cohl brand across Canada, he had to deal with the formidable rock promoter Donald K. Donald. The two had worked together at arm's length. For a Bee Gees concert tour, Cohl had promoted in Hamilton, Toronto and London, while Donald had promoted in Ottawa, Montreal and Halifax. The Bee Gees agent decided he wanted only one promoter for all of Canada, which led to a bidding war between Cohl and Donald.

Cohl came in at $12,500 a night.

Donald bid $15,000.

Cohl bid $17,500.

Donald bid $18,500.

"It was a Thursday," said Cohl, "so I told the Bee Gees agent, 'Give me the weekend to think about it.' Then I picked up the phone and called Donald. When he said, 'Hello,' I replied, 'Hello, partner, how are you?' Donald later told me he literally fell off his chair laughing, because he knew exactly what I was talking about. We made a deal, fifty-fifty. Any tour he had, I would have a chance to buy fifty percent. Any tour I had, he would have a chance to buy fifty per cent. I would keep Toronto and he would keep Montreal."

Together, Cohl and Donald not only cornered rock promotion in Canada, but their nationwide tour circuits began attracting American booking agents.

Meanwhile, Cohl's private life was headed downhill. "I was floundering. I had a terrible marriage, and I was not a happy guy. I didn't like dating, and then this goddess took a liking to me." Her name was Lori McGoran, his former secretary. Now, after more than three decades and four children, Lori told me in interview, "Michael is really serious, but he also has a lighthearted side, so maybe I just helped bring that out a little bit with him."

Together, they turned Michael's career into a family business. While I was filming Michael in Miami, their son, Jake, was shooting the Stones tour and their son Eli was working as a stage carpenter. Chase and Liam, though still in school, were also interested in show-business careers. All four kids liked their parents a lot. "There's great chemistry between them," said Eli. "I mean, they're best friends and they've been that way for as long as I can remember."

Jake agreed. "They're incredibly natural. They're in sync on everything, even though they're two completely different people."

"I love her, that's all," said Cohl. "She's fabulous. It's like, oh, my God, she's the funniest person I've ever met. She's the best person I've ever met. And she's hot."

A happy man is an undistracted man. Cohl expanded into the United States, creating Concert Productions International, the world's largest and most profitable concert promoter. "I noticed that everything entertaining was sponsored, except for concerts," he said.

"I talked to Molson's, I talked to Coca-Cola, but no one was interested in my concerts."

Cohl's contact at Molson gave him a hint. "We love hockey. If you have any sporting events come see us."

Cohl blurted out, "How about tennis?"

Three years later, Cohl was promoting the Molson Tennis Challenge at Maple Leaf Gardens. His main motivation was to get on the company's inside track, and, sure enough, he swung a long-term deal with Molson to sponsor concerts. At the same time, sports promotion—begun as a ploy—became a new way for Cohl to make money. Basketball, skating and boxing followed. He later dropped these ventures for an unexpected reason. "Athletes were way more difficult to deal with than rock stars," said Cohl. "I didn't want to know about all their petulant behaviour."

Though live theatre had been the Waterloo for many a well-heeled dreamer, Cohl cracked that one too with his hugely successful tours of *Les Misérables* and *Cats*. He succeeded in part by adding cities that had never hosted a large touring Broadway show before. Later, he would produce Toronto's *The Lion King*, Broadway's *Spamalot* and the critically lambasted *Lord of the Rings* and *Spider-Man* musicals.

Cohl was now ready for his next big thing on the band circuit: *Why tour only in North America when you could tour all over the world?* The key to opening that lock was Cohl's acquisition of Brockum, the company that controlled merchandising for global tours. This was another ploy. As King Cohl put it, "If I could be the guy doing the merchandise, then my people and I would be on the road, in the building, in the hotel, at the restaurant, in the dressing room with the acts. Every single night. That was my theory."

Bill Ballard added, "We didn't invent T-shirts, we didn't invent pay-TV, but Michael definitely was the master of putting together all the ingredients to get the perfect gig."

He sure was. And Cohl's pleasure in acquiring the Michael Jackson tour has not diminished over the years. "So here we go . . . We gave Michael Jackson three million dollars for the merchandising rights to the tour, and so I was on the tour. I wasn't there as a promoter. I was there as a T-shirt guy. Three weeks into the tour, a horrible rumour was going around about the promoter being in trouble. I started having heart palpitations. If this tour went down, I was going down. Getting my money back would take years, if I could ever do it. So, I went to Chuck Solomon, who was running the tour, and I told him, 'I understand you're in trouble and I can fix it for you. Let me see your contract.' It was just a fluke of all flukes that the dates of October 6, 7 and 8 were available at the CNE Stadium. I told Solomon, 'I can book you in Toronto, where you weren't planning to go, and then you're going to love me.' We set up the three shows. They were a huge success, and that was that. We sat down, the lawyers worked all night. By breakfast, we had a contract for me to take over."

So, Cohl had the Michael Jackson *Thriller* tour, but trouble was brewing on his doorstep. The *Toronto Star* ran a damaging front-page story alleging that Cohl, the biggest name in rock promotion, was scalping his own tickets. "The story was about how few tickets were going on sale to the public," said Cohl, "and, in particular, how few of these were for the best seats. I'm absolutely certain that not all of the best seats went on sale to the public at the Roman Coliseum either. It's simply the way business is done. Say Harold Ballard is having an event in his building and calls to say, 'Put two hundred tickets away for me.' Warner Brothers, the record label, says, 'Put two hundred tickets away for Warner.' Mick Jagger is the singer. 'Put two hundred tickets away for Mick Jagger.' And on and on down the line. Somehow, the paper decided that was a crime."

New York rock promoter Ron Delsener agreed that the practice was universal. "You get that all the time when you're in the public eye. Probably nothing is wrong, but everybody is thinking here's a scam."

"Let's face it," said Cohl. "Wealthy people like music too, and a lot of those old hippies have done really well, allowing us to get ten per cent of the audience to pay for the fact that the other tickets are still cheap."

Martin Onrot, another concert promoter, added, "Michael may have been the first promoter with whom I had this conversation: 'How much can you charge? What is the ceiling?' I followed him. He recognized that the audience would pay more for tickets."

Ray Waddell, author of *This Business of Concert Promotion and Touring: A Practical Guide to Creating, Selling, Organizing, and Staging Concerts*, said, "Michael brought one hundred dollar tickets, two hundred dollar tickets and now five hundred dollar tickets to rock and roll, whatever kind of legacy that is. He'll argue with you all day long that those tickets pay for the cheaper tickets—he was the one who broke that glass ceiling."

"It's entertainment, it's for the love of music, it's for connecting with people and it's a business," declared Cohl.

Though Cohl occasionally looked like a sideman with the Grateful Dead, he thought like a corporate executive. He understood that if you built a bridge between entertainment and corporations in sponsorship deals, then you could make an unbelievable amount of money. He did that by selling 45 per cent of his company, Concert Productions International, to Labatt. "They had always said for the right deal, money isn't the issue. So I believed them," said Cohl. He was now after bigger fish: the Moby Dick of show business.

Bill Ballard said, "We always felt that the Rolling Stones would be the epitome of rock royalty to take on tour."

That wasn't necessarily obvious in 1988. "They hadn't toured since '82," said Cohl, "and they were badgering the crap out of each other, fighting and bickering."

If Cohl wanted the Stones, he would have to poach them from the biggest self-promoter in the business. Bill Graham was flamboyant, larger than life and likely the most powerful concert promoter of all time. He put the legendary San Francisco Fillmore on the map and the Stones didn't make a move without him. "Bill Graham loved the spotlight," said promoter Marty Onrot. "He enjoyed putting himself up on a par with his attraction."

"Bill was entirely different than Michael Cohl," agreed promoter Ron Delsener. "He was a great offstage actor, striding around with rolled-up sleeves, carrying a clipboard and instructing, 'All right, put him on now!' Michael was the opposite. He'd come in, low-key, dressed like he'd been sleeping on a park bench."

Cohl's first critical step was to get the Stones' business manager, Prince Rupert, onside. He phoned him in London. "I'd heard about Cohl," said Rupert. "I knew him as a very successful Canadian local promoter." Cohl talked money upfront: forty million dollars for forty shows. He could do that because he now had Labatt's money. Rupert quickly replied, "You've got my vote." Then he added. "Now you have to convince Mick and Keith."

That startled Cohl. "Oh, God, I thought that was the manager's job."

The Stones were in Barbados making their *Steel Wheels* album. Wisely, Cohl went courting with his Labatt's certified cheque. "I remember picking it up, putting it in my little pocket, then flying to Barbados, while checking every five minutes to see it was still there."

Despite his reputation for offhand dress, Cohl walked into his first meeting with the Stones looking like an advertisement for what he could do for them. "I put on my leather Pink Floyd jacket, an expensive six hundred dollar item, which we'd persuaded Pink Floyd to go for. While I was wondering what the Stones' first question might be, Mick exclaimed, 'That's exactly what I'm talking about!' He turned to Keith. 'See that jacket? That's what we should have been doing all these years!'"

Cohl calmly talked numbers, outlining in a quiet way his version of a Rolling Stones tour, emphasizing all the money they could make by marketing themselves effectively. As Exhibit A, he waved that certified cheque—the kind of money rock and roll had never seen before. Keith Richards later told me, "Michael was away ahead of the game in seeing how to bring everything together for us."

He was also a behind-the-scenes guy who knew that the talent should be front and centre. As Mick Jagger explained, "Bill Graham was larger than life, and it was sometimes quite a strain working with him. In 1989, we decided not to do that anymore."

Riley O'Connor, a member of the Cohl team who was present at that meeting, said, "It was like a tickertape parade in the office, you know, with streams of paper coming down. We were like, 'Wow! This is something.'"

An embittered Bill Graham later told the press, "Today I watched my lover become a whore."

To which Cohl replied, "Sour grapes."

Cohl cut out everyone between himself and the Stones for the band's 1989 tour: one tour, one promoter. He also proved that he understood what the ancient Romans meant when they produced a spectacle. He foresaw and took advantage of every conceivable way to wring money from the Rolling Stones sponge. This included multimillion-dollar pay-TV deals, unprecedented sponsorship agreements and, yes, $450 bomber jackets like the one he'd worn to impress the Stones.

"We hadn't toured for a long time," said Jagger, "and the whole business had undergone somewhat of a revolution, but we—and the numbers—were very big for those days. Michael and I were in agreement that if we were going to do this, we had to make it an event."

"Michael was everywhere," said Richards. "He took care of the crew. He gave a lot of thought to the teamwork, which is incredibly important in this game."

The tour grossed more than $260 million, an industry record. All at little risk for Cohl, and none for the Stones. "That broke the touring business wide open," said Riley O'Connor.

Cohl promoted four more tours for the Stones. After that, U2 came knocking. And he already had Pink Floyd. In one busy year, King Cohl's company promoted three events a day. He was a producer, a TV broadcaster, a record man and a T-shirt man, rolled into one. He changed the business.

Though Cohl avoided the spotlight, its glare sometimes struck him in a way he found abhorrent. His hometown paper, the *Toronto Star*, again went after him, this time alleging that, under the guise of a provincial sales tax, Cohl was skimming off 10 per cent of the gate from each of his bands. "They called me a scumbag and a liar and a thief," protested Cohl.

He challenged Kevin Donovan, the *Star*'s lead investigator, saying, "So why don't we go to Peter Moore, a civic employee who runs the CNE, and ask him to put in writing that they keep the tax, that they've been fully paid, and that the tax exemption is only for the CNE? We got that in writing, and the *Star* wrote the story anyway. Now they also called Peter a liar. We knew that we were helping to keep the CNE alive. We knew that we were making a contribution to the city of Toronto, so that something that had cost the government money year after year was now contributing money. I thought, 'I may as well live in Florida. Why should I have any ties to this city anymore?' I phoned everybody, and I said, 'Here's my address, bring whatever auditors you want, bring whatever accountants you want. Here's where our records are kept, here's my office. Come and open every file, talk to anyone you want. There was no phony tax, or tax scheme or fraud.'"

Riley O'Connor saw it this way: "I come from a nice, rich, Irish Montreal Catholic background, and I thought the attack was kind of anti-Semitic. Here's a guy who lived and breathed the essence of Toronto. That whole CNE thing was crushing."

Dusty Cohl agreed. "The *Star* definitely tried to interfere with Michael's relationship with his acts. This was just one paper, the *Toronto Star* only."

Cohl's family also felt the pain. "This attack was devastating for Michael," said his wife Lori.

"I was thirteen years old," said Jake Cohl. "When I got to school, some kid, whom I was kinda friends with, was like, 'So is your dad going to jail?' After this, you would never, ever see a *Toronto Star* anywhere near our house again."

The *Toronto Star*, which stood by its story, declined by email to be interviewed for my Michael Cohl documentary. Donovan had actually wanted to go on film but said that his legal team feared Cohl and had to pass. In 2002, Cohl was inducted into the Canadian Music Hall of Fame, and in 2005 he was given a star on Canada's Walk of Fame.

"What a job it's been!" he reminisced. "Forty years of travelling around the world with U2, Pink Floyd, the Rolling Stones, watching the fans explode with love every night, watching the bands perform, and thinking, *I get a percentage of this too?*"

Keith Richards summed up the experience in these words: "Michael's motto should be Adapt, Improvise and Overcome."

Cohl now wanted to give something back, even to the hometown that had once treated him shabbily. In 2003, Toronto tourism was still suffering from the '90s recession when the city was hit by the SARS epidemic. After a spring outbreak of this highly infectious disease, the World Health Organization (WHO) issued an advisory warning to travellers to stay away. The international media carried photos of Torontonians lined up for blocks, some wearing face-masks, awaiting their vaccination, and of hospital staff garbed head-to-toe like astronauts visiting a toxic planet. Hotel occupancy was way down, conventions were being cancelled and fear kept even locals away from shops and restaurants, with an estimated revenue loss to the city of $600 million.

Even after the WHO lifted its advisory, Toronto remained tainted. How to convince the world that the city was once again a safe and dynamic destination?

Bring in the Rolling Stones, that's how!

The Stones knew Toronto because it was where Cohl rehearsed them. He would rent a school, or some other venue closed for the summer, along with residences for the Stones. When Cohl was approached with the idea of producing a SARS benefit concert to show the world that Toronto was once again open for business, no persuasion was necessary. "My team and the Stones were proud to come to the rescue," recalled Cohl. "When I told Keith, 'SARS. Toronto. Pain. We can help.' He looked surprised, then said these exact words, 'They think we can help? Then, of course, we have to do it.' He knew he was speaking for the others."

The venue for the all-day rock fest called Molson Canadian Rocks for Toronto (or SARSfest among the fans) was Downsview Park in north Toronto. The date was July 30. In the buildup to the event, Mick Jagger and the other Stones appeared in TV ads, assuring the world that Toronto was now the place to be—no face-masks or other protective gear necessary.

Most of the pressure for the event fell on Michael Cohl. "I was a nervous wreck all that day," he confessed. "I woke up that morning at the Four Seasons Hotel, and I looked in the mirror as I was brushing my teeth, running tomorrow's imaginary newspaper headline through my brain, 'COHL KILLS FOUR.' That's because every time you produce one of these shows, with five hundred thousand people, somebody dies, somebody gives birth, twelve people are hospitalized or have heart attacks."

Bill Ballard agreed. "That was a big problem for Michael. A problem for all of us. I was proud to be his partner."

SARSfest turned out to be the loud, flamboyant and fabulous triumph everyone had hoped for. Actor/singer Dan Aykroyd hosted the event. There were performances by AC/DC, the Guess Who, Justin Timberlake, Rush, Tom Cochrane, Blue Rodeo and many others.

"I spent most of the day walking around, worried," said Cohl. "I

was repeating to myself, 'My God, it's really working, it's fantastic and nobody's dead yet, nobody's been shot. What's happening here?'"

The Rolling Stones closed with a ninety-minute set. This was three years before I began filming my Cohl documentary, but my ad agency was working for the Stones, and Dusty Cohl had arranged for me to have a backstage pass. We were transported with the band and the crew in special buses to the Four Seasons Hotel, and then to Downsview Park along the Don Valley Parkway, which had been shut down for us. We went backstage and ate with the Stones and all the VIPs, and it was quite something. Dusty said, "Let's go on stage before the Stones to see the audience from their perspective."

As expected, the concert had attracted between 450,000 and 500,000 people, making it the largest outdoor ticketed event in Canadian history, and one of the largest in North America. Dusty and I walked to the edge of the stage as the fans waited for the Stones. You could feel the immense energy in the air. If I hadn't had my feet firmly planted, I'm sure I would have been sucked into the crowd. I stood in the wings as the Stones came out. Michael Cohl patted each on the back as a send off. It was mind-blowing.

I now know from watching the Stones in Miami while filming my doc that Mick Jagger would have run a treadmill for forty-five minutes before the show to get his metabolism moving, followed by a massage. He was in such outrageous shape. Keith Richards didn't do any of that stuff.

Once on stage, the Stones gave and gave and gave. When they came off, they were soaked in sweat, Mick especially, because of the way he moved and danced, so that he had to change his silk shirt. I can't remember how many pounds he lost every show, but that was one of the reasons he was so thin.

Thanks to Dusty, I had also been to intimate, private concerts that the Stones gave in Toronto after rehearsing and before going on tour. The Stones would perform at Palais Royale, or the Phoenix, a small nightclub on Sherbourne Street in Toronto. After these privileged experiences, sitting in an audience of 100,000 as just another fan had no attraction for me.

Both Cohl and the Stones were happy. "I think it was the biggest crowd we'd ever played to," said Cohl. "I don't think there'd been a crowd this big, you know, for a one-day event, ever."

Instead of trying to top himself, Cohl made a sweet and sentimental return to the music that had moved him as a teenager: he did a show in New York with the Weavers.

"These last few years have been the best time ever," he told me, "when I could sit in a meeting with Harold Leventhal, the Weavers' long-time manager, and say, 'I didn't even know the Weavers were back together, and here they're playing Carnegie Hall, and of course you're filming it.' He said, 'No, of course we're not.' I asked, 'Why not?' He said, 'We don't have the money.' I told him, 'You do now.' That night I informed my kids, 'I just blew half your inheritance. Too bad.' You know, if you make all this money, it's best to put it to some good use instead of just keeping a pile around."

The sentimental forays were fun but for Michael Cohl the main event was always the Stones. He took them on the road again for 2005's *Bigger Bang* tour, and in 2006, he produced the largest rock concert in history, The Rolling Stones in Rio. And here's the kicker: those tickets were free.

That event had a dauntingly slow start. From Cohl's hotel room overlooking the beach and the stage, they could see that by 10 a.m. only two or three hundred thousand people had turned up—small by Stones' standards. "Goodness gracious," joked Mick. "That's a lot of people. Any excuse for a party."

But the fans kept flooding in. By evening, they stretched about a mile along Copacabana beach and there were two hundred boats anchored in the harbour, including a cruise ship. The official police count was two million. Cohl was jubilant. Once again, he could say, "Nobody died, and fewer than three hundred were taken to the hospital or arrested. We went from the Super Bowl, which looked like our all-time highlight, and two weeks later we were in Brazil, which proved to be our absolutely all-time highlight."

Along with Cohl's phenomenal success, which is reflected in the numbers, he brought to show business a piece of wisdom that protected him from the spectacular tumbles typical of so many others: *If you want to keep the ones you love, you have to hold them close.* Where Cohl went, so did his wife and kids. And it seemed to work. For this, Cohl credits his wife.

"Because we've toured for so many years, the kids became really comfortable with it," said Lori. "They liked living in hotels. They liked room service. They seemed to get their schoolwork done. We tried all the food, we went to places to dance, we went to museums, we went to beaches, we went on trains and on boats. We tried to give our kids a good experience, and because the Rolling Stones have kids of similar ages, everybody came along and got along."

"We've all grown up together," said Chase Cohl. "We've shared experiences with these kids that no one else could understand, and I think it's so cool that we've been able to live this crazy life. At the same time, our parents have always kept things under control, and taught us really strong values."

"I don't think anybody close to us would ever deny that with us our family comes first," agreed Jake Cohl.

"Since all our kids have travelled on the road for extended periods," said Michael, "they now jump in and out because they have their own lives. They all seem down-to-earth, great kids. It's shocking. Lori managed to do it. I don't know how. In my wildest dreams, I would never have come close to imagining what's actually happened. Everything is way beyond anything I ever expected."

Is this the moral of my documentary on Michael Cohl? A happy showbiz story without huge losses, big regrets or a downward spiral? It seems so. A week before *Satisfaction* was to air, I screened the film for Michael at his Rosedale home. He loved it. He was uncharacteristically emotional, and then asked for a copy to show his mother. Since I was still on a high, I gave it to him. Big mistake. No Jewish mother is willing to accept the slightest criticism of her son.

Three days before the film was to air, Michael called me. "I want all that *Toronto Star* tax stuff out."

"I can't do that. The network has it. We're done."

After that, I received a vicious email from Michael, saying he only did the film because of Dusty's ego, and demanding the changes be made so he wouldn't embarass his mother.

I received this while I was at a press event connected to the Stratford Festival and it floored me. I left the conference abruptly and walked the city for five hours. I thought that I had made a great film, full of inside information about rock and roll. So had Michael, before this silliness.

I finally wrote my answer. "I'm sorry that you're upset, and that the film didn't please you, but at the end of the day, if your mother isn't proud of your accomplishments, then fuck it. It stays the way it is, and that's it."

Because I'm notorious for shooting off emails without reflection, I checked in with Eddie Greenspan before sending it. It was 11 p.m., but I knew Eddie would be in his office, and he was. After talking me off the ledge, he told me, "Send it."

I pressed the send key, heard the blip and the deed was done.

Michael responded immediately. "I guess I should have looked at the film earlier, and good luck with it."

Satisfaction aired while I was in Los Angeles working on another project. My cellphone rang. It was Michael's assistant. "Hi, Barry. I have Michael Cohl for you."

I asked in a flat voice, "What does he want?"

"He really wants to speak with you."

"I'm on a project, and if he has an issue, or is disgruntled, I don't want to listen to him. I'm just not fucking interested."

"Hi, Barry, it's Michael."

"Hi." I'm cold as ice.

"So, what are the ratings like?"

People had been calling Michael, saying the film was fantastic, so now he wanted to know how many people had seen it?

Typical showbiz, but I couldn't relish the moment, because I was still too angry at his earlier explosion. I calmed down after a few days when Dusty said to me, "Kid, this is his way of saying sorry. Toughen up."

Chapter Twenty

UNAUTHORIZED: THE HARVEY WEINSTEIN PROJECT

I'm not sure what attracts me to making films about moguls. It could be their Faustian exercise of power, often leading to a tragic downfall. It could be the glittering world that—at least for a time—they create around them. When I was filming Lew Wasserman, whom I called *The Last Mogul*, the name *Harvey Weinstein* kept surfacing. The entertainment industry had grown so exponentially since Wasserman that no single person could hope ever again to hold it in such an iron grip. Yet, Weinstein, operating from both America's east and west coasts, changed movies in ways that others scrambled to copy. He was a self-described outsider and yet everyone in the industry knew him by his first name. As a producer, he had the ambition of a tyrant and the eye of an artist. His films captured an unprecedented 303 Oscar nominations and more than seventy-five wins.

Like Lew Wasserman, Harvey Weinstein defined an era that would never be repeated. And like Wasserman, my introduction to him came through my advertising work with Echo. Alliance had the rights to distribute Miramax Films, founded in 1979 by Harvey and Bob Weinstein, and this made me the marketing guy for Miramax in Canada. Occasionally I would be on conference calls with Alliance and Harvey or his marketing people, and he'd be asking, "What are we doing in Canada? No, no, no! You gotta buy more media."

My access gave me an insight into Harvey's savvy at picking up small movies and turning them into blockbusters. After distributing Quentin Tarantino's first film, *Reservoir Dogs*, Miramax went on to break the indie record in 1994 with Tarantino's *Pulp Fiction*, which grossed more than $200 million worldwide. *Pulp Fiction* also won the Palme d'Or and seven Academy Award nominations, resulting in an Oscar for best screenplay. After that, Harvey gave Tarantino a blank cheque and creative autonomy, leading the director to make more successful films, including *Jackie Brown*, *Kill Bill 1* and *Kill Bill 2*.

Once again, Dusty Cohl was instrumental first in urging me to do a Weinstein documentary, and then in getting me to Harvey through personal emails and phone calls. I said repeatedly to Weinstein, "I'd like to make a film about you," and he replied each time with increasing force, "No, I don't want you to do it right now." Eventually, he added, "I shouldn't tell you this, but Quentin Tarantino is already filming a documentary on my life."

I replied, "Harvey, I find that hard to believe. He's working on *Kill Bill 3*."

I knew another filmmaker—certainly not Tarantino—had tried to document Weinstein. Weinstein had pushed him right out of the business. But Harvey also had sent me a pleasant note about *The Last Mogul*. So, maybe?

When I contacted him again, he sounded more conciliatory. "Barry, I'm not ready to make the film, but when I do, you're the guy."

I knew that he never meant it to happen, but by now enough buzz had been created by my attempts to get it started that the *New York*

Times approached me for a story. I replied, "Let me get the financing in place first, or I'll look like an idiot if this unravels."

I did get the financing, and then I sold domestic rights to HBO Canada and international rights to High Point Media, a UK distributor. After that, the *New York Times* did a major story, "DOCUMENTARIAN ATTEMPTS TO CLIMB MOUNT WEINSTEIN."

Michael Cohl called me as soon as the story hit the newsstands. In the early days, Michael and Harvey had known each other because both promoted concerts. Later, they had partnered to produce Broadway shows.

Michael began by saying, "Harvey asked me to speak to you." *Was he going to wave a flag, or swing a bat?* "Harvey doesn't want your film made, so if he doesn't want it, don't make it. There are all kinds of other films you can do."

"Michael, I'm making the Harvey movie."

"I'm asking you not to. Harvey doesn't want it. Take a cheque, go and meet him and maybe he'll finance one of your other films."

I became cagey. "What kind of cheque are we talking about? In 1989, you offered the Rolling Stones forty million dollars to walk away from Bill Graham. If I'm going to be a whore, what's the payoff?" Michael couldn't answer because he wasn't supposed to be negotiating. Instead, he became somewhat aggressive. After I started setting up key interviews, word again got back to Harvey, and I received another call from Cohl. "Barry, don't be an idiot. Stop making the film."

"Here's the deal, Michael. Set up a meeting with Harvey. Let me sit down with him, and let's see what we come up with." Michael passed on my message, and Harvey agreed.

I flew down to Los Angeles on the weekend of the 2011 Oscars. We were to meet at 10 a.m. at the Montage Hotel in Beverly Hills. Even though I'd brought my friend, Todd White, a savvy criminal lawyer and a former partner of Eddie Greenspan, I was trembling.

The notepad I'd just purchased said *Carpe Diem*, and Seize the Day was exactly what I hoped to do.

Harvey was sitting in the middle of an otherwise empty dining room with a group of associates. It was like a scene from *The Godfather*, as if he had taken over the entire restaurant for his meetings. When he finished the first conversation, he came over to my table. He glanced at Todd.

"Who is this?" he asked.

"Todd White, a friend."

"Okay, then do you mind if I have a friend join us?"

"No. That's fine."

I don't remember who that friend was, but I do remember that Harvey immediately began working me over with his charm offensive. "Barry, I'm not ready to do this film, I've got a family, you know, and I'm building my new business. Let's do something else together. Do you want to make a film about Martin Scorsese? I can get that done."

"Not really. That film has already been made." I went back to first principles. "Harvey, when I made *The Last Mogul*, you told me—"

"Fantastic film! Could I have another DVD of it?"

"Sure. I'll send it."

"How about making a movie about Arthur Krim. Great story!"

"Who?"

"Arthur Krim. He created Orion Pictures and was an adviser to Lyndon Johnson."

Another dead man. "Harvey, fewer people will go to that film than a film about you."

That seemed to encourage him. "So, we're going to agree that a film about me is not worth doing. Now, do you want something for breakfast, or a Diet Coke or anything?"

"No, no, I don't want anything."

"Okay, then let's agree to keep talking about this."

"Sure, we can agree about that."

"Anything else you want?"

I decided to go for something better than a Diet Coke. "I'd love to attend your famous post-Oscar party."

"Done!"

I walked out of the restaurant, knowing I was still going to make the Harvey Weinstein story, and still trembling.

I wasn't attending the ceremony, but I had an invitation to Elton John's Oscar party, along with clients and a friend. After that, we attended Harvey's party at the Chateau Marmont. Quentin Tarantino was there, and a few other celebrities, along with Harvey's mother, Miriam, and his kids. I asked myself, What am I doing here? It felt too private so we left.

The Page Six gossip column of the *New York Post* printed a story saying I was moving ahead with the Weinstein project. Harvey contacted me again. "I need to talk to you about this movie. I'm getting annoyed here."

We set up a telephone appointment for the next Saturday morning.

Before that could happen, I called my friend, Jim Sherry, who had worked at Miramax, for advice.

He told me, "Barry, there are three phases with Harvey. He's going to tell you what an unbelievable filmmaker you are and try to convince you not to make the film." Check. "He's going to try to buy you out by promising you money to make another movie." Check. "Then, he's going to try to destroy you." Okay.

Next, I called Eddie Greenspan. "I don't know how to handle this. Can you listen in quietly on my phone call with Harvey and take notes?"

Eddie agreed.

On Saturday morning, Harvey launched into familiar territory. "Barry, I've asked you over and over and over not to make this movie. You're making the movie and I'm not happy. I've offered you things, and you're still making the movie."

"So, you want me to make a movie about somebody else? Wire a million dollars into my account tomorrow, and we can get into a development deal together."

Silence. Then, "Are you going through with this film, or not?"

"Yes."

"How would you feel if I showed up on your doorstep Monday morning with a film crew to make a movie about you?"

"Harvey, I'm not telling the stories that maybe you think I'm telling. People have told me some salacious stories, but I'm not going down that road. This is a film about you and your movies, so you have nothing to worry about."

"Barry, this is not over. I don't want you to make the film, and I'm not through with you."

"I hear you, but I'm making the film."

We hung up. Eddie said, "You handled it well. You went back at him. It's fine, keep going."

Harvey Weinstein hadn't yet declared war. It was still cat and mouse. When the *New York Times* contacted him for another story about the film, he told them, "Barry is a great filmmaker."

After that, he kept checking in on me. He tried coercion. He tried threats. He recommended people to interview for the film. He contacted people I'd already lined up and compelled them to pull out. Periodically, he would even ignore me.

When my mother, who knew about the threats over the Wasserman film, heard I was making a documentary about Harvey Weinstein, she asked, "Can't you pick another dead one so at least he can't kill you personally?"

My mother—an overnight Harvey Weinstein expert—was almost right, but it wasn't me Harvey was determined to destroy. Just my documentary.

★

Harvey Weinstein was born in 1952 in Flushing, New York. He grew up to be a tough, flamboyant brawler. His loyal brother, Bobby, two years younger, was quieter and more self-contained. Physically, they were not impressive: two fat guys raised in a six-storey, rent-controlled apartment building. Their father, Max, was a diamond cutter who had health problems; their mother, Miriam, was the family's driving force.

Miriam instilled in the brothers the desire to make money and acquire status. Max developed their artistic taste by taking them every Saturday to the Mayfair Theater, which showed foreign films by directors such as Fellini, Visconti and Rossellini. Harvey would later claim that François Truffaut's *400 Blows* had the greatest impact on him. At fourteen, he took brother Bob and six friends to see it at the Mayfair, thinking they were going to see a pornographic movie. When the lights came on, Harvey and Bob were the only ones left in the theatre. As well as being mesmerized by the film, Harvey considered its provocative title a lesson in marketing.

Max taught his sons another strategy vital for their film career: the art of display—something my father had taught me too. One diamond looked like another until you placed it on a black velvet cushion. Then, it became the only diamond anyone wanted to see.

Given a choice between the Vietnam War and college, Harvey left New York City in 1969 to attend the University of Buffalo. Like Wasserman and Cohl, he began his career as a concert promoter by bringing music acts to the city. He eliminated competition at the university, reportedly by using cutthroat tactics, and then started a concert company with his classmate, Corky Burger. Five years later, Harvey and Corky Presents was producing 2,000 concerts a year. Harvey dropped out of college and acquired a run-down, 2,000-seat theatre called The Century, which he used for concerts and Saturday-night movies. His brother, Bob, gave early promise of his marketing shrewdness when he conceived of the idea of showing three movies for the price of one.

In 1979, when he was twenty-seven, Harvey sold his shares in the concert company and moved back to New York City to start a film company with Bob. They called it Miramax after their parents Miriam and Max, and defined its mission with reference to *Star Trek*: "To boldly go where no one has gone before."

Soon after setting up an office, Harvey was smitten with his stunning, socially prominent secretary, Eve Chilton. His relentless wooing of her upset the company's small staff but he persisted and married Eve within the year. The two eventually had three daughters.

In 1969, *Easy Rider* had exploded onto movie screens. Its success heralded a wave of films by independent and innovative directors, such as Peter Bogdanovich, Mike Nichols, Stanley Kubrick and Francis Ford Coppola, in a movement that became known as The New Hollywood. By the 1980s, however, the big studios had once again pushed aside these story-driven films with blockbusters like *Jaws* and *Raiders of the Lost Ark*. In 1986, Miramax, with twenty employees, was still struggling for focus and barely staying afloat. The Weinstein brothers sold 45 per cent of Miramax to the UK bank, Midland Montagu, for $3.5 million and a $10 million line of credit. Harvey and Bob used the cash, combined with the film savvy they acquired as boys watching art films at the Mayfair, to finally find their métier. Harvey acquired the Italian movie *Cinema Paradiso*, which he reshaped and repositioned for a mainstream North American audience. He had a fixed idea about how long anyone would sit for a movie, and this led him to cut forty-five minutes from the film. He was right. The film, which had been poorly received in its original version, grossed more than $12 million, won a Special Jury Prize at the Cannes Film Festival and Best Foreign Language Film at the Oscars in 1989.

A year later, Harvey did much the same for the independently produced *Sex, Lies, and Videotape*, which won an Audience Award at the Sundance Film Festival. Instead of relying on reviews, small ads and word of mouth, which was typical for indies, Miramax spent an unheard-of $2.5 million on a TV campaign. The film ultimately grossed more than $54 million worldwide and won a Palme d'Or at the 1989 Cannes Film Festival. It also brought director Steven Soderbergh into prominence, while also highlighting the importance of Robert Redford's Sundance Festival.

The British drama *The Crying Game* failed in its 1992 UK and New York releases. Miramax created for its North American release the most talked about film-marketing campaign ever. He demanded that moviegoers promise—on their honour—never to reveal the shocking twist. That film grossed $63 million; received six Academy Awards nominations, including Best Picture; and won a Best Original Screenplay for writer and director Neil Jordan. Miramax had found a winning formula: acquire indie and foreign films, repackage them as mainstream blockbusters and use aggressive advertising to take them from art houses to the suburbs.

The Weinstein brothers were riding high in the entertainment business, but you wouldn't have known it by the manner in which it was conducted. Their staff worked in a stuffy, fluorescent-lit two-bedroom New York apartment-office, in an atmosphere some described as a hothouse of anger and fear. Bob hunkered down in one bedroom, Harvey in the other, and everyone else was packed into the living room among filing cases and small desks.

"It was high pressure and unforgiving," recalled Eamonn Bowles, now president of Magnolia Pictures. "At first, it was also bracing. Everyone was very smart, and there wasn't much backstabbing because we all seemed united in avoiding Harvey's and Bob's wrath."

Their episodes of rage apparently included tearing phones out of walls and using anything else that was handy as a potential weapon.

Director George Hickenlooper vividly recalled working with Harvey on his film *Factory Girl*. "He would call me in the middle of the night, and shout into the phone, 'Why are you sleeping? You're a loser, loser, loser!' I'd say, 'Huh, huh? What did I do?' 'You're a fucking idiot. I'm going to take out an ad in *Variety*, full page, and say don't ever hire Hickenlooper. He's a loser!'"

Harvey was especially keen on reshooting a sex scene between Sienna Miller and Hayden Christensen. Before the cameras rolled, Hickenlooper claimed Harvey had instructed Hayden, "You're going to hump her and hump her and hump her and hump her, and then you're going to flip her over and do her the other way. Then she's going to get on top of you, and then there's going to be a tear running down her cheek, and the whole audience is going to tear up with her. That's how it's going to be done."

Following orders, Hickenlooper sent Harvey a video playback, leading to another call five hours later on set. "He shouted, 'Where's my wide shot? Where's my wide shot?' I told him, 'We were in a confined space. I couldn't go wider.' 'You're lying to me! You're a liar! You're lying to Harvey Weinstein. I'm going to take another ad out in *Variety* and say George Hickenlooper lied to Harvey Weinstein. You're fired!'"

Not knowing where he stood on the film, before packing up his belongings to vacate the set, Hickenlooper decided he might as well eat the free catered lunch. Word got back to Harvey that George was leaving the set and he called him on his cell. "Harvey came shouting at me, 'What are you doing? Get the fuck back in there!' He was like an alcoholic patriarch with everyone in constant fear of being spanked, or beaten or talked down to."

Harvey justified the abuse by pointing to his record of success. As Hickenlooper recalled, he would shout, "'Do you know how many Oscars I've won? Do you know how many Golden Globes?' Gee, Harvey, do you know how many Boy Scout badges I've won, plus an Emmy?"

Meryl Poster, a long-time Harvey stalwart, surprised me by agreeing to be interviewed. After starting out as Harvey's second assistant, Poster rose through the ranks of Harvey's various enterprises before branching out on her own. *Why was she showing up?* I decided she must be Harvey's eyes and ears. My suspicions were confirmed when she arrived with an assistant and a tape recorder. I told her, "I don't want to lose you, Miss Poster, but no taping of the interview, and your assistant has to go. You can, of course, say no to any of my questions."

She surprised me by giving in to my conditions. She confirmed stories about Harvey's temper tantrums, as many others would do. "I quit after the second week, but he begged me to come back. I told him he needed anger management. He would blow up and then feel badly."

Harvey emailed me to ask, "How did the Meryl Poster interview go?"

As if he didn't know.

The late *New York Times* writer David Carr, recalled, "Harvey would tell me again and again, 'I've mellowed. I've got my blood sugar under control.' If you typed in 'mellow' and 'Harvey Weinstein' your search engine would blow up because of all the times he's said that. He's very volatile, but he's also very accessible, a fun, smart guy to talk to about books, films or television shows."

Like everyone else I interviewed, Mark Urman, an indie film distributor and former Miramax employee, agreed that Harvey had been a game changer in the film business: the outsider who became the ultimate insider. "I think Harvey understood very early that he would have to turn some of his liabilities into assets," said Urman. "Harvey was always sloppy, but famously so. His clothing was always stained, sometimes so egregiously that you could only scratch your head and wonder, 'How is it possible that there is so much sauce on that shirt?'"

Film historian and author Peter Biskind, who wrote the definitive book on the indie film business of the '90s, *Down and Dirty Pictures*, called Harvey a Reverse Waldo. "Once you saw him in a room you couldn't see anyone else. That happened with me even before I knew who he was."

Harvey's spectacular success with *Sex, Lies, and Videotapes* and *The Crying Game* had not gone unnoticed by the big studios. Many set up their own divisions to chase indies. Spurred on by this new competition, Harvey began scooping up films he didn't want just to keep them from the competition, inflating prices and leaving him cash-starved once again.

"It became a trend to use Hollywood stars in independent films," said Peter Biskind. "Finally, they began to cost as much as low-budget Hollywood movies."

Harvey also became known as Mr. Scissorhands for the way he recut films. Independent directors began to say, "The good news is that we sold our film to Miramax. The bad news is that we sold our film to Miramax." Peter Biskind reported, "Sometimes Harvey would have students cutting the films of famous directors. One told me that he was in a dentist's chair having his teeth drilled when he heard Harvey was cutting his film. He didn't know which was worse, the drilling or the cutting."

I was excited when James Ivory of the famous Merchant Ivory team agreed to be interviewed. After waiting ninety minutes with my crew, I phoned him. "Hello, it's Barry Avrich. We're wondering where you are."

"I can't do this."

"Why not?"

"Well, there may be one more film I want to make, and if I do your interview, Harvey won't green-light it."

"Mr. Ivory, you've made a commitment to me, in the same way you make a commitment to actors and others on a film. I have a crew ready to roll here." He knew I was right, and he agreed to come.

Ivory explained that his connection with Harvey began while he was riding a subway, trying to figure out how to get the next Ismail Merchant/James Ivory movie financed. "Suddenly, it became clear. For a certain kind of film, all subways and roads head in one direction—to Harvey Weinstein's office." But as almost every director discovered, working with Harvey came at a price. "Harvey had a carnivorous appetite for dismembering his films," said Ivory. "With *Mr. & Mrs. Bridge*, Harvey wanted us to do things to the film that we didn't want to do, and he began ranting and raving and charging around his office. Ismail had a very heavy briefcase, and he slammed it against a big glass partition. There was this loud cracking sound, and it shattered. Then, the two of them were going to take the fight into the street."

Ivory and Merchant showed their version of the film to their stars, Paul Newman and Joanne Woodward. "Paul told Harvey, 'That's the film I'll do the publicity for, not another,' and that settled Harvey down." The two filmmakers and Harvey didn't speak to each other for two years. Then they tried another collaboration in 2000 with *The Golden Bowl*. This time, when Harvey brandished his scissors, the British filmmakers insisted on buying back their film rights, which they then sold to Lionsgate Films.

Harvey often spent huge amounts of money on marketing and acquisitions, while counting on the next hit to cover the deficit. Meanwhile, brother Bob would bring in money with horror and controversial films. Harvey sometimes was accused of deliberately seeking an X-rating to stir up controversy and create box-office interest. "I remember doing a television clip of Helen Mirren walking around in her underwear," said Mark Urman. "It aired all over the news. We had been looking at small images, but when these were blown up, we discovered Helen Mirren wasn't wearing any panties. She had on a garter belt, and what we thought was black lace was Helen Mirren."

Despite the controversies, that same year Miramax picked up a Best Picture Oscar for *My Left Foot*, an inspirational movie about a young man with cerebral palsy, played by Daniel Day-Lewis, who won Best Actor.

In 1993, the Weinstein brothers sold Miramax Films to the Walt Disney Company for $60 million. The agreement called for both Harvey and Bob to stay on until 2005. Now able to play for higher stakes, Harvey diversified, with investments in the fashion house Halston, the cable network Ovation, a long list of restaurants, the Bravo hit *Project Runway* and dozens of Broadway productions. In 1998, he hired former *Vanity Fair* editor Tina Brown to launch a magazine called *Talk*. That venture alone eventually lost him $50 million.

Taking a leaf from Lew Wasserman's playbook, Harvey became a strong supporter of Bill Clinton, and then of Hillary Clinton, donating $750,000 and raising another $14 million.

The prestigious awards continued to pile up. In 1996, Miramax received nine Oscars, including Best Picture for the epic film *The English Patient*, in which Harvey invested $30 million for a gross of $78 million. The dénouement was not so good. The film's producer, Saul Zaentz, claimed he had been cheated out of millions in profits, while Harvey adamantly insisted the film was not profitable due to high marketing costs. Zaentz said, "Harvey is a pushcart peddler who puts his thumb on the scale when the old woman is buying meat." More accounting questions were raised over *Good Will Hunting*, which was nominated in 1997 for Best Picture. For an investment of $20 million, the film grossed over $200 million. Matt Damon and Ben Affleck, who had written and developed the film, were left feeling shortchanged by millions of dollars, while co-star Robin Williams, with a different contract, made more than $20 million. "Matt and Ben shamed Harvey into giving them each one million dollars," said Biskind. "As a gesture, Harvey dumped a bag of fake money onto a bed. He could have given them forty-five million dollars and still made out like a bandit."

In 1998, at the height of his power, Harvey launched an all-out military-style campaign to win Best Picture for *Shakespeare in Love*.

He succeeded, unexpectedly beating out Steven Spielberg's *Saving Private Ryan*. "No vote was too obscure to pursue," said Biskind, referring to the votes of members of the Academy. "He did screenings at retired actors' homes, mailed out cassettes and sent stars and directors on the road. Harvey knew that just as you could win by one vote, you could also lose by one vote."

Despite such successes, Miramax entered a phase in which the company floundered, while other distributors were successfully releasing indie films using their formula. By 2002, Miramax had laid off 15 per cent of its staff.

More serious trouble was brewing. When Disney chairman, Jeffrey Katzenberg, a Harvey ally, departed the company, the Weinsteins were forced to deal with his heir, the less pliable Michael Eisner. The deterioration of the Disney/Miramax relationship came as no surprise to many in the industry. Disney was a corporate monolith, which had built its success on children's animated features and theme parks. Miramax had built its success on risk-taking, both in deals and in content. Tarantino's 1994 iconoclastic *Pulp Fiction* included scenes that featured hypodermic needles and anal rape. In *Priest*, which also was released in 1994, priests were portrayed in both heterosexual and homosexual encounters. This led directly to a boycott by the Catholic League, a stockholders' revolt and the picketing of Walt Disney World. *Kids*, in 1995, was about a day in the life of sexually uninhibited, drug-taking New York teenagers with a suggestion of child pornography. These were not the kinds of films with which Disney was usually associated.

Gangs of New York, at $90 million, was Harvey's most expensive film. Directed by Martin Scorsese, it was supposed to reestablish his prestige and remake his fortune. Though it had a 2003 Best Picture nomination, it was only a modest box-office success.

I interviewed Martin Scorsese in England and asked him about his rumoured production battles with Harvey. It was clear to me that

Scorsese had a sort of chip implanted in his brain, which prevented him from going all out either to praise Harvey or condemn him. "Before *Cinema Paradiso*, audiences had an aversion to films with subtitles, but Harvey changed that," he said. "When you take chances on subject matter, sometimes it works, and sometimes it doesn't. Harvey has a touch of sensationalism, like a DeMille." In 2004, Harvey and Scorsese worked together again on *The Aviator*, which had a much better reception and also received a Best Picture nomination.

With *Chicago* in 2002, Harvey acquired the hit he needed. The modestly budgeted musical became Miramax's highest-grossing film and had a domestic box office of $171 million. It also won six Oscars, including one for Best Picture. With *Chicago*, it seemed that Harvey had dodged a bullet.

That same year, Harvey signed filmmaker Michael Moore, who had won an Oscar for his documentary, *Bowling for Columbine*, in which Moore blamed America's culture of guns and violence for the mass killing spree at a Colorado high school and similar atrocities. Moore's next film, *Fahrenheit 9/11*, shot under conditions of secrecy, was unsparing in its criticism of George W. Bush and the War on Terror. When CEO Michael Eisner refused to release it under the Disney label, Harvey bought it back. He released it in 2004 through Lionsgate Films, earning $100 million on a $6 million investment, and picking up a Palme d'Or in Cannes. The big question following this public fissure was this: would Disney renew the Weinstein brothers' employment contracts, which ran out in 2005? On March 30, 2005, the corporation announced that it would not.

The Weinstein brothers were out of a job. Harvey ranted, "We have shelves full of Oscars, two billion dollars in assets and hundreds of millions in profits, and still Michael Eisner won't renew?"

Five years later, Disney would close down Miramax, lay off eighty people and shelve many unreleased films. Despite a furious ten-month battle, Disney also refused to let the Weinsteins buy back the Miramax name and library. Disney had purchased it for $60 million; the Weinsteins offered $600 million; Disney accepted a rival bid for a reported $675 million. Like Lew Wasserman and Garth Drabinsky before him, Harvey learned the hard way: *Don't sell off your mother company and expect to remain in control.*

The Weinsteins' wings had been clipped, but they were far from being grounded. They partnered with Goldman Sachs and two other financiers to launch The Weinstein Company, with $500 million in equity and another $500 million in scrutinized debt. The company's first two years were unimpressive. Instead of focusing on film, Harvey tried to be the next Rupert Murdoch, making investments in Internet, cable and fashion. That last purchase was personal. He had divorced his wife of eighteen years and was now married to English fashion designer and actress, Georgina Chapman. He then made sure his Oscar nominees wore his new wife's creations.

By 2009, The Weinstein Company was in trouble. Of the seventy films the Weinsteins released in four years, 25 per cent failed to make $1 million at the box office, while thirteen took in less than $100,000. Kevin Smith, one of Harvey's protege directors, commented that Harvey had impeccable taste when he was hungry, but had lost it, now that he was starving and desperate. Although Tarantino's long-awaited *Inglourious Basterds* lost out to *The Hurt Locker* at the 2009 Academy Awards, it earned an outstanding worldwide gross of $313 million—a reprieve for the beleaguered Weinstein Company. In 2010, Harvey and Bob scored Best Picture for *The King's Speech*, and in 2011 they repeated with *The Artist*. Though perhaps not the dominant force they once had been, the Weinsteins were back in business.

When, despite Harvey's harassment, I finally had all the interviews I needed for the film, I brought in the same editor I had hired for *The*

Last Mogul. This turned out to be a mistake: as I watched him work, I felt that he wasn't unlocking the story properly. I was feeling frustrated when his young assistant confessed to me, "I've been secretly editing. Can I show you my cut?" Hers was terrific. I gave her the job.

Word began to circulate through the industry that I had a rough cut worth seeing. In September 2010, IFC Films, an influential NY-based distribution company, asked for a screening. They were enthusiastic. They offered me more money for a documentary than I had ever seen in a deal that included release through their own theatre and television network. *Wow*. Since they were in a hurry to get the deal done, I bought out my international contract with UK-based High Point Media so IFC could announce their acquisition. Neither I nor my lawyers stopped to ask, *Why the rush?* Hell, they even had me sign the contract on the hood of a stranger's Ferrari in front of Yorkville's Sassafraz restaurant.

With the deal in my pocket, I thought my only problem was to finish the film. Among other things, that meant hiring the right narrator. Like everything else involving Harvey, this proved to be more difficult than it should have been. My friend Peter Fonda was my first choice. "I'd love to do it," he told me. Then his agent got involved, warning him, "Look, Peter, you make the same kind of movies Harvey does. Take this job and you won't get hired."

Next, I asked Tony-winning Frank Langella. We worked out a deal, then he told me, "Harvey nixed it." Frank pulled out.

Christopher Plummer told me, "I live two houses away from Harvey in Connecticut. I'm not going to mess with him."

Alan Alda refused as well. Same reason.

Canadian uber agent Perry Zimel recommended William Shatner. Then IFC chimed in, "He's not the right voice for the film."

After I thought about that, I agreed.

Finally, I settled on Albert Shultz, who runs Toronto's Soulpepper Theatre Company. He had narrated for me before, and he was fantastic.

So, back to the editing room. When IFC saw my rough cut, I was told, "Harvey objects to that Hickenlooper humping scene and he wants it cut."

I was flabbergasted. "Why is Harvey calling the shots?"

"Well, Barry, IFC does business with Harvey. We buy his films."

"But he's not a partner in this film."

"No, but IFC now owns the movie, and these are the changes we want to make."

That was when I realized I had reached Act III in my negotiations with Harvey Weinstein, as my friend had predicted. True, Harvey hadn't killed me, as my mother feared, but he had sucker-punched me. IFC was owned by the Dolan family, who owned Madison Square Gardens and Radio City Music Hall. The Dolans and Harvey were reputed to be close friends. *Had Harvey instructed IFC to buy my film to control it?* In the case of the Hickenlooper *Factory Girl* humping scene, I managed to save the anecdote by cutting Harvey's instructions down from six humps to four.

I worried that my film was essentially dead. Those fears were briefly allayed in a heady IFC party following its premiere at the Toronto International Film Festival, when IFC's head of acquisitions told me *Unauthorized* would be entered into other key international festivals. This would be followed by a few high-end screenings in New York and Los Angeles before its mainstream launch. Great! Had my previous dealings with Harvey made me unnecessarily paranoid?

I flew to New York to speak to Jonathan Sehring, President of IFC Entertainment, about release dates. He said, "Barry, I have to tell you that Harvey sent a team to Toronto to see the film, and here's his list of changes they want." He took a sheaf of paper from his drawer. "If you aren't going to trim the film, we will."

So apparently I hadn't been paranoid enough. Harvey had final cut.

We fought over every snip. I won a few battles but lost most. *Unauthorized* was in danger of becoming *Authorized*. When I continued to press for a distribution plan, I received a passionately articulated promise from Sehring about the importance of the film to them, and how they planned to use it to launch their new Netflix-like service. I breathed a sigh of relief.

Too soon.

Follow-up conference calls and meetings appeared to be vintage theatre designed to keep me distracted. For the next year, IFC broke promises on screenings and marketing campaigns, probably hoping I would go away. Then, after months of avoiding my calls, Sehring and his acquisition flunky nearly dropped their champagne glasses when they found me seated at a table next to them at the May 2011 Cannes Film Festival. Later, I ran into Weinstein himself on the terrace of the Hôtel du Cap. Typically, he was surrounded by stars: Jane Fonda, Leonardo DiCaprio and Robert De Niro. When Peggy Siegal, the go-to person for getting celebrities to parties, recognized me, she called out, "Barry, do you know Harvey Weinstein?"

Harvey said, "I understand you made a good movie about me."

I responded, "My cut was way better."

By now I was pretty sure IFC had bought my film in order to bury it. I wanted to buy it back, but my lawyer said, "That's ludicrous. Walk away. Make another movie."

I was losing every round. I rallied when the *New York Times* ran an online article in October 2011 asking, *What happened to the Harvey Weinstein film?* When questioned, IFC went on the record by saying the film would be released. On October 7, 2011, they played *Unauthorized* on their obscure download service, sundancenow.com, with zero publicity and marketing. You had to be a tracker dog with a keen nose to find it.

Even after this knock-down, I was still in the ring. IFC had refused to run my film in their New York theatre. I called up the director of Film Studies at New York University and asked, "How would you like to screen the Harvey Weinstein film that everyone's talking about and that nobody has seen? I'll come with great stories about the making of this film and show an uncensored cut." He was enthusiastic. "I'd like to open the screening up to the public," I told him, "so I'm taking an ad in the *New York Times.*"

He liked that even more.

As it turned out, of course, the *Times* refused my ad because they were afraid of pissing off Harvey. Harvey placed a lot of ads for his films in the *Times.* As he once reportedly bragged to the media, "I'm the fucking Sheriff of New York!" I called the *Times* editorial division and told them that their ad department had turned me down. I essentially embarrassed the *Times* into taking my ad after all. IFC was furious.

Good.

I invited key players from New York and L.A., intent on becoming an irritant if that's what it took to get the film noticed. The NYU theatre was packed, and my panel did a great job for my moment of glory. Afterwards, I received a slew of emails and calls from insiders and luminaries, such as director Oliver Stone, who thought the film was amazing. Ron Meyer, chairman of Universal Studios, also called to say that it was a perfect follow-up to my earlier film on Wasserman.

The professional critics weren't as kind. I had tried to create a well-balanced documentary for the general public. As usual, however, I attracted the asshole factor: *Where's the sleaze? Where's the inside story that's never before been told? Where's the Michael Moore exposé?*

I'm proud of the film. It was finally released intact in Canada in February 2011. We subsequently created a Mogul Box Set of my films including *Unauthorized.* I sent one to Weinstein.

Harvey keeps in touch. He answers my emails almost immediately. When I asked him for a copy of *The Imitation Game* to show for the Floating Film Festival in January 2015, he said, "Yes, but I'm going to need a favour in return."

"Okay. What's the favour?"

"I don't know yet."

Typical Harvey.

Chapter Twenty-One

AMERIKA IDOL:
A TRUE STORY

Zitiste, a village in Serbia, having endured 1,200 years of bad luck, dreamed of a better future. Its three thousand residents had seen floods and famine. They'd been trampled on by armies and exploited by warlords. The tribulations visited upon the village over the centuries were of nearly Biblical proportions. Even people in the rest of Serbia thought Zitiste had been cursed. Beautiful Belgrade was just fifty-five kilometres away, but no tourists came to Zitiste. The village, with its wheat fields, its horse carts and a complete absence of shops, was of another time.

The villagers decided they needed an extraordinary tourist attraction to reverse their luck. Disneyland Serbia wasn't likely to happen and they had no money. What if they raised the statue of a public hero? Would tourists then flock to Zitiste?

Perhaps . . . but that would depend on the hero.

When the village elders examined their history and folklore, they found only warlords and politicians, such as the infamous former

Serbian president, Slobodan Milošević. They considered looking beyond their borders to figures such as the Dalai Lama, Mahatma Gandhi and Mother Teresa, but they decided those figures had been sufficiently celebrated elsewhere. What they needed was a larger-than-life hero who epitomized the spirit of their village.

Enthusiasm crystallized around one man—an underdog who picked himself up every time he was knocked down. A man who was ready to overcome every new obstacle placed in his path, just as Zitiste had always done. The mayor and the village council took a vote. Finally, Zitiste had its hero: Rocky Balboa.

Rocky, as surely everyone in the civilized world must know, was the boxing champion created by Sylvester Stallone for his *Rocky* film franchise. Surely Rocky, with all his courage and clout, would change Zitiste's fortune. Surely, his statue would draw global recognition to their *Field of Dreams*. Create him, and the tourists will come. Right?

When Zitiste's Friends of Rocky wrote to Sylvester Stallone asking for permission to raise a statue in his honour, they received no response. Undaunted, they wrote to A. Thomas Schomberg, designer of the famous bronze Rocky Balboa statue, with its upflung arms, that once stood at the top of the steps to the Philadelphia Museum of Art. As fans of the Rocky films know, when Balboa is training for his big fight in the first film, he does a victory run up those seventy-two steps to the triumphal strains of the big anthem, "Gonna Fly Now." And, yes, Rocky had flung up his arms. Though the run was referenced in all of the Rocky films, the statue was created for *Rocky III*.

So iconic was this scene in popular imagination that as long as the statue remained at the top of the museum's stairs, tourists ran up to have their pictures taken with it. The statue was featured in the torch relay preceding the Atlanta Olympic Games in 1996. It was parodied in *The Simpsons*, when Lisa, sweatsuited like Rocky, ran up the steps when training for a spelling bee.

This mixed attention had created controversy among Philadelphians: "Why do we have a Hollywood prop on the steps of an art museum?" they asked. "Is it really art?"

The Rocky statue was shunted to the South Philadelphia Sports Complex. That is, until—power to the people!—a petition bearing 100,000 signatures caused it to be hauled back. Not to the top of the museum steps, but to a pedestal near the foot.

Not only did Rocky, the Hollywood champ, reflect Zitiste's up-and-down history, the bronze statue did too. No wonder the Friends of Rocky Balboa in Zitiste were thrilled when the statue's designer, Thomas Schomberg, endorsed their plan. Unfortunately, his suggested commission—$1.5 million—was beyond their resources. When the sculptor understood the villagers' situation, he generously gave them the right to reproduce the statue themselves. Now—full steam ahead!—they hired a local Croatian artist, who planned to build it out of cement, coat it with shiny wax or varnish it to make it appear like bronze.

It was at this point that Melissa Coghlan, with whom I'd worked on dozens of films at Alliance, suggested that we make a film based on Zitiste's Rocky project. She had read about it in the *New York Times*. I knew Melissa was keen to work in film, so I agreed. Why not?

I decided to make a short, self-financed documentary, and since I was busy, I told Melissa, "I'll direct it, but you'll have to produce it." That meant she had to line up everything.

The enterprising Melissa found a guy in Toronto who spoke Serbian. He contacted Zitiste's Rocky Balboa Association. They gave us the go-ahead, and we flew to Belgrade aboard Air Serbia. On the flight, I noticed something peculiar. I asked Melissa, "Do you smell cigarette smoke?" She did. I called the steward to report what I thought to be an international infraction.

The steward replied, "Oh, it's the pilot."

Melissa Coghlan and Barry Avrich on
the set of *Amerika Idol* in Serbia, 2007
from the personal collection

The cockpit door was wide open, and, indeed, the pilot was having a cigarette.

Belgrade was beautiful, and so were some of its residents. It is noted as a site for scouting models. We spent the night at the fabulous Hyatt Regency, then the next day drove to Zitiste.

We were met by the mayor, the council and the head of the Rocky Balboa Association, whose membership included about seventy supporters. Everyone was excited. It was as if a big Hollywood film crew had flown in to take over their village.

That evening, the Zitiste Hunting Association hosted a feast for us at their forest lodge. Because almost nobody spoke English, I asked for an interpreter. Then, unable to resist, I began asking questions, such as, "How many Jews lived in this village?"

Though I later found the answer to be sixteen, my interpreter replied, "I'm not answering that." The topic was verboten because of the Nazi-inspired events of World War II.

Then I asked, "What are we eating?"

My interpreter replied, "Bambi."

I threw up in my mouth, then stuffed myself with cucumbers. After that, I was presented with the Rocky Balboa Award.

Melissa and I were to spend the night in Zitiste, and to begin filming the next day. We were taken to the village's only motel, which was actually an old military barracks. My room contained a row of six military cots, a shower and a toilet—which, by the way, was located *inside* the shower. Melissa's room had a TV but no signal. There was nothing to watch.

Suddenly, in the night, I heard a scream. Melissa! I rushed into her room to see what was wrong. On her bed was a cockroach the size of a Buick.

She was prepared to stay anyway. Not me. I said, "We're leaving." It was 3:30 a.m.

"Where are we going?"

"I don't know. Just get dressed."

We tiptoed down the stairs to the lobby. I don't know why we tiptoed. The stairs were made of concrete, but that's how they do it in the movies. We discovered the entire town was already up, waiting for us, their celebrities. It was like a crowd scene from *Young Frankenstein*. I found the interpreter. I told him we weren't comfortable—a gross understatement—and he drove us to someone's home an hour away. He was probably mumbling to himself something about pretentious Hollywood filmmakers for whom no cockroach is small enough.

On our first day of filming, members of the Rocky Balboa Association introduced us to the statue's artist, Boris Staparac. He had been installed behind police headquarters in a studio that had once been a stable. Boris had been given $12,000 in advance. We watched as he applied cement, working up from Rocky's bones to his muscles and skin, cutting and sanding. He was proud of his work and happily showed us his other creations—bizarre, erotic statues of women with big breasts and spread legs. Though he didn't speak English, he sounded gay. How can you sound gay in a foreign language surrounded by erotic female statues? I'm not sure, but he did.

Over the next few days, we talked to the village priest and then went on to an elementary school, where the kids had been taught a song about Rocky Balboa. We also questioned and filmed some townspeople, the mayor and members of the Rocky Balboa Association. Suddenly, key people stormed out of the room. I was mystified. I turned to the interpreter and he told me they thought I was making fun of them, the way Sacha Baron Cohen, as a fake journalist, had satirized Kazakhstan in *Borat*.

Production was halted. I had a problem. I begged my interpreter, "Bring them back. Let's talk."

Once they had reassembled, I tried to set their minds at ease. "I came here thinking I was going to make a comedy," I told them. "I mean, you live in this tiny town, and you're worshipping this idol, which is why the film is called *Amerika Idol*. I began by thinking this was comic, but then I came here and was charmed by the whole town."

I got quite emotional. I was on the verge of tears. "This experience has changed my life, as well as changing yours, and I came to understand that this was a story the world had to learn."

They wept along with me, and finally decided to let me go ahead with the film. Mostly, what I said was what I needed to say to finish the film. After all, the situation was ridiculous—how could I not laugh? But I also knew these were wonderful people. And they had welcomed us as friends. Later that night, Melissa and I ended up in Club Rocky. Rocky's friends had made a giant cake for us with a Canadian flag on it.

By now, I wanted to go home. I was beginning to feel claustrophobic, as if I had been imprisoned in a Communist detention camp, or Treblinka. The villagers had another idea. They wanted us to stay one more night so we could attend the international press conference they'd arranged for the next day. I agreed, but I spent the night in Belgrade. I'd had enough of Zitiste's guest accommodation.

Before the press conference, Melissa, our crew and I were invited to a high-level council meeting in the government building. In a room in which we were surrounded by flags of state and country, the city council formally passed a motion honouring us. They regarded us as Hollywood, the real deal, people who would put Zitiste on the cultural map. I was reminded of that wonderful David Mamet film, *State and Main*, in which a glitzy Hollywood crew seduces a small town.

The press conference took place in the lobby of the army barracks–like motel, and it was packed, mostly with media from Eastern Europe. The mayor and the head of tourism were present, but they sat me down at the table to field all the questions.

Will Sylvester Stallone show up for the unveiling?

Will this film open in Hollywood?

Will it bring tourists to Zitiste?

Afterwards, my gang was invited to another feast, during which Rocky Balboa statuettes were presented to Melissa and me, as if this were the Academy Awards and *Amerika Idol* had already won. Then, and only then, were we free to leave the country, which we did.

★

We filmed Stallone before we returned to Zitiste for the unveiling. Melissa had set up the encounter through some powerful Hollywood connections. Sly's people laid down one surprising and disappointing condition: no woman would be allowed in the interview room. Melissa was my producer but I had to tell her she could not come in.

I interviewed him at his editing facility where he was editing the fourth Rambo film. I told him, "Sly, a group of people in Zitiste, Serbia, want to raise a statue of you as their town hero."

This was news to Stallone. I showed him some of my footage, and he was overwhelmed. He kept saying, "Who knew? It's so great."

He played the interview absolutely straight, with the ego of a Hollywood star who understood that, of course, a Rocky statue would be exactly right to attract tourists to a village in Serbia. "To the people of Zitiste. You've taken concrete and you've made it into something great. When people find something worth living for, they start to live."

It was a tear-jerker of a speech, and, of course, it made the film.

In 2007, when our crew returned to Zitiste, we discovered the unveiling would take place during the village's annual Agroziv Chicken Fest. This, apparently, was a condition of the statue's existence, because the sculptor's work had been financed by Agroziv, the largest chicken-processing plant in Eastern Europe. All they did was kill chickens. Which is why we had filmed the head of the company.

Let me set the scene. The Agroziv's boardroom was like something out of the 1950s. The president and his executives—all men, of course—were sitting around the table, smoking. That part was expected. Everybody in Zitiste, in fact everybody in Belgrade, smoked (along with the pilots of Air Serbia). It was a national pastime. This next part, however, was new: Around the boardroom were posters of chickens, as if this were a chicken casting agency, showing off its roster of beautiful clients. Those hens eyed me. I eyed them right back. Were they looking at me in a suggestive way, or did they just want to kill me? Either answer seemed plausible.

On the boardroom table were about nine large platters of cold chicken, each processed in different ways, along with toothpicks so we could sample them. There were chicken cutlets, smoked chicken, chicken sausages, and so on, some rolled up, some in squares, some twisted like origami into swans. Now I knew the chickens in the posters would be putting out a contract on me, but I was hungry, so I ate some of their relatives, and I have to tell you, they were good.

Afterwards, we were taken into the plant, which made me regret that I had eaten. Even from the outside, we could hear those chickens screaming. They sprayed us with disinfectant before they let us inside. I urged the sprayers to disinfect the motel/barracks where Melissa and I had been booked on our first night when they were finished here. That building also belonged to Agroziv. They had plans to turn it into a fancy spa. The Rocky Balboa Spa?

For the sake of the film, I asked the Agroziv people some pertinent questions through my interpreter, such as, "Why did Agroziv want to finance the Rocky statue?" And I got the kind of answers you would expect. "From a sense of community," they said. "This is a great project for us to be involved in, it's what Zitiste needs," and so on. Blah blah.

Eventually, the perverse side of me took control.

"How many chickens do you kill in a day?" I asked.

"Okay," they told the interpreter. "This interview is over."

That answer, by the way, was 8,000—*an hour!*

About 100,000 people showed up for the giant Rockypalooza Chicken Festival. There were rock bands, and strong-men contests with guys pulling trucks. When, at last, it was time for the Rocky Balboa unveiling, people danced around it wearing giant chicken costumes. When the cover came off, fireworks shot into the sky, and the crowd went crazy. You'd have thought their new tourist attraction was more momentous than the Shroud of Turin. Zetiste's dream had been realized. Their moment had arrived.

We screened the film for them, and they mostly liked it, even though they must have known that I was sometimes poking fun at them. Basically, they saw it as a good experience, something to cheer about, which was what they had hoped for.

Amerika Idol got good reviews at Toronto's Hot Docs Festival. It also got great press in the United States. Somehow, the making and showing of this film had turned into a win-win situation: both its makers and subjects were happy. This still seems so bizarre to me, that it continues to play in my mind as if in real time.

Rocky Balboa, in cement, continues to loom over Zetiste. In fact, the artist did a fantastic job. I believe the village saw a spike in tourism, mostly from Eastern Europe. When we later filmed interviews in Belgrade, everyone had heard about it. Feelings were divided. Some thought it a good idea, while others asked, "Why are we worshipping an American hero when the U.S. bombed the shit out of Belgrade during the Kosovo War?"

To which I can only answer, I have no idea.

★ *Chapter Twenty-Two* ★

AN UNLIKELY OBSESSION: THE UNTOLD STORY OF CHURCHILL AND THE JEWS

The documentary about Winston Churchill's role in the founding of Israel was not on my lifetime to-do list. This period of history was mostly unknown to me and the challenge of addressing it reminded me of the day, almost two decades earlier, when I filmed the great economist John Kenneth Galbraith. Each interview brought on a wave of trepidation and a case of butterflies. I know my Hollywood but now I was dancing with the giants of the past.

My cast included members of the Churchill family, a Duke no less, a Lord (before his fall from grace), Winston Churchill's official biographer, one of the most respected historians in the world and a legendary criminologist. The setting was no less intimidating. It included the graceful halls of Oxford University; Blenheim Palace, which is the principal residence of the Dukes of Marlborough and birthplace of Winston Chrurchill; Churchill House in Westminster; the National Churchill Museum; and Stornoway House, which once was owned by Lord Beaverbrook, who was a great supporter and friend of the wartime prime minister. So our backdrop was truly *Game of Thrones*.

I shot a series of three interviews with Sir Martin Gilbert, who was easily the world's most renowned authority on Churchill. I was worried that he would be too stuffy and musty for my audience. He was the opposite—a great storyteller and wonderfully elegant, yet accessible. He ended up as the film's sensational thread and powerful voice. He was as nervous about making the film as I was, but for a different reason. He was concerned that the attempt to cram a story that spanned nearly eight decades into ninety minutes was too great a challenge. When I showed him the cut, he was beyond thrilled. I really enjoyed my adventure with this warm and scholarly man. Sadly, just a few years after we made a film, Gilbert suffered a stroke and died.

My interview with Celia Sandys, Churchill's granddaughter, was illuminating. She was candid about the unpopularity of supporting Jews and the notion of Israel in mid-twentieth century England. She also understood filmmaking and how to provide a memorable sound bite. She had ideas of her own too: for months after shooting the film, she pursued me to finance and direct a miniseries about famous women who flirted with power and scandal.

The randy Duke of Marlborough, John Spencer Churchill, was a less rewarding interview subject. While he provided us with the best setting ever, Blenheim Palace, and a few good sound bites, he refused to talk about Churchill's connection to Israel. He wouldn't even acknowledge it. Each time I brought it up, he would say, "My boy, did I tell you that Churchill was born in this very room? There is the baby carriage!" When the interview was over, the spirited eighty-five-year-old asked if my mother, who had accompanied me on this adventure, was single. My mother, eighty-three years old at the time, *was* single. The Duke was not.

Two of the most interesting interviews were with Conrad Black and Margaret MacMillan, filmed separately in Oxford, England, and

Palm Beach. Black, for all of his flaws, was a damn good historian and I wanted his perspective, especially with regard to Roosevelt's position on the Jews and the death camps. Equally thrilling to interview was Margaret MacMillan, a noted historian and professor at Oxford University. MacMillan's grandmother was the daughter of David Lloyd George, the prime minister of the UK from 1916 to 1922. Her recounting of history for my film was invaluable. However, it was fascinating to see Black who had a history of being extraordinarily critical of MacMillan's writing, differ on the account of FDR's role in supporting the Jews who were looking for a new home during the Holocaust and the UK's plans to bomb the rail lines into the death camps. Both historians were courteous and restrained in their comments, but you can sense the tension between them.

The making of this film was one of my proudest accomplishments. I didn't think I could pull it off and I did.

It was the agent, Michael Levine, who gave me a copy of Sir Martin Gilbert's book, *Churchill and the Jews*. In it, Gilbert described how Winston Churchill had used his political power, both as British prime minister and in lesser political posts, to counter anti-Semitism on the world stage and to help the Jews fulfill their historical destiny. It became Churchill's unlikely obsession.

Throughout his life, Churchill remained attuned to what he called "the hereditary antipathy to the Jewish race." To his critics, he was a man who was too fond of the Jews. I was fascinated by this largely unexplored side of England's great leader. Churchill, after all, was celebrated primarily for his role in the Second World War, not for this. But I was not fascinated enough to want to turn a book into a film. I told Michael, "I'm not Tsipi Reibenbach, who does all these Israeli documentaries. You've got the wrong guy."

Michael persisted, as Michael does. He said, "Come with me to London to meet the author. Then make up your mind."

We visited Sir Martin Gilbert in his home in Oxford. Among the more than eighty books he had written, about thirty were on Winston Churchill. We chatted over honeycake, and Gilbert and Michael persuaded me, one nibble at a time, that a film on Churchill and Israel, from a layman's perspective, would be better than a documentary made dreary with historical data.

That was the theory.

When I make a documentary with my producing partner Jonas Prince, I start by creating a "war wall" on which I post file cards that map out a timeline. I shoot a lot of footage, and then I do what I call a paper edit, in which I watch the footage and write down the best lines uttered by the people I interviewed. I post these comments on my wall, and then I break them down first into themes, and then into acts, moving them all around as I search for the most effective narrative arc. But I struggled to make the system work with the Churchill story. Every time I thought I had a handle on it, I found another tough-to-cover event that demanded to be included. British history was not exactly within my comfort zone, and no matter how well prepared I was, or thought I was, I increasingly felt out of my depth. What was I doing, questioning Sir Martin, or Churchill's heirs, in an attempt to follow the great man's path through the twentieth century?

I did, finally, finish the interviews. I also found the story arc I was looking for and wrote my narrator's script. I signed on Gordon Pinsent as my narrator, and then took pleasure in correcting him on his pronunciation of Jewish names. At least here was an area in which I had some expertise. During our recording sessions, Pinsent would do imitations of Churchill's impassioned rhetoric, so distinctive it had bred the adjective "Churchillian." That part was fun. The rest was a steep learning curve for this Jewish boy from Montreal. Churchill's obsession became mine too.

★

Winston Leonard Spencer-Churchill was born on November 30, 1874, into a life of aristocratic privilege at Blenheim Palace, the ancestral home of the Dukes of Marlborough since 1724. His Brooklyn-born mother, Jennie Jerome, was a free-spirited woman fiercely supportive of young Winston. His father, Randolph, whom Winston admired, exposed his impressionable son not only to powerful political players, but also to a select group of distinguished Jews. These included Nathan Rothschild, the first Jew to serve in the House of Lords, Baron de Hirsch and the banker Sir Ernest Cassel. They became almost like godfathers to young Winston.

"Churchill loved the Bible, and was intrigued by the Jewish ethic, not just the historical narrative," said Sir Martin. "He held in high regard how Moses had moulded a disputatious tribe into a body of high moral standards, which he considered to be the basis of modern ethics."

John Forster, the Blenheim Palace archivist, told me, "Young Winston could recite yards and yards of the Bible, which was the focus of his awareness of Jewish history."

While yearning for adventure, Churchill also read military history, and the history of his own family. "He felt placed on this earth to do something important," said Celia Sandys.

Churchill attended the Royal Military College, and then joined a cavalry regiment. In 1898, at the battle of Omdurman, he participated in a cavalry charge. Churchill next set his sights on a political career. After being elected as a Member of Parliament for Oldham as a Conservative, he crossed the floor to the Liberal side, and subsequently represented a constituency in North West Manchester. His part of the city had a significant Jewish population. Among them was an individual, Nathan Laski, who solicited Churchill's support in fighting the Aliens Bill of 1904 with its potential for severely restricting Jewish immigration. Churchill was amenable. He favoured controls over immigration but argued against any that smacked of anti-Semitism.

In 1905, Churchill was part of a new Liberal government as Undersecretary for Colonial Affairs. This was the first British government in which Jews—who often were regarded by the establishment as pushy, money-grubbing and too ambitious—played an integral role. Though Churchill was criticized for the company he kept, he liked to associate with clever people, and didn't care where they came from.

"Churchill admired the Jews and invited them home for dinner, which was not done," confirmed Sir Martin.

This was at a time when politicians such as Leo Amery found it prudent to hide their Jewish origins.

Canadian-born Oxford historian Margaret MacMillan said, "Churchill's Jewish associations were unusual for his class at a time when casual anti-Semitism was enormously pervasive."

The idea of Zionism was born out of the desperate search for a safe haven by Jews fleeing persecution in Eastern Europe. In 1896, an Austro-Hungarian journalist, Theodor Herzl, had published *The Jewish State*, which argued persuasively for a Jewish homeland in the ancestral land of Palestine.

The bullet that assassinated Archduke Franz Ferdinand of Austria on June 28, 1914, set off a chain of events that ultimately led to the start of the First World War. During that five-year conflict, Britain faced a dire shortage of explosives. As Minister of Munitions, Churchill appealed for assistance to Chaim Weizmann, a research chemist at the University of Manchester. Apart from his academic and war work, Weizmann had been inspired by Herzl's dream of creating a Jewish state. Thanks, in part, to Weizmann's synthetic explosives, Britain and her allies defeated their enemies. A grateful government was anxious to reward Dr. Weizmann who, as head of what was now a worldwide

Zionist movement, had a clear and persistent desire to establish a Jewish homeland in Palestine.

The Ottoman Empire now lay in ruins, and the Middle East, including Palestine, became the responsibility of the British Military Administration. This made Britain the largest ruler of Muslims on earth. Nevertheless, many in London saw the advantages in Weizmann's plan. Even before the war's end, British policy had gradually become committed to the Zionist cause. After discussions in the British cabinet, a letter was written by Arthur James Balfour to Lord Rothschild, recognizing Zionist aspirations. Though the Balfour letter became the founding document of a Jewish homeland, it was not at first seen that way.

Churchill noted that Jewish soldiers in the British army had won over 1,500 medals for bravery. "This record is a great one, and British Jews can look back with pride on the part they played in winning the Great War." Churchill also declared that a national homeland was not a gift to the Jewish people but an act of restitution, in that it gave back to the Jews something that had been stolen from them in the early days of the Christian era.

Weizmann's proposed Jewish state stretched almost to Damascus in the North, Amman to the East and south to the Gulf of Aqaba. Privately, Churchill had doubts about the division of the region, fearing a long and costly conflict. He wrote to Prime Minister David Lloyd George, saying, "The Jews, whom we are pledged to introduce into Palestine, take it for granted that the local population will be cleared out to suit their convenience."

Despite his concerns, Lloyd George remained committed to the Balfour Declaration, and the establishment of a Jewish homeland in Palestine.

"Churchill liked the idea, but thought it unwise to talk about a Jewish state at that time, preferring to call it a homeland," said Margaret MacMillan. "He worried that Germany, where the Jews were well integrated, might come up with an alternative plan that would cause them to be seen as the protector of the Jews. He was always looking out for Jewish interests, though he knew this could cause him trouble down the road. He also had obligations as a British statesman."

"The debates in the Commons over the Jewish state were difficult, and Churchill was warned not to ask for too much," said Sir Martin.

When the Bolsheviks, headed by Lenin and Trotsky, marched into St. Petersburg and took over the Russian empire, Churchill published an article in the *Sunday Herald*. "There should be created in our own lifetime by the banks of the Jordan," he wrote, "a Jewish state under the protection of the British Crown, which might be comprised of 3 or 4 million Jews, which would, from every point-of-view, be beneficial and in harmony with the truest interest of the British Empire."

"People protested that the Russian pogroms were a long way away," said Sir Martin. "Churchill spoke powerfully, stating it was a moral issue."

Britain's interests in the Middle East went far beyond an obligation to the Palestinian Mandate. The Suez Canal was a crucial lifeline to the far eastern colonies and to India, often referred to as the jewel in the British Crown. Churchill convened a conference in Cairo with Arab and Jewish leaders, and his own advisors, Herbert Samuel and T.E. Lawrence.

"When Churchill travelled through the streets of Gaza, an Arab city, he was met with cheering crowds of a kind he'd never heard before," said Sir Martin. "When he asked the translator what the Arabs were crying out, he was told, 'Long live the British minister and death to the Jews!' Then, at the conference, instead of the Arab leaders saying, 'This our our vision,' they said, 'We want the Jews out.' The Jews, by contrast, presented their vision of what the area could become with irrigation."

Churchill told them, "The Zionist ideal is a very great ideal, and I confess for myself it is one that claims my keen personal sympathy."

Before leaving Jerusalem, Churchill visited the site of the future Hebrew University on Mount Scopus, where he reminded the Jews of their responsibility to all Palestinians. When the Arabs pressed for representational government, Churchill resisted. He understood that their intent was to restrict Jewish immigration.

"The Arabs were farming the land in all the old ways, whereas the Jews were bringing in all these technologies for irrigation and electrification," said Margaret MacMillan. "With any concession to the Arabs, the Jews objected, and with everything that seemed to favour the Jews, the Arabs objected."

"The Jews brought access to Western technology," agreed Harvard law professor Alan M. Dershowitz. "If only the Arabs had used that to transform their land, they would have benefitted by allowing the Jews to return."

While Churchill argued for an understanding of Zionism based on idealism, as the fulfillment of the Jews' historic destiny, Lord Curzon, the Foreign Secretary, argued that whatever might be done for the Jewish people was without legal foundation and based entirely on sentimental grounds. This encouraged Churchill's enemies to renew their attacks.

Churchill's White Paper was approved by the League of Nations in July 1922. It stated that Jews were in Palestine by right and not on sufferance. However, four months later, his government was defeated, and Churchill lost his seat in Parliament. Ramsay MacDonald's Labour government immediately moved to water down the policy outlined in the White Paper.

Fuelled by the rising pressure of Nazism, Jewish immigration to Palestine soared, so that by 1939, Jews made up one-third of the population. The British Colonial Secretary, Malcolm MacDonald, authored another white paper, which later became known as the

Black Paper, because it placed further restrictions on Jewish immigration. Prime Minister Neville Chamberlain added his voice: "If we must offend one side, let us offend the Jews rather than the Arabs."

The MacDonald bill was passed in Parliament by a strong majority, temporarily ending the dream of a Jewish state in Palestine.

Churchill had visited Munich in 1932 and witnessed first-hand Hitler's Brownshirt parades. Yet, the Chamberlain government remained reluctant to confront Hitler. For two nights in November 1938, Nazi storm troopers attacked Jewish homes and businesses, also setting fire to thousands of synagogues. Over 30,000 Jews were subsequently deported to concentration camps. Thousands of German Jews were desperately looking for refuge, but even Churchill's close friend, Lord Beaverbrook, was strongly opposed to accepting them into the United Kingdom.

"One of the things often held against Churchill was that he would not leave anything alone," said Margaret MacMillan. "He was often cast down by lack of support, but he always rallied. Kristallnacht was a watershed in public opinion, especially the cynicism of the Nazis in making the Jews pay for the damage inflicted upon them."

By May 1940, Hitler had overrun Europe and was poised to invade Britain. Neville Chamberlain was forced to resign and Winston Churchill became prime minister. In regard to Zionism, he was told he had no right to change legislation already passed by Parliament. As Nazi persecution increased, however, the British people came to understand that it wasn't just the Jews, but also the Poles and the French who were being killed. "Whole areas of Europe had become a prison camp," said Sir Martin. "Churchill allowed a single British passport to be sufficient for perhaps three hundred people who had arrived on a boat, or all those that arrived on a train. As the war came to an end, Churchill spelled out in stark terms that the Nazi leaders must be tried as war criminals."

With Germany's surrender in 1945, Britain's wartime government

coalition was dissolved. Although Churchill remained personally popular, Clement Attlee's Labour party was elected, putting
Churchill out of office. Meanwhile, violence in Palestine continued
to escalate. On May 14, 1948, the day before the expiration of the
British Mandate, Israel proclaimed its independence, with David
Ben-Gurion as its first prime minister. The following day, the armies
of four Arab countries—Egypt, Syria, Lebanon and Iraq—attacked
the Jewish state, launching the 1948 Arab-Israeli War. After a year
of fighting, a ceasefire was declared, and temporary borders, known
as the Green Line, were established. Jordan annexed what became
known as the West Bank and East Jerusalem, while Egypt took control of the Gaza Strip.

Two years passed before the British government recognized the
state of Israel. "Churchill had become ambivalent about Zionism
toward the end of the war," said Margaret MacMillan. "His legacy to
the Jews was to keep their hopes alive."

Sir Winston Churchill died, age ninety, on January 24, 1965.

In his eulogy, Israeli Prime Minister David Ben-Gurion did not
hold back his praise. "Churchill was the perfect combination of a
great man at a great hour," he said. "He joined battle and he prevailed. Churchill belonged to the entire world. His memory will light
the way for generations to come in every corner of the globe."

"Many Jews themselves were anti-Zionist," said Alan Dershowitz.
"American Jews wanted to be recognized as a well-integrated part
of America, not as people with loyalty to a different state. Jews are
always proud of their accomplishments. If you asked most of them
who was responsible for the state of Israel, they'd give you all sorts
of Jewish names, but without Churchill, there wouldn't be an Israel
today. There should be a gigantic statue to Churchill in Jerusalem."

Chapter Twenty-Three

SHOW STOPPER: THE THEATRICAL LIFE OF GARTH DRABINSKY

Garth, like the other moguls whose careers I documented, did his best to keep me from making a film about him. He was handicapped in his attempts to interfere by his enforced residence in a prison cell, but even that didn't make him helpless. *Show Stopper: The Theatrical Life of Garth Drabinsky* was scheduled to premiere in the fall of 2012 at the Toronto International Film Festival. In TIFF's bible, a thick book of listings, Garth was described as a thief. This inspired him to make one last attempt to prove he still had power, and to squeeze out one last drop of drama. Legal letters were sent to TIFF, claiming the description of Garth was damaging and libellous. He threatened to sue unless the wording was changed and the program reprinted. He also insisted that TIFF's director and CEO, Piers Handling, send letters to all TIFF buyers, correcting the offence and apologizing.

Piers and his COO Michele Maheux consulted me. "Okay," he said, "how shall we handle this?"

"Number one," I said, "I will write a letter, through my lawyer indemnifying TIFF from all potential legal action. Number two, I suggest you also get your own legal opinion."

Legal letters were sent from TIFF and from me to Garth, essentially saying that he was in prison, convicted of a crime, without much moral clout, and the TIFF program, which had cost a fortune to produce, could not be reprinted. It was then mutually agreed that the word "thief" in the description of the film would be changed to "loathsome character," a change we hoped would give Garth some comfort. Even that amendment would appear only online. He oddly accepted "loathsome character" over "thief."

The TIFF premiere of *Show Stopper* was a red-carpet affair held at the Bell Lightbox theatre. There was a lot of press interest, both because of Garth's stature in Toronto's entertainment business and because of his imprisonment. I had interviewed many Torontonians, including critics Richard Ouzounian and Brian D. Johnson. I had spoken to former *Maclean's* editor Peter Newman, whom Garth had once attempted to sue over an article, a revelation that naturally created some high-energy foyer chatter. People were calling it a Livent reunion. James Earl Jones, the voice of *Show Boat*, was there, as was Broadway octogenarian, Elaine Stritch, also from *Show Boat*. She refused to fly, so I hired my long-time New York driver, a Russian named Gregori, to bring her to Toronto. Midway through the journey, he phoned me: "I don't know who this woman is," he said, "but she's driving me crazy. She insisted that all the headrests be removed so she could see out, then I'm driving too fast, then it's too slow. I'd rather be back in Siberia in a death camp than in a car with this woman."

Driving Miss Daisy: The Sequel? I think not.

Elaine joined me on stage. She described *Show Stopper* as a great story about a great character "who's in the clink," which received a big laugh, releasing the tension in the room.

I watched the audience as the film was screened, as my dad had taught me. No one was yawning, no one was coughing or sneaking a peek at their watch.

The film began, fittingly and ironically, with Garth at TIFF, only a year before, walking the red carpet at the premiere of his film, *Barrymore*, with Christopher Plummer. That was on a Saturday night. By Monday, Garth was in Toronto's Don Jail.

I had footage of Garth as a child born into a modest North York family, then of him stricken with polio in 1953. "I was running through the garden, and it was a hot summer day, and in my next recollection, I'm in a taxicab with my father on the way to Sick Kids Hospital. Hours later, they said I had polio."

Garth's next seven summers were spent in hospitals, where he underwent six gruelling operations on his leg. "Was I angry? Sure. Frustrated? Sure. Did I ask why? Many times. Everyone has the ability to rationalize."

Garth's entrepreneurial debut was with movie magazines, and then with moviemaking: *The Silent Partner* in 1978 with Christopher Plummer, then *Tribute*, which earned Jack Lemmon a 1980 Oscar nomination. *The Changeling*—his attempt to make a Hitchcockian thriller—was one of the most expensive movies ever made in Canada, with lead actor, George C. Scott receiving an astonishing US$1 million, at that time the highest salary in Canadian film history.

Garth made a noisy Broadway debut in 1978 with the redundantly named *A Broadway Musical*, backed by a group of high-profile Toronto investors to whom he had guaranteed profits. Bad reviews shut down the show after its opening night performance.

Garth secured investment in multiscreen theatres he branded as Cineplexes. Recession, plus his inability to book blockbusters like *Jaws* and *Star Wars* on their small screens, led to a loss of $15 million. It was then that Garth persuaded Toronto broker Myron Gottlieb to join him in buying back a million dollars' worth of stock to save the company. The Bronfman family later bought 23 per cent of Cineplex. Garth purchased the Odeon theatre chain's 297 screens for a bargain basement price of $22 million. The newly branded Cineplex Odeon soon hit box-office gold with *Ghostbusters*, reporting a record profit of $12 million. Drabinsky quickly gobbled up as many Canadian independent movie theatre chains as he could. Eventually, he had 1,800 screens in 500 locations in North America and the UK. He spared no expense in buying buildings and renovating them with fancy Italian-marble floors and bold art. Every theatre had to be bigger than the last one.

By the time he was thirty-six, Garth had built one of the largest cinema circuits in North America, acquiring in the process a stunning debt of over $300 million. The need for new partners took him to Hollywood, to MCA chairman Lew Wasserman and President Sid Sheinberg, whom he persuaded to invest $150 million for 50 per cent of the company. Eventually, Garth chipped away at the rest of his company until he owned only 7 per cent—a long way down from control.

With thousands of screens at his disposal, and against the explicit orders of MCA, Garth returned to film production, making critically acclaimed, box-office disappointments such as *Madame Sousatzka* with Shirley MacLaine, *Talk Radio* directed by Oliver Stone and *The Glass Menagerie*, directed by Paul Newman and starring Joanne Woodward. When he pumped $8 million into Martin Scorsese's controversial film *The Last Temptation of Christ*, angry religious mobs picketed MCA offices. Lew Wasserman wanted—and got—Garth's head. But not without a struggle. Garth raised $127 million to buy out the Bronfmans. Wasserman countered with a legal manoeuvre that forced Garth into either buying him out as well, or being forced out. That meant Drabinsky needed to raise a monumental $1.3 billion. He came close, but failed.

Garth walked out of Cineplex's offices with a golden handshake of $4.5 million, but also with the right to buy the Pantages Theatre, along with *Phantom of the Opera*, for $88 million, a bargain price for a show that would gross Garth $600 million in Canada alone.

Sid Sheinberg called Garth a "madman," but some of his other comments were quite forgiving: "I knew as soon as I met Garth that his ambition was to have my job. He wanted to be the major player in Canada, on his way to becoming the major player in North America. This was not Rabbi Drabinksy, but a very entrepreneurial person who, once he set out to do something, would get it done, but not necessarily in the best way. I felt sorry for him. Maybe I was too forgiving."

As for the talent Garth had overpaid to star in his productions, they all had a warm feeling for him. I get that.

Diahann Carroll: "One moment he was a child, and the next he was the most exquisite and profound producer."

Chita Rivera: "I thought others were jealous of him, this young, big hotshot producer."

Elaine Stritch: "We're talking about a powerhouse. It breaks my heart. He walked the way Bette Davis walked, 'Step aside, and don't think I'm just being bossy. I'm bringing something, and I need room and I want it, and this musical deserves it.'"

Garth's toughest critic was theatre columnist Michael Riedel of the *New York Post*, who said of Garth, "He was a tyrant, cruel and unpleasant and nasty and brutal—the kind of obnoxious boor who went into a restaurant and, if his table wasn't ready, would demand, 'Do you know who I am?' He didn't raise money on each show, but in selling stock. I remember going to the opening of *Show Boat*. At the end of the production, Garth brought everybody who'd participated onto the stage—every usher, every stagehand. I was sitting beside this very experienced old producer, and he was looking at everyone, and costing out what each was being paid. In my interview, I told Garth, 'I don't see how you could be making money on *Show Boat* and *Ragtime*.' Garth banged his fist on the desk, 'I am the most investigated man on Broadway. Everything I do is monitored,' and he's pounding his desk and my table recorder is jiggling, then after this explosion he collapses, 'You know, Michael, all I want to do is create great shows.' He ran these shows all over the world because it was only when they closed that he had to declare a loss. He deserved to go to jail."

I held a private dinner in the Shangri-La Hotel after the premiere of *Show Stopper*, where Elaine Stritch praised the film as a "smartass doc," then claimed she couldn't wait until Garth got out of the clink to do another show with him. The prevailing view of those at my party seemed to echo Garth's own: that he might yet have a third act. I never for a minute believed that Garth started Cineplex or Livent to defraud people. These were significant businesses. For him, the cooked books served a greater ideal: to keep Livent going so he could mount the perfect musical. Even when he was sitting in jail, Garth was a man full of dreams.

Garth was released on day parole in February 2013, having served about 30 per cent of his sentence. He then announced to all who would listen that Barry Avrich was Public Enemy #1. He claimed that his parole had been substantially delayed because of the attention that was given to the film, which he insisted he hadn't seen. He also claimed that his fellow inmates gave him a rough time over it.

Friends who visited Garth in prison told me a different story. They said that, according to Garth, his fellow inmates had seen the documentary on HBO and given him a standing ovation when he walked into the dining hall the next morning. He was their hero.

I was thrilled to learn that HBO was available in prison. I also found it hard to believe that Garth hadn't seen *Show Stopper*. I could more easily imagine him rifling through local papers and *Variety* looking for reviews.

In January 2014, Garth was granted full parole until the fall of

Elaine Stritch, Barry Avrich and James Earl Jones,
at the *Show Stopper* TIFF premiere, 2012
from the personal collection

2016. Once he was released from prison, I felt he lost his opportunity to rebuild his reputation through teaching or establishing any kind of give-back to the theatre community. I understood that we would likely never speak again, but as his biographer, I didn't expect to be eating cake at the same table. Others have suffered a similar fate. Political journalist Peter Newman told me how his 2005 book, *The Secret Mulroney Tapes*, ended his relationship with the former prime minister. After helping to convict Michael Skakel, the nephew of Ethel Skakel Kennedy, Dominick Dunne did not expect to be invited to the Kennedy Compound at Hyannis Port. And Truman Capote found all of New York's golden doors forever closed to him after he wrote *Answered Prayers*.

Conclusion: I'll never speak with Garth again, unless he needs something from me. Then, I'll be back on The List.

Chapter Twenty-Four

FILTHY GORGEOUS: THE BOB GUCCIONE STORY

Why make a documentary about Bob Guccione, a pornographer who made a fortune but died penniless in a hospital in Plano, Texas? The inspiration came from *Playboy* publisher Hugh Hefner, archrival of Guccione and Guccione's raunchier magazine, *Penthouse*.

I was at the Palm Springs Festival in 2005 for the premiere of *The Last Mogul* when my assistant told me, "Hugh Hefner is on the line."

I thought it must be a joke, so I greeted my caller in an overly ballsy manner, "Hi, Hef, how ya doing?"

He replied, "I've just read a terrific review of *The Last Mogul* in the *New York Times*. I'd like to show it at the Playboy Mansion. Would you come and present it?"

"Yeah, yeah, sure."

"Barry. It *is* Hugh Hefner."

Whoa! "I'm sorry, Mr. Hefner."

"No, it's Hef—you were right about that."

When word circulated among my friends about my impending

trip to Bunnyland, they teased my wife Melissa. "I can't believe you're going to let him go."

"If he wants to hang out with the bunnies, then he'd better get it out of his system," replied Melissa. Except she expressed her thoughts more crudely and decisively.

When you arrive at the gates of the Playboy Mansion in Holmby Hills between Beverly Hills and Bel Air, a rock with a built-in speaker and microphone says, "Yes?" You say your name, identify your car and the gates fly apart as if by magic.

You drive up a very steep hill, where you come to a yield sign: "Caution, Bunnies at Play." Eventually, you find yourself at a Tudor-Gothic mansion which, for a guy like me who grew up with *Playboy*, appears mysterious and mystical. A valet takes your car. You enter Hef's domain, and automatically you're a VIP.

During repeat visits to the Playboy Mansion, I now know the movie-night ritual: Fridays are for previously released popular films, Saturdays are for Hef's curated films and Sundays are for newly released films.

With *The Last Mogul*, I was Saturday night . . . Hef's choice.

He hadn't come downstairs yet from his private suite, but his three favourite bunnies—Kendra, Holly and Bridget, all bodacious, stunning, long-haired blondes—greeted me. Since this was California, they were casually dressed in UGGS and sweatpants instead of their bunny armour. All three fawned over me, and it was pretty exciting.

KH&B took me on a tour. Hef's place is valued at more than $55 million. It has a wine cellar with a Prohibition-era secret door, a basement gym and a sauna. The games room was actually a separate building with a pool table, a jukebox, pinball machines and other '70s-style arcade favourites. Outside was a fountain, a walkway inset with a duplicate of Hef's Hollywood Star, a pool, and a waterfall and Grotto, where a long list of celebrities have romped. Because Hef was nuts about animals, he had a huge zoo, with peacocks and flamingos that wandered among the tree ferns and redwoods. The original servants' wing had been converted into *Playboy*'s editorial offices.

Meanwhile, other guests were arriving at the mansion: '70s TV star Robert Culp, '50s singing sensation Vic Damone, '70s actor James Caan, '60s *Get Smart* star Don Adams and the late Benny Goodman's lead trumpet player, Ray Anthony, who, at ninety-two years old, has been a fixture at the mansion for half a century. Despite the many young, beautiful women floating around, Hef's drawing room looked more like a scene from *Cocoon* than the setting for an orgy. Years later, a friend, whom I brought to one of Playboy Mansion's movie nights, dubbed it "Bunnies at Baycrest"—a reference to the Toronto Jewish old-age home. Even my presence probably lowered the average age of the attending males by a few years.

An odd buffet was served: fried chicken and broccoli. Whatever. Then, at 6:15, Hef descended in his silk pyjamas and silk robe. He greeted everyone and sat down at the dining table, where people lined up to give him little gifts. Next, he introduced me and I took photos of Hef wearing a *Mogul* hat. We filed into the screening room with its pipe organ, and I introduced my film. Servants brought Hef some cake and a glass of milk. Afterwards, I did a Q & A.

When I left the mansion, Hef told me he loved my movie. He added, "I want you to know that my house is your house. Visit me any time you want, but since I'm not young anymore, you better come soon and come often."

Over the next decade, I visited Hef and the mansion dozens of times and received a Ph.D. in movie classics with a minor in hedonism. In 2015, I was saddened to read former Playmate and Hefner girlfriend Holly Madison's memoir *Down the Rabbit Hole*. It was a mean and desperate account of her life with Hef that was an exercise

in humiliation and revisionism. I had met Holly many times over the years I visited, and I found her vapid and self-absorbed. In the book, she exposes her sex life with Hef, his other eccentricities and how awful her life was in the Mansion. It was so awful that she lived there for over seven years and begged to be Playmate in the magazine but never won the ultimate prize of being Mrs. Hefner. She used the book to paint Hefner in such unflattering light, that I felt a profound sadness for a legendary character that was now over ninety years old. Why do this now? I saw it as a last gasp of glory as Holly's fifteen minutes were just about up. Why else revisit such an allegedly horrible part of your life, unless you had not achieved success beyond the Playboy years? Fade to pink quickly, please.

★

But now, Guccione . . .

The visit to Playboy Mansion reminded me of one of my favourite movies, Bob Fosse's *Star 80*, which was about Playboy Playmate of the Year, Dorothy Stratten, who was murdered by her estranged husband. I also became super-aware of how masterfully Hugh Hefner had been marketed as a brand. When I left the mansion that first time, I was presented with Playboy pads and pens and Playboy water. Any time after that, whenever I walked into Hef's fiefdom, a staff photographer took my picture; on my next visit I would be handed a print—like I needed a dozen pictures of myself with Hef? Similarly, everywhere Hef went, he was photographed with celebrities and with his current version of KH&B. As an ad man, I was fascinated by how carefully constructed the Hugh Hefner persona was, all of which had me thinking about Bob Guccione.

Unlike Hefner, Guccione had fallen completely off the radar. This had happened well before his death in 2010, when he was seventy-nine. No book had been written about him, no movie had been made. Despite the fact that *Penthouse* had outsold *Playboy*, nothing remained of that empire. He had been a billionaire, with one of the world's best art collections. He had presided over a massive publishing empire in which *Penthouse* was just one of the properties. He had all this, and then Guccione had experienced one of the classic mogul falls.

One day, when I was brooding about my next documentary, I googled Guccione. I learned he had a son, Bob Jr. I emailed him, identified myself, and said, "I'd like to make a film about your father. Is there anything already in the works that I should know about?" Bob Jr. emailed me right back. "We haven't had meetings with anybody that we've liked. I'm teaching this year at University of Mississippi's journalism and media school. Why don't you come here so we can talk?"

I didn't necessarily believe that there had been other meetings about a Guccione project: sometimes people say these things as a negotiating ploy. But I flew to Oxford, Mississippi, which, I discovered, was not an easy destination to get to. Over fried pigs' ears—a Mississippi delicacy that would frighten my mother—I told Bob Jr., "I can't promise you this film will be a love letter to your father, but I'll provide balance."

He replied, "I'm happy to tell my father's story, warts and all."

We cut a deal, for which I hired Bob Jr. and his younger brother, Nick, as consultants. That's the way business is done, and the sons also brought great insight into their father's life. Our working relationship developed an interesting dynamic, as the two of them played off against their sister, who refused to be in the film, and Guccione's widow—his fourth wife, April—who sent me vicious Facebook messages saying she knew I would completely distort Bob's life. All of them wanted to know how much money they'd make from the film, and I had to say, "Guys, it's a documentary. There won't be a big payday. This is about your father's legacy."

Filthy Gorgeous turned out to be the easiest of all my documentaries to sell: the rights were picked up by EPIX and HBO Canada while retired hedge-fund manager and now entrepreneur, Jeremy Frommer, bought for the international market. It was *Penthouse*, and it was Bob Guccione, who was unmined territory, so everyone nodded, *Of course*. After I began my research, my good luck turned phenomenal. Frommer reached out and told me he had purchased a distressed locker, the size of an airplane hanger, contents unknown, which turned out to contain the remains of Bob Guccione's estate. Apparently, when Guccione was forced out of his magnificent NY townhouse, he threw all his personal stuff into this locker, then lost control of it.

Frommer said, "I think you'll want to come and see the contents."

I told him, "I'm on my way."

Once the locker was opened, I found myself staring at the motherlode. Guccione had kept everything: the guestbook for his Madison Avenue mansion with signatures of everyone from astronaut John Glenn to Henry Kissinger to Harvard civil-rights professor Alan M. Dershowitz; dry-cleaning receipts; all his old cameras; all his own paintings; nude photos of Madonna and model Lauren Hutton, and anyone else he'd photographed. There also was footage of his infamous 1979 movie, *Caligula*, which I fondly remembered as the first porn film I'd ever seen. I had snuck into a Montreal theatre, age thirteen, walking in backwards to avoid being caught.

As rights payment for turning over the locker's contents, Frommer wanted to be my executive producer and to attend the film's premiere at the Toronto International Film Festival. I quickly agreed.

I spent hours sorting through Guccione's remarkable archive. I think Frommer hoped the documentary would relaunch Guccione as an artist, because he had so many of his original paintings, but that didn't happen. While having eye-appeal, Guccione's art seemed only brilliantly derivative of the French masters he idolized. Sadly, it was not as a pornographer, nor even as a publisher that Guccione had hoped to become famous. He wanted to be known for his art.

Robert Charles Joseph Edward Sabatini Guccione was born on December 17, 1930, the son of a Sicilian accountant. He grew up in New Jersey, surrounded by a big, devoted family, and was especially close to his mother, Nina. He would later say that she shaped his attitude toward women: "She taught me that everyone you meet is someone's daughter or mother or sister."

Guccione spent a year in a seminary studying to be a priest. "After I got over that, I decided to follow my passion to be a painter."

While still a teenager, he married his girlfriend, Lilyan, who was already pregnant with his first child, Tonina. He then moved his family to Rome where he tried, without success, to sell his paintings. He took small parts in Italian movies and read palms for gullible tourists near the Spanish Steps. His priorities were clear: "If I had only enough money to buy dinner for the family or paintbrushes and canvas, the paintbrushes and canvas would win." Lilyan, however, got tired of being an obstacle to Guccione's dreams, and took Tonina back to America.

He was on his own now and hungry for adventure. He travelled around Europe and North Africa, sketching tourists in cafés. In Morocco, he met Muriel Hudson, an English singer. They were married in 1955, and subsequently had four children: Bob Jr., Nina, Anthony and Nick.

In 1957, Guccione moved his family to London, where he tried to relaunch his career as a painter and to sell cartoons. Inspired by the popularity of *Playboy*, he conceived of *Penthouse*, which was initially designed for a British audience, but failed to sell his idea to potential backers. As a teaser for potential subscribers, Bob and Muriel massmailed pin-up photos, each accompanied by a personal letter signed "Robert Gucci," in which he offered ten more pictures for $2. As a further inducement, "Gucci" wrote, "I have dozens of other young Italian girls, but I chose a girl whose voluptuous and perfect beauty made me turn to photography. I hope you will buy my new magazine."

Their mailing list was exceptionally broad-based. It ranged from shop workers and bartenders to doctors and nurses, nuns and priests, MPs and maybe even the Queen. Every day in the House of Commons one or another politician would rise to complain about the avalanche of pornography sweeping the nation. Bob Jr. remembered seeing a billboard in front of a news kiosk with the headline, "Sex Maniac To Be Deported." Curious, he moved closer to identify this pervert: *Dad?*

Guccione blamed the backlash on the fact that he was not only an American, but an *Italian*-American. He was charged for obscenity and paid his £100 fine, then used his pin-up profits to launch the magazine for which he had already pre-sold thousands of subscriptions. First, he needed someone to teach him how to use a camera properly—to improve on his previous amateur attempts. Then, he had to teach himself how to photograph with artistry. He developed a soft-focus style, skillfully utilizing light and shadow, a look that became a *Penthouse* signature.

Sometimes he took several days for a single shoot, always striving for more natural, more realistic photos than those in *Playboy*. Since "more realistic" meant no airbrushing, that also meant more risqué.

Guccione's models often reported that they enjoyed being photographed. As Divina Celeste, the February 1982 Penthouse Pet, enthused, "He created this beautiful person I wasn't expecting to see. It was so inspiring. I wish I could give one *Penthouse* day to every woman."

Guccione described a typical shoot this way: "The first day, my models would think, 'What a marvellous guy. He didn't take one step toward me.' The second day, they would think, 'He's a funny guy. He didn't lay a hand on me.' The third day, they would make a move to prove themselves, and I would have to leave till they cooled down."

Jane Homlish, Guccione's personal assistant, verified his version. "All the girls were crazy about Bob, and he'd have to come in and get me."

As well as pin-ups, *Penthouse*—like *Playboy*—attempted to provide sophisticated, well-written editorial content by the smartest authors of the day. As Lynn Barber, a *Penthouse* editor, irreverently explained, "It was for connoisseurs of fine wine, connoisseurs of fine cars, connoisseurs of beautiful women with big tits."

Penthouse was launched in Britain in 1965, outsold *Playboy* in its first week, then kept right on going. Guccione's pride was palpable. "When I held the first copy in my hand, I said, 'This is like a father holding a child for the first time,' and I knew I would take this magazine out of England to the U.S. and do battle with *Playboy*."

Guccione attributed the magazine's success to its crystallization of changing attitudes. Bob Jr. agreed. "At that time in society, most men's first experience with sex was in marriage. My dad understood that men wanted their guilty feelings lifted."

Shortly after the launch, Guccione met the woman who would shape his personal and professional life for the next several decades. Kathy Keeton was nine years his junior. She had moved from South

Africa to London at the age of thirteen to study ballet. Fifteen years later, she met Guccione while working as a burlesque dancer in London's West End. He was impressed by the fact that her dressing room contained books on science and the *Financial Times*. She was impressed by Guccione's entrepreneurial skills and by his dreams. "I was bored to tears with dancing, and I didn't see any future in it," said Keeton. "If I'd had a chance, I would have been a biologist, but girls didn't do that in those days."

Keeton told Guccione that she wanted to give up the stage to sell ads for *Penthouse*. When she brought in high-end clients such as Pernod, Barclay's Bank and Riviera cigarettes, he made her his president and COO. They were well matched: Keeton was tough and cool while Guccione was warm and creative.

"My imagination has a career," said Guccione. "I'm just tagging along."

Keeton became the architect of Guccione's business success, and ultimately his third wife. Under her leadership, *Penthouse* became one of the few magazines in the world almost exclusively run by women. Keeton called them "an unexploited resource." She wasn't bothered by his frequent affairs. "She knew Bob would come home to her and their relationship was more than just physical," said Jane Homlish.

One of Guccione's long-term affairs was with Penthouse Pet Victoria Lynn Johnson. "I was in love with him. So was everyone— his staff, his secretary, and I was ready to go for it. He exuded sexuality through his lens and his voice. He could make a woman melt like a scoop of ice cream. I was in the running with four models for Penthouse Pet, August 1976, which meant I'd be going to London with this man, and staying in the same apartment a whole day to work out this fantasy. Afterwards, he said, 'I have cooked spaghetti for us.' We had pasta and wine. We talked. He walked me to my room. I turned to say goodnight, to kiss him on the cheek. I never made it to his cheek. Making love to Bob was an experience. I never felt like I was his mistress, or one of the girls. I think he loved to give pleasure as much as to receive it, and maybe even more."

I interviewed Victoria in Houston, Texas. While we were watching footage of her interview, she asked her boyfriend, a Houston dentist, "Would you mind leaving the room. I need to do this alone." I stood up to leave as well, but Victoria stopped me. "Oh, no, you can stay." And she began describing what it was like to make love with Bob Guccione. She described this in great detail, losing herself in the experience, till I felt like I was in a 190°F room. It was like Bertolucci's X-rated *Last Tango in Paris*, with Marlon Brando and Maria Schneider making raw, erotic love in an empty apartment. Since the character played by Maria shot Brando after having told him too much, this was a bit worrisome. When my scene with Victoria was over, I was still alive. Sweating, but alive.

I also interviewed a bona fide insider on the Gucionne-Keeton marriage: Xaviera Hollander, a New York madam who gained fame in the '70s because of scandals that connected her with political figures. She described it all in her memoir *The Happy Hooker*. After her exile, for legal reasons, from New York, Guccione hired her to write a column for *Penthouse*, titled "Call Me Madam." She poetically described her readers' letters to me as, "Penis too big, penis too small. I'm coming too quick, I can't come at all." And, the edgier ones: "If I like seeing my wife and my boss making out, am I a homo?"

Hollander agreed to be interviewed if I would come to Amsterdam. I did as requested, soon discovering that she was a one-person Dutch industry. She owned dozens of bed and breakfasts, plus she was a playwright and producer who invested in the theatre. She owned a multimillion-dollar house in Amsterdam, which she called a Bed & Brothel. Her conditions: I was to pay her five hundred euros and to stay two nights. What was I getting into?

I explained the deal to Ken Ng, my lead cameraman, and added, "I'll pay her, but I'm only staying one night."

Xaviera answered her own door. A robust seventy-five, she was larger than life, both personally and figuratively. She grabbed, hugged and kissed me, saying, "Barry, I'm so happy!" She then identified herself as a Jew to make us simpatico. Her husband was sitting at a table covered with marijuana, from which he was removing the seeds.

Xaviera told me, "You can help yourself."

"Okay." When in Rome, savour the grapes.

Her walls were plastered with erotica. "We'll do the interview later," she announced. "You're going to stay tonight and tomorrow night, right?"

"I can't stay tomorrow night. I'm sorry but I have to leave."

"Do you have the five hundred euros?"

I gave Xaviera an envelope, which I thought contained only the money. As it turned out, it also contained my boarding pass and airplane ticket for my return flight. Fortunately, I managed to take those back before she saw them.

While we waited for Xaviera's makeup person, Ken set up his cameras.

She asked him, "What are you, Ken—Asian?"

"Yes."

"Small penis."

"No, that's not true."

"Yes it is. I've been with other Chinese movie stars, but a small penis—that's okay."

Ken said, "I don't have a small penis." Understandably, he was now in a bad mood. I had to wonder if my film would be in focus.

Xaviera's makeup person arrived, and we did the interview.

I asked Xaviera a question to which I expected a connoisseur's answer: "What was it like making love with Bob Guccione?"

She grumped, "Boring." Xaviera also claimed to have had a three-way with Kathy Keeton: "Boring again. I don't think she'd ever had an orgasm."

Xaviera's conversation then turned to specifics, but as it turned out, she was more interested in the quality of Guccione's Italian shoes than his genitalia or his fabled sexual prowess. Afterwards, Xaviera wanted to take Ken and me out for dinner. That part was great, but next came the part where we had to sleep in her Bed & Brothel. By way of self-defence, I told her, "I'm sorry but I have to leave at three a.m. to catch my flight."

She replied, "I can arrange a taxi for you. It will be fifty euros to the airport."

I managed to finagle Xaviera's detached coach house, leaving Ken to sleep in a room upstairs in Bed & Brothel. He was half-convinced he would be jumped in the night by someone with a tape measure. Even in the relative security of the coach house, I stayed up all night. I was waiting outside with my bag at 3 a.m.

Who turned up to take me to the airport? Xaviera's husband.

The instant I climbed in his car, he said, "fifty euros." I was happy to pay, simply to get the hell out of there.

Guccione launched *Penthouse* in the U.S. in 1969. At first, he was intimidated at the sight of Hef's omnipresent tall-eared bunny logo—on nightclubs, on keychains, on the Playboy jet. Nevertheless, he made his intentions clear in an ad in the *New York Times* entitled, "We're Going Rabbit Hunting." It showed a silhouette of the Playboy bunny, head riddled by ten bullet holes. According to the ad's designer, George Lois, when Guccione saw it, he did an Irish jig. The warning that Hefner might sue over trademark infringement only made Guccione happier. "Do you think he would? That would be great!" His own cartoon doodles included a *Playboy* rabbit with a tear dripping from one eye, and a pair of bunny ears sticking out of a toilet bowl.

Guccione described his assault on *Playboy* magazine as comparable to Hannibal's attack on Rome, through the Alps, the snow and the ice, with elephants and troops ready to fight like guerrillas. It was an assault that hit *Playboy*, quite literally, below the belt, in what became known as The Pubic Wars. In earlier issues of *Penthouse*, the crotch between the spread legs of the Penthouse Pets had been covered. However, one issue featured a small side photo of a naked woman, strolling down a beach with a just-visible curl of black pubic hair. "When no one complained, our next issue had more pubic hair," said art director Joe Brooks. "Then, when critics did jump in, Guccione used the previous issue as a precedent."

He defended his first pubic-haired centrefold on the grounds of female liberation. "We repudiate that guilt-inspiring attitude that a woman's genitals need to be hidden. Nothing is more beautiful than a woman's body." Bob Jr. supported his father's decision. "Millions of American men were now seeing anuses and vaginas for the first time. My father was like a single-combat warrior for them, coming out like Batman in cape and boots."

A shocked Hugh Hefner told *Time* magazine, "There will be no pubic hair in *Playboy*—ever." Nine months later, a wisp of pubic hair made its first appearance in Hef's magazine. There was no going back.

By 1980, *Penthouse* had caught up to *Playboy* in circulation, and was grossing $140 million a year. Guccione—well-built and handsome, with dark, curly hair—became a '70s celebrity, and then a caricature. That was partly to do with his uniform. He wore tight Italian leather pants, high boots and open shirts that revealed a hairy, tanned chest, and so many gold chains that they jingled as he walked. Those chains meant more than mere wealth to Guccione. The first one had been given to him by his mom, who exuded pride in her notorious son.

"I wore my shirt open to school once," confessed an aspiring Bob Jr., "but never again."

Along with *Penthouse*'s sensational visuals, Guccione featured tougher, more investigative articles than *Playboy* and other men's magazines. Political scandals, government corruption, even the Mafia's misdeeds were catnip to him. He was a tireless supporter of Vietnam veterans, and printed article after article about their shabby treatment because of the unpopularity of that war. He even opened a Washington office specifically to lobby for their support.

"My fondest memories of working for *Penthouse* were visiting veterans' hospitals," said Penthouse Pet Davina Celeste. "I tried to visit every person in the hospital—privates, generals, sergeants. Bob was devastated about how they were being pushed around and forgotten."

A scandal erupted in 1984 when Guccione printed erotic, lesbian, bondage photos of Vanessa Williams, the first black woman to be crowned Miss America. These nude photos, taken much earlier in Vanessa's career, forced her to give up her Miss America crown. Since I had become friendly with Vanessa while shooting commercials for *Kiss of the Spider Woman*, I approached her to appear in the Guccione film. Her agent replied with a rude note which could be summed up as, "Are you out of your mind?"

I argued, "Vanessa Williams became a star overnight as a result of the scandal. Certainly, her career is safe enough to look back on this and comment."

No way.

As Bob Jr. recalled, "We thought we'd sell maybe fifty thousand copies of Vanessa. Instead, we sold seven million. We couldn't get paper to print them fast enough. People were paying a couple of hundred dollars for an issue, five dollars for a Xerox, one dollar for a look. Half of America had masturbated to Miss America, and now the pageant wanted to take it out on someone. I believe *Penthouse* was forever besmirched." Hugh Hefner went on record to express his shock. "This is an invasion of Vanessa Williams' personal life, and that is immoral."

Guccione invested $US17 million of his own money to finance the epic movie, *Caligula*, with the intention of changing modern

Western culture by showing Rome at its most erotically decadent. As *Caligula*, he cast Malcolm McDowell, with Helen Mirren, John Gielgud and Peter O'Toole in supporting roles. Gore Vidal was the original scriptwriter, but later withdrew his name. For the orgy scenes, with their lavish production values, the casting director was charged with finding big-breasted women who didn't mind being naked, and men with large penises. Helen Mirren later described the film as "an irresistible mix of art and genitals." Everything about the making of the film was controversial, including the editing. Guccione later lamented, "I had to steal my own film back, two hundred miles [of film] stuffed into luggage. Instead of the feature I wanted, the editor had created one that could be shown anywhere."

Guccione also had to purchase his own New York theatre, which he renamed the Penthouse East, to show it. The more disgusted the reviewers, the longer the lineups. It played for a year, and had a limited release in other cities.

In 1982, *Forbes* ranked Guccione in their list of the world's 400 wealthiest people, with a reported $400 million net worth. Along with his burgeoning success, he had adopted a luxurious lifestyle, expressed prophetically in his motto, "It's easy to go down, so live it up." His new 22,000-square-foot, Madison Avenue office and residence was outfitted like an Imperial Roman palace. Italian and French artisans were imported to install mosaic tiles, stately pillars and arches, a sumptuous pool with wall medallions, tons of marble and gilt (even on a toilet seat), along with Judy Garland's gold piano. Guccione had also initiated what would become a world-class art collection, including works by Modigliani, Dürer, Picasso, El Greco, Pissarro, Renoir, van Gogh, Chagall, Matisse and Botticelli. "Visitors would stop and stare," said art director Joe Brooks. "They would exclaim, 'Is that a Holbein?'"

Of special significance was a painting by Edgar Degas of a woman disrobing with her back to the viewer. As a young boy, Guccione had fallen in love with a reproduction of that picture, which he had cut from a magazine and carried in his pocket. "One day, I am going to own this picture."

Instead of the orgies once associated with Playboy Mansion, the centrepiece of Guccione's mansion was a long, marble table, around which he collected scientists such as Carl Sagan, financiers like Malcolm Forbes, promising young artists and athletes, as well as the requisite beautiful women. A great compliment to his guests was when their host, a remarkably good chef, cooked the dinner.

Guccione's social interests along with his business empire distracted him from being an involved father. "We kids just dealt with the fact that Dad wasn't going to be there for us a lot," said Nick, his youngest son. "Most of the time he was at a long table full of people, always at that distance, but we got through that."

As for the Penthouse Pets always hanging about the mansion, Nick added, "My hormones were flying, but Dad told all these beautiful girls, 'Don't go near the kids,' and he told us the same. The Pets were taboo." Nevertheless, Nick confessed during our interview to sometimes scoring with them outside the mansion. This aroused the belated envy of Bob Jr., "My hero!"

Guccione became a voracious empire-builder. His General Media not only published *Penthouse*, but dozens of other magazines, including *Forum*, which provided advice on sex and relationships, and *Omni*, which featured scientific articles. "We were all looking for answers as to why we were here, and where we were going," he said. "The church hadn't moved ahead as quickly as it could. Only science was answering these questions."

Guccione launched Anna Wintour's career as a fashion editor at his *Viva* magazine. He also made Bob Jr. editor of his alternative rock magazine, a decision that led to a painful father-and-son scrap over ownership. The two were estranged because of the dispute for many years.

After pouring millions into a fusion energy plant that was never built, Guccione rolled the dice on his biggest gamble. He started construction on a $150 million casino in Atlantic City without first obtaining either a casino licence or the financing. In 1987, Guccione tried to sell the rusting steel framework of the unbuilt casino to the Sands Hotel in Las Vegas, which would make the Sands then a competitor to Donald Trump's Atlantic City project. When Trump tried to block the sale, *Penthouse* threatened to expose his affair with Marla Maples. Trump ultimately won the battle, bought the property and built a new casino, making Guccione one of the biggest losers in gambling's history.

Guccione was still one of America's richest men. He liked to boast that *Penthouse*, with its monthly circulation of 4.7 million in 16 countries, had started with a bank loan of $1,700 and had grossed $4 billion over its 30-year history. However, all that money could not save Guccione from what happened next: His wife and business partner, Kathy Keeton, was diagnosed in 1997 with galloping breast cancer. When she died, age fifty-eight, Guccione's personal world collapsed. "Losing her blew out my lamps," confessed Guccione. "I was never the same again." His professional world was also about to nosedive.

Guccione had always lived beyond his means. No matter how much money poured in, everything he owned was mortgaged to the hilt. For a man obsessed by scientific developments in the realms of space exploration and energy production, he was surprisingly out of touch when it came to technological changes in his own field. First video and then the Internet were making pornography available in ways that print media couldn't match. *Penthouse* was losing its status as the primary, most available source of sexually explicit material. Guccione responded with sensational offerings. He proposed that the infamous Unabomber write a column. He published nude photographs of Madonna. He tried to get Monica Lewinsky to pose for the magazine. To *Penthouse*'s now routinely exposed vulvas and anuses, he added sexual fetishes, such as photos of women urinating. This scared away advertisers without boosting circulation. Predictably, it also aroused the indignation of America's religious right, leading to censorship problems under the Reagan administration.

Guccione responded to such attacks with righteous indignation of his own. *Penthouse* took great pleasure in exposing the sexual hypocrisy of TV evangelists Jimmy Swaggart and James Bakker, helping to end their ministries. In defending the American First Amendment right to freedom of speech, Guccione insisted, "Reagan's presidency couldn't deliver the prayer issue or abortion to the evangelists, who delivered his election, but they could deliver censorship."

Now, with a circulation of just 400,000, *Penthouse* could no longer support Guccione's other ventures. In 1984, Bob Jr. told his father, "The sexual revolution is over, Dad. You won. My friends and I don't buy *Penthouse* anymore. We buy *Sports Illustrated*. The girls have clothes on—not many, but they do."

Having interviewed '70s Penthouse Pets, who described how exposure in *Penthouse* had launched them on respectable careers, I wanted to interview women who had posed for *Penthouse* after it became a hardcore failing magazine. I phoned Mark Spiegler, an L.A. agent for pornographic film stars, and told him, "I'd like to interview your client, Dana DeArmond, who once posed for *Penthouse* and was now directing her own sex films for *Penthouse*'s video division, for a documentary I'm doing on Bob Guccione."

He replied, "She doesn't do anal."

I repeated, "It's for a Guccione documentary."

He said, "It's six hundred dollars an hour, and I just want to remind you that she doesn't do anal."

"Listen, I've been on your website, and she does do anal, but that's not why I need her."

I agreed to the $600, and Dana DeArmond came to the Sunset Marquis Hotel where I was filming. She caused a stir in my crew when she walked in. She was gorgeous. She was also a businesswoman who had made millions marketing her brand; not a coked-up porn star, but a pro who directed her own scenes. She was insightful, not only about the Guccione years, but about the porn industry. When I asked her what her parents thought of her career, she responded in a way that didn't quite make it into the film.

She asked, "Do you have a daughter?"

I said, "Yes."

"You know, at some point you're going to get a call saying your daughter skipped school, that your daughter was caught smoking in the washroom and so on. My parents got a call saying, 'You know what? Your daughter takes two cocks in the ass.' And I figured out, 'So, what's the difference?'" Dana pointed out the obvious advantages of Internet porn. "When buying online, you don't have to look over your shoulder to see who's watching." She also made this rather contradictory statement: "You also need the element of taboo, because if everyone is taking two cocks in the ass, then it's boring."

Dana was intimidating, fascinating, sexy, the whole package. I asked her off-camera, "How do you handle ordinary dates with men?"

She replied, "When I answer the door, and my boyfriend is on the other side, I am expecting him to bring his best game."

In 2003, General Media was forced into bankruptcy. Guccione had to sell off his beloved art collection to pay $100 million in back taxes. Jane Homlish removed each painting from the wall and handed it to the auctioneers. But she did more than that. "After we lost our very last one, I spent all night till sun-up, hanging Bob's own paintings in their place. When he finally came downstairs, he could see that they looked beautiful."

It was also Jane who picked up the first phone call from General Media's new owners: "Is this Jane? I just phoned to let you know that you and Bob are fired."

Guccione lost his mansion to his mortgage holder that same year. He also underwent surgery for throat cancer, losing in the operation his ability to swallow solid food along with his sense of taste. Though it made it difficult for him to talk, he still managed to say, "I probably desire food more than sex."

Before Kathy Keeton died in 1997, she had decided that Guccione should not live alone, and suggested that he marry her friend, April Warren, a model from Texas. "April was extremely aggressive about living with Bob," said Homlish. "Bob needed to be entertained, and thought this would help him to get over Kathy. I don't think that worked, but I believe she made him feel alive again."

Guccione appointed Warren creative director of *Penthouse*, and married her in 2006. She was with Guccione in 2010 when he died, age seventy-nine, of lung cancer in a Plano, Texas, hospital. By then, both Bob Jr. and Nick had made peace with their father.

"It was shocking to see Dad wind up in a crap hospital in the middle of nowhere," said Nick.

"I think he just gave up," said Bob Jr.

People kept bringing up the name of Al Goldstein when I was conducting interviews for the film. When you talk about freedom of expression in the '60s and '70s, especially when the subject is sex, you talk about Hugh Hefner, you talk about Bob Guccione and you talk about Al Goldstein. It was Goldstein who produced the radical tabloid with the self-explanatory title *Screw*. In its twenty-five-year history, the tabloid's most sensational scoops were nude pictures of Jacqueline Kennedy and an article entitled, "Is J. Edgar Hoover a Fag?"

Goldstein was very much a New York kind of guy who, at the height of his notoriety wore Rolex watches and diamond bling and had homes all over the world. He oozed sleaze. And, like Guccione, he experienced a precipitous fall, living homeless for a while in Central Park. My research team finally found him in a nursing home for veterans in Queens. When I phoned him, he said, "I loved Bob. I'll do an interview. It will cost you five hundred dollars."

We made a date. I kept phoning to confirm that it was on until he said, "Why are you calling? It's done. Bring the five hundred dollars."

The more serious problem was getting permission from the hospital to take in a film crew. Because they never answered my request, I told my people, "We're going to do this guerrilla-style." We walked into the home with our film equipment hidden in our coats, pockets and bags. When a guard asked whom we were visiting, I said, "Mr. Goldstein." He replied, "Ward seven, third floor, room sixty-eight."

I'm not good at hospitals, as I've said many times, and this place was like something out of Scorsese's *Shutter Island* combined with *The Shining*. Even Ken, who'd survived Xaviera and filming in jungles, was getting shaky. Just as we arrived at Goldstein's room, a nurse came out wearing rubber gloves and a neck-to-toe rubber apron. I told her, "I'm here to see Mr. Goldstein."

"Well, I have to finish cleaning him up. He's made a mess. Why don't you wait in the reception area?"

When we got to reception, another nurse asked who we were visiting. I repeated, "Mr Goldstein."

"Oh yes, he's a very nice guy, very mild-mannered."

Nice? Mild-mannered? I told her, "That doesn't quite fit what I know of Al Goldstein."

"Oh, I was talking about *Dave* Goldstein. *Al* Goldstein is in Ward eight. You go down to the basement then take the tunnel . . . Is somebody escorting you?"

"No."

"Oh." She seemed both pensive and surprised.

We went down to the basement and it was the most frightening underground walk ever. People were wandering around like zombies, and we could hear strange noises. When we took the elevator up to Ward 8, this was now Destitute Island, where people had been left to rot. I'd seen bad stuff before, but this sad case of lost souls' decline really bothered me. I put on my blinders, and we found a room with "Al Goldstein" on the door. I knocked and he yelled, "Enter and fuck you!" He was sitting in a wheelchair, wearing shorts with a T-shirt pulled above his belly. It was tattooed with the words, "Let's Fuck." Goldstein greeted me, "Good Shabbat," a Jewish greeting reserved for Friday nights. He added, "I'm ready to go. Do you have the five hundred dollars? I'm sorry to ask but I need it."

We closed the door to set up the cameras, and it was boiling hot. The *New York Times* book section and other signs that Goldstein was a voracious and cultured reader, were scattered about the room. He wanted to know, "Is Côte Basque restaurant still around? I'd love to get out and have a good lunch with you and smoke some weed."

It was Ken's job to put the microphone up Goldstein's T-shirt, a task he clearly wasn't looking forward to. This man hadn't washed in God knows how long, but when we started the interview, he was charming. Unfortunately, he'd had a series of strokes, so he'd start a great story, then lose it, then repeat it, provide another nibble or moment of brilliance, and then say something like, "Have you ever had a Thai woman? They're the best." Or he'd talk about having to be satisfied with nursing manuals to masturbate. He also kept taking out his teeth because he felt he could talk better that way. It was a crazy interview, and it was sad. I didn't want to exploit him, but I thought it was important to put him in the film. The best I could get was his assertion, "I could jerk off to *Penthouse*."

Goldstein died on December 19, 2013, aged seventy-seven, from renal failure at a nursing home in Cobble Hill, Brooklyn.

I premiered *Filthy Gorgeous: The Bob Guccione Story* at the 2013 Toronto International Film Festival, to which I invited both Jane Homlish and Victoria Lynn Johnson. These two women were a study in opposites:

Victoria was the still-beautiful, long-time mistress; Jane was the love-lorn, long-suffering personal assistant and loyal confidante, who remained sexually invisible to him. Jane had never had her fifteen minutes with Bob, ever. Victoria, a Penthouse Pet, who had travelled the world, was used to the red-carpet treatment, which Jane resented. Jane kept complaining that Victoria was hogging the spotlight, and that her stories weren't true. Finally I had to tell her, "Jane, this is a film to celebrate Bob's legacy. If you say one more negative thing, you're going back on the plane to New Jersey, so go ahead and test me."

As for Xaviera Hollander, now that I was her best friend, who'd immortalized her in the Guccione film, she told me, "Barry, I'd love to come to Toronto for the festival, but I have an outstanding legal issue."

"What is it, Xaviera? I know the best criminal attorney in the world, so maybe he can make it go away."

"In the seventies, when I lived in Toronto, I was having a *ménage à trois* with brothers of a prominent retail family. They dared me to go to a store owned by a rival retailer and to steal a negligee. I did, and I got caught shoplifting."

I told Eddie Greenspan. He asked, "How many years ago was this? I don't think it will be an issue." But then he looked into it and found Xaviera's problem was an outstanding tax issue, not a shoplifting one, so she couldn't attend the premiere.

I sold the documentary internationally, and it did well. Not unexpectedly, it met with a mixed critical reception, because I had taken a man who exploited women and told the story of his life from the standpoint of insiders instead of exposing him as a scumbag. I was angry, because I thought the film was a fantastic story about the rise and fall of a business empire. I didn't see it as a tragedy, the way his sons saw it, because Bob Guccione had lived most of his life the way he wanted. He just had a bad Act III. Some people are unlucky that way.

★

I continued to visit Playboy Mansion when I was in L.A., mainly because I loved the movies. (My friends refused to believe this; they think it's like saying, "I read *Playboy* magazine for the articles.") I'd go for the 6:30 screening, then join other friends for dinner.

While making the Guccione documentary, I had taken Hef aside to ask him if he would participate. He replied, "Barry, I have never gone on record about *Penthouse* magazine, and I'm not going to do it now. I don't need to do it. It's over. *Penthouse* was an imitator, *Playboy* was the real deal." I think Hef just forgot about the documentary, but the friends I had made at the mansion did not. They kept egging me on when it was finished. "You've got to have Hef show your film here."

I remembered how Hef always sat down at his magnificent dining-room table at 6:15, to greet his guests, who sometimes gave him gifts before the screening. With trepidation, I joined the lineup, gave him a DVD of *Filthy Gorgeous*, then beat it to the door, where I could see how he reacted while in a position to escape before being thrown out. Hef picked up the DVD, looked at it for a moment, then called to his assistant. I heard him say, "Take this upstairs to the bedroom."

I've since returned to the mansion. Hef has never said a word about the film. So I don't know how he felt about that famous ad with the silhouette of his Playboy bunny, riddled with bullet holes, or the film's take on The Pubic Wars.

Chapter Twenty-Five

QUALITY BALLS: THE DAVID STEINBERG STORY

As a Jewish kid from Montreal, I grew up watching Winnipeg's David Steinberg—another Jewish kid like me—develop a great standup career.

An earlier generation of comedians, such as Bob Hope, George Burns and Jack Benny, shot well-rehearsed, rapid-fire, one-line zingers. Steinberg was different: he led a new wave of comedians who told stories. Like Richard Pryor, Lily Tomlin and George Carlin, he was willing to give up the fast laugh to invest in a bigger climax five minutes up the road. He wasn't afraid to improvise, and he was political in the way Jon Stewart is today. Steinberg was on fire in the '60s. He made more than 130 appearances on Johnny Carson's *The Tonight Show*, second only to Bob Hope. After that, he launched a second career, directing sitcoms like *Seinfeld*, *Friends*, *Mad About You* and *Curb Your Enthusiasm*.

I grew up wanting to be like David Steinberg, so working with him was a dream come true. In 2006, I hired him to do a series of humorous commercials for a wealth management company. We shot the ads over four or five days in Palm Springs and had dinner together every night. We traded jokes. We were like two old comedic souls who'd fallen in love on a first date.

Five years later, when HBO green-lit a documentary about Steinberg, he and producer Debbie Nightingale suggested that I direct it. Could life be any sweeter? I signed a contract with the production company as a director-for-hire, not as a producer, which was my usual dual role.

David and I met several times to talk about the arc of the film. My brainchild was to shoot David performing standup, which he hadn't done in thirty-five years. I attempted to pitch this idea to him over lunch at Il Pastaio, one of his favourite Beverly Hills restaurants. As I discovered, David and his wife, Robyn, had become very particular about what they would eat. At first, it was funny, but then it became wearing: *We will have the poppy seed, but it has to be washed in mineral water. Does the waitress have a cold? Is this table too near the UV lighting? Has somebody walked by who might some day get Ebola?*

Izzy, the Steinbergs' giant standard poodle, was also present. I liked Izzy. He was a well-mannered dog, but he was treated as if he were a person who appeared to be taller than me. Everything at that lunch came down to two imperatives: preserving David's health so he would live to be 190, and catering to Izzy's every imagined whim.

David loved my standup idea, but was understandably nervous about performing before an audience after so many years. What would his new act be about? How would he prepare his material? I suggested honing his performance in La Jolla, down the coast from L.A. Billy Crystal performed there over seven hundred Sundays before taking his show to Broadway, where it enjoyed massive success. Billy had worked with Des McAnuff, a Tony Award–winning director and former artistic director of Stratford. Since Des and I had worked together on *The Tempest* and *Caesar and Cleopatra*, I felt confident recommending the idea. David also brought in a well-known *Saturday Night Live* director and the brilliant writer, Alan Zweibel.

As David was honing his show, I was attempting to set up interviews with people who had worked with him. I kept asking David to arrange access to well-known comedians like Jerry Seinfeld, Larry David from *Curb Your Enthusiasm*, Paul Reiser from *Mad About You*, but nothing was happening. When David contacted me to say he wanted to see me, I flew to L.A. for another lunch. After the usual fuss about the food, he told me, "Barry, I've been thinking, and I believe we should bring in someone else instead of you to interview the comics."

Since this film was already off-track, and I was still working on my Guccione film, I didn't get as insulted as I might have done. "So, you want to bring in someone else. Why is that?"

"Yeah, I've been thinking that it would be better if another comedian interviewed a comedian instead of you. You'd be there to direct. I think we'd get better stuff that way."

Still keeping my cool, I replied, "You know, David, I couldn't disagree with you more. A comic interviewing a comic is going to be masturbation. We're not going to get anything in-depth. It's just going to be one big love affair, back and forth. If you're questioning my skills, I've interviewed everybody from Mick Jagger to studio heads and moguls. I know how to do that."

"No, it's not that."

"I get it. What you really want is to direct this film about you, so why don't you direct it?" I got up to leave.

"Where you going?"

"I'm walking. *You* direct the film."

I called the producer, Debbie Nightingale, in Toronto. "Debbie, I'm out of the film. Pay out my contract and take my name off it. I don't want to do this."

Debbie was responsible for delivering the documentary to the network. She was understandably apoplectic, but I stood firm. "I'm not being allowed to do what I need to do, so I want out."

She protested, "But David and Robyn are invested in this film and they're executive producers."

"What?" This was news. I became even more suspicious. "So who has final cut?"

A pause. "Well, they do."

"And you've never told me that? So . . . this is a bar mitzvah film. Now I *really* don't want to be a part of it."

"Let me try to fix this for you."

"Here's the way it's going to be fixed. If David has final cut, I'm stuck with that contractually, but let me finish the film the way I need to finish it, and give me a new contract that says I'm allowed to take my name off it."

An agreement was reached. I was back on the film.

I always like to interview around the subject so I know what questions to ask later. While I was filming around David, he was simultaneously doing the cable-TV series *Sit Down Comedy with David Steinberg*, in which he chatted informally with other comics such as Mike Myers, Larry David, Bob Newhart, Martin Short, Jerry Seinfeld, who were exactly the people I wanted to interview. Whenever I approached David with a request, he said he didn't want to impose on that comic for me because then that comic might not also want to come on his *Sit Down* show.

I tried to understand David's attitude. When you've been on top in Hollywood as a standup comedian, and everyone knows who you are, that's a big high. Then, when you go behind the camera, and you're not Steven Spielberg, even though you're a sought-after sitcom director, it's not the same. The industry certainly knew who David Steinberg was, but maybe he didn't feel as sought-after now that heads didn't turn when he walked into a restaurant. Maybe he had reverted to being an insecure Canadian.

After all the wrangling, I sometimes found it necessary to remind myself why I had wanted to do this film in the first place.

David Steinberg was born on August 9, 1942, of immigrant parents. Or, as he liked to put it, "My parents came from Russia in the late twenties, early thirties. The Jewish Agency met them in Halifax. They said, 'Okay, how can we find a place more hellish than where they came from?' Hello, Winnipeg."

He was the youngest of four children born to Yasha and Ruth Steinberg. "I was a big surprise so, basically, my parents were finished parenting. This was the best thing that could have happened to a kid like me. I did whatever I wanted."

David's father, his uncle and his aunt all owned grocery stores. "My uncle and aunt's store had a big radio. I first heard Jack Benny and Fred Allen on the radio because they could get the American programs. I had a dog, a black-and-white dog. I called him Spotty, which was an indication of the kind of creativity that was going to burst forth from me in later years. I told stories a lot. I easily could get laughs. It was just so comfortable for me."

David's father also ran a little synagogue. "Gentiles, to my father, were people who, although intelligent, would sell their children for whiskey."

At age fifteen, David left Winnipeg on a scholarship to a theological school in Israel. Since he didn't want to be a rabbi like his father, he left to study English literature at the University of Chicago. "There were eight, maybe nine, pretty women on campus, and, across from the coffee shop, there was a door. It led to some steps. Six of the pretty girls every day went in that door and walked up those steps. One day, I just followed them. They were going to the University of Chicago theatre, and there was a sign on the door: 'Auditions for chamber theatre production of *Candide*.' This guy, Robert Benedetti, who ran the theatre, asked, 'What are you doing here?' I said, 'I'm auditioning for *Candide*.' He said, 'Well, what role in *Candide*?' I didn't know if Candide was a guy, a lead or a building. I said, 'Just, you know, one of the Candidian parts.' And he said, 'Well, I haven't seen you here before. What brings you here?' Of course, he knew all those gorgeous girls had just left. I said, 'Well, I'm a big fan of chamber theatre.' He said, 'Oh, that's so interesting. Chamber theatre is a term we came up with today.'"

Benedetti and Steinberg became friends and their friendship led to Steinberg's stage debut. "I didn't play any leading role. But he had me playing, you know, a horse. I played inanimate objects. I was just, literally, there because of the girls."

One day, Benedetti phoned Steinberg at home to tell him, "I want you to get here early because there's a show at Mandel Hall I want you to see."

The show was Second City, and it left Steinberg gobsmacked. "Here was this most incredible group of people, Barbara Harris, Mike Nichols, Elaine May, Alan Arkin, all who became comedy gods in their own way." Their humour was sharp, cool and cerebral, often with lofty punchlines: "Let's get back to football, shall we? We have a left guard and a right guard, but no Kierkegaard." Steinberg was enthralled. "I'd never seen anything like that before, and somewhere in the middle of that routine, I said to myself, *I do that! What they're doing, I do that.* I wanted to follow them like a kid follows a circus."

After a few appearances, the word got out and he was invited to perform with the group. His comedic style proved to be a great fit for their style of quick-thinking, topical improvisation. As he explained it, "You had to know what movies were playing. You had to know what was happening politically so when the audience suggested a topic you could do it."

Steinberg created recurring characters such as the psychiatrist who was nuttier than his patients, and the preacher who delivered satirical sermons with faux profundity. The sermons were convincing because of Steinberg's own detailed biblical knowledge as the son of a rabbi: "Tonight's sermon deals with the exciting personalities Moses, Solomon, Noah and Job, all of whom had a wonderful rapport with God, whom I'm sure you'll all remember from last week's sermon. And God looked down and saw that things were bad. Every time God looks down, things are bad. Maybe if He wouldn't look down so much, things would pick up?

"God appeared to Solomon in a dream. He said, 'Solomon, if you could have anything your heart desires, what would that be?' Solomon said. 'Oh, Lord, grant me wisdom that I might be the wisest king of all.'

"God gave him this anthropomorphic zap, and Solomon became all wise and knowing. And at that moment, he knew he should have asked for money."

After appearing in two Broadway plays, which closed in the first week, David did standup in a New York club called The Bitter End. "When I had a big audience, it was a Gray Line bus tour, and they hated me. One night, there were only six people, so the club manager, with that commitment that managers have, said, 'You've got three more days, and you're out.' I just wanted to get to sleep as fast as I could."

Next morning, Steinberg was awakened by a phone call from his friend, singer Carly Simon. "David, have you seen the *New York Times?* Go get it." He flipped to the Entertainment section. "There was a review by a man named Dan Sullivan—a name I will never forget. He was one of the six people who turned up, and he said, 'David Steinberg is a cross between Woody Allen and Lenny Bruce.' And I was away!"

The hippest, most controversial TV show at the time was *The Smothers Brothers Comedy Hour.* The brothers had their own musical comedy act, which they supplemented by inviting other comedians and musicians to join them. Pete Seeger and Joan Baez, who were opposed to the Vietnam War and critical of the U.S. presidency, were among their guests. Considering how provocative the anti-war material was, it was ironic that one of David Steinberg's sermons finally caused CBS to close down the show.

"Moses was wandering in The Wilderness when he saw a bush that was burning, yet it would not consume itself," he told viewers on his first guest appearance. "A voice came out of the heavens. 'Moses, take off your shoes from off of your feet,' God said in his redundant way, "for the land that you are standing upon is Holy Land.' Well, Moses took his shoes off, approached the burning bush, and burned his feet, and God went, 'Ah-ha, third one today!'"

In 1969, that was more than irreverent. It was shocking.

"Comedy is about bringing down authority," said writer Billy Grundfest. "Who's the biggest authority? God!"

When Steinberg returned to the L.A. studio two weeks later, Tommy Smothers told him, "Come. I want to show you something." He opened a door, revealing stacks of boxes.

"What's that?" Steinberg asked,

"It's your hate mail," said Smothers. Then he added, "You should be happy about this."

CBS was not. The corporation warned the Smothers Brothers that, if they ever had Steinberg back, he must never do another sermon. Tommy Smothers not only invited David back, but specifically asked him to do a sermon. Steinberg's monologue contained these immortal words, "The Old Testament scholars say that Jonah was swallowed by a whale. The Gentiles, the New Testament scholars, say, 'Hold it, Jews, no, that's not true.' They literally grabbed the Jews by the Old Testament." The series was cancelled before the Jonah segment could be aired. "*The Smothers Brothers* was the No. 1 show in America," marvelled Steinberg. "Just imagine, financially, what cancelling it meant."

"Tommy Smothers completely supported David," said Grundfest. "I personally would do anything for David Steinberg. I would walk on fire for David Steinberg. I would eat pork for David Steinberg, but get your show cancelled for David Steinberg? Are you out of your fucking mind?"

That same year, 1969, marked the beginning of the Richard Nixon presidency. Steinberg became relentlessly, fearlessly, as some would say, political. "Well, I will tell you something about President Nixon. Once I've told it to you, you are never going to see him the same way again, because what I am going to tell you is the truth, and the strange, mystical thing about the truth is, once you've heard it, it remains lodged in your memory forever. And that is simply this, President Nixon has a face that looks like a foot." Steinberg polarized his audiences in what became a one-man crusade. He was ridiculing the presidency in a way that had never been done before.

"When you write comedy, you start with what pisses you off," said Grundfest. "Well, nothing pissed David off. He's Canadian. But Nixon got to the point where even David was pissed off."

One day, an hour before a show, Steinberg received a knock on his door at the Plaza Hotel. Two men, who identified themselves as FBI agents, told him, "You've had an assassination threat that came through our switchboard. If you do your Nixon material tonight, someone is going to take a shot at you, but don't worry. We FBI guys will be standing around the whole room." Steinberg's initial response was gratitude. "I thought, this is an amazing country. These guys are going to protect me." He went on stage, he did his Nixon material, and then he added a sermon. "I got up on a chair, even flaunting myself, because I knew, as a comedian, that if I didn't, I would never have any edge ever again."

But wait: "It turned out these two guys were basically just investigating me, and I kept on seeing them everywhere that I went, and when Watergate occurred, they were sitting behind Donald Segretti."

Segretti was one of the Watergate Plumbers crew that had been hired to run a campaign of dirty tricks against the Democrats. "I realized they had just been trying to stop me, and it was amazing to know that Nixon's people were paying attention to what I was saying and doing in nightclubs."

In 1974, Steinberg, Richard Pryor and Lily Tomlin were slated for the cover of *Newsweek* as an example of new wave humorists. "I was there by virtue of my Nixon material, and then that bastard resigned, and knocked us off the cover."

With his face. Like a foot.

Steinberg later discovered that he was on Nixon's famous enemies list—a badge of honour in the minds of other comics.

While all this archival and interview material was great, I kept complaining to executive producer Debbie Nightingale that I needed access to high-profile comics. At last, she told me that I was invited to bring a crew onto the set of *Curb Your Enthusiasm*. This seemed like a breakthrough. The largely improvised show, with Larry David playing a misanthropic version of himself, had become a critical favourite. In one classic scene, Jeff Greene, a close friend of Larry's, played by Jeff Garlin, persuaded Larry to help him cover up his marital infidelities.

> JEFF: Shh, shh. I got in a lot of trouble with Susie. I need your help so bad. She found a pair of panties in my glove compartment.

> LARRY: *Oy vey iz mir.* Are you kidding me?

> JEFF: No, I am not kidding you.

LARRY: How the hell did you do that?

JEFF: I forgot they were even in there. I forgot. But here's where I need your help. Man, oh man. I told her they were your panties . . .

When I arrived at the California house that was the set for the TV show, I soon discovered that my enthusiasm was about to be curbed. I was informed upfront by Steinberg's people that I couldn't interview anyone. All I could do was to film David directing. This is what is known in the industry as the B-roll, meaning secondary footage useful for filling in gaps when you're editing. David's neurosis was at work again.

While I was sitting by my cameras, without much to do, Larry David walked by.

He asked, "Hello, who are you?" in that Larry David way.

"Barry Avrich. I'm shooting a documentary about David Steinberg."

"Don't you want to interview anyone?"

"Yes, but David told me not to bother you."

"Well, that's ridiculous. Set up a studio in the kitchen and I'll bring people over."

So that's what we did. I interviewed Larry David, who had cocreated *Seinfeld* with Jerry Seinfeld. Like every comic I spoke with, he confirmed that Steinberg was a comic's comic. "David sort of set the template for the way a lot of comedians wanted to work, myself included," Larry David told me. "We work well together because we like the same things and we hate the same things. We share the same values."

In one scene over which they were at odds, Larry wanted to complain about having a pubic hair stuck in his throat. Steinberg only reluctantly agreed. Now, buoyed up, Larry wanted to do the pubic hair in every scene. Steinberg drew the line. "We'll do it in every second scene." Steinberg thought he'd lost that battle but he won the war: he ended up receiving an Emmy nomination and a Director's Guild for that episode.

"For its time, David's comedy was outrageous to close-minded people," said Jeff Garlin. "To open-minded people, it was cool. My career aspiration is to be a director, and David's a mentor."

The show's executive producer, Larry Charles, was another *Seinfeld* alumnus, and the director of *Borat*. Charles, with his big beard, was almost Hasidic. He talked about coming to California to find fame and fortune, but ending up as a valet at David's health club. "I recognized him as a big star, and one of the original, brilliant visionaries of modern humour. He had a vision. He had a point of view. He had a voice that was completely unique for the time."

Larry Charles would leave jokes in Steinberg's car, and sometimes he'd find a leftover joint in David's ashtray, which he'd smoke. "When I would get his car, I would talk to him about comedy. He was very nice, very generous, and he gave me a lot of time and some good tips." Later, when Charles was doing *Seinfeld*, he returned the favour by suggesting that David direct an episode.

The interviews I collected in that kitchen were great, but I still needed more interview subjects, so I continued to nag people in Steinberg's camp. Eventually, they hired a talent-wrangler, whose job it was to line up subjects. The ones she brought often gave me good interviews, but I was flying to NY and L.A. to speak to B- and C-level players in David's life, such as Vidal Sassoon, who cut David's hair during his halcyon standup days. I had to keep asking, *Where are the super-famous people everyone expects to see in a documentary about David Steinberg?* I was running out of time.

I continued to find archival footage that we could license. This included a treasure trove of material with Johnny Carson on *The Tonight Show*. Carson was every comic's ticket to instant fame in those days. "Comedians talked about this all the time," he told me. "When did you get to sit down next to Johnny?"

Steinberg was announced as a guest four times and then cut each time because the show was running too long. The fourth time looked like a cinch: only Tony Bennett and Steinberg were booked for the whole ninety minutes. After Bennett sang as expected, he sat down with Carson to talk. "Tony Bennett is not exactly Mr. Words," said Steinberg. "That night he was George Bernard Shaw. He was waxing eloquent. You've never heard such mellifluous tones and dialogue and language. It was phenomenal. He went on for three segments, telling stories about his childhood."

The fifth invitation to *The Tonight Show*, in 1968, proved the charm. "Next day, I remember walking down the street in New York, and one out of every four people, it seemed, said, 'Oh, I saw you last night.'"

Carson and Steinberg had made an instant connection, which they played out over subsequent shows over many years. A favourite topic of Steinberg's was his Jewishness. "If the business is run by Jews, then why does Rob Lowe get one million dollars a picture, and I have to open for Robert Goulet at The Aladdin? And if the business is run by Jews, why does Mickey Rourke get to make endless love to Kim Basinger, and I'm up for the part as the panicky rabbi who gets slapped around by George Kennedy in *Airport '88*?

"The Italians, they like to play. You know, they have a good time. They're dancing. They have the concertina. When the Jews arrive, it's like a ward from Cedars of Sinai Hospital, you know? They come in with the hats and the pills. Don't barbecue the meat. You could get cancer. Don't eat before you go into the water. Don't eat after you go into the water. If they had a bumper sticker it would say FUN KILLS.

"A Jewish princess, to me, is the kind of girl that makes love with her eyes closed because she can't bear to see another person's pleasure.

"I also get a lot of hostile mail, but I can determine the difference a little quicker now than I could before. A letter that starts 'Dear

Kike—' That's a pretty good indication that they're not going to like the show I did previously."

Most anything was fodder for Steinberg's comic talent. "It's really hard to cry in a film, you know? Like, Rod Steiger pulls his nose hairs and that brings a little tear. And then they say, 'What a sensitive, poetic performance.' But I care too much about my nose to do such a thing to it."

The rapport between Carson and Steinberg was so intuitive that Carson sometimes hit David's punchlines at the same time as he did.

STEINBERG: You know, I have a sort of capsulized philosophy now. Success is so relative. When you're a baby, success is not wetting your bed.

CARSON: I guess that could be considered, yes.

STEINBERG: When you're a teenager, success is going all the way. When you're a young man, success is making money. When you're middle aged, success is being happy. When you're an old man, success is going all the way. And when you're really old. . .

BOTH TOGETHER: . . . it's not wetting your bed.

On Steinberg's second appearance on *The Tonight Show*, Carson offered him a chance to host. He was only twenty-six, the youngest person to pinch-hit for Johnny. His first guest was singer Paul Simon. After Steinberg had sweated through the all-important monologue, which referenced the satirical sermons for which he had become famous, Simon commented during the commercial break, "You know, David, I watched your monologue. When you said, 'I had a wonderful rapport with God,' it would have been better if you had said 'a connection with God.'" Steinberg responded, "You know, I was just thinking, when you sing, it would be better to do 'Bridge Over Meshuggeneh Waters.'"

Steinberg and Carson became friends offscreen as well as on. "Johnny invited me to see a screening in his office, and there were just the two of us, and in the middle of that, I thought *My God, this is Johnny Carson and me.*"

Steinberg embarked on his second career as a director thanks in part to Burt Reynolds. Reynolds, then one of Hollywood's biggest stars, insisted that Steinberg direct his next movie. Steinberg said, "It's hard to imagine that he had more clout than Barry Diller and Mike Eisner, who were running Paramount, but that's what happened."

Though *Paternity* (1981), about a bachelor looking for a woman to bear his baby, was forgettable, Steinberg emerged with new ambition. At a time when TV wasn't taken seriously as a director's medium, Steinberg got in early, putting him in line for the shows with the best scripts. He was directing *Mad About You* (1992–99), which featured New York newlyweds, Paul and Jamie, played by Paul Reiser and Helen Hunt, when Steinberg seized the opportunity to seize the limelight once again, this time as a scripted actor. His character was eulogizing at a funeral when it became clear the corpse was someone he had never known or even met:

BAD EULOGIZER [STEINBERG]: The world is poorer today, for having lost Marty Brekman.

JAMIE, correcting him from a front pew: Buchman. It's Buchman.

BAD EULOGIZER: Buchman. I am poorer. You, his friends, are poorer. His loving family is poorer. Let me introduce them. His nephew, Bill . . .

JAMIE: Burt.

BAD EULOGIZER: Burt. His nephew, Amon . . .

JAMIE: Arnold.

BAD EULOGIZER: Arnold. And their wives, Celia . . .

JAMIE: Sylvia.

BAD EULOGIZER: Sylvia. And Rose . . .

JAMIE: Blossom.

BAD EULOGIZER: Blossom and Sylvia. And their children, Pete, Janice, Arthur, Sheila, Darcy and Douglas.

JAMIE gives a thumbs-up for this unexpected accuracy.

All this incredibly rich archival material, showcasing David at his boldest and best, worked its magic on me. By the time I flew to La Jolla for David's show, I was excited once again. Two of his producers picked me up at the San Diego airport, and drove me to La Jolla. On the way, I reminded them, "I want a shot of David walking from the dressing room to the stage. I need that lonely, wonderful shot."

One replied, "We asked him, but he doesn't want to do it."

"Why not?"

"He just doesn't want to do it."

"Okay." But I was pissed off. "I also want a meeting with the cameramen who are shooting the show. I want them on headsets so I can give them direction."

"David doesn't want the cameramen to wear headsets. It's too distracting. You'll be able to get what you need without that."

I saw too clearly where this was going. "Take me back to the airport. I'm tired of this bullshit."

Now, they were panicked. They contacted David, who said he wanted a meeting with me.

I went to David's hotel room, and he was with his wife, who had finished wiping down the entire room for germs. Izzy, the dog, whom I had liked, was not present. He had probably been sent to the airport to kill me, but had killed another Jew by mistake.

The first thing David said after we were seated was, "So, you want a shot of me walking from the dressing room to the stage? Sounds like a great idea. We can do that." His tone shifted. "But, Barry, I don't want the cameramen wearing headsets."

"I *need* to direct them."

"The theatre is so small we're going to get all the coverage we can use."

Fine, so win one, lose one. Except, of course, they didn't do the dressing-room shot either, so it was a double loss for me.

My crew shot three of David's performances, and they were good. I only wanted to use a little of this footage to bookend the documentary, but I filmed the whole show for them to use as they wanted.

I once again brought on Tiffany Beaudin, who had cut the Harvey Weinstein film so brilliantly, to edit the documentary. What I didn't know was that David had another editor sending her notes, instructing her to remove anything he considered negative. In my films, I try to be fair and balanced, then let viewers decide what kind of person is featured, which means I show everything I get. Now, I learned the film was being sanitized behind my back. This led to yet another argument—a big one.

David said, "I've seen your films and many are tragic stories about someone's rise and fall, and I don't want that."

"You haven't had a fall, but there are periods in your life when things weren't going so well, like before Burt Reynolds resurrected your career by asking for you to direct his movie."

"I don't want to talk about that."

We were fighting over sequencing and everything else, and David won most of those battles, because I knew he had final cut. I wanted to keep a funny line that went back to *Rowan & Martin's Laugh-In* days. The mother of Judy Carne, the "Sock it to me" girl, disliked David, so she told Judy, "Fine, he can come to dinner, but he only gets the dark meat." David wanted that out. More significantly, I wanted to include David's beautiful daughters, but because they came from his difficult first marriage? Out.

There was a hilarious scene in which David talked about directing Bea Arthur for the first time on *The Golden Girls*. Bea liked to have a gin and tonic after each show, usually with the director. She asked David, while in a mellow mood, "Why is it that people take such an instant dislike to me?" David replied, "It just saves time."

David wanted that out, but I needed at least one win, so I dug in my heels. "It has to stay." David finally agreed.

Vidal Sassoon talked about what he knew best about David—his beautiful hair. In fact, all of David's friends talked about his great hair. Out. In the '70s, rock stars got the women, not comics. Except for David Steinberg. He had this fantastic ability to attract them. Partly because of his great hair. As writer Alan Zweibel said, "Back then, comedy people were never good-looking. There's a nose. There's something's crooked. There's bad hair, but David was this really sexy guy, and he was accessible because of that."

"Most people think Carly Simon's 'You're So Vain' was about Warren Beatty," said Ziggy Steinberg. "It was about David."

"One morning, I went up to David's apartment and rang the bell, and Tuesday Weld opened the door," said Broadway producer Bill Gerber.

Everyone agreed: no one had more women than David.

Unfortunately, David requested this entire theme be cut out of the film. It was tragic, given how funny it was. Whom was he protecting? He was a single guy on the road. Oy.

David and I had one more raging argument. It was about the film's title. I wanted to call it *Quality Balls: The David Steinberg Story*. That came from Jerry Seinfeld, who'd said about David, "When I was just thinking of comedy, he was already doing it. And he was such an idol of mine. He really had, you know, quality balls."

David was incensed. He wanted to call the film *It Might Be Something Big, It Might Not*—the name of his new standup comedy tour, which I'd all but set up for him by suggesting he return to standup for the film. That was another one I managed to win. However, at a private New York screening, to which I was not invited, David told his celebrity friends, "I wanted to call the film *Quality Balls*." His version was printed in the *New York Post*, and later David repeated it on *Late Night with Jimmy Fallon*. Incidentally, he also mispronounced "Avrich" by using a short-a sound, as in "average," instead of a long-a sound as in "ace."

Quality Balls premiered in Toronto at the 2013 Hot Docs Festival, and David flew up for the sold-out show. We did a Q&A on stage, jockeying for the best lines, and keen to tell our version of the story. The reviews were quite good, but of course the critics complained that the film was too flattering: *Where's the tough stuff?* In this case, on the cutting-room floor.

I still see David from time to time. The film has played tremendously well. I've received many compliments on it, and I'm proud of it, though I would have done some of it differently. There's no bad blood between David and myself that I'm aware of. Our film experience was a typical case of a director trying to direct a film about himself, while treating me, the putative director, as staff. If I had known the rules going in, I might have made a different decision about whether or not to be involved. What I learned was this, I am the only person who can make projects happen for me. The Steinberg film was the first—and last—time I will work as a director-for-hire.

Chapter Twenty-Six

IT'S A WRAP!

My desperate need to entertain led to my two-track career, in advertising and making films. Even as I write these words, I'm exactly where I want to be, in the centre of sheer pandemonium. I am in post-production for a planned filmed adaptation of a staged version of *Hamlet*, my seventh Shakespeare film. As the kid who was blown away by Stratford's *School for Scandal* when I was eight, I'm in Heaven. On the documentary front I'm developing a slew of films, including biopics of the legendary comedian, Rodney Dangerfield, and American singer-songwriter Marvin Gaye. I'm also working on a film about the Bronfman dynasty. There's never a shortage of projects.

My dad would have been pleased about the Dangerfield project. My dad and I adored him. We saw him at his club when I was ten, on one of those trips we made to New York City, and my dad bravely took me up to introduce me. He told Dangerfield I was his biggest fan. Rodney's reply? "Look what it is: a midget!" Cue rim shot.

Dangerfield complained that he got no respect. I sometimes have felt the same way, that there's something about how Canadians choose not to honour their own. The critic Richard Ouzounian calls it the "tall poppy syndrome." Grow too tall and it's off with your head! I once shared this feeling with Robert Evans. He said, "Barry, you're the kid who won't leave the picture and never should." I could have kissed him for that. Except that we were lying together on his mink-covered bed, which is where he took his meetings. Cue the rim shot again.

I have lost friends by death and by design. I can't bring back the friends who have died. As for the others, some friendships just have an expiration date, no matter how long they endured. But for the friends who are no longer a part of my life, because of ego or temper or even lack of focus, know that I miss you, and I'm sorry that we have yet to make right what is so wrong.

For the assholes and the monsters, I harbour no anger. From ex-bosses, dishonest partners, a few psychotic clients and a couple of society wannabes, I thank all of you as well for being part of the DNA that has allowed me to live and love the life I have been given. I have been blessed.

Dad, you told me to never blend in. I am grateful for that advice and I miss you every day.

ACKNOWLEDGMENTS

None of this adventure was possible without the mentors, characters and assholes who carved out the path for me, got in my way, or forced me to think smarter. Thank you. And especially my thanks go out to those who inspired me.

I miss my mentors every day: my father and my great friend Dusty Cohl. I am indebted to my muses for life: Max (Melissa) and Sloan. They liberate me and make me laugh. My gratitude for making this book soar goes to Sylvia Fraser, Jack David, Erin Creasey, Jennifer Hale for her editorial genius, Crissy Calhoun, Malcolm Lester, Jonathan Webb and Michael Levine who pushed me to get it done. For their unyielding loyalty: Todd White, Michael Schwartz, Michael Korman, Jonas Prince, Heidi Kaplan, Dusty Cohl, Eddie Greenspan, Suzie Goodman, Antoni Cimolino, Robert Pattillo, Paul Godfrey, Bill Goldberg, Ken Rosenstein, Myrna and Jack Daniels, Ralph Lean, Robin Mirsky, Paul Bronfman, Ellis Jacob, Gary Slaight and too many others I will forget. To those who believed in my work and happily shared the adventure: Tori Laurence (my beloved partner), Ken Borden, John Tory, David Peterson, Piers Handling, Michele Maheux, Anita Gaffney, Ivan Fecan, Sheldon Levy, Patricia Rozema, Nat Brescia (where ever you are), Patrice Theroux, Robert Lantos, Heather Conway, Bob Richardson, Jack Gardner, Devon Macgregor, Tony Mark, Jennifer Dettman, Aubie Greenberg, George Anthony, Shinan Govani, Jyl Rosenfeld, Richard Gere, Ron Meyer, Helga Stephenson, Virginia Kelly, Scott Henderson, Richard Crouse, Rob Lamb, Mary Pat Gleeson, Alexander Neefe, Janice Price, Richard Ouzounian, Martin Knelman, David Brown, Helen Gurley Brown, Parky and Peter Fonda, Paul Nagle, Tina Santoro, David Barnes, Howard Kerbel, James Earl Jones, Robert Evans, Dominick Dunne, the extraordinary concierge team at the Sunset Marquis Hotel who always said yes as a setting for most of my films, and even Harvey Weinstein. And to that one person who inspired me to love art and everything cultural: Faye Avrich. Thanks, Mom.

INDEX

A note on the index: page numbers followed by a "p" indicate that the subject appears in a photograph on that page.

9 1/2 Weeks 30
20th Century Fox 211, 220
77 Sunset Strip 102
400 Blows 276

Academy Awards 9, 271, 272, 274, 278, 286
Accidental Tourist, The 104
AC/DC 264
A Chorus Line 12, 38
Adams, Don 11, 322
Adele 128
Adler, Joey 105–06, 110–11
Affleck, Ben 109, 283
Affluent, The Society 189
Aird & Berlis LLP 157–58

Airport 220
Albany Club 242
Alda, Alan 287
Alfred Hitchcock Presents 211
Ali, Muhammad 89
Allen, Fred 349
Allen, Woody 3, 177, 351
Alliance 75, 77, 78, 85, 270, 294
Alliance Atlantis 78
All That Jazz 67
Alonso, María Conchita 54
American Capitalism 189
American Express 78, 116–17
American Gigolo 107, 181
American Graffiti 220
Amerika Idol 292–301
Amery, Leo 307
Amiel, Barbara "Lady Black" 123–24, 244
Amsterdam Theatre 65

An Inconvenient Woman 193
Ann-Margret 101–02
Answered Prayers 319
Anthony, George 88
Anthony, Ray 322
Antoinette Perry Award for Excellence
   in Theatre, see Tony Award
Antony and Cleopatra 122, 145, 148
Apollo Theater 65, see also Ford
   Center for the Performing Arts
   (New York)
Architectural Digest
Arkin, Alan 350
Armstrong, Louis 42
Arthur, Bea 362
Artist, The 286
Ash Wednesday 196
Aspects of Love 51
Astaire, Fred 42, 89, 210
As You Like It 122, 144
Atlee, Simon 107
Attlee, Clement 312
Avedon, Richard 29
Aviator, The 285
Avrich (née Wahler), Cindy 10, 12, 16,
   17, 21, 24
Avrich, Faye (née Garellek) vii, xv,
   4, 7–8, 9–10, 14, 16–17, 20–21, 24,
   28, 29, 36, 96, 97, 128–29, 134, 143,
   161, 191p, 275, 303, 325
Avrich, Irving vii, xv, 3, 4, 5p, 5–6,
   7–13, 14, 16–17, 20–24, 27–28, 71,
   87, 103, 134, 143, 175, 179, 231, 247,
   248, 276, 315, 365, 366
Avrich, Melissa (née Manly) iii, 35, 65,
   90–97, 91p, 103, 123, 125, 141, 156,
   192, 247, 248–49, 321
Avrich, Sloan iii, 12, 95–97, 97p, 103,
   176, 190–91, 191p, 247, 248
Avrich, Sol 6, 23, 28, 103

Aykroyd, Dan 264
Aznavour, Charles 84p

Bacall, Lauren 99–100, 194
Bacharach, Burt 4
Baez, Joan 352
Bailey, F. Lee 236, 240
Bailey, Pearl 12
Bakker, James 338
Balfour, Arthur James 308
Ballard, Bill 254, 257, 259, 264
Ballard, Harold 253–54, 258
Barber, Lynn 328
Barker, Michael 113
Barnum, P.T. 146
Barris, Chuck 176
Barrymore 71–72, 148, 315
Barrymore, John 148
Base, Ron 113
Basinger, Kim 357
Bastian, Michael 229
Battleship Potemkin 177, 178
BDO 160
Beatles 127, 137, 252
Beaudin, Tiffany 361
Beauty and the Beast 78
Beckerman, Henry 209
Bee Gees 255
Behind the Mask 49, see also *The
   Phantom of the Opera*
Beker, Jeanne 33
Belafonte, Harry 129–30
Bellair Café 180
Bell, Bert 55
Bell Lightbox Theatre 314
Benedetti, Robert 350
Ben-Gurion, David 312
Ben-Hur 183
Bennett, Tony 3, 80–81, 81p, 357
Benny, Jack 89, 345, 349

Benotto, Mary Lou 71
Bergen, Polly 213
Bergman, Ingrid 100
Bertolucci, Bernardo 330
Best Buddies 98, 120
Best Buddies Gala 98–105
Between Friends 63
Beverly Hills Hotel 119, 182
Bilbao Film Festival 186
Biskind, Peter 280–81, 283–84
Black, Conrad 123–26, 243–46, 245p,
    248–49, 303–04
Black Robe 76–77,
    see also Brian Moore
Blondie 181
Blood Simple 184
Bloor Cinema 182
Blue Rodeo 264
Bluhdorn, Charles 119
B'nai Brith Camp 16–17
Bob Newhart Show, The 217
Body Heat 104
Bogart, Humphrey 100
Bogdanovich, Peter 277
Bono 106
Borat 356
Bordertown 85
Borden, Ken 37–43, 46, 182, 183
Botticelli, Sandro 335
Bowles, Eamonn 278
Bowling for Columbine 285
Bradshaw, Richard 109
Braga, Sonia 82
Brando, Marlon 88, 211, 330
Branson, Richard 116–17
Bravo 192, 283
Brickman, Samantha 105–06, 111,
    116
Broadway Musical, A 315
Brockum 257

Bronfman (family) 30, 45, 114, 212,
    316, 365
Bronfman, Edgar, Jr. 206, 222
Bronson, Charles 232
Brooks, Joe 333, 335
Brooks, Mel 3, 233
Brown, David 117–19, 199–200,
    211, 220
Brown, Helen Gurley 117–19
Brown, Tina 197, 200, 283
Bruce, Lenny 351
BT/A 159, 162
Buck Owens and the Buckaroos 253
Burger, Corky 276
Burns, George 345
Burton, Richard 144, 196
Bush, George W. 285
Bus Riley's Back in Town 102
Buxbaum, Hanna 241
Buxbaum, Helmuth 241
Bye Bye Birdie 102

Caan, James 322
Cabaret 82
Caesar and Cleopatra 11, 71, 148, 342
Caligula 326, 334–35
Campbell, Cherri 77
Campbell, Graeme 48
Camp Naivelt 112
Canada's Walk of Fame 79, 90, 263
Canadian Centre for Diversity (CCD)
    129–30, 131
    Emerging Leadership Award 130;
    International Diversity Award 129
Canadian Council of Christians and
    Jews, see Canadian Centre for
    Diversity
Canadian Music Hall of Fame 263
Canadian National Exhibition Stadium
    (CNE) 255, 258, 262

Canadian Tenors 165
Candide 62, 350
Cannes Film Festival 89, 113, 228,
    277, 289
    Palme d'Or 271, 278, 285
Capitol Records 127
Capone, Al 209
Capote, Truman xvi, 201–02, 319
Capra, Frank 89
Carlin, George 345
Carlton Hotel 89, 113
Carnal Knowledge 102
Carnegie Hall 128, 267
Carne, Judy 362
Carousel 12
Carr, David viii, 201–03, 280
Carroll, Diahann xiii, 62, 317
Carson, Joanne 194
Carson, Johnny 11, 88, 137, 214, 219,
    345, 356–59
Carter, Billy 216
Carter Center 216
Carter, Graydon 200–01
Carter, Jimmy 216–17
Carver, Brent 53
Casablanca 100
Cassavetes, John 88
Cassavetes, Nick 88
Cassel, Ernest 306
Casual Togs 6
Cat on a Hot Tin Roof 104
Cats 257
Cavett, Dick 88–89
CBC 85, 241
CBC-TV 205, 237
CBS 201, 352
Celeste, Divina 328, 334
CFRB (radio) 38–39
Chagall, Marc 335
Chamberlain, Neville 311

Chameroy, Dan 146
Changeling, The 315
Chapman, Georgina 286
Charles, Larry 356
Charlie's Angels 62
Château Frontenac 21–22
Chekhov, Anton 183
Chicago (film) 285
Chicago (stage) 82, 138
Chioran, Juan 53
Christy, George 71–72
Chrysalis Records 181
Chow, Olivia 170–71
Christensen, Hayden 279
Churchill and the Jews 124, 304
Churchill, John Spencer 303
Churchill, Randolph 306
Churchill, Winston 126, 215, 302,
    304–12
Cimolino, Antoni 147–48
Cincinnati Kid, The 102
Cinema Paradiso 277, 285
Cineplex Odeon xiii, 39, 43, 44–45, 48,
    49, 72, 136, 179, 316, 318
Cirque du Soleil 165
Citadel Theatre (Edmonton) 52
Citizen Kane 10
City Lights 193
City-TV 181, 193
Clarkson, Wayne 112
Clinton, Bill 127, 189, 216, 217, 283
Clinton, Hillary 283
Clift, Montgomery 211
Clockwork Orange, A 62
Clooney, George 169
Clooney, Rosemary 213
Close, Glenn 62
Closer to the Sun 73–74
CNN 58
Cochran, Johnnie 198–200

Cochrane, Tom 264
Coen brothers 184
Coghlan, Melissa 294–98, 295p, 300
Cohen, Sacha Baron 297
Cohl, Chase 256, 267–68
Cohl, Dusty xvi, 79, 87–90, 92, 111–15, 115p, 123, 230–31, 248, 250, 252, 262, 265, 268–69, 271
Cohl, Eli 256, 267
Cohl, Jake 256, 263, 267–68
Cohl, Joan (née Carin) 89
Cohl, Liam 256, 267
Cohl, Michael "King Cohl" xvi, 43, 64, 79, 87, 129, 152, 250–69, 253p, 272, 276
   documentary on: see *Satisfaction*
Cohon, George 34
Collier, Jacob 128
Colosimo, Big Jim 209
Concert Productions International 256–57, 259
Condit, Gary 205
Cooper, Michael 84
Copacabana 80–82
Coppola, Francis Ford 277
Cordis, Maria 187
Corea, Chick 128
Corky Presents 276–77
Cosmopolitan 117
Court TV USA 192, 205
Coward, Noel 193
CPI Theatre 64
Crash 77
Creative Artists Agency (CAA) 221, 226
Crewson, Gregory 222
Crispo, John 32
Cronenberg, David 77, 179–80
Crouse, Richard 181
Crouter, Wally 39

Cruise, Tom 221
Crying Game, The 278, 281
Crystal, Billy 346
CSS Stellar 151, 153
Culp, Robert 322
Curb Your Enthusiasm 345, 347, 354
Curzon, George 310

Daily News, see *New York Daily News*
Dalai Lama 54, 293
Dale, Cynthia 146
Dalí, Salvador 88
Dalitz, Moe 209
Dallaire, Roméo 232
Damon, Matt 106, 109, 112, 121p, 161, 283
Damone, Vic 322
Dangerfield, Rodney 365–66
Daniels, John 133p, 136
Daniels, Myrna 133p, 136
Darrow, Clarence 237
David, Larry 347, 348, 354–56
Davis, Bette 89, 317
Davis, Clive 206
Day-Lewis, Daniel 282
Dear Love 105
DeArmond, Dana 338–39
Death Wish 232
Decca Records 211
de Cordova, Fred 219
de Cordova, Janet 219–20
Degas, Edgar 335
de Hirsch, Baron 306
de Kooning, Willem 222
De Niro, Robert 289
Delsener, Ron 258, 260
Del Tredici, Bob 177–78
Demeter, Christine 238
Demeter, Peter 238–41
Dershowitz, Alan M. 310, 312, 325

Desrosiers Dance Theatre 33
Diamond, Jack 109
DiCaprio, Leonardo 289
Diller, Barry 359
Dion, Céline 78–79
Disney, see Walt Disney Company
Doctorow, E.L. 65
Dolan family 288
Donald, Donald K. 255–56
Donato, Andy 244
Donovan, Kevin 262–63
Dorsey, Tommy 210
Dos Equis 236
Douglas, Kirk 195
Douglas, Michael 221, 232
Down and Dirty Pictures 280
Down the Rabbit Hole 322–23
Drabinsky, Cyril 71
Drabinsky, Garth ix–xiv, xvi, 39, 43–46,
    47–74, 75, 82, 83, 84p, 94, 99, 105,
    143, 149, 179–80, 183, 184, 185, 213,
    222–23, 233, 250, 286, 313–19
    autobiography: see *Closer to the Sun*
    documentary on: see *Show Stopper*
    incarceration: Beaver Creek
    Institution ix–x, xiii; Kingston
    Penitentiary x–xi
    polio: 71, 73
Dracula 143
Dragnet 211
DreamWorks 136
Dubai Film Festival 107
Dunne, Alex 195, 196
Dunne, Dominick viii, xvi, 118, 192–
    207, 212, 244, 319
Dunne, Dominique 195, 196–97
Dunne, Griffin 195, 196, 201
Dürer, Albrecht 335
Duvall, Robert 212
Dynasty 62

Easy Rider 220, 277
Eaton Centre 27, 31–32
Ebb, Fred, see Kander and Ebb
Ebert, Roger 113
Echo 43, 47–48, 63–64, 68–70, 75,
    76–77, 79, 85–86, 87, 89, 150–53,
    183, 250, 270
    see also Len Gill
Eckman, Jan 58
Ed Sullivan Show, The 137
Eisenstein, Sergei 178
Eisner, Michael 284–85, 359
Elgin Theatre (Toronto) 52, 57, 114
El Greco 335
Endeavor 153–62, 168
English Patient, The 283
Empry, Gino 38–39, 43
Enrico, Robert 54
eOne Entertainment 78
EPIX 325
Evans, Robert 119–21, 120p, 212, 366

Faces 88
Factory Girl 278–79, 288
Fahrenheit 9 /11 285
Falk, Peter 88
Famous Players 44
Faulkner, William 187
Fecan, Ivan 72, 111–12
Federal Communications Commission
    (FCC) 215, 216
Felder, Raoul 140–41
Fellini, Federico 82, 120, 276
Ferdinand, Franz 307
Fiddler on the Roof 12, 57, 183
Film Society of Lincoln Center 234
Filthy Gorgeous 324–26, 342, 344
Fitzgerald, Ella 3
Floating Film Festival viii, 32, 87,
    115, 291

Follies, see Florenz Ziegfeld
Fonda, Henry viii, 196, 210
Fonda, Jane 289
Fonda, Parky 103
Fonda, Peter vii–viii, 103, 287
Forbes (magazine) 250, 335
Forbes, Chris "Skip" 117
Forbes, Malcolm 117, 336
Ford Centre for the Performing Arts
    (North York, now Toronto Centre
    for the Arts) 62
Ford Center for the Performing Arts
    (New York) 65
Ford, Doug 170–72
Ford, Rob 169–71
Forster, John 306
Forsythe, John 62–63
Fortune (magazine) 250
Forum 336
Fosse, Bob 67, 138, 324
Four Seasons (restaurant) 206–07
Four Seasons Centre for the
    Performing Arts 109, 112
Four Seasons Hotel
    New York 64, 96
    Toronto 92, 94, 96, 102, 103, 120, 265
Francey, Peter 168
Fred's Not Here 44
Freshly Squeezed 138
Friday the 13th 76
Friedrich, Hans 181
Friendly, Lynda 44–45, 55–56, 83
Friends 345
Frommer, Jeremy 325, 326

Gabor, Zsa Zsa 127
Galbraith, John Kenneth 188–90, 216,
    302
Gaffney, Anita 143, 148
Gangs of New York 284

Garbo, Greta 119, 125–26, 210, 215
Garellek, Jack 15
Garellek Kosher Meat Market 15
Garellek, Louis "Zadie" 8–9, 15
Garellek, Manny xv, 17–18, 19, 30
Garellek, Minnie "Aunt Minnie" 9
Garellek, Steven 15
Garellek, Sylvia 28, 37–38
Garland, Judy 83, 88, 335
Garlin, Jeff 354, 356
Gates, Henry Louis, Jr. 59
Gaye, Marvin 128, 365
Gazzara, Ben 88
General Electric Theater 211, 215
General Media 336, 339
Genson, Edward 243
Gerber, Bill 363
Gere, Richard 107–09, 179–82
Gershwin, George 32
Gershwin Theatre (New York) 53, 59
Get Smart 11, 322
Ghomeshi, Jian 122
Ghostbusters 316
Gielgud, John 144, 335
Gilbert, Martin 124, 302–03, 304–05,
    306–07, 309, 311
Gill, Len 43, 46, 47–48, 63–64, 68–70,
    87, 150–53, 155, 186
Giller Prize 123
Glass Menagerie, The 316
Gleeson, Mary Pat 76–77, 85
Glengarry Glen Ross 23–24
Glenn, John 325
Globe and Mail 52, 246
Gloria 88
Godard, Jean-Luc 82
Godfather, The 108, 119, 212
Goldberg, Bill 42
Golden Bowl, The 282
Golden Girls, The 362

Golden Globes 98
Goldman Sachs 286
Goldstein, Al 340–42
Goldwyn, Sam 221
Gong Show, The 176
Goodbye, Columbus 178
Goodis, Jerry 40
Goodman, Benny 210, 322, 345
Goodman, Ned 141–42
Good Will Hunting 283
Gorme, Eydie 79
Gottlieb, Bonnie xii
Gottlieb, Myron xii, 59, 64, 68, 70–72, 316
Goulet, Robert 357
Grace (singer) 128
Graduate, The 220
Graham, Bill 259–60, 261, 272
Graham, Laurie 38–39
Grammy Awards 126, 128
Grant, Cary 221
Grateful Dead 212, 252, 259
Grauman's Chinese Theatre 41–42
Greenglass, Daniel 135
Greenspan, Brian 238, 240
Greenspan, Edward "Eddie" xiii, xvi, 88, 113–14, 124, 136, 156–57, 160, 199, 204–05, 228, 230–49, 245p, 269, 272, 274–75, 343
Greenspan, Emma 237
Greenspan, Joseph 237, 242
Greenspan, Julianna 238, 241, 247, 248, 249
Greenspan, Samantha 238, 241
Greenspan, Suzy (née Dahan) 236, 237–38, 242
Griffin, Ellen 195
Grundfest, Billy 352–53
Guccione, Anthony 327

Guccione, April (née Warren) 325, 340
Guccione, Bob "Robert Gucci" xv, 320, 324–44
    documentary on: see *Filthy Gorgeous*
Guccione, Bob, Jr. 324–25, 327, 333, 334, 336, 338, 340
Guccione, Lilyan (née Becker) 326
Guccione, Muriel (née Hudson) 327
Guccione, Nick 325, 327, 336, 340
Guccione, Nina (Bob's daughter) 327
Guccione, Nina (Bob's mother) 326
Guccione, Tonina 325
Guess Who 252, 264
Guilty Pleasure 192–207
Guinness, Alec 88
Guthrie, Woody 252

Haddad, Mary Jo 134–35
Hain, Rob 153
Hamlet 144, 148, 365
Hammerstein, Oscar II 57
Hana, Jeanette 168
Handling, Piers 113, 313
Happy Hearts Fund 106–07
Happy Hooker, The 330
Harris, Barbara 350
Hawaiian Eye 102
Hayward, Leland viii
Hazelton Hotel, The 123
HBO 220, 318, 346
HBO Canada 272, 325
Hearst, Patty 240
Hecht, Ben 210
Hee Haw 253
Hefner, Hugh 320, 321–23, 323p, 324, 332–34, 340
Hello, Dolly! 12
Henderson, Paul 32–33

Hepburn, Audrey 196
Hepburn, Katharine 88
Heppner, Ben 109
Herzl, Theodor 307
Herzliah High School 176
Heston, Charlton 182–83
Hickenlooper, George 278–79, 288
High Point Media 272, 287
Hills, Beverly 38, 42
Hippodrome Movie House 209
Hitler, Adolf 311
Hoffman, Dustin 221
Holbein, Hans 335
Holbrook, Hal 232
Hollander, Xaviera 330–32, 341, 343
Hollinger Inc. 243–45
Hollywood Reporter 71, 228
Holosko, John 83
Homlish, Jane 328, 329, 339, 340, 342–43
Hoover, J. Edgar 340
Hope, Bob 345
Hosanna 145
Hospital for Sick Children's Daniels Hollywood Theatre 124, 133p
Hot Docs Festival 301, 363
Hôtel-Dieu Hospital 21–22
Hôtel du Cap 289
House of Chan 156
Hudson, Kate 106, 116
Hunt, Helen 359
Hunter, Holly 77
Hurt Locker, The 286
Hurt, William 82
Hutt, William 144–45
Hutton, Lauren 326

Ides of March, The 169
IFC Entertainment 289

IFC Films 287–90
Imitation Game, The 290
Imperial Room, see Royal York Hotel
Imperial Six 44, 45, see also Pantages Cinema
Inglourious Basterds 286
In Praise of Older Women 76
Intercontinental Hotel 55, 158
Island, The 70, 73
Ivory, James 281–82

Jackie Brown 271
Jackson, Michael 127, 128, 250
  tours: *Thriller* 258
Jacob, Ellis 136
Jacobi, Lou 3
Jagger, Mick 151, 251, 252, 258, 260, 261, 264, 265p, 266, 267, 347
Jaws 117, 220–21, 277, 315
Jazz Singer, The 209
Jean, Wyclef 109–10
Jefferson Airplane 252
Jerome, Jennie 306
Jersey Boys 147
Jewison, Norman 101, 102, 135, 232
Joe Allen Restaurant 55–56, 139
Joel, Billy 176
John, Elton 127, 274
Johns, Jasper 222
Johnson, Brian D. 314
Johnson, Lyndon B. (LBJ) 189, 215–16, 217, 224, 273
Johnson, Victoria Lynn 329–30, 342–43
Jolie, Angelina 193
Jolson, Al 209
Jonas, George 241
Jones, James Earl 58, 99, 103, 314, 319p
Jones, Quincy 126–29
Jordan, Neil 278

Joseph and the Amazing Technicolor Dreamcoat 54–55, 56–57, 60, 73
Joshua Then and Now 76
Julía, Raúl 82
J. Walter Thompson 37

Kaczynski, Ted "Unabomber" 337
Kander and Ebb 82
Kander, John, see Kander and Ebb
Kaplan, Heidi 177–79
Kaplan, Van 81
Karnofsky family 42
Katzenberg, Jeffrey 136, 284
Kay Kyser and His College of Musical Knowledge 210
Keeton Guccione, Kathy 328–31, 337, 340
Kelly, Sean 153
Kennedy, Jacqueline "Jackie" 340
Kennedy, John F. (JFK) 172, 189, 211, 215
Kennedy, Robert "Bobby" 203, 211, 214
Kennedy Shriver family 98
Kerkorian, Kirk 212
Kern, Jerome 57
Kids 284
Kid Stays in the Picture, The 119
Kill Bill (1 and 2) 271
Kind, Richard 184–85
King Edward Hotel, The 83, 100–01, 161
King, Larry 200, 205, 212
King Lear 148
King of Yorkville, The 179–81
Kings Row 210
King's Speech, The 286
Kinski, Nastassja 30
Kissinger, Henry 206, 217, 325
Kiss of the Spiderwoman (stage) 53–54, 57, 60, 73, 82, 84p, 334
    awards: Tony Award 53–54, 65
    book: 82, see also Manuel Puig
    film: 82

Kitt, Eartha 3
Kitten with a Whip 102
Korshak, Sidney 212, 214, 215, 220
Kosoy, David 160
Kotcheff, Ted 112
Kreviazuk, Chantal 101, 106, 135
Krim, Arthur 273
Kubrick, Stanley 62, 277
Kurosawa 177
Kyser, Kay 225

Labatt 259–60
Ladies' Room, The 179, 181–82
Lancaster, Burt 88
Lane, Nathan 66
Langella, Frank 287
Lansky, Meyer 212
Lantos, Robert 72, 75–78, 123, 228
Larry King Live 198, 199, 205
Laski, Nathan 306
Lastman, Dale 160
Lastman, Mel 33
Last Mogul, The xv, 77, 119, 208, 213, 219, 225–29, 270, 271, 273, 275, 286–87, 320, 321, see also Lew Wasserman
Last Tango in Paris 330
Last Temptation of Christ, The 316
Late Night with Jimmy Fallon 363
Latowsky, Larry 152–55, 157
Laughing Room Only 138, 139
Laurence, Craig 162
Laurence, Tori 86, 153, 157, 159–60, 162, 163–64, 167, 188, 239
Lawrence, T.E. 309
Lawrence, Steve 79
Lead Belly 252
Lean, Ralph 247
Lee, Peggy 39
Leigh, Janet 213

Lemmon, Jack 23–24, 42, 315
Lenin, Vladimir 309
Leopard, The 230
Les Misérables 43, 48, 235, 257
Let's Kill All the Lawyers 182
Leventhal, Harold 266–67
Levine, Michael 304–05
Levitan, Jerry 56, 182
Levy, Chandra Ann 205
Lewinsky, Monica 337
Life and Times 205, 237
Linehan, Brian 193
Lion King, The 12, 65–66, 257
   awards: Tony Award 65
Lionsgate Films 282, 285
Livent, Inc. 45, 48, 50, 52, 53, 55–58,
   60, 61, 63–64, 67, 68–71, 78, 150,
   223, 314, 318
Lloyd George, David 304, 308
Loewy, Victor 39, 75–78
Lord Beaverbrook 302–03, 311
Lord of the Rings (musical) 257
Lombardi, Johnny 187
Los Angeles Times 229
Love Boat, The 80
Love Story 119
Lowe, Rob 357
Lucas, George 220
Luminato 165
Lustig, Hailey 119–20
Lyric Theatre 65, see also Ford Center
   for the Performing Arts (New York)

Macbeth 122
Maccabi 141–42
Macdonald, Darryl 225
MacDonald, Malcolm 310
MacDonald, Ramsay 310
MacGraw, Ali 178
MacLaine, Shirley 10, 105, 316

MacLaren McCann 37
Maclean's 314
MacLeod, Gavin 80
MacMillan, Margaret 303–04, 307,
   308–09, 310, 311, 312
MacMillan, Michael 78
Macpherson, Elle 106
Mad About You 184, 345, 347, 359–60
Madame Sousatzka 316
Madison, Holly 321, 322–23, 324
Madness of King Richard, The 143, 147,
   see also Richard Monette
Madness of Method, The 183–86
Madonna 67, 123, 326, 337
Magnolia Pictures 278
Mahatma Gandhi 293
Maheux, Michele 313
Make-A-Wish Foundation 103
*Mamas and the Papas of the Next
   Generation, The* 4
Mamma Mia! 235
Mame! 10
Mamet, David 298
Mancini, Henry 221
Manilow, Barry 80–82
   see also *Copacabana*
Manly, Doreen 92–95, 96
Manly, Melissa, see Melissa Avrich
Manly, Sheldon 93, 96
Maple Leaf Gardens 79, 253–55, 257
Maples, Marla 337
Maraden, Marti 147
Margulies, Alan 101
Marquardt, Bridget 321, 324
Martin, Dean 211
Marshall, Bill 89, 113
Martin, Tony 210
Marx Brothers
   film festival in Saratoga Springs 9
Marx, Groucho 88–89

Mason, Jackie 137–42
Matisse, Henri 335
Matsushita 222
Matter of Principle, A 246
May, Elaine 350
Mayfair Casino 209
Mayfair Theatre 276–77
McAnuff, Des 52, 147, 346–47
MCA Universal xiii, 45, see also
 Universal Studios, Music
 Corporation of America
McDaniel, Hattie 210
McDowell, Malcolm 62, 335
McGoran, Lori 256, 267–68
McGowen, Ken 34
McGrath, Jim 225
McGuinty, Dalton 167
McLuhan, Marshall 32
McNally, Terrence 53
McQueen, Steve 102
Meara, Anne 139
Measure for Measure 122
Medina, Ernest 240
Meehan, Denise 40
Mehta, Deepa 130
Meiler, Gregori 314
Mendicino, Frank 77
Menendez, Erik 194, 197, 198
Menendez, Lyle 194–95, 197, 198
Merchant, Ismail 281–82
Merchant Ivory 281–82
Meyer, Ron 221, 226–27, 228, 290
Midsummer Night's Dream, A 122, 143
Mighty Heart, A 193
Miller, David 167
Miller, Joey 4
Miller, Sadie 3
Miller, Sam 3–4, 5
Miller, Sienna 279
Minnelli, Liza 82–83

Minnelli, Vincente 83
Minskoff Theatre 60
Miramax Films 77, 271, 274, 277–78,
 280–86
Mirren, Helen 282, 335
Mirsky, Robin 213
Mirvish (empire/family) xi, 143
Mirvish, David 29, 43, 48
Mirvish, Ed 29, 38, 43, 64, 187
Mister Roberts 102
Mitchell, Adelaide ix
Models 177–78
Modigliani, Amedeo 335
Molson 257
Molson Canadian Rocks for Toronto
 (SARSfest) 264–66
Monette, Mark 144
Monette, Maurice 144
Monette, Richard 143–47, 148–49
Montage Hotel 272
Montreal Star 16
Montreux Jazz Festival 128
Moore, Brian 76
Moore, Michael 285, 290
Moore, Peter 262
Morrison, Van 179
Moscow on the Hudson 54
Moskovic, Steve 140
Mostel, Zero 233
Mother Teresa 293
Motion Picture Association of
 America 215
Mounteer, David 123
Mount Royal Hotel 6, 23
Moxley, Dorthy 203–04
Moxley, Martha 202–04
Mr. & Mrs. Bridge 282
Much Ado About Nothing 122
Mulroney, Brian 125
Mulroney government 232

Murderball 228
Music Corporation of America
  (MCA) 209–13, 214, 215, 220, 221,
  222, 224, 316
Music Man, The 49p
Myers, Mike 348
My Left Foot 282

Neeson, Liam 121
Nehru, Jawaharlal 189
Nelligan, Kate 29
Nemcova, Petra 106–07, 116, 126, 136
Ness, Eliot 209
Network 170
Newhart, Bob 217, 348
New Hollywood, The 277
New Industrial State, The 189
New Line Cinema 77
Newman, Paul 195, 282, 316
Newman, Peter 314, 319
Newsweek 354
Newton, Helmut 119
New York Daily News 65
New York Post 317, 363
  Page Six 274
New York Stock Exchange 85–86
New York Times viii, 120, 195, 201,
  271–72, 275, 280, 289, 290, 294,
  332, 342, 351
  reviews: *Aspects of Love* 51;
  The Last Mogul 226, 229, 320;
  Show Boat 59
Ng, Ken 330–32, 341–42
Niccolini, Julian 206–07
Nichols, Mike 206, 277, 350
Nightingale, Debbie 346, 347–48, 354
Niven, David 193, 195
Nixon, Richard 89, 353–54
North York Performing Arts Centre
  57, 58–59

Notarile, Crescenzo 67
Notebook, The 88
NY Erotic Film Festival 76
NYSE, see New York Stock Exchange

Obama, Barack 142
Obama, Michelle 164
Ocean's Eleven 106
O'Connor, Donald 39
O'Connor, Riley 261, 262
Ogilvy, David 18
Oh! Calcutta! 145
Olegnowicz, Alex 166–67
Olivier, Laurence 144
Omni 336
Once a Thief 85
One Angry Man 140–41
ONEXONE 105–12, 116
Onrot, Martin 259, 260
O'Regan, Seamus 123
Orion Pictures 273
ORT 236
Orwell, George 208
Osmond, Donny 55, 56
O'Toole, Peter 335
Outrageous 87, 123
Out There 105
Ouzounian, Richard 314, 366
Ovation 283
Ovitz, Michael viii, 67, 68, 221–24, 226

Pacino, Al 212, 245
Page Six, see *New York Post*
Palais Royale 266
Palance, Jack 65
Paley, Barbara "Babe" 201–02
Paley, William S. 201
Palme d'Or, see Cannes Film Festival
Palm Springs Festival 225–26
Pan Am/Parapan Am Games 163–69

Pandora's Box 252
Pantages Cinema 44, 45, 53
Pantages Theatre 316
Paramount Pictures 119, 215, 359
Parker, Dorothy 210
Paternity 359
Pattillo, Robert 85, 161
Patton, George S. 164
Pearl, Ken 160
Peggy Sue Got Married 104
Peninsula Hotel 229
Penthouse 320, 324, 325, 327–30, 332–34, 336–38, 342
Penthouse East 335
People Like Us 197, 202
Pete & Marty's 180
Peterson, David 163–65, 167–69, 170
Petrillo, James Caesar 209–10, 221
Phantom Express 49–50, see also *The Phantom of the Opera*
Phantom of the Opera, The 45, 48–51, 52, 54, 57, 73, 317
    awards: Tony Award 53–54; see also *Behind the Mask* and Phantom Express
Phillips, Robin 51–52
Phoenix, The 266
Picasso, Pablo 222, 335
Pickett, Denise 116
Pink Floyd 67, 250, 260, 262, 263
Pinsent, Gordon 39, 305
Pisello, Salvatore "Big Sal" 224–25
Pissarro, Camille 335
Pitre, Louise 235
Pitt, Brad 106
Planned Parenthood 103
Playboy 320, 321, 322, 324, 327, 328, 332–34, 344
Playboy Mansion 320–23, 324, 336, 344
Plaza Hotel 60, 353

Pleshette, Suzanne viii, 217–19
Plummer, Christopher xiii, 11, 71–72, 122, 145, 146–47, 148–49, 287, 315
Pocketful of Miracles 102
Politically Incorrect 138
Polo, Roberto 193
Pomerant, Joe 239–40
Pomerant & Pomerant 238
Poppell, Karen 68
Poster, Meryl 279–80
Powell, Ucal 234–35
Presley, Elvis 137
Priest 284
Prince 250
Prince Charles 131–34, 132p
Prince, Hal 53, 57, 60, 62, 83
Prince, Jonas 143, 305
Prince of Wales Charitable Foundation 131
Prince's Charities Canada (PCC) 131–32
Princess Diana 134
Prizzi's Honor 104
Producers, The 233–34
Project Runway 283
Pryor, Richard 345, 354
Puig, Manuel 82
Pulp Fiction 271, 284
Pump Up the Volume 76

Quality Balls 346–49, 360–64, see also David Steinberg
Queen Elizabeth II 134
Queen Noor of Jordan 193

Radio City Music Hall 66, 288
Radler, David 244
Ragtime 65–66, 317
Raiders of the Lost Ark 220, 277
Ramer, Henry 62–63
Raña, Mario Vázquez 166–68

Rawls, Lou 65
Reagan, Nancy 195, 207, 216
Reagan, Ronald 195, 210–11, 215–16,
    217, 221, 338
    administration: 338
Red Alert 190
Red Cross 103
Redford, Robert 278
Reel Justice 231–32
Regan, Gerald 241
Reibenbach, Tsipi 304
Reiser, Paul 347, 359
Renoir, Pierre-Auguste 335
Rent A Fan Club 33–35, 154
Reservoir Dogs 271
Revue Productions 210
Reynolds, Burt 101, 120, 359, 362
Rhapsody in Blue 32
Richard III 122
Richards, Keith 251, 260, 261, 263,
    264, 266
Richardson, Bob 163–64, 166–67,
    169–70
Rickles, Don 137
Riedel, Michael 317–18
Ritz-Carlton Hotel 235
Rivera, Chita xiii, 39, 53, 317
Rocky (films) 293
    Rocky Balboa 293–94, 297, 298
    Rocky Balboa Association 294–97
    Rocky Balboa Award 296
    Rocky Balboa Spa 300
    Rocky Balboa statue 293–94,
    296–97, 299, 300, 301
Rodriguez, Alfredo 127–28
Rogen, Seth 182
Rogers, Ginger 210
Rolling Stones 151, 152, 250, 256,
    259–68, 272
    albums: *Steel Wheels* 260

tours: A Bigger Bang Tour 255p,
    265p, 267; The Rolling Stones in
    Rio 267; Stones Wheels Tour 251
Romancing the Stone 104
Roosevelt, Franklin Delano (FDR)
    189, 243, 304
Roots 211
Rosenfeld, Jyll 138–40
Rosenstein, Ken 157–59
Rossellini, Roberto 276
Rothschild, Nathan 306, 308
Rourke, Mickey 357
Rowan & Martin's Laugh-In 362
Rowlands, Gena 10, 88
Royal Alexandra Theatre 29, 37, 38,
    39, 43
Royal York Hotel, The 122–23
    Imperial Room at 38, 39
Rupert, Prince 260
Rush 254, 264
Rush, Geoffrey 72
Russell, Craig 87
Russell, Rosalind 10
Ryerson Polytechnical Institute 28–29,
    31, 36, 179, 181

Sackman, Jeff 39, 44–45, 179–83,
    228–29
Sagan, Carl 336
Saget, Bob 254–55
Samuel, Herbert 309
Sandys, Celia 303, 306
San Francisco Fillmore 260
Sarah, Duchess of York 131
SARSfest, see Molson Canadian Rocks
    for Toronto
Sassafraz 287
Sassoon, Vidal 356, 362
Satisfaction (film) 251, 253p, 265, 266,
    268–69, see also Michael Cohl

Saturday Evening Post 211
Saturday Night Live 347
Saving Private Ryan 284
Scales of Justice 241
Scheider, Roy 67
Schell, Maximilian 211
Scherman, Tony 125–26
Schneider, Maria 330
Schomberg, A. Thomas 293–94
School for Scandal 11, 365
Scorsese, Martin 273, 284–85, 316, 341
Scotiabank 85
Scott, George C. 315
Screen Actors Guild (SAG) 210
Screw 340
Scullion, Bridget 177–78
Season in Purgatory, A 203
Sebbag, Steph 77
Second City 350–51
Secret Mulroney Tapes, The 319
Seeger, Pete 252, 352
Segretti, Donald 353
Sehring, Jonathan 288–89
Seinfeld 139, 345, 355, 356
Seinfeld, Jerry 347, 348, 355, 363
Selling the Sizzle 118
Selznick, David O. 196
Serendipity Point Films 78
Seven Samurai 177
Sex and the Single Girl 117
Sex, Lies, and Videotape 277–78, 281
Shakespeare in Love 283–84
Shakira 109–10
Shangri-La Hotel 318
Share the Dream 165, 167, see also Pan
    Am/Parapan Am Games
Shatner, William 287
Shearer, Norma 119
Sheen, Charlie 158
Sheinberg, Sid xiii, 316, 317

Sheplee's 31–32
Sheppard, Sam 240
Sherman, Marilyn 76
Sherrington, Amanda 129–30, 131
Sherry, Jim 274
Shetty, Shilpa 108–09
Shining, The 123, 341
Shipley, Don 147
Short, Martin 348
Show Boat 57–60, 64, 314, 317
Show Stopper ix, xi, xiii, xiv, 233,
    313–15, 318–19
Shrek the Third 135, 136
Shrimp Kitchen 33
Shultz, Albert 287
Shutter Island 341
Shutters Hotel 105
Sick Kids, see Toronto Hospital for
    Sick Children
Siegal, Peggy 289
Silent Movie Theatre, The 227
Silent Partner, The 315
Silent Syndicate 209
Simon, Carly 351, 362
Simon, Paul 358–59
Simpson, Nicole Brown 192, 194
Simpson, O.J. 192, 194, 197–99, 202, 240
Sinatra, Frank 79–80, 127, 128, 212, 250
Sit Down Comedy with David Steinberg
    348
Six Feet Under 222
Skakel Kennedy, Ethel 203, 319
Skakel, Michael 202–04, 319
Skakel, Rushton "Rush" 203–04
Skakel, Thomas 202–04
Skydome 255
Slater, Christian 76
Slobodan Milošević 293
Slumdog Millionaire 130
SmartTrack 170, see also John Tory

Smitherman, George 169–70
Smith, Kevin 286
Smith, Maggie 122
Smith, Rex 62
Smith, Roger 102
Smith-Spencer, Rachel 122–23
Smith, William Kennedy 193
Smothers Brothers Comedy Hour, The
    351–52
Smothers, Tommy 352–53
Snitzer, Herb 42
Soderbergh, Steven 278
Solomon, Chuck 258
Soltys, Marty 180–81
Soulpepper Theatre 287
Spader, James 77
Spamalot 257
Special Olympics 103
Spider-Man (musical) 257
Spiegler, Mark 338
Spielberg, Steven 220–21, 284, 348
Spoils of War 29
Sports Illustrated 338
Stackhouse, John 246
Stallone, Sylvester "Sly" 293, 298–99
Stalmaster, Lynn 183
Staparac, Boris 296–97
Star 80 324
Star Chamber, The 232
Star Wars 220, 315
State and Main 298
Steiger, Rod 358
Stein, Jules C. viii, 209–10, 221
Steinberg, David 345–64,
    documentary on: see Quality Balls
Steinberg, Robyn 346, 348, 361
Steinberg, Ruth 349
Steinberg, Yasha 349
Steinberg, Ziggy 362
Stephenson, Helga 112–13

Stern, Jeremy 178
St. Eve, Amy J. 244
Stewart, Jimmie viii
Stewart, Jon 345
Stiller, Jerry 139
Sting, The 117, 220
Stone, Oliver 107–08, 290, 316
Strasberg, Lee 183
Stratford Festival 10–11, 121, 143–47,
    269, 346, 365
Stratten, Dorothy 324
Streisand, Barbra 221, 250
Stritch, Elaine xiii, 314–15, 317, 318,
    319p
Stymiest, Barbara 85
Sullivan & Cromwell 244
Sullivan, Dan 351
Sullivan, Ed 11, 137
Sun Always Sets, The 32
Sundance Film Festival 113, 225, 277
Sun Life Financial Canada 85
Sunset Boulevard 10, 61–62, 88
Sunset Marquis Hotel 214, 218, 254, 338
Sutton Agency 203
Swaggart, Jimmy 338
Swanson, Gloria 10

Tabarrok, Rey 90, 91
Talk (magazine) 283
Talk Radio 316
Taming of the Shrew, The 11, 145
Tarantino, Quentin 271, 274, 284, 286
Taylor, Elizabeth 63, 195, 196
Taylor, Robert 88
Tempest, The 11, 71, 148, 149, 346
The Movie Network (TMN) 192
ThinkFilm 227, 228
This Business of Concert Promotion and
    Touring 259
Thomas, Jackie 95–96

TIFF, see Toronto International Film
  Festival
Timberlake, Justin 264
Time (magazine) 15, 333
Time Inc. 220
Titanic 189
Tomlin, Lily 345, 354
Tommy, see *The Who's Tommy*
Tonight Show, The 219, 345, 356–59
Tony Award 53–54, 60, 65–66
Toronto Hospital for Sick Children
  134–36, 315
Toronto International Film Festival
  (TIFF) xiv, 23, 71–72, 87, 89, 99,
  105, 106, 113, 114, 122–23, 165, 176,
  190, 233, 288, 313–15, 326, 342
Toronto Star 113, 258, 262–63, 268
Toronto Stock Exchange 85–86
Toronto Sun 244
Tory, John 169–72, 171p
Townshend, Pete 52
Tremblay, Michel 145
Tribute 315
Triple Sensation 70
Trotsky, Leon 309
Truffaut, François 276
Truman, Harry 189
Trump, Donald 337
TSE, see Toronto Stock Exchange
Tucker, Sophie 210
Turner, Kathleen 10, 103–04
Two Mrs. Grenvilles, The 197

U2 250, 262, 263
UforChange 131–32
Ultimate Jew, The 139–40
Unauthorized (film) 270, 286–91, 361,
  see also Harvey Weinstein
Unforgettable: 100 Years Remembered
  186–90

Universal City 211, 223
Universal Pictures 220
Universal Studios 211, 214, 216,
  226–27, 290
University of Toronto 32–33, 36
Unlikely Obsession, An 124, 302–12,
  see also *Churchill and the Jews*
Untouchables, The 209
Urman, Mark 280, 282

Valenti, Jack 214–15, 221, 224
van der Rohe, Mies 212
van Gogh, Vincent 335
Vanier College 27, 177–79
Vanity Fair 118, 192, 194, 197, 198, 200–
  01, 204, 205, 212, 227, 244, 283
Van Susteren, Greta 198
Variety (magazine) 11, 231, 279, 318
vaudeville 3, 6
Vidal, Gore 195, 335
Visconti, Luchino 230, 276
Viva 336
Viva Films 76
Viva Las Vegas 102
Virgin Unite 116
Voltaire 62
von Bülow, Claus 197
von Furstenberg, Diane 194

Waddell, Ray 259
Wagner, Robert 195
Wall Street 44, 158
Walsh, M. Emmet 184–86
Walt Disney Company 65–66, 78, 283,
  284–86
Walters, Barbara 194, 206
Wasserman, Casey 214
Wasserman, Edie (née Beckerman) 209,
  212–13, 217–19, 221, 226, 227, 229
Wasserman, Isaac (née Weiserman) 208

Wasserman, Lew viii, xiii, xv, 45, 208–29, 270, 276, 283, 286, 316
    documentary on: see *The Last Mogul*
Wasserman, Minnie (Weiserman) 208
Weavers 252, 266–67
Webber, Andrew Lloyd 45, 51, 54, 61
Weinstein, Bob "Bobby" 271, 276, 277, 278, 282, 283, 286
Weinstein Company, The 286
Weinstein, Eve (née Chilton) 277
Weinstein, Harvey 77, 113, 228, 270–91, 361
    documentary on: see *Unauthorized*
Weinstein, Max 276, 277
Weinstein, Miriam 274, 276, 277
Weinzweig, John 187
Weiss, Rachel Ann 104–05
Weizmann, Chaim 307–08
Weld, Tuesday 363
Weller, Michael 29
Welles, Orson 10, 89
Welsh, Ken 39–40
Weston, Galen 131
West Side Story 53, 143
Whitehead, Edward 18
White, Todd 228, 272–73
The Who 52
The Who's Tommy 52–53, 64, 102, 147
Wilder, Billy 62, 210

Wilkinson, Colm 48, 70
Wilkinson, Kendra 321, 324
William Morris (agency) 227
Williams, Robin 283
Williams, Vanessa 54, 334
Winford, Elizabeth 72
Wintour, Anna 336
Woman Under the Influence, A 88
Wood, Natalie 195
Woodward, Joanne 282, 316
Wonder, Stevie 250
Worth, Irene 144
Wortsman, Irving 32
Wortsman, Sylvia 32

Young Lions, The 211
Young, Loretta 195
Young Presidents Organization (YPO) 150, 152

Zaentz, Saul 283
Zanuck, Richard 220
Zeiger, Scott 119
Zeta-Jones, Catherine 138
Ziegfeld, Florenz 3, 166
    Follies 3
Zimel, Perry 287
Znaimer, Moses 123
Zweibel, Alan 347, 362